Communications
in Computer and Information Science　　1723

More information about this series at https://link.springer.com/bookseries/7899

Sun-Yuan Hsieh · Ling-Ju Hung · Ralf Klasing ·
Chia-Wei Lee · Sheng-Lung Peng (Eds.)

New Trends in Computer Technologies and Applications

25th International Computer Symposium, ICS 2022
Taoyuan, Taiwan, December 15–17, 2022
Proceedings

Editors
Sun-Yuan Hsieh (iD)
National Cheng Kung University
Tainan, Taiwan

Ling-Ju Hung (iD)
National Taipei University of Business
Taoyuan, Taiwan

Ralf Klasing
CNRS and University of Bordeaux
Talence, France

Chia-Wei Lee (iD)
National Taitung University
Taitung, Taiwan

Sheng-Lung Peng (iD)
National Taipei University of Business
Taoyuan, Taiwan

ISSN 1865-0929   ISSN 1865-0937 (electronic)
Communications in Computer and Information Science
ISBN 978-981-19-9581-1   ISBN 978-981-19-9582-8 (eBook)
https://doi.org/10.1007/978-981-19-9582-8

This Springer imprint is published by the registered company Springer Nature Singapore Pte Ltd.
The registered company address is: 152 Beach Road, #21-01/04 Gateway East, Singapore 189721, Singapore

Preface

The International Computer Symposium (ICS 2022) was held at National Taipei University of Business, Taoyuan, Taiwan during December 15–17, 2022. ICS is one of the largest joint international IT symposia held in Taiwan. Founded in 1973, it is intended to provide a forum for researchers, educators, and professionals to exchange their discoveries and practices, and to explore future trends and applications in computer technologies. The biannual symposium offers a great opportunity to share research experiences and to discuss potential new trends in the IT industry.

The technical program of ICS 2022 included 7 workshops addressing emerging pervasive technologies, covering an extensive landscape of the research topics involving new trends in computer technologies:

– Workshop on Algorithms, Bioinformatics, and Computation Theory
– Workshop on Cloud Computing and Big Data
– Workshop on Computer Vision and Image Processing
– Workshop on Cryptography and Information Security
– Workshop on Electronics and Information Technology
– Workshop on Mobile Computation and Wireless Communication
– Workshop on Ubiquitous Cybersecurity and Forensics

The technical program of the conference included 58 regular papers selected by the Program Committee from 137 full submissions received in response to the call for papers. All the papers were peer reviewed by three Program Committee members or external reviewers on average.

The program also included 4 keynote talks, given by Prof. Oscar Castillo (Tijuana Institute of Technology, Mexico), Prof. Nilanjan Dey (Techno International New Town, India), Prof. Peter Rossmanith (RWTH Aachen University, Germany), and Prof. Dong Xiang (Tsinghua University, China). Abstracts or extended versions of their talks are included in this volume.

We thank the Conference Chairs for giving us the opportunity to serve as Program Chairs of ICS 2022, and for the responsibilities of selecting the Program Committee, the conference program, and publications.

We gratefully acknowledge additional financial support from the following Taiwanese institutions: Ministry of Education of Taiwan, National Science and Technology Council, National Taipei University of Business, Academic Sinica, National Center for High-performance Computing, and Taiwan Association of Cloud Computing (TACC).

We thank everyone who made this meeting possible: the authors for submitting papers, the Program Committee members, and external reviewers for volunteering their time to review conference papers. We thank Springer for publishing the proceedings in the Communications in Computer and Information Science series. We would also like to extend special thanks to the workshop chairs and other chairs and the conference Organizing Committee for their work in making ICS 2022 a successful event.

Finally, we acknowledge the use of the EasyChair system for handling the submission of papers, managing the review process, and generating these proceedings.

December 2022

Sun-Yuan Hsieh
Ling-Ju Hung
Ralf Klasing
Chia-Wei Lee
Sheng-Lung Peng

Organization

Honorary Chairs

Wen-Chung Pan	Ministry of Education, Taiwan
Tsung-Tsong Wu	National Science and Technology Council, Taiwan
Lichung Jen	National Taipei University of Business, Taiwan

Conference Chairs

Cheng-Hsuan Li	Ministry of Education, Taiwan
Sheng-Lung Peng	National Taipei University of Business, Taiwan

Advisory Committees

Oscar Castillo	Tijuana Institute of Technology, Mexico
Nilanjan Dey	Techno International New Town, India
Dac-Nhuong Le	Hải Haiphong University, Vietnam
Le Hoang Son	Vietnam National University, Vietnam
Pankaj Srivastava	Motilal Nehru National Institute of Technology Allahabad, India
Dong Xiang	Tsinghua University, China

Program Chairs

Sun-Yuan Hsieh	National Cheng Kung University, Taiwan
Ling-Ju Hung	National Taipei University of Business, Taiwan
Ralf Klasing	CNRS and University of Bordeaux, France
Chia-Wei Lee	National Taitung University, Taiwan

Workshop Chairs

Workshop on Algorithms, Bioinformatics, and Computation Theory

Jou-Ming Chang	National Taipei University of Business, Taiwan
Sun-Yuan Hsieh	National Cheng Kung University, Taiwan
Ling-Ju Hung	National Taipei University of Business, Taiwan
Ralf Klasing	CNRS and University of Bordeaux, France
Chia-Wei Lee	National Taitung University, Taiwan

Workshop on Cloud Computing and Big Data

Wu-Chun Chung   Chung Yuan Christian University, Taiwan
Ching-Hsien Hsu   Asia University, Taiwan

Workshop on Computer Vision and Image Processing

Chuan-Yu Chang   National Yunlin University of Science and
                                 Technology, Taiwan
Chia-Hung Yeh   National Taiwan Normal University, Taiwan

Workshop on Cryptography and Information Security

Chin-Chen Chang   Feng Chia University, Taiwan
Wen-Chung Kuo   National Yunlin University of Science and
                                 Technology, Taiwan
Ching-Nung Yang   National Dong Hwa University, Taiwan
Kuo-Hui Yeh   National Dong Hwa University, Taiwan

Workshop on Electronics and Information Technology

Iuon-Chang Lin   National Chung Hsing University, Taiwan
Min-Shiang Hwang   Asia University, Taiwan
Cheng-Ying Yang   University of Taipei, Taiwan

Workshop on Mobile Computation and Wireless Communication

Yao-Chung Chang   National Taitung University, Taiwan
Jiann-Liang Chen   National Taiwan University of Science and
                                 Technology, Taiwan

Workshop on Ubiquitous Cybersecurity and Forensics

Jen-Chun Chang   National Taipei University, Taiwan
Jung-San Lee   Feng Chia University, Taiwan
Tzu-Wei Lin   Feng Chia University, Taiwan
Shiuh-Jeng Wang   Central Police University, Taiwan

PC Members

Jemal Abawajy   Deakin University, Australia
Matthias Bentert   TU Berlin, Germany
Hans-Joachim Böckenhauer   ETH Zurich, Switzerland
Arnaud Casteigts   University of Bordeaux, France
Shi-Cho Cha   National Taiwan University of Science and
                                 Technology, Taiwan

Che-Cheng Chang	Feng Chia University, Taiwan
Jou-Ming Chang	National Taipei University of Business, Taiwan
Yue-Shan Chang	National Taipei University, Taiwan
Yao-Chung Chang	National Taitung University, Taiwan
Hsuan-Ting Chang	National Yunlin University of Science and Technology, Taiwan
Ing-Chau Chang	National Changhua University of Education, Taiwan
Chuan-Yu Chang	National Yunlin University of Science and Technology, Taiwan
Chin-Chen Chang	Feng Chia University, Taiwan
Ching-Chun Chang	National Institute of Informatics, Japan
Shih-Hao Chang	National Taipei University of Science and Technology, Taiwan
Tzung-Shi Chen	National University of Tainan, Taiwan
Hsin-Tzu Chen	Chinese Culture University, Taiwan
Ying-Nong Chen	National Central University, Taiwan
Ho-Lin Chen	National Taiwan University, Taiwan
Po-An Chen	National Yang Ming Chiao Tung University, Taiwan
Chia-Mei Chen	National Sun Yat-sen University, Taiwan
Jiann-Liang Chen	National Taiwan University of Science and Technology, Taiwan
Yen-Hung Chen	University of Taipei, Taiwan
Yu-Chi Chen	National Taipei University of Science and Technology, Taiwan
Shih-Yeh Chen	National Taitung University, Taiwan
Min-Xiou Chen	National Dong Hwa University, Taiwan
Chi-Yuan Chen	National Ilan University, Taiwan
Mei-Juan Chen	National Dong Hwa University, Taiwan
Shih-Yu Chen	National Yunlin University of Science and Technology, Taiwan
Eddie Cheng	Oakland University, USA
Chen-Yang Cheng	National Taipei University of Technology, Taiwan
Wen-Huang Cheng	National Yang Ming Chiao Tung University, Taiwan
Wei-Che Chien	National Dong Hwa University, Taiwan
Hung-Yu Chien	National Chi Nan University, Taiwan
Hsin-Hung Cho	National Ilan University, Taiwan
Jerry Chou	National Tsing Hua University, Taiwan
Hsin-Hung Chou	National Chi Nan University, Taiwan
Wu-Chun Chung	Chung Yuan Christian University, Taiwan
I-Hsin Chung	IBM, USA

Stelvio Cimato	University of Milan, Italy
Christophe Cérin	University of Paris 13, France
Beniamino DiMartino	University of Campania, Italy
Thomas Erlebach	Durham University, UK
Jianxi Fan	Soochow University, China
Chun-I Fan	National Sun Yat-sen University, Taiwan
Florent Foucaud	LIMOS - Université Clermont Auvergne, France
Leszek Gąsieniec	University of Liverpool, UK
Jing-Ming Guo	National Taiwan University of Science and Technology, Taiwan
Lein Harn	University of Missouri-Kansas City, USA
Bingsheng He	National University of Singapore, Singapore
Wing-Kai Hon	Nation Tsing Hua University, Taiwan
Hung-Chang Hsiao	National Cheng Kung University, Taiwan
Sun-Yuan Hsieh	National Cheng Kung University, Taiwan
Yi-Zeng Hsieh	National Taiwan University of Science and Technology, Taiwan
Jun-Wei Hsieh	National Yang Ming Chiao Tung University, Taiwan
Hsi-Chin Hsin	National United University, Taiwan
Ching-Hsien Hsu	Asia University, Taiwan
Wei-Wen Hsu	National Taitung University, Taiwan
Min-Chun Hu	National Tsing Hua University, Taiwan
Wu-Chih Hu	National Penghu University of Science and Technology, Taiwan
Jheng-Jia Huang	National Taiwan University of Science and Technology, Taiwan
Shih-Yun Huang	National Dong Hwa University, Taiwan
Ling-Ju Hung	National Taipei University of Business, Taiwan
Che-Lun Hung	National Yang Ming Chiao Tung University, Taiwan
Ngoc Tu Huynh	Ton Duc Thang University, Viet Nam
Min-Shiang Hwang	Asia University, Taiwan
Ren-Hung Hwang	National Yang Ming Chiao Tung University, Taiwan
Bahman Javadi	Western Sydney University, Australia
Yao-Chiang Kan	Yuan Ze University, Taiwan
Li-Wei Kang	National Taiwan Normal University, Taiwan
Sanpawat Kantabutra	Chiang Mai University, Thailand
Hung-Yu Kao	National Cheng Kung University, Taiwan
Cheonshik Kim	Sejong University, Korea
Ralf Klasing	CNRS and University of Bordeaux, France
Chien-Chuan Ko	National Chiayi University, Taiwan

Anna Kobusinska	Poznan University of Technology, Poland
Christian Komusiewicz	Philipps-Universität Marburg, Germany
Wen-Chung Kuo	National Yunlin University of Science and Technology, Taiwan
Kuan-Chou Lai	National Taichung University of Education, Taiwan
Ying Hsun Lai	National Taitung University, Taiwan
Chun-Ming Lai	TungHai Univeristy, Taiwan
Van Bang Le	Universität Rostock, Germany
Che-Rung Lee	National Tsing Hua University, Taiwan
Jung-San Lee	Feng Chia University, Taiwan
Chia-Wei Lee	National Taitung University, Taiwan
Lai-Chung Lee	Minghsin University of Science and Technology, Taiwan
Guan-Ling Lee	National Dong Hwa University, Taiwan
Hui Lei	IBM T. J Watson Research Center, USA
Li-Hua Li	Chaoyang University of Technology, Taiwan
Wen-Hwa Liao	National Taipei University of Business, Taiwan
Chung-Shou Liao	National Tsing Hua University, Taiwan
Tzu-Wei Lin	Feng Chia University, Taiwan
Cheng-Kuan Lin	National Yang Ming Chiao Tung University, Taiwan
Jason Lin	National Chung Hsing University, Taiwan
Chuang-Chieh Lin	Tamkang University, Taiwan
Yu-Shan Lin	National Taitung University, Taiwan
Iuon-Chang Lin	National Chung Hsing University, Taiwan
Chih-Yang Lin	Yuan Ze University, Taiwan
Tzu-Chun Lin	Feng Chia University, Taiwan
Chun-Yuan Lin	Asia University, Taiwan
Chien-Chou Lin	National Yunlin University of Science and Technology, Taiwan
Guo-Shiang Lin	National Chin-Yi University of Technology, Taiwan
Wei-Yang Lin	National Chung Cheng University, Taiwan
Pang-Feng Liu	National Taiwan University, Taiwan
Wei-Min Liu	National Chung Cheng University, Taiwan
Nai-Wei Lo	National Taiwan University of Science and Technology, Taiwan
Jung-Wen Lo	National Taichung University of Science and Technology, Taiwan
Shou-Chih Lo	National Dong Hwa University, Taiwan
Jia-Ning Luo	Chung Cheng Institute of Technology, Taiwan

Yi-Wei Ma	National Taiwan University of Science and Technology, Taiwan
Tobias Mömke	University of Augsburg, Germany
Kung-Jui Pai	Ming Chi University of Technology, Taiwan
Syu-Jyun Peng	Taipei Medical University, Taiwan
Tomasz Radzik	King's College London, UK
Rajiv Ranjan	Newcastle University, UK
Peter Rossmanith	RWTH Aachen University, Germany
Yung-Hoh Sheu	National Formosa University, Taiwan
Shyong Jian Shyu	Ming Chuan University, Taiwan
Chien-Hsing Su	National Taipei University of Business, Taiwan
Po-Chyi Su	National Central University, Taiwan
Chunhua Su	University of Aizu, Japan
Hung-Min Sun	National Tsing Hwa University, Taiwan
Minghan Tsai	Feng Chia University, Taiwan
Ming-Feng Tsai	National Chengchi University, Taiwan
Chia-Wei Tsai	National Taitung University, Taiwan
Fan-Hsun Tseng	National Cheng Kung University, Taiwan
Vincent Tseng	National Yang Ming Chiao Tung University, Taiwan
Chih-Hung Wang	National Chiayi University, Taiwan
Wei-Jen Wang	National Central University, Taiwan
Shiuh-Jeng Wang	Central Police University, Taiwan
Dajin Wang	Montclair State University, USA
Hung-Lung Wang	National Taiwan Normal University, Taiwan
Chuan-Ju Wang	Academia Sinica, Taiwan
Cho-Li Wang	The University of Hong Kong, Hong Kong
Chien-Erh Weng	National Kaohsiung University of Science and Technology, Taiwan
Jan-Jan Wu	Academia Sinica, Taiwan
Chao-Chin Wu	National Changhua University of Education, Taiwan
Weili Wu	University of Texas at Dallas, USA
Jules Wulms	TU Wien, Austria
Feng Xia	RMIT University, Australia
Dong Xiang	Tsinghua University, China
Tomoyuki Yamakami	University of Fukui, Japan
Ching-Nung Yang	National Dong Hwa Uniersity, Taiwan
Cheng-Ying Yang	University of Taipei, Taiwan
Wuu Yang	National Yang Ming Chiao Tung University, Taiwan
Wu-Chuan Yang	I-Shou University, Taiwan

Cheng-Hsing Yang	National Pintung University, Taiwan
Chao-Tung Yang	Tunghai University, Taiwan
Ming-Hour Yang	Chung Yuan Christian University, Taiwan
Jenq-Foung Yao	Georgia College & State University, USA
Kuo-Hui Yeh	National Dong Hwa University, Taiwan
Chia-Hung Yeh	National Sun Yat-sen University, Taiwan
Yun-Shuai Yu	National Formosa University, Taiwan
Chia-Mu Yu	National Yang Ming Chiao Tung University, Taiwan
Shuming Zhou	Fujian Normal University, China

Sponsors

Abstracts of Invited Talks

Optimization of Type-2 Fuzzy Systems and Perspectives for Type-3: Theory and Applications

Oscar Castillo

Tijuana Institute of Technology, Tijuana, Mexico

Type-2 fuzzy systems are powerful intelligent models based on the theory of fuzzy sets, originally proposed by Prof. Zadeh. Most real-world applications up to now are based on type-1 fuzzy systems, which are built based on the original (type-1) fuzzy sets that extend the concept of classical sets. Type-2 fuzzy sets extend type-1 fuzzy sets by allowing the membership to be fuzzy, in this way allowing a higher level of uncertainty management. Even with the current successful applications of type-1 fuzzy systems, now several papers have shown that type-2 is able to outperform type-1 in control, pattern recognition, manufacturing and other areas. The key challenge in dealing with type-2 fuzzy models is that their design has a higher level of complexity, and in this regard the use of bio-inspired optimization techniques is of great help in finding the optimal structure and parameters of the type-2 fuzzy systems for particular applications, like in control, robotics, manufacturing and others. Methodologies for designing type-2 fuzzy systems using bio-inspired optimization in different areas of application are presented as illustration. In particular, we will cover Bee Colony Optimization, Particle Swarm Optimization, Gravitational Search and similar approaches to the optimization of fuzzy systems in control applications, robotics and pattern recognition. Finally, the prospects for the future trends and applications of type-3 fuzzy logic will be discussed.

Knowledge-Based XAI on Small Data

Nilanjan Dey

Department of Computer Science and Engineering,
Techno International New Town, Kolkata, India

Data is the principal part of all data analytics, machine learning, and artificial intelligence. Popularity of Big data has grown in recent years, and Small data is now the "new big data". Both are critical in data science. Small data can be defined as small samples that are accessible, clear, and practical for making individual decisions and is widely used in marketing, healthcare, cybersecurity, space, postal services, etc. Small data can also provide insights into data- and knowledge-based approaches. However, it faces the following challenges:

(I)   How can small data explain or interpret the results of the model?
(II) How can small data focus on bimodal features (e.g., numbers or pictures)?
(III) Does small data help experts or decision-makers understand the meaning of the features and the uncertainty of the model etc.?

Researchers, experts, and stakeholders in various fields have applied various machine learning techniques to small data to predict model outcomes. However, because these machine-learning approaches are black-box concepts, they do not explain how they work. Therefore, experts, clinicians, systems analysts, and decision-makers do not know how the small data is processed and how it relates to features. Without a proper interpretation in any area, these machine learning methods do not gain confidence. Explainable AI (XAI) approaches provide multiple capabilities to address the challenges of small data as follows:

(I)   Various XAI approaches (i.e., LIME, SHAP, LINDABN, and BRB) can explain the black box model, which helps experts and decision-makers understand how the model works.
(II) LIME and SP-LIME can help explain the features of the bi-model from both local and global perspectives.
(III) LINDA-BN and the BRB approach help identify linked features of the small data and address the uncertainty of the model, which increases the confidence of the model. This talk will highlight different challenges, issues and solutions for knowledge-based XAI on Small data.

Transformations Between Probability Distributions

Fabian Frei[1], Peter Rossmanith[2] and David Wehner[1]

[1] Department of Computer Science, ETH Zurich, Switzerland
[2] Department of Computer Science, RWTH Aachen, Germany

Generating certain probability distributions is a well studied problem and has important applications in both theory and practice. For example, many algorithms rely on random bits that independent and are 0 or 1 with a probability of exactly $\frac{1}{2}$. Such a random bit is often called a *fair coin* and we call the possible outcomes not 0 and 1, but *heads* and *tails*. In contrast to a fair coin a *biased coin* has a heads-probability different from $\frac{1}{2}$. Can we simulate a fair coin if we only have a biased coin at our disposal? John von Neumann solved this problem in his pioneering paper "Various techniques used in connection with random digits" in 1951 as follows: Throw the biased coin twice. If the two outcomes are different (head–tails or tails–head) then announce the result of the first throw as the outcome of your simulated fair coin. If the two outcomes are identical, just start over. It is easy to see that this procedure simulates a fair coin.

Similarly, we can simulate a coin with a given heads-probability p if the number p is computable. An extensive body of research exists on these and similar simulations. An important question addressed is usually to investigate how many coin tosses you need to simulate a given coin. The question is important because true randomness is a precious resource, but is needed in many areas like cryptographical protocols.

A related question has been investigated less: What transformations between probability distributions are computationally feasible? This question occurs for example in the design of reductions in the area of average case complexity. In its simplest form we can ask for which functions f can we simulated a coin with heads-probability $f(p)$ given a coin with heads-probability p? This question is easy to answer for certain functions. For example for $f(p) = p/2$ we can first simulate a fair coin with von Neumann's trick, announce tails with a probability of $\frac{1}{2}$ and otherwise announce heads with a probability of p.

We investigate for which functions f such a transformation is algorithmically possible. It turns out an approximate simulation is possible if basically the variation of f is bounded. If the simulation needs to work just for finitely many different values of p, then an exact solution is possible with some pathological exceptions. If, on the other hand, we want to solve the general problem for all meaningful values of p, it turns out that many transformations are infeasible. An example is $f(p) = 2p$, which makes sense for $0 < p < \frac{1}{2}$. There is no algorithm that is capable of this transformation, which stays true even if we restrict f to any countable infinite domain. The same holds true for many other functions f and the non-existence proof is absolute: It does not need any complexity theoretic assumption. Surprisingly, the proof uses results from complex analysis.

High-Radix Interconnection Networks

Dong Xiang

School of Software, Tsinghua University, Beijing, China

Interconnection networks fall into two different classes: (1) low-radix networks, and (2) high-radix networks. High-radix networks mainly include fat-tree networks, and dragonfly related networks. Dragonfly related networks include the 1D dragonfly networks, 2D Slingshot networks, dragonfly+ networks and others. The 1D dragonfly networks consist of completely connected router groups, where each pair of router groups has one or multiple global optical connection. Each pair of routers in the same router group has a single local connection. The Slingshot networks replace the router group with a flattened butterfly 2D connected group, where every two groups can be connected by one or multiple global connections. The dragonfly+ network is an enhanced 1D dragonfly network, where each router group contains two sub-groups of switches: one called leaf switches, and the other are spine switches. The spine switches are directly connected to the spine switches of the other router groups while the leaf switches are connected to the spine switches in the same group and the servers. The speaker presents efficient routing algorithms, network connection schemes, and collective communication operations in different high-radix networks.

Contents

Cloud Computing and Big Data

Computer Vision and Image Processing

Cryptography and Information Security

Electronics and Information Technology

Mobile Computation and Wireless Communication

Ubiquitous Cybersecurity and Forensics

Invited Paper

High-Radix Interconnection Networks

Dong Xiang[✉]

School of Software, Tsinghua University, No. 1, Tsinghua Garden Street,
Beijing 100084, China
dxiang@tsinghua.edu.cn

Abstract. Interconnection networks fall into two different classes: (1) low-radix networks, and (2) high-radix networks. High-radix networks mainly include fat-tree networks, and dragonfly related networks. Dragonfly related networks include the 1D dragonfly networks, 2D Slingshot networks, dragonfly+ networks and others. The 1D dragonfly networks consist of completely connected router groups, where each pair of router groups has one or multiple global optical connection. Each pair of routers in the same router group has a single local connection. The Slingshot networks replace the router group with a flattened butterfly 2D connected group, where every two groups can be connected by one or multiple global connections. The dragonfly+ network is an enhanced 1D dragonfly network, where each router group contains two sub-groups of switches: one called leaf switches, and the other are spine switches. The spine switches are directly connected to the spine switches of the other router groups while the leaf switches are connected to the spine switches in the same group and the servers. The speaker presents efficient routing algorithms, network connection schemes, and collective communication operations in different high-radix networks.

1 Introduction

Interconnection networks are the most important components of supercomputers [5,11–16]. Economical optical signaling enables high-radix topologies with long channels, which are less expensive than the short electrical channels. The use of high-radix routers attracts more interests than those of low-radix ones by maintaining a small number of ports and increasing the bandwidth per port. Dragonfly networks [1–4,6–13] have been popular in the past decade. It consists of a number of router groups, where each group contains completely connected routers for 1D router groups. Any pair of groups are connected by at least one global channel. Each router group can also be connected as a 2D flattened butterfly [2,9]. Each router has multiple global links that are connected to other groups.

The original dragonfly network is presented in Sect. 2. The Slingshot network is presented in Sect. 3. The dragonfly+ network is presented in Sect. 4. The paper is concluded in Sect. 5.

S.-Y. Hsieh et al. (Eds.): ICS 2022, CCIS 1723, pp. 3–9, 2022.
https://doi.org/10.1007/978-981-19-9582-8_1

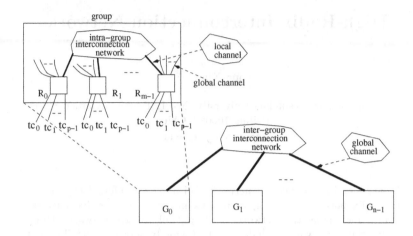

Fig. 1. The dragonfly interconnection network.

2 The Original Dragonfly Networks

Connection of the global links has an impact on the performance of the network. We use the same scheme to connect the global channels for the dragonfly networks as presented in [15]. Let each group have m routers R_0, R_1, ..., R_{m-1}. The groups are labeled as G_0, G_1, G_2, ..., G_{n-1}, while for $i \in \{0, 1, 2, ..., n-2\}$, the last router of G_i is connected to the first router of G_{i+1} for $0 < i < n - 1$. Figure 2 presents the global connections between any pairs of adjacent groups for a system with nine groups and each group contains four routers.

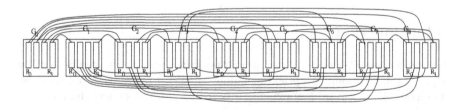

Fig. 2. Connecting the global links for the dragonfly networks.

There are n router groups G_0, G_1, ..., G_{n-1}, where each group contains m routers R_0, R_1, ..., R_{m-1}. Let each router be connected to $g = m/2$ global links, therefore, each group has $m \cdot g$ global links. Our method connects the first group G_0 to any other group G_j $(j \geq 2)$ from $j = 2$ to $n-1$ in the following way: the router in G_0 with the highest ID, that has an available slot, is connected to the router in G_j with the lowest ID and an available slot. The group G_1 is then connected with all other groups G_j $(j \geq 3)$ in the same way. This process continues until G_{n-3} has connected a global link with G_{n-1} finally.

For each pair of groups that are not adjacent, $R_v \in G_i$ and $R_{v'} \in G_j$ with $i + 1 < j$, R_v is connected to $R_{v'}$. Let $R_v \in G_i$ be connected to $R_{v'} \in G_j$. We have the following equations for the IDs of the routers R_v and $R_{v'}$.

$$v = m - 1 - \lfloor \frac{j - i - 2}{g} \rfloor, \tag{1}$$

$$v' = \lceil \frac{i + 2}{g} \rceil - 1. \tag{2}$$

Figure 2 presents the global link connections in a dragonfly network with nine groups, where each group contains four routers. Each router can be connected to up to $g = 2$ separate groups. Figure 2 presents the global link connections between any pair of groups. All local connections in the same group are not presented. The scheme to connect global channels for 1D dragonfly networks can be applied to dragonfly networks with each group established by a 2D flattened butterfly, such as, the Cray Cascade system [2] and Slingshot [9].

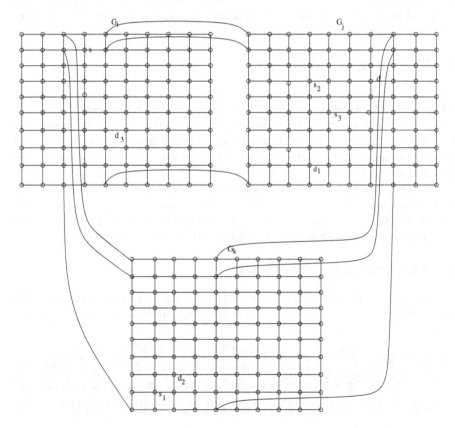

Fig. 3. Connecting the global channels in Slingshot network for safe paths among groups with $i < j < k$.

We give each unidirectional link a unique label plus or minus by the identities (IDs) of source and sink. Each router can be represented by a 2-element tuple (a, b), where a and b are the group ID, and router ID, respectively. A link (s, d) with s (a_1, b_1), and d (a_2, b_2) in the same group is *plus* if $b_1 < b_2$, otherwise it is *minus*. A global link (s, d), that connects nodes $s \in G_{a_1}$ and $d \in G_{a_2}$, is *plus* if $a_1 < a_2$; otherwise, the global link (s, d) is *minus*.

The minus-first routing (MFR) algorithm was proposed in [11, 15] for dragonfly networks without any VCs. Assume that the dragonfly network is connected as stated above. The main idea of the MFR algorithm is: any packet cannot be delivered across a plus hop unless all minus hops have been traversed.

The MFR algorithm is a partially adaptive routing scheme, which can be enhanced to a minimum routing by using a simple flow control scheme. Each input port for local link contains two indistinguishable buffers, which is enough to keep the whole packet. Our method classifies packets as safe or unsafe: A safe packet at a router can be delivered to the destination by the baseline routing scheme MFR provided hops; otherwise, the packet is unsafe. The flow controlled minimum routing requires two buffers that are indistinguishable. A message is delivered along an MFR path if it is delivered across one or more minus hops first, followed by one or more plus hops.

3   The Slingshot Network

The Slingshot interconnection networks have been used in many supercomputers in USA [2, 9]. However, the routing techniques are not satisfied. At least four virtual channels are used, which supports misrouting. The key for a slingshot network is, connection of the network, the routing scheme, and collective communication techniques. All the above techniques can have great impact on the performance and congestion avoidance.

Figure 3 presents a new global optical link connection scheme, where multiple connections are added to each pair of router groups. Based on the above connection technique, we can propose a new routing algorithm with a single virtual channel to support both minimum routing and adaptive misrouting.

4   The Dragonfly+ Network

The dragonfly+ network is an enhanced 1D dragonfly network, where each router group contains two sub-groups of switches: one called leaf switches, and the

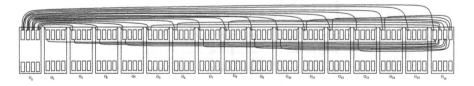

Fig. 4. Connecting the global links in a dragonfly+ network with $m = 4$, $g = 4$, $p = 4$, and $n = 17$.

other are spine switches. The spine switches are directly connected to the spine switches of the other router groups while the leaf switches are connected to the spine switches in the same group and the servers.

Dragonfly+ networks are popular for AI clusters and CPU clusters [8,10], which is far more scalable than the original 1D dragonfly networks. We use a similar global link connection scheme for dragonfly+ networks. As shown in Fig. 4, we present a dragonfly+ network with $m = 4$, $g = 4$, $p = 4$, and $n = 17$, where m, g, p, and n are the number of routers in the same router group (the same as the number of spine and leaf switches), the number of global channels connected to a single spine switch, the number of servers connected to a single leaf switch, and the number of router groups, respectively.

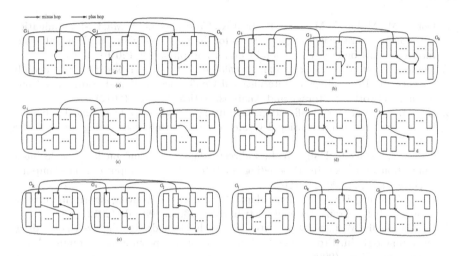

Fig. 5. Misrouting cases, (a) $k > j > i$ and $s \in G_i$, (b) $k > j > i$ and $s \in G_j$, (c) $i < k < j$ and $s \in G_i$, (d) $k < i < j$ and $s \in G_i$, (e) $k < i < j$ and $s \in G_j$, (f) $i < k < j$, and $s \in G_j$.

There are three different routing schemes as proposed in [10]. The general scheme used two virtual channels to support misrouting. There is only a single global channel between each pair of groups, therefore, we must propose an efficient misrouting scheme. We can present a cost-effective routing scheme with a single virtual channel to support minimum and misrouting. Figure 5 presents six different misrouting cases, the whole routing paths conform to the MFR paths in the last four cases. In the first two cases, all packets can still always advance. Therefore, no deadlock can be introduced.

5 Conclusions

High-radix networks mainly include fat-tree networks, and dragonfly related networks. Dragonfly related networks include the 1D dragonfly networks, 2D Slingshot networks, dragonfly+ networks and others. The fat-tree networks can be only special cases of dragonfly+ networks. The 1D dragonfly networks, and dragonfly+ networks connect two router groups with a single global channel. The dragonfly+ networks can connect any two router groups with multiple global channels just like [10]. More efficient routing, network connections, and collective communication schemes can be proposed than those in [2,4,6,8–10].

References

1. Dorier, M., Mubarak, M., Ross, R., Li, J.K., Carothers, C.D., Ma, K.-L.: Evaluation of topology-aware broadcast algorithms for dragonfly networks. In: Proceedings of International Conference on Cloud Computing, pp. 40–49 (2016)
2. Faanes, G., et al.: Cray cascade: a scalable HPC system based on a dragonfly network. In: Proceedings of International Conference on High-Performance Computing, Networking, Storage and Analysis, Article No. 103 (2012)
3. Garcia, M., et al.: On-the-fly adaptive routing in high-radix hierarchical networks. In: Proceedings of International Conference on Parallel Processing, pp. 280–288 (2012)
4. Jiang, N., Kim, J., Dally, W.J.: Indirect adaptive routing on large scale interconnection networks. In: Proceedings of International Symposium on Computer Architecture, pp. 220–231 (2009)
5. Luo, W., Xiang, D.: An efficient adaptive deadlock-free routing algorithm for torus networks. IEEE Trans. Parallel Distrib. Syst. **23**(5), 800–808 (2012)
6. Kim, J., Dally, W.J., Scott, S., Abts, D.: Technology-driven, highly-scalable dragonfly topology. In: Proceedings of International Symposium on Computer Architecture, pp. 77–88 (2008)
7. Maglione-Mathey, G., et al.: Scalable deadlock-free deterministic minimal-path routing engine for infiniband-based dragonfly networks. IEEE Trans. Parallel Distrib. Syst. **29**(1), 183–197 (2018)
8. Ponce, M., et al.: Deploying a top-100 supercomputer for large parallel workloads: the niagara supercomputer. In: Proceedings of PEARC 2019 in Conjunction with International Conference on Proceeding Series, pp. 1–8 (2019)
9. De Sensi, D., Di Girolamo, S., McMahon, K.H., Roweth, D., Hoefler, T.: An in-depth analysis of the slingshot interconnect. In: Proceedings of International Conference on High-Performance Computing, Networking, Storage and Analysis (2020). https://doi.org/10.1109/SC41405.2020.00039
10. Shpiner, A., Haramaty, Z., Eliad, S., Zdornov, V., Gafni, B., Zahavi, E.: Dragonfly+: low cost topology for scaling datacenters. In: Proceedings of IEEE 3rd International Workshop on High-Performance Interconnection Networks in the Exascale and Big-Data Era, pp. 1–8 (2017)
11. Xiang, D., Zhang, Y., Shan, S., Xu, Y.: A fault-tolerant routing algorithm design for on-chip optical networks. In: Proceedings of Symposium on Reliable Distributed Systems, pp. 1–9 (2013)
12. Xiang, D., Liu, X.: Deadlock-free broadcast routing in dragonfly networks without virtual channels. IEEE Trans. Parallel Distrib. Syst. **27**(9), 2520–2532 (2016)

13. Xiang, D., Li, B., Fu, Y.: Fault-tolerant adaptive routing in dragonfly networks. IEEE Trans. Dependable Secur. Comput. **16**(2), 259–271 (2019)
14. Xiang, D., Chakrabarty, K., Fujiwara, H.: Multicast-based testing and thermal-aware test scheduling for 3D ICs with a stacked network-on-chip. IEEE Trans. Comput. **65**(9), 2767–2779 (2016)
15. Xiang, D., Zhang, Y., Pan, Y.: Practical deadlock-free fault-tolerant routing based on the planar network fault model. IEEE Trans. Comput. **58**(5), 620–633 (2009)
16. Xiang, D.: Fault-tolerant routing in hypercube multicomputers using local safety information. IEEE Trans. Parallel Distrib. Syst. **12**(9), 942–951 (2001)

Algorithms, Bioinformatics, and Computation Theory

String Editing Under Pattern Constraints

Robert D. Barish$^{(\boxtimes)}$ and Tetsuo Shibuya

Division of Medical Data Informatics, Human Genome Center, Institute of Medical
Science, University of Tokyo, 4-6-1 Shirokanedai, Minato-ku, Tokyo 108-8639, Japan
`rbarish@ims.u-tokyo.ac.jp`, `tshibuya@hgc.jp`

Abstract. We introduce the novel Nearest Pattern Constrained String
($NPCS$) problem of finding a minimum set Q of character mutation,
insertion, and deletion edit operations sufficient to modify a string x
to contain all contiguous words in a pattern set $\mathcal{P}$ and no contiguous words in a forbidden pattern set $\mathcal{F}$. Letting Σ be the alphabet of allowed characters, and letting η and Υ be the longest string
length and sum of all string lengths in $\mathcal{P} \cup \mathcal{F}$, respectively, we show
that $NPCS$ is fixed-parameter tractable in $|\mathcal{P}|$ with time complexity
$\mathcal{O}\left(2^{|\mathcal{P}|} \cdot \Upsilon \cdot |\Sigma| \cdot (|\mathcal{P}| + \eta)(|x| + 1)\right)$.

Keywords: Combinatorics on words · Combinatorial pattern
matching · String editing · Fixed-parameter tractability ·
Parameterized complexity

1 Introduction

Determining the existence of a pattern in a noise contaminated string, be it one
or more contiguous or non-contiguous permutations of characters that must or
must not occur, has been a fundamental problem in the information sciences
since at least Shannon's work on data transmission through a finite-state noisy
channel [19]. Beyond the example of automated spelling checkers [16], this is
the task of decoders for Hamming [12], Reed-Solomon [17], and numerous other
error-correcting codes, employed in contexts ranging from compact disc readers
[22], to biometric authentication protocols [13] and deep space communication
networks [22]. In the other direction of embedding patterns in strings, there is
the well-known local search problem of minimally perturbing a string to insert a
steganographic pattern [23] such as a watermark [6,18], or to secretly obfuscate
suspected steganographic patterns hidden in media by malicious actors [9,20].

  In this work, we introduce what we denote the Nearest Pattern Constrained
String ($NPCS$) problem. Here, provided a string x, a character alphabet Σ, a set
of required contiguous pattern words $\mathcal{P}$, and a set of contiguous forbidden pattern

This work was supported by JSPS Kakenhi grants {20K21827, 20H05967, 21H04871},
and JST CREST Grant JPMJCR1402JST.

words $\mathcal{F}$, the objective is to return a minimum set $\mathcal{Q}$ of character mutations, insertions, and deletions that convert the input string $x \in \Sigma^*$ into a string $x' \in \Sigma^*$ with at least one substring matching each element of $\mathcal{P}$ and no substrings matching any element of $\mathcal{F}$.

Observing the reduction from the Shortest Common Superstring (SCStr) problem to an instance of $NPCS$ where $\mathcal{F} = \emptyset$ and x is the empty string, and that the SCStr problem is NP-hard even for binary alphabets [10] as well as APX-hard to approximate [5], in general we have that no polynomial time algorithm can exist for the $NPCS$ problem (unless $P = NP$). However, letting η be the length of the longest word in $\mathcal{P} \cup \mathcal{F}$, and letting Υ be the sum of the word lengths in $\mathcal{P} \cup \mathcal{F}$, we prove (Theorem 1) that $NPCS$ is Fixed-Parameter Tractable (FPT) in the cardinality of the pattern set $\mathcal{P}$, admitting a solution with time complexity $\mathcal{O}\left(2^{|\mathcal{P}|} \cdot \Upsilon \cdot |\Sigma| \cdot (|\mathcal{P}| + \eta)(|x| + 1)\right)$. We furthermore show (Corollary 1.1) that a variation on $NPCS$ where we allow for individually specified integer edge weights of size at most C_{mid} for each editing operation can be solved in time $\mathcal{O}\left(2^{|\mathcal{P}|} \cdot \Upsilon \cdot (|\Sigma| \cdot (|\mathcal{P}| + \eta) + C_{mid})(|x| + 1)\right)$.

2   Related Literature

Restricted variants of our $NPCS$ problem have indirectly arisen in various contexts. A notable example is Guo et al.'s [11] Local Search Shortest Common Superstring ($LSSCS_{TR}$) problem, where, provided a superstring S for a set of strings $\mathcal{T}$ and a parameter k, one is tasked with deciding if $\leq k$ mutations can yield a new superstring of length $|S| - 1$ for the words in $\mathcal{T}$. There is also a rather extensive body of work on Constrained Longest Common Subsequence (C-LCSeq) problems, originally due to Tsai [21], where the objective is to find an LCSeq for a set of two or more strings under occurrence or non-occurrence constraints for one of more pattern subsequences or substrings.

Other examples come from the class of *string sanitization* problems [2–4]. In particular, Bernardini et al. [2] introduced the *Combinatorial String Dissemination* (CSD) model for publishing data encoding strings under opposing privacy and utility constraints. Here, they developed [2] (and subsequently improved upon and extended [3,4]) a polynomial time algorithm for editing a string x to produce the shortest possible string x' without substrings in a sensitive pattern set (preserving privacy), while approximately preserving the order of appearance and frequency of non-sensitive substrings (preserving utility). However, we remark that a fundamental difference between our $NPCS$ problem and these string sanitization problems is the requirement in $NPCS$ to generate new patterns in a specified set $\mathcal{P}$, and that this novelty leads to the problem's polynomial time intractability (unless $P = NP$).

3   Preliminaries and Clarifications

3.1   Fixed-Parameter Tractability

A problem is Fixed-Parameter Tractable (FPT) if it has time complexity $f(k) \cdot |x|^{\mathcal{O}(1)}$, where x is a string encoding the problem instance, k is some specified parameter, and $f(k)$ is any computable function.

3.2   Aho-Corasick Automaton

An Aho-Corasick automaton [1] is a finite-state machine generally used for matching strings in a given input text to words in a preprocessed dictionary. Here, let Σ be some specified alphabet, and let $w_1, w_2, \ldots, w_{|D|} \in D$ be an arbitrary collection of words composing a dictionary. To construct an Aho-Corasick automata from D, which can be done in $\mathcal{O}\left(\sum_{i=1}^{|D|} |w_i| \cdot |\Sigma|\right)$ time [1], we create a set of states S_{AC} corresponding to all distinct prefixes for all words $w_i \in D$ as well as a root node ϕ standing in for the empty string (abusing notation we treat the elements of S_{AC} as the strings they correspond to). As is standard, we allow for a transition $s_i \to s_j$ between a pair of states $s_i, s_j \in S_{AC}$ if and only if s_j is the longest proper suffix for $s_i c_k$ in S_{AC}.

3.3   String Terminology

Concerning terminology, for a tuple X or string 's' we write $X[i]$ and $s[i]$ to refer to the element and character, respectively, at the i-th index (assuming 1-indexing), and refer to X as an n-tuple if $|X| = n$. Finally, we define $Append\,(X, q)$ as a function which appends an element q to the end of X.

3.4   Computation Model and Data Structures

For the algorithms in the current work, we everywhere use the RAM (Random Access Machine) model of computation where we assume $\mathcal{O}\,(1)$ costs for reading or moving pointers. In the framework of analyzing the time complexity of operations on sets or tuples of elements, it should be understood that we are treating sets and tuples of pointers to the elements in question.

4   A Fixed-Parameter Tractable Algorithm for NPCS

Theorem 1. *For input string x, alphabet Σ of allowed characters, required pattern set $\mathcal{P}$, forbidden pattern set $\mathcal{F}$, η equal to the longest word length in $\mathcal{P} \cup \mathcal{F}$, and Υ equal to the sum of word lengths in $\mathcal{P} \cup \mathcal{F}$, NPCS admits a FPT algorithm for parameter $|\mathcal{P}|$ with time complexity $\mathcal{O}\left(2^{|\mathcal{P}|} \cdot \Upsilon \cdot |\Sigma| \cdot (|\mathcal{P}| + \eta)(|x| + 1)\right)$.*

Proof. We will proceed by detailing a procedure (Algorithm 1) to solve an arbitrary instance ψ of $NPCS$ with the stated time complexity.

At a very high level of abstraction, after an initialization step where we specify costs for edit operations and remove patterns from $\mathcal{P}$ that are implied by others (Step 0), we will first construct an Aho-Corasick [1] automaton $\mathcal{A}$ from the dictionary $\mathcal{P} \cup \mathcal{F}$ (Step 1). Letting $V_{\mathcal{A}}$ be the list of states for $\mathcal{A}$, the idea will be to prune away states that imply matches to words in $\mathcal{F}$ to generate a new automaton with state set $B_{\mathcal{A}} \subseteq V_{\mathcal{A}}$ (Step 2). This latter automaton will then be used to construct a digraph G, where paths initiated at a specified source node, v_{source}, encode the trajectories through the states $B_{\mathcal{A}}$ that occur as one sequentially steps through all $|x| + 1$ possible positions before, between, and after the characters c_i in the input string x, as well as the set of words in $\mathcal{P}$ that have occurred along the trajectory (Step 3). Here, at each position prior to a character c_i in x (or prior to an empty "" character at the end of x), there will be edges in G whose traversal will decide whether to accept c_i, mutate c_i to some other character $c_k \in \Sigma$, or insert some character $c_k \in \Sigma$ immediately prior to c_i. We remark that, while we necessarily allow for multiple instances of the aforementioned character insertions prior to a character c_i in x, at most $\mathcal{O}(|x|)$ insertions will occur in a given witness for the NPCS problem.

We can now observe that by weighting the aforementioned edges according to the cost of the edit operation they correspond to, or assigning a weight of 0 if the edge accepts a character in the input string, we can reduce the problem of finding a witness for the NPCS problem to that of finding a shortest path in G. Here, by using an appropriate variation on Dijkstra's algorithm [8], we can find such a shortest path (Step 4), and use this path to reconstruct a witness for the original NPCS problem (Step 5).

More specifically, (Step 0) through (Step 5) are as follows:

- (Step 0; Algorithm 1, lines 1–2; $\mathcal{O}(\Upsilon)$ time) specification of the weights $(c_m, c_i, c_d) = (1, 1, 1)$ for mutation, insertion, and deletion edit operations, and a call to an auxiliary function $PruneAffixes(\mathcal{P})$ to remove all elements of the pattern set $\mathcal{P}$ that are affixes of another element (e.g., using a suffix tree constructed via the algorithm of McCreight [15]);
- (Step 1; Algorithm 1, line 3; $\mathcal{O}(\Upsilon \cdot |\Sigma|)$ time) the construction of an Aho-Corasick [1] automaton $\mathcal{A}$ from the dictionary $\mathcal{P} \cup \mathcal{F}$;
- (Step 2; Algorithm 1, line 4; $\mathcal{O}(\Upsilon \cdot |\Sigma|)$ time) the use of an auxiliary function $ForbiddenSubstringPrune(V_{\mathcal{A}}, \mathcal{F}, \Sigma)$ to prune of all states in $\mathcal{A}$ possessing affixes matching strings in the forbidden pattern set $\mathcal{F}$, the result being a new automaton with state set $B_{\mathcal{A}} \subseteq V_{\mathcal{A}}$;
- (Step 3; Algorithm 1, lines 5–9; $\mathcal{O}(2^{|\mathcal{P}|} \cdot \Upsilon \cdot |\Sigma| \cdot (|\mathcal{P}| + \eta)(|x| + 1))$ time) the use of the automaton constructed in the prior step (with state set $B_{\mathcal{A}} \subseteq V_{\mathcal{A}}$) to reduce ψ to a minimum weight path problem on a digraph G with binary edge weights, $|V_G| \in \mathcal{O}(2^{|\mathcal{P}|} \cdot \Upsilon \cdot (|x| + 1))$ vertices, and $|E_G| \in \mathcal{O}(2^{|\mathcal{P}|} \cdot \Upsilon \cdot (|x| + 1) \cdot |\Sigma|)$ edges;

- (Step 4; Algorithm 1, line 10; $\mathcal{O}\left(|V_G| + |E_G|\right)$ time) the use of Dial's small weight-range optimization [7] of Dijkstra's algorithm [8] to find a minimum weight path, $minPath$, from a source vertex $v_{source} \in V_G$ to sink vertex $v_{sink} \in V_G$;
- (Step 5; Algorithm 1, lines 11–12; $\mathcal{O}\left(|E_G| \cdot \eta\right)$ time) the use of $minPath$ to compute and return a minimum set $\mathcal{Q}$ of mutations, insertions, and deletions corresponding to a witness for ψ.

Following the initialization (Step 0), for (Step 1) we call an auxiliary function in (Algorithm 1, line 3) to construct an Aho-Corasick automaton $\mathcal{A}$ with worst-case time complexity $\mathcal{O}\left(\Upsilon \cdot |\Sigma|\right)$ [1]. The auxiliary function then returns $\mathcal{A}$ along with the tuples: (1) $V_{\mathcal{A}}$, corresponding to the states for $\mathcal{A}$ where vertex IDs are equal to their automaton state's prefix; (2) $E_{\mathcal{A}}$, corresponding to automaton transitions in the form of directed edges; (3) $L_{\mathcal{A}}$, where the character at the ith index in $L_{\mathcal{A}}$ induces the transition corresponding to the ith edge in $E_{\mathcal{A}}$.

Algorithm 1: Algorithm for $NPCS$ that is FPT for parameter $|\mathcal{P}|$.

---

1   $(c_m, c_i, c_d) \leftarrow (1, 1, 1)$
2   $\mathcal{P} \leftarrow PruneAffixes\,(\mathcal{P})$
3   $(\mathcal{A}, V_{\mathcal{A}}, E_{\mathcal{A}}, L_{\mathcal{A}}) \leftarrow ConstructACA\,(\mathcal{P} \cup \mathcal{F}, \Sigma)$
4   $B_{\mathcal{A}} \leftarrow ForbiddenSubstringPrune\,(V_{\mathcal{A}}, \mathcal{F}, \Sigma)$
5   $E_G \leftarrow \{(v_{source} \rightarrow (1, 1, 1), 0)\}$
6   **foreach** $j \in [1, |B_{\mathcal{A}}|]$ **do**
7      $\big|$ $E_G \leftarrow Append\big(E_G, \big((|x| + 1, j, 2^{|\mathcal{P}|}) \rightarrow v_{sink}, 0\big)\big)$
8   **end**
9   $E_G \leftarrow BuildDigraph(x, \Sigma, \mathcal{P}, \mathcal{A}, B_{\mathcal{A}}, E_G, c_m, c_i, c_d)$
10   $minPath \leftarrow FindMinWeightPath\,(E_G, v_{source}, v_{sink})$
11   $\mathcal{Q} \leftarrow MinPathToStringEdits\,(minPath)$
12   **return** $\mathcal{Q}$

Subsequently, (Step 2; Algorithm 1, line 4) calls the auxiliary function $ForbiddenSubstringPrune\,(V_{\mathcal{A}}, \mathcal{F}, \Sigma)$ to generate the tuple $B_{\mathcal{A}}$ from $V_{\mathcal{A}}$ by using an Aho-Corasick automaton to prune all vertices with IDs corresponding to words with a substring in $\mathcal{F}$ (line 4). Accordingly, $B_{\mathcal{A}}$ will correspond to the subset of $V_{\mathcal{A}}$ with IDs corresponding to all proper prefixes in $\mathcal{F}$ and all not necessarily proper prefixes in $\mathcal{P}$ that do not contain a word in $\mathcal{F}$ as a substring. Letting $\Upsilon_{V_{\mathcal{A}}}$ and $\Upsilon_{\mathcal{F}}$ be the sum of all string lengths in $V_{\mathcal{A}}$ and $\mathcal{F}$, respectively, the asymptotic time complexity for $ForbiddenSubstringPrune\,(V_{\mathcal{A}}, \mathcal{F}, \Sigma)$ will be $\mathcal{O}\left(\Upsilon_{\mathcal{F}} \cdot |\Sigma| + \Upsilon_{V_{\mathcal{A}}} \cdot \ln\left(|\Sigma|\right)\right) \in \mathcal{O}\left(\Upsilon \cdot |\Sigma|\right)$.

In (Step 3; Algorithm 1, lines 5–9), Algorithm 1 generates a digraph G defined by a weighted edge set E_G. Letting v_a and v_b be an arbitrary pair of vertices, and letting $q \in \{0, 1\}$ be some edge weight (or letting $q \in \mathbb{N}_0$ for more general mutation, insertion, and deletion edit costs), we remark that elements in E_G are tuples of the form $(v_a \rightarrow v_b, q)$. We remark also that, aside from a special source node v_{source} and sink node v_{sink}, the vertices of G have IDs of the form

(α, β, γ), where α specifies one of the $|x| + 1$ positions preceding or proceeding characters in the input string x, β represents the index of an element of $B_{\mathcal{A}}$, and γ represents the index of a set in a lexicographically ordered powerset (i.e., set of all subsets including the empty set and the identity) for $\mathcal{P}$.

To build G, we begin by adding weight 0 initialization edges $v_{source} \rightarrow (1, 1, 1)$ and $(|x| + 1, j, 2^{|\mathcal{P}|}) \rightarrow v_{sink}$ for all $j \in [1, |B_{\mathcal{A}}|]$. To explain the subsequent step, first let $kthPowersetTuple\,(X, k)$ be an auxiliary function which accepts a tuple X and an index $k \in [1, 2^{|X|}]$, then returns the kth tuple in the powerset for the elements of X in accordance with their ordering in X. This can be done in $\mathcal{O}\,(|X|)$ time by generating a binary string s_k corresponding to the integer $k - 1$, creating a string s'_k by prepending $(|X| - |s_k|)$ '0' characters to s_k, and then using s'_k as a bit-mask for X. Additionally, let $NextState\,(\mathcal{A}, p, c)$ be an auxiliary function which accepts an Aho-Corasick automaton $\mathcal{A}$, a prefix string p, and a character c, then returns in $\mathcal{O}\,(|p| \cdot \ln\,(|\Sigma|))$ time the prefix string q according to the transition in $\mathcal{A}$ associated with appending the character c to p (which may be the empty string 'ϕ' or "Fail" if the state was pruned by the auxiliary function $ForbiddenSubstringPrune\,(\ldots)$).

Finally, let $MatchingSuffix\,(\mathcal{P}, B_{\mathcal{A}}[\beta_2])$ be an auxiliary function which returns a suffix of $B_{\mathcal{A}}[\beta_2]$ matching an element of $\mathcal{P}$ (or otherwise the empty set $\emptyset$ otherwise), and let $NewPattern\,(\mathcal{P}, B_{\mathcal{A}}, \beta_2, Z_x, Z_y)$ be an auxiliary function which evaluates "True" if and only if, letting $Z_x = kthPowersetTuple\,(\mathcal{P}, \gamma_1)$ and $Z_y = kthPowersetTuple\,(\mathcal{P}, \gamma_2)$, we have that $Z_x \cup MatchingSuffix\,(\mathcal{P}, B_{\mathcal{A}}[\beta_2])$ and Z_y have the same sets of unique elements. Note that we need to consider all not necessarily proper suffixes of $B_{\mathcal{A}}[\beta_2]$ rather than simply the string $B_{\mathcal{A}}[\beta_2]$ due to the possibility that $ForbiddenSubstringPrune\,(V_{\mathcal{A}}, \mathcal{F}, \Sigma)$ may make some states unreachable, requiring us to consider states implying the existence of a new pattern in $\mathcal{P}$.

In this context, the auxiliary function $BuildDigraph(\ldots)$ called in (Algorithm 1, line 9) constructs G by adding a directed arc from a vertex with ID $(\alpha_1, \beta_1, \gamma_1)$ to a vertex with ID $(\alpha_2, \beta_2, \gamma_2)$ in the following four cases (each corresponding to a distinct edge "type" with a meaning in terms of modifying input string x):

- (Case 1; "Acceptance" edges; weight 0) $\alpha_1 + 1 = \alpha_2 \wedge$
  $NextState(\mathcal{A}, B_{\mathcal{A}}[\beta_1], x[\alpha_1]) = B_{\mathcal{A}}[\beta_2] \wedge NewPattern\,(\mathcal{P}, B_{\mathcal{A}}, \beta_2, Z_x, Z_y)$,
  corresponding to the acceptance of the character immediately proceeding the index $x[\alpha_1]$;
- (Case 2; "Mutation" edges; weight $c_m = 1$) $\alpha_1 + 1 = \alpha_2 \wedge \exists c \in \Sigma$ s.t.
  $NextState\,(\mathcal{A}, B_{\mathcal{A}}[\beta_1], c) = B_{\mathcal{A}}[\beta_2] \wedge NewPattern\,(\mathcal{P}, B_{\mathcal{A}}, \beta_2, Z_x, Z_y)$, corresponding to the mutation of the character at index $x[\alpha_1]$ in the input string to a character $c \in \Sigma$;
- (Case 3; "Insertion" edges; weight $c_i = 1$) $\alpha_1 = \alpha_2 \wedge \beta_1 \neq \beta_2 \wedge$
  $\exists c \in \Sigma$ s.t. $NextState\,(\mathcal{A}, B_{\mathcal{A}}[\beta_1], c) = B_{\mathcal{A}}[\beta_2] \wedge$
  $NewPattern\,(\mathcal{P}, B_{\mathcal{A}}, \beta_2, Z_x, Z_y)$, corresponding to the insertion of a character $c \in \Sigma$ before character at index $x[\alpha_1]$ in the input string;

– (Case 4; "Deletion" edges; weight $c_d = 1$) $\alpha_1 + 1 = \alpha_2 \;\wedge\; \beta_1 = \beta_2 \;\wedge$ $NewPattern\,(\mathcal{P}, B_{\mathcal{A}}, \beta_2, Z_x, Z_y)$, corresponding to the deletion of the character at index $x[\alpha_1]$ in the input string.

Immediately prior to returning E_G, $MinWeightSimplification\,(E_G)$ is invoked to simplify G by deleting all parallel arcs but the one of lowest weight. Observing now that $|B_{\mathcal{A}}| \leq \Upsilon + 1$ and that $|E_G| \in \mathcal{O}\left(2^{|\mathcal{P}|} \cdot \Upsilon \cdot |\Sigma| \cdot (|x| + 1)\right)$, a straightforward analysis shows that the total time complexity of (Step 3) is given by $\mathcal{O}\left(2^{|\mathcal{P}|} \cdot \Upsilon \cdot |\Sigma| \cdot (|\mathcal{P}| + \eta)\,(|x| + 1)\right)$.

In the subsequent (Step 4; Algorithm 1, line 10), we make an auxiliary function call $FindMinWeightPath\,(E_G, v_{source}, v_{sink})$ to either find and return a minimum weight path, $minPath$, connecting the vertices v_{source} and v_{sink} in G, or return "Fail" if no such path exists. This is accomplished in $\mathcal{O}\,(|E_G|) \implies$ $\mathcal{O}\left(2^{|\mathcal{P}|} \cdot \Upsilon \cdot |\Sigma| \cdot (|x| + 1)\right)$ time by using Dial's small weight-range optimization [7] of Dijkstra's algorithm [8].

Finally, in (Step 5; Algorithm 1, lines 11–12), we return the output of the auxiliary function $MinPathToStringEdits\,(minPath)$, which either returns "Fail" if $minPath = Fail$, or else iterates over the length of $minPath$ in $\mathcal{O}\,(|E_G| \cdot \eta) \implies \mathcal{O}\left(2^{|\mathcal{P}|} \cdot \Upsilon \cdot |\Sigma| \cdot \eta \cdot (|x| + 1)\right)$ time to determine if each path edge is an "acceptance", "mutation", "insertion", or "deletion" edge, and then generates and returns the set $\mathcal{Q}$ of these editing operations.

Putting everything together, we have a final (Step 3; Algorithm 1, lines 5–9) dominated time complexity of $\mathcal{O}\left(2^{|\mathcal{P}|} \cdot \Upsilon \cdot |\Sigma| \cdot (|\mathcal{P}| + \eta)\,(|x| + 1)\right)$.   □

Corollary 1.1. *Allowing weights (c_m, c_i, c_d) for mutations, insertions, and deletions to be arbitrary positive integers of size at most C_{mid}, the time complexity for Algorithm 1 becomes $\mathcal{O}\left(2^{|\mathcal{P}|} \cdot \Upsilon \cdot (|\Sigma| \cdot (|\mathcal{P}| + \eta) + C_{mid})\,(|x| + 1)\right)$.*

Proof. If we assume that $max\{c_m, c_i, c_d\} \leq C_{mid}$, Dial's algorithm [7] will have a time complexity of $\mathcal{O}\,(C_{mid} \cdot |V_G| + |E_G|)$. Adding this contribution to the time complexity for Algorithm 1 yields the corollary.   □

5   Implementation Details for the NPCS Algorithm (Algorithm 1)

In this section, we provide additional implementation details for the $NPCS$ algorithm via Algorithm 2 and Algorithm 3. Here, Algorithm 2 corresponds to a slightly modified version of Algorithm 1, and Algorithm 3 corresponds to pseudocode for the auxiliary function $BuildDigraph(\ldots)$. As an important clarification, unlike the case for Algorithm 1, we will be treating the output edge set E_G for $BuildDigraph(\ldots)$ as an ordered tuple. We will also be separately storing the weights for edges in an ordered tuple W_G with the same indexing as E_G, and in places will specify W_G as input to auxiliary functions.

As in the case of Algorithm 1, Algorithm 2 takes as input a string x, a character alphabet tuple Σ, a tuple of contiguous pattern words $\mathcal{P}$ (in any order), and a tuple of contiguous forbidden pattern words $\mathcal{F}$ (in any order). The algorithm then returns a minimum cost set $\mathcal{Q}$ of mutation, insertion, and deletion editing operations that suffice to convert the input string $x \in \Sigma^*$ into a string $x' \in \Sigma^*$, with at least one substring matching each element of $\mathcal{P}$ and no substrings matching any element of $\mathcal{F}$.

Algorithm 2: Algorithm for $NPCS$ that is FPT for parameter $|\mathcal{P}|$.

---

1 $(c_m, c_i, c_d) \leftarrow (1, 1, 1)$
2 $\mathcal{P} \leftarrow PruneAffixes\,(\mathcal{P})$
3 $(\mathcal{A}, V_\mathcal{A}, E_\mathcal{A}, L_\mathcal{A}) \leftarrow ConstructACA\,(\mathcal{P} \cup \mathcal{F}, \Sigma)$
4 $B_\mathcal{A} \leftarrow ForbiddenSubstringPrune\,(V_\mathcal{A}, \mathcal{F}, \Sigma)$
5 $(E_G, W_G) \leftarrow ((v_{source} \rightarrow (1, 1, 1)), (0))$
6 **foreach** $j \in [1, |B_\mathcal{A}|]$ **do**
7 $\quad\big|\quad E_G \leftarrow Append\Big(E_G, (|x| + 1, j, 2^{|\mathcal{P}|}) \rightarrow v_{sink}\Big)$
8 $\quad\big|\quad W_G \leftarrow Append\,(W_G, 0)$
9 **end**
10 $(E_G, W_G) \leftarrow BuildDigraph(x, \Sigma, \mathcal{P}, \mathcal{A}, B_\mathcal{A}, E_G, W_G, c_m, c_i, c_d)$
11 $minPath \leftarrow FindMinWeightPath\,(E_G, W_G, v_{source}, v_{sink})$
12 $\mathcal{Q} \leftarrow MinPathToStringEdits\,(minPath)$
13 **return** $\mathcal{Q}$

We will make use of the following auxiliary functions (some of which were earlier defined in the Theorem 1 proof argument):

– *Append* (X, q), which appends q to the end of a tuple X in $\mathcal{O}\,(1)$ time.
– *ConstructACA* (D, Σ), a function which constructs an Aho-Corasick automaton $\mathcal{A}$, with a trie-like data structure, for a set of input words (i.e., a dictionary) $w_1, w_2, \ldots, w_{|D|} \in D$ and alphabet Σ in $\mathcal{O}\left(\sum_{i=1}^{|D|} |w_i| \cdot |\Sigma|\right)$ time [1], then returns the result as the 4-tuple $(\mathcal{A}, V_\mathcal{A}, E_\mathcal{A}, L_\mathcal{A})$. Here, $V_\mathcal{A}$ is a tuple of vertices corresponding to the states of $\mathcal{A}$ where vertex IDs are equal to their automaton state's prefix, $E_\mathcal{A}$ is a tuple of directed edges corresponding to automaton transitions where the transition $v_i \rightarrow v_j$ for some $v_i, v_j \in V_\mathcal{A}$ is represented as the 2-tuple (v_i, v_j), and $L_\mathcal{A}$ is a tuple of characters from the alphabet Σ where we have that the character at the ith index in $L_\mathcal{A}$ induces the automaton transition corresponding to the edge at the ith index in $E_\mathcal{A}$.
– *FindMinWeightPath* $(E, W, v_{source}, v_{sink})$, a function which accepts a digraph G specified by the tuple (E, W), where E is a tuple of edges for G, W is a tuple of positive integer edge weights having the same indices as the edges they correspond to in E, v_{source} is a specified source vertex for a directed path, and v_{sink} is a specified sink vertex for a directed path. Letting V be the vertex set for G, the function uses Dial's algorithm [7] to either return a tuple of vertices X corresponding a minimum weight path between v_{source} and v_{sink}, or return "Fail" if no such path exists, in $\mathcal{O}\,(|V| + |E|)$ time.

Algorithm 3: $BuildDigraph(x, \Sigma, \mathcal{P}, \mathcal{A}, B_{\mathcal{A}}, E_G, W_G, c_m, c_i, c_d)$

---

1   Preprocess $TupleIndex_{X=\mathcal{P}}(X, q)$, $TupleIndex_{X=B_{\mathcal{A}}}(X, q)$,
    $PowersetTupleIndex_{X=\mathcal{P}}(X, Y)$, $TupleInsert_{U=\mathcal{P}}(X, U, y)$,
    $MatchingSuffix_{X=\mathcal{P}}(X, y)$

2   **foreach** $k \in \left[1, 2^{|\mathcal{P}|}\right]$ **do**

3      $Z \leftarrow kthPowersetTuple(\mathcal{P}, k)$

4   Preprocess $TupleIndex_{X=Z}(X, q)$

5   **end**

6   **foreach** $i \in [1, |x|+1]$, $j \in [1, |B_{\mathcal{A}}|]$, $k \in \left[1, 2^{|\mathcal{P}|}\right]$ **do**

7   **if** $i \leq |x|$ **then**

8         $E_G \leftarrow Append(E_G, (i, j, k) \rightarrow (i+1, j, k))$

9         $W_G \leftarrow Append(W_G, c_d)$

10   **end**

11     $p_0 \leftarrow B_{\mathcal{A}}[j]$

12     $Z \leftarrow kthPowersetTuple(\mathcal{P}, k)$

13   **foreach** $\sigma \in \Sigma$ **do**

14        $p_1 \leftarrow NextState(\mathcal{A}, p_0, \sigma)$

15   **if** $TupleIndex_{X=B_{\mathcal{A}}}(B_{\mathcal{A}}, p_1) \neq Fail$ **then**

16          $In.p_1 \leftarrow TupleIndex_{X=B_{\mathcal{A}}}(B_{\mathcal{A}}, p_1)$

17          $Z^* \leftarrow TupleInsert_{U=\mathcal{P}}(Z, \mathcal{P}, MatchingSuffix(\mathcal{P}, p_1))$

18          $In.ns \leftarrow PowersetTupleIndex_{X=\mathcal{P}}(\mathcal{P}, Z^*)$

19          $E_G \leftarrow Append(E_G, (i, j, k) \rightarrow (i, In.p_1, In.ns))$

20          $W_G \leftarrow Append(W_G, c_i)$

21   **if** $i \leq |x|$ **then**

22            $E_G \leftarrow Append(E_G, (i, j, k) \rightarrow (i+1, In.p_1, In.ns))$

23   **if** $\sigma = x[i]$ **then**

24              $W_G \leftarrow Append(W_G, 0)$

25   **end**

26   **else**

27              $W_G \leftarrow Append(W_G, c_m)$

28   **end**

29   **end**

30   **end**

31   **end**

32   **end**

33   $(E_G, W_G) \leftarrow MinWeightSimplification(E_G, W_G)$

34   **return** (E_G, W_G)

– $ForbiddenSubstringPrune(X, S, \Sigma)$, which takes a set of strings X, a set of words corresponding to forbidden substring patterns $s_1, s_2, \ldots, s_{|S|} \in S$, and an alphabet Σ of characters for the words in X and S, then constructs an Aho-Corasick automaton $\mathcal{Q}_S$ for the words in S via the auxiliary function call $ConstructACA(S, \Sigma)$. It subsequently uses $\mathcal{Q}_S$ to generate and return the set X' of words in X without a substring in S. Letting Υ_S and Υ_X be the sum of all string lengths in S and X, respectively, the asymptotic time complexity for this procedure will be $\mathcal{O}\left(\Upsilon_S \cdot |\Sigma| + \Upsilon_X \cdot \ln(|\Sigma|)\right)$.

- $kthPowersetTuple\,(X,k)$, which accepts a tuple X and an index $k \in [1, 2^{|X|}]$, then returns the kth tuple in the powerset for the elements of X in accordance with their ordering in X, where $k = 1$ always returns the empty set and $k = 2^{|X|}$ always returns the set of all elements. This can be done in $\mathcal{O}\,(|X|)$ time by generating a binary string s_k corresponding to the integer $k - 1$, creating a string s'_k by prepending $(|X| - |s_k|)$ '0' characters to s_k, and then using s'_k as a bit-mask for X.
- $MatchingSuffix_{X=\Gamma}\,(X,y)$, a function which accepts a tuple of strings X and a string y, then either returns a not necessarily proper suffix of y matching a string in X or the empty set $\emptyset$. The subscript "$X = \Gamma$" indicates that an initial preprocessing step was performed for the case $X = \Gamma$ to allow for a time complexity of $\mathcal{O}\,(|y|)$.
- $MinPathToStringEdits\,(minPath)$, a function identical to the one called in (Algorithm 1, line 11) and elaborated upon in the Theorem 1 proof argument.
- $MinWeightSimplification\,(E,W)$, a function which accepts a digraph G specified by the tuple (E,W), where E is tuple of edges for G and W is a tuple of positive integer edge weights having the same indices as the edges they correspond to in E. It then creates a graph G' by converting all parallel arcs in G to a single arc having the lowest weight among the parallel arcs, and returns G' specified in the same manner as the input via the tuple (E', W'). Assuming that vertex IDs are strings of length at most L, and that weights are integers of size at most C, the most naive implementation of this function will have a time complexity of $\mathcal{O}\,(L \cdot C \cdot |E|)$. Here, we simply iterate through the edges, hash each edge $v_a \to v_b$ with a key generated deterministically from the ordered pair (v_a, v_b), and whenever a collision occurs for a pair of edges e_a and e_b having weights w_a and w_b, respectively, update the stored weight with the value $min\{w_a, w_b\}$.
- $NextState\,(\mathcal{A}, p, c)$, a function which accepts an Aho-Corasick automaton $\mathcal{A}$ as defined in the description of $ConstructACA\,(D, \Sigma)$, a prefix string p, and a character c, then either returns the prefix string q according to the transition in $\mathcal{A}$ associated with appending the character c to p, or "Fail" if no such transition exists (due to the state being pruned by the $ForbiddenSubstringPrune\,(\ldots)$ auxiliary function). Letting Σ be the alphabet for $\mathcal{A}$, this procedure will have a time complexity of $\mathcal{O}\,(|p| \cdot \ln\,(|\Sigma|))$.
- $PowersetTupleIndex_{X=\Gamma}\,(X,Y)$, a function which accepts a pair of tuples X and Y, where $Y \subset X$, then returns the integer k inducing the output $kthPowersetTuple\,(X,k) = Y'$, where Y' is equivalent to Y up to a permutation of its elements. The subscript "$X = \Gamma$" indicates that an initial preprocessing step was performed for the case $X = \Gamma$ to allow for a time complexity of $\mathcal{O}\,(|Y|)$. If X is a tuple of strings and L is the longest string length, then a variety of approaches yield an $\mathcal{O}\,(L \cdot |X|)$ preprocessing time (e.g., the generation of a trie data structure to give the bit-mask pattern used by $kthPowersetTuple\,(X,k)$ to generate Y).
- $PruneAffixes\,(X)$, a function which accepts a set of strings $s_1, s_2, \ldots, s_{|X|} \in X$ and returns a set of strings $X' \subseteq X$ generated by removing all words that are affixes (i.e., a prefix, infix, or suffix) of any other word.

Making use of a suffix tree (e.g., constructed using the algorithm of McCreight [15]), and letting Υ_X be the sum of all string lengths in X, this can be accomplished in time $\mathcal{O}\left(\Upsilon_X\right)$.

- $TupleInsert_{U=\Gamma}\left(X, U, y\right)$, a function which accepts a pair of tuples $X \subseteq Y$, where elements of X are sorted in the manner they occur in Y, and a string $y \in U$. The function then returns a tuple generated by either inserting y in X at an index that preserves the relative ordering of the elements in U, or returns X if $y \in X$. Here, the subscript "$U = \Gamma$" indicates that an initial preprocessing step was performed for the case $U = \Gamma$ to allow for a time complexity of $\mathcal{O}\left(|y| + |X|\right)$.

- $TupleIndex_{X=\Gamma}\left(X, q\right)$, which returns the first index where the element q (assumed to be a string) occurs in a tuple X, or "Fail" if no instance of q exists. The subscript "$X = \Gamma$" indicates that an initial preprocessing step (e.g., hashing) was performed for the case $X = \Gamma$ to allow for a time complexity of $\mathcal{O}\left(|q|\right)$.

We can observe that the time complexity of (Step 3; Algorithm 1, lines 5–9), or in the current context (Algorithm 2, lines 5–10), is a function of the terms: $t_1 \in \mathcal{O}\left(\Upsilon \cdot |\Sigma|\right)$ (Algorithm 2, lines 5–10); $t_2 \in \mathcal{O}\left(\Upsilon + (\eta \cdot |\mathcal{P}|)\right)$ (Algorithm 3, line 1); $t_3 \in \mathcal{O}\left(2^{|\mathcal{P}|} \cdot \Upsilon \cdot |\mathcal{P}|\right)$ (Algorithm 3, lines 2–5); $t_4 \in \mathcal{O}\left(2^{|\mathcal{P}|} \cdot \Upsilon \cdot |\Sigma| \cdot (|x| + 1)\right)$ (Algorithm 3, lines 6 & 13); $t_5 \in \mathcal{O}\left(|\mathcal{P}|\right)$ (Algorithm 3, line 12); $t_6 \in \mathcal{O}\left(\eta + |\mathcal{P}|\right)$ (Algorithm 3, lines 14–30); and $t_7 \in \mathcal{O}\left(\eta \cdot \left(2^{|\mathcal{P}|} \cdot \Upsilon \cdot |\Sigma| \cdot (|x| + 1)\right)\right)$ (Algorithm 3, line 33). Putting everything together, we have a total time complexity of $(t_1 + t_2 + t_3 + t_4 \cdot (t_5 + t_6) + t_7) \in \mathcal{O}\left(2^{|\mathcal{P}|} \cdot \Upsilon \cdot |\Sigma| \cdot (|\mathcal{P}| + \eta) (|x| + 1)\right)$, corresponding to the stated time complexity in Theorem 1.

6   Concluding Remarks

As remarked upon in the introduction of the current work, outside of the case where the set of required patterns $\mathcal{P}$ is of bounded size, we have that the Nearest Pattern Constrained String (NPCS) problem is NP-hard (even for binary alphabets), as well as APX-hard to approximate. However, we consider it an interesting open question as to whether an algorithm exists which achieves a reasonable approximation ratio of around $\approx 2 - 4$. Here, we can observe that the reduction from the SCStr problem is currently known to only rule out anything better than a $\left(\frac{333}{332}\right)$-approximation algorithm unless $P = NP$ [14], implying the same bound on the efficient approximability of NPCS.

References

1. Aho, A.V., Corasick, M.J.: Efficient string matching: an aid to bibliographic search. Commun. ACM **18**(6), 333–340 (1975)
2. Bernardini, G., et al.: String sanitization: a combinatorial approach. In: Proceedings of 2019 European Conference on Machine Learning and Principles and Practice of Knowledge Discovery in Databases (ECML PKDD), pp. 627–644 (2019)

3. Bernardini, G., et al.: Combinatorial algorithms for string sanitization. ACM Trans. Knowl. Discov. Data **15**(1), 1–34 (2021)
4. Bernardini, G., et al.: String sanitization under edit distance. In: Proceedings of 31st Annual Symposium on Combinatorial Pattern Matching (CPM), pp. 1–14 (2020)
5. Blum, A., Jiang, T., Li, M., Tromp, J., Yannakakis, M.: Linear approximation of shortest superstrings. J. ACM **41**(4), 630–647 (1994)
6. Cox, I.J., Miller, M.L.: Review of watermarking and the importance of perceptual modeling. In: Proceedings of SPIE 3016. Conference on Human Vision and Electronic Imaging II, pp. 92–99 (1997)
7. Dial, R.B.: Algorithm 360: shortest-path forest with topological ordering. Commun. ACM **12**(11), 632–633 (1969)
8. Dijkstra, E.W.: A note on two problems in connexion with graphs. Numer. Math. **1**, 269–271 (1959)
9. Fisk, G., Fisk, M., Papadopoulos, C., Neil, J.: Eliminating steganography in internet traffic with active wardens. In: Proceedings of 5th International Workshop on Information Hiding (IH), pp. 18–35 (2002)
10. Gallant, J., Maier, D., Astorer, J.: On finding minimal length superstrings. J. Comput. Syst. Sci. **20**(1), 50–58 (1980)
11. Guo, J., Hermelin, D., Komusiewicz, C.: Local search for string problems: brute-force is essentially optimal. Theoret. Comput. Sci. **525**, 30–41 (2014)
12. Hamming, R.W.: Error detecting and error correcting codes. Bell Syst. Tech. J. **29**(2), 147–160 (1950)
13. Hao, F., Anderson, R., Daugman, J.: Combining crypto with biometrics effectively. IEEE Trans. Comput. **55**(9), 1081–1088 (2006)
14. Karpinski, M., Schmied, R.: Improved inapproximability results for the shortest superstring and related problems. In: Proceedings of 19th Computing: The Australasian Theory Symposium (CATS), pp. 27–36 (2013)
15. McCreight, E.M.: A space-economical suffix tree construction algorithm. J. ACM **23**(2), 262–272 (1976)
16. Peterson, J.L.: Computer programs for detecting and correcting spelling errors. Commun. ACM **23**(12), 676–687 (1980)
17. Reed, I.S., Solomon, G.: Polynomial codes over certain finite fields. J. Soc. Ind. Appl. Math. **8**(2), 300–304 (1960)
18. Rizzo, S.G., Bertini, F., Montesi, D.: Content-preserving text watermarking through unicode homoglyph substitution. In: Proceedings of 20th International Database Engineering and Applications Symposium, pp. 97–104 (2016)
19. Shannon, C.E.: A mathematical theory of communication. Bell Syst. Tech. J. **27**(3), 379–423 (1948)
20. Smith, C.B., Agaian, S.S.: Denoising and the active warden. In: Proceedings of 2007 IEEE International Conference on Systems, Man and Cybernetics (SMC), pp. 3317–3322 (2007)
21. Tsai, Y.T.: The constrained longest common subsequence problem. Inf. Process. Lett. **88**(4), 173–176 (2003)
22. Wicker, S.B., Bhargava, V.K. (eds.): Reed-Solomon Codes and Their Applications, 1st edn. IEEE Press, Piscataway (1994)
23. Zielińska, E., Mazurczyk, W., Szczypiorski, K.: Trends in steganography. Commun. ACM **57**(3), 86–95 (2014)

Priority Algorithms with Advice
for Disjoint Path Allocation Problems
(Extended Abstract)

Hans-Joachim Böckenhauer[1] , Fabian Frei[1(✉)] , and Silvan Horvath[2]

[1] Department of Computer Science, ETH Zürich, Zürich, Switzerland
`fabian.frei@inf.ethz.ch`
[2] Department of Mathematics, ETH Zürich, Zürich, Switzerland

Abstract. We analyze the Disjoint Path Allocation problem (DPA) in the priority framework. Motivated by the problem of traffic regulation in communication networks, DPA consists of allocating edge-disjoint paths in a graph. Like an online algorithm, a priority algorithm receives its input sequentially and must output irrevocable decisions for individual input items before having seen the entire input. However, in contrast to the online setting, a priority algorithm may choose an order on the set of all possible input items and the actual input is then presented according to this order. A priority algorithm is thus a natural model for the intuitively well-understood concept of a greedy algorithm.

Mainly motivated by their application for proving lower bounds, we also consider priority algorithms with advice, thus measuring the necessary amount of information about the yet unknown parts of the input.

Besides considering the classical variant of the DPA problem on paths and the related problem of Length-Weighted DPA, we mainly focus on DPA on trees. We show asymptotically matching upper and lower bounds on the advice necessary for optimality in LWDPA and generalize the known optimality result for DPA on paths to trees with maximal degree at most 3. On trees with higher maximal degree, we prove matching upper and lower bounds on the approximation ratio in the advice-free priority setting as well as upper and lower bounds on the advice necessary to achieve optimality.

Keywords: Disjoint path allocation · Priority algorithms · Advice complexity · Greedy algorithms

1 Introduction

Priority Algorithms. Priority algorithms, a more powerful variant of online algorithms, were originally conceived by Borodin, Nielsen, and Rackoff [11] with the goal of modeling greedy algorithms. Online algorithms receive their input sequentially in the form of individual *requests*, where an irrevocable decision for each request must be made before the subsequent request is revealed. While this

© The Author(s), under exclusive license to Springer Nature Singapore Pte Ltd. 2022
S.-Y. Hsieh et al. (Eds.): ICS 2022, CCIS 1723, pp. 25–36, 2022.
https://doi.org/10.1007/978-981-19-9582-8_3

constraint already forces the online algorithm into some degree of greediness, actual greedy algorithms often operate by preprocessing their input to ensure a certain order among the individual requests. They then operate in an online fashion on the preprocessed data, such that requests are presented in the predetermined order. This idea of exploiting the presentation order is captured in the priority model.

Like a classical online algorithm, a priority algorithm is presented with its input in a sequential fashion and has to output a decision for each request before being fed the next one. However, unlike in the classical online setting, a priority algorithm imposes a *priority order* (denoted by $\prec$) on the set, or *universe*, of all possible requests. The subset of the universe comprising the actual input is then fed to the priority algorithm according to this order.

We further distinguish *fixed-priority* algorithms from the more general class of *adaptive-priority* algorithms. Both types choose a priority order before being presented with the first request. While this initial priority order persists during the entire operation of a fixed-priority algorithm, an adaptive priority algorithm may change the order after each processed request. For example, Prim's algorithm for finding a minimum spanning tree is a classical greedy algorithm that can only be modeled in the adaptive-priority framework.

Priority algorithms have been studied for a range of optimization problems, such as set cover [1], vertex cover, independent set, and colorability [7], auctions [10], scheduling [11], and satisfiability [21].

Advice. For many optimization problems, one notices that the quality of a solution produced by an online algorithm is much worse than that of an optimal solution. This of course stems from the fact that an online algorithm is oblivious of the remaining input when making its decision for each request, i.e., it lacks information. To analyze this information deficiency, Dobrev et al. [16] introduced the measure of the *advice complexity* of an online problem, a concept that was refined by Emek et al. [17], by Hromkovič et al. [19], and by Böckenhauer et al. [5], whose model we assume in this paper.

Intuitively, advice complexity is the amount of information about the input an online algorithm needs in order to produce a solution of certain quality. More concretely, an *online algorithm with advice* is given an *advice tape* – an infinite binary string – that contains information about the specific input the algorithm has to operate on. The advice tape can be thought of as being provided by an oracle that has unlimited computational power, knows the entire input as well as the inner workings of the algorithm, and cooperates with it. The advice complexity is the number of bits of the advice tape the algorithm accesses during its runtime in the worst case. An overview of results in the advice framework can be found in the survey by Boyar et al. [12] and in the textbook by Komm [20].

The concept of advice has recently been extended to the priority framework by Borodin et al. [8] and by Boyar et al. [13]. There are multiple possible models of priority algorithms with advice. While an online algorithm with advice only uses the advice string to make decisions for requests, a priority algorithm must also decide what priority order to use. It is subject to modeling whether or not the priority order should also be allowed to depend on the advice. Boyar et al. [13] distinguish four possible models with different priority-advice dependencies. However, since both our upper and our lower bounds hold in all four models, we will not assume any specific one of them.

Disjoint Path Allocation. The Disjoint Path Allocation problem (DPA) is a standard online optimization problem. Motivated by the real-world problem of routing calls in communication networks, it consists in allocating edge-disjoint paths between pairs of vertices in a graph. More concretely, the input of an online algorithm for DPA consists of some graph G in a fixed class of graphs – we will mainly consider the classes of paths and trees – followed by a sequence of vertex pairs in G, which are revealed one after the other. For each request, i.e., vertex pair $[x, y]$, that is revealed, the online algorithm must immediately decide whether to *accept* or *reject* it. If the algorithm accepts $[x, y]$, it must allocate an x-y-path in G not sharing an edge with any previously allocated path.[1] The decision for $[x, y]$ may only depend on previously received vertex pairs and on the graph G. The goal is to accept as many vertex pairs as possible.

The classical DPA problem (also simply referred to as DPA) considers the problem on the graph class of paths. Generalizing DPA to trees results in the so-called CAT problem (*Call Admission on Trees*). Note that these versions of the problem allow to somewhat simplify the setting, since there is only one x-y-path between every vertex pair $[x, y]$ in a tree. Thus, an online or priority algorithm for DPA on trees and paths must essentially only make a binary decision for each request, namely whether to accept or reject it.

The DPA problem is well-studied in the online framework with and without advice. Advice-free online DPA on various graph classes is discussed in Chapter 13 of the textbook by Borodin and El-Yaniv [9]. Online algorithms with advice for DPA on paths are analyzed by Böckenhauer et al. [5], by Barhum et al. [2], and discussed in Chap. 7 of the textbook by Komm [20]. Böckenhauer et al. analyze online algorithms with advice for DPA on the graph class of trees [3] and on the graph class of grids [6]. We also consider the Length-Weighted DPA Problem (LWDPA), a natural variant introduced by Burjons et al. [14]. Inspired by the real-world problem of trying to maximize a meeting room's occupancy, the goal in LWDPA consists not in maximizing the number of accepted paths, but rather their total length.

In Sect. 3, we discuss the classical DPA problem on paths and in Sect. 4, we consider the related problem of Length-Weighted DPA. Our main contributions lie in Sect. 5, where we analyze DPA on trees. Finally, in Sect. 6, we very briefly discuss DPA on the class of grids. Some proofs are omitted in this extended abstract.

---

[1] If the underlying graph G is itself a path, the pair $[x, y]$ can be interpreted as the closed interval between x and y – thus the use of square brackets. We identify $[x, y]$ with $[y, x]$.

2   Preliminaries

There is a certain subtlety that must be considered when applying the priority framework to the online problem DPA. Namely, we do not want what we informally consider to be the first input item a priority algorithm for DPA receives – the underlying graph G on which the given instance is defined – to be a request to which a priority can be assigned. We thus define requests of the priority problem DPA to be of the form $[x, y]^G$, where $G = (V, E)$ is some graph, $x \neq y \in V$, and we identify $[x, y]^G$ with $[y, x]^G$. Hence, the underlying graph does not need to be communicated to the algorithm separately. Informally, we will still think of G as being the first input item that is presented, even though we technically assume that it is only revealed together with the first request.

As mentioned previously, we typically distinguish different variants of the DPA problem with respect to the graph class from which the underlying graph is chosen, e.g., the class of paths or the class of trees. Thus, we define the universe of all possible requests to be the set $\mathcal{U} := \{ [x, y]^G \mid G \in \mathcal{G}, \ x \neq y \in V(G) \}$, where $\mathcal{G}$ is some arbitrary graph class. An *instance* of DPA on $\mathcal{G}$ is then simply a subset $I \subseteq \mathcal{U}$ with $[x, y]^G, [v, w]^H \in I \Rightarrow G = H$. Note that the same request cannot appear twice in an instance.

As explained above, a priority algorithm for DPA chooses a priority order $\prec$ on $\mathcal{U}$ and an instance I is then presented to the algorithm according to this order – such that $\max_{\prec} I$ is presented first. A fixed-priority algorithm chooses a fixed order, while an adaptive-priority one chooses a new order after each request. Note that we assume that $\prec$ is total in order to simplify notation – but we never care about the order relation between requests defined on distinct graphs, because such requests never appear in the same instance. In fact, we often do not even require the order on the subsets of $\mathcal{U}$ that correspond to sets of requests belonging to the same graph to be total. Since, by the Szpilrajn extension theorem [22], every partial order on a set can be extended to a total order, we will thus only define partial orders on $\mathcal{U}$.

On a further note, as explained earlier, we may simplify the setting if every graph $G \in \mathcal{G}$ is cycle-free. Since paths in such a graph are uniquely determined by their end points, we can identify the request $[x, y]^G$ with the unique x-y-path in G. The algorithm must then only decide whether to accept or reject the path $[x, y]^G$. Furthermore, this identification allows us to use certain helpful terminology – such as that two requests $[x, y]^G$ and $[v, w]^G$ *intersect* if the corresponding paths edge-intersect. If $[x, y]^G$ cannot be accepted because it intersects the previously accepted request $[v, w]^G$, we say that $[v, w]^G$ *blocks* $[x, y]^G$.

For a priority algorithm ALG and an instance I, we define $\mathrm{ALG}(I) \subseteq I$ to be the set of requests accepted by ALG and $\mathrm{OPT}(I) \subseteq I$ to be an optimal solution for I. If ALG uses the advice string Φ, we write $\mathrm{ALG}^{\Phi}(I)$. For the DPA problem, we denote by $|\mathrm{ALG}(I)|$ and $|\mathrm{OPT}(I)|$ the sizes of the corresponding sets, i.e., the number of requests accepted by ALG and the optimal solution, respectively. For the related problem of LWDPA – where the goal consists in maximizing the total length of the accepted paths – we denote that quantity by

$|\text{ALG}(I)|$ or $|\text{OPT}(I)|$. We refer to $|\text{ALG}(I)|$ and $|\text{OPT}(I)|$ as the *gains* on I of ALG and the optimal solution, respectively.

We say that ALG is *strictly c-competitive* for some $c : \mathcal{G} \to \mathbb{R}_{\geq 1}$ if, for every $G \in \mathcal{G}$ and every instance I defined on G, $|\text{OPT}(I)| / |\text{ALG}(I)| \leq c(G)$. The *strict competitive ratio* or *approximation ratio* of ALG is the pointwise infimum over all c for which ALG is strictly c-competitive. ALG is optimal if it has a strict competitive ratio of 1.

Regarding priority algorithms with advice, we say that such an algorithm is strictly c-competitive with advice complexity $b : \mathcal{G} \to \mathbb{N}$ if, for every $G \in \mathcal{G}$ and every instance I defined on G, there exists an advice string Φ such that $|\text{OPT}(I)| / |\text{ALG}^{\Phi}(I)| \leq c(G)$ and each of the algorithm's decisions only depends on the first $b(G)$ bits of Φ.

Note that the study of online algorithms is often centered around the analysis of their *non-strict* competitive ratio (sometimes just called competitive ratio), where ALG is (non-strictly) c-competitive for some $c \in \mathbb{R}_{\geq 1}$ if there is a constant $\alpha \in \mathbb{R}$ such that, for every instance I, $|\text{OPT}(I)| \leq c \cdot |\text{ALG}(I)| + \alpha$. The additive constant α allows ALG to be c-competitive even if there are finitely many instances I for which $|\text{OPT}(I)| / |\text{ALG}(I)| > c$. However, since there are only finitely many instances of DPA defined on the same underlying graph and since we want to analyze competitiveness with respect to that graph, we focus on analyzing the strict competitive ratio. Note however that all lower bounds on the strict competitive ratio presented in this paper can be translated into lower bounds on the non-strict competitive ratio if we dispense with letting the latter depend on the underlying graph.

3   DPA on Paths

We begin by reviewing the classical variant of the DPA problem – namely DPA on the graph class of paths, $\mathcal{P}$. DPA on paths is essentially a discrete variant of interval scheduling with unit profit on a single machine – an optimization problem already studied in the priority framework by Borodin et al. [11]. Both problems are solved optimally by a fixed-priority algorithm without advice, a fact independently shown by Carlisle and Lloyd [15] and by Faigle and Nawijn [18].

Theorem 1 (Carlisle and Lloyd [15] and Faigle and Nawijn [18]). *There is an optimal fixed-priority algorithm without advice for DPA on paths.*

Essentially, the algorithm achieving optimality is a greedy algorithm – accepting every unblocked request. As shown in Sect. 5, the above result generalizes. Namely, the DPA problem on trees with maximum degree at most 3 is also solved optimally by a fixed-priority greedy algorithm requiring no advice.

In contrast to this optimality result, there is a tight lower bound of l – the length of the underlying path graph – on the strict competitive ratio for DPA on paths in the standard online setting, as shown by Borodin and El-Yaniv [9].

4 Length-Weighted DPA

We observe that LWDPA is related to the interval scheduling problem with proportional profits on a single machine. This optimization problem was also studied in the advice-free priority setting by Borodin et al. [11]. The tight bound of 3 on the approximation ratio for the latter problem corresponds to an upper bound of $(3 - 3/l)$ and a lower bound of $(3 - \mathcal{O}(l^{-1/3}))$ for LWDPA.

Theorem 2. *There is a strictly $(3 - 3/l)$-competitive fixed-priority algorithm without advice for LWDPA.*

Theorem 3. *The approximation ratio of any adaptive-priority algorithm without advice for LWDPA is at least $(3 - \mathcal{O}(l^{-1/3}))$.*

This asymptotically tight bound stands in contrast to a lower bound of l in the standard online framework proved by Burjons et al. [14].

Regarding priority algorithms with advice for LWDPA, we begin with an upper bound on the number of advice bits necessary to achieve optimality. We use a similar strategy to the one used by Burjons et al. [14] for their optimal online algorithm with advice for LWDPA. The strategy is to fix an optimal solution for the given instance and to encode this optimal solution in the advice string. Burjons et al. do this by conveying to the algorithm for every vertex in the graph whether or not this vertex is a *transition point*, i.e., a start point or end point of a path contained in the fixed optimal solution. The algorithm then simply checks for each path it is presented whether or not its start point and end point are consecutive transition points and accepts only if they are. The algorithm thus reproduces the fixed optimal solution.

Using this strategy yields that $(l - 1)$ advice bits are sufficient for an online algorithm to be optimal since whether or not a vertex is a transition point needs to be conveyed for all but the first and the last vertex in the graph. However, if we instead consider this strategy in the more powerful priority framework, we find that fewer advice bits are sufficient. Importantly, in our setting we do not convey any fixed optimal solution to the priority algorithm, but the one we will refer to as the *greediest* optimal solution.

Definition 1. *Let I be an instance of DPA or of LWDPA and $\prec$ a fixed-priority order for the problem at hand. Write $I = \{r_1, r_2, \ldots, r_n\}$, where $r_1 \succ r_2 \succ \ldots \succ r_n$. Inductively define, for $1 \leq k \leq n$ and $S_0 := \emptyset$,*

$$S_k := \begin{cases} S_{k-1} \cup \{r_k\} & \text{if there is an } R \subseteq \{r_{k+1}, r_{k+2}, \ldots, r_n\} \text{ such that } S_{k-1} \\ & \cup \{r_k\} \cup R \text{ is an optimal solution for } I, \text{ and} \\ S_{k-1} & \text{otherwise.} \end{cases}$$

Define the greediest optimal solution *of I to be $\mathrm{OPT}_{\mathrm{Gr}}(I) := S_n$.*

It is clear that $\mathrm{OPT}_{\mathrm{Gr}}(I)$ is in fact an optimal solution for I. More informally, it is the solution produced by an optimal offline algorithm that first computes all optimal solutions for a given instance and then operates on it in a sequential fashion (according to the priority order), accepting a request whenever possible, i.e., never rejecting a request if it could also arrive at an optimal solution by accepting that request.

By conveying the greediest optimal solution of the given instance of LWDPA via the advice string, we obtain the following result.

Theorem 4. *There is an optimal fixed-priority algorithm for* LWDPA *reading* $3\lceil l/4 \rceil$ *advice bits.*

Proof Sketch. The strategy is to convey the greediest optimal solution of the instance at hand to the priority algorithm. We use a fixed-priority order ordering paths primarily by non-increasing length and secondarily by their position on the underlying path graph, from left to right. However, instead of encoding all transition points in the advice, it suffices for the algorithm to know only the starting points of the requests in the greediest optimal solution. Furthermore, the starting points of requests with length 1 do not need to be communicated but can be accepted greedily by the algorithm.   □

With this upper bound on the amount of advice necessary to achieve optimality, we continue with a corresponding lower bound. However, instead of simply giving a lower bound for optimality, the following theorem bounds the advice complexity of priority algorithms for LWDPA for a whole range of small approximation ratios from below. This is achieved by reducing the online problem of binary string guessing with known history (2-SGKH) to the priority problem LWDPA. The binary string guessing problem was introduced by Böckenhauer et al. [4] with the aim of deriving such lower bounds for online algorithms. Reducing 2-SGKH to a priority problem rather than to an online problem makes the construction slightly more complicated.

Definition 2 (2-SGKH). *The input of* 2-SGKH *is a parameter* $n \in \mathbb{N}$*, followed by binary values* $d_1, d_2, \ldots, d_n \in \{0, 1\}$ *which are revealed one-by-one (in an online fashion). Before reading* d_i*,* $i \in \{1, 2, \ldots, n\}$*, an online algorithm solving* 2-SGKH *outputs* $y_i \in \{0, 1\}$*. The gain of the solution produced by the algorithm is the number of* i *in* $\{1, 2, \ldots, n\}$ *with* $y_i = d_i$*.*

In other words, an online algorithm solving 2-SGKH tries to guess n binary values $d_1, d_2, \ldots, d_n$. Importantly, the algorithm knows the number n of values to guess before making the first guess and is informed whether it guessed correctly after each guess. Böckenhauer et al. [4] proved the following theorem:

Theorem 5 (Böckenhauer et al. [4, Corollary 1]). *Let* $1/2 \leq \varepsilon < 1$*. An online algorithm for* 2-SGKH *guessing more than* εn *out of a total of* n *bits correctly needs to read at least* $(1 - \mathcal{H}(\varepsilon))n$ *advice bits, where* $\mathcal{H}(x) = -x \log(x) - (1 - x) \log(1 - x)$ *is the binary entropy function.*

This theorem allows us to prove the following lower bound by reduction. A similar, more general construction was used by Boyar et al. [13] and applied to a wide range of problems.

Theorem 6. *Let* $1/2 \leq \varepsilon < 1$. *The advice complexity of any adaptive-priority algorithm for* LWDPA *with an approximation ratio smaller than* $3/(2 + \varepsilon)$ *is at least* $(1 - \mathcal{H}(\varepsilon)) \lfloor l/3 \rfloor$.

The core idea is to translate guessing the bit d_i into guessing whether a certain LWDPA request should be accepted or not. The challenge lies in ensuring that this request is presented in accordance with the given priority order.

5   DPA on Trees

We denote by $\mathcal{T}$ the graph class of trees. As in the previous sections, we identify the request $[x, y]^T$, $T \in \mathcal{T}$, with the unique x-y-path in T. Since T is always clear from the context, we will omit it as the superscript of $[x, y]$. As is common, we denote by $\deg(x)$ the degree of the vertex x and by $d(x, y)$ the distance between the vertices x and y, i.e., the length of the unique x, y-path in T.

Theorem 7. *There is a strictly 2-competitive fixed-priority algorithm without advice for* DPA *on trees.*

Proof Sketch. We again consider the algorithm GREEDY that accepts every unblocked request. Here, GREEDY uses a priority order that orders paths primarily by non-increasing distance to the root of the tree T on which the given instance is defined. More formally, choose, for each $T \in \mathcal{T}$, some arbitrary leaf w as its root and define, for each path p in T, its *peak* to be the vertex $s_p := \arg\min_{v \in p} d(v, w)$, i.e., p's vertex closest to the root. It is easy to show that s_p is unique. We choose a fixed-priority order $\prec$ such that, for each $T \in \mathcal{T}$ and all requests p and p' defined on T,

$$d(s_p, w) > d(s_{p'}, w) \implies p \succ p'.$$

With this priority order, it follows that GREEDY is strictly 2-competitive.   □

By slightly refining the priority order we defined above, we obtain the generalization of the result in Theorem 1 mentioned earlier. This refinement consists in additionally requiring that $p \succ p'$ whenever $s_p = s_{p'}$ and s_p is an end-vertex of p but not of p'.

Proposition 1 (Generalization of Theorem 1). *There is an optimal fixed-priority algorithm without advice for* DPA *on the graph class of trees with maximum degree at most* 3.

Having established this optimality result for the subclass of $\mathcal{T}$ containing trees with maximum degree at most 3, it remains to show a lower bound for the class of trees with maximum degree at least 4.

Theorem 8. *The approximation ratio of any adaptive-priority algorithm without advice for* DPA *on trees with maximum degree at least* 4 *is at least* 2.

With this tight bound we now turn to the advice setting.

We begin with an optimal fixed-priority algorithm reading advice. As in the proof of Theorem 4, the advice string is going to encode some optimal solution for the instance at hand, which the algorithm is going to decode. This fixed optimal solution will in fact again be the *greediest* optimal solution, as defined in Definition 1.

At first, our result might seem surprising in that the number of advice bits the algorithm requires does not directly depend on the size of the tree on which the given instance is defined. However, this makes intuitive sense, considering that the DPA problem on paths – or, more generally, on trees with maximum degree at most 3 – is optimally solvable without advice. We might thus expect the amount of advice necessary to achieve optimality on a certain tree to be small if it contains large subtrees without vertices of degree greater than 3.

Theorem 9. *There is an optimal fixed-priority algorithm for* DPA *on trees with advice complexity* $(\theta_1(T) - \theta_3(T) - 2) \left\lceil \log \frac{\Delta(T)}{2} \right\rceil$, *where* $\theta_1(T)$ *denotes the number of leaves in the tree* T, $\theta_3(T)$ *the number of vertices of degree 3 and* $\Delta(T)$ *the maximum degree in* T.

Proof. The proofs of all subsidiary claims are omitted.

We are again extending the partial order on $\mathcal{U}$ that we initially defined in the proof of Theorem 7 and already extended once for Proposition 1. We pose the additional condition that all requests in the given instance that share the same peak are presented consecutively to our algorithm. To achieve this, we choose some arbitrary total order $<_T$ on the set $V(T)$ for each $T \in \mathcal{T}$ and define, for each $T \in \mathcal{T}$ and all requests p, p' defined on T,

$$d(s_p, w) > d(s_{p'}, w) \implies p \succ p',$$

$$d(s_p, w) = d(s_{p'}, w) \text{ and } s_p >_T s_{p'} \implies p \succ p',$$

$$s_p = s_{p'} \text{ and } (s_p \text{ is an end-vertex of } p \text{ but not of } p') \implies p \succ p',$$

and extend this partial order to some total order on $\mathcal{U}$. With this priority order, the algorithm we define below will again be a quasi-greedy algorithm, as in the proof of Theorem 4.

Let $\mathrm{OPT}_{\mathrm{Gr}}(I)$ again be the greediest optimal solution for the instance I with respect to $\prec$. In DPA, we have a simple characterization of $\mathrm{OPT}_{\mathrm{Gr}}(I)$. Namely, for all $p \succ p' \in I$ with $p' \in \mathrm{OPT}_{\mathrm{Gr}}(I)$ and $p \notin \mathrm{OPT}_{\mathrm{Gr}}(I)$, it holds that the set $(\mathrm{OPT}_{\mathrm{Gr}}(I) \cup \{p\}) \setminus \{p'\}$ is not a valid solution for I, i.e., it contains intersecting paths. This is because if it were a valid solution, it would in fact be an optimal solution, since it has the same size as $\mathrm{OPT}_{\mathrm{Gr}}(I)$. This, however, means that p should have been included in $\mathrm{OPT}_{\mathrm{Gr}}(I)$ by Definition 1.

Claim 1. Let $p \in I$ be a path such that its peak s_p is an end-vertex of p and such that p does not intersect a path in $\mathrm{OPT}_{\mathrm{Gr}}(I)$ with higher priority. It holds that $p \in \mathrm{OPT}_{\mathrm{Gr}}(I)$.

Claim 2. Let $p \in I$ be a path such that $\deg(s_p) \leq 3$ and such that p does not intersect a path in $\mathrm{OPT}_{\mathrm{Gr}}(I)$ with higher priority. It holds that $p \in \mathrm{OPT}_{\mathrm{Gr}}(I)$.

Thus, our algorithm can operate greedily on requests whose peaks coincide with one of their end points or have degree at most 3. More precisely, if our algorithm must decide whether to accept or reject a request p and we assume that its partial solution on the requests preceding p agrees with $\mathrm{OPT}_{\mathrm{Gr}}(I)$, accepting p if it is not yet blocked and rejecting it otherwise extends this partial solution in such a way that it still agrees with $\mathrm{OPT}_{\mathrm{Gr}}(I)$, given that s_p is an end-vertex of p or that $\deg(s_p) \leq 3$.

We now use the following strategy: We partition the instance I into disjoint phases, such that phase I_v contains all paths with peak v. Due to our condition on the priority order that all requests with peak v are presented consecutively, the algorithm knows that the previous phase is finished and the new phase I_v starts as soon as it first receives a request with the new peak v.

If v has degree at most 3, the algorithm operates greedily during the entire phase I_v without reading advice. If v has degree greater than 3, the algorithm first greedily accepts all unblocked paths in I_v with end point v, again requiring no advice. For the remaining requests in I_v, the algorithm needs advice:

Similarly to the advice strategy used by Böckenhauer et al. [3], the basic idea is that the advice string communicates to the algorithm which pairs of edges incident to v belong to the same optimal request in the remainder of I_v. More precisely, we first fix an ordering of the remaining edges $e_v^1, e_v^2, \ldots, e_v^{n_v}$ between v and its children. Remaining edges are those edges that are not yet blocked by accepted requests with end point v. Note that $n_v \leq \deg(v) - 1$ since we chose a leaf as the root in the proof of Theorem 7 and thus all vertices with degree greater than 3 have a parent. Now, the edges $e_v^1, e_v^2, \ldots, e_v^{n_v}$ each receive a label to denote which of them are part of the same path in $\mathrm{OPT}_{\mathrm{Gr}}(I)$.

This is done by first labeling edges that are not part of any optimal path belonging to I_v with 0. There are two kinds of such edges: On the one hand, those that are not part of any optimal path at all, on the other hand, there possibly is one edge that is part of an optimal path belonging to a later phase.

There now remain $n_v' \leq n_v$ edges, constituting $n_v'/2$ pairs of edges belonging to the same optimal path in I_v. These edges receive labels in $\{1, 2, \ldots, n_v'/2\}$, such that two edges receive the same label if and only if they are contained in the same optimal path.

Having the labels for phase I_v, the algorithm checks for each unblocked path $p \in I_v$ whether its edges incident to v are labeled identically with a strictly positive label and accepts p only if they are. If p is blocked, the algorithm naturally rejects it.

Claim 3. If the algorithm's partial solution on the requests preceding p agrees with $\mathrm{OPT}_{\mathrm{Gr}}(I)$, this will still be true after accepting or rejecting p according to this rule.

Inductively, we thus know that the algorithm perfectly recreates $\mathrm{OPT}_{\mathrm{Gr}}(I)$ if it has the labels. It remains to bound the length of the advice string necessary to convey them. We omit the derivation. □

Lastly, we again use a reduction of the online binary string guessing problem to derive lower bounds on the advice complexity of priority algorithms for DPA on trees with small approximation ratios. We need the following lemma.

Lemma 1. *Let T be a tree. T contains at least $\left\lceil \frac{1}{2} \sum_{v \in V(T)} \left\lfloor \frac{\deg(v)}{4} \right\rfloor \right\rceil$ pairwise edge-disjoint subtrees isomorphic to $K_{1,4}$ (the star tree S_4).*

Using the construction central to the proof of Theorem 8 on each such subtree allows us to prove the following theorem.

Theorem 10. *Let $1/2 \leq \varepsilon < 1$. The advice complexity of any adaptive-priority algorithm for DPA on trees with an approximation ratio smaller than $\frac{2}{1+\varepsilon}$ is at least $(1 - \mathcal{H}(\varepsilon)) \left\lceil \frac{1}{2} \sum_{v \in V(T)} \left\lfloor \frac{\deg(v)}{4} \right\rfloor \right\rceil$.*

6   Remarks on DPA on Grids

The DPA problem on grids – another generalization of DPA on paths – has already been analyzed in the online framework by Böckenhauer et al. [6]. The complication lies in the fact that requests no longer correspond to unique paths, i.e., that an online or priority algorithm has multiple options to satisfy a request.

It is quite easy to show a lower bound of 3/2 on the approximation ratio of any adaptive-priority algorithm without advice for DPA on grids – but only on a specific graph.

Theorem 11. *An adaptive-priority algorithm without advice for DPA on grids cannot be better than strictly 3/2-competitive on all grids.*

The proof uses a construction on the (3×3)-grid. We conjecture that this lower bound holds for all grids – except, of course, for the $1 \times n$ grid, $n \in \mathbb{N}$, since this is simply the path of length $n - 1$, on which DPA is optimally solvable by Theorem 1. While this lower bound might be difficult to prove in the general case, proving it for specific grid sizes should be possible in a manner similar to how we prove it for the (3×3)-grid. It is simply a matter of distinguishing finitely many cases, which can be done by a computer.

References

1. Angelopoulos, S., Borodin, A.: The power of priority algorithms for facility location and set cover. Algorithmica **40**(4), 271–291 (2004)
2. Barhum, K., et al.: On the power of advice and randomization for the disjoint path allocation problem. In: Geffert, V., Preneel, B., Rovan, B., Štuller, J., Tjoa, A.M. (eds.) SOFSEM 2014. LNCS, vol. 8327, pp. 89–101. Springer, Cham (2014). https://doi.org/10.1007/978-3-319-04298-5_9

3. Böckenhauer, H.-J., Corvelo Benz, N., Komm, D.: Call admission problems on trees with advice. In: Colbourn, C.J., Grossi, R., Pisanti, N. (eds.) IWOCA 2019. LNCS, vol. 11638, pp. 108–121. Springer, Cham (2019). https://doi.org/10.1007/978-3-030-25005-8_10

4. Böckenhauer, H.J., Hromkovič, J., Komm, D., Krug, S., Smula, J., Sprock, A.: The string guessing problem as a method to prove lower bounds on the advice complexity. Theor. Comput. Sci. **554**, 95–108 (2014)

5. Böckenhauer, H.J., Komm, D., Královič, R., Královič, R., Mömke, T.: Online algorithms with advice: the tape model. Inf. Comput. **254**, 59–83 (2017)

6. Böckenhauer, H.-J., Komm, D., Wegner, R.: Call admission problems on grids with advice (extended abstract). In: Epstein, L., Erlebach, T. (eds.) WAOA 2018. LNCS, vol. 11312, pp. 118–133. Springer, Cham (2018). https://doi.org/10.1007/978-3-030-04693-4_8

7. Borodin, A., Boyar, J., Larsen, K.S., Mirmohammadi, N.: Priority algorithms for graph optimization problems. Theor. Comput. Sci. **411**(1), 239–258 (2010)

8. Borodin, A., Boyar, J., Larsen, K.S., Pankratov, D.: Advice complexity of priority algorithms. Theory Comput. Syst. **64**(4), 593–625 (2020)

9. Borodin, A., El-Yaniv, R.: Online Computation and Competitive Analysis. Cambridge University Press, Cambridge (1998)

10. Borodin, A., Lucier, B.: On the limitations of greedy mechanism design for truthful combinatorial auctions. ACM Trans. Econ. Comput. **5**(1), 2:1–2:23 (2016)

11. Borodin, A., Nielsen, M.N., Rackoff, C.: (Incremental) priority algorithms. Algorithmica **37**(4), 295–326 (2003)

12. Boyar, J., Favrholdt, L.M., Kudahl, C., Larsen, K.S., Mikkelsen, J.W.: Online algorithms with advice: a survey. ACM Comput. Surv. **50**(2), 19:1–19:34 (2017)

13. Boyar, J., Larsen, K.S., Pankratov, D.: Advice complexity of adaptive priority algorithms. Technical report (2019)

14. Burjons, E., Frei, F., Smula, J., Wehner, D.: Length-weighted disjoint path allocation. In: Böckenhauer, H.-J., Komm, D., Unger, W. (eds.) Adventures Between Lower Bounds and Higher Altitudes. LNCS, vol. 11011, pp. 231–256. Springer, Cham (2018). https://doi.org/10.1007/978-3-319-98355-4_14

15. Carlisle, M.C., Lloyd, E.L.: On the k-coloring of intervals. Discret. Appl. Math. **59**(3), 225–235 (1995)

16. Dobrev, S., Královič, R., Pardubská, D.: How much information about the future is needed? In: Geffert, V., Karhumäki, J., Bertoni, A., Preneel, B., Návrat, P., Bieliková, M. (eds.) SOFSEM 2008. LNCS, vol. 4910, pp. 247–258. Springer, Heidelberg (2008). https://doi.org/10.1007/978-3-540-77566-9_21

17. Emek, Y., Fraigniaud, P., Korman, A., Rosén, A.: Online computation with advice. Theor. Comput. Sci. **412**(24), 2642–2656 (2011)

18. Faigle, U., Nawijn, W.M.: Note on scheduling intervals on-line. Discret. Appl. Math. **58**(1), 13–17 (1995)

19. Hromkovič, J., Královič, R., Královič, R.: Information complexity of online problems. In: Hliněný, P., Kučera, A. (eds.) MFCS 2010. LNCS, vol. 6281, pp. 24–36. Springer, Heidelberg (2010). https://doi.org/10.1007/978-3-642-15155-2_3

20. Komm, D.: An Introduction to Online Computation: Determinism, Randomization, Advice. Springer, Cham (2016). https://doi.org/10.1007/978-3-319-42749-2

21. Poloczek, M.: Bounds on greedy algorithms for MAX SAT. In: Demetrescu, C., Halldórsson, M.M. (eds.) ESA 2011. LNCS, vol. 6942, pp. 37–48. Springer, Heidelberg (2011). https://doi.org/10.1007/978-3-642-23719-5_4

22. Szpilrajn, E.: Sur l'extension de l'ordre partiel. Fundam. Math. **1**(16), 386–389 (1930)

On Two Variants of Induced Matchings

Juhi Chaudhary[1]([✉]) and B. S. Panda[2]

[1] Department of Computer Science, Ben-Gurion University of the Negev,
Beersheba, Israel
juhic@post.bgu.ac.il
[2] Department of Mathematics, Indian Institute of Technology Delhi,
New Delhi, India
bspanda@maths.iitd.ac.in

Abstract. A matching M in a graph G is an *induced matching* if the subgraph of G induced by M is the same as the subgraph of G induced by $S = \{v \in V(G) \mid v$ is incident on an edge of $M\}$. Given a graph G and a positive integer k, INDUCED MATCHING asks whether G has an induced matching of cardinality at least k. An induced matching M is *maximal* if it is not properly contained in any other induced matching of G. Given a graph G, MIN-MAX-IND-MATCHING is the problem of finding a maximal induced matching M in G of minimum cardinality. Given a bipartite graph $G = (X \uplus Y, E(G))$, SATURATED INDUCED MATCHING asks whether there exists an induced matching in G that saturates every vertex in Y. In this paper, we study MIN-MAX-IND-MATCHING and SATURATED INDUCED MATCHING. First, we strengthen the hardness result of MIN-MAX-IND-MATCHING by showing that its decision version remains NP-complete for perfect elimination bipartite graphs, star-convex bipartite graphs, and dually chordal graphs. Then, we show the hardness difference between INDUCED MATCHING and MIN-MAX-IND-MATCHING. Finally, we propose a linear-time algorithm to solve SATURATED INDUCED MATCHING.

Keywords: Matching · Induced matching · Minimum maximal induced matching · NP-completeness · Linear-time algorithm

1 Introduction

All graphs considered in this paper are simple, finite, connected, and undirected. For a graph G, let $V(G)$ denote its vertex set, and $E(G)$ denote its edge set. A matching M in a graph G is an *induced matching* if $G[M]$, the subgraph of G induced by M, is the same as $G[S]$, the subgraph of G induced by $S = \{v \in V(G) \mid v$ is incident on an edge of $M\}$. An induced matching M is *maximal* if M is not properly contained in any other induced matching of G. Given a graph G, MIN-MAX-IND-MATCHING asks to find a maximal induced matching M of minimum cardinality in G. Formally, the decision version of MIN-MAX-IND-MATCHING is defined as follows:

S.-Y. Hsieh et al. (Eds.): ICS 2022, CCIS 1723, pp. 37–48, 2022.
https://doi.org/10.1007/978-981-19-9582-8_4

DECIDE-MIN-MAX-IND-MATCHING:
Input: A graph G and a positive integer $k \leq |V(G)|$.
Question: Does there exist a maximal induced matching M in G such that $|M| \leq k$?

The *induced matching number* of G is the maximum cardinality of an induced matching among all induced matchings in G, and we denote it by $\mu_{\text{in}}(G)$. The *minimum maximal induced matching number* of G is the minimum cardinality of a maximal induced matching among all maximal induced matchings in G, and we denote it by $\mu'_{\text{in}}(G)$. It is also known as the *lower induced matching number* of G [8]. For an example, consider the graph G with vertex set $V(G) = \{a, b, c, d, e\}$ and edge set $E(G) = \{ab, bc, cd, de\}$. $M_1 = \{bc\}$ and $M_2 = \{ab, de\}$ are two maximal induced matchings of G and M_1 is a minimum maximal induced matching of G. Therefore, $\mu'_{\text{in}}(G) = 1$.

When we restrict INDUCED MATCHING by applying a constraint, which is to saturate one of the partitions of the bipartite graph, then we obtain SATURATED INDUCED MATCHING. The motivation for SATURATED INDUCED MATCHING comes directly from the applications of INDUCED MATCHING, which are secure communication networks, VLSI design, risk-free marriages, etc. One possible application of SATURATED INDUCED MATCHING in the secure communication channel is as follows: Suppose we have a bipartite graph $G = (X \uplus Y, E(G))$ where the partitions X and Y represent broadcasters and receivers, respectively, and the edges represent the communication capabilities between broadcasters and receivers. Now, we want to select $|Y|$ edges such that all receivers should get the information, and that too from a unique broadcaster. Moreover, there should be no edge between any two active channels (i.e., edges) to avoid any interception or leakage.

Related Work. MIN-MAX-IND-MATCHING is known to be polynomial-time solvable for graph classes like chordal graphs, circular-arc graphs, and AT-free graphs [15]. The weighted version of MIN-MAX-IND-MATCHING is known to be linear-time solvable for trees [11]. MIN-MAX-IND-MATCHING for random graphs has been studied in [6]. A graph G is *bi-size matched* if there exists $k \geq 1$ such that $|M| \in \{k, k+1\}$ for every maximal induced matching M in G. For bi-size matched graphs, DECIDE-MIN-MAX-IND-MATCHING is shown to be NP-complete in [16]. From the approximation point of view, MIN-MAX-IND-MATCHING cannot be approximated within a ratio of $n^{1-\epsilon}$ for any $\epsilon > 0$ unless P = NP [15]. The MIN-MAX version of other variants of matchings, like acyclic matching and uniquely restricted matching, have also been considered in the literature [4,5,12].

Our Contribution. In Sect. 3, we discuss MIN-MAX-IND-MATCHING. In particular, in Subsect. 3.1, we strengthen the hardness result of MIN-MAX-IND-MATCHING by showing that DECIDE-MIN-MAX-IND-MATCHING remains NP-complete for perfect elimination bipartite graphs, star-convex bipartite graphs, and dually chordal graphs. In Subsect. 3.2, we show the hardness difference between INDUCED MATCHING and MIN-MAX-IND-MATCHING by giving a graph class where one problem is polynomial-time solvable while the other problem is APX-hard, and vice-versa. In Sect. 4, we introduce SATURATED INDUCED MATCHING and propose a linear-time algorithm for the same.

2   Preliminaries

For a positive integer k, let $[k]$ denote the set $\{1, \ldots, k\}$. Given a graph G and a matching M, we use the notation V_M to denote the set of M-saturated vertices and $G[V_M]$ to denote the subgraph induced by V_M. In a graph G, the open and closed neighborhood of a vertex $v \in V(G)$ are denoted by $N(v)$ and $N[v]$, respectively, and defined by $N(v) = \{w \mid wv \in E(G)\}$ and $N[v] = N(v) \cup \{v\}$. The degree of a vertex v is $|N(v)|$ and is denoted by $d_G(v)$. When there is no ambiguity, we do not use the subscript G. If $d(v) = 1$, then v is a *pendant vertex*. For a graph G, the subgraph of G induced by $S \subseteq V(G)$ is denoted by $G[S]$, where $G[S] = (S, E_S)$ and $E_S = \{xy \in E(G) \mid x, y \in S\}$. A graph G is a *k-regular* graph if $d(v) = k$ for every vertex v of G. Let K_n and P_n denote a *complete graph* and a *path graph*, respectively. A graph G is a *bipartite graph* if its vertex set $V(G)$ can be partitioned into two sets, X and Y, such that every edge of G joins a vertex in X to a vertex in Y. We use the notation $G = (X \uplus Y, E(G))$ to represent the bipartite graph with vertex partitions X and Y. An edge xy of G is a *bisimplicial edge* if $N(x) \cup N(y)$ induces a complete bipartite subgraph of G. Let $\sigma = (x_1 y_1, x_2 y_2, \ldots, x_k y_k)$ be a sequence of pairwise nonadjacent edges of G. Let $S_j = \{x_1, x_2, \ldots, x_j\} \cup \{y_1, y_2, \ldots, y_j\}$ and $S_0 = \emptyset$. Then, σ is a *perfect edge elimination ordering* for G if each edge $x_{j+1} y_{j+1}$ is bisimplicial in $G_{j+1} = G[(X \uplus Y) \setminus S_j]$ for $j = 0, 1, \ldots, k-1$ and $G_{k+1} = G[(X \uplus Y) \setminus S_k]$ has no edge. A bipartite graph for which there exists a perfect edge elimination ordering is a *perfect elimination bipartite graph*. Introduced by Golumbic and Goss, the class of perfect elimination bipartite graphs is considered to be a bipartite counterpart of chordal graphs and can be recognized in polynomial time [9].

A bipartite graph G is a *tree-convex bipartite graph*, if a tree $T = (X, E^X)$ can be defined on the vertices of X, such that for every vertex y in Y, the neighborhood of y induces a subtree of T. Tree-convex bipartite graphs are recognizable in linear time, and an associated tree T can also be constructed in linear time [2]. A tree with at most one non-pendant vertex is called a *star*. If the tree T in a tree-convex bipartite graph G is a star, then G is a *star-convex bipartite graph*. The following proposition is a characterization of star-convex bipartite graphs.

Proposition 1 (Pandey and Panda [14]). *A bipartite graph $G = (X \uplus Y, E(G))$ is a star-convex bipartite graph if and only if there exists a vertex $x \in X$ such that every vertex $y \in Y$ is either a pendant vertex or is adjacent to x.*

A vertex $u \in N_G[v]$ in a graph G is a *maximum neighbor* of v if for all $w \in N_G[v]$, $N_G[w] \subseteq N_G[u]$. An ordering $\alpha = (v_1, \ldots, v_n)$ of $V(G)$ is a *maximum neighborhood ordering*, if v_i has a maximum neighbor in $G_i = G[\{v_i, \ldots, v_n\}]$ for all $i \in [n]$. A graph G is a *dually chordal graph* if it has a maximum neighborhood ordering. These graphs are a generalization of strongly chordal graphs and a superclass of interval graphs. Furthermore, note that dually chordal graphs can be recognized in linear time [1].

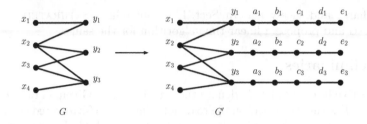

Fig. 1. An illustration of the construction of G' from G.

3 Minimum Maximal Induced Matching

3.1 NP-completeness Results

In this subsection, we first show that DECIDE-MIN-MAX-IND-MATCHING is NP-complete for perfect elimination bipartite graphs.

Theorem 2. DECIDE-MIN-MAX-IND-MATCHING *is* NP-*complete for perfect elimination bipartite graphs.*

Proof. Given a perfect elimination bipartite graph G and a matching M, it is easy to observe that DECIDE-MIN-MAX-IND-MATCHING is in NP. Next, we prove that DECIDE-MIN-MAX-IND-MATCHING is NP-hard for perfect elimination bipartite graphs by establishing a polynomial-time reduction from DECIDE-MIN-MAX-IND-MATCHING for bipartite graphs, which is known to be NP-hard [15].

Given a bipartite graph $G = (X \uplus Y, E(G))$, where $X = \{x_1, \ldots, x_p\}$ and $Y = \{y_1, \ldots, y_l\}$, an instance of DECIDE-MIN-MAX-IND-MATCHING, construct a graph $G' = (X' \uplus Y', E(G'))$, an instance of DECIDE-MIN-MAX-IND-MATCHING for perfect elimination bipartite graphs in the following way: For each $y_i \in Y$, introduce a path $P_i = y_i, a_i, b_i, c_i, d_i, e_i$ of length 5. Formally, $X' = X \cup \bigcup_{i \in [l]} \{a_i, c_i, e_i\}$, $Y' = Y \cup \bigcup_{i \in [l]} \{b_i, d_i\}$ and $E(G') = E(G) \cup \bigcup_{i \in [l]} \{y_i a_i, a_i b_i, b_i c_i, c_i d_i, d_i e_i\}$. See Fig. 1 for an illustration of the construction of G' from G. Note that G' is a perfect elimination bipartite graph as $(e_1 d_1, \ldots, e_l d_l, c_1 b_1, \ldots, c_l b_l, a_1 y_1, \ldots, a_l y_l)$ is a perfect edge elimination ordering of G'. Now, the following claim is sufficient to complete the proof of the theorem.

Claim 3. *G has a maximal induced matching of cardinality at most k if and only if G' has a maximal induced matching of cardinality at most $k + l$.*

Proof. Let M be a maximal induced matching in G of cardinality at most k. Define a matching $M' = M \cup \bigcup_{i \in [l]} \{b_i c_i\}$ in G'. By the definition of an induced matching, note that M' is a maximal induced matching in G' and $|M'| \leq k + l$.

Conversely, let M be a minimum maximal induced matching in G' of cardinality at most $k + l$. Since M is maximal, $|M \cap \{b_i c_i, c_i d_i, d_i e_i\}| \geq 1$ for each $i \in [l]$. Furthermore, since M is an induced matching, $|M \cap \{b_i c_i, c_i d_i, d_i e_i\}| \leq 1$ for each $i \in [l]$. Thus, for each $i \in [l]$, $|M \cap \{b_i c_i, c_i d_i, d_i e_i\}| = 1$.

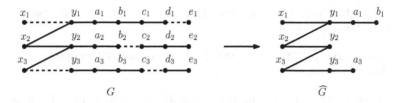

Fig. 2. An illustration of the construction of $\widehat{G}$ from G'. Here, the dashed edges show a minimum maximal induced matching in G'.

Now, we label each $y_i \in Y$ as either Type-I vertex, Type-II vertex or Type-III vertex depending on whether $b_i c_i, c_i d_i$ or $d_i e_i$ belongs to M. For every $i \in [l]$, if y_i is a Type-I vertex, remove the vertices a_i, b_i, c_i, d_i, e_i from G', if y_i is a Type-II vertex, remove the vertices b_i, c_i, d_i, e_i from G', and if y_i is a Type-III vertex, remove the vertices c_i, d_i, e_i from G'. After removing all the desired vertices, let us call the graph so obtained as $\widehat{G}$. See Fig. 2 for an illustration of the construction of $\widehat{G}$ from G'. Let M be the restriction of M to $\widehat{G}$. Clearly, $\widehat{M}$ is a maximal induced matching in $\widehat{G}$ and $|\widehat{M}| = (k + l) - l = k$. Now, we claim that there exists a maximal induced matching in G of cardinality at most k. If $\widehat{M} \subset E(G)$, then we are done, as $\widehat{M}$ will be a desired maximal induced matching in G of cardinality at most k. So, let us assume that $\widehat{M}$ contains an edge from the path P_j for some fixed $j \in [l]$.

If $y_j a_j \in \widehat{M}$ and y_j is a Type-II (or Type-III) vertex, then we claim that one of the following conditions will hold:

i) $(\widehat{M} \setminus \{y_j a_j\}) \cup \{y_j x_k\}$ is a maximal induced matching in $\widehat{G}$ for some $x_k \in N(y_j)$.
ii) $\widehat{M} \setminus \{y_j a_j\}$ is a maximal induced matching in $\widehat{G} \setminus \{a_j\}$ or $\widehat{G} \setminus \{a_j, b_j\}$ depending on whether y_j is a Type-II vertex or a Type-III vertex, respectively.

If Condition i) holds, then we are done. So, let us assume that $(\widehat{M} \setminus \{y_j a_j\}) \cup \{y_j x_k\}$ is not a maximal induced matching in $\widehat{G}$ for any $x_k \in N(y_j)$. This implies that the edges incident on y_j (except $y_j a_j$) are dominated by edges from the edge set $E(G) \cap \widehat{M}$. So, in other words, if we remove the edge $y_j a_j$ from $\widehat{M}$, then all edges except $y_j a_j$ will be dominated by the rest of $\widehat{M}$. This further implies that $\widehat{M} \setminus \{y_j a_j\}$ is a maximal induced matching in $\widehat{G} \setminus \{a_j\}$ or $\widehat{G} \setminus \{a_j, b_j\}$ depending on whether y_j is a Type-II or a Type-III vertex. Similarly, if $a_j b_j \in \widehat{M}$, then we claim that either $(\widehat{M} \setminus \{a_j b_j\}) \cup \{y_j a_j\}$ is a maximal induced matching in $\widehat{G}$ or $\widehat{M} \setminus \{a_j b_j\}$ is a maximal induced matching in $\widehat{G} \setminus \{a_j, b_j\}$. So, we have proved that every edge $e \in \widehat{M} \cap P_j$ can either be replaced by an edge in $E(G)$ or can be removed without disturbing the maximality of the matching restricted to $E(G)$. Therefore, G has a maximal induced matching of cardinality at most k. □

Hence, DECIDE-MIN-MAX-IND-MATCHING is NP-complete for perfect elimination bipartite graphs. □

Next, we show that DECIDE-MIN-MAX-IND-MATCHING is NP-complete for star-convex bipartite graphs.

Theorem 4. DECIDE-MIN-MAX-IND-MATCHING *is* NP-*complete for star-convex bipartite graphs.*

Proof. Given a star-convex bipartite graph G and a matching M, it is easy to observe that DECIDE-MIN-MAX-IND-MATCHING is in NP. Next, we prove that DECIDE-MIN-MAX-IND-MATCHING is NP-hard for star-convex bipartite graphs by establishing a polynomial-time reduction from DECIDE-MIN-MAX-IND-MATCHING for bipartite graphs, which is known to be NP-hard [15].

Given a bipartite graph $G = (X \uplus Y, E(G))$, where $X = \{x_1, \ldots, x_p\}$ and $Y = \{y_1, \ldots, y_q\}$ for $q \geq 3$, an instance of DECIDE-MIN-MAX-IND-MATCHING, we construct a star-convex bipartite graph $G' = (X' \uplus Y', E(G'))$, an instance of DECIDE-MIN-MAX-IND-MATCHING in the following way:

- Introduce a vertex x_0 and make x_0 adjacent to y_i for each $i \in [q]$.
- Introduce the vertex set $\{\overline{y}_1, \ldots, \overline{y}_q\}$ and make x_0 adjacent to $\overline{y}_i$ for each $i \in [q]$.
- Introduce the edge set $\bigcup_{i,j \in [q]} \{x_{ij} y_{ij}\}$. For each $i \in [q]$, make $\overline{y}_i$ adjacent to x_{ij} for every $j \in [q]$.

Formally, $X' = X \cup \{x_0\} \cup \bigcup_{i,j \in [q]} \{x_{ij}\}$ and $Y' = Y \cup \bigcup_{i \in [q]} \{\overline{y}_i\} \bigcup_{i,j \in [q]} \{y_{ij}\}$. See Fig. 3 for an illustration of the construction of G' from G. Note that every vertex in Y' is either adjacent to x_0 or is a pendant vertex. So, by Proposition 1, it is clear that the graph G' is a star-convex bipartite graph. Now, the following claim is sufficient to complete the proof of the theorem.

Claim 5. *G has a maximal induced matching of cardinality at most k if and only if G' has a maximal induced matching of cardinality at most $k + q$.*

Proof. Let M be a maximal induced matching in G of cardinality at most k. Define a matching M' in G' as follows: $M' = M \cup \bigcup_{i \in [q]} \{\overline{y}_i x_{ii}\}$. Clearly, M' is a maximal induced matching in G' and $|M'| \leq k + q$.

Conversely, let M be a minimum maximal induced matching in G' of cardinality at most $k + q$. Let M_G denote a maximum induced matching in G. Note that $|M_G| \leq q$. Now consider the following matching: $M' = \bigcup_{i \in [q]} \{\overline{y}_i x_{ii}\} \cup M_G$. Note that M' is a maximal induced matching in G' of cardinality at most $2q$. Thus, $|M| \leq 2q$. Now, we will show that there exists a maximal induced matching in G of cardinality at most k.

If $x_0 \overline{y}_i \in M$ for some fixed $i \in [q]$, then $\overline{y}_k x_{kj} \notin M$ for any $k, j \in [q]$. Also, $x_0 \overline{y}_k \notin M$ for any $k \in [q] \setminus \{i\}$. So, edges of the form $x_{kj} y_{kj}$ must belong to M for every $k \in [q] \setminus \{i\}$ and $j \in [q]$. Thus, $|M| \geq q(q-1) + 1$, which is a contradiction to the fact that $|M| \leq 2q$. Therefore, $x_0 \overline{y}_i \notin M$ for any $i \in [q]$. Now, there are two possibilities. If $x_{ij} y_{ij} \in M$ for some $i \in [q]$, then $x_{ij} y_{ij} \in M$ for every $j \in [q]$. On the other hand, if for each $i \in [q]$ there exists some $j \in [q]$ such that $\overline{y}_i x_{ij} \in M$, then only q edges will suffice to make M maximal. So, in

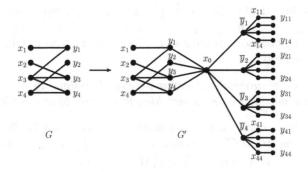

Fig. 3. An illustration of the construction of G' from G.

any minimum maximal induced matching M, it is always better to choose edges of the form $\overline{y}_i x_{ij}$ in M for all $i, j \in [q]$. Thus, M restricted to $E(G)$ is a desired maximal induced matching in G of cardinality at most k.   □

Hence, by Claim 5, DECIDE-MIN-MAX-IND-MATCHING is NP-complete for star-convex bipartite graphs.   □

As the class of tree-convex bipartite graphs is a superclass of star-convex bipartite graphs, the following corollary is a consequence of Theorem 4.

Corollary 6. DECIDE-MIN-MAX-IND-MATCHING *is* NP-*complete for tree-convex bipartite graphs.*

Next, we show that DECIDE-MIN-MAX-IND-MATCHING is NP-complete for dually chordal graphs. Note that the reduction is similar to the reduction given for star-convex bipartite graphs.

Theorem 7. DECIDE-MIN-MAX-IND-MATCHING *is* NP-*complete for dually chordal graphs.*

Proof. Given a dually chordal graph G and a subset $M \subseteq E(G)$, it can be checked in polynomial time whether M is a maximal induced matching in G or not. So, DECIDE-MIN-MAX-IND-MATCHING belongs to the class NP for dually chordal graphs. To show the NP-hardness, we give a polynomial-time reduction from DECIDE-MIN-MAX-IND-MATCHING for general graphs, which is already known to be NP-complete [15].

Given a graph G, where $V(G) = \{v_1 \dots, v_n\}$ and $n \geq 3$, an instance of DECIDE-MIN-MAX-IND-MATCHING, we construct a dually chordal graph G', an instance of DECIDE-MIN-MAX-IND-MATCHING in the following way:

– Introduce a vertex v_0 and make v_0 adjacent to v_i for each $i \in [n]$.
– Introduce the vertex set $\{w_1, \dots, w_n\}$ and make v_0 adjacent to w_i for each $i \in [n]$.
– Introduce the edge set $\bigcup_{i,j \in [n]} \{p_{ij} q_{ij}\}$. For each $i \in [n]$, make w_i adjacent to p_{ij} for every $j \in [n]$.

Clearly, G' is a dually chordal graph as $(q_{11}, \ldots q_{1n}, q_{21}, \ldots q_{2n}, \ldots, q_{n1}, \ldots$ $q_{nn}, p_{11}, \ldots p_{1n}, p_{21}, \ldots p_{2n}, \ldots, p_{n1}, \ldots p_{nn}, w_1, w_2, \ldots, w_n, v_1, v_2, \ldots, v_n, v_0)$ is a maximum neighborhood ordering of G'. Now, the following claim is sufficient to complete the proof.

Claim 8. *G has a maximal induced matching of cardinality at most k if and only if G' has a maximal induced matching of cardinality at most $k + n$.*

Proof. Let M be a maximal induced matching in G of cardinality at most k. Define a matching M' in G' as follows: $M' = M \cup \bigcup_{i \in [n]} \{w_i p_{ii}\}$. Clearly, M' is a maximal induced matching in G' and $|M'| \leq k + n$.

Conversely, let M be a minimum maximal induced matching in G' of cardinality at most $k + n$. Now, we will show that there exists a maximal induced matching in G of cardinality at most k. Let M_G denote a maximum induced matching in G. Note that $|M_G| \leq \frac{n}{2}$.

If $v_0 w_i \in M$ for some fixed $i \in [n]$, then $w_k p_{kj} \notin M$ for any $k, j \in [n]$. Also, $v_0 w_k \notin M$ for any $k \in [n] \setminus \{i\}$. So, edges of the form $p_{kj} q_{kj}$ must belong to M for each $k \in [n] \setminus \{i\}$ and $j \in [n]$. Thus, $|M| \geq n(n-1) + 1$, which is a contradiction as $M' = \bigcup_{i \in [n]} \{w_i p_{ii}\} \cup M_G$ is a maximal induced matching in G' of cardinality at most $\frac{n}{2} + n$ and cardinality of M cannot be greater than the cardinality of M'. Therefore, $v_0 w_i \notin M$ for any $i \in [n]$. Now, there are two possibilities. If $p_{ij} q_{ij} \in M$ for some $i, j \in [n]$, then $p_{ik} q_{ik} \in M$ for every $k \in [n]$. On the other hand, if for each $i \in [n]$ there exists some $j \in [n]$ such that $w_i p_{ij} \in M$, then only n edges will suffice to make M maximal. So, in any minimum maximal induced matching M, it is always better to choose edges of the form $w_i p_{ij}$ in M for all $i, j \in [n]$. Thus, M restricted to $E(G)$ is a desired maximal induced matching in G of cardinality at most k.   □

Hence, DECIDE-MIN-MAX-IND-MATCHING is NP-complete for dually chordal graphs.   □

3.2   Hardness Difference Between Induced Matching and Minimum Maximal Induced Matching

In this subsection, we show that MIN-MAX-IND-MATCHING and INDUCED MATCHING differ in hardness; that is, there are graph classes in which one problem is polynomial-time solvable while the other is APX-hard, and vice versa. For this purpose, consider the following definition.

Definition 9 (GC_3 graph). *A graph H is a GC_3 graph if it can be constructed from some graph G, where $V(G) = \{v_1, \ldots, v_n\}$ in the following way: For each vertex v_i of G, introduce a cycle v_i, a_i, b_i, v_i of length 3 in H. Formally, $V(H) = V(G) \cup \bigcup_{i \in [n]} \{a_i, b_i\}$ and $E(H) = E(G) \cup \bigcup_{i \in [n]} \{v_i a_i, a_i b_i, v_i b_i\}$.*

Now, consider the following straightforward observation that follows from the definition of maximal induced matching.

Observation 10. *Let M be an induced matching in a GC_3 graph H. Then, M is maximal in H iff for each $i \in [n]$, either v_i is saturated by M or $a_i b_i \in M$.*

Now, we will show that INDUCED MATCHING is polynomial-time solvable for GC_3 graphs, and MIN-MAX-IND-MATCHING is APX-hard for GC_3 graphs.

Theorem 11. *Let H be a GC_3 graph constructed from a graph G, where $V(G) = \{v_1, \ldots, v_n\}$, as in Definition 9. Then, $\mu_{\text{in}}(H) = n$.*

Proof. Let $M = \bigcup_{i \in [n]} \{a_i b_i\}$. It is easy to see that $|M| = n$ and $G[V_M]$ is a disjoint union of $K_2's$. So, M is an induced matching in H. Hence, $\mu_{\text{in}}(H) \geq n$.

Next, consider a maximum induced matching, say M_{in} in H. If $|M_{in}| > n$, then M_{in} must contain at least one edge from the edge set $E(G)$, i.e., $v_i v_j \in M_{in}$ for some $i, j \in [n]$. Define $M = (M_{in} \setminus \{v_i v_j\}) \cup \{a_i b_i, a_j b_j\}$. By Observation 10, M is an induced matching in H and $|M| > |M_{in}|$, which is a contradiction as M_{in} is a maximum induced matching in H. Thus, $\mu_{\text{in}}(H) \leq n$. □

Proposition 12 (Gotthilf and Lewenstein [10]). *Let G be a graph with maximum degree Δ. Then, $\mu_{\text{in}}(G) \geq \frac{|E(G)|}{1.5\Delta^2 - 0.5\Delta}$.*

Proposition 13 (Duckworth et al. [7]). INDUCED MATCHING *is APX-complete for r-regular graphs for every fixed integer $r \geq 3$.*

Theorem 14. MIN-MAX-IND-MATCHING *is APX-hard for GC_3 graphs.*

Proof. Given a 3-regular graph G, an instance of INDUCED MATCHING, we construct a GC_3 graph H, an instance of MIN-MAX-IND-MATCHING by attaching a cycle v_i, a_i, b_i, v_i of length 3 to each $v_i, i \in [n]$. Next, let Type-A edges $= \bigcup_{i \in [n]} \{a_i b_i\}$ and Type-B edges $= E(G)$. Now, consider the following claim whose proof follows from Observation 10 and the fact that every edge of the form $v_i a_i$ or $v_i b_i$ (where $i \in [n]$) can be replaced with $a_i b_i$.

Claim 15. *For every maximal induced matching M in a GC_3 graph H, there exists a maximal induced matching M' such that $|M'| = |M|$ and M' contains edges of Type-A and Type-B only.*

Claim 16. *Let M_B^* be a minimum maximal induced matching in H and M_A^* be a maximum induced matching in G. Then, $|M_B^*| = n - |M_A^*|$.*

Proof. Since M_A^* is a maximum induced matching in G, this implies that $2|M_A^*|$ vertices are saturated, and $n - 2|M_A^*|$ vertices are unsaturated by M_A^* in G. Define a matching $M_B = M_A^* \cup \{a_i b_i \mid v_i \text{ is unsaturated by } M_A^*\}$ in H. By Observation 10, M_B is a maximal induced matching in H. Since $|M_B| = (|M_A^*| + n - 2|M_A^*|) = n - |M_A^*|$, $|M_B^*| \leq n - |M_A^*|$.

By Claim 15, there exists a minimum maximal induced matching M_B^* in H such that M_B^* contains edges of Type-A and Type-B only. Let $T^* \cup S^*$ be a partition of M_B^* such that T^* contains Type-A edges and S^* contains Type-B edges. Since M_B^* is maximal, $|T^*| = n - 2|S^*|$. This implies that $|M_B^*| = |S^*| + (n - 2|S^*|) = n - |S^*|$. Since $S^* \subset M_B^*$, S^* is an induced matching in G and $|S^*| \leq |M_A^*|$. As $|S^*| = n - |M_B^*|$, $n - |M_B^*| \leq |M_A^*|$. This completes the proof of Claim 16. □

We now return to the proof of Theorem 14. By Proposition 12, we know that any 3-regular graph G satisfies the inequality $|M_A^*| \geq \frac{n}{8}$. Therefore, we have $|M_B^*| = n - |M_A^*| \leq 8|M_A^*| - |M_A^*| = 7|M_A^*|$. Further, let M be a maximal induced matching in H. By Claim 15, there exists a maximal induced matching in H such that $|M_B| = |M|$ and M_B contains edges of Type-A and Type-B only. Let $T_B \cup S_B$ be a partition of M_B such that T_B contains Type-A edges and S_B contains Type-B edges. Since M_B is maximal, $|T_B| = (n - 2|S_B|)$. Hence, $|M_B| = n - |S_B|$. Here, S_B is a desired induced matching in G. Let $S_B = M_A$. Now, $|M_A^*| - |M_A| = |M_A^*| - |M_A| + n - n = (n - |M_A|) - (n - |M_A^*|) \leq |(|M_B^*| - M_B)|$. From these two inequalities and Proposition 13, it follows that it is an L-reduction with $\alpha = 7$ and $\beta = 1$. Thus, MIN-MAX-IND-MATCHING is APX-hard for GC_3 graphs.   □

Next, consider the following definition.

Definition 17 (Gx_0 graph). *A bipartite graph $G' = (X' \uplus Y', E(G'))$ is a Gx_0 graph if it can be constructed from a bipartite graph $G = (X \uplus Y, E(G))$, where $Y = \{y_1, \ldots, y_l\}$ in the following way: Introduce a new vertex x_0 and make x_0 adjacent to each $y_i \in Y$. Formally, $X' = X \cup \{x_0\}, Y' = Y$, and $E(G') = E(G) \cup \{x_0 y_i \mid y_i \in Y\}$.*

Now, we show that MIN-MAX-IND-MATCHING is polynomial-time solvable for Gx_0 graphs, and INDUCED MATCHING is APX-hard for Gx_0 graphs.

Theorem 18. *Let $G' = (X' \uplus Y', E(G'))$ be a Gx_0 graph constructed from a bipartite graph $G = (X \uplus Y, E(G))$, where $Y = \{y_1, \ldots, y_l\}$, as in Definition 17. Then, $\mu'_{in}(G') = 1$.*

Proposition 19 (Panda et al. [13]). *Let G' be a Gx_0 graph constructed from an r-regular ($r \geq 3$) bipartite graph G by introducing a vertex x_0 and making x_0 adjacent to every vertex in one of the partitions of G. Then, G has an induced matching of cardinality at least k if and only if G' has an induced matching of cardinality at least k.*

Now, we are ready to prove the following theorem by giving a polynomial-time reduction from INDUCED MATCHING.

Theorem 20. INDUCED MATCHING *is APX-hard for Gx_0 graphs.*

Proof. Given an r-regular graph G, an instance of INDUCED MATCHING, we construct a Gx_0 graph H, an instance of INDUCED MATCHING by introducing a vertex x_0 and making it adjacent to every vertex of G (see Definition 17). Now, we have the following claim from Proposition 19.

Claim 21. *If M_B^* is a maximum induced matching in G' and M_A^* is a maximum induced matching in G, then $|M_B^*| = |M_A^*|$.*

We now return to the proof of Theorem 20. By Claim 21, it is clear that $|M_B^*| = |M_A^*|$. Further, let M_B be an induced matching in G'. By Proposition 19,

---

Algorithm 1. ALGO-SIM(G)

Input: A bipartite graph $G = (X \uplus Y, E(G))$;
Output: A saturated induced matching M_S or a variable reporting that G has no saturated induced matching;
$M_S \leftarrow \emptyset$;
for *every* $y \in Y$ **do**
  if (*there exists some* $x \in N(y)$ *such that* $d(x) = 1$) **then**
    $\lfloor$ $M_S \leftarrow M_S \cup \{xy\}$;
  else
    $\lfloor$ **return** 0;
return M_S;

---

there exists an induced matching M_A in G such that $|M_A| \geq |M_B|$. By Claim 21, it follows that $|M_A^*| - |M_A| \leq |M_B^*| - M_B|$. From these two inequalities, it follows that it is an L-reduction with $\alpha = 1$ and $\beta = 1$. Therefore, MIN-MAX-IND-MATCHING is APX-hard for Gx_0 graphs. $\square$

4   Saturated Induced Matching

In this section, we will first introduce SATURATED INDUCED MATCHING and then propose a linear-time algorithm to solve it.

SATURATED INDUCED MATCHING:
Input: A bipartite graph $G = (X \uplus Y, E(G))$.
Question: Does there exist an induced matching in G that saturates each vertex of Y?

It is well-known that INDUCED MATCHING is NP-complete for bipartite graphs [3]. However, when we restrict INDUCED MATCHING to SATURATED INDUCED MATCHING, then the problem becomes linear-time solvable. To prove this, consider the following lemma.

Lemma 22. *Let M_S be an induced matching in a bipartite graph $G = (X \uplus Y, E(G))$ that saturates all vertices of Y. Then, an edge $x_i y_j \in M_S$ only if $d(x_i) = 1$.*

Proof. Targeting a contradiction, let us suppose that there exists an edge $x_i y_j \in M_S$ such that $d(x_i) > 1$. Let $y_k \in Y \setminus \{y_j\}$ be such that $x_i y_k \in E(G)$. Now, since $x_i y_j \in M_S$, therefore $x_i y_k \notin M_S$ (as $x_i y_k$ and $x_i y_j$ are adjacent). However, since M_S is a saturated induced matching, this implies that there is an edge incident on y_k that belongs to M_S. This, in turn, implies that the edge $x_i y_k$ is dominated twice, a contradiction to the fact that M_S is an induced matching. $\square$

Based on Lemma 22, we have Algorithm 1 that finds a saturated induced matching M_S in a given bipartite graph, if one exists. Since we are just traversing the adjacency list of every vertex in the X partition of the bipartite graph G, we have the following theorem.

Theorem 23. *Given a bipartite graph G, the* SATURATED INDUCED MATCHING *problem can be solved in* $\mathcal{O}(|V(G)| + |E(G)|)$ *time.*

5   Open Problems

Exploring the parameterized complexity of MIN-MAX-IND-MATCHING is an interesting future direction.

References

1. Brandstädt, A., Dragan, F.F., Chepoi, V.D., Voloshin, V.: Dually chordal graphs. SIAM J. Discrete Math. **11**(3), 437–455 (1998)
2. Bao, F.S., Zhang, Y.: A review of tree convex sets test. Comput. Intell. **28**, 358–372 (2012)
3. Cameron, K.: Induced matchings. Discrete Appl. Math. **24**(1–3), 97–102 (1989)
4. Chaudhary, J., Mishra, S., Panda, B. S.: On the complexity of minimum maximal acyclic matching. In: Zhang, Y., Miao, D., Möhring, R. (eds.) Computing and Combinatorics. COCOON 2022. LNCS, vol. 13595, pp. 106–117. Springer, cham (2022). https://doi.org/10.1007/978-3-031-22105-7_10
5. Chaudhary, J., Panda, B.S.: On the complexity of minimum maximal uniquely restricted matching. Theor. Comput. Sci. **882**, 15–28 (2021)
6. Clark, L.: The strong matching number of a random graph. Australas. J. Comb. **24**, 47–58 (2001)
7. Duckworth, W., Manlove, D.F., Zito, M.: On the approximability of the maximum induced matching problem. J. Discrete Algorithms **3**(1), 79–91 (2005)
8. Goddard, W., Hedetniemi, S.M., Hedetniemi, S.T., Laskar, R.: Generalized subgraph-restricted matchings in graphs. Discrete Math. **293**(1–3), 129–138 (2005)
9. Golumbic, M.C., Goss, C.F.: Perfect elimination and chordal bipartite graphs. J. Graph Theory **2**(2), 155–163 (1978)
10. Gotthilf, Z., Lewenstein, M.: Tighter approximations for maximum induced matchings in regular graphs. In: Erlebach, T., Persinao, G. (eds.) WAOA 2005. LNCS, vol. 3879, pp. 270–281. Springer, Heidelberg (2006). https://doi.org/10.1007/11671411_21
11. Lepin, V.V.: A linear algorithm for computing of a minimum weight maximal induced matching in an edge-weighted tree. Electron. Notes in Discrete Math. **24**, 111–116 (2006)
12. Panda, B.S., Pandey, A.: On the complexity of minimum cardinality maximal uniquely restricted matching in graphs. In: Arumugam, S., Bagga, J., Beineke, L.W., Panda, B.S. (eds.) ICTCSDM 2016. LNCS, vol. 10398, pp. 218–227. Springer, Cham (2017). https://doi.org/10.1007/978-3-319-64419-6_29
13. Panda, B.S., Pandey, A., Chaudhary, J., Dane, P., Kashyap, M.: Maximum weight induced matching in some subclasses of bipartite graphs. J. Comb. Optim. **40**, 1–20 (2020)
14. Pandey, A., Panda, B.S.: Domination in some subclasses of bipartite graphs. Discrete Appl. Math. **252**, 51–66 (2019)
15. Orlovich, Y.L., Finke, G., Gordon, V., Zverovich, I.: Approximability results for the maximum and minimum maximal induced matching problems. Discrete Optim. **5**(3), 584–593 (2008)
16. Orlovich, Y.L., Zverovich, I.E.: Maximal induced matchings of minimum/maximum size. Technical report, DIMACS TR 2004-26 (2004)

A Tree Structure for Local Diagnosis in Multiprocessor Systems Under Comparison Model

Meirun Chen[1], Cheng-Kuan Lin[2(✉)], and Kung-Jui Pai[3]

[1] School of Mathematics and Statistics, Xiamen University of Technology,
Xiamen, China
mrchen@xmut.edu.cn

[2] Department of Computer Science, National Yang Ming Chiao Tung University,
Hsinchu, Taiwan
cklin@nycu.edu.tw

[3] Department of Industrial Engineering and Management, Ming Chi University
of Technology, New Taipei City, Taiwan
poter@mail.mcut.edu.tw

Abstract. If we only care about the status of a particular vertex, instead of doing global diagnosis, Hsu and Tan introduced the concept of local diagnosis and proposed an extended star structure to diagnose a vertex under comparison model. Usually, there is a gap between the local diagnosability and the lower bound guaranteed by the extended star structure mentioned above. In this paper, we propose a new testing structure and corresponding diagnosis algorithm to diagnose a vertex under comparison model to better evaluate the local diagnosability. The local diagnosability of a vertex is upper bounded by its degree in the system. If the local diagnosability of each vertex equals to its degree in the system then we say this system has the strong local diagnosability property. Based on the new structure, we show that the n-dimensional star graph S_n with faulty links has the strong local diagnosability property provided that each vertex connects to at least three fault-free links. Simulations are presented to show the performance of our tree structure.

1 Introduction

As the number of processors increases, the communication link between processors becomes more and more complex. Therefore, one cannot avoid some processors failure. How to identify the faulty processors accurately is the key to ensure the normal operation of the network. System-level diagnostics is to distinguish each processor failure or not, and then replace the faulty processors by fault-free ones to ensure the reliable operation of the system. A system is called t-diagnosable if all faulty processors can be identified without replacement as long as the number of faulty processors does not exceed t [11]. The diagnosability of a system is the maximum value of t such that it is t-diagnosable [11]. That is, the maximum number of faulty processors that can be identified in this system.

S.-Y. Hsieh et al. (Eds.): ICS 2022, CCIS 1723, pp. 49–60, 2022.
https://doi.org/10.1007/978-981-19-9582-8_5

To diagnose a multiprocessor system, several different models have been proposed [11]. One major method is called the comparison model, which was proposed by Maeng and Malek [8]. Under this model, the system performs diagnosis using a one-to-two testing: each processor sends two identical signals to each pair of its distinct neighbors and compares their responses. The result of the comparison depends on whether the two responses are agreed or not. Collecting all the comparison results, the system can decide the status of each node.

If we only want to know the state of a special node, Hsu and Tan [6] introduced the concept of local diagnosis. A local structure called an extended star was presented for guaranteeing a processor's local diagnosability. Occasionally, the local diagnosability guaranteed by the extended star is optimal. Usually, it is underestimated. In order to better evaluate the local diagnosability of a node, in this work we propose a tree structure and evaluate the local diagnosability of a node by the existence of this structure.

The rest of this paper is organized as follows: Sect. 2 provides preliminaries and background of system diagnosis. Section 3 introduces a new tree structure and the related algorithm. Section 4 considers the strong local diagnosability property of star graphs with faulty links. Simulations are presented in Sect. 5. In Sect. 6, we draw a conclusion.

2   Preliminaries

For standard graph-theoretic terminology, we follow [2,7]. In this paper, we use a finite and undirected graph $G(V, E)$ to represent a multiprocessor system where V is the node set of processors of the system and E is the edge set of communication links between two processors.

A graph H is a subgraph of a graph G if $V(H) \subseteq V(G)$ and $E(H) \subseteq E(G)$. Let S be a subset of $V(G)$. We say that H is a subgraph of G induced by S if $V(H) = S$ and $E(H) = \{(u, v) \mid u, v \in V(S) \text{ and } (u, v) \in E(G)\}$. Let u be any node in G. The neighborhood of u in G, $N_G(u) = \{v \mid (u, v) \in E(G)\}$, is the set of nodes adjacent to u. The degree of u in G, $\deg_G(u) = |N_G(u)|$, is the number of edges incident with u in G. We use $\delta(G) = \min_{v \in V(G)}\{\deg_G(v)\}$ to denote the minimum degree of the nodes of G. A path is a distinct vertex sequence $v_0 v_1 \cdots v_k$ such that v_i is adjacent to v_{i+1} for any $i \in \{0, 1, \ldots, k - 1\}$. A vertex sequence $v_0 v_1 \cdots v_k v_0$ forms a cycle if $v_0, v_1, \ldots, v_k$ are mutually distinct and v_i is adjacent to v_{i+1} for any $i \in \{0, 1, \ldots, k\}$ where $v_{k+1} = v_0$. For any two vertices $u, v \in V(G)$, the distance between u and v denoted by $dist_G(u, v)$ is the number of the edges in a shortest path connects u and v. The girth $g(G)$ of a graph G is the number of the edges in a shortest cycle of G. The diameter of a graph G is $\max\{dist_G(u, v) \mid u, v \in V(G)\}$.

A graph G is bipartite if the vertex set $V(G)$ can be partitioned into two subsets V_1 and V_2 such that each edge of G has one endpoint in V_1 and the other endpoint in V_2. A subset M of $E(G)$ is called a matching in G if its elements are edges and no two are adjacent in G. We say a vertex u is independent to a matching M if u is not the endpoint of any element of M. A vertex subset $V' \subseteq V(G)$ is independent if no two vertices of V' are adjacent.

Let A and B be any two sets. The difference set for A and B, $A - B$, is $\{x \mid x \in A$ and $x \notin B\}$, and the symmetric difference of A and B is $A \Delta B = (A - B) \cup (B - A)$.

A graph G is called t-diagnosable if the number of faulty nodes does not exceed t then all faulty nodes in G can be identified without replacement [11]. The diagnostic strategy of MM* model are proposed as follows.

Comparison-based diagnosis [5, 9] requests a node to allocate the same system tasks to two distinct nodes and compare their responses. Let w, x and y be any three distinct nodes which $(w, x), (w, y) \in E(G)$. We use $\sigma_w(x, y)$ to represent the result of w compare the responses of x and y. Suppose that w is fault-free. If both x and y are fault-free, then $\sigma_w(x, y) = 0$; otherwise, $\sigma_w(x, y) = 1$. Suppose w is faulty. Then the test result is unreliable, that is, $\sigma_w(x, y) \in \{0, 1\}$ no matter x and y are faulty or not. That is, if F is the set of faulty nodes then the outcome of a test result under comparison model is

$$
\sigma_w(x, y) = \begin{cases} 0, & \text{if } \{w, x, y\} \cap F = \emptyset \\ 1, & \text{if } w \notin F \text{ and } \{x, y\} \cap F \neq \emptyset \\ 0 \text{ or } 1, & \text{if } w \in F \end{cases}
$$

The necessary and sufficient conditions to identify if a pair of distinct faulty node subset under comparison model is distinguishable or not, follow.

Theorem 1. *[12] For any two distinct node subsets F_1 and F_2 of a graph G, (F_1, F_2) is a distinguishable pair of G if and only if one of the following conditions is satisfied:*

(1) There are two nodes $w, u \in V(G) - (F_1 \cup F_2)$ and there is a node $v \in F_1 \Delta F_2$ such that $(w, u) \in E(G)$ and $(w, v) \in E(G)$;

(2) There are two nodes $u, v \in F_1 - F_2$ and there is a node $w \in V(G) - (F_1 \cup F_2)$ such that $(w, u) \in E(G)$ and $(w, v) \in E(G)$;

(3) There are two nodes $u, v \in F_2 - F_1$ and there is a node $w \in V(G) - (F_1 \cup F_2)$ such that $(w, u) \in E(G)$ and $(w, v) \in E(G)$.

It follows from the definition of t-diagnosable and Theorem 1 that the following lemma holds.

Lemma 2. *A system G is t-diagnosable if and only if for each distinct pair F_1 and F_2 of subsets of $V(G)$ with $\max\{|F_1|, |F_2|\} \leq t$, F_1 and F_2 are distinguishable.*

In contrast to the global sense in system diagnosis, Hsu and Tan present a local concept called the local diagnosability of a given node in a system. This method requires only the correct identification of the faulty or fault-free status of a single node. Below are two definitions that introduce the concept of local diagnosability.

Definition 3 *[4]. A system $G(V, E)$ is locally t-diagnosable at the node u, if given a test syndrome σ_F produced by the system under the presence of a set of faulty nodes F containing node u with $|F| \leq t$, every set of faulty nodes F' consistent with σ_F and $|F'| \leq t$, must also contain node u.*

Definition 4 *[4]. The local diagnosability $t_l(u)$ of a node u in a system $G(V, E)$ is defined to be the maximum number of t for G being locally t-diagnosable at u, that is, $t_l(u) = \max\{t \mid G \text{ is locally t-diagnosable at } u\}$.*

The relationship between the local diagnosability and the traditional diagnosability is stated as follows.

Lemma 5 *[4]. A system $G(V, E)$ is t-diagnosable if and only if G is locally t-diagnosable at every node.*

Lemma 6 *[4]. The diagnosability $t(G)$ of a system $G(V, E)$ is equal to the minimum value among the local diagnosability of every node in G, that is, $t(G) = \min\{t_l(u) \mid u \in V(G)\}$.*

Under the comparison diagnosis model, an extended star structure for guaranteeing the local diagnosability of a given node is stated as below.

Definition 7 *[4]. Let u be a node in a graph $G(V, E)$. An extended star $ES(u; n)$ of order n at node u is defined as $ES(u; n) = (V(u; n), E(u; n))$, where the set of nodes $V(u; n) = \{u\} \cup \{v_{i,j} \mid 1 \leq i \leq n, 1 \leq j \leq 4\}$, the set of edges $E(u; n) = \{(u, v_{k,1}), (v_{k,1}, v_{k,2}), (v_{k,2}, v_{k,3}), (v_{k,3}, v_{k,4}) \mid 1 \leq k \leq n\}$ and $n \leq deg_G(u)$. (See Fig. 1 for an illustration.)*

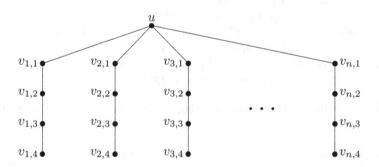

Fig. 1. The extended star $ES(u; n)$

Chiang and Tan showed that the local diagnosability of u is at least n if there exists an extended star $ES(u; n)$ at u. The order n at a node u is usually less than the degree of u. In order to better evaluate the local diagnosability of u, we propose a tree structure $T(u; a, b, c, d)$ around u in this paper.

3   Local Diagnosis Algorithm

In this section, we first propose a tree structure to better evaluate the local diagnosability of a vertex. We provide the corresponding algorithm to diagnose a vertex based on the tree structure and the syndrome output by this structure.

Definition 8. *Let u be a vertex in a graph $G(V, E)$. For $a+b+c+d \leq \deg_G(u)$, a tree structure $T(u; a, b, c, d)$ of order $a + b + c + d$ at the vertex u is defined as $T(u; a, b, c, d) = (V(T(u; a, b, c, d)), E(T(u; a, b, c, d)))$.*

- $V(T(u; a, b, c, d)) = \{u\} \cup V_a \cup V_b \cup V_c \cup V_d$, *where*
  $V_a = \{x_{i,j} \mid 1 \leq i \leq a, 1 \leq j \leq 4\}, V_b = \{y_{i,j} \mid 1 \leq i \leq b, 1 \leq j \leq 3\}$,
  $V_c = \{z_{i,j} \mid 1 \leq i \leq c, 1 \leq j \leq 2\}, V_d = \{v_{i,j}, w_i \mid 1 \leq i \leq d, 1 \leq j \leq 3\}$;
- $E(T(u; a, b, c, d)) = E_a \cup E_b \cup E_c \cup E_d$, *where*
  $E_a = \{(u, x_{k,1}), (x_{k,1}, x_{k,2}), (x_{k,2}, x_{k,3}), (x_{k,3}, x_{k,4}) \mid 1 \leq k \leq a\}$,
  $E_b = \{(u, y_{k,1}), (y_{k,1}, y_{k,2}), (y_{k,2}, y_{k,3}) \mid 1 \leq k \leq b\}$,
  $E_c = \{(u, z_{k,1}), (z_{k,1}, z_{k,2}) \mid 1 \leq k \leq c\}$,
  $E_d = \{(u, v_{k,1}), (v_{k,1}, v_{k,2}), (v_{k,2}, v_{k,3}), (v_{k,1}, w_k) \mid 1 \leq k \leq d\}$.

(See Fig. 2 for an illustration.)

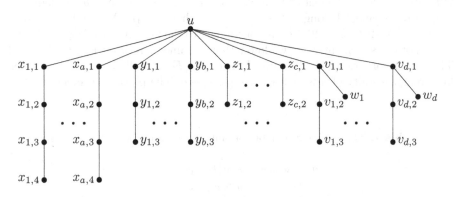

Fig. 2. The tree structure $T(u; a, b, c, d)$

There are four different types of branches start from u. From left to right, we call them Type a, Type b, Type c and Type d. That's, for any $k \in \{1, \ldots, a\}$, we call the connected branch induced by $\{(u, x_{k,1})\} \cup \{(x_{k,i}, x_{k,i+1}) \mid 1 \leq i \leq 3\}$ Type a.

Theorem 9. *Let u be a vertex in a graph $G(V, E)$. The local diagnosability of u is at least $a + \lfloor \frac{b+c}{2} \rfloor + d$ if there exists a tree structure $T(u; a, b, c, d) \subseteq G$ at u.*

Proof. Let t be a positive integer and $t \leq a + \lfloor \frac{b+c}{2} \rfloor + d$. We show that u is t-diagnosable. Let F_1, F_2 be two subsets of $V(G)$ such that $u \in F_1 \Delta F_2$ and $|F_1|, |F_2| \leq t$. Let $|F_1 \cap F_2| = p$, by assumption, we know that $0 \leq p \leq t - 1$. Delete $F_1 \cap F_2$ from G, we consider the connected component u belongs to, denote it by C_u. After deleting $F_1 \cap F_2$ from G, among the $a+b+c+d$ branches around u there are at least $(a+b+c+d) - p$ complete branches in $T(u; a, b, c, d) - F_1 \cap F_2$. Notice that there are at most $2t - 2p$ vertices in $F_1 \Delta F_2$.

The matching $M = \{(x_{i,1}, x_{i,2}), (x_{i,3}, x_{i,4}), (y_{j,1}, y_{j,2}), (z_{k,1}, z_{k,2}), (v_{l,1}, w_l), (v_{l,2}, v_{l,3}) \mid 1 \leq i \leq a, 1 \leq j \leq b, 1 \leq k \leq c, 1 \leq l \leq d\}$ in the structure $T(u; a, b, c, d)$ of size $2a + b + c + 2d$ is independent to u. Next we show that after deleting $F_1 \cap F_2$ from $T(u; a, b, c, d)$ there is at least one element of M left in C_u with both endpoints belong to $V(G) - (F_1 \cup F_2)$. This edge can be connected to u by $F_1 \Delta F_2$. Thus, Theorem 1 condition (1) holds. Therefore, F_1, F_2 is distinguishable.

We consider two cases.

Case 1. $p \geq a + d$. Among the $2a + b + c + 2d$ elements of M, at least $b + c - (p - a - d)$ elements left in C_u. Claim that at least one element belong to $G - (F_1 \cup F_2)$. Otherwise, every element has at least one endpoint belongs to $F_1 \Delta F_2$ and $u \in F_1 \Delta F_2$. So $|F_1 \Delta F_2| \geq 1 + (b+c) - (p-a-d) \geq 1 + (t-p) + \lfloor \frac{b+c}{2} \rfloor = 1 + (t-p) + (t-a-d) > 2t - 2p$. It contradicts to the fact that $|F_1 \Delta F_2| \leq 2t - 2p$.

Case 2. $p < a + d$. Among the $2a + b + c + 2d$ elements of M, at least $2(a+d-p) + b + c$ elements left in C_u. Among the $2(a+d-p) + b + c$ elements, at least one element belong to $G - (F_1 \cup F_2)$. Otherwise, $|F_1 \Delta F_2| \geq 1 + 2(a+d-p) + b + c \geq 1 + 2(t-p) > 2t - 2p$. It contradicts to the fact that $|F_1 \Delta F_2| \leq 2t - 2p$.

Denote this element by e, we know that e connects to u by $F_1 \Delta F_2$. We find Theorem 1 condition (1) structure. Hence, (F_1, F_2) is t-distinguishable. So the local diagnosability of u is at least $a + \lfloor \frac{b+c}{2} \rfloor + d$. The proof is complete. □

Table 1. The minimum number of faulty vertices in the set $\{z_{i,1}, z_{i,2}\}$

$(\sigma_{z_{i,1}}(u, z_{i,2}))$	$\min |F \cap \{z_{i,1}, z_{i,2}\}|$	
	$u \in F$	$u \notin F$
(0)	1	0
(1)	0	1

Denote the number $|\{i \mid (\sigma_{z_{i,1}}(u, z_{i,2})) = (j), 1 \leq i \leq c, 0 \leq j \leq 1\}|$ by c_j. Notice that $c_0 + c_1 = c$. If u is faulty and $\sigma_{z_{i,1}}(u, z_{i,2}) = 0$, then $z_{i,1}$ is faulty. If u is faulty and $\sigma_{z_{i,1}}(u, z_{i,2}) = 1$, then the number of faulty vertices in the set $\{z_{i,1}, z_{i,2}\}$ is uncertain. If u is fault-free and $\sigma_{z_{i,1}}(u, z_{i,2}) = 0$, then the number of faulty vertices in the set $\{z_{i,1}, z_{i,2}\}$ is uncertain. If u is fault-free and $\sigma_{z_{i,1}}(u, z_{i,2}) = 1$, then at least one faulty vertex in the set $\{z_{i,1}, z_{i,2}\}$. So we have Table 1.

Table 2. The minimum number of faulty vertices in the set $\{y_{i,1}, y_{i,2}, y_{i,3}\}$

$(\sigma_{y_{i,1}}(u, y_{i,2}), \sigma_{y_{i,2}}(y_{i,1}, y_{i,3}))$	$\min |F \cap \{y_{i,1}, y_{i,2}, y_{i,3}\}|$	
	$u \in F$	$u \notin F$
$(0,0)$	2	0
$(1,0)$	0	1
$(0,1), (1,1)$	1	1

We set $B_0 = \{(0,0)\}$, $B_1 = \{(1,0)\}$, $B_2 = \{(0,1),(1,1)\}$. Denote $|\{i \mid (\sigma_{y_{i,1}}(u, y_{i,2}), \sigma_{y_{i,2}}(y_{i,1}, y_{i,3})) \in B_j, 1 \leq i \leq b\}|$ by b_j for $j \in \{0, 1, 2\}$. We know that $b_0 + b_1 + b_2 = b$. Similar to the analysis in the previous paragraph, we have the information for the minimum number of faulty vertices in the set $\{y_{i,1}, y_{i,2}, y_{i,3}\}$ as shown in Table 2.

Table 3. The minimum number of faulty vertices in the set $\{x_{i,1}, x_{i,2}, x_{i,3}, x_{i,4}\}$

$(\sigma_{x_{i,1}}(u, x_{i,2}), \sigma_{x_{i,2}}(x_{i,1}, x_{i,3}), \sigma_{x_{i,3}}(x_{i,2}, x_{i,4}))$	$\min |F \cap \{x_{i,1}, x_{i,2}, x_{i,3}, x_{i,4}\}|$	
	$u \in F$	$u \notin F$
$(0,0,0)$	3	0
$(1,0,0)$	0	2
$(0,0,1), (0,1,0), (0,1,1), (1,0,1), (1,1,0), (1,1,1)$	1	1

Let $A_0 = \{(0,0,0)\}$, $A_1 = \{(1,0,0)\}$, $A_2 = \{(i_1, i_2, i_3) \mid i_1, i_2, i_3 \in \{0,1\}\} - (A_0 \cup A_1)$. Denote the number $|\{i \mid (\sigma_{x_{i,1}}(u, x_{i,2}), \sigma_{x_{i,2}}(x_{i,1}, x_{i,3}), \sigma_{x_{i,3}}(x_{i,2}, x_{i,4})) \in A_j, 1 \leq i \leq a\}|$ by a_j for $j \in \{0, 1, 2\}$. Notice that $a_0 + a_1 + a_2 = a$. The analysis of the number of faulty vertices in the set $\{x_{i,1}, x_{i,2}, x_{i,3}, x_{i,4}\}$, we refer to [4]. We have Table 3.

Table 4. The minimum number of faulty vertices in the set $\{v_{i,1}, v_{i,2}, v_{i,3}, w_i\}$

$(\sigma_{v_{i,1}}(u, w_i), \sigma_{v_{i,1}}(u, v_{i,2}), \sigma_{v_{i,2}}(v_{i,1}, v_{i,3}))$	$\min |F \cap \{v_{i,1}, v_{i,2}, v_{i,3}, w_i\}|$	
	$u \in F$	$u \notin F$
$(0,0,0)$	2	0
$(1,1,0)$	0	2
$(0,0,1), (0,1,0), (0,1,1), (1,0,0), (1,0,1), (1,1,1)$	1	1

Let $D_0 = \{(0,0,0)\}$, $D_1 = \{(1,1,0)\}$, $D_2 = \{(i_1, i_2, i_3) \mid i_1, i_2, i_3 \in \{0,1\}\} - (D_0 \cup D_1)$. Denote the number $|\{i \mid (\sigma_{v_{i,1}}(u, w_i), \sigma_{v_{i,1}}(u, v_{i,2}), \sigma_{v_{i,2}}(v_{i,1}, v_{i,3})) \in D_j, 1 \leq i \leq d\}|$ by d_j for $j \in \{0,1,2\}$. Notice that $d_0 + d_1 + d_2 = d$. Similarly, we get the number of faulty vertices in the set $\{v_{i,1}, v_{i,2}, v_{i,3}, w_i\}$ as shown in Table 4.

We propose the algorithm **LDAT** (see Algorithm 1) for the tree structure $T(u; a, b, c, d)$ and prove it can identify the state of u correctly under comparison model if the number of faulty vertices is at most $a + \lfloor \frac{b+c}{2} \rfloor + d$.

Algorithm 1: Local diagnosis algorithm for tree structure (**LDAT**)

Input: A tree structure $T(u; a, b, c, d)$.
Output: The value is 0 or 1 if u is fault-free or faulty, respectively.

1 **begin**

2 $\quad a_1 \leftarrow |\{i \mid (\sigma_{x_{i,1}}(u, x_{i,2}), \sigma_{x_{i,2}}(x_{i,1}, x_{i,3}), \sigma_{x_{i,3}}(x_{i,2}, x_{i,4})) = (1,0,0), 1 \leq i \leq a\}|$;

3 $\quad a_2 \leftarrow |\{i \mid (\sigma_{x_{i,1}}(u, x_{i,2}), \sigma_{x_{i,2}}(x_{i,1}, x_{i,3}), \sigma_{x_{i,3}}(x_{i,2}, x_{i,4})) \in A_2, 1 \leq i \leq a\}|$;

4 $\quad b_1 \leftarrow |\{i \mid (\sigma_{y_{i,1}}(u, y_{i,2}), \sigma_{y_{i,2}}(y_{i,1}, y_{i,3})) = (1,0), 1 \leq i \leq b\}|$;

5 $\quad b_2 \leftarrow |\{i \mid (\sigma_{y_{i,1}}(u, y_{i,2}), \sigma_{y_{i,2}}(y_{i,1}, y_{i,3})) \in \{(0,1),(1,1)\}, 1 \leq i \leq b\}|$;

6 $\quad c_1 \leftarrow |\{i \mid \sigma_{z_{i,1}}(u, z_{i,2}) = 1, 1 \leq i \leq c\}|$;

7 $\quad d_1 \leftarrow |\{i \mid (\sigma_{v_{i,1}}(u, w_i), \sigma_{v_{i,1}}(u, v_{i,2}), \sigma_{v_{i,2}}(v_{i,1}, v_{i,3})) = (1,1,0), 1 \leq i \leq d\}|$;

8 $\quad d_2 \leftarrow |\{i \mid (\sigma_{v_{i,1}}(u, w_i), \sigma_{v_{i,1}}(u, v_{i,2}), \sigma_{v_{i,2}}(v_{i,1}, v_{i,3})) \in D_2, 1 \leq i \leq d\}|$;

9 $\quad$ **if** $2a_1 + a_2 + b_1 + b_2 + c_1 + 2d_1 + d_2 \leq a + \lfloor \frac{b+c}{2} \rfloor + d$ **then return** 0;

10 $\quad$ **else return** 1;

11 **end**

Theorem 10. *Let $T(u; a, b, c, d)$ be a tree of order $a+b+c+d$ at a vertex u, let F be any faulty vertex set of G. If $|F| \leq a + \lfloor \frac{b+c}{2} \rfloor + d$ then Algorithm 1 can identify the state of u correctly. That is, u is fault-free if $2a_1 + a_2 + b_1 + b_2 + c_1 + 2d_1 + d_2 \leq a + \lfloor \frac{b+c}{2} \rfloor + d$; otherwise, u is faulty.*

Proof. We prove this Theorem by contradiction.

Suppose that u is faulty and $2a_1 + b_1 + c_1 + 2d_1 + a_2 + b_2 + d_2 \leq a + \lfloor \frac{b+c}{2} \rfloor + d$. According to Tables 1, 2, 3 and 4, we have $|F| \geq 1 + 3a_0 + 2b_0 + c_0 + 2d_0 + a_2 + b_2 + d_2 = 1 + 3(a - a_1 - a_2) + 2(b - b_1 - b_2) + (c - c_1) + 2(d - d_1 - d_2) + a_2 + b_2 + d_2 = 1 + 3a + 2b + c + 2d - 3a_1 - 2a_2 - 2b_1 - b_2 - c_1 - 2d_1 - d_2 \geq 1 + 3a + 2b + c + 2d - a_1 - a_2 - b_1 - 2a_1 - a_2 - b_1 - b_2 - c_1 - 2d_1 - d_2 \geq 1 + 2a + b + c + 2d - (a + \lfloor \frac{b+c}{2} \rfloor + d) \geq 1 + a + \lfloor \frac{b+c}{2} \rfloor + d$ which contradicts to $|F| \leq a + \lfloor \frac{b+c}{2} \rfloor + d$. Thus, u is fault-free if $2a_1 + b_1 + c_1 + 2d_1 + a_2 + b_2 + d_2 \leq a + \lfloor \frac{b+c}{2} \rfloor + d$.

Suppose that u is fault-free and $2a_1 + a_2 + b_1 + b_2 + c_1 + 2d_1 + d_2 \geq 1 + a + \lfloor \frac{b+c}{2} \rfloor + d$. According to Tables 1, 2, 3 and 4, we have $|F| \geq 2a_1 + a_2 + b_1 + b_2 + c_1 + 2d_1 + d_2 \geq 1 + a + \lfloor \frac{b+c}{2} \rfloor + d$ which contradicts to $|F| \leq a + \lfloor \frac{b+c}{2} \rfloor + d$. Thus, u is faulty if $2a_1 + a_2 + b_1 + b_2 + c_1 + 2d_1 + d_2 \geq 1 + a + \lfloor \frac{b+c}{2} \rfloor + d$. $\qquad \square$

4   Local Diagnosis of Star Graphs with Faulty Edges

If the local diagnosability of each vertex is equal to its degree then we say the graph has the strong local diagnosability property. In this section, we give a sufficient condition for a star graph to have the strong local diagnosability property.

Star graph is the well-known interconnection network of multiprocessor systems. The star graph is proposed in [1]. The n-dimensional star graph is an attractive topology in parallel computers and distributed systems because of its recursive structure, vertex and edge symmetric. The vertex set of an n-dimensional star graph S_n is $\{u_1 u_2 \cdots u_n \mid u_1 u_2 \cdots u_n \text{ is a permutation of } 1, 2, \ldots, n\}$. Thus $|V(S_n)| = n!$. The adjacency is defined as follows: $u = u_1 u_2 \cdots u_i \cdots u_n$ is adjacent to $v = v_1 v_2 \cdots v_i \cdots v_n$ through an edge of dimension i with $2 \leq i \leq n$ if $v_j = u_j$ for $j \notin \{1, i\}$, $v_1 = u_i$ and $v_i = u_1$. Hence the degree of every vertex in S_n is $n - 1$. The star graph is bipartite with girth six and diameter $\lfloor \frac{3(n-1)}{2} \rfloor$.

Before we present the main result of this section, we need the following known result.

Theorem 11. *Suppose that $G = (V_1 \cup V_2, E)$ is a bipartite graph with $|V_1| \leq |V_2|$. If every vertex from V_1 has at least t neighbors in V_2 and every vertex from V_2 has at most t neighbors in V_1 for some $t \geq 1$. Then G has a matching saturating every vertex of V_1.*

In [3], they proved that the n-dimensional star graph has the strong local diagnosability property if there are at most $n - 3$ faulty edges. In our work, we show that the star graph with faulty edges has the strong local diagnosability property if the remaining graph has minimum degree at least three no matter how many edges are faulty.

Theorem 12. *Let S_n be an n-dimensional star graph with $n \geq 5$ and $S \subset E(S_n)$ be a faulty set of edges such that $\delta(S_n - S) \geq 3$. Then $S_n - S$ has the strong local diagnosability property.*

Proof. For any vertex $u \in V(S_n)$, let $L_i(u) = \{v \in V(S_n) : dist_{S_n-S}(u, v) = i\}$. Since the star graph is bipartite, so both $L_1(u)$, $L_2(u)$ and $L_3(u)$ are independent. Label the vertices in $L_1(u)$ by $v_{1,1}, v_{2,1}, \ldots, v_{d,1}$, where $|L_1(u)| = d$. Since $L_1(u)$ is independent and $\delta(S_n - S) \geq 3$, so each $v_{i,1}$ $(1 \leq i \leq d)$ has at least two neighbors in $L_2(u)$. We pick two neighbors for each $v_{i,1}$ and denote them by $v_{i,2}, w_i$. Since the girth of $S_n - S$ is at least six, we know that $\{v_{i,2}, w_i\} \cap \{v_{j,2}, w_j\} = \emptyset$ for any $i \neq j, 1 \leq i, j \leq d$.

Consider the bipartite graph induced by $\{v_{i,2} \mid 1 \leq i \leq d\}$ and $L_3(u)$. Each vertex $v_{i,2}$ has exactly one neighbor in $L_1(u)$ and at least two neighbors in $L_3(u)$. According to the definition of S_n, each vertex from $L_3(u)$ has at most two neighbors in $L_2(u)$. By Theorem 11, we know that there is a matching saturating every vertex of $\{v_{i,2} \mid 1 \leq i \leq d\}$. Denote the matching by $M = \{(v_{i,2}, v_{i,3}) \mid 1 \leq i \leq d\}$. We get the $T(u; 0, 0, 0, d)$ as follows: $V(T(u; 0, 0, 0, d)) = \{u\} \cup L_1(u) \cup \{v_{i,2}, v_{i,3}, w_i \mid 1 \leq i \leq d\}$, $E(T(u; 0, 0, 0, d)) = \{(u, v_{i,1}), (v_{i,1}, v_{i,2}), (v_{i,2}, v_{i,3}), (v_{i,1}, w_i) \mid 1 \leq i \leq d\}$ and $d = \deg_{S_n - S}(u) = |L_1(u)|$. So u is $\deg_{S_n - S}(u)$-diagnosable. $\square$

Next, we show that $S_n - S$ might not keep this strong local diagnosability property if $\delta(S_n - S) \leq 2$.

Example 13. *Let u be a vertex of S_n and $uvwxyzu$ be a six cycle of S_n. Let the edges adjacent to v, w, x, y, z except the edges in the six cycle are faulty. Then we know $|S| = 5(n - 3)$. Let $F_1 - F_2 = \{u, v\}$, $F_2 - F_1 = \{x, y\}$ and $F_1 \cap F_2 = N(u) - \{v, z\}$. We know that $\delta(S_n - S) = 2$, $|F_1| = |F_2| = n - 1$ and (F_1, F_2) is indistinguishable. So $t_l(u) \leq n - 2$. By our structure, we get a $T(u; 1, 0, 0, n - 3)$ or a $T(u; 0, 1, 1, n - 3)$ or a $T(u; 0, 0, 2, n - 3)$. Hence $t_l(u) \geq n - 2$. Therefore, $t_l(u) = n - 2 = \deg_{S_n - S}(u) - 1$.*

5   Simulation Results

In this section, we show the performance of our algorithm on $T(u; a, b, c, d)$. In order to evaluate our algorithm, we introduce the confusion matrix $\begin{pmatrix} \text{TP} & \text{FP} \\ \text{FN} & \text{TN} \end{pmatrix}$.

The four parameters TP, TN, FP and FN are explained as follows:

True Positive (TP): A test result that correctly indicates the presence of a condition or characteristic.

True Negative (TN): A test result that correctly indicates the absence of a condition or characteristic.

False Positive (FP): A test result which wrongly indicates that a particular condition or attribute is present.

False Negative (FN): A test result which wrongly indicates that a particular condition or attribute is absent.

Then the accuracy of the diagnosis of our algorithm is defined as:

$$\text{Accuracy} = \frac{\text{TP} + \text{TN}}{\text{Tot. N}}$$

where Tot. N strands for the total number of experiments.

The positive predictive value (PPV) and negative predictive value (NPV) are defined as:

$$\text{PPV} = \frac{\text{TP}}{\text{TP} + \text{FP}}, \text{NPV} = \frac{\text{TN}}{\text{FN} + \text{TN}}.$$

First, we explore the influence of Type a and Type d on Accuracy, PPV and NPV. We set $b = c = 1$, $a + d = 30$ and $a \equiv 1 \pmod 4$. In each case, the system generates 1,000,000 instances. So the sum of TP, FP, FN and TN in each row is 1,000,000. In each instance, we set the failure probability of each vertex to be 0.4. The item "under Diag." means the proportion of the number of simulations with faulty vertices in $T(u; a, b, c, d)$ less than $a + \lfloor \frac{b+c}{2} \rfloor + d$ and 1,000,000.

Table 5. The influence of different a and d on Accuracy, PPV and NPV

under Diag.	a	b	c	d	TP	FP	FN	TN	Accuracy	PPV	NPV
0.000315	1	1	1	29	517416	30	82501	400053	0.9175	0.9999	0.8290
0.000279	5	1	1	25	525049	73	74907	399971	0.9250	0.9999	0.8423
0.000267	9	1	1	21	531117	113	67814	400956	0.9321	0.9998	0.8553
0.000284	13	1	1	17	539923	169	60919	398989	0.9389	0.9997	0.8675
0.000028	17	1	1	13	545113	303	54247	400337	0.9455	0.9994	0.8807
0.000296	21	1	1	9	552151	579	48207	399063	0.9512	0.9990	0.8922
0.000317	25	1	1	5	558631	1033	41440	398896	0.9575	0.9982	0.9059
0.000286	29	1	1	1	564688	1923	35474	397915	0.9626	0.9966	0.9181

It is easy to see from Table 5 that $a + d$ and $|V(T(u; a, b, c, d))|$ are constant. The Accuracy and NPV increases as a increases and d decreases. On the other hand, PPV decreases as a increases and d decreases. If a branch can be both Type a and Type d and we look forward for higher Accuracy then we can determine it to be Type a. In some circumstances, the price for processors is not expensive, and we can not afford the price for a faulty processor to be misdiagnosed to be fault-free. That is, we pursue higher PPV, then we choose it to be Type d.

Table 6. The influence of different b and c on Accuracy, PPV and NPV

under Diag.	a	b	c	d	TP	FP	FN	TN	Accuracy	PPV	NPV
0.000314	1	1	57	1	506118	0	93967	399915	0.9060	1	0.8097
0.000127	1	5	53	1	455201	0	145168	399631	0.8548	1	0.7335
0.000045	1	9	49	1	389047	0	210289	400664	0.7897	1	0.6558
0.000017	1	13	45	1	314730	0	285793	399477	0.7142	1	0.5829
0.000009	1	17	41	1	235582	0	364227	400191	0.6358	1	0.5235
0.000001	1	21	37	1	163754	0	436767	399479	0.5632	1	0.4777
0	1	25	33	1	103946	0	495755	400299	0.5042	1	0.4467
0.000001	1	29	29	1	59934	0	539787	400279	0.4602	1	0.4258

Second, we compare the influence of Type b and Type c on Accuracy, PPV and NPV. We set $a = d = 1$, $b + c = 58$, $b \leq c$ and $b \equiv 1(\mathrm{mod}4)$. In each case, the system generates 1,000,000 instances. In each instance, we set the failure probability of each vertex to be 0.4. We can see from Table 6 that the Accuracy and NPV decrease as b increases and c decreases. In each case, PPV keeps 1 which means the faulty processors can't hide. In conclusion, we can consider Type b to be Type c if $b \leq c$.

6   Conclusion

In this paper, we propose a tree structure and the related algorithm to better evaluate the local diagnosability of a graph under comparison model. Based on this structure, we show that the star graph with faulty edges has the strong local diagnosability property if the remaining graph has minimum degree at least three. In future, we will consider the local diagnosability of star graph with faulty edges and minimum degree less than three. We will explore more structures to depict the local diagnosability and conditional diagnosability [10] of multiprocessor systems.

Acknowledgment. This work was supported by Shin Kong Wu Ho Su Memorial Hospital National Yang Ming Chiao Tung University Joint Research Program (111-SKH-NYCU-03) and Fujian Provincial Department of Science and Technology (2020J01268).

References

1. Akers, S.B., Krishnameurthy, B.: Group-theoretic model for symmetric interconnection networks. IEEE Trans. Comput. **38**(4), 555–566 (1989)
2. Bondy, J.A., Murty, U.S.R.: Graph Theory. Springer, New York (2008)
3. Chiang, C.F., Hsu, G.H., Shih, L.M., Tan, J.J.M.: Diagnosability of star graphs with missing edges. Inf. Sci. **188**, 253–259 (2012)
4. Chiang, C.F., Tan, J.J.M.: Using node diagnosability to determine t-diagnosability under the comparison diagnosis model. IEEE Trans. Comput. **58**(1), 251–259 (2009)
5. Chwa, K.-Y., Hakimi, S.L.: Schemes for fault tolerant computing: a comparison of modularly redundant and t-diagnosable systems. Inf. Control **49**, 212–238 (1981)
6. Hsu, G.H., Tan, J.J.M.: A local diagnosability measure for multiprocessor systems. IEEE Trans. Parallel Distrib. Syst. **18**, 598–607 (2007)
7. Hsu, L.-H., Lin, C.-K.: Graph Theory and Interconnection Networks. CRC Press, Boca Raton (2009)
8. Maeng, J., Malek, M.: A comparison connection assignment for diagnosis of multiprocessor systems. In: Proceedings of the 11th International Symposium on Fault-Tolerant Computing, pp. 173–175 (1981)
9. Malek, M.: A comparison connection assignment for diagnosis of multiprocessor systems. In: Proceedings of the 7th Annual Symposium on Computer Architecture, pp. 31–35 (1980)
10. Peng, S.-L., Lin, C.-K., Tan, J.J.M., Hsu, L.-H.: The g-good-neighbor conditional diagnosability of hypercube under PMC model. Appl. Math. Comput. **218**(21), 10406–10412 (2012)
11. Preparata, F.P., Metze, G., Chien, R.T.: On the connection assignment problem of diagnosable systems. IEEE Trans. Electron. Comput. **16**(12), 848–854 (1967)
12. Sengupta, A., Dahbura, A.T.: On self-diagnosable multiprocessor systems: diagnosis by the comparison approach. IEEE Trans. Comput. **41**(11), 1386–1396 (1992)

Multiagent Learning for Competitive Opinion Optimization (Extended Abstract)

Po-An Chen[1(✉)], Chi-Jen Lu[2], Chuang-Chieh Lin[3(✉)], and Ke-Wei Fu[1]

[1] Institute of Information Management, National Yang Ming Chiao Tung University,
Hsinchu, Taiwan
{poanchen,andrewfu.mg09}@nycu.edu.tw
[2] Institute of Information Science, Academia Sinica, Taipei, Taiwan
cjlu@iis.sinica.edu.tw
[3] Department of Computer Science, Tamkang University, New Taipei, Taiwan
josephcclin@gms.tku.edu.tw

Abstract. From a perspective of designing or engineering for opinion formation games in social networks, the *opinion maximization (or minimization)* problem has been studied mainly for designing subset selecting algorithms. We define a two-player zero-sum Stackelberg game of competitive opinion optimization by letting the player under study as the leader minimize the sum of expressed opinions by doing so-called "internal opinion design", knowing that the other adversarial player as the follower is to maximize the same objective by also conducting her own internal opinion design. We furthermore consider multiagent learning, specifically using the Optimistic Gradient Descent Ascent, and analyze its convergence to equilibria in the simultaneous version of competitive opinion optimization.

Keywords: Competitive opinion optimization · Multiagent learning · Optimistic gradient descent ascent

1 Introduction

The opinion forming process in a social network can be naturally thought as opinion influencing and updating dynamics. This already attracted researchers' interest a while ago in mathematical sociology, and recently in theoretical computer science. Bindel et al. [3] viewed it as each player updating her expressed opinion to minimize her quadratic individual cost function, which consists of the disagreement between her expressed opinion and those of her friends, and the difference between her expressed and internal opinions. They analyzed how socially good or bad the system can be at equilibrium compared to the optimum

P.-A. Chen—Supported in part by MOST 110-2410-H-A49-011.
C.-C. Lin—Supported in part by MOST 110-2222-E-032-002-MY2.

solution in terms of the price of anarchy [13]. For directed graphs, we also had a price-of-anarchy result in a general class of graphs where no node is influencing others much more than being influenced [5].

From a perspective of designing or engineering, *opinion maximization (or minimization)* has been studied for seeding algorithms in [2,9]. With a *linear* objective of the sum of expressed opinions, opinion maximization seeks to find a k-subset (for a fixed size k) of nodes to have their expressed opinions fixed to 1 to maximize the objective. Opinion minimization can be similarly defined to minimize the objective. A seeding algorithm chooses what subset of nodes to fix their expressed opinions (to 1 if to maximize the objective), and it turns out that opinion maximization is NP-hard [9]. Thus, greedy algorithms [2,9] have been designed to approximate the maximum with the help of the submodularity of such a social cost of the expressed opinion sum.

It is obvious to see that controlling the expressed opinions is not the only way to optimize the objective. It is natural to consider changing the intrinsic (or equivalently, internal) opinions of some subset to optimize the objective. Notice that setting a selected subset of nodes to have certain assigned internal opinions does not prohibit later deciding their expressed opinions by the influence and update dynamics while controlling the expressed opinions of the chosen subset is definitive. In this sense, such an "internal opinion designing" approach is relatively more relaxed, compared to the "expressed opinion control" [9].

Our Results: Online and Multiagent Learning for Competitive Opinion Optimization. We then define the game of *competitive opinion optimization* as follows. One can think of a competitive scenario of two players, one with the goal to minimize (or maximize) the objective and the other adversarial player trying to do the opposite thing. In such competitive opinion optimization, a zero-sum game is formed by these two players with all the possible combination of influence values added on nodes subject to a capacity constraint as the strategy set and each optimizing the same objective in the opposite direction. The min player minimizes the sum of expressed opinions, i.e., doing internal opinion design discussed above, knowing that the max player as the follower is to maximize the same objective by also her own internal opinion design, and similarly for the max player. Even if a node is influenced by a player for its intrinsic opinion design, its internal opinion would still be influenced by the other player. Thus, a node's expressed opinion will be decided by its designed internal opinion (possibly by both players) and the update dynamic.

We first ask the problem of coming up with the min player's Stackelberg strategy against the max player's adversarial strategy as an online optimization problem in essence, specifically an online linear optimization one. From this idea, we design a randomized algorithm simply using the *follow-the-perturbed-leader* (FTPL) algorithm [11] to produce candidate strategies that are distributed according to the underlying probability distribution of mixed strategies and output a randomized strategy at some uniformly chosen time step. To uniformly randomize over the strategies at different time steps, the min player has to self-simulate playing FTPL, which requires obtaining every step's loss that depends on the other adversarial player's play. Then, we show that the strategy output by the randomized algorithm for the min player converges to an approximate min strategy against the other adversarial player mainly taking advantage of the no-regret property in Sect. 3. Note that the FTPL that we adopt uses uniformly random perturbation in each dimension, which is called the additive version, instead of the multiplicative version [11] or another version using Gumbel distributed perturbation leading to essentially the multiplicative weights algorithm [14]. The efficiency of our proposed randomized algorithm is inherently guaranteed and, moreover, its no-regret property can be used for our equilibrium strategy analysis.

Furthermore, we view our problem of coming up with the *minimax* strategy and the *maximin* strategy as *multiagent extension of online learning/online convex optimization*. Note that using generic or specific no-regret algorithms to play is also a common approach to reach certain equilibria *on average* in repeated games [15, Chapter 4]. Finally, we adapt the Optimistic Gradient Descent Ascent algorithm for the specific problem structure of competitive opinion optimization to derive the dynamics for both the min and max players and analyze the convergence to equilibria in the simultaneous version of competitive opinion optimization with a convergence rate in Sect. 4.

Relate Work

Seed Selection Algorithms for Opinion Maximization. Using the sum of expressed opinions as the objective, opinion maximization seeks to find a k-subset of nodes to have their expressed opinions fixed to 1 to maximize the objective. Greedy algorithms have been designed to approximate the optimum with the help of the submodularity of such social cost [2,9]. We can view opinion maximization as a single-player problem compared with our competitive opinion optimization.

Connection to Combinatorial Online Optimization. Online learning algorithms have been designed for making "structured" decisions that are composed of components [12], i.e., combinatorial online optimization problems. There could be an exponential number of decisions in terms of the number of components. To apply the well-known hedge algorithm [7,8] to the combinatorial expert setting, the experts are chosen as the structured decisions, which is called the extended hedge algorithm [12]. Obviously, one of the problems of this approach is to maintain exponentially many weights. Learning with structured decisions has also been dealt with in the bandit setting where only the loss for the structured decision selected is available, which is called a combinatorial bandits problem [4].

2 Preliminaries

Our game is based on the opinion formation game and its equilibrium. First, we introduce the fundamentals in opinion formation games. Then, we proceed with preliminaries of our competitive opinion optimization in Sect. 2.1. The performance measure for convergence will be introduced in Sect. 2.2.

We describe a social network as a weighted graph $(G, \mathbf{w})$ for directed graph $G = (V, E)$ and weight matrix $\mathbf{w} = [w_{ij}]_{ij}$. The node set V of size n represents the selfish players, and the edge set E corresponds to the relationships between a pair of nodes. The edge weight $w_{ij} \geq 0$ is a real number and represents how much player i is influenced by player j; note that weight w_{ii} can be seen as a self-loop weight, i.e., how much player i influences (or is influenced by) herself. Each (node) player has an internal opinion s_i, which is unchanged and not affected by opinion updates. An opinion formation game can be expressed as an instance $(G, \mathbf{w}, \mathbf{s})$ that combines weighted graph $(G, \mathbf{w})$ and vector $\mathbf{s} = (s_i)_i$. Each player's strategy is an expressed opinion $z_i \in [-1, 1]$, which may be different from her $s_i \in [-1, 1]$ and gets updated. Both s_i and z_i are real numbers. The individual cost function of player i is $C_i(\mathbf{z}) = w_{ii}(z_i - s_i)^2 + \sum_{j \in N(i)} w_{ij}(z_i - z_j)^2$, where $\mathbf{z}$ is the strategy profile/vector and $N(i)$ is the set of the neighbors of i, i.e., $\{j : j \neq i, w_{ij} > 0\}$. Each node minimizes her cost C_i by choosing her expressed opinion z_i. We analyze the game when it stabilizes, i.e., at equilibrium. In a *(pure) Nash equilibrium* $\mathbf{z}$, each player i's strategy is z_i such that given $\mathbf{z}_{-i}$ (i.e., the opinion vectors of all players except i) we have $C_i(z_i, \mathbf{z}_{-i}) \leq C_i(z_i', \mathbf{z}_{-i})$ for any other z_i'.

In an opinion formation game, computing Nash equilibrium can be done by using *absorbing random walks* [9]. In a random walk on a directed graph $H = (Z, R)$ with its weight matrix W, a node in Z is an absorbing node if the random walk can only enter this node but not exit from it, and each entry $w_{i,j} \in R$ is the weight on edge (i, j). Let $B \subseteq Z$ be the set of all *absorbing* nodes, and the remaining nodes $U = Z \setminus B$ are *transient* nodes. Given the *transition matrix* P (from the weight matrix W) whose entry $P_{i,j}$ represents the probability transiting from node i to node j in this random walk, a $|U| \times |B|$ matrix Q_{UB} can be computed where each entry $Q_{UB_{i,j}}$ is *the probability that a random walk starting at transient state $i \in U$ is absorbed at state $j \in B$* (see [9] for details). If a random walk starting from transient node i gets absorbed at an absorbing node j, we assign to node i the value b_j associated with node j. With Q_{UB}, the expected value of node i is then $f_i = \sum_{j \in B} Q_{UB_{i,j}} b_j$. Let f_U be the vector of the expected values for all $i \in U$ and f_B the vector of values b_j for all $j \in B$. We have that $f_U = Q_{UB} f_B$.

Thus, computing the expressed opinion vector at Nash equilibrium for an opinion formation game can be done by taking advantage of $f_U = Q_{UB} f_B$ on a graph $H = (Z, R)$ constructed for our purpose as follows. The weighted graph $(G, \mathbf{w})$ with original internal opinions $\mathbf{s}$ gives $U = V$ and $B = V'$ for the random walk on H, where each $u_i \in V$ has a distinct copy $u_i' \in V'$ and $R = E \cup \{(u_i, u_i') : u_i \in V, u_i' \in V'\}$ with each weight $w_{u_i u_i'} = 1$ and $f_B = \mathbf{s}$ so $\mathbf{z} = Q_{UB} \mathbf{s}$.

Remark 1. The expressed opinion vector at Nash equilibrium can be computed in polynomial time in terms of the number of nodes.

Our competitive *internal opinion design* will be introduced in Sect. 2.1. There, when using absorbing random walks for arriving at stable states, $U = V$

and $B = V'$ along with the weighted edges remain as mentioned in the last paragraph yet with f_B being the internal opinion after manipulation. Note that the matrix computations involved in computing f_U (computing Q_{UB} included) can done in polynomial time in terms of the number of states in the random walk by Remark 1.

2.1 Competitive Opinion Optimization

A two-player *competitive opinion optimization* can be described as an instance $((G, \mathbf{w}), \mathbf{s}, \mathcal{X}, \mathcal{Y}, f)$. We will elaborate each component one by one. Knowing $\mathbf{y}$, let the min player's strategy be a vector $\mathbf{x} = (x_i)_i \in \mathbb{R}^n$ with $\|\mathbf{x}\|_1 \leq k$. Knowing $\mathbf{x}$, the max player's strategy is a vector $\mathbf{y} = (y_i)_i \in \mathbb{R}^n$ with $\|\mathbf{y}\|_1 \leq k$. Let $\mathcal{X} = \{\mathbf{x} \in \mathbb{R}^n : \|\mathbf{x}\|_1 \leq k\}$ and $\mathcal{Y} = \{\mathbf{y} \in \mathbb{R}^n : \|\mathbf{y}\|_1 \leq k\}$ denote the strategy sets for the min player and the max player, respectively. Thus, for a node i, after its internal opinion is affected by the min player and the max player, its internal opinion becomes *a modified value* $s_i + x_i + y_i$ *clipped between* -1 *and* 1. That is, for the min player, when $x_i < -1 - a_i$ for $a_i = s_i + y_i$, the modified opinion $s_i + x_i + y_i$ stays at -1; for the max player, when $y_i > 1 - b_i$ for $b_i = s_i + x_i$, the modified opinion $s_i + x_i + y_i$ stays at 1. Note that the expressed opinions are still influenced by $\mathbf{s} + \mathbf{x} + \mathbf{y}$ and get updated to the value at stable state by the dynamic, using absorbing random walks (applying Eq. (2)). We consider an objective $C(\mathbf{z}) = \sum_i z_i$ that is the sum of all nodes' expressed opinions z_i.

The min player minimizes her cost function over all $\mathbf{x}$'s, which the max player maximizes, $f(\mathbf{x}, \mathbf{y}) = C(Q_{UB}(\mathbf{s} + \mathbf{x} + \mathbf{y})) = \ell^{\mathbf{T}}(\mathbf{s} + \mathbf{x} + \mathbf{y})$ for $U = V$ and $B = V'$ and a vector $\ell = (\sum_i Q_{UB}(i, j))_j$.

Online Linear/Convex Optimization. In the setting of online convex optimization, we describe an online game between a player and the environment. The player is given a convex set $\mathcal{K} \subset \mathbb{R}^d$ and has to make a sequence of decisions $\mathbf{x}^{(1)}, \mathbf{x}^{(2)}, \ldots \in \mathcal{K}$. After deciding $\mathbf{x}^{(t)}$, the environment reveals a convex reward function $f^{(t)}$ and the player obtains $f^{(t)}(\mathbf{x}^{(t)})$. Which is closely related to our problem is a more specific problem of online linear optimization where the reward functions are linear, i.e., $f^{(t)}(\mathbf{x}) = \langle F^{(t)}, \mathbf{x} \rangle$ for some $f^{(t)} \in \mathbb{R}^d$.

We define the player's adaptive strategy $\mathcal{L}$ as a function taking as input a subsequence of loss vectors $F^{(1)}, \ldots, F^{(t-1)}$ and returns a point $\mathbf{x}^{(t)} \leftarrow \mathcal{L}(F^{(1)}, \ldots, F^{(t-1)})$ where $\mathbf{x}^{(t)} \in \mathcal{K}$. The performance of the player is measured by *regret* defined in the following.

Definition 1. *Given an online linear optimization algorithm $\mathcal{L}$ and a sequence of loss vectors $F^{(1)}, F^{(2)}, \ldots \in \mathbb{R}^n$, let the regret* $\text{Regret}(\mathcal{L}; F_{1:T})$ *be defined as* $\sum_{t=1}^{T} \langle F^{(t)}, \mathbf{x}^{(t)} \rangle - \min_{\mathbf{x} \in \mathcal{K}} \sum_{t=1}^{T} \langle F^{(t)}, \mathbf{x} \rangle.$[1]

A desirable property that one would want an online linear optimization algorithm to have is a regret which scales sublinearly in T. The *no-regret* property above is useful in a variety of contexts. For example, it is known (e.g., [1,

---

[1] For a player maximizing her total reward given a sequence of reward vectors, the regret can also be defined accordingly.

Section 3]) that two players playing $o(T)$-regret algorithms $\mathcal{L}_{\mathcal{X}}$ and $\mathcal{L}_{\mathcal{Y}}$, respectively, in a zero-sum game with a cost function $f : \mathcal{X} \times \mathcal{Y} \to R$ of the form $f(\mathbf{x}, \mathbf{y}) = \mathbf{x}^T M \mathbf{y}$ for some $M \in \mathbb{R}^{n \times m}$ give a version of minmax equilibrium. This standard technique and result have been existing for playing generic no-regret algorithms in a zero-sum $n \times m$ matrix game. One can view the argument as something we would like to do on a high level but with different technical details for coping with our game.

For our competitive opinion optimization, one can first notice that the strategies of the two players interact with each other and matrix Q_{UB}, which corresponds to the cost matrix M, in a very different way from the standard result just mentioned. For example, we have $Q_{UB}(\mathbf{s} + \mathbf{x} + \mathbf{y})$ here instead of $\mathbf{x}^T M \mathbf{y}$. Given the strategy sets $\mathcal{X}$ and $\mathcal{Y}$, our competitive opinion optimization takes a cost function $f : \mathcal{Z} = \mathcal{X} \times \mathcal{Y} \to R$. The min player imagines engaging herself in an online optimization problem and the max player in the other online optimization problem, where at time t the min player chooses $\mathbf{x}^{(t)}$ and the max player chooses $\mathbf{y}^{(t)}$. In one online optimization, *the min player chooses her strategies according to the play of a* no-regret *algorithm, assuming that the max player in response maximizes the value of the objective each time step, and in the other online optimization, the max player does similarly.* These two directions of optimization can actually be done jointly and simultaneously (see Sect. 4).[2]

2.2 Performance Measure for Convergence

For the notation $\mathcal{Z}$, which is a concatenation of $\mathcal{X}$ and $\mathcal{Y}$, and accordingly $\mathcal{Z}^*$ is also a concatenation of $\mathcal{X}^*$ and $\mathcal{Y}^*$ only for convenience. For a point, $(\mathbf{x}, \mathbf{y})$ as a strategy profile can be directly represented by $\mathbf{z} \in \mathcal{Z}$, and define $F(\mathbf{z}) = (\nabla_{\mathbf{x}} f(\mathbf{x}, \mathbf{y}), -\nabla_{\mathbf{y}} f(\mathbf{x}, \mathbf{y}))$. In a minimax equilibrium game, there are unique distances which are often used to estimate the convergence rate. The duality gap, defined as $\alpha_f(\mathbf{z}) = \max_{\mathbf{y}' \in \mathcal{Y}} f(\mathbf{x}, \mathbf{y}') - \min_{\mathbf{x}' \in \mathcal{X}} f(\mathbf{x}', \mathbf{y})$, which is always a positive value. This term has been used in many works, either for theorem proof or numerical experiments. The notation dist $(\mathbf{z}, \mathcal{Z}^*)$ is the squared distance between $\mathbf{z}$ and $\mathcal{Z}^*$, which can be formulated as $\|\mathbf{z} - \Pi_{\mathcal{Z}^*}(\mathbf{z})\|^2$, and we denote by $\Pi_{\mathcal{Z}^*}(\mathbf{z}) := \operatorname{argmin}_{\mathbf{z} \in \mathcal{Z}^*} \operatorname{dist}(\mathbf{z}, \mathcal{Z}^*)$ the projection of $\mathbf{z}$ onto $\mathcal{Z}^*$.

3 Randomized Algorithm for the Leader's Strategy

Being aware of the differences between our game and standard results discussed in Sect. 2.1, in this section we henceforth design algorithms for computing an approximate equilibrium strategy of the min player (against the adversarial player), and focus on efficient computation of the adversary's strategy as well as

---

[2] In particular, for a node i, after its internal opinion is affected by the min player and the max player, *without* clipping its modified internal opinion value $s_i + x_i + y_i$ clipped to the range $[-1, 1]$ every node's equilibrium strategy would result in a *dominant strategy* solution, which is a special Nash equilibrium and less interesting to look for since the strategies of both players would not be mutually entangled.

the equilibrium strategy analysis only for the min player, instead of characterizing equilibrium, i.e., equilibrium strategies for both players (since the adversarial player can overwrite the min player's selection and we do not have a symmetric structure such as $\mathbf{x}^T M \mathbf{y}$ in our problem).

Given the strategy sets $\mathcal{X}$ and $\mathcal{Y}$, our Stackelberg opinion optimization game takes a cost function $f : \mathcal{X} \times \mathcal{Y} \to R$ defined in Sect. 2.1. The min player imagines engaging herself in an online optimization problem, where at time t the min player chooses $\mathbf{x}^{(t)}$ and the adversarial (max) player chooses $\mathbf{y}^{(t)}$. In such online optimization, *the min player chooses her strategies according to simulating the play of a* no-regret *algorithm, assuming that the adversarial player in response maximizes the value of the objective each time step.* Also, the min player can select a strategy of some time $T_{\min}$, chosen uniformly at random, and this randomized subset will be shown to be an approximate equilibrium strategy.

3.1 Simulating the Play of the FTPL Algorithm

Specifically, transforming our problem of finding the leader's strategy into an online linear optimization, we simulate playing the additive version of the FTPL algorithm [11] to obtain a sequence of "randomized" (fractional) strategies; we then get an "average" (over time steps) randomized (fractional) strategy as the output of our randomized algorithm.

For every time step t, the (fractional) strategy of the leader $\mathbf{x}^{(t)} \leftarrow \mathcal{L}_{\mathcal{X}}(f^{(1)}(\cdot), \ldots, f^{(t-1)}(\cdot))$ can be rounded into the integral strategy $\mathbf{x}^{(t)}$, noting $\mathcal{X} = \{\mathbf{x} \in \mathbb{R}^n : \|\mathbf{x}\|_0 \leq k, 0 \leq \bar{x}_i \leq 1\}$ and $\mathcal{L}_{\mathcal{X}}$ is the additive version of the FTPL algorithm, and estimating $\mathbf{y}^{(t)} \simeq \arg\max_{\mathbf{y} \in \mathcal{Y}} f(\mathbf{E}[\mathbf{x}^{(t)}], \mathbf{y})$.

Algorithm Design. We are now ready to specify simulating the play of the additive version of the FTPL algorithm to get a randomized strategy $\mathbf{x}^{(t)}$ at each time step t: the min player's (fractional) strategy at time step t is $\mathbf{x}^{(t)} = \arg\min_{\mathbf{x} \in \mathcal{X}} L^{(t-1)}(\mathbf{x}) = \arg\min_{\mathbf{x} \in \mathcal{X}} (\sum_{\tau=1}^{t-1} f^{(\tau)}(\mathbf{x}) + R_t^\top \mathbf{x})$.

for a random vector $R_t \in [0, \sqrt{T}]^n$ uniformly distributed in each dimension. Since $L^{(t-1)}$ is affine in $\mathbf{x} \in \mathcal{X}$ and the constraints forming $\mathcal{X}$ are linear as well, the minimizer $\mathbf{x}^{(t)}$ can be computed efficiently.

Actually, $\mathbf{E}_{\mathbf{x}^{(t)} \sim X^{(t)}}[\mathbf{x}^{(t)}]$ can be estimated by sampling $\mathbf{x}^{(t)}$ enough times, which we will use and explain in the full version. Thus, we conclude that our randomized algorithm outputs a (randomized) pure strategy in a uniformly random time step $T_{\min}$ for the min player against the adversarial player who ideally is to play $\arg\max_{\mathbf{y} \in \mathcal{Y}} g(\mathbf{E}_{\mathbf{x}^{(t)} \sim X^{(t)}}[\mathbf{x}^{(t)}], \mathbf{y})$ at each time step t.

Proposition 1. *We can estimate this strategy of the adversary as accurately as possible with high probability. That is, with high probability*

$$f(\mathbf{E}_{\mathbf{x}^{(t)} \sim X^{(t)}}[\mathbf{x}^{(t)}], \mathbf{y}^{(t)}) \geq \max_{\mathbf{y} \in \mathcal{Y}} f(\mathbf{E}_{\mathbf{x}^{(t)} \sim X^{(t)}}[\mathbf{x}^{(t)}], \mathbf{y}) - \epsilon,$$

where $\epsilon > 0$ is an error from estimation, which can be made as small as desired.

We show that such strategy $\mathbf{y}^{(t)}$ of the adversary can be found efficiently in the full version. The randomized algorithm simulates the FTPL algorithm up to time step $T_{\min}$. Our main result is to show that the randomized pure strategy indeed approaches an approximate minimax equilibrium strategy (see Sect. 3.2). The randomized algorithm is summarized as follows.

Algorithm 1. Randomized algorithm for the leader's strategy

1: Choose $T_{\min}$ uniformly at random from $\{1, \ldots, T\}$
2: **for** $t = 1$ to $T_{\min}$ **do**
3:    $\mathbf{x}^{(t)} = \arg\min_{\mathbf{x} \in \mathcal{X}} (\sum_{\tau=1}^{t-1} f^{(\tau)}(\mathbf{x}) + R_t^\top \mathbf{x})$ for a uniformly random (in each dimension) vector $R_t \sim U[0, \sqrt{T}]^n$, where the adversary's $\mathbf{y}^{(\tau)}$ can be efficiently computed.
4:    Estimating the adversary's strategy $\mathbf{y}^{(t)}$ to achieve Proposition 1.
5: **end for**

3.2 Equilibrium Strategy Analysis

Let the min player play the strategy output by the randomized algorithm and the adversarial player's strategy be the one maximizing the loss, given the min player's chosen strategy. First, it can be shown that the play output by the randomized algorithm is "nearly" $O(\frac{n^{3/2}}{\sqrt{T}})$-average regret with high probability (see the proof of Lemma 1). This is achieved naturally in the sense of expected losses of the min player since there is a random vector R_t as a random source that produces the distribution $X^{(t)}$. The proof is deferred to the full version.

Lemma 1. *For the min player, the FTPL algorithm is nearly $\frac{2(1+\delta)n^{3/2}}{\sqrt{T}}$-average regret w.r.t. her respective loss functions depending on the adversary's strategy $\mathbf{y}^{(t)}$'s.*

Since the randomized algorithm chooses time step $T_{\min}$ uniformly at random from $1, \ldots, T$, we let

$$\mathbf{E}_{T_{\min} \in \{1,\ldots,T\}, \mathbf{x}^{(T_{\min})} \sim X^{(T_{\min})}}[\mathbf{x}^{(T_{\min})}] = \frac{\sum_{t=1}^{T} \mathbf{E}_{\mathbf{x}^{(t)} \sim X^{(t)}}[\mathbf{x}^{(t)}]}{T}.$$

Then, we are ready to state the main result.[3]

Theorem 1. *The strategy $\mathbf{x}^{(T_{\min})}$ output by the randomized algorithm for the min player against the adversarial player is a $(1 + \delta, \frac{\sqrt{\ln T} + 2(1+\delta)n^{3/2}}{\sqrt{T}})$-approximate equilibrium strategy for $(1 + \delta)$ multiplicative approximation and $(\frac{\sqrt{\ln T} + 2(1+\delta)n^{3/2}}{\sqrt{T}})$ additive approximation with probability of at least $1 - \frac{2}{T}$ for some constant $0 < \delta \leq 1$.*

---

[3] The whose proof is detailed in the full version.

4 Optimistic Mirror Descent Ascent for Simultaneous Competitive Opinion Optimization

Combining the play of a specific no-regret algorithm, say *the optimistic mirror descent, for the min player* and that of a specific no-regret algorithm, say *the optimistic mirror ascent, for the max player*, we propose to adapt the Optimistic Mirror Descent Ascent (OMDA) algorithm [6,10,16], which guarantees the last-iterate convergence, including bimatrix and convex-concave settings. OGDA plays a crucial role in computing $\mathbf{x}_t, \hat{\mathbf{x}}_{t+1}$ via gradient of $f(\mathbf{x}_{t-1}, \mathbf{y}_{t-1})$ and $f(\mathbf{x}_t, \mathbf{y}_t)$ (and similarly $\mathbf{y}_t, \hat{\mathbf{y}}_{t+1}$, using gradient of $f_{\mathbf{y}}(\mathbf{x}_{t-1}, \mathbf{y}_{t-1})$ and $f_{\mathbf{y}}(\mathbf{x}_t, \mathbf{y}_t)$). At the end of each iteration t, the objective function $\sum_i(\sum_j Q_{UB}(i,j)\cdot\mathbf{clip}_j(s_j + x_j + y_j)) = (\sum_j(\sum_i Q_{UB}(i,j))\cdot\mathbf{clip}_j(s_j + x_j + y_j))$ is updated to attain the convergence to the minimax equilibrium in our competitive opinion optimization.

Algorithm 2. OGDA for Competitive Opinion Optimization

1: **Parameters** : i (index of a node), $\eta > 0$, vector $\mathbf{s} = (s_i)_i$, $|i| \times |j|$ matrix Q_{UB}
2: **Initialization** : $\mathbf{x}_0, \hat{\mathbf{x}}_1, (x_i)_i \in \mathbb{R}^n, \|\mathbf{x}\|_1 \leq k$; $\mathbf{y}_0, \hat{\mathbf{y}}_1, (y_i)_i \in \mathbb{R}^n, \|\mathbf{y}\|_1 \leq k$.
3: **for** $t = 1, \ldots, T$ **do**
4:   if (GDA): $\widehat{\mathbf{x}_{t+1}} = \mathbf{x}_t$, $\widehat{\mathbf{y}_{t+1}} = \mathbf{y}_t$,
5:   Update the min player's strategy and the max player's strategy:

$$\mathbf{x}_t = \Pi_{\mathbf{x}}\left(\hat{\mathbf{x}}_t - \eta\nabla_{\mathbf{x}}\bar{f}(\mathbf{x}_{t-1}, \mathbf{y}_{t-1})\right), \quad \widehat{\mathbf{x}_{t+1}} = \Pi_{\mathbf{x}}\left(\hat{\mathbf{x}}_t - \eta\nabla_{\mathbf{x}}\bar{f}(\mathbf{x}_t, \mathbf{y}_t)\right),$$
$$\mathbf{y}_t = \Pi_{\mathbf{y}}\left(\hat{\mathbf{y}}_t + \eta\nabla_{\mathbf{y}}\bar{f}(\mathbf{x}_{t-1}, \mathbf{y}_{t-1})\right), \quad \widehat{\mathbf{y}_{t+1}} = \Pi_{\mathbf{y}}\left(\hat{\mathbf{y}}_t + \eta\nabla_{\mathbf{y}}\bar{f}(\mathbf{x}_t, \mathbf{y}_t)\right).$$

6:   The gradient vector of $\bar{f}$ w.r.t. the min player's strategy is computed as follows:

$$\left(\begin{cases} \sum_i Q_{UB}(i,j) = \ell_j, & \text{if } \mathbf{x}_t(j) > -1 - (s_j + \mathbf{y}_t(j)) \\ \text{non-differentiable}, & \text{if } \mathbf{x}_t(j) = -1 - (s_j + \mathbf{y}_t(j)) \\ 0, & \text{if } \mathbf{x}_t(j) < -1 - (s_j + \mathbf{y}_t(j)) \end{cases} \right),$$

where $\beta \cdot \sum_i Q_{UB}(i,j)$ for any $\beta \in [0,1]$ is a subgradient w.r.t. node j's strategy if $\mathbf{x}_t(j) = -1 - (s_j + \mathbf{y}_t(j))$. The max player's strategy is computed similarly.
7: **end for**

4.1 Convergence Results for OGDA

Therefore, using the objective function of each dimension ($\ell_i\cdot\mathbf{clip}_i(s_i + x_i + y_i)$), we approximate the original three-piecewise functions to strongly convex and strongly concave functions. The following proposition makes the approximation between $f_{\mathbf{y}}(\mathbf{x})$ (original three-piecewise linear function) and $\bar{f}_{\mathbf{y}}(\mathbf{x})$ (two-piecewise linear function), from the coordinate diagram, in which the x-axis is the value of x_i, and the y-axis is the value of $\ell_i \cdot \mathbf{clip}_i(s_i + x_i + y_i)$, we can obtain the distance bound between the two functions at most k (capacity limit) which is much smaller than n. The proof is in deferred in the full version.

Proposition 2 ($\bar{f}$ as an approximation of f). *Given* $\mathbf{y}$, *we have* $\bar{f}_\mathbf{y}(\mathbf{x}) - f_\mathbf{y}(\mathbf{x}) \le k$ *for all* $\mathbf{x}$.

The next proposition makes the approximation between $\tilde{f}_\mathbf{y}(\mathbf{x})$ (convex function) and $\bar{f}_\mathbf{y}(\mathbf{x})$ (two-piecewise linear function), we characterize the distance between the two functions in Proposition 3.

Proposition 3 ($\tilde{f}$ as an approximation of $\bar{f}$). *For* $\mathbf{x}$ *with* $\|\mathbf{x}\|_1 \le k$, *we have*

$$\tilde{f}_\mathbf{y}(\mathbf{x}) - \bar{f}_\mathbf{y}(\mathbf{x}) = \sum_i \tilde{f}_\mathbf{y}^{(i)}(x_i) - \sum_i \bar{f}_\mathbf{y}^{(i)}(x_i)$$

$$\le \sum_i \bar{f}_\mathbf{y}\left(x_q(i)\right) - \left(\tilde{f}_\mathbf{y}^{(i)}\left(x_p(i)\right) + \left\langle \nabla \tilde{f}_\mathbf{y}^{(i)}\left(x_p(i)\right), x_q(i) - x_p(i)\right\rangle\right),$$

where $x_q(i) = -1 - (s_i + y_i)$ *and* $x_p(i)$ *is a minimizer of* $\tilde{f}_\mathbf{y}^{(i)}(x_i)$. *And for* $\mathbf{y}$ *with* $\|\mathbf{y}\|_1 \le k$, $\sum_i \tilde{f}_\mathbf{x}^{(i)}(y_p(i)) + \langle \nabla \tilde{f}_\mathbf{x}^{(i)}(y_p(i)), y_q(i) - y_p(i)\rangle - \tilde{f}_\mathbf{x}^{(i)}(y_q(i))$ *represents the maximum overall distance between* $\bar{f}_\mathbf{x}(\mathbf{y})$ *and* $\tilde{f}_\mathbf{x}(\mathbf{y})$, *where* $y_q(i) = 1 - (s_i + x_i)$ *and* $y_p(i)$ *is a maximizer of* $\tilde{f}_\mathbf{x}^{(i)}(y_i)$.

Given a differentiable convex function $\tilde{f}_\mathbf{y}^{(i)}(x_i)$, we assume that the linear approximation of $\tilde{f}_\mathbf{y}^{(i)}(x_i)$ is the line that lies flat in $\bar{f}_\mathbf{y}^{(i)}(x_i)$. We can find in the range of x_i that the largest distance between $\bar{f}_\mathbf{y}^{(i)}(x_i)$ and $\tilde{f}_\mathbf{y}^{(i)}(x_i)$ is at its turning point, $-1 - (s_i + y_i)$ in our game, to the intersection of its vertical line with $\tilde{f}_\mathbf{y}^{(i)}(x_i)$, which is exactly the Bregman Divergence by definition.

We further derive the following proposition proved in the full version for the strong convexity of $\tilde{f}(\mathbf{x}', \mathbf{y})$ and also the strong concavity of $\tilde{f}(\mathbf{x}, \mathbf{y}')$.

Proposition 4 (Strong convexity of $\tilde{f}$, fixing y). *We have*

$$\tilde{f}(\mathbf{x}, \mathbf{y}) - \tilde{f}(\mathbf{x}^*, \mathbf{y}) \le \nabla_\mathbf{x} \tilde{f}(\mathbf{x}, \mathbf{y})^\top (\mathbf{x} - \mathbf{x}^*) - \gamma \|\mathbf{x} - \mathbf{x}^*\|^2 / 2$$

for all $\mathbf{x}$, *where* γ_i *satisfies for all* i

$$\tilde{f}(\mathbf{x}, \mathbf{y}) - \tilde{f}(x_i^*, \mathbf{x}_{-i}, \mathbf{y}) \le \nabla_{x_i} \tilde{f}(\mathbf{x}, \mathbf{y})^\top (x_i - x_i^*) - \gamma_i |x_i - x_i^*|^2 / 2.$$

In the rest of this subsection we further derive the convergence result of our game. First, the average-iterate convergence can be derived using a standard technique.[4] Then, we elaborate on the last-iterate convergence.

Last-Iterate Convergence. Here, with a further approximation $\tilde{f}$ of a proper approximation $\bar{f}$ of f by Proposition 3 and 2, we can further derive results that are similar to those in [16] but specific to the technical details of the competitive opinion optimization game.

We make the assumption that f is L-smooth, which is in place with $\|F(\mathbf{z}) - F(\mathbf{z}')\| \le L \|\mathbf{z} - \mathbf{z}'\|$ and also $\|\mathbf{z} - \mathbf{z}'\| \le 1$ for any $\mathbf{z}, \mathbf{z}' \in \mathcal{Z}$, and recall SP-RSI-2 (Definition 1 of [16]) here, which is a general condition according to $f(\mathbf{x}, \mathbf{y})$ and $\mathcal{Z}$ to obtain the results of last-iterate convergence.

---

[4] This part is deferred to the full version.

Definition 2 Definition 1 (Generalized Saddle-Point Restricted Secant Inequality (SP-RSI)) of [16]). *Condition SP-RSI-2 is defined as: for any $\mathbf{z} \in \mathcal{Z}$ with $\mathbf{z}^* = \Pi_{\mathcal{Z}^*}(\mathbf{z})$, where a point $\mathbf{z} = (\mathbf{x}, \mathbf{y}) \in \mathcal{Z}$, and $\mathcal{Z} = \mathcal{X} \times \mathcal{Y}$,*

$$(SP\text{-}RSI\text{-}2) \qquad F(\mathbf{z})^\top (\mathbf{z} - \mathbf{z}^*) \geq C \, \|\mathbf{z} - \mathbf{z}^*\|^{\beta+2}$$

holds for some parameters $\beta \geq 0$ and $C > 0$.

Lemma 2 (Theorem 6 of [16]). *If f is strongly convex in $\mathbf{x}$ and strongly concave in $\mathbf{y}$, then SP-RSI-2 holds with $C = \frac{\gamma}{2}$ and $\beta = 0$.*

Under the SP-RSI-2 condition with a value of $\beta = 0$, we can have a last-iterate convergence guarantee which is analogous to Theorem 8 of [16].

Lemma 3 (Theorem 8 of [16]). *For any learning rate $\eta \leq \frac{1}{8L}$, if SP-RSI-2 holds with $\beta = 0$, then OGDA guarantees linear last-iterate convergence:*

$$\text{dist}\left(\mathbf{z}_t, \mathcal{Z}^*\right) \leq 96 \left(1 + \frac{15 \min\left\{\eta^2 C^2, 1\right\}}{81(1+\beta) \cdot 2^\beta}\right)^{-t}.$$

Based on the existing convergence result of Lemma 3, we can also get a convergence guarantee for $\alpha_{\tilde{f}}(\mathbf{z}_t)$ (duality gap of $\mathbf{z}_t$) when f is Lipschitz continuous. This is because, for $(\mathbf{x}^*, \mathbf{y}^*) = \Pi_{\mathcal{Z}^*}(\mathbf{z}_t)$, we have

$$\alpha_{\tilde{f}}(\mathbf{z}_t) \leq \max_{\mathbf{x}', \mathbf{y}'} f(\mathbf{x}_t, \mathbf{y}') - f(\mathbf{x}^*, \mathbf{y}') + f(\mathbf{x}', \mathbf{y}^*) - f(\mathbf{x}', \mathbf{y}_t)$$
$$\leq \mathcal{O}\left(\|\mathbf{x}_t - \mathbf{x}^*\| + \|\mathbf{y}_t - \mathbf{y}^*\|\right) = \mathcal{O}\left(\sqrt{\text{dist}(\mathbf{z}_t, \mathcal{Z}^*)}\right). \qquad (1)$$

Theorem 2. *Algorithm 2 with $\eta \leq \frac{1}{8L}$ where SP-RSI-2 only holds with $\beta = 0$ guarantees linear last-iterate convergence with certain approximation errors:*

$$\alpha_f(\mathbf{z}_t) \leq \mathcal{O}\left(\sqrt{\text{dist}(\mathbf{z}_t, \mathcal{Z}^*)}\right)$$
$$+ \sum_i \bar{f}_{\mathbf{y}}\left(x_q(i)\right) - \left(\tilde{f}_{\mathbf{y}}^{(i)}\left(x_p(i)\right) + \langle \nabla \tilde{f}_{\mathbf{y}}^{(i)}\left(x_p(i)\right), x_q(i) - x_p(i)\rangle\right)$$
$$+ \sum_i \tilde{f}_{\mathbf{x}}^{(i)}(y_p(i)) + \langle \nabla \tilde{f}_{\mathbf{x}}^{(i)}\left(y_p(i)\right), y_q(i) - y_p(i)\rangle - \tilde{f}_{\mathbf{x}}^{(i)}(y_q(i)) + 2k.$$

By Theorem 2, the duality gap converges at the rate $\mathcal{O}\left(\sqrt{\text{dist}(\mathbf{z}_t, \mathcal{Z}^*)}\right)$, which is bounded by Lemma 3 and Proposition 3. Note that the capacity k is much smaller than n in Proposition 2.

5 Discussions and Future Work

As future directions, we can generalize competitive opinion optimization to multi-player non-zero-sum games with different (linear) objectives in terms of expressed opinions for different players each optimizing her own objective. Playing certain no-regret algorithms, the average strategy of each player then might converge to certain more permissive equilibrium (Nash equilibrium, correlated equilibrium, etc.). It does not really make sense in a zero-sum game to ask about the price of anarchy. Nevertheless, the price-of-anarchy type of questions becomes interesting and meaningful in a non-zero-sum game setting again.

References

1. Abernethy, J., Bartlett, P.L., Hazan, E.: Blackwell approachability and no-regret learning are equivalent. In: Proceedings of Conference on Learning Theory (2011)
2. Ahmadinejad, A., Mahini, H.: How effectively can we form opinions? In: Proceedings of International World Wide Web Conference (2014)
3. Bindel, D., Kleinberg, J., Oren, S.: How bad is forming your own opinion? In: Proceedings of 52nd Annual IEEE Symposium on Foundations of Computer Science (2011)
4. Cesa-Bianchi, N., Lugosi, G.: Combinatorial bandits. In: Proceedings of 22nd Annual Conference on Learning Theory (2009)
5. Chen, P.-A., Chen, Y.-L., Lu, C.-J.: Bounds on the price of anarchy for a more general class of directed graphs in opinion formation games. Oper. Res. Lett. **44**, 808–811 (2016)
6. Chiang, C.-K., Yang, T., Lee, C.-J., Mahdavi, M., Lu, C.-J., Zhu, S.: Online optimization with gradual variations. In: Proceedings of Conference on Learning Theory (2012)
7. Freund, Y., Schapire, R.E.: A decision theoretic generalization of on-line learning and an application to boosting. J. Comput. Syst. Sci. **55**(1), 119–139 (1997)
8. Freund, Y., Schapire, R.E.: Adaptive game playing using multiplicative weights. Games Econ. Behav. **29**, 79–103 (1999)
9. Gionis, A., Terzi, E., Tsaparas, P.: Opinion maximization in social networks. In: Proceedings of 13th SIAM International Conference on Data Mining (2013)
10. Golowich, N., Pattathil, S., Daskalakis, C.: Tight last-iterate convergence rates for no-regret learning in multi-player games. In: Proceedings of the 34th Conference on Neural Information Processing Systems (2020)
11. Kalai, A., Vempala, S.: Efficient algorithms for online decision problems. J. Comput. Syst. Sci. **71**, 291–307 (2005)
12. Koolen, W., Warmuth, M., Kivinen, J.: Hedging structured concepts. In: Proceedings of 23rd Annual Conference on Learning Theory (2010)
13. Koutsoupias, E., Papadimitriou, C.: Worst-case equilibria. In: Proceedings of 17th Annual Symposium on Theoretical Aspects of Computer Science (1999)
14. Lee, C.: Analysis of perturbation techniques in online learning. Doctoral Dissertation, the Department of Computer Science and Engineering, the University of Michigan (2018)
15. Nisan, N., Roughgarden, T., Tardos, E., Vazirani, V.V. (eds.): Algorithmic Game Theory. Cambridge University Press, Cambridge (2007)
16. Wei, C.-Y., Lee, C.-W., Zhang, M., Luo, H.: Linear last-iterate convergence in constrained saddle-point optimization. In: Proceedings of 9th International Conference on Learning Representations (2021)

The MAXIMUM ZERO-SUM PARTITION Problem

Guillaume Fertin[1(✉)][iD], Oscar Fontaine[2], Géraldine Jean[1][iD],
and Stéphane Vialette[3][iD]

[1] Nantes Université, CNRS, LS2N, UMR 6004, 44000 Nantes, France
{guillaume.fertin,geraldine.jean}@univ-nantes.fr
[2] Ecole Normale Supérieure PSL, DMA, 75230 Paris, France
oscar.fontaine@ens.psl.eu
[3] LIGM, CNRS, Université Gustave Eiffel, 77454 Marne-la-Vallée, France
stephane.vialette@univ-eiffel.fr

Abstract. We study the MAXIMUM ZERO-SUM PARTITION problem (or MZSP), defined as follows: given a multiset $\mathcal{S} = \{a_1, a_2, \ldots, a_n\}$ of integers $a_i \in \mathbb{Z}^*$ such that $\sum_{i=1}^{n} a_i = 0$, find a maximum cardinality partition $\{S_1, S_2, \ldots, S_k\}$ of $\mathcal{S}$ such that, for every $1 \le i \le k$, $\sum_{a_j \in S_i} a_j = 0$. Solving MZSP is useful in genomics for computing evolutionary distances between pairs of species. Our contributions are a series of algorithmic results concerning MZSP, in terms of complexity, (in)approximability, with a particular focus on the fixed-parameter tractability of MZSP with respect to either (i) the size k of the solution, (ii) the number of negative (resp. positive) values in $\mathcal{S}$ and (iii) the largest integer in $\mathcal{S}$.

1 Introduction

In this paper, we study the MAXIMUM ZERO-SUM PARTITION (or MZSP).

MAXIMUM ZERO-SUM PARTITION (MZSP)
Instance : A multiset $\mathcal{S} = \{a_1, a_2, \ldots, a_n\}$ of numbers $a_i \in \mathbb{Z}^*$ s.t. $\sum_{i=1}^{n} a_i = 0$.
Output : A maximum cardinality partition $S = \{S_1, S_2, \ldots, S_k\}$ of $\mathcal{S}$ such that, for every $1 \le i \le k$, $\sum_{a_j \in S_i} a_j = 0$.

This problem emerged in bioinformatics, where determining the distance between two genomes was studied [1]. The distance formula in that context depends on a parameter to be optimized, which directly relates to answering MZSP. However, the MZSP problem in itself was not central to the results in [1], and thus has not been studied *per se* in that paper. Hence, the goal of the present paper is to extensively study the MZSP problem from an algorithmic point of view.

Definitions and Notations. For any integer n, $[\![1, n]\!]$ denotes the set of integers from 1 to n. Given a (multi)set S of integers and an integer p, we say that S *sums to p* when the sum of the elements of S is equal to p. When $p = 0$, we say that S is a *zero-sum (multi)set*. For any instance $\mathcal{S}$ of MZSP, we let neg (resp. pos) denote the number of negative (resp. positive) integers in $\mathcal{S}$ and $m = \min\{\mathsf{neg}, \mathsf{pos}\}$. We denote by n^* the number of distinct values in $\mathcal{S}$, by $b = \sum_{i=1}^{n} \lceil \log_2 (|a_i|) \rceil$ the number of bits needed to encode $\mathcal{S}$ (e.g. when $\mathcal{S}$ is stored as a list, in which each element is binary encoded), and by $B = \max_{i \in [1,n]}\{|a_i|\}$. The cardinality of an optimal partition of $\mathcal{S}$, i.e. the size of the solution, is denoted by k. For example, if $\mathcal{S} = \{-7, -7, -7, -1, -1, -1, 2, 3, 3, 4, 4, 4, 4\}$, then $n = 13$, $\mathsf{neg} = 6$, $\mathsf{pos} = 7$, $m = 6$, $n^* = 5$, $B = 7$ and it can be seen that the optimal solution is $k = 4$: for instance, $S_1 = S_2 = \{-7, 4, 3\}$, $S_3 = \{-7, -1, 4, 4\}$ and $S_4 = \{-1, -1, 2\}$ form a solution. UNARY MZSP denotes MZSP for which unary encoding of the input instance is used. For any positive integer p, p-MZSP denotes the decision version of MZSP, in which, given p and a zero-sum integer multiset $\mathcal{S}$, we ask whether there exists a zero-sum partition S of $\mathcal{S}$ such that $|S| \geq p$. We will also often use the O^* notation, as frequently done in parameterized complexity: for a given problem whose size of the input is n and parameter is k, $O^*(f(k))$ stands for $O(f(k) \cdot poly(n))$. In other words, O^* only describes the exponential part of the running time (in k) and discards the polynomial factor (in n).

First Observations. Note that if we denote by $-\mathcal{S}$ the multiset $\mathcal{S}$ to which all signs have been switched, then $-\mathcal{S}$ is a valid instance for MZSP, and both $\mathcal{S}$ and $-\mathcal{S}$ have the same optimum k. Consequently, any result that applies to neg (resp. pos) applies to pos (resp. neg), and thus to m. Note also that an m-size zero-sum partition of $\mathcal{S}$ is necessarily optimal, since at least one positive (resp. negative) element of $\mathcal{S}$ needs to be present in any S_i from the partition. In other words, we always have $k \leq m$. For any given $p \in \mathbb{N}^*$, a YES-instance for p-MZSP is also a YES-instance for p'-MZSP as long as $p' \in [1, p]$. Indeed, merging any two sets in a size-p zero-sum partition of $\mathcal{S}$ yields a size-$(p-1)$ zero-sum partition of $\mathcal{S}$. Finally, observe that if an integer a and its opposite $-a$ both belong to $\mathcal{S}$, then there always exists an optimal solution $S = \{S_1, S_2, \ldots, S_k\}$ in which $S_i = \{-a, a\}$ for some $i \in [1, n]$. Indeed, suppose $-a$ and a both belong to $\mathcal{S}$, and observe an optimal solution $S = \{S_1, S_2, \ldots, S_k\}$ in which $S_i \neq \{-a, a\}$ for every $i \in [1, k]$. Clearly, no S_i is such that $\{-a, a\} \subset S_i$, otherwise we could partition S_i into $\{-a, a\}$ and $S_i \backslash \{-a, a\}$, both summing to zero, contradicting the optimality of S. Thus $-a \in S_x$ and $a \in S_y$ for some $1 \leq x \neq y \leq k$. Now consider the following partition $S' = \{S_1', S_2', \ldots, S_k'\}$ of $\mathcal{S}$: (i) $S_i' = S_i$ for every $i \in [1, k]$ such that $i \neq x$ and $i \neq y$, (ii) $S_x' = \{-a, a\}$ and (iii) $S_y' = (S_x \cup S_y) \backslash \{-a, a\}$. Every S_i', $i \in [1, k]$, sums to zero, and $|S| = |S'| = k$.

In this paper, we study the MZSP problem under an algorithmic viewpoint, and, in particular, discuss its computational complexity, approximability and fixed-parameter tractability with respect to n, n^*, m, B and k (see Table 1).

2   Computational Complexity of MZSP

Theorem 1. MZSP *is strongly NP-complete, even if each S_i in the solution S contains at most four elements.*

Proof. The proof is by reduction from 3-PARTITION, which has been proved to be strongly NP-complete [3], and whose definition is as follows.

Table 1. Summary of our main results, in relation to parameters n, m, k, n^*, B and b.

Parameter	Results
n	Strongly NP-complete (Theorem 1)
	No $2^{o(n)}b^{O(1)}$ algorithm unless ETH fails (Theorem 4)
	FPT (Theorem 5)
	No approximation within ratio $O(n^{1-\epsilon})$ (Theorem 7)
m	NP-complete, even if bounded (Theorem 2)
k	NP-complete, even if bounded (Theorem 2)
m	W[1]-hard (Theorem 8)
Unary encoded instance	XP (Corollary 2)
k	W[1]-hard (Corollary 1)
Unary encoded instance	XP (Theorem 9)
n^*	No $2^{o(n^*)}b^{O(1)}$ algorithm unless ETH fails (Theorem 10)
	XP (Theorem 11)
B	FPT (Theorem 13)
n^*+k	FPT (Theorem 12)

3-PARTITION

Instance : An integer C, a multiset $X = \{x_1, x_2, \ldots, x_{3p}\}$ of integers such that
(i) $\sum_{i=1}^{3p} x_i = C \cdot p$ and (ii) $\forall x_i \in X, \frac{C}{4} < x_i < \frac{C}{2}$.
Question : Does there exist a partition $\{X_1, X_2, \ldots, X_p\}$ of X such that, for every $i \in [\![1,p]\!]$, $\sum_{x_j \in X_i} x_j = C$?

Let $I = (C, X)$ be an instance of 3-PARTITION, and let $\mathcal{S}$ be the multiset such that $\mathcal{S} = \{x_1, \ldots, x_{3p}, -C, \ldots, -C\}$, where $-C$ appears p times in $\mathcal{S}$. Note that, by definition of 3-PARTITION, the sum of all elements in $\mathcal{S}$ is equal to zero, hence $\mathcal{S}$ is an instance of MZSP. We now show that $I = (C, X)$ is a YES-instance for 3-PARTITION iff MZSP (with instance $\mathcal{S}$) has a solution of cardinality p.

($\Rightarrow$) If I is a YES-instance for 3-PARTITION, there exists $t_j = (x_{i_{j,1}}, x_{i_{j,2}}, x_{i_{j,3}})$, $j \in [\![1,p]\!]$, such that $x_{i_{j,1}} + x_{i_{j,2}} + x_{i_{j,3}} = C$. In particular, for every $j \in [\![1,p]\!]$, $S_j = \{x_{i_{j,1}}, x_{i_{j,2}}, x_{i_{j,3}}, -C\}$ is a size-p partition of $\mathcal{S}$ in which every S_j sums to zero. Moreover, such partition is optimal: since neg $= p$, no zero-sum partition of $\mathcal{S}$ can contain strictly more than p sets.

($\Leftarrow$) Suppose there exists a solution of MZSP of cardinality p, say $S = \{S_1, S_2, \ldots, S_p\}$. Since any zero-sum subset in S contains at least one negative element from $\mathcal{S}$, every S_j, $j \in [\![1,p]\!]$, contains *exactly* one negative element, namely $-C$. Since, in 3-PARTITION, every x_i satisfies $\frac{C}{4} < x_i < \frac{C}{2}$, exactly 3 such elements are required to sum to C. Thus, any S_j, $j \in [\![1,p]\!]$, contains 3 elements of the form x_i, together with $-C$. Since each S_j sums to zero, $\{x_1, \ldots, x_{3p}\}$ can be partitioned in triplets, each summing to C, i.e. $I = (C, X)$ is a YES-instance for 3-PARTITION.

In unary, 3-PARTITION and MZSP are both encoded in $\Theta(p \cdot C)$ space. As 3-PARTITION is strongly NP-complete, MZSP is also strongly NP-complete. $\square$

As discussed above, finding a solution S to MZSP where every zero-sum set S_i in S satisfies $|S_i| = 2$ (if such a solution exists) is easy: look for two opposite values, combine them, and iterate. Theorem 1 proves that solving MZSP when every S_i contains 4 elements is (strongly) NP-complete, which rules out parameter "maximum size of an S_i" for FPT considerations. Note that the case $|S_i| = 3$ (or equivalently $|S_i| \leq 3$) has been shown to be strongly NP-complete in [1].

Theorem 2. *MZSP is NP-complete, even when k and m are bounded.*

Proof. We show NP-completeness of MZSP in the specific case $m = k = 2$, by reduction from PARTITION which is known to be NP-complete [8].

PARTITION
Instance : A multiset $X = \{x_1, x_2, \ldots, x_n\}$ of integers from $\mathbb{N}^*$.
Question : Does there exist a partition $\{X_1, X_2\}$ of X s.t. $\sum_{x_i \in X_1} x_i = \sum_{x_j \in X_2} x_j$?

Let X be an instance of PARTITION. We can always assume $\sum_{i=1}^{n} x_i$ to be even, otherwise we have a NO-instance. Thus assume $\sum_{i=1}^{n} x_i = 2N$. The MZSP instance we build from X is $S = X \cup \{-N, -N\}$. We show that X is a YES-instance for PARTITION iff MZSP yields a size-2 zero-sum partition for S.

($\Rightarrow$) Suppose there exists a partition $\{X_1, X_2\}$ of X such that $\sum_{x_i \in X_1} x_i = \sum_{x_j \in X_2} x_j$. We thus have $\sum_{x_i \in X_1} x_i = \sum_{x_j \in X_2} x_j = N$, and $\{X_1 \cup \{-N\}, X_2 \cup \{-N\}\}$ is a zero-sum partition of S. Moreover, this partition is optimal since $m = \mathsf{neg} = 2$ and $k \leq m$.

($\Leftarrow$) Suppose there exists a zero-sum partition of cardinality $k = 2$ of S, say $S = \{S_1, S_2\}$. Because $\mathsf{neg} = 2$, we know that S_1 (resp. S_2) contains exactly one negative integer; thus, both in S_1 and S_2, this integer is $-N$. Assume $S_1 = X_1 \cup \{-N\}$ and $S_2 = X_2 \cup \{-N\}$. In that case, $\{X_1, X_2\}$ is a partition of X, and because both S_1 and S_2 sum to zero, we have $\sum_{x_i \in X_1} x_i = \sum_{x_j \in X_2} x_j = N$. Thus X is a YES-instance for PARTITION. $\square$

Although we just showed that MZSP is strongly NP-complete in general, and remains NP-complete when k is bounded, we show there exists a pseudo-polynomial algorithm that solves MZSP in the case $k = 2$.

Theorem 3. *2-MZSP can be solved in pseudopolynomial time.*

The following result gives two lower bounds on the time to solve MZSP, both based on the Exponential-Time Hypothesis (ETH, see e.g. [4] for a definition). Recall that b is the size of the input S, assuming it is binary encoded.

Theorem 4. *Unless ETH fails, MZSP cannot be solved (i) in $2^{o(n)} \cdot b^{O(1)}$ or (ii) in $2^{o(\sqrt{b})}$.*

We now show that the above ETH bound based on n is essentially tight.

Theorem 5. *MZSP is solvable in $O^*(2^n)$.*

Proof. We solve MZSP by dynamic programming. Given an instance $\mathcal{S}$ of MZSP, we create a dynamic programming 1-dimensional table T indexed by the subsets of $\mathcal{S}$. We set $T[\emptyset]$ to 0. Then, for increasing $i \in [\![1,n]\!]$, and for every size-i subset P_i of $\mathcal{S}$, we fill $T[P_i]$ using the following rule:

$$T[P_i] = \begin{cases} \max_{a \in P_i}\{T[P_i\backslash\{a\}]\} & \text{if } P_i \text{ does not sum to } 0 \\ \max_{a \in P_i}\{T[P_i\backslash\{a\}]\} + 1 & \text{otherwise} \end{cases}$$

The optimal value k for MZSP is then found in $T[\mathcal{S}]$, and an optimal zero-sum partition of $\mathcal{S}$ can be found by backtracking from that value. The space and time complexity of the above algorithm is $O^*(2^n)$, since it takes polynomial time to fill any of the 2^n elements in T. It remains to show correctness. For this, for any subset P of $\mathcal{S}$, we denote by k_P the cardinality of a maximum zero-sum subpartition of P, where the term *subpartition* describes a partition of a subset of P. Our goal is to show that for any P, $T[P] = k_P$. This is done by induction on $i = |P|$. When $i = 0$, this trivially holds as $T[\emptyset]$ is set to 0. Suppose now that for some $i \in [\![0, n-1]\!]$, any P such that $|P| = i$ satisfies $T[P] = k_P$. Let us now observe a set P of cardinality $i + 1$. If P does not sum to zero, let us consider a maximum cardinality zero-sum subpartition of P, say $(A_1, \ldots, A_{k_P})$. Since P does not sum to zero, there exists $a \in P$ such that $a \notin \bigcup_{i=1}^{k_P} A_i$. Thus $(A_1, \ldots, A_{k_P})$ is a maximum cardinality zero-sum subpartition of $P\backslash\{a\}$, otherwise this would contradict the cardinality maximality of $(A_1, \ldots, A_{k_P})$. Thus $k_{P\backslash\{a\}} = k_P$. Since $T[P\backslash\{a\}] = k_{P\backslash\{a\}}$, we have $T[P] \geq k_P$ by definition of $T[P]$. Conversely, if $a \in P$ and $(A_1, \ldots, A_{k_{P\backslash\{a\}}})$ is a zero-sum subpartition of $P\backslash\{a\}$, then $(A_1, \ldots, A_{k_{P\backslash\{a\}}})$ is a zero-sum subpartition of P. Thus $k_{P\backslash\{a\}} \leq k_P$, which means $T[P\backslash\{a\}] \leq k_P$ and thus implies $T[P] \leq k_P$. Altogether, we have $T[P] = k_P$. Now if P sums to zero, let $(A_1, \ldots, A_{k_P})$ be a maximum cardinality zero-sum partition of P. We thus have $P = \bigcup_{j=1}^{k_P} A_j$. Let $a \in A_{k_P}$ (note that a exists, since A_{k_P} is non-empty). Thus $(A_1, \ldots, A_{k_P-1})$ is a maximum zero-sum subpartition of $P\backslash\{a\}$, and hence $k_P = k_{P\backslash\{a\}} + 1$, which implies $T[P] \geq k_P$. Conversely, if $a \in P$, then $a \in A_j$ for a given $j \in [\![1, k_P]\!]$. Using similar arguments as previously, we can prove that $k_P = k_{P\backslash\{a\}} + 1$, and thus $T[P] \leq k_P$. Altogether, we have $T[P] = k_P$. We conclude that $T[P] = k_P$ for any $P \subseteq \mathcal{S}$. In particular, $T[\mathcal{S}]$ contains a maximum cardinality zero-sum partition of $\mathcal{S}$. By backtracking in T, the sought partition can be found in polynomial time, which solves MZSP. $\square$

The previous theorem is based on the fact that the number of distinct subsets in $\mathcal{S}$ is upper bounded by $O(2^n)$. It is also possible to upper bound this number by a function of b, the number of bits needed to binary encode $\mathcal{S}$.

Theorem 6. MZSP *is solvable in* $2^{O\left(\frac{b}{\log b}\right)}$.

Proof. Let us partition $\mathcal{S}$ into $S_p = \{a_i \in \mathcal{S} \text{ s.t. } |a_i| \leq \sqrt{b}\}$ and $S_q = \{a_i \in \mathcal{S} \text{ s.t. } |a_i| > \sqrt{b}\}$. Let us also denote, for any multiset E, by $\mathcal{P}(E)$ the *set* of subsets of E (e.g. $\mathcal{P}(\{2,3,3\}) = \{\emptyset, \{2\}, \{3\}, \{2,3\}, \{3,3\}, \{2,3,3\}\}$). In that case, we have $|\mathcal{P}(S_p)| \leq (b+1)^{2\sqrt{b}}$: indeed, by definition any element $a \in S_p$

satisfies $|a| \leq \sqrt{b}$. Moreover, a appears at most b times in S_p, since any a needs at least one bit to be encoded, while b bits are enough to encode S. Thus S_p contains at most $2\sqrt{b}$ different numbers, each of them appearing at most b times in S_p. Hence $|\mathcal{P}(S_p)| \leq (b+1)^{2\sqrt{b}} \leq 2^{2\sqrt{b}\log(b+1)} \leq 2^{2\frac{b}{\log b}}$. On the other hand, S_q contains elements of size at least $\sqrt{b}$. Then S_q cannot be of cardinality greater than $2\frac{b}{\log b}$, otherwise encoding S_q would require more than b bits ; thus $|\mathcal{P}(S_q)| \leq 2^{2\frac{b}{\log b}}$. Since S_p and S_q form a partition of S, we have that $|\mathcal{P}(S)| = |\mathcal{P}(S_p)| \cdot |\mathcal{P}(S_q)| \leq 2^{4\frac{b}{\log b}}$. Since the dynamic programming algorithm from proof of Theorem 5 solves MZSP and has running time in $O^*(|\mathcal{P}(S)|)$, we conclude that MZSP can be solved in $2^{O\left(\frac{b}{\log b}\right)}$, which proves the theorem.   □

We now end this section by turning our attention to the inapproximability of MZSP, in Theorem 7 below.

Theorem 7. *Unless P=NP, MZSP cannot be approximated within ratio $O(n^{1-\epsilon})$ for any $\epsilon > 0$.*

Proof. As for Theorem 2, we prove the result by reduction from PARTITION, which is known to be NP-complete [8]. Let $X = \{x_1, x_2, \ldots, x_\ell\}$ be an instance of PARTITION, and let $\sum_{i=1}^{\ell} x_i = 2N$ with $N \geq 1$. We can indeed assume $\sum_{i=1}^{\ell} x_i$ to be non-zero and even, otherwise the problem is trivially answered. The reduction is as follows: let $q \geq 1$ be any integer, and let us recursively build a set $\{p_0, p_1, \ldots, p_q\}$ of integers. More precisely, we set $p_0 = 1$, and $p_i = (2iN + 1)p_{i-1}$ for any $i \in [\![1, q]\!]$. We note that for any $0 \leq j < i \leq q$, p_j divides p_i. Based on X and on the values $p_0, p_1, \ldots, p_q$, we now construct the multiset $S = \bigcup_{i=0}^{q}\{p_i X, -Np_i, -N\sum_{i=0}^{q} p_i\}$ where, for any $i \in [\![0, q]\!]$, $p_i X$ denotes the values obtained by multiplying each element of X by p_i. It can be seen that S sums to zero, and is thus a valid instance of MZSP. It can also be seen that the above reduction takes polynomial-time, as long as q remains polynomial in the input size of PARTITION. Intuitively, the above reduction consists in "copying", a certain amount of times, an (expanded) instance X of PARTITION, so that the solution size of MZSP on S increases, while maintaining the property that the different "expanded copies" of X in S do not mutually interact.

Let us now prove correctness of our reduction, by showing the following: (i) X is a YES-instance for PARTITION iff (ii) MZSP for S yields a partition of cardinality $q + 2$ iff (iii) MZSP for S yields a partition of cardinality 2.

$((i) \Rightarrow (ii))$ Suppose X is a YES-instance for PARTITION. Then there exists $P \subset X$ such that $\sum_{a \in P} a = N$. By construction, for every $i \in [\![0, q]\!]$, $\sum_{a \in P} p_i a = Np_i$. Hence, for every negative number $-s$ in S (s being either $-Np_i$ for some $i \in [\![0, q]\!]$, or $-N\sum_{i=0}^{q} p_i$), it is possible to find a subset of S summing to Np_i, and moreover any pair of such sets is mutually disjoint. Hence S can be partitioned into zero-sum subsets, and the cardinality of such a partition is $q+2$.

$((ii) \Rightarrow (iii))$ If MZSP for S yields a partition of cardinality $q + 2$, and since $q + 2 \geq 2$ then, by merging any $q + 1$ sets in this partition, we obtain a size-2 zero-sum partition.

$((iii) \Rightarrow (i))$ Suppose there exists a zero-sum partition of MZSP for $\mathcal{S}$, of cardinality 2. In that case, there exists a non-empty zero-sum (multi)set $P \subset \mathcal{S}$ that does not contain the negative integer $-N\sum_{i=0}^{q} p_i$. Let us denote i_0 the smallest index $i \in [\![0,q]\!]$ such that $-Np_i$ belongs to P. Note that for all $i \in [\![0, i_0 - 1]\!]$, we have $p_i X \cap P = \emptyset$: indeed, suppose by contradiction that this is not the case, and let A be the sum of the elements of $\left(\bigcup_{i=0}^{i_0-1} p_i X \right) \cap P$. Then we have $A \leq (1 + p_1 + \cdots + p_{i_0-1}) \cdot 2N$, hence $A \leq i_0 \cdot 2N \cdot p_{i_0-1}$, which yields $A < p_{i_0}$. In particular, p_{i_0} does not divide A, since $A \neq 0$. As p_{i_0} divides every other element of P, we conclude that $A = 0$, which is the sought contradiction.

Now, let us consider $P' = P \bmod p_{i_0+1}$. From the above, the only elements from P that induce non zero elements in P' are the elements of $p_{i_0} X \cap P$, together with $-Np_{i_0}$. We thus conclude there exists a (multi)set $K \subset X$ such that $\sum_{a \in K} p_{i_0} a \equiv Np_{i_0} \bmod p_{i_0+1}$. Since $p_{i_0+1} > 2Np_{i_0}$, $\sum_{a \in K} p_{i_0} a = Np_{i_0}$, and thus $\sum_{a \in K} a = N$. In other words, we have a YES-instance for PARTITION.

Now we have proved correctness of our reduction, let us turn to proving our inapproximability result. Let ϵ be any strictly positive value, and suppose that there exists an approximation algorithm $\mathcal{A}$ for MZSP, of ratio $\rho = O(n^{1-\epsilon})$ with $n = |\mathcal{S}|$. Take now an instance X of PARTITION, and recall that $\ell = |X|$. Let C be a constant such that $\rho \leq Cn^{1-\epsilon}$ for sufficiently large n. We let $q = \max(C^{\frac{1}{1-\epsilon}} - 1, (C^{\frac{1}{1-\epsilon}}(\ell+1)+1)^{\frac{1}{\epsilon}-1}-1)$, and we proceed with the above mentioned reduction by building the MZSP instance $\mathcal{S}$ based on X and on parameter q. We have that $n = |\mathcal{S}| = (\ell + 1)(q + 1) + 1$.

Then, $\frac{q+1}{C^{\frac{1}{1-\epsilon}}} \geq 1$ and $(q+1)^{\frac{1}{1-\epsilon}-1} - C^{\frac{1}{1-\epsilon}}(\ell+1) \geq 1$ which yields $\frac{q+1}{C^{\frac{1}{1-\epsilon}}} \cdot ((q+1)^{\frac{1}{1-\epsilon}-1} - C^{\frac{1}{1-\epsilon}}(\ell+1)) \geq 1$ and $C((\ell+1)(q+1)+1)^{1-\epsilon} \leq q+1$. We thus conclude that $Cn^{1-\epsilon} \leq q + 1$. We now apply $\mathcal{A}$ on $\mathcal{S}$, and solve it polynomially within factor $\rho \leq Cn^{1-\epsilon}$. Thus we obtain $\rho \leq q+1$, hence $\rho < q+2$. However, we know from the above that if we have a YES-instance for PARTITION, then there exists a zero-sum partition of $\mathcal{S}$ of cardinality $q+2$. In that case, the solution provided by the approximation algorithm $\mathcal{A}$ is a zero-sum partition of $\mathcal{S}$ of cardinality $c \geq \frac{q+2}{\rho} > 1$. Conversely, if $\mathcal{A}$ provides a zero-sum partition of cardinality $c > 1$, then such zero-sum partition shows that X is a YES-instance for PARTITION.

Altogether, if there exists an approximation algorithm $\mathcal{A}$ for MZSP of ratio $\rho = O(n^{1-\epsilon})$, it is possible to polynomially solve PARTITION: a contradiction, unless P=NP, to the fact that PARTITION is NP-complete [8]. □

3   Parameterized Complexity of MZSP

Parameters k and m. We first consider fixed-parameterized complexity of MZSP with respect to the size k of the solution. On the way, we will also discuss parameter $m = \min\{\mathsf{neg}, \mathsf{pos}\}$, as we always have $m \geq k$. By Theorem 2, we know that, unless P=NP, MZSP is not FPT with respect to parameter k (resp. m), since MZSP is NP-complete even in the case where both these values are constant. The following theorem and corollary show W[1]-hardness of UNARY MZSP with respect to the same parameters.

Theorem 8. UNARY MZSP *parameterized by m is W[1]-hard.*

Theorem 8 implies the following corollary, as we always have $m \geq k$.

Corollary 1. UNARY MZSP *parameterized by k is W[1]-hard.*

Proof. (of Theorem 8) Let us assume that integers are encoded in unary. We reduce from UNARY BIN-PACKING, which is known to be W[1]-hard with respect to parameter "size of the solution" [6], to UNARY MZSP. We first recall the definition of BIN-PACKING (presented here in its decision version):

BIN-PACKING
Instance : a multiset of strictly positive integers $P = \{w_1, \ldots, w_n\}$, an integer W, an integer t.
Question : Does there exist a partition $\{J_1, \ldots, J_t\}$ of P such that $\sum_{w_j \in J_i} w_j \leq W$ for every $i \in [\![1, t]\!]$?

As mentioned above, UNARY BIN-PACKING is BIN-PACKING in which all integers are assumed to be encoded in unary; besides, UNARY BIN-PACKING, parameterized by the number t of bins, is known to be W[1]-hard [6]. Let $I = (P, W, t)$ be an instance of UNARY BIN-PACKING. Moreover, assume $\sum_{i=1}^{n} w_i = tW$, since UNARY BIN-PACKING remains W[1]-hard parameterized by the number t of bins under this condition [6]. Let us now construct the following instance of MZSP: $S = \{w_1, \ldots, w_n, \underbrace{-W, \ldots, -W}_{t}\}$. Note that we have $m = t$. We now show that MZSP admits a t-size zero-sum partition iff $I = (P, W, t)$ is a YES-instance for UNARY BIN-PACKING.

($\Rightarrow$) Suppose (P, W, t) is a YES-instance for UNARY BIN-PACKING. Thus there exists a partition $\{J_1, \ldots, J_t\}$ of P such that $\sum_{w_j \in J_i} w_j \leq W$ for every $i \in [\![1, t]\!]$. However, since we assume $\sum_{i=1}^{n} w_i = tW$, we conclude that every J_i, $i \in [\![1, t]\!]$, is such that $\sum_{w_j \in J_i} w_j = W$. Hence, $\{A_1, A_2, \ldots, A_t\}$, where $A_i = J_i \cup \{-W\}$ for every $i \in [\![1, t]\!]$, is a t-size zero-sum partition of S.

($\Leftarrow$) Conversely, suppose there exists a t-size zero-sum partition $\{A_1, A_2, \ldots, A_t\}$ of S. Since S contains exactly t negative numbers, this implies that every A_i, $i \in [\![1, t]\!]$, contains exactly one occurrence of $-W$. Thus $\{J_1, J_2, \ldots, J_t\}$, where $J_i = A_i \backslash \{-W\}$ for every $i \in [\![1, t]\!]$, is a partition of P. Moreover, since each A_i sums to zero, we know that each J_i sums to W, which ensures that (P, W, t) is a YES-instance for UNARY BIN-PACKING.

The above reduction is a valid parameterized reduction, since parameter t for UNARY BIN-PACKING is strictly equal to parameter m for UNARY MZSP. Moreover, the instance S of UNARY MZSP that we built satisfies $k = m$.   □

Theorem 8 suggests that, even encoded in unary, MZSP admits no FPT algorithm parameterized by k. What we can show, in the following theorem, is that MZSP encoded in unary is in XP when parameterized by k.

Theorem 9. UNARY MZSP *is in XP parameterized by k.*

Since we always have $m \geq k$, Theorem 9 implies the following corollary.

Corollary 2. UNARY MZSP *is in* XP *when parameterized by* m.

Parameter number of distinct values n^*. We now discuss parameter n^*, for which we first provide a complexity lower bound based on ETH. Recall that b is the (binary encoded) size of the input instance $\mathcal{S}$.

Theorem 10. *Unless* ETH *fails,* MZSP *cannot be solved in* $2^{o(n^*)}b^{O(1)}$.

Proof. The proof is based on a combination of (i) a reduction from 3-SAT to SUBSET-SUM presented in [7] and inspired from [10] and (ii) the reduction from SUBSET-SUM to MZSP from proof of Theorem 4. More precisely, starting from any instance of 3-SAT with n variables and m clauses, an instance of SUBSET-SUM containing $n' = 2n + 2m$ integers, among which $2n + m$ are pairwise distinct, is constructed. Moreover, in proof of Theorem 4, the instance $\mathcal{S}$ of MZSP built from SUBSET-SUM contains $n'' = n' + 2 = 2n + 2m + 2$ integers, among which $n^* = 2n + m + 2$ are pairwise distinct. Under ETH, 3-SAT cannot be solved in $2^{o(n)}$. If we combine this information with the sparsification method [5] (which allows to consider only 3-SAT instances for which $m = O(n)$) and the above argument, we conclude that, under ETH, MZSP cannot be solved in $2^{o(n^*)}b^{O(1)}$. $\quad\square$

Concerning parameterized complexity with respect to n^*, we suspect MZSP to be W[1]-hard parameterized by n^*, but the question remains open. Meanwhile, we are able to prove (see Theorem 11) that the problem is in XP with respect to n^*. The rationale for this result is that the multisets that constitute any maximum zero-sum partition of $\mathcal{S}$ are few, and that we can efficiently compute them. In order to prove Theorem 11, we need to introduce several definitions, and first prove two propositions (Propositions 1 and 2).

Let us suppose that $\mathcal{S}$ is a multiset containing n^* distinct values, denoted $a_1, \ldots, a_{n^*}$. We introduce several notions: given any multiset $\mathcal{M}$ built from $a_1, \ldots, a_{n^*}$, we call *multiplicity multiset* of $\mathcal{M}$ the multiset $\{u_1, u_2, \ldots, u_{n^*}\}$ representing the mutiplicities of each a_i in $\mathcal{M}$: more precisely, for any $i \in [\![1, n^*]\!]$, $u_i \in \mathbb{N}$ is the number of times a_i appears in $\mathcal{M}$. With this notation, we can define a partial order $\leq$ on multiplicity multisets as follows: let $u = \{u_1, u_2, \ldots, u_{n^*}\}$ and $v = \{v_1, v_2, \ldots, v_{n^*}\}$ be two multiplicity multisets; we write $u \leq v$ whenever $u_i \leq v_i$ for every $i \in [\![1, n^*]\!]$. Now let $s = \{s_1, s_2, \ldots, s_{n^*}\}$ be the multiplicity multiset of $\mathcal{S}$. We first define two sets, respectively named K and D: K is the set of irreducible multiplicity multisets of $\mathcal{S}$ leading to zero-sum subsets of $\mathcal{S}$, and D is the set of all zero-sum subsets of $\mathcal{S}$. In the following, for simplicity we write $u = 0$ for any vector u whenever all its coordinates are equal to 0. Formally, K and D are defined as follows:

$$K = \left\{ u \in \mathbb{N}^{n^*} \,\middle|\, \textstyle\sum_{i=1}^{n^*} u_i a_i = 0, u \neq 0 \text{ and} \right.$$
$$\left. \forall v \in \mathbb{N}^{n^*}, v \leq u \text{ and } \textstyle\sum_{i=1}^{n^*} v_i a_i = 0 \Rightarrow v = 0 \text{ or } v = u \right\} \text{ and}$$
$$D = \left\{ u \in \mathbb{N}^{n^*} \,\middle|\, u \leq s, u \neq 0 \text{ and } \textstyle\sum_{i=1}^{n^*} u_i a_i = 0 \right\}.$$

Any maximum zero-sum partition of S is induced by elements of $K \cap D$ only. We define a third set Z as follows: $Z = \left\{ u \in \mathbb{N}^{n^*} \mid u \neq 0 \text{ and } \sum_{i=1}^{n^*} u_i a_i = 0 \right\}$. Note that both K and D are included in Z. We are now interested in two properties, related to the above definitions. We begin with Proposition 1.

Algorithm 1. XP algorithm for solving MZSP, parameterized by n^*

1: Compute D
2: Initialize T
3: **for** every $i \in [\![1, n]\!]$ **do**
4:    **for** every $u \in D$ **do**
5:       **for** every $v \in D$ **do**
6:          **if** $v + u \in D$ **then**
7:             $T[v + u] = \max(T[v] + 1, T[v + u])$
8:          **end if**
9:       **end for**
10:    **end for**
11: **end for**
12: **return** $T[s]$

Proposition 1. *Let U be a subset of Z such that $K \cap D \subseteq U$. There exists a size-p zero-sum partition of S iff there exists $\ell \geq p$ elements of U, say $u^1, u^2, \ldots, u^\ell$ such that $\sum_{i=1}^{\ell} u^i = s$.*

For solving p-MZSP, it thus suffices to compute $K \cap D$, and to test whether it is possible to reach s, using p or more elements of $K \cap D$. Before that, we discuss the maximum cardinalities of K and D (see Proposition 2), which will be useful to evaluate the time complexity to generate these sets.

Proposition 2. $D \subseteq [\![0, n]\!]^{n^*}$ and $K \subseteq [\![0, n^*B - 1]\!]^{n^*}$.

In order to compute D (resp. K), it thus suffices to generate each element of $[\![0, n]\!]^{n^*}$ (resp. $[\![0, n^*B - 1]\!]^{n^*}$), and check for each of them whether it belongs to D (resp. K). For each element of $[\![0, n]\!]^{n^*}$, checking its membership to D can be achieved in $O(n^2 \log B)$, thus D can be computed in $O(n^{n^*+2} \log(B))$. Concerning K, testing if an element of $[\![0, n^*B - 1]\!]^{n^*}$ sums to zero can be done in $O(n^* \log(n^*B))$, and by dynamic programming, we can check if it is irreducible in $O((n^*B)^{n^*})$; thus K can be computed in $O((n^*B)^{2n^*})$.

The set K (and its computation) will be useful later for proving Theorem 13. In the following, we first focus on set D, whose cardinality is denoted c_D. Indeed, starting from D, Algorithm 1 shows that MZSP can be solved in $O(nc_D^2 n^* \log n + n^{n^*+2} \log B)$. Since, by Proposition 2 above, c_D is in $O(n^{n^*})$, this shows that MZSP is XP relatively to parameter n^*, as stated by the following theorem.

Theorem 11. *MZSP is in XP when parameterized by n^*.*

Proof. We provide an algorithm that runs in time $O(nc_D^2 n^* \log n + n^{n^*+2} \log B)$. The proof derives from Algorithm 1, in which T is an array indexed by the elements of D and which is initialized as follows: $T[0] = 0$, and for every other vector $v \in D$, $T[v] = -\infty$. We also recall that s is the multiplicity multiset of S.

Clearly, Algorithm 1 runs in $O(nc_D^2 n^* \log n)$ where $c_D = |D|$, since nc_D^2 additions on vectors are realized, each taking $O(n^* \log n)$ time. To this complexity, $O(n^{n^*+2} \log B)$ should be added for the precomputation of D. We now show that Algorithm 1 is correct. At the end of the algorithm, for any $v \in D$, $T[v]$ represents the largest number of elements of D that we can sum to obtain v. Let us denote w_v this value (thus $T[v] = w_v$). For any $i \in [\![1, n]\!]$, let $\mathcal{P}(i)$ be the following property: for every $v \in D$, $T[v] = w_v$ if $w_v \in [\![0, i]\!]$. Our goal is to prove, by induction on i, that $\mathcal{P}(i)$ holds for any $i \in [\![1, n]\!]$. First, $\mathcal{P}(0)$ is true since $w_v = 0$ implies $v = 0$. Now let $i \geq 0$, and let us assume $\mathcal{P}(i)$ holds. Let $v \in D$. If $w_v \leq i$, then by induction hypothesis, we have $T[v] = w_v$. If not, then there exists $u \in D$ such that $w_{v-u} = i$, and hence $T[v - u] = i$. Hence, by construction of T, $T[v] = i + 1 = w_v$, which consequently proves that $\mathcal{P}(i + 1)$ holds. By induction, $\mathcal{P}(i)$ holds for any $i \in [\![1, n]\!]$. In particular, $T[s]$ represents the largest number of elements from D that can be summed in order to obtain s. By Proposition 1, there exists ℓ elements of D whose sum is s iff there exists a zero-sum partition of S, of cardinality ℓ. Thus the cardinality of a maximum zero-sum partition of S is $T[s]$, which shows correctness of Algorithm 1.   □

As mentioned before, we conjecture MZSP to be W[1]-hard parameterized by n^*. In contrast, we have the following result.

Theorem 12. *MZSP is FPT when parameterized by* $n^* + k$.

Parameter maximum absolute value B. Recall that B is the greatest integer (in absolute value) in an instance S of MZSP.

Theorem 13. *MZSP is FPT when parameterized by B.*

Proof. In order to prove the result, we will provide an ILP model for our problem. We will then show that the number of variables of our ILP is a function of n^* and B only, which, combined with the fact that ILP is FPT parameterized by its number of variables [2,9] and the fact that $n^* \leq 2B$, allows us to conclude. Given an integer k, we are interested in solving k-MZSP, which asks whether a size-k zero-sum partition of S exists. Let (S, k) be an instance of k-MZSP. Let us number the n^* distinct values in S $a_1, \ldots, a_{n^*}$ and let $s_1, \ldots, s_{n^*}$ be their respective multiplicities in S. Let $c_K = |K|$, where K is the set defined previously, and let us compute K – recall that c_K, by Proposition 2 and the discussion that follows, satisfies $c_K = O((n^*B)^{n^*})$ –, and that K can be computed in $O((n^*B)^{2n^*})$. Our ILP based on the following c_K variables x_u, $u \in K$, where x_u represents the number of times element u appears in a zero-sum partition of S of cardinality at least k. The ILP formulation of the problem is as follows.

---

k-MZSP (ILP model):

$$\text{C.1 } \forall u \in K \qquad\qquad x_u \geq 0$$
$$\text{C.2 } \forall i \in [\![1, n^*]\!] \ \textstyle\sum_{u \in K} u_i x_u = s_i$$
$$\text{C.3 } \qquad\qquad\qquad \textstyle\sum_{u \in K} x_u \geq k$$

We now show correctness of our ILP model, by proving that there exists a zero-sum partition of MZSP of cardinality k iff the above ILP formulation admits a solution.

($\Rightarrow$) Suppose $\mathcal{S}$ admits a size-k zero-sum partition. Then, by Proposition 1, we know there exist $\ell \leq k$ elements of K which sum to s, that we will call $u^1, \ldots, u^\ell$. For $u \in K$, let x_u denote the number of times u appears in $(u_1, \ldots, u_\ell)$. Then, by definition, $\forall u \in K, x_u \geq 0$, $\sum_{u \in K} x_u u = s$ and $\sum_{u \in K} x_u = \ell \geq k$. Thus our ILP formulation admits a solution.

($\Leftarrow$) Conversely, suppose there exists x_u for $u \in K$, which is a solution to the above ILP formulation. Let us build $(u^i)_{i \in [\![1, \ell]\!]}$, where element u appears exactly x_u times. Then, from C.2, $\sum_{i=1}^{\ell} u^i = s$. Moreover, from C.3, $\ell \geq k$. Thus, from Proposition 1, there exists a size-k zero-sum partition of $\mathcal{S}$.

Since $n^* \leq 2B$, and since ILP, parameterized by the number x of variables, is FPT and can be solved in $O^*\left(x^{2.5x + o(x)}\right)$ [2,9], and since here $x = c_K = O((n^* B)^{n^*})$, the result follows. $\qquad\qquad\square$

4 Conclusion

We provided diverse algorithmic results concerning the MZSP problem: hardness, (in)approximability and fixed-parameterized complexity considerations with respect to parameters n, m, k, n^* and B. Some questions about MZSP remain unanswered. In particular, we conjecture MZSP to be W[1]-hard parameterized by the number n^* of distinct values in $\mathcal{S}$; (dis)proving it remains open.

Acknowledgments. We thank Ton van der Zanden for his suggestions, in particular those concerning parameter b.

References

1. Fertin, G., Jean, G., Tannier, E.: Algorithms for computing the double cut and join distance on both gene order and intergenic sizes. Algorithms Mol. Biol. **12**(1), 16:1–16:11 (2017)
2. Frank, A., Tardos, É.: An application of simultaneous diophantine approximation in combinatorial optimization. Combinatorica **7**(1), 49–65 (1987)
3. Garey, M.R., Johnson, D.S.: Computers and intractability: a guide to the theory of NP-completeness. Bell Telephone Laboratories (1979)
4. Impagliazzo, R., Paturi, R.: On the complexity of k-SAT. J. Comput. Syst. Sci. **62**(2), 367–375 (2001)
5. Impagliazzo, R., Paturi, R., Zane, F.: Which problems have strongly exponential complexity? J. Comput. Syst. Sci. **63**(4), 512–530 (2001)

6. Jansen, K., Kratsch, S., Marx, D., Schlotter, I.: Bin packing with fixed number of bins revisited. J. Comput. Syst. Sci. **79**(1), 39–49 (2013)
7. Jansen, K., Land, F., Land, K.: Bounding the running time of algorithms for scheduling and packing problems. In: Dehne, F., Solis-Oba, R., Sack, J.-R. (eds.) WADS 2013. LNCS, vol. 8037, pp. 439–450. Springer, Heidelberg (2013). https://doi.org/10.1007/978-3-642-40104-6_38
8. Karp, R.M.: Reducibility among Combinatorial Problems. In: Miller, R.E., Thatcher, J.W., Bohlinger, J.D. (eds.) Complexity of Computer Computations, pp. 85–103. Springer, Boston (1972). https://doi.org/10.1007/978-1-4684-2001-2_9
9. Lenstra, H.W.: Integer programming with a fixed number of variables. Math. Oper. Res. **8**(4), 538–548 (1983)
10. Wegener, I.: Complexity Theory. Springer, Heidelberg (2005). https://doi.org/10.1007/3-540-27477-4

Combined Bayesian and RNN-Based Hyperparameter Optimization for Efficient Model Selection Applied for autoML

Ruei-Sing Guan[1(✉)] [iD], Yu-Chee Tseng[1,2,3] [iD], Jen-Jee Chen[1] [iD], and Po-Tsun Kuo[1,4] [iD]

[1] College of AI, National Yang Ming Chiao Tung University, Hsinchu, Taiwan
{rs.guan.ai09,jenjee}@nycu.edu.tw, yctseng@cs.nycu.edu.tw,
Paul.Kuo@advantech.com.tw
[2] Academia Sinica, Taipei, Taiwan
[3] Kaohsiung Medical University, Kaohsiung, Taiwan
[4] Advantech Co., Ltd., Taipei, Taiwan

Abstract. The field of hyperparameter optimization (HPO) in auto machine learning (autoML) has been intensively studied, mainly in auto model selection (AMS), which finds the best set of hyperparameters, and neural architecture search (NAS), which optimizes the architecture of deep learning networks. In HPO, the two most significant problems are the demand of high level computational resources and the need of enormous computational time (GPU hours). In particular, the computational resources spent on HPO for complex deep learning networks are extremely high. Therefore, this paper augments HPO by adding recurrent neural networks (RNNs) to traditional statistical model-based algorithms to reduce the number of iterations of statistical models and eventually achieve the goal of lowering required computational resources. This paper's main contribution is combining traditional statistical model-based algorithms and recurrent neural network models to reduce the computational time when doing HPO with deep learning.

Keywords: Bayesian Optimization (BO) · Hyperparameter Optimization (HPO) · autoML · Recurrent Neural Network (RNN)

1 Introduction

With the advancement of computing devices, deep learning applications are becoming increasingly popular, and artificial intelligence (AI) engineers are in short supply. To alleviate this problem, one of the most popular solutions is automated Machine Learning (autoML) [8]. So, autoML is increasingly essential, and hyperparameter optimization (HPO) [3] has become a crucial issue in autoML.

In autoML, HPO is one of the core technologies in both neural architecture search (NAS) [1] and auto model selection (AMS) [2]. Several mathematical

S.-Y. Hsieh et al. (Eds.): ICS 2022, CCIS 1723, pp. 86–97, 2022.
https://doi.org/10.1007/978-981-19-9582-8_8

methods are often used to complete the HPO task, such as Bayesian Optimization (BO) [4], and Gradient-based Optimization [5]. Among them, BO is the most mainstream method.

The computational resources required for BO are actually considerable. Before exploiting this problem in more detail, we have to first know that there are two kinds of hyperparameters. One is the selective-kind hyperparameter, such as optimizer, and the other is the numerical-kind hyperparameter, such as learning rate, dropout rate, etc.

Because selective-kind hyperparameters would inherit from the prior iteration rounds, BO uses few resources to optimize them in the latter iteration rounds. For each iteration round, the number of attempts (or sampling) is fixed. BO takes more computing resources on numerical-kind hyperparameters optimization in the latter iteration rounds. We usually could find that BO is effective and converges very fast. From the experiments, we could see the performance improvement of BO for HPO in latter iterations is relatively limited. So BO for hyperparameter optimization is very effective, but the computing and exploration cost per iteration round is extremely high. In short, we can see two properties in BO: (1) As the number of iterations and explorations increases, the selective-kind hyperparameters converge because of the inheritance relationship. So the computational resources in the latter iterations are mostly spent on the numerical-kind hyperparameter exploration. (2) In the latter iteration rounds, the performance gradually converges, and more and more exploration is concentrated in specific local areas. In such a case, BO does lots of unnecessary computation, because it evaluates the whole global area. So, some lightweight methods can be considered to replace BO in the latter iteration rounds when BO gradually converges to speed up the HPO task.

Therefore, this paper proposes an RNN-based Hyperparameter Generator. For the BO task, BO is still adopted in the initial iteration rounds for effective hyperparameter prediction. When BO converges, we interrupt BO and let the RNN-based Hyperparameter Generator continue the hyperparameter optimization task. Experiments show that our new method can reach the best hyperparameter optimization with the same iteration rounds and significantly reduce the total time of the HPO task compared to pure BO methods.

2   Related Work

2.1   Bayesian Optimization and Hyperband (BOHB)

Bayesian Optimization (BO) is a statistical model, where BO is commonly used in HPO for autoML. There are two major components in BO: the prior function and the acquisition function. The statistical method, Gaussian Process (GP) [7], is often used in the prior function. Although the performance of GP is good, it is hard to well approximate the target function and predict the interval probability distribution of unsampled intervals with small sample points. Therefore, in BOHB [4], the typical GP is replaced by Hyperband [6] to solve this problem.

The input BO includes the Target Model, Target Dataset, and training budget b. When we want to increase the training cost on the indicated project, we would fix the number of iteration round and increase the training budget b. The evaluation criteria of HPO is the target model's performance by using the conducted hyperparameter, e.g., validation accuracy. The better the performance of the target model, the better the performance of the hyperparameters.

2.2 Optuna

Optuna [9] is a popular HPO tool in the autoML field because of its lightweight and cross-platform architecture. Since Optuna has been developed as an API that can be used without a deep background in artificial intelligence, it is a well-known success story in autoML. Optuna claims that it can handle any number of hyperparameters, but when the kinds of hyperparameters increase, the complexity of optimal hyperparameter-set search increases exponentially. So in practice, a few kinds of hyperparameters are preferred. Since it is necessary to reduce the search space hyperparameter importance ranking is often used, i.e., Functional Analysis of Variance (fANOVA) [14] technique, to give a statistic score for each kind of hyperparameter to represent its importance. We could learn fANOVA to give hyperparameters a ranking and prioritize high-ranking hyperparameters when doing HPO tasks.

2.3   Neural Architecture Search (NAS).

Neural Architecture Search (NAS) [1] not only optimizes the model's hyperparameters but modifies the model architecture of the target model according to the developer's setting rules. To avoid unlimited searching, a limited search space for the target model is given in NAS. Then, a search strategy performs calculation and model ontology modification. For each candidate structure of the target model, NAS would validate and evaluate its performance. Usually, a deep learning-based model would be optimized in the search strategy part and some hidden layers specified in the search space would be tried by adding or removing them from the model. In the end, NAS would decide on a final target model structure after a series of appropriate changes.

3   RNN-BO Hyperparameter Optimization Framework

3.1   Overall Framwork

Our proposed framework combines statistical models (or BO) and deep learning networks for hyperparameter exploration and optimization.

In our framework, BO is used as the statistic model to sample and evaluate initial hyperparameter sets (Fig. 1 (1)). The user sets the number of iteration rounds k to be performed by BO and all the hyperparameter sets selected and sampled by BO within the k iteration rounds will be recorded. The records include all n hyperparameter set samples for k different iteration rounds, i.e., there are $n \cdot k$ hyperparameter set samples, and their corresponding hyperparameter values (or the validation result) for each hyperparameter set sample.

The results and records from BO are than forwarded to Hyperparameter-Kind Importance Ranking (Fig. 1 (2)) to calculate the importance of each hyperparameter kind.

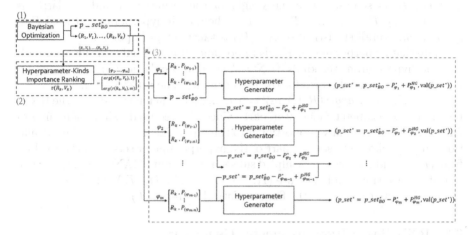

Fig. 1. Model flowchart

Finally, according to the ranking result, our framework continues optimizing each hyperparameter kind in sequence from the most important one to the least (Fig. 1 (3)). That is, the samples of the most important hyperparameter-kind in R_k, i.e., $(R_k.P_{\phi_1,1}), ..., (R_k.P_{\phi_1,n})$, and the best performance hyperparameter-set gained from BO, i.e., $p\_set_{BO}{}^*$, are put into the RNN-based Hyperparameter Generator for single hyperparameter prediction and optimization. The optimization is carried out one by one according to the ranking obtained from the importance ranking of hyperparameter-kinds.

Since the RNN-based Hyperparameter Generator only deals with one single kind of hyperparameter at a time, the time complexity is much lower than BO but the order of the kind of hyperparameter to be optimized does matter. Our framework designs the Hyperparameter-Kinds Importance Ranking module to rank the importance of all hyperparameter-kinds and then decides the optimization sequence of the hyperparameter kinds by referring to the ranking results.

3.2 Hyperparameter-Kinds Importance Ranking

Functional analysis of variance (fANOVA) [14] is a standard application to rank the individual and joint importances of hyperparameter-kind in the autoML domain. We exploit fANOVA in our Hyperparameter-Kinds Importance Ranking module. The inputs of fANOVA are $(R_1, ..., R_k)$ and $(V_1, ..., V_k)$ generated during BO. Then, fANOVA comes out the Individual Importance I and Total Importance T. I is the set of individual statistical scores of all hyperparameter-kinds for the target model, i.e., $I = [((P_1), f_{(P_1)}(\theta_{P_1})), ..., ((P_m), f_{(P_m)}(\theta_{P_m}))],$

where each element in I is a key and value pair, hyperparameter-kind (P_i) is the key and its statistical score $f_{P_i}(\theta_{P_i})$ is the value. T is the set of statistical scores of various combinations of hyperparameter-kinds, i.e., $T = [((P_1, P_2), f_{(P_1,P_2)}(\theta_{(P_1,P_2)})), ..., ((P_1, P_2, ..., P_m), f_{(P_1,P_2,...,P_m)}(\theta_{(P_1,P_2,...,P_m)}))]$. Then, we calculate the overall statistical score of each hyperparameter-kind P_i, $i = 1, ..., m$, by the weighted summation of its individual statistical score and all its related joint statistical scores, where the weight of the former is α and the latter is $(1 - \alpha)$, i.e., $g(P_i) = I_i \cdot \alpha + T_i \cdot (1 - \alpha)$. Then, each hyperparameter-kind P_i's, $i = 1, ..., m$, overall statistical score $g(P_i)$ is taken as its Importance.

Note that Hyperparameter-Kinds Importance Ranking only considers numerical-kind hyper-parameter-kinds. fANOVA computes only numerical-kind hyperparameters' statistical scores for the target model. The ranking result $r(R, V) = [arg(r(R, V), 1), ..., arg(r(R, V), m)] = [\phi_1, ..., \phi_m]$ is then forwarded to the RNN-based Hyperparameter Generator part. Since the required calculation time of fANOVA is exponentially proportional to the input size. So, to limit the calculation time, we choose to sample part of the hyperparameter sets with their values from (R, V) and then use the sampled subset as the input of fANOVA. This will be repeated for n times and generate $(I_1, T_1), (I_2, T_2), ..., (I_n, T_n)$. Then we average all these results to compute the final statistical scores (I, T).

3.3   RNN-Based Hyperparameter Generator

In this section, we will explain how to use the samples and information generated by BO to train the hyperparameter generator deep learning network to reduce computational costs.

In the following, two important issues are illustrated and then explained in order: (1) Why use an RNN-based deep learning model to perform HPO and how to train it? (2) How the RNN-based Hyperparameter Generator work.

This paper uses the Recurrent Neural Network (RNN)-based [13] deep learning network as the model of the hyperparameter generator, called RNN-based Hyperparameter Generator. Because of the recurrent nature of RNN, the RNN-based Hyperparameter Generator is trained to predict a better hyperparameter set by considering previous samples to fit the value curve when performing numerical prediction.

We select the Long Short-Term Memory (LSTM) [12] method from the RNN family as the RNN-based Hyperparameter Generator training model for two main reasons. The first is that the RNN-based Hyperparameter Generator only deals with numerical-kind hyperparameters. So, the amount of hyperparameter-kinds waiting to be optimized is limited. Second, since the core objective of this framework is to replace the high-cost BO prediction iteration round after a fixed k iteration round(s) (which is set by the user) with a low-cost deep learning method to reduce the computational complexity, a relatively lightweight LSTM-based model is used as the model of our RNN-based Hyperparameter Generator. Numerical prediction uses LSTM widely, such as stock market analysis [10], sales volume analysis [11], etc.

After obtaining the importance ranking of hyperparameter-kinds $[\phi_1, ..., \phi_m]$, we iteratively take the specified value-set of the hyperparameter-kind $\phi_i, i =$

$$
val(\varphi_i) = \begin{bmatrix} R_k \cdot P_{(\varphi_{i,1})} \\ \vdots \\ R_k \cdot P_{(\varphi_{i,n})} \end{bmatrix} \longrightarrow \begin{bmatrix} \begin{bmatrix} R_k \cdot P_{(\varphi_{i,1})} \\ \vdots \\ R_k \cdot P_{(\varphi_{i,(n-l))}} \end{bmatrix} \longrightarrow D = \begin{bmatrix} R_k \cdot P_{(\varphi_{i,1})}, \dots, R_k \cdot P_{(\varphi_{i,l})} \\ \vdots \\ R_k \cdot P_{(\varphi_{i,(n-2l))}}, \dots, R_k \cdot P_{(\varphi_{i,(n-l-1))}} \end{bmatrix} \\ \begin{bmatrix} R_k \cdot P_{(\varphi_{i,(n-2l+1))}} \\ \vdots \\ R_k \cdot P_{(\varphi_{i,n})} \end{bmatrix} \longrightarrow P = \begin{bmatrix} R_k \cdot P_{(\varphi_{i,(n-2l+1))}}, \dots, R_k \cdot P_{(\varphi_{i,(n-l))}} \\ \vdots \\ R_k \cdot P_{(\varphi_{i,(n-l+1))}}, \dots, R_k \cdot P_{(\varphi_{i,(n))}} \end{bmatrix} \end{bmatrix}
$$

Fig. 2. RNN-based Hyperparameter Generator inputs

$1 \dots m$, from R_k and the updated best hyperparameter-set p_set^*(it is $p\_set^*_{BO}$ when $i = 1$), as the input to the ith iteration round of RNN-based Hyperparameter Generator (as shown in Fig. 1 (3)).

Figure 2 shows how we select and prepare datasets to train the core LSTM model in the RNN-based Hyperparameter Generator. The specified numerical-kind hyperparameter values of hyperparameter kind ϕ_i from the kth BO iteration round are split into the LSTM training dataset D and the LSTM prediction dataset P. The final expected prediction and lookback value is l.

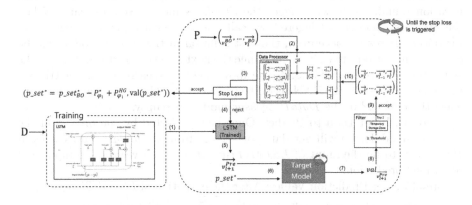

Fig. 3. RNN-based Hyperparameter Generator flowchart

In the following, the whole workflow of the RNN-based Hyperparameter Generator is illustrated, where the overall flow is composed of ten steps. Figure 3 shows the flowchart of the RNN-based Hyperparameter Generator.

Step (1). Get Trained $LSTM(Trained)$ Model: The $LSTM(Trained)$ model is the core prediction model of the RNN-based Hyperparameter Generator.

Step (2). Define Next Input Data: In $DataProcessor$, we will have two data resources. One is from P and the other is from the prediction of the RNN-based Hyperparameter Generator. After each iteration of the execution of the generator, we will get two predictions $(\overrightarrow{v_1^1}, \dots, \overrightarrow{v_{l-1}^1}, \overrightarrow{v_l^1})$ and $(\overrightarrow{v_1^2}, \dots, \overrightarrow{v_{l-1}^2}, \overrightarrow{v_l^2})$ from the last process of the generator (Fig. 3 (10)). $DataProcessor$ will cut them to be two sub-vectors $(\overrightarrow{v_1^1}, \dots, \overrightarrow{v_{l-1}^1})$ and $(\overrightarrow{v_1^2}, \dots, \overrightarrow{v_{l-1}^2})$. And then, concatenate the two sub-vectors $[(\overrightarrow{v_1^1}, ..., \overrightarrow{v_{l-1}^1}), (\overrightarrow{v_1^2}, ..., \overrightarrow{v_{l-1}^2})]$ and the next prediction data $\overrightarrow{v_l^{BO}}$ from P to be $[(\overrightarrow{v_1^1}, ..., \overrightarrow{v_{l-1}^1}, \overrightarrow{v_l^{BO}}), (\overrightarrow{v_1^2}, ..., \overrightarrow{v_{l-1}^2}, \overrightarrow{v_l^{BO}})]$. So we will get four vectors $(\overrightarrow{v_1^1}, ..., \overrightarrow{v_{l-1}^1}, \overrightarrow{v_l^1}), (\overrightarrow{v_1^2}, ..., \overrightarrow{v_{l-1}^2}, \overrightarrow{v_l^2}), (\overrightarrow{v_1^1}, ..., \overrightarrow{v_{l-1}^1}, \overrightarrow{v_l^{BO}}), (\overrightarrow{v_1^2}, ..., \overrightarrow{v_{l-1}^2}, \overrightarrow{v_l^{BO}})$, in total. Note that if we only get one prediction from the last process of the previous iteration round, we will get only two vectors after data processing. In the end, we will put these one pair (two vectors) or two pairs (four vectors), the first pair is $[(\overrightarrow{v_1^1}, ..., \overrightarrow{v_{l-1}^1}, \overrightarrow{v_l^1}), (\overrightarrow{v_1^1}, ..., \overrightarrow{v_{l-1}^1}, \overrightarrow{v_l^{BO}})]$, and the other pair is $[(\overrightarrow{v_1^2}, ..., \overrightarrow{v_{l-1}^2}, \overrightarrow{v_l^2}), (\overrightarrow{v_1^2}, ..., \overrightarrow{v_{l-1}^2}, \overrightarrow{v_l^{BO}})]$ into the *Candidate Data* set as the data source for next iteration of prediction in the recursive loop of the RNN-based Hyperparameter Generator.

Step (3). Early Stop or not: The latest prediction values, $\overrightarrow{v_l^1}$, $\overrightarrow{v_l^2}$, and $\overrightarrow{v_l^{BO}}$, will be entered into *StopLoss* module to evaluate whether to end the execution of the RNN-based Hyperparameter Generator or not. The *StopLoss* module will make a judgment based on the input vector from *CandidateData*. If the previous iteration round does not perform well, no predicted vector will enter the *CandidateData*, and it will cause the *CandidateData* to be empty. So the *CandidateData* will not pass any vector into the *StopLoss* module during this iteration round, which will trigger the *StopLoss* module to stop early. When the *StopLoss* module is triggered, we call that yes (or accept); otherwise is no (or reject). If yes (or accepted), the best solution in the overall process will be output; if no (or rejected), it will continue the next cycle (or next iteration) of the generator. Note that in addition to the above-mentioned early stop which triggers the generator to stop, the RNN-based Hyperparameter Generator naturally stops when the buffer P in the *DataProcessor* module is empty.

Step (4). Input Data to Predict: Once being rejected by the process of the *StopLoss* module, we will get data (or vector) from *CandidateData* (in *Data Processor*) to be the input of $LSTM(Trained)$ until all vectors are input and performed prediction.

Step (5). Get Prediction Values: After the execution of $LSTM(Trained)$, we will get the number of t prediction values $\overrightarrow{v_{l+1}^{Pre_1}}, ..., \overrightarrow{v_{l+1}^{Pre_t}}$ when we input each vector from *CandidateData*. In an iteration round, we would input up to four vectors (two pairs) from *CandidateData*, so we would get $(4 \cdot t)$ prediction values.

Step (6). Validate the Prediction Values: In order to validate the t predicted values obtained from $LSTM$ $(Trained)$, t candidate hyperparameter sets will be created by setting $p\_set_{cad} = p\_set^* - P_{\phi_i}^* + v_{l+1}^{Pre_k}$, $k = 1...t$. Then these candidate hyperparameter sets will be tried and evaluated in the target model for validation.

Step (7). Get the Validation Result: After the validation over the target model, a set of validation values, $val_{\overrightarrow{v_{l+1}^{Pre_1}}}$, ..., $val_{\overrightarrow{v_{l+1}^{Pre_t}}}$, corresponding to each of the candidate hyperparameter set are conducted.

Step (8). Filter the Predictions: A set of performance validation results, $val_{\overrightarrow{v_{l+1}^{Pre_k}}}$, $k = 1...t$, obtained in the previous step is entered into the *Filter* module. If a validation value $val_{\overrightarrow{Pre_k}\atop v_{l+1}}$, $k = 1...t$, is greater than or equal to the predefined threshold, the corresponding prediction $v_{l+1}^{\overrightarrow{Pre_k}}$ and its input $(\overrightarrow{v_1}, ..., \overrightarrow{v_l})$ is stored in temporal storage; otherwise, drop the prediction value and no action is taken.

Step (9). Get the Output of this Cycle: If there is ≥ 2 predicted data left in the *temporarystoragezone*, select the top-2 according to the validation results; otherwise, output the remaining results.

Step (10). Prepare to Execute Next Iteration Round: Cut and enter the hyperparameter-sets $(\overrightarrow{v_2}, \overrightarrow{v_3}, ..., v_{l+1}^{\overrightarrow{Pre_k}})$s with their corresponding validation results $val_{\overrightarrow{Pre_k}\atop v_{l+1}}$s from step (9) into *DataProcessor*. This process is the last step in an iteration round. Note that we will get zero to two prediction vectors after the execution of each iteration round of the RNN-based Hyperparameter Generator. We will put these prediction vectors to *DataProcessor* to be part of the candidate input resource of the next iteration round of the generator.

Note that the *Filter* module only leaves at most two best lists of hyperparameter values in the *TemporaryStorageZone* by playing the threshold checking and the mutual comparison.

4   Experimental Results

In this chapter, an HPO comparison between the traditional statistic model, BO, and our proposed framework, RNN-BO Hyperparameter Optimization Structure, is conducted. The following experiments are conducted to measure the performance of the methods.

In BO, the selective hyperparameter is inherited from the previous iteration round. With the inheritance relationship, the numerical hyperparameters can gain more resources for evaluation so that a set of more stable hyperparameters can be obtained.

When the selective hyperparameter is converged, increasing the number of iteration rounds only increases the number of predictions, but does not improve the accuracy of each BO prediction. However, increasing the budget will allow BO to obtain more accurate validation values for subsequent predictions.

In the following, we design two experiments, Experiment 1 and Experiment 2. Experiment 1 does pure numerical hyperparameter optimization by given a set of fixed selective hyperparameters (refer to Subsect. 4.1), and Experiment 2 considers all adjustable kinds of hyperparameters, i.e., all numerical and selective hyperparameters (refer to Subsect. 4.2). After the two experiments, we discuss the efficiency and generalization ability of the overall model architecture (refer to Subsect. 4.3) based on the experiments' results.

4.1 Pure Numerical Hyperparameter Optimization

Table 1. Experiment 1 Result Table of VGG-16 with CIFAR-10.

Model	Val. Acc.	Total Time (min)	Time of the Last Round (min)	Efficiency Comparison
BO (1 round)	0.7844	189	–	–
BO (2 rounds)	0.7446	378	189	–
RNN-BO (BO R1) (Ours)	0.7797	312	**123**	**34.92%**
BO (3 rounds)	0.7903	567	189	–
RNN-BO (BO R2) (Ours)	0.7621	501	**123**	**34.92%**
BO (4 rounds)	0.8117	756	189	–
RNN-BO (BO R3) (Ours)	**0.8215**	696	129	31.75%

"R" is the short of "Round".

By given a set of fixed setting selective hyperparameters, this section focuses on pure numerical hyperparameter optimization. In the experiment, the common BOHB will be used to represent the traditional statistic model and for each iteration round, the Training Budget $b = 60$. The RNN-BO Hyperparameter Optimization Structure first applies BOHB for k iteration rounds, $k = 1, 2, or 3$, and then executes the RNN-based Hyperparameter Generator to optimize each hyperparameter one by one. The LSTM model used in the RNN-based Hyperparameter Generator is a two layer model architecture, look back value $l = 5$, Optimizer = Adam. In Experiment 1, the framework is PyTorch 1.10.1 with CUDA 11.6, and all sub-experiments run on Intel(R) Core(TM) i9-10900KF CPU @ 3.70GHz and NVIDIA GeForce RTX 3090 graphics card.

In the experiment, we use VGG-16 [15] to be the target model and the CIFAR-10 to be the target dataset. We summarize Experiment 1 by Table 1. RNN-BO (BO Rk) outperforms BO ($k + 1$ rounds) in most cases and the former tasks less time. Our model prediction is worse when $k = 2$ due to the instability of BO (2 rounds) for pure numerical hyperparameter optimization.

4.2 All Hyperparameter Optimization

In this section, both selective hyperparameters and numerical hyperparameters are optimized in BO. In the experiment, the same BOHB is used as the statistic model and for each iteration round, the Training Budget $b = 100$. The RNN-BO Hyperparameter Optimization Structure first applies BOHB for k iteration rounds, $k = 1, 2, or 3$, and then executes the RNN-BO Hyperparameter Generator to further optimize each numerical hyperparameter one by one. The embedded LSTM model in the RNN-based Hyperparameter Generator sets the look back value $l = 5$, Optimizer = Adam, and is a two layers model architecture.

In Experiment 2, the framework is PyTorch 1.10.1 with CUDA 11.6, and all sub-experiments run on Intel(R) Xeon(R) W-2235 CPU @ 3.80GHz and NVIDIA GeForce RTX 3090 graphics card.

Table 2. Experiment 2 Result Table of CNN with MNIST as the target model.

Model	Val. Acc.	Total Time (min)	Time of the Last Round (min)	Efficiency Comparison
BO (1 round)	0.966471354	75	–	–
BO (2 rounds)	0.967122396	150	75	–
RNN-BO (BO R1) (Ours)	0.965820313	101	26	65.33%
RNN-BO (BO R1)$^{(*)}$ (Ours)	0.970377604	106	31	58.67%
BO (3 rounds)	0.967773438	225	75	–
RNN-BO (BO R2) (Ours)	0.965169271	177	27	64.00%
RNN-BO (BO R2)$^{(*)}$ (Ours)	0.970703125	177	27	64.00%
BO (4 rounds)	0.970377604	300	75	–
RNN-BO (BO R3) (Ours)	0.968098958	246	**21**	**72.00%**
RNN-BO (BO R3)$^{(*)}$ (Ours)	**0.971354167**	252	27	64.00%

In this experiment, the target model is a Convolutional Neural Network (CNN) and the MNIST (Modified National Institute of Standards and Technology database) [16] to be the target dataset. Since the performance of the top-3 results calculated by BO is usually close to each other, and the performance is evaluated with limited time, in order to avoid missing the best hyperparameter set among the top-3 candidate hyperparameter sets, RNN-BO (BO Rk)$^{(*)}$ method is added and it reserves the top-3 results generated by BO, not only the best result. In RNN-BO (BO Rk)$^{(*)}$, the top-3 results obtained from BO are revalidated in the target model and each for three times. Then the average performance of the top-3 candidates are ranked and the first ranking one is taken as the $p\_set^*_{BO}$, one of the input of the subsequent RNN-based models.

Table 2 summarizes and experiments in this subsection, we can see that RNN-BO (BO R3)$^{(*)}$ performs the best. The RNN-based Hyperparameter Generator indeed improves BO's results further with limited extra execution time, i.e., RNN-BO (BO Rk)$^{(*)}$ always performs better than BO (k rounds). An iteration round of RNN-based hyperparameter optimization is only about one third of execution time of one round of BO. So our proposed model saves more time.

4.3   Model Efficiency and Generalization Ability

In Fig. 4, we compare the model efficiency of the last iteration round's hyperparameter optimization of the three methods. We can see that the time cost of BO is much higher than RNN-BO and RNN-BO$^{(*)}$. The time efficiency of RNN-BO$^{(*)}$ (an improved version of RNN-BO) is also obviously better than BO. Therefore,

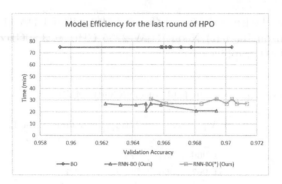

Fig. 4. Model Efficiency for the last round of hyperparameter optimization

if there is a severe time cost consideration, RNN-BO$^{(*)}$ is a time-efficient choice than BO and can get a better result.

BO is the most widely used hyperparameter optimization statistic model, and the RNN-based Hyperparameter Generator is different from the statistic model, which is based on the prediction results of BO and then continues optimizing hyperparameters. The RNN-based Hyperparameter Generator in RNN-BO uses a numerically analyzing and predicting method, which is a very general approach, to find a better hyperparameter set p_set^* than the best BO solution $p\_set^*_{BO}$. Therefore, in model generalization ability, RNN-BO can apply in all cases where BO can effectively perform hyperparameter optimization.

5   Conclusion

With the popularity of artificial intelligence, hyperparameter optimization is a critical issue in the field of automated machine learning. In both NAS and AMS, HPO plays a significant role in the autoML business. In the past, the primary optimization method of HPO is the statistic model, which is mature and stable, but its required computational resource is considerable. In this paper, we propose an RNN-based Hyperparameter Generator. With the RNN-based Hyperparameter Generator, the RNN-BO framework is then developed which integrates BO, fANOVA, and RNN-based Hyperparameter Generator to better optimize hyperparameters with the less computational resource. Experiments show that RNN-BO can not only reduce the computational resource but also better hyperparameters for the target model. As future work, we plan to implement RNN-BO as a service to help users or non-AI engineers to optimize their target AI models on the specified data type.

Acknowledgement. This research is co-sponsored by ITRI, Pervasive Artificial Intelligence Research (PAIR) Labs, and the National Science and Technology Council (NSTC). This work is also financially supported by the Higher Education Sprout Project of the National Yang Ming Chiao Tung University (NYCU) and the Ministry of Education (MOE), Taiwan.

References

1. Elsken, T., Metzen, J.H., Hutter, F.: Neural architecture search: a survey. JMLR **20**(1), 1997–2017 (2019)
2. Laredo, D., Qin, Y., Schütze, O., Sun, J.-Q.: Automatic Model Selection for Neural Networks. arXiv:1905.06010 (2019)
3. Thornton, C., Hutter, F., Hoos, H.H., Leyton-Brown, K.: Auto-WEKA: combined selection and hyperparameter optimization of classification algorithms. In: 19th ACM SIGKDD International Conference on Knowledge Discovery and Data Mining, pp. 847–855 (2013)
4. Falkner, S., Klein, A., Hutter, F.: BOHB: robust and efficient hyperparameter optimization at scale. In: ICML (2018)
5. Bengio, Y.: Gradient-based optimization of hyperparameters. Neural Comput. **12**(8), 1889–1900 (2000)
6. Li, L., Jamieson, K.G., DeSalvo, G., Rostamizadeh, A., Talwalkar, A.: Hyperband: bandit-based configuration evaluation for hyperparameter optimization. In: ICLR (2017)
7. Ebden, M.: Hyperband: Gaussian Processes: A Quick Introduction. arXiv:1505.02965 (2015)
8. He, X., Zhao, K., Chu, X.: AutoML: a survey of the state-of-the-art. Knowl.-Based Syst. **212**, 106622 (2021)
9. Akiba, T., Sano, S., Yanase, T., Ohta, T., Koyama, M.: Optuna: a next-generation hyperparameter optimization framework. In: 25th ACM SIGKDD International Conference on Knowledge Discovery & Data Mining, pp. 2623–2631 (2019)
10. Nelson, D.M., Pereira, A.C., De Oliveira, R.A.: Stock market's price movement prediction with LSTM neural networks. In: International Joint Conference on Neural Networks (IJCNN) (2017)
11. Dai, Y., Huang, J.: A sales prediction method based on LSTM with hyperparameter search. In: Journal of Physics Conference Series, vol. 1756 (2021)
12. Hochreiter, S., Schmidhuber, J.: Long short-term memory. Neural Comput. **9**(8), 1735–1780 (1997)
13. Wang, J.: Analysis and design of a recurrent neural network for linear programming. IEEE Trans. Circuits Syst. I: Fundam. Theory Appl. **40**(9), 613–618 (1993)
14. Hutter, F., Hoos, H., Leyton-Brown, K.: An efficient approach for assessing hyperparameter importance. In: ICML (2014)
15. Simonyan, K., Zisserman, A.: Very Deep Convolutional Networks for Large-Scale Image Recognition. arXiv:1409.1556 (2014)
16. Open Source Dataset, LeCun, Y., Cortes, C., Burges, C.J.C.: Modified National Institute of Standards and Technology database (MNIST). http://yann.lecun.com/exdb/mnist/. Accessed 1998

Adiabatic Quantum Computation for Cyber Attack and Defense Strategies

Sanpawat Kantabutra[✉]

The Theory of Computation Group and Center of Excellence in Quantum Technology, Faculty of Engineering, Chiang Mai University, Chiang Mai 50200, Thailand
sanpawat@alumni.tufts.edu

Abstract. Cyber security has become increasingly important in today's world widely connected by the Internet. Many important problems in the cyber security domain can be framed as optimization problems. Recently there has been much progress in applying quantum annealing to solve optimization problems in various application domains. In this article quantum annealing is shown to solve hard problems in cyber security from the perspectives of both attack and defense. In the process a few new techniques for QUBO construction are also illustrated and can potentially be used to solve problems in other application domains.

Keywords: Cyber security · Adiabatic computation · Cyber attack and defense

1 Introduction

Cyber security has become increasingly important in today's world widely connected by the Internet because it encompasses everything that relates to protecting our data from cyber attackers who want to steal this information and abuse it to cause harm or damages. Many important problems in cyber security can be framed as optimization problems [12,31,36,40]. In general, optimization problems are known to be hard to solve exactly and efficiently. There is not a single "perfect" classical method that solves every optimization problem. The best we can do is to invent a host of complementary methods, each being suited for specific tasks or instances of problems [39]. With the advent of quantum computation, optimization problems can be solved using a totally different set of principles. In particular, quantum annealing (QA) is a generic algorithm aimed at solving optimization problems by exploiting the quantum tunneling effect that does not exist in the classical world and by framing any optimization problem as an energy minimization problem. The energy of the problem is represented by a Hamiltonian. The Hamiltonian of a problem represents the total energy of the system; the sum of the kinetic and potential energies of all particles associated

Supported by Thailand Research Fund grant number RSA6080029.

S. Kantabutra—Ineligible for the best student paper award.

with the system. The Hamiltonian can take different forms. In this article we consider only the Hamiltonian that is used in a quantum annealer such as those of D-Wave systems. The Hamiltonian is the sum of the initial Hamiltonian and the final Hamiltonian. The lowest energy state of the initial Hamiltonian is when all qubits are in a superposition state of 0 and 1. On the other hand, the lowest energy state of the final Hamiltonian is the answer to the problem to be solved. The final state is a classical state, and includes the qubit biases and the couplings between qubits. In quantum annealing, the system begins in the lowest energy eigenstate of the initial Hamiltonian. As it anneals, it introduces the problem Hamiltonian, which contains the biases and couplers, and it reduces the influence of the initial Hamiltonian. At the end of the anneal, it is in an eigenstate of the problem Hamiltonian. Ideally, it has stayed in the minimum energy state throughout the quantum annealing process so that at the end it is in the minimum energy state of the problem Hamiltonian and therefore has an answer to the problem to be solved. The method was originally proposed as an algorithm for numerical computation [20] inspired by simulated annealing (SA) [22] and exchange Monte-Carlo simulation [18]. Additionally, quantum annealing has the advantage of solving an optimization problem formulated with discrete variables. A well-known example is searching for the ground state of the spin-glass model, which corresponds to various types of optimization problems, such as the traveling salesman problem and satisfiability problem [25–27]. The protocol of QA is realized in an actual quantum device using present technology and is called the quantum annealer. Many optimization problems in various domains such as portfolio optimization [33], protein folding [32], molecular similarity problem [16], computational biology [23], job scheduling [37], traffic flow optimization [29], election forecast [15], machine learning [6], and automated guided vehicles [30] were successfully solved using the quantum annealer. When compared with the classical simulated annealing, the quantum version was reported to achieve better solutions [4,34,38]. This major advantage stems possibly from the quantum tunneling effect penetrating the valley of the potential energy. Quantum annealing has also recently been applied in the cyber security domain [9,17,21]. In this article we show how to apply quantum annealing to solve optimization problems in cyber security. We focus on a layered security model. In this model we use a rooted tree to represent a security system. Each edge has an associated penetration cost and each node has an associated prize. We can look at cyber security from the perspectives of attack or defense. Agnarsson et al. [1] were the first to study such a system. An attacker who comes with a budget enters the system via the root of the tree, encounters an edge and pays an associated cost to collect a prize in the corresponding vertex, and continues to traverse the tree until the budget is no longer enough to cover any cost. The objective of the attacker is to maximize the sum of prizes under the given budget. The authors proved that the general version of the problem is intractable, but does admit a polynomial time approximation scheme. Building on the work done in Agnarsson et al. [1], the same authors also studied a layered security from the defense perspective [2]. Instead of having given associated penetration costs for edges and associated prizes for vertices, the objective is now to assign penetration costs and prizes so as to minimize the amount of total prize the attacker with a budget can obtain from the system. The authors showed that in general it is not possible to develop an optimal security system for a given cyber security model. Their results give us some mathematical insights into how layered security defenses should be organized. Formally, we define a model and an attack in the security system as follows. All of our definitions are borrowed from the original works by Agnarsson et al. [1, 2] and Mukdasanit and Kantabutra [28].

Definition 1. [CYBERSECURITY MODEL] *A cybersecurity model M is given by a three-tuple $M = (C, P, T)$, where $T = (V, E)$ is a tree rooted at r having $n \in \mathbb{N}$ non-root vertices, C is a set of penetration costs $c_1, \ldots, c_n \in \mathbb{Z}^+$, and P is a set of prizes $p_1, \ldots, p_n \in \mathbb{Z}^+$. The attack always begins at the root r and the root always has prize 0.*

Definition 2. [SECURITY SYSTEM] *A security system (c, p, T) with respect to a cybersecurity model $M = (C, P, T)$ is given by two functions $c : E(T) \to C$ and $p : V(T) \setminus \{r\} \to P$. A system attack in (c, p, T) is given by a subtree τ of T that contains the root r of T. The cost of a system attack τ with respect to (c, p, T) is given by the cost $cst(c, \tau) = \sum_{e \in E(\tau)} c(e)$. The prize of a system attack τ with respect to (c, p, T) is given by the prize $pr(p, \tau) = \sum_{u \in V(\tau)} p(u)$. For a given budget $B \in \mathbb{Z}^+$ the maximum prize $pr^*(c, p, B)$ with respect to B is defined by $pr^*(c, p, B) = \max\{pr(p, \tau)|$ for all $\tau \subseteq T$, where $cst(c, \tau) \leq B\}$. A system attack τ whose prize is maximum with respect to a given budget B is called an optimal attack. Every system attack τ is maximal.*

Definition 3. [OPTIMAL ATTACK OPTIMIZATION PROBLEM]
INSTANCE: *A security system $S = (c, p, T)$ associated with M and a budget $B \in \mathbb{Z}^+$.*
INSTRUCTION: *Compute the maximum total prize $pr^*(c, p, B)$.*

Every system attack, or simply attack, is required to be maximal because an attacker wants to have as high total prize as possible in a real situation. On the defense, a security measure represented by a cost strictly greater the budget is given with a security system in the model. We would like to find an edge in the system to place this security measure so that the maximum total prize from an attack is minimized. Formally, we define the defense problem as follows.

Definition 4. [INFINITY PLACEMENT OPERATION] *Given a cyber security model M, let $S = (c, p, T)$ be a security system associated with M and (c', p, T) be a security system in the model after the infinity placement operation has taken place. We say that an infinity placement operation replaces an edge cost $c(e)$ with ∞ if for all edges $e' \in E(T) \setminus \{e\}$, $c'(e') = c(e')$ and $c'(e) = \infty$.*

In a real-life situation security measures may have various strengths and can be either hardware and software devices or rules and policies. Examples of security measures are passwords, firewalls, virtual private networks (VPNs), intrusion detection/prevention systems, antivirus software, or role-based access control policies. Each of these measures may have various strengths. A shorter password with only lowercase English characters obviously has less strength than a longer password with uppercase and lowercase English characters plus numbers and special characters. A virtual private network without an access restriction of IP addresses obviously has less strength than another virtual private network with an IP address access restriction. In this article we define the *strongest* security measure to be any security measure that prohibits any access to the part of the system that it is used to protect. This is also equivalent to removing an edge in a graph. In terms of mathematical notation we use *infinity cost* to represent the strongest security measure in the model and defines it to be any integer number *strictly greater* than a given budget.

Definition 5. [INFINITY PLACEMENT OPTIMIZATION PROBLEM]
INSTANCE: *A security system* $S = (c, p, T)$ *associated with* M *and a budget* $B \in \mathbb{Z}^+$.
INSTRUCTION: *Find an edge* $e \in E(T)$ *such that* $pr^*(c', p, B)$ *is minimized after the infinity placement operation has been performed.*

The OPTIMAL ATTACK OPTIMIZATION PROBLEM and the INFINITY PLACE-MENT OPTIMIZATION PROBLEM are known to be *NP*-hard [1] and *coNP*-hard [28], respectively. Therefore, it is very unlikely that polynomial-time exact algorithms for both problems exist unless $P = NP$. The best known classical exact solutions are the $O(G^2 n)$-time algorithm to compute an optimal attack and the $O(G^2 n^2)$-time algorithm to determine such an optimal edge placement, where $G = \sum_{p_i \in P} p_i$ is the total prize in the model, while the best known classi-cal approximate solutions are a (1-ϵ) FPTAS with the time bound $O(\frac{1}{\epsilon^2} n^3 \log G)$ and a (1+ϵ) FPTAS with the time bound $O(\frac{1}{\epsilon^2} n^4 \log G)$ for the first and second problems, respectively [28]. In recent years there has been much interest in the possibility of using adiabatic quantum optimization (AQO) to solve *NP*-hard optimization problems and other problems in the similar classes of hardness [24]. At the same time much debate has been going on whether such an adia-batic quantum optimization would run significantly faster than their classical counterpart [24]. Even though most quantum computer scientists believe that it is very unlikely that *NP*-complete problems can be solved in polynomial time by AQO, the hidden constant in the time complexity may be smaller than that of the known classical algorithms. There is also another advantage by quantum tunneling where a better solution can be expected from the AQO [24]. Because the OPTIMAL ATTACK OPTIMIZATION PROBLEM and the INFINITY PLACEMENT OPTIMIZATION PROBLEM are hard to solve classically, we can expect to have both advantages of the AQO.

Our contributions in this article are threefold. First, given a rooted tree, we show how to invent a quadratic unconstrained binary optimization (QUBO) that constructs rooted subtrees. Second, we show how to invent a QUBO for the OPTIMAL ATTACK OPTIMIZATION PROBLEM and, third, a QUBO for the INFIN-ITY PLACEMENT OPTIMIZATION PROBLEM. A few other techniques for QUBO construction are also discussed. These techniques can potentially be applied to solve problems in other application domains.

2   Results

2.1   QUBO for Rooted Subtrees

Because an attack in a security system in the model is defined as a rooted subtree, we need a QUBO that generates legitimate rooted subtrees. Given a rooted tree T, our goal is to generate all possible rooted subtrees of T. Let q_u and q_v be two binary variables representing an edge $\{u, v\} \in E(T)$ where u is the vertex closer to the root. Both q_u and q_v are each set to 1 if and only if $\{u, v\}$ is in a rooted subtree of T. Hence, we would like to have all rooted subtrees of 1's. More precisely, T' is a rooted subtree of T if and only if for each path $u_0 u_1 \ldots u_l$ in T and $u_0 = r$ there exists $0 \leq k \leq l$ such that $u_0, u_1, \ldots, u_k \in V(T')$ and $u_0 u_1 \ldots u_k$ forms a path in T' and (possibly empty list) $u_{k+1}, u_{k+2}, \ldots, u_l \notin V(T')$. A rooted subtree T' of 1's is where $q_{u_0} = q_{u_1} = \ldots = q_{u_k} = 1$ and $q_{u_{k+1}} = q_{u_{k+2}} = \ldots = q_{u_l} = 0$ for each such a path. From this point on, we call a rooted subtree T' of 1's simply a rooted subtree T' when there is no confusion. Consider an edge $\{u, v\} \in E(T)$ and the following behavior of the binary variables in Table 1.

Table 1. Desired behavior of two binary variables

q_u	q_v	H_{uv}
0	0	0
0	1	1
1	0	0
1	1	0

Using the most general form of a two-binary variables QUBO $H_{uv} = aq_u + bq_v + cq_u q_v$ and solving this equation, we have $H_{uv} = q_v - q_u q_v$ for representing the behavior of the edge $\{u, v\}$. To create a QUBO for each edge in the given tree, we sum H_{uv} over all edges in $E(T)$.

Lemma 1. *Let $H_A = \sum_{\{uv\} \in E} H_{uv} = \sum_{\{uv\} \in E} (q_v - q_u q_v)$. The QUBO H_A is 0 if and only if all edges $\{u, v\} \in E(T)$ are either $q_u = 0$ and $q_v = 0$, $q_u = 1$ and $q_v = 0$, or $q_u = 1$ and $q_v = 1$.*

At this point we have filtered out all edges $\{u, v\}$ with $q_u = 0$ and $q_v = 1$. We now need to connect the remaining edges to form rooted subtrees of 1's. We achieve this by adding $H_B = 1 - q_0$, where q_0 is the binary variable corresponding to the root vertex of T. Note that $H_B = 0$ if and only if $q_0 = 1$.

Lemma 2. *Let $H_A = \sum_{\{uv\} \in E} H_{uv} = \sum_{\{uv\} \in E} (q_v - q_u q_v)$ and $H_B = 1 - q_0$. The QUBO $H_A + H_B = 0$ if and only if there exists a nonempty consecutive bit sequence of 1's followed by a (possibly empty) consecutive bit sequence of 0's for each path from the root binary variable q_0.*

We say that a configuration $\{q_v\}$ satisfies $H_A + H_B = 0$ if and only if restricting T to edges $\{\{u, v\} \in E(T) | q_u = q_v = 1\}$ produces a rooted subtree T' of T.

2.2   QUBO for the Optimal Attack

In this section we extend $H_A + H_B$ to cover both costs and prizes of each rooted subtree. By Definition 2, each vertex $v \in V(T)$ is associated with prize $p_v = p(v)$ and each edge $\{u,v\} \in E(T)$ is associated with cost $c_{uv} = c(\{u,v\})$. Furthermore, let y_i and z_j be binary variables for picking the values i, j for a total prize and a total cost respectively and $q_v = 1$ if and only if $v \in V(T)$ is chosen to be in a rooted subtree. Let H_P and H_C be the Hamiltonians representing the total prize and the total cost, respectively. Lastly, let $AP = \sum_{v \in V(T)} p(v)$ and $AC = \sum_{\{u,v\} \in E(T)} c_{uv}$.

$$H_P = (1 - \sum_{i=1}^{AP} y_i)^2 + (\sum_{i=1}^{AP} i y_i - \sum_{v \in V(T)} p_v q_v)^2$$

$$H_C = (1 - \sum_{j=1}^{AC} z_j)^2 + (\sum_{j=1}^{AC} j z_j - \sum_{\{u,v\} \in E(T)} c_{uv} q_u q_v)^2$$

Observe that $H_P = 0$ is forced to have only a single total prize and similarly $H_C = 0$ is forced to have only a single total cost. We combine both together by setting $H_{PC} = H_P + H_C$. For now, H_C is not in the QUBO format. We will shortly describe a standard technique to turn H_C into an equivalent QUBO.

Lemma 3. $H_A + H_B + H_{PC} = 0$ *if and only if the annealing process produces a rooted subtree of T with a corresponding total prize $i y_i$ and a corresponding total cost $j z_j$.*

We say that a configuration $\{q_v\}$, $\{y_i\}$, $\{z_j\}$ satisfies $H_A + H_B + H_{PC} = 0$ if and only if the subtree determined by $\{q_v\}$ has a total prize i and a total cost j and $y_i = z_j = 1$. We next want to maximize the total prize and make sure that the total cost does not exceed a given budget B. To maximize the total prize, we do the following.

$$H_D = - \sum_{v \in V(T)} p_v q_v$$

Observe that by making it negative, we are turning a maximization problem into a minimization problem. To make sure that the total cost is no greater than a given budget B, we do the following.

$$H_E = (1 - \sum_{i=0}^{AC} b_i)^2 + (\sum_{\{u,v\} \in E(T)} c_{uv} q_u q_v + \sum_{i=0}^{AC} i b_i - B)^2$$

Observe that $H_E = 0$ if and only if exactly one b_i in the first term is set to be 1 and $\sum_{\{u,v\} \in E(T)} c_{uv} q_u q_v + i b_i = B$ and that $H_E \geq 0$. Once again, H_E is currently not in the QUBO format. We will transform it into an equivalent QUBO shortly. Let H_{attack} be as follows.

$$H_{attack} = H_A + H_B + H_{PC} + H_D + H_E$$

$$= \sum_{\{u,v\} \in E} (q_v - q_u q_v) + 1 - q_0 + (1 - \sum_{i=1}^{AP} y_i)^2$$

$$+ (\sum_{i=1}^{AP} i y_i - \sum_{v \in V(T)} p_v q_v)^2 + (1 - \sum_{j=1}^{AC} z_j)^2 + (\sum_{j=1}^{AC} j z_j - \sum_{\{u,v\} \in E(T)}^{AC} c_{uv} q_u q_v)^2$$

$$- \sum_{v \in V(T)} p_v q_v + (1 - \sum_{i=0}^{AC} b_i)^2 + (\sum_{\{u,v\} \in E(T)} c_{uv} q_u q_v + \sum_{i=0}^{AC} i b_i - B)^2$$

We remark here that $H_A + H_B + H_{PC} + H_E$ is at least 0 for all solutions whose costs are no greater than B.

Theorem 1. *Let $H_{attack} = L_1(H_A + H_B + H_{PC} + H_E) + L_2(H_D)$, where L_1, L_2 are constants such that $L_1 > L_2 p_{max}$. H_{attack} yields $-L_2 \times$ an optimal solution to the OPTIMAL ATTACK OPTIMIZATION PROBLEM at the end of the anneal, assuming the ideal annealing process.*

We note here that if a constraint in $H_A + H_B + H_{PC} + H_E$ is violated, a solution we will obtain is no longer a solution to the OPTIMAL ATTACK OPTI-MIZATION PROBLEM. However, if a constraint in H_D is violated, i.e., some p_v should have been included but is not, and no constraint in $H_A + H_B + H_{PC} + H_E$ is violated, a solution we will obtain is a feasible solution to the OPTIMAL ATTACK OPTIMIZATION PROBLEM. Observe that $L_1(H_A + H_B + H_{PC} + H_E)$ is at least zero. We want to obtain a solution when $L_1(H_A + H_B + H_{PC} + H_E) = 0$ and $L_2(H_D)$ is at minimum. For each violation of a constraint in $L_1(H_A + H_B + H_{PC} + H_E)$, we have a penalty of at least L_1 and we have a penalty of $L_2 p_v$ for each violation of a constraint in $L_2(H_D)$. Therefore, we set $L_1 > L_2 p_{max}$ where p_{max} is the largest prize in P. Because $L_1 > L_2 p_{max}$, each constraint in $L_1(H_A + H_B + H_{PC} + H_E)$ is less preferable to be violated because the energy penalty is higher.

2.3   QUBO for the Optimal Defense

In this section we discuss a solution to the INFINITY PLACEMENT OPTIMIZATION PROBLEM according to Definition 5. The idea is to reuse H_{attack} d times with d different placements of infinity, where d is the degree of the root vertex of T. We would then like to identify the attack with the minimum total prize within a given budget. First, we need to have a QUBO for exactly one placement of infinity.

Lemma 4. *Let s_i be a binary variable. For any integer $d \geq 1$, $H_d^\infty = -\sum_{i=1}^{d} s_i + 2\sum_{i=1}^{d-1} \sum_{j>i}^{d} s_i s_j + 1 = 0$ if and only if exactly one s_i is set to 1.*

At this point we have a mechanism that sets exactly one s_i to 1 if and only if $H_d^\infty = 0$. We can incorporate H_d^∞ into H_{attack} to produce a QUBO for the optimal defense. The idea is to have d instances of the same given security system with d different placements of ∞ on each of the d edges adjacent to the root vertex. Let ∞ be any value strictly greater than a given budget B. We can define this value because the budget B is given as part of the input instance. We make two observations. First, the optimal edge for the infinity placement is always the one among all d edges adjacent to the root vertex r for otherwise we can always move infinity upward to reduce a total prize from an attack. Second, the infinity placement has the same effect as removing the edge with the infinity cost and all other edges below it (i.e., the subtree). Hence, instead of placing the infinity, we remove the subtree from the input instance to save qubits. Let $H_{defense} = -\sum_{i=1}^{d} s_i H_{attack}^{i} + H_d^{\infty}$ such that H_{attack}^{i} is the QUBO for the optimal attack on the input instance in which the edge i adjacent to the root vertex r is removed along with its corresponding subtree. Observe that $H_{defense}$ is now not in the QUBO form. We will change it into the equivalent QUBO form shortly. For now, we show that $H_{defense}$ works as intended.

Theorem 2. *Let H_d^{∞} be according to Lemma 4 and $H_{defense} = -\sum_{i=1}^{d} s_i H_{attack}^{i} + H_d^{\infty}$, where H_{attack}^{i} is the QUBO for the optimal attack of the security system in Theorem 1 with the placement of infinity on the edge i adjacent to the root vertex r. $H_{defense}$ produces $L_2 \times$ the minimum of d maximum total prizes if and only if $H_{defense}$ is at the minimum energy level.*

We are now ready to discuss a way to turn $H_{defense}$ into a corresponding QUBO form. We use a standard technique called *polynomial reduction by minimum selection* [35]. To reformulate a non-quadratic higher-degree polynomial to QUBO, substitute a term in the form of $a s_i q_u q_v$, where a is a real number, with one of the following quadratic terms, depending on whether a is negative or positive. Let w be an ancillary binary variable. If $a < 0$, let $a s_i q_u q_v = a w (s_i + q_u + q_v - 2)$. If $a > 0$, let $a s_i q_u q_v = a \{ w(s_i + q_u + q_v - 1) + (s_i q_u + q_u q_v + q_v s_i) - (s_i + q_u + q_v) + 1 \}$. This technique exploits the identities $s_i q_u q_v = \max_{w} \{ w(s_i + q_u + q_v - 2) \}$ for the case $a < 0$ and $s_i q_u q_v = \min_{w} \{ w(s_i + q_u + q_v - 1) + (s_i q_u + q_u q_v + q_v s_i) - (s_i + q_u + q_v) + 1 \}$ for the case $a > 0$. Tables 2 and 3 illustrate the transformation from a triplet of variables to an equivalent QUBO form when $a < 0$ and $a > 0$, respectively. We repeatedly substitute such terms until no such term is left.

Table 2. Triplet transformation into QUBO when $a < 0$

s_i, q_u, q_v	$s_i q_u q_v$	$s_i + q_u + q_v - 2$	$\max\limits_{w}\{w(s_i + q_u + q_v - 2)\}$
0,0,0	0	-2	$0|_{w=0}$
0,0,1	0	-1	$0|_{w=0}$
0,1,0	0	-1	$0|_{w=0}$
0,1,1	0	0	$0|_{w=0,1}$
1,0,0	0	-1	$0|_{w=0}$
1,0,1	0	0	$0|_{w=0,1}$
1,1,0	0	0	$0|_{w=0,1}$
1,1,1	1	1	$1|_{w=1}$

Table 3. Triplet transformation into QUBO when $a > 0$

s_i, q_u, q_v	$s_i q_u q_v$	$s_i + q_u + q_v - 1$	$\min_w \{w(s_i+q_u+q_v-1)+(s_iq_u+q_uq_v+q_vs_i)$ $- (s_i + q_u + q_v) + 1\}$
0,0,0	0	-1	$0\vert_{w=1}$
0,0,1	0	0	$0\vert_{w=0,1}$
0,1,0	0	0	$0\vert_{w=0,1}$
0,1,1	0	1	$0\vert_{w=0}$
1,0,0	0	0	$0\vert_{w=0,1}$
1,0,1	0	1	$0\vert_{w=0}$
1,1,0	0	1	$0\vert_{w=0}$
1,1,1	1	2	$1\vert_{w=0}$

Observe that columns 2 and 4 produce the same numbers in each table. Hence, the transformations are correct. We do a similar transformation with H_C and H_E whose interaction involves 4 variables. An interaction involving 4 or more variables can be reduced to pairwise by sequentially introducing new ancillary variables and reducing the degree of the interaction by 1 at each step.

3   Discussion

Thailand is presently not on the list of countries with access to D-Wave quantum computer. With the absence of such access, we instead show mathematical proofs of correctness of QUBOs. Our main contributions are the QUBOs for the optimal attack and the optimal defense. We also provided a few important general techniques for constructing a QUBO for rooted subtrees and a QUBO for selecting exactly one choice. These techniques could be useful in constructing other QUBOs for other problem domains. All of our QUBO's were proved correct using mathematical reasoning. In this section we will discuss quality of solutions and resources such as time and qubits for such QUBOs and real-life applications of the problems. Quantum annealing is commonly used with optimization problems whose objective functions are multidimensional. In the quantum annealing process there exists a quantum phenomenon called quantum tunneling that helps avoid local minima and does not require an approximation to a wave function [11,20]. Therefore, the quality of solutions is expected to be better than its classical annealing process. If we prepare a quantum system to be in the ground state H_0 and then adiabatically change the Hamiltonian for a time T according to the following equation.

$$H(t) = (1 - \frac{t}{T})H_0 + \frac{t}{T}H_P \tag{1}$$

where H_P is the problem Hamiltonian. By the adiabatic theorem, T must be large enough and H_P does not commute with H_0 in order to be effective. The whole quantum system will then remain in the ground state at all times. When $t = T$, the quantum system will return a solution of our problem when it is measured. There has been ongoing debate whether a quantum adiabatic computation is any faster than its classical algorithmic counterpart [3,7,8,10,13,14,19], due to the fact that if the problem has size N, it is usually the case that

$$T = O(\exp(\alpha N^{\beta})) \tag{2}$$

in order for the system to remain in the ground state, for positive coefficients α and β, as $N \to \infty$. This is a consequence of the requirement that exponentially small energy gaps between the ground state of $H(t)$ and the first excited state, at some intermediate time, not lead to Landau-Zener transitions into excited states [5]. Even though most researchers do not believe that adiabatic quantum computation will give an exponential speedup over its classical algorithm on NP-complete problems and problems with similar hardness, the coefficients α and β may be smaller than those of known classical algorithms [24]. Hence, adiabatic computation may still have some advantages on some classes of problems including the OPTIMAL ATTACK OPTIMIZATION PROBLEM and the INFINITY PLACEMENT OPTIMIZATION PROBLEM. In addition to time, we also need to consider the number of qubits in each QUBO formulation. For H_{attack}, the total number of qubits is at most the sum of the number n of vertices of T, the total prize AP, the total cost AC and the budget B. We can reduce the number of qubits for each of AP, AC, and B to $\log(AP)$, $\log(AC)$, and $\log(B)$, respectively using the standard method in the work by Lucas [24]. Hence, the total number of qubits for H_{attack} is $O(n + \log(AP) + \log(AC) + \log(B))$. For $H_{defense}$, the total number of qubits equals $d \times$ the number of qubits in H_{attack} plus the number of additional qubits for H_d^{∞}. Hence, the total number of qubits for $H_{defense}$ is $d \times O(n + \log(AP) + \log(AC) + \log(B)) + d$. For H_{attack}, we have $O(n \log(AC)) + O(n^2)$ of non-quadratic terms of degree 3 and $O(n^2)$ of non-quadratic terms of degree 4 from H_C and, similarly, $O(n \log(AC)) + O(n^2)$ of non-quadratic terms of degree 3 and $O(n^2)$ of non-quadratic terms of degree 4 from H_E. For each term of degree 4, we introduce one ancillary variable to reduce each term to that of degree 3. Hence, there is a total of $O(n^2)$ ancillary variables in this stage. According to Table 2 and Table 3, we have at most 6 new terms of degree 2 for each term of degree 3 that has been reduced. The number of terms with degree 3 now becomes $6 \times O(n^2) = O(n^2)$. At this point we have $O(n^2) + O(n \log(AC))$ terms of degree 3. For each term of degree 3, we introduce one ancillary variable. Hence, there is a total of $O(n^2) + O(n \log(AC))$ ancillary variables for making H_{attack} QUBO-appropriate. For each H_{attack}^i that has already been transformed, the number of ancillary variables equals the number of the original terms with degree 2 plus the number of new terms with degree 2. This number is at most $[O(n^2 + n \log(AP) + \log^2(AC) + \log^2(AP))] + [O(n^2) + O(n \log(AC))] = O(n^2 + n \log(AP) + n \log(AC) + \log^2(AP) + \log^2(AC))$. Therefore, the total number of ancillary variables for $H_{defense}$ is $d \times O(n^2 + n \log(AP) + n \log(AC) + \log^2(AP) + \log^2(AC))$. To save qubits even more, we can use a hybrid classical-quantum approach for $H_{defense}$ by running H_{attack} d times on quantum annealer, keeping the smallest one so far, and adjusting each input in each iteration by classical computer. We can save d qubits. Both OPTIMAL ATTACK OPTIMIZATION PROBLEM and INFINITY PLACEMENT OPTIMIZATION PROBLEM can potentially be applied in real life. A tree T can be a representation of an actual layered security network. A prize can be viewed as some valuable thing or information that is kept in the security network. A penetration cost can be viewed as a security measure or a security device. In real life we would need an expert to define prizes and costs for us. Given this corresponding real-life configuration of a security network, a solution to the OPTIMAL ATTACK OPTIMIZATION PROBLEM becomes an attack strategy that maximizes the total valuable thing/information and a solution to the INFINITY PLACEMENT OPTIMIZATION PROBLEM becomes a defense strategy that indicates the portion of the security system that allows users to minimize the total asset an attacker can obtain.

References

1. Agnarsson, G., Greenlaw, R., Kantabutra, S.: On cyber attacks and the maximum-weight rooted-subtree problem. Acta Cybernet. **22**, 591–612 (2016)
2. Agnarsson, G., Greenlaw, R., Kantabutra, S.: The structure of rooted weighted trees modeling layered cyber-security systems. Acta Cybernet. **22**(4), 25–59 (2016)
3. Altshuler, B., Krovi, H., Roland, J.: Anderson localization makes adiabatic quantum optimization fail. Proc. Natl. Acad. Sci. U.S.A. **107**, 12446–50 (2010)
4. Baldassi, C., Zecchina, R.: Efficiency of quantum vs. classical annealing in nonconvex learning problems. Proc. Natl. Acad. Sci. **115**(7), 1457–1462 (2018)
5. Bapst, V., Foini, L., Krzakala, F., Semerjian, G., Zamponi, F.: The quantum adiabatic algorithm applied to random optimization problems: the quantum spin glass perspective. Phys. Rep. **523**(3), 127–205 (2013)
6. Crawford, D., Levit, A., Ghadermarzy, N., Oberoi, J.S., Ronagh, P.: Reinforcement learning using quantum Boltzmann machines, vol. 18, no. 1–2, pp. 51–74 (2018)
7. van Dam, W., Mosca, M., Vazirani, U.: How powerful is adiabatic quantum computation? In: Proceedings 42nd IEEE Symposium on Foundations of Computer Science, pp. 279–287 (2001)
8. Dickson, N., Amin, M.: Does adiabatic quantum optimization fail for NP-complete problems? Phys. Rev. Lett. **106**(5), 050502 (2011)
9. Dixit, V., et al.: Training a quantum annealing based restricted Boltzmann machine on cybersecurity data. IEEE Trans. Emerg. Top. Comput. Intell. **6**, 417–428 (2022)
10. Farhi, E., Goldstone, J., Gosset, D., Gutmann, S., Shor, P.: Unstructured randomness, small gaps and localization. Quantum Inf. Comput. **11**(9–10), 840–854 (2011)
11. Finnila, A., Gomez, M., Sebenik, C., Stenson, C., Doll, J.: Quantum annealing: a new method for minimizing multidimensional functions. Chem. Phys. Lett. **219**, 343–348 (1994)
12. Ganesan, R., Jajodia, S., Cam, H.: Optimal scheduling of cybersecurity analysts for minimizing risk. ACM Trans. Intell. Syst. Technol. **8**, 1–32 (2017)
13. Gilyén, A., Hastings, M.B., Vazirani, U.: (Sub)Exponential advantage of adiabatic quantum computation with no sign problem, pp. 1357–1369. Association for Computing Machinery, New York (2021)

14. Hen, I., Young, A.: Exponential complexity of the quantum adiabatic algorithm for certain satisfiability problems. Phys. Rev. E **84**, 061152 (2011)
15. Henderson, M., Novak, J., Cook, T.: Leveraging quantum annealing for election forecasting. J. Phys. Soc. Jpn. **88**(6), 061009 (2019)
16. Hernandez, M., Aramon, M.: Enhancing quantum annealing performance for the molecular similarity problem. Quantum Inf. Process. **16**(5), 1–27 (2017). https://doi.org/10.1007/s11128-017-1586-y
17. Hu, F., et al.: Quantum computing cryptography: finding cryptographic boolean functions with quantum annealing by a 2000 qubit D-wave quantum computer. Phys. Lett. A **384**(10), 126214 (2020)
18. Hukushima, K., Nemoto, K.: Exchange Monte Carlo method and application to spin glass simulations. J. Phys. Soc. Jpn. **65**(6), 1604–1608 (1996)
19. Jörg, T., Krzakala, F., Semerjian, G., Zamponi, F.: First-order transitions and the performance of quantum algorithms in random optimization problems. Phys. Rev. Lett. **104**, 207206 (2010)
20. Kadowaki, T., Nishimori, H.: Quantum annealing in the transverse ising model. Phys. Rev. E **58**, 5355–5363 (1998)
21. Keplinger, K.: Is quantum computing becoming relevant to cyber-security? Netw. Secur. **2018**(9), 16–19 (2018)
22. Kirkpatrick, S., Gelatt, C.D., Vecchi, M.P.: Optimization by simulated annealing. Science **220**(4598), 671–680 (1983)
23. Li, R., Di Felice, R., Rohs, R., Lidar, D.: Quantum annealing versus classical machine learning applied to a simplified computational biology problem. NPJ Quantum Inf. **4**, 14 (2018)
24. Lucas, A.: Ising formulations of many np problems. Front. Phys. **2** (2014)
25. Mezard, M., M.A.: Information, Physics, and Computation, p. 569. Oxford University Press Inc., Oxford (2009)
26. Monasson, R.: Optimization problems and replica symmetry breaking in finite connectivity spin glasses. J. Phys. A: Math. Gen. **31**(2), 513–529 (1998)
27. Monasson, R., Zecchina, R.: Statistical mechanics of the random k-satisfiability model. Phys. Rev. E **56**, 1357–1370 (1997)
28. Mukdasanit, S., Kantabutra, S.: Attack and defense in the layered cyber-security model and their $(1 \pm \varepsilon)$-approximation schemes. J. Comput. Syst. Sci. **115**, 54–63 (2021)
29. Neukart, F., Compostella, G., Seidel, C., Von Dollen, D., Yarkoni, S., Parney, B.: Traffic flow optimization using a quantum annealer. Front. ICT **4**, 1–6 (2017)
30. Ohzeki, M., Miki, A., Miyama, M.J., Terabe, M.: Control of automated guided vehicles without collision by quantum annealer and digital devices. Front. Comput. Sci. **1**, 1–9 (2019)
31. Okimoto, T., Ikegai, N., Inoue, K., Okada, H., Ribeiro, T., Maruyama, H.: Cyber security problem based on multi-objective distributed constraint optimization technique. In: 2013 43rd Annual IEEE/IFIP Conference on Dependable Systems and Networks Workshop (DSN-W), pp. 1–7 (2013)
32. Perdomo-Ortiz, A., Dickson, N., Drew-Brook, M., Rose, G., Aspuru-Guzik, A.: Finding low-energy conformations of lattice protein models by quantum annealing. Sci. Rep. **2**, 571 (2012)
33. Rosenberg, G., Haghnegahdar, P., Goddard, P., Carr, P., Wu, K., de Prado, M.L.: Solving the optimal trading trajectory problem using a quantum annealer. IEEE J. Sel. Top. Signal Process. **10**(6), 1053–1060 (2016)
34. Santoro, G.E., Martoňák, R., Tosatti, E., Car, R.: Theory of quantum annealing of an ising spin glass. Science **295**(5564), 2427–2430 (2002)

35. D-Wave Systems Inc.: D-Wave Problem-Solving Handbook. D-Wave Systems Inc
36. Vamvoudakis, K.G., Hespanha, J., Kemmerer, R., Vigna, G.: Formulating cyber-security as convex optimization problems. In: Tarraf, D. (ed.) Control of Cyber-Physical Systems, vol. 449, pp. 85–100. Springer, Heidelberg (2013). https://doi.org/10.1007/978-3-319-01159-2_5
37. Venturelli, D., Marchand, D., Rojo, G.: Quantum annealing implementation of job-shop scheduling, pp. 25–34 (2016)
38. Martoňák, R., Santoro, G.E., Tosatti, E.: Quantum annealing of the traveling-salesman problem. Phys. Rev. E **70**, 057701 (2004)
39. Weise, T., Zapf, M., Chiong, R., Nebro, A.J.: Why is optimization difficult? In: Chiong, R. (ed.) Nature-Inspired Algorithms for Optimisation, pp. 1–50. Springer, Heidelberg (2009). https://doi.org/10.1007/978-3-642-00267-0_1
40. Zhang, Y., Malacaria, P.: Optimization-time analysis for cybersecurity. IEEE Trans. Dependable Secure Comput. **19**, 2365–2383 (2022)

Computation Offloading Algorithm Based on Deep Reinforcement Learning and Multi-Task Dependency for Edge Computing

Tengxiang Lin[1,2], Cheng-Kuan Lin[3], Zhen Chen[1], and Hongju Cheng[1,2]($\boxtimes$)

[1] College of Computer and Data Science, Fuzhou University, Fuzhou 350108, China
{200327171,chenzhen,cscheng}@fzu.edu.cn
[2] Fujian Provincial Key Laboratory of Network Computing and Intelligent Information Processing, Fuzhou University, Fuzhou 350108, China
[3] Department of Computer Science, National Yang Ming Chiao Tung University, Hsinchu 300, Taiwan
cklin@nycu.edu.tw

Abstract. Edge computing is an emerging promising computing paradigm that brings computation and storage resources to the network edge, significantly reducing service latency. In this paper, we aim to divide the task into several sub-tasks through its inherent interrelation, guided by the idea of high concurrency for synchronization, and then offload sub-tasks to other edge servers so that they can be processed to minimize the cost. Furthermore, we propose a DRL-based Multi-Task Dependency Offloading Algorithm (MTDOA) to solve challenges caused by dependencies between sub-tasks and dynamic working scenes. Firstly, we model the Markov decision process as the task offloading decision. Then, we use the graph attention network to extract the dependency information of different tasks and combine Long Short-term Memory (LSTM) with Deep Q Network (DQN) to deal with time-dependent problems. Finally, simulation experiments demonstrate that the proposed algorithm boasts good convergence ability and is superior to several other baseline algorithms, proving this algorithm's effectiveness and reliability.

Keywords: Computation offloading · Edge computing · Dependency · Deep reinforcement learning · Multiple tasks

1 Introduction

The technological development of smartphones, tablets, and wearables drives new services and applications with high computing capacities, such as virtual reality (VR), augmented reality (AR), face recognition, and mobile health care. IoT devices often suffer from limited computing power due to minor physical size and tight production cost constraints. Edge Computing (EC) [1,2] is a promising

S.-Y. Hsieh et al. (Eds.): ICS 2022, CCIS 1723, pp. 111–122, 2022.
https://doi.org/10.1007/978-981-19-9582-8_10

solution and has attracted widespread attention. Its core idea is to deploy servers and storage devices at the network's edge to guarantee powerful computing and storage capabilities.

Most existing literature uses Directed Acyclic Graph(DAG) to model the computation offload problem with dependencies. Unfortunately, due to the complexity and diversity of the DAG structure, the computation offload problem based on it becomes NP-hard [3]. So most of the previous papers mainly used heuristic algorithms to solve this problem [4]. Since the edge server's link state and computing capacity change dynamically in edge computing, the heuristic algorithm cannot meet the requirements of real-time dynamic decision-making in the virtual environment and lacks generality [5]. To solve this dilemma, references [6] proposed a method to solve the DAG task offloading scheduling decision through deep reinforcement learning (Deep Reinforcement Learning, DRL) and used the strong representation ability [7] of DRL to learn the vast state space of the DAG offloading decision problem.

However, using DRL to solve the DAG-based offloading scheduling problem will face the problem that the neural network is only suitable for Euclidean processing space [8] data. In the computer field, images and texts belong to Euclidean space data, while DAG is a kind of structured data. In order to better extract the dependencies between sub-tasks and the features of these sub-tasks, this paper adopts the Graph Attention Network(GAT) [9] to process DAG. In a natural environment, due to the complexity of the problem and the limitation of perception, it is difficult for the system to obtain the actual state of the current time step directly. This paper intends to combine LSTM with DQN to settle time-dependent problems. The main contributions of this paper are as follows:

- We model EC scenarios, including task dependency, communication, and cost models. We Utilize MDP to describe the offloading problem in MEC and aims to minimize the transmission and computing costs.
- An MTDOA algorithm based on DRL is proposed. In order to optimize the task offloading strategy, a graph attention network is used to capture the characteristics of DAG and LSTM to improve the deep reinforcement learning algorithm.
- The experimentations adopt the generated data and compare the algorithm's performance in this paper with some existing algorithms. Experiments show that our method outperforms the heuristic baseline algorithm and can achieve near-optimal results in dynamic MEC scenarios.

2   Related Work

Qiao et al. [10] studied the joint optimization problem of computation offloading and content caching in the vehicular edge network. He et al. [11] proposed a method of dynamic joint arrangement of network, cache and computing resources in the dynamic MEC environment. For the optimization problem of energy consumption, Yu et al. [12] modeled it as a linear programming problem, and proposed a task offloading algorithm based on Lyapunov's optimization theory. Wang et al.

[13] use the graph coloring method to allocate the computing resources of the edge computing server to the user's terminal device. Xu *et al.* [14] considered dynamic service caching and task offloading, and proposes an efficient online decentralized computation offloading algorithm. Dai *et al.* [15] proposed a heuristic computational offload scheduling algorithm under the scenario of multi-user and multi-MEC server to achieve the optimization goal of minimizing the average processing delay of tasks.

When considering the internal dependencies of offloaded tasks, Lin *et al.* [16] represented a mobile application as a task graph and proposed a heuristic-based algorithm to solve the task offloading problem in MEC. Neto *et al.* [17] proposed a user-level online offloading scheme for MEC, which makes offloading decisions based on the estimation of the energy and execution time of the relevant tasks. Yan *et al.* [18] proposed a reduced-complexity Gibbs sampling algorithm is proposed to obtain the optimal offloading decision by considering the task dependency among users. Chen *et al.* [19] used linear integer programming and heuristics such as first-fit and online first to optimize the delay and energy consumption problems in task offloading.

3   System Model

The scenario considered in this paper includes multiple micro base stations (SBSs) and multiple tasks on a selected micro base station. $N = \{N_1, N_2, \ldots, N_n\}$ denotes the set of edge servers, and $|N|$ denotes their number. $N_i.f$, $N_i.p$, $N_i.b$, and $N_i.p^{tr}$ denote the computing power, computing cost, transmission bandwidth, and transmission power of the edge server N_i, respectively.

$T = \{T_1, T_2, \ldots, T_i\}$ denotes the set of tasks, $|T|$ denotes the number of tasks, and T_i denotes the tasks produced by user i. $T_i.d$, $T_i.a$, $T_i.g$, $T_i.t^{max}$, $T_i.e$ and $T_i.n$ represent the data size of task T_i, the set of subtasks, the DAG graph, the upper limit of execution time, the edge server where the set of tasks is located, and the number of subtasks, respectively.

Denote by $T_i.n$ the number of subtasks in task T_i and T_i^j the jth subtask of task T_i. The set of all subtasks is denoted by $T_i.a = \left\{T_i^j | j \in [1, T_i.n]\right\}$. $T_i^j.in$, $T_i^j.out$, $T_i^j.c$, $T_i^j.k$, $T_i^j.p$, and $T_i^j.s$ represent the input data amount, the output data amount, the average computation density, the offloading to the edge server k processing, the predecessor task set, and the successor task set of the subtask T_i^j respectively.

3.1   Task Dependency Model

In this paper, the dependency between different subtasks in a task is modeled as a DAG, denoted by $G = (\nu, \varepsilon)$, where ν and ε represent the vertex set and the edge set, respectively. Each edge of the graph in this paper represents the data dependency between the subtasks, for example, a directed edge $\left(T_i^j, T_i^{j'}\right)$ represents that the subtask T_i^j will transmit the data to the subtask $T_i^{j'}$ after the execution, and the $T_i^{j'}$ must receive the data before it can continue to execute.

3.2 Communication Model

Users need to offload the task data to the edge server where the task set is located through wireless resources. The user and the edge server are connected through a wireless link. According to the Shannon formula, the maximum transmission rate from the user i to the edge server e where the task set is located can be defined as:

$$R_{i,e}^{off} = B_i \log_2 \left(1 + \frac{p_i^{tr} h_{i,e}}{\varpi^2} \right), \tag{1}$$

in (1), B_i represents the available transmission bandwidth of user i, p_i^{tr} represents the transmission power of user i, $h_{i,e}$ is the channel gain from user i to the edge server e where the task set is located. According to (1), the transmission delay of user i offloading task T_i to edge server $T_i.e$ can be calculated as follows:

$$t_i^{ue\_off} = \frac{T_i \cdot d}{R_{i,T_i.e}^{off}}. \tag{2}$$

After the last subtask $T_i^{T_i.n}$ is executed, the calculation result needs to be transmitted to user i. The transmission delay of the calculation result of the subtask $T_i^{T_i.n}$ at the edge server k back to the user i is t_i^{dr}.

Similarly, the transmission delay for the edge server $T_i.e$ to offload any T_i^j to the edge server k can be calculated as $t_{i,j}^{mec\_off}$.

If subtask T_i^j and $T_i^{j'}$ are executed on the same edge server, the communication delay between them is 0. When the subtask T_i^j is a direct predecessor task of the subtask $T_i^{j'}$, the data transmission delay of the edge server $T_i^j.k$ where the subtask T_i^j is located transmitting the output data to the edge server $T_i^{j'}.k$ where the subtask $T_i^{j'}$ is located can be expressed as $t_{i,j,j'}^{com}$.

3.3 Cost Model

Assuming that the communication cost per unit time between user i and the edge server is β_i, the transmission cost of the task offloaded from the device to the edge server where the task set is located and the calculation result returned to the user can be calculated as:

$$Cost_i^{ue\_tran} = \beta_i \left(t_i^{ue\_off} + t_i^{dr} \right). \tag{3}$$

If the subtask T_i^j is offloaded to the edge server $T_i^j.k$ for calculation, assuming that the calculation capability of the edge server $T_i^j.k$ is $T_i^j.k.f$, the execution time of the subtask T_i^j on the edge server $T_i^j.k$ can be obtained:

$$t_{i,j}^{exe} = \frac{T_i^j.c \cdot T_i^j.in}{T_i^j.k.f}. \tag{4}$$

The cost of offloading the subtask T_i^j to the edge server $T_i^j.k$ consists of three parts, the transmission cost of the subtask offloading, the cost of the edge server $T_i^j.k$ executing the subtask T_i^j, and the communication cost of the immediate successor task transmitting its result to the subtask T_i^j. Assuming that the unit cost for the edge server k to execute the task is $N_i.p$, and the communication cost per unit time between the edge servers is β_k, the cost for offloading the subtask T_i^j to the edge server $T_i^j.k$ calculation can be obtained as:

$$Cost_{i,j}^{mec} = t_{i,j}^{mec\_off} \cdot \beta_k + t_{i,j}^{exe} \cdot N_i.p + \sum_{T_i^{j'} \in T_i^j.s} \frac{T_i^j.out}{R_{T_i^j.k,T_i^{j'}.k}^{off}} \cdot \beta_k. \qquad (5)$$

Therefore, the total cost of completing all tasks is:

$$Cost^{total} = \sum_{i=1}^{|\mathcal{M}|} Cost_i^{ue\_tran} + \sum_{i=1}^{|\mathcal{M}|} \sum_{j=1}^{|T_i.n|} Cost_{i,j}^{mec}. \qquad (6)$$

3.4 Problem Definition

In this section, the task scheduling decision problem is formalized as a 0-1 programming problem.

Defining the scheduling decision variable $x_{i,j,k}$:

$$x_{i,j,k} = \begin{cases} 1, \text{ if } T_i^j \text{ can be executed on MEC server } k \\ 0, \text{ otherwise} \end{cases} \qquad (7)$$

Considering that each subtask can only be calculated on one edge server, the task scheduling shall meet the following constraints: $\sum_{k=1}^{|N|} x_{i,j,k} = 1$.

Using the variable $y_{j,j'}$ to describe the task scheduling sequence:

$$y_{j,j'} = \begin{cases} 1, \text{ if task } j \text{ is scheduled before task } j' \\ 0, \text{ otherwise} \end{cases} \qquad (8)$$

Considering that there is a certain dependency between the subtasks, before executing the subtask T_i^j, all its predecessor tasks need to be scheduled. Let $AST_{i,j}$ and $AFT_{i,j}$ denote the actual start execution time and the actual completion time of the subtask T_i^j, respectively. The actual start time of the task is calculated recursively from the entry task node:

$$AST_{i,j} = \max \left\{ t_{i,j}^{mec\_off}, \max_{T_i^j \in T_i^j.p} \left(AFT_{i,j'} + t_{i,j,j'}^{com} \right) \right\}, \qquad (9)$$

where $T_i^{j'} \in T_i^j.p$ represents the set of all task predecessors of the subtask T_i^j, $AFT_{i,j'}$ represents the actual completion time of the subtask at the edge server, and $t_{i,j,j'}^{com}$ represents the communication delay for transmitting the calculation result of the subtask $T_i^{j'}$ to the subtask T_i^j. Next, the actual completion time $AFT_{i,j'}$ of the immediate predecessor task $T_i^{j'}$ of the subtask T_i^j is calculated:

$$AFT_{i,j'} = \min \left\{ t_{i,j'}^{exe} + AST_{i,j'} \right\} \tag{10}$$

When $T_i^j.k = T_{i'}^{j'}.k$, denote by $AFT_{i',j'}$ the completion time of the subtask $T_{i'}^{j'}$ on the edge server $T_{i'}^{j'}.k$, then the earliest start time $AST_{i,j}$ of the subtask T_i^j on the edge server $T_i^j.k$ should satisfy the following constraint:

$$AST_{i,j} \geq x_{i,j,T_i^j.k} \cdot x_{i',j',T_i^j.k} \cdot y_{j',j} \cdot AFT_{i',j',T_i^j.k}. \tag{11}$$

In this paper, $T_i.t^{max}$ is used to denote the upper bound of the processing delay of task T_i, that is $t_i^{AFT} \leq T_i.t^{max}$.

Therefore, the following optimization problem can be obtained:

$$\min \left(\sum_{i=1}^{|\mathcal{M}|} Cost_i^{ue\_tran} + \sum_{i=1}^{|\mathcal{M}|} \sum_{j=1}^{|T_i.n|} x_{i,j,T_i^j.k} Cost_{i,j}^{mec} \right). \tag{12}$$

4   MTDOA Dependent Task Offloading Algorithm

In this paper, we propose an MTDOA algorithm based on DRL and Graph Attention Network (GAT) for the DAG task offloading problem with dependencies, as shown in Fig. 1. First, calculating the task's latest start time yields the task's priority queue. The algorithm must unload the task following that priority queue. The state space requires the relevant task data to construct the MDP model. In order to retrieve the data from the DAG graph's vertices, the GAT network is utilized to extract the DAG graph's features. The LSTM network enhances the DQN algorithm to address the timing-dependent issue.

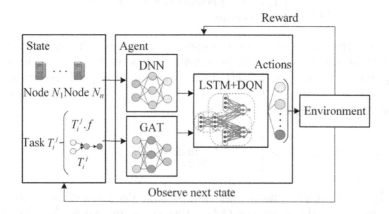

Fig. 1. Multi-task with dependency offloading algorithm

4.1   Task Scheduling Priority

If more than one task needs to be executed, multiple tasks need to be prioritized first. Then the latest start time of each subtask can be estimated according to the latest finish time of all subtasks, and a task priority queue T_{PQ}.

Letting $LCT_{i,j}$ denote the latest completion time allowed for the task T_i^j. Therefore, the latest completion time $LCT_{i,j}$ allowed for the subtask T_i^j can be expressed as:

$$LCT_{i,j} = \min_{T_i^{j'} \in T_i^j.s} \left\{ LCT_{i,j'} - t_{i,j'}^{exe} + t_{i,j,j'}^{com} \right\}. \tag{13}$$

The latest start time $LST_{i,j}$ allowed for the subtask T_i^j can be calculated according to the above equation:

$$LST_{i,j} = LCT_{i,j} - \min_{T_i^j \in T_i} \left(t_{i,j}^{exe} \right). \tag{14}$$

4.2   State Space

For the node N_n, the computation capacity $N_n.f$, the computation cost $N_n.p$, the transmission bandwidth $N_n.b$, and the transmission power $N_n.p^{tr}$ are all necessary information for the decision, Then the state of node N_n can be expressed as $S_{N_n} = \{N_n.f, N_n.p, N_n.b, N_n.p^{tr}\}$. And the state of S_N of all nodes can be expressed as $S_N = \{S_{N_1}, S_{N_2}, \ldots, S_{N_n}\}$. For task T_i, its state can be expressed as $S_{T_i} = \{T_i.d, T_i.a, T_i.g, T_i.t^{max}, T_i.e, T_i.n\}$, Then all tasks $S_T = \{S_{T_1}, S_{T_2}, \ldots, S_{T_i}\}$.

A DAG $G_i = (\nu_i, \varepsilon_i)$ is used to represent all subtasks and dependencies of task T_i, where $\nu_i = T_i.n$ and ε_i represents dependencies. There is a profile $T_i^j.f$ for each subtask T_i^j in the task T_i. The characteristics of task T_i can be summarized as follows: $h_i = \left[T_i^1.f; T_i^2.f; \ldots; T_i^{T_i.n}.f \right]$.

The goal of this paper is to produce a task-level output $Z_i \in R^{T_i.n \times F}$, where F is the number of output features for each task, with h_i and M_i as inputs. Each row Z_i^j of Z_i represents an embedding of a subtask T_i^j of task T_i. Softmax is used to normalize the neighbor nodes of the central node to get $\alpha_i^{jj'}$.

The final output of the attention layer is a new set of node features: $h' = \{h_1, h_2, \ldots, h_i\}$, then the output $Z_i = h_i$ of the task T_i can be obtained, so the embedded expression of the subtask T_i^j can be calculated as $V_{S_{T_i^j}} = f \left(\sum_{T_i^{j'} \in T_i^j.s} Z_i^{j'} \right)$, where $Z_i^{j'}$ is the embedded feature of the subtask $T_i^{j'}$ extracted from Z_i, and $f(\cdot)$ is a nonlinear activation function.

To sum up, the state of the system at time t can be expressed as: $S_t = \left[S_N, S_{T_i^j} \right] \in S$. The state embedding can be expressed as: $V_{S_t} = \left[V_{S_N}, V_{S_{T_i^j}} \right]$.

4.3 Action Space

For any arriving task, the decision goal is to find a suitable node to unload the task, so the scope of the action is the set of all nodes, defined as:

$$A_t \in \{N_1, N_2, \ldots, N_n\} = A. \tag{15}$$

4.4 Reward Function

A node receives a reward r_t immediately after performing an action at time t. The goal of this paper is to minimize the transmission cost and computation cost of a task. The transmission cost includes the transmission cost of the task and the calculation result, and the calculation cost is generated by the calculation task of the node, so the reward function can be expressed as:

$$r_t = -Cost^{total}. \tag{16}$$

4.5 The Proposed MTDOA

DQN is a deep reinforcement learning algorithm based on value iteration, whose goal is to estimate the Q value of the optimal policy. The algorithm uses deep neural network to calculate the approximate value function, and turns the update problem of Q-Table into a function fitting problem, so that it can get similar output actions according to similar States. In order to solve the shortcomings of traditional Q-Learning algorithm in high-dimensional and continuous problems. The objective of the training process is to minimize the loss, which is defined as:

$$\begin{cases} L(\theta) = E\left[\left(y(t) - \hat{Q}\left(s_t, a_t; \theta\right)\right)^2\right] \\ y(t) = r_{t+1} + \gamma \max_{a'} \hat{Q}\left(s_{t+1}, a'; \theta^-\right) \end{cases} \tag{17}$$

After using LSTM to improve the DQN algorithm, the observed state Z_t and action a_t at the current time step can be obtained to form a state-action pair, which can be integrated with the output value in LSTM to deduce the real environmental state s_t, and then imported into the deep neural network for training. The specific algorithm is shown in Algorithm 1. At the beginning of the algorithm, the agent of DQN receives the task set, DAG graph, environmental data and other information to be unloaded and scheduled, generates the node representation of each task node, initializes the cumulative reward and action space to 0 and $\emptyset$ respectively, and creates an experience playback buffer D. The algorithm first determines the scheduling priority of all tasks, and then makes the unloading decision of the tasks in descending order of the priority of the subtasks. When making a decision for each task, the agent uses Algorithm 1 to evaluate the q value of each action, obtains the q value of each action, selects the action according to the ε greedy strategy, obtains the action state pair (z_t, a_t) and deduces the real environment state s_t, and the system enters the next state after implementing the selected action. And the system stores (z_t, a_t, r_t) into an experience playback buffer area for training the neural network and updating parameters.

Algorithm 1. Multi-Task Dependency Offloading Algorithm(MTDOA).

Input:
　　Environment E, task set T_i, policy network weight θ;
Output:
　　Offloading action a_t;
　1: Initialize agent and D, $s_t \leftarrow \{\emptyset\}$, $a_t \leftarrow \{\emptyset\}$, $a_t \leftarrow 0, M \leftarrow 10000$;
　2: Arranging all tasks in ascending order of their $LST_{i,j}$ to get the priority sequence T_{PQ};
　3: **while** $T_{PQ} \neq \emptyset$ **do**
　4: 　　Obtaining the subtask T_i^j and calculate the q value of the action a_t;
　5: 　　Action a_t to be taken is selected according to the ε greedy algorithm;
　6: 　　Obtaining the observed state z_t and the action a_t at the current time step constitutes a state-action pair (z_t, a_t);
　7: 　　Combining the state action pair to generate the real environment state s_t, update the action a_t, and obtain the immediate reward r_t;
　8: 　　**if** s_{j+1} is terminated **then**
　9: 　　　y_j can be represented by r_j;
　10: 　　**else**
　11: 　　　y_j is equal to $y(t)$ in equation 17;
　12: 　　**end if**
　13: 　　Updating parameter θ using stochastic gradient descent algorithm SGD;
　14: 　　Copying the weight θ of the policy network to the target network$\theta^- = \theta$ regularly;
　15: **end while**

5　Result and Discussion

5.1　Simulation Environment and Hyperparameters

Consider a typical task offload scheduling scenario: the CPU power of the UE is 1–2 GHz, the maximum transmission power is 100 mW, and the available transmission bandwidth is 8 MHz. The CPU computing power of the MEC server is 5–10 GHz, the maximum transmission power is 1000 mW, and the available transmission bandwidth is 10–15 MHz. The computational cost and data transmission cost of the edge server are set to 1 and modified during the experiment.

The experiment uses the DAG generator to generate 5000 DAGs for training and 1000 DAGs for testing according to the number of tasks $\{10, 20, 30, 40, 50\}$ of the graph. The discount coefficient of deep reinforcement learning is defined as $\gamma = 0.9$, the memory space size is defined as $M = 10000$, Adam is selected as the optimizer in the training process, the learning rate is 10^{-4}, the batch learning size is BatchSize $= 64$, and for the deep reinforcement learning algorithm based on LSTM improvement, its time window is set as 20.

5.2　Experimental Results and Analysis

First, under the simulation parameters described above, 5000 DAG samples are randomly generated for training. At the end of each training period, the test

DAG is input into the current policy network to obtain the unloading scheduling scheme for the batch of samples. Then, the scheduling scheme is used to simulate the scheduling of the batch of samples in the same simulation environment, and the cumulative rewards obtained by the batch of samples are recorded. As shown in Fig. 2, the total reward represents the sum of all rewards for executing the offloading strategy at each iteration. The cumulative reward of this batch of samples gradually tends to be stable after 2000 iterations, which proves that the algorithm has good convergence.

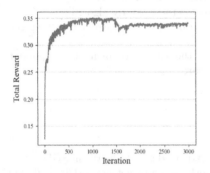
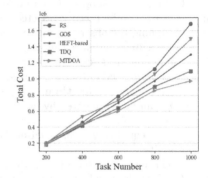

Fig. 2. MTDOA algorithm training process cumulative reward

Fig. 3. Total cost changes with the number of tasks

Four baseline algorithms are set to compare with the MTDOA algorithm:

- Random Scheduling (RS): The scheduling decision is randomly determined for all tasks in the DAG graph.
- Greedy Offload Strategy (GOS): According to the generated DAG graph, tasks are selected from the start node to the exit node in turn, and assigned to the device with the lowest cost for execution.
- HEFT-based scheduling: Tasks are first prioritized according to their earliest completion time, and then the prioritized tasks are scheduled to the resource with the earliest estimated completion time.
- Traditional DQN algorithm (TDQ): This algorithm does not consider the task dependencies.

Then, based on the optimization goal of minimizing the total execution cost of tasks, the execution cost of DAGs with different number of tasks is compared in the default environment. Figure 3 shows the experimental results. The total cost on the y-axis represents the sum of the costs required to offload all tasks and calculate. When the number of tasks increases, the total execution cost of the first three heuristics is relatively large, the trend of the total execution cost of RS is larger. In most cases, the total cost of TDQ and MTDOA is lower than the baseline algorithm. Compared with TDQ algorithm, MTDOA has better performance because it considers the dependencies between tasks, can reduce the total execution cost by parallel processing of subtasks.

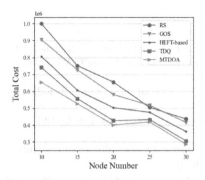

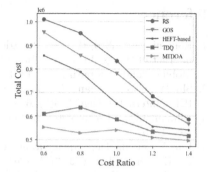

Fig. 4. Total cost changes with the number of tasks

Fig. 5. Total cost changes with the number of nodes

Next, as shown in Fig. 4, with the increase of the number of nodes, the total amount of computing resources in the system also increase. Although the performance of all algorithms is almost the same in the case of sufficient resources, in the case of limited resources, compared with several other baseline algorithms, The MTDOA algorithm has the minimum total task execution cost.

Finally, the performance of each algorithm will be verified under the condition of varying the communication cost and the computation cost, as shown in Fig. 5. For the three heuristics, when the ratio of communication cost to computation cost is less than 1, the computation cost is so significant that the total cost of task execution is considerable. In contrast, the MTDOA algorithm can adjust the offloading strategy according to the dynamic changes in communication cost and computing cost to maintain a better offloading scheduling effect.

6 Conclusion

This paper studies the multitasking dependent computation offloading problem in edge computing, aiming to minimize the total cost of task execution. The computational offloading process adopts a graph attention network (GAT) to extract the dependencies of tasks; then the offload scheduling is modeled as an MDP process, and LSTM and DQN are combined to deal with timing-dependent problems; finally, by combining four The comparison of the baseline algorithms proves the effectiveness of using the MTDOA algorithm to solve the multi-task dependency offloading computing problem in edge computing scenarios.

Acknowledgements. This work is supported in part by the Science Foundation of Fujian Province of China under Grand No. 2019J01245, and the National Natural Science Foundation of China under Grand No. 83419114.

References

1. Bonomi, F., Milito, R., Zhu, J., Addepalli, S.: Fog computing and its role in the internet of things. In: Proceedings of the First Edition of the MCC Workshop on Mobile Cloud Computing, pp. 13–16 (2012)
2. Shi, W., Cao, J., Zhang, Q., Li, Y., Xu, L.: Edge computing: vision and challenges. IEEE Internet Things J. **3**(5), 637–646 (2016)
3. Ullman, J.D.: NP-complete scheduling problems. J. Comput. Syst. Sci. **10**(3), 384–393 (1975)
4. Liu, Y., et al.: Dependency-aware task scheduling in vehicular edge computing. IEEE Internet Things J. **7**(6), 4961–4971 (2020)
5. Lin, L., Liao, X., Jin, H., Li, P.: Computation offloading toward edge computing. Proc. IEEE **107**(8), 1584–1607 (2019)
6. Yan, J., Bi, S., Zhang, Y.J.A.: Offloading and resource allocation with general task graph in mobile edge computing: a deep reinforcement learning approach. IEEE Trans. Wireless Commun. **19**(8), 5404–5419 (2020)
7. Li, Y.: Deep reinforcement learning: an overview. arXiv preprint arXiv:1701.07274 (2017)
8. Scarselli, F., Gori, M., Tsoi, A.C., Hagenbuchner, M., Monfardini, G.: The graph neural network model. IEEE Trans. Neural Networks **20**(1), 61–80 (2008)
9. Veličković, P., Cucurull, G., Casanova, A., Romero, A., Lio, P., Bengio, Y.: Graph attention networks. arXiv preprint arXiv:1710.10903 (2017)
10. Qiao, G., Leng, S., Maharjan, S., Zhang, Y., Ansari, N.: Deep reinforcement learning for cooperative content caching in vehicular edge computing and networks. IEEE Internet Things J. **7**(1), 247–257 (2019)
11. He, Y., Zhao, N., Yin, H.: Integrated networking, caching, and computing for connected vehicles: a deep reinforcement learning approach. IEEE Trans. Veh. Technol. **67**(1), 44–55 (2017)
12. Yu, B., Pu, L., Xie, Y., Jian, Z.: Joint task offloading and base station association in mobile edge computing. J. Comput. Res. Dev **55**, 537–550 (2018)
13. Wang, C., Yu, F.R., Liang, C., Chen, Q., Tang, L.: Joint computation offloading and interference management in wireless cellular networks with mobile edge computing. IEEE Trans. Veh. Technol. **66**(8), 7432–7445 (2017)
14. Xu, J., Chen, L., Zhou, P.: Joint service caching and task offloading for mobile edge computing in dense networks. In: IEEE INFOCOM 2018-IEEE Conference on Computer Communications, pp. 207–215. IEEE (2018)
15. Dai, Y., Xu, D., Zhang, K., Maharjan, S., Zhang, Y.: Deep reinforcement learning and permissioned blockchain for content caching in vehicular edge computing and networks. IEEE Trans. Veh. Technol. **69**(4), 4312–4324 (2020)
16. Lin, X., Wang, Y., Xie, Q., Pedram, M.: Task scheduling with dynamic voltage and frequency scaling for energy minimization in the mobile cloud computing environment. IEEE Trans. Serv. Comput. **8**(2), 175–186 (2014)
17. Neto, J.L.D., Yu, S.Y., Macedo, D.F., Nogueira, J.M.S., Langar, R., Secci, S.: ULOOF: a user level online offloading framework for mobile edge computing. IEEE Trans. Mob. Comput. **17**(11), 2660–2674 (2018)
18. Yan, J., Bi, S., Zhang, Y.J., Tao, M.: Optimal task offloading and resource allocation in mobile-edge computing with inter-user task dependency. IEEE Trans. Wireless Commun. **19**(1), 235–250 (2019)
19. Chen, W., Wang, D., Li, K.: Multi-user multi-task computation offloading in green mobile edge cloud computing. IEEE Trans. Serv. Comput. **12**(5), 726–738 (2018)

A Comparison Diagnosis Algorithm for Conditional Fault Local Diagnosis of Multiprocessor Systems

Yali Lv[1] , Cheng-Kuan Lin[2,3,4](✉) , D. Frank Hsu[5], and Jianxi Fan[6]

[1] School of Information Technology, Henan University of Chinese Medicine, Zhengzhou, China
[2] Department of Computer Science, National Yang Ming Chiao Tung University, Hsinchu, Taiwan
cklin@nycu.edu.tw
[3] Undergraduate Degree Program of Systems Engineering and Technology, National Yang Ming Chiao Tung University, Hsinchu, Taiwan
[4] Computer Science and Information Engineering, Chung Cheng Institute of Technology, NDU, Taoyuan City, Taiwan
[5] Department of Computer and Information Science, Fordham University, New York, USA
[6] School of Computer Science and Technology, Soochow University, Suzhou, China

Abstract. An efficient diagnosis is very important for a multiprocessor system. In this paper, we present a (α, β)-trees combination $S(u, X, \alpha, \beta)$ and give some conclusions about the local diagnosis. Based on the (α, β)-trees combination, we give a conditional fault local diagnosis algorithm to identify the fault or fault-free status of each processor correctly under the MM* model when the number of faulty nodes does not exceed $\alpha + 2\beta - 3$ and every node has at least one fault-free neighboring node. According to our results, a connected network with a (α, β)-trees combination $S(u, X, \alpha, \beta)$ for a node u is conditionally locally $(\alpha + 2\beta - 3)$-diagnosable at node u and the time complexity of our algorithm to diagnose u is $O(\alpha^2\beta + \alpha\beta^2)$. As an application, we show that our algorithm can identify all the faulty nodes of n-dimensional star graph S_n if the faulty node number does not exceed $3n - 8$. Compared with existing algorithms, our algorithm allows more faulty node in a multiprocessor system.

Keywords: Comparison diagnosis model · Conditional diagnosis · Local diagnosability · Diagnosis algorithm

1 Introduction

As a typical application of parallel computing, multiprocessor systems have gained rapid development. A multiprocessor system consists of processors and communication links between processors. In a high-speed multiprocessor system, processor failures are inevitable. Fault tolerance is always a hot topic in

S.-Y. Hsieh et al. (Eds.): ICS 2022, CCIS 1723, pp. 123–134, 2022.
https://doi.org/10.1007/978-981-19-9582-8_11

the research of multiprocessor systems [17,18,25]. It is hoped that the fault processors could be identified and replaced in time to guarantee that the system can work properly. Identifying all the faulty processors in a system is said to be system-level diagnosis. In system-level diagnosis theory, researchers created various models to identify faulty processors [1,3,12,21,31]. The classical diagnostic models are the PMC model [22] and the MM model [20]. In the PMC model, the result of the diagnosis is achieved through two linked processors testing each other. In the MM model, the result of the diagnosis is achieved through a processor sending the same task to two of its neighbors, and comparing their responses. Sengupta and Dahbura [24] proposed a further modification of the MM model, called the MM* model, in which each processor must test another two processors, if they are adjacent to it. The diagnosability of a system is the maximum number of faulty processors that can be correctly identified. It is unlikely to determine whether or not a processor is faulty if all its neighboring processors happen to be faulty simultaneously. So the diagnosability of a system is upper bounded by the minimum degree of the system. Lai et al. [10] proposed a new measure of diagnostic capability ——conditional diagnosability, by restricting that for each processor in a system, all its neighboring processors do not fail at the same time. The conditional diagnosability has been studied widely [2,6,11,26–28,30]. Hsu and Tan [7] presented a novel measure of diagnosability, called local diagnosability, which is concerned with the status of a single processor instead of the whole system. Many scholars have researched the local diagnosis of different systems [16,19,29]. According to the concept of conditional diagnosability, Kung et al. [9] presented the conditional local diagnosability, which restrains that all the neighbor processors of each processor from being faulty at the same time. Lin et al. [13,14,16] presented some sufficient conditions to estimate the conditional local diagnosability of a given processor based on certain structures and gave corresponding algorithms.

Note that the conditional diagnosability of star graph S_n is $3n - 7$ under the MM* model [15]. Yuan et al. [29] presented an algorithm $A^*(T(u; \alpha, \alpha - 1, \beta))$ can identify the status of each node u of S_n correctly provided the node number of conditional fault set is not more than $3n - 9$. In this paper, we present a new conditional fault local diagnosis algorithm where the node number of conditional fault set is not more than $3n - 8$.

In this paper, we present a (α, β)-trees combination $S(u, X, \alpha, \beta)$ and give some conclusions about the local diagnosis. Based on the (α, β)-trees combination, we give a conditional fault local diagnosis algorithm to identify the fault or fault-free status of each processor correctly under the MM* model when the number of faulty nodes does not exceed $\alpha + 2\beta - 3$ and every node has at least one healthy neighboring node. As an application, we show that our algorithm can identify all the faulty nodes of n-dimensional star graph S_n if the faulty node number does not exceed $3n - 8$.

The rest of this paper is organized as follows. In Sect. 2, we give some definitions and existing results about diagnosis. In Sect. 3, we provide two classes of tree structures and arrive some conclusions in these tree structures. In Sect. 4, we define the (α, β)-trees combination $S(u, X, \alpha, \beta)$ and give a diagnosis algorithm to determine the status of a given node and show a sufficient condition for a given node to be conditionally locally $(\alpha + 2\beta - 3)$-diagnosable. In Sect. 5, we apply the algorithm in star graph S_n. Conclusions are presented in Sect. 6.

2 Preliminaries

In this paper, we follow [8] for the graph-theoretical terminology and notation not defined here. The underlying topology of a multiprocessor system is usually modeled as an undirected simple graph $G(V, E)$, whose node set $V(G)$, and edge set $E(G)$ represent the set of all processors, and the set of all links between processors, respectively. We say u is a neighbor of v if the nodes u and v are adjacent nodes. For each node u, we define the neighborhood $N_G(u)$(or $N(u)$ for convenience) of u in G to be the set of nodes adjacent to u. The degree $d_G(u)$ of node u is the number of edges incident with u. A path P, denoted by $\langle u_1, u_2, \ldots, u_n \rangle$, is a sequence of adjacent nodes where all nodes are distinct except possibly $u_1 = u_n$. A cycle is a path that begins and ends with the same node. A hamiltonian cycle is a cycle which includes all nodes of G. A graph G is hamiltonian if it has a hamiltonian cycle. A graph H is a subgraph of G if $V(H) \subseteq V(G)$ and $E(H) \subseteq E(G)$.

Under the MM model, the comparison scheme of the system G is modeled as a multigraph $M(V(G), C)$, where C is a labeled-edge set. A labeled edge $(u, v)_w \in C$, represents a comparison performed by a node w between its two neighbors u and v. The complete result of all comparisons is called a syndrome of diagnosis, denoted by σ. The result of the comparison $(u, v)_w$ is denoted by $\sigma_w(u, v)$. If the outputs of u and v agree, we have $\sigma_w(u, v) = 0$, otherwise, $\sigma_w(u, v) = 1$. If $\sigma_w(u, v) = 0$ and w is fault-free, then u and v are fault-free; otherwise, at least one of u, v and w must be faulty. If w is faulty, the result of the comparison is unreliable, and the status of u and v are unknown. In the MM* model, all comparisons of a graph G must be performed, so $(u, v)_w$ in C if u and v are two neighbors of w. A faulty node set $F \subseteq V(G)$ is said to be consistent with σ if $\sigma_w(u, v) = 1$ when $\{u, v\} \cap F \neq \emptyset$, $w \in V(G)/F$, and $\sigma_w(u, v) = 0$ when $\{u, v, w\} \cap F = \emptyset$ for any $(u, v)_w \in C$. Note that a given set F of faulty nodes may be consistent with different syndromes. Let $\sigma(F) = \{\sigma | F$ is consistent with $\sigma\}$. Then two distinct fault sets $F_1, F_2 \subset V$ are distinguishable if $\sigma(F_1) \cap \sigma(F_2) = \emptyset$, otherwise F_1, F_2 are indistinguishable. We use $F_1 \triangle F_2$ to denote the set $(F_1 \setminus F_2) \cup (F_2 \setminus F_1)$.

Sengupta and Dahbura [24] gave a necessary and sufficient condition for a pair of faulty node sets to be distinguishable under the MM* model.

Theorem 1. *[24] For any two distinct vertex subsets F_1 and F_2 of graph G, F_1 and F_2 is a distinguishable pair if and only if at least one of the following conditions is satisfied.*

(1.) $\exists \ u, w \in V - (F_1 \cup F_2)$ *and* $\exists \ v \in F_1 \triangle F_2$ *such that* $(u, v)_w \in C$.
(2.) $\exists \ u, v \in F_1 - F_2$ *and* $\exists \ w \in V - (F_1 \cup F_2)$ *such that* $(u, v)_w \in C$.

(3.) $\exists~u, v \in F_2 - F_1$ and $\exists~w \in V - (F_1 \cup F_2)$ such that $(u, v)_w \in C$.

In [9], Kung et al. gave the concept of conditional local diagnosis.

Definition 1. *[9] Let u be any node in graph G. The node u is conditionally locally t-diagnosable in G if any pair of distinct conditional sets of faulty nodes F_1, F_2 with $|F_1| \le t$, $|F_2| \le t$ and $u \in F_1 \triangle F_2$, are distinguishable.*

Definition 2. *[9] The conditional local diagnosability of node u is the maximum integer of t such that u is conditionally locally t-diagnosable.*

Kung et al. [9] show that a graph G is conditionally t-diagnosable if and only if u is conditionally locally t-diagnosable for each node $u \in V(G)$.

3 Two Tree Structures

In this section, we first give three facts and then propose two tree structures and give some properties of each structure.

Fact 1. Let P be any path. If there is a test result equal to 1 in P. Then there is at least one faulty node in P.

Fact 2. Let P be any path. If all test results equal to 0 in P and the first node is a faulty node. Then there are at least $|V(P)| - 1$ faulty nodes in P.

Fact 3. Let P be any path. If the first test result is 1, the others test results equal to 0 in P and the first node is fault-free. Then there are at least $|V(P)| - 3$ faulty nodes in P.

Let $\langle n \rangle = \{1, 2, 3, \ldots, n\}$. Let $X = \{x_1, x_2, \ldots, x_\alpha\}$ be α distinct neighbors of node u. A balanced (α, β)-tree rooted at u with neighbor set X, $T_0(u; X; \alpha, \beta)$, is a tree with

- $V(T_0(u; X; \alpha, \beta)) = \{u\} \cup X \cup \{y_{i,j,k} \mid i \in \langle \alpha \rangle, j \in \beta, k \in \langle \alpha + 2\beta + 1 \rangle\}$, and
- $E(T_0(u; X; \alpha, \beta)) = E_0 \cup E_1 \cup E_2$
  where
- $E_0 = \{ux_i \mid i \in \langle \alpha \rangle\}$
- $E_1 = \bigcup_{i \in \langle \alpha \rangle} \{x_i y_{i,j,1} \mid j \in \langle \beta \rangle\}$
- $E_2 = \bigcup_{i \in \langle \alpha \rangle, j \in \langle \beta \rangle} \{y_{i,j,k} y_{i,j,k+1} \mid k \in \langle \alpha + 2\beta \rangle\}$

The Fig. 1 show the structure. For the structure $T_0(u; X; \alpha, \beta)$, we first give two definitions.

- For $i \in \langle \alpha \rangle$, if there is an index j, $j \in \langle \beta \rangle$, such that $\sigma_{y_{i,j,1}}(x_i, y_{i,j,2}) = 0$ and $\sigma_{y_{i,j,k}}(y_{i,j,k-1}, y_{i,j,k+1}) = 0$ for each $k \in \langle \alpha + 2\beta \rangle - \{1\}$, we call that i satisfies $PathD(00)$.
- For $i \in \langle \alpha \rangle$, if there is an index j, $j \in \langle \beta \rangle$, such that $\sigma_{y_{i,j,1}}(x_i, y_{i,j,2}) = 1$ and $\sigma_{y_{i,j,k}}(y_{i,j,k-1}, y_{i,j,k+1}) = 0$ for each $k \in \langle \alpha + 2\beta \rangle - \{1\}$, we call that i satisfies $PathD(10)$.

We set $A = \{i \mid i \in \langle \alpha \rangle$ and i satisfies $PathD(00)\}$ and $B = \{i \mid i \in \langle \alpha \rangle$ and i satisfies $PathD(10)\}$. In $T_0(u; X; \alpha, \beta)$, if $|F| \leq \alpha + 2\beta - 3$, we can arrive some conclusions as follows.

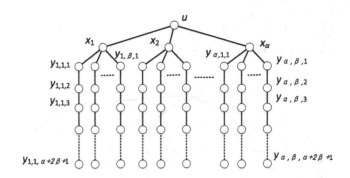

Fig. 1. $T_0(u; X; \alpha, \beta)$

Theorem 2. *If there is an index i in A, then x_i is fault-free. Moreover, $y_{i,j,1}$ is fault-free if $\sigma_{y_{i,j,1}}(x_i, y_{i,j,2}) = 0$ and $\sigma_{y_{i,j,k}}(y_{i,j,k-1}, y_{i,j,k+1}) = 0$ for each $k \in \langle \alpha + 2\beta \rangle - \{1\}$.*

Proof. Suppose that $y_{i,j,1}$ is faulty. By Fact 2, there are at least $\alpha + 2\beta$ faulty nodes in the structure. It is contradictory with $|F| \leq \alpha + 2\beta - 3$. That is $y_{i,j,1}$ is fault-free. Since $\sigma_{y_{i,j,1}}(x_i, y_{i,j,2}) = 0$ and $y_{i,j,1}$ is fault-free, we have x_i is fault-free.

Similarly we can arrive Theorem 3.

Theorem 3. *If there is an index i in B, then x_i is faulty.*

Based on Theorems 2 and 3, we know that $A \cap B = \emptyset$.

Theorem 4. *If $|A| = 0$, then $|B| \geq \alpha - 2$.*

Proof. Suppose that $|B| < \alpha - 2$. By Fact 1 and Theorem 3, there are at least $|B| + (\alpha - |B|)\beta$ faulty nodes. Since $|B| < \alpha - 2$, $|B| + (\alpha - |B|)\beta = \alpha\beta - (\beta - 1)|B| > \alpha\beta - (\beta - 1)(\alpha - 2) > \alpha + 2\beta - 2$. It is contradictory with $|F| \leq \alpha + 2\beta - 3$. So $|B| \geq \alpha - 2$.

Theorem 5. *If $|A| = 0$ and $|B| = \alpha - 2$, then u is fault-free.*

Proof. Suppose that u is faulty. By Fact 1, there are at least $|B| + (\alpha - |B|)\beta + 1 = \alpha + 2\beta - 1$ faulty nodes. It is contradictory with $|F| \leq \alpha + 2\beta - 3$. So u is fault-free.

Then we give the structure of a remain (α, β, γ)-tree, $T_\gamma(u; X; \alpha, \beta)$, rooted at u with neighbor set X, $X = \{x_1, x_2, \ldots, x_\alpha\}$, $\gamma \in \langle \alpha \rangle$. A remain (α, β, γ)-tree rooted at u with neighbor set X, $T_\gamma(u; X; \alpha, \beta)$, is a tree with

- $V(T_\gamma(u; X; \alpha, \beta)) = \{u\} \cup X \cup \{p_{\gamma,i} \mid i \in \langle \beta \rangle\} \cup \{q_{\gamma,i,j,k} \mid i \in \langle \beta \rangle, j \in \langle \beta \rangle, k \in \langle \beta \rangle + 2\}$, and
- $E(T_\gamma(u; X; \alpha, \beta)) = E_0 \cup E_1 \cup E_2 \cup E_3$, where
  - $E_0 = \{ux_i \mid i \in \langle \alpha \rangle\}$
  - $E_1 = \{x_\gamma p_{\gamma,i} \mid i \in \langle \beta \rangle\}$
  - $E_2 = \bigcup_{i \in \langle \beta \rangle} \{p_{\gamma,i} q_{\gamma,i,j,1} \mid i,j \in \langle \beta \rangle\}$
  - $E_3 = \bigcup_{i \in \langle \beta \rangle, j \in \langle \beta \rangle} \{q_{\gamma,i,j,k} q_{\gamma,i,j,k+1} \mid k \in \langle \beta + 2 \rangle\}$

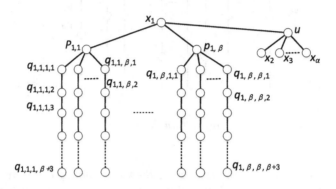

Fig. 2. $T_1(u; X; \alpha, \beta)$

A remain $(\alpha, \beta, 1)$-tree $T_1(u; X; \alpha, \beta)$ is shown in Fig. 2. For the structure $T_\gamma(u; X; \alpha, \beta)$, we first give two definitions.

- Give an integer i, $i \in \langle \beta \rangle$, for an index j, $j \in \langle \beta \rangle$, if $\sigma_{\gamma,i,j,1}(p_{\gamma,i}, q_{\gamma,i,j,2}) = 0$ and $\sigma_{\gamma,i,j,k}(q_{\gamma,i,j,k-1}, q_{\gamma,i,j,k+1}) = 0$ for each $k \in \langle \beta + 2 \rangle - \{1\}$, we call that j satisfies $PathD_\gamma(i; 00)$.
- Give an integer i, $i \in \langle \beta \rangle$, for an index j, $j \in \langle \beta \rangle$, if $\sigma_{\gamma,i,j,1}(p_{\gamma,i}, q_{\gamma,i,j,2}) = 1$ and $\sigma_{\gamma,i,j,k}(q_{\gamma,i,j,k-1}, q_{\gamma,i,j,k+1}) = 0$ for each $k \in \langle \beta + 2 \rangle - \{1\}$, we call that j satisfies $PathD_\gamma(i; 10)$.

For each i in $\langle \beta \rangle$, we set $A_{\gamma,i} = \{j \mid j \in \langle \beta \rangle$ and j satisfies $PathD_\gamma(i; 00)\}$, and let $B_{\gamma,i} = \{j \mid j \in \langle \beta \rangle$ and j satisfies $PathD_\gamma(i; 10)\}$. In the structure $T_\gamma(u; X; \alpha, \beta)$, if $|F| \leq \alpha + 2\beta - 3$ and x_γ is fault-free, x_m is faulty for each $m \in \langle \alpha \rangle - \{r\}$, we can arrive some theorems as follows.

Theorem 6. *If there is an integer i in $\langle \beta \rangle$ such that $|A_{\gamma,i}| \geq \max\{|B_{\gamma,i}|, 1\}$, then $p_{\gamma,i}$ is fault-free.*

Proof. Suppose that $p_{\gamma,i}$ is faulty. By Fact 1 and Fact 2, there are at least $(\alpha - 1) + |A_i| \times (\beta + 2) + 1 + (\beta - |A_i| - |B_i|)$ faulty nodes. Since $(\alpha - 1) + |A_i| \times (\beta + 2) + 1 + (\beta - |A_i| - |B_i|) \geq \alpha + 2\beta - 1 > \alpha + 2\beta - 3$, It is contradictory with $|F| \leq \alpha + 2\beta - 3$. So $p_{\gamma,i}$ is fault-free.

Similarly we can proof Theorem 7 and Theorem 8.

Theorem 7. *If there is an integer i in $\langle \beta \rangle$ such that $|B_{\gamma,i}| > |A_{\gamma,i}|$, then $p_{\gamma,i}$ is faulty.*

Theorem 8. *If there is an integer i in $\langle \beta \rangle$ such that $|A_{\gamma,i}| = |B_{\gamma,i}|$ and $|B_{\gamma,m}| > |A_{\gamma,m}|$ for each $m \in \langle \beta \rangle - \{i\}$, then $p_{\gamma,i}$ is fault-free.*

4   A Conditional Fault Local Diagnosis Algorithm

Let $S(u, X, \alpha, \beta)$ be a graph of the (α, β)-trees combination if

1. there is a balanced (α, β)-tree rooted at u with neighbor set X, $T_0(u; X; \alpha, \beta)$, and
2. there is a remain (α, β, γ)-tree rooted at u with neighbor set X, $T_\gamma(u; X; \alpha, \beta)$ for each $\gamma \in \{1, 2, \ldots, \alpha\}$.

In this section, we propose an effective conditional fault local diagnosis algorithm (**CFLDA**) which can identify the status of u in the graph $S(u, X, \alpha, \beta)$ when the number of faulty nodes presented does not exceed $\alpha + 2\beta - 3$ and every node has at least one healthy neighboring node.

Based on Theorem 2, if we can be sure that x_i and $y_{i,j,1}$ are fault-free, then the status of u can be determined by the value of $\sigma_{x_i}(u, y_{i,j,1})$ (See line 4 to line 11 of Algorithm 1). Suppose that we can not ensure x_i and $y_{i,j,1}$ are fault-free in the line 11 of Algorithm 1. Based on Theorems 3 and 4, we can arrive that $|S| = 2$ or $|S| = 1$ through line 14 of Algorithm 1. If $|S| = 2$, based on Fact 1 there are at least $(\alpha - 2) + \beta + \beta = \alpha + 2\beta - 2$ faulty nodes in $V(T_0(u; X; \alpha, \beta)) - \{u\}$, so u is fault-free (See line 15 of Algorithm 1). From line 16 to line 35, we discuss the case $|S| = 1$. That means there is only one fault-free node x_s among the neighbors of u. From line 17 to line 30, we collect A_i and B_i for each $i \in \langle \beta \rangle$. Based on Theorem 6, the status of u can be determined by the value of $\sigma_{x_s}(u, p_{s,i})$ when $p_{s,i}$ is fault-free (See line 29 of Algorithm 1). Suppose that we can not ensure $p_{s,i}$ is fault-free in the line 31. Then we consider that $|R| = 0$ or $|R| = 1$ from line 32 to line 35. Note if $|R| \geq 2$, then there are at least $2\beta + (\alpha - 1)$ faulty nodes. It is contradictory with $|F| \leq \alpha + 2\beta - 3$. If $|R| = 0$ for each $i \in \langle \beta \rangle$, $p_{s,i}$ is faulty, then u is fault-free since every node has at least one healthy neighboring node (See line 32). If $|R| = 1$, based on Theorem 8, $p_{s,m}$ is fault-free. We set $r \in R$. And the status of u can be determined by the value of $\sigma_{x_s}(u, p_{s,r})$ (See line 34). So the algorithm can identify the status of u correctly. Moreover, the time complexity of the algorithm is $O(\alpha^2 \beta + \alpha \beta^2)$.

Theorem 9. *Let G be a graph, a subgraph $S(u, X, \alpha, \beta)$ of G is a (α, β)-trees combination. Let $|F| \leq \alpha + 2\beta - 3$ and F be a conditional fault set in the subgraph. Then the algorithm 1 can identify the status of u correctly.*

Algorithm 1: Conditional fault local diagnosis algorithm (**CFLDA**)

Input: Node u, integers α and β, a balanced (α, β)-tree $\mathtt{T}(u; \mathtt{X}; \alpha; \beta)$, and remain (α, β, γ)-trees $T_r(u; X; \alpha; \beta)$, $\gamma \in \langle \alpha \rangle$.

Output: The value is 0 or 1 if u is fault-free or faulty, respectively.

```
 1 begin
 2     S ← {1, 2, ..., α};
 3     R ← {1, 2, ..., β};
 4     for i = 1 to α do
 5         for j = 1 to β do
 6             temp ← 0;
 7             for k = 2 to α + 2β do
 8                 if σ_{y_{i,j,k}}(y_{i,j,k-1}, y_{i,j,k+1}) = 1 then temp ← 1
 9             end
10             if temp = 0 then
11                 if σ_{y_{i,j,1}}(x_i, y_{i,j,2}) = 0 then return σ_{x_i}(u, y_{i,j,1}) else
                      S ← S - {j}
12             end
13         end
14     end
15     if |S| = 2 then return 0 else
16         choose an element s from S;
17         for i = 1 to β do
18             A_i ← ∅;
19             B_i ← ∅;
20             temp ← 0;
21             for j = 1 to β do
22                 for k = 2 to α + 2β do
23                     if σ_{y_{i,j,k}}(y_{i,j,k-1}, y_{i,j,k+1}) = 1 then temp ← 1
24                 end
25                 if temp = 0 then
26                     if σ_{q_{s,i,j,1}}(p_{s,i}, q_{s,i,j,2}) = 0 then A_i ← A_i ∪ {j} else
                          B_i ← B_i ∪ {j}
27                 end
28             end
29             if |A_i| ≥ max{|B_i|, 1} then return σ_{x_s}(u, p_{s,i}) if |B_i| > |A_i| then
                  R = R - {i}
30         end
31     end
32     if |R| = 0 then return 0 else
33         choose an element r from R;
34         return σ_{x_s}(u, p_{s,r});
35     end
36 end
```

5   Conditional Fault Local Diagnosis of Star Graph

The n-dimensional star graph S_n is an undirected graph [4,5,23]. The nodes of S_n are in a one-to-one correspondence with the permutations $[p_1, p_2, \ldots, p_n]$ of the set $\langle n \rangle$. Two nodes of S_n are connected by an edge if and only if the permutation of one node can be obtained from the other by interchanging the first symbol p_1 with the ith symbol p_i, $2 \leq i \leq n$. For a node $u = [p_1, p_2, \ldots, p_n]$, let u_i denote the figure p_i, and let $(u)^i$ denote the node $u' = [p_i, p_2, \ldots, p_{i-1}, p_1, p_{i+1}, \ldots, p_n]$, obtained by transposition i on u. Let $S_n^{i,j}(u)$ is subgraph of S_n, with $V(S_n^{i,j}(u)) = \{v | v \in V(S_n),\ v_i = u_1,\ v_1 = u_j,\ v_j = u_i$ and $j \neq i\}$, $E(S_n^{i,j}(u)) = \{wv | w, v \in V(S_n^{i,j}(u))$ and $wv \in E(S_n)\}$. Note that $S_n^{i,j}(u)$ is isomorphic with S_{n-2}. So in the subgraph $S_n^{i,j}(u)$, there is a hamiltonian cycle as $< ((u)^i)^j, v_1, v_2, \ldots, v_{(n-2)!-1}, ((u)^i)^j >$. Then the path $< ((u)^i)^j, v_1, v_2, \ldots, v_{3n-5} >$, denoted by $PT(((u)^i)^j)$, can be a path of length $3n - 4$ beginning with the node $((u)^i)^j$.

For each node u in S_n, we can construct $T_0(u; X; n - 1, n - 2)$ in star graph S_n as follows (see Fig. 3).

- $V(T_0(u; X; n - 1, n - 2)) = V_1 \cup V_2 \cup V_3$
  - $V_1 = \{u\}$
  - $V_2 = \{(u)^i \mid i \in \langle n \rangle - \{1\}\}$
  - $V_3 = \{v \mid v \in V(PT(((u)^i)^j)), i, j \in \langle n \rangle - \{1\}$ and $j \neq i\}$
- $E(T_0(u; X; n - 1, n - 2)) = E_1 \cup E_2 \cup E_3$
  - $E_1 = \{u(u)^i \mid i \in \langle n \rangle - \{1\}\}$
  - $E_2 = \{(u)^i((u)^i)^j \mid i \in \langle n \rangle - \{1\}, j \in \langle n \rangle - \{1\}$ and $j \neq i\}$
  - $E_3 = \{e \mid e \in E(PT(((u)^i)^j)), i, j \in \langle n \rangle - \{1\}$ and $j \neq i\}$

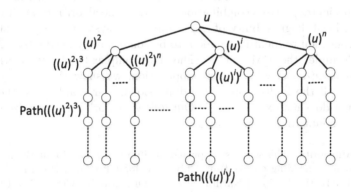

Fig. 3. $T_0(u; X; n - 1, n - 2)$ in S_n

Note that there is no same node in the tree $T_0(u; X; n - 1, n - 2)$.

Similarly we can construct the remain $T_\gamma(u; X; n - 1, n - 2)$-trees for $\gamma \in \langle n \rangle - \{1\}$.

Let $S_n^{\gamma,j,k}(u)$ be a subgraph of S_n, with $V(S_n^{\gamma,j,k}(u)) = \{z \mid z \in V(S_n), z_j = u_\gamma, z_k = u_j$ and $j \neq \gamma$ and $k \neq j\}$, $E(S_n^{\gamma,j,k}(u)) = \{wv \mid w,v \in V(S_n^{\gamma,j,k}(u))$ and $wv \in E(S_n)\}$. Note that $S_n^{\gamma,j,k}(u)$ is isomorphic with S_{n-2}. So in the subgraph $S_n^{\gamma,j,k}(u)$, there is a hamiltonian cycle as $\langle(((u)^\gamma)^j)^k, v_1, v_2, \ldots, v_{(n-2)!-1}, (((u)^\gamma)^j)^k\rangle$. Then the path $\langle(((u)^\gamma)^j)^k, v_1, v_2, \ldots, v_n\rangle$, denoted by $PT((((u)^\gamma)^j)^k)$, can be a path of length $n+1$ beginning with the node $(((u)^\gamma)^j)^k$.

For each node u in S_n, we can construct $T_\gamma(u; X; n-1, n-2)$ for $\gamma \in \langle n\rangle - \{1\}$ in a star graph S_n as follows.

- $V(T_0(u; X; n-1, n-2)) = V_1 \cup V_2 \cup V_3 \cup V_4$
  - $V_1 = \{u\}$
  - $V_2 = \{(u)^i \mid i \in \langle n\rangle - \{1\}\}$
  - $V_3 = \{((u)^\gamma)^j \mid j \in \langle n\rangle - \{1\}$ and $j \neq \gamma\}$
  - $V_4 = \{v \mid v \in V(PT((((u)^\gamma)^j)^k)), j, k \in \langle n\rangle - \{1\}, j \neq \gamma$ and $k \neq j\}$
- $E(T_0(u; X; n-1, n-2)) = E_1 \cup E_2 \cup E_3 \cup E_4$
  - $E_1 = \{u(u)^i \mid i \in \langle n\rangle - \{1\}\}$
  - $E_2 = \{(u)^\gamma((u)^\gamma)^j \mid j \in \langle n\rangle - \{1\}$ and $j \neq \gamma\}$
  - $E_3 = \{((u)^\gamma)^j(((u)^\gamma)^j)^k \mid j, k \in \langle n\rangle - \{1\}$ and $j \neq \gamma, k \neq j\}$
  - $E_4 = \{e \mid e \in E(PT((((u)^\gamma)^j)^k)), j, k \in \langle n\rangle - \{1\}$ and $j \neq \gamma, k \neq j\}$

By Theorem 9, for a star graph S_n and a node u in S_n, the algorithm 1 can identify the status of u correctly if $|F| \leq 3n - 8$ and F is a conditional fault set.

6   Conclusion

In this paper, we construct a conditional fault local diagnosis algorithm with the help of a special (α, β)-trees combination. Based on the algorithm, we discuss the conditional local diagnosability of a multiprocessor system, and present a new sufficient condition to identify a node u to be conditionally locally $(\alpha + 2\beta - 3)$-diagnosable under the MM* model. The time complexity of our algorithm to diagnose u is $O(\alpha^2\beta + \alpha\beta^2)$. As an application, we show that our algorithm can identify all the faulty nodes of n-dimensional star graph S_n if the faulty node number does not exceed $3n - 8$. Our following work is to optimize the tree structure to adapt to more networks.

Acknowledgments. This work is supported by Shin Kong Wu Ho Su Memorial Hospital National Yang Ming Chiao Tung University Joint Research Program (No. 111-SKH-NYCU-03), the National Natural Science Foundation of China (No. 61902113, 62172291) and the Doctoral Research Foundation of Henan University of Chinese Medicine (No. BSJJ2022-14).

References

1. Barsi, F., Grandoni, F., Maestrini, P.: A theory of diagnosability of digital systems. IEEE Trans. Comput. **25**(6), 585–593 (1976)
2. Chang, N.W., Hsieh, S.Y.: Conditional diagnosability of augmented cubes under the PMC model. IEEE Trans. Dependable Secure Comput. **9**(1), 46–60 (2010)
3. Friedman, A.D., Simoncini, L.: System-level fault diagnosis. Comput. J. **13**(3), 47–53 (1980)
4. Gu, Q.P., Peng, S.: Node-to-set disjoint paths problem in star graphs. Inf. Process. Lett. **62**, 201–207 (1997)
5. Gu, Q.P., Peng, S.: Cluster fault-tolerant routing in star graphs. Inf. Process. Lett. **35**, 83–90 (2000)
6. Hsieh, S.Y., Kao, C.Y.: The conditional diagnosability of k-ary n-cubes under the comparison diagnosis model. IEEE Trans. Comput. **62**(4), 839–843 (2013)
7. Hsu, G.H., Tan, J.J.: A local diagnosiability measure for multiprocessor systems. IEEE Trans. Parallel Distrib. Syst. **18**(5), 598–607 (2007)
8. Hsu, L.H., Lin, C.K.: Graph Theory and Interconnection Networks. CRC Press, Boca Raton (2008)
9. Kung, T.L., Teng, Y.H., Lin, C.K., Chen, H.C.: A localized fault detection algorithm for mobility management in the strongly t-diagnosable wireless ad hoc network under the comparison model. EURASIP J. Wirel. Commun. Netw. **2016**, 218–228 (2016)
10. Lai, P.L., Tan, J.J.M., Tsai, C.H., Hsu, L.H.: The diagnosability of the matching composition network under the comparison diagnosis model. IEEE Trans. Comput. **53**, 1064–1069 (2004)
11. Li, D., Lu, M.: The g-good-neighbor conditional diagnosability of star graphs under the PMC and mm* model. Theoret. Comput. Sci. **674**, 53–59 (2017)
12. Li, X., Fan, J., Lin, C.K., Jia, X.: Diagnosability evaluation of the data center network DCell. Comput. J. **60**, 129–143 (2018)
13. Lin, C.K., Kung, T.L., Tan, J.J.: Conditional-fault diagnosability of multiprocessor systems with an efficient local diagnosis algorithm under the PMC model. IEEE Trans. Parallel Distrib. Syst. **22**(10), 1669–1680 (2011)
14. Lin, C.K., Kung, T.L., Tan, J.J.: An algorithmic approach to conditional-fault local diagnosis of regular multiprocessor interconnected systems under the pmc model. IEEE Trans. Comput. **62**(3), 439–451 (2013)
15. Lin, C.K., Tan, J.J.M., Hsu, L.H., Cheng, E., Lipták, L.: Conditional diagnosability of Cayley graphs generated by transposition trees under the comparison diagnosis model. J. Interconnect. Netw **9**, 83–97 (2008)
16. Lin, C.K., Teng, Y.H., Tan, J.J., Hsu, L.H.: Local diagnosis algorithms for multiprocessor systems under the comparison diagnosis model. IEEE Trans. Reliab. **62**(4), 800–810 (2013)
17. Lv, Y., Fan, J., Hsu, D.F., Lin, C.K.: Structure connectivity and substructure connectivity of k-ary n-cube networks. Inf. Sci. **433**(10), 115–124 (2018)
18. Lv, Y., Lin, C.K., Fan, J., Jia, X.: Hamiltonian cycle and path embeddings in 3-ary n-cubes based on $k_{1,3}$-structure faults. J. Parallel Distrib. Comput. **120**, 148–158 (2018)
19. Lv, Y., Lin, C.K., Wang, G.: An exchanged 3-ary n-cube interconnection network for oarallel computation. Int. J. Found. Comput. Sci. **32**, 235–252 (2021)
20. Maeng, J., Malek, M.: A comparison connection assignment for self-diagnosis of multiprocessor systems. In: Proceedings of 11th International Symposium on Fault-Tolerant Computing, pp. 173–175 (1981)

21. Mallela, S., Masson, G.M.: Diagnosable system for intermittent faults. IEEE Trans. Comput. **27**(6), 461–470 (1978)
22. Preparata, F., Metze, G., Chien, R.: On the connection assignment problem of diagosis systems. IEEE Trans. Electr. Comput. **16**(6), 848–854 (1967)
23. Rouskov, Y., Latifi, S., Srimani, P.K.: Conditional fault diameter of star graph networks. J. Parallel Distrib. Comput. **33**, 91–97 (1996)
24. Sengupta, A., Dahbura, A.: On self-diagnosable multiprocessor system diagnosis by the comparison approach. IEEE Trans. Comput. **41**(11), 1386–1396 (1992)
25. Wang, G., Lin, C.K., Fan, J., Cheng, B., Jia, X.: A novel low cost interconnection architecture based on the generalized hypercube. IEEE Trans. Parallel Distrib. Syst. **31**, 647–662 (2020)
26. Wang, S., Wang, Z., Wang, M., Han, W.: g-good-neighbor conditional diagnosability of star graph networks under PMC model and mm* model. Front. Math. China **12**, 1221–1234 (2017)
27. Yuan, J., Liu, A., Ma, X., Liu, X., Qin, X., Zhang, J.: The g-good-neighbor conditional diagnosability of k-ary n-cubes under the PMC model and mm model. IEEE Trans. Parallel Distrib. Syst. **26**(4), 1165–1177 (2015)
28. Yuan, J., Liu, A., Qin, X., Zhang, J., Li, J.: g-good-neighbor conditional diagnosability measures for 3-ary n-cube networks. Theoret. Comput. Sci. **626**, 144–162 (2016)
29. Yuan, J., Qiao, H., Liu, A., Wang, X.: Measurement and algorithm for conditional local diagnosis of regular networks under the mm* model. Discret. Appl. Math. **309**, 46–67 (2022)
30. Zhou, S.: The conditional fault diagnosability of (n, k)-star graphs. Appl. Math. Comput. **218**(19), 9742–9749 (2012)
31. Zhou, S., Lin, L., Xu, L.: The t/k-diagnosability of star graph networks. IEEE Trans. Comput. **64**(2), 547–555 (2015)

Novel Ways of Enumerating Restrained Dominating Sets of Cycles

Sushmita Paul[1]([⊠]), Ratanjeet Pratap Chauhan[2], and Srinibas Swain[2][ID]

[1] National Institute of Technology Meghalaya, Shillong, India
sushmita.nitm@gmail.com
[2] Indian Institute of Information Technology Guwahati, Guwahati, India
{ratanjeet.chauhan,srinibas}@iiitg.ac.in

Abstract. Let $G = (V, E)$ be a graph. A set $S \subseteq V$ is a restrained dominating set (RDS) if every vertex not in S is adjacent to a vertex in S and to a vertex in $V - S$. The restrained domination number of G, denoted by $\gamma_r(G)$, is the smallest cardinality of a restrained dominating set of G. Finding the restrained domination number is NP-hard for bipartite and chordal graphs. Let G_n^i be the family of restrained dominating sets of a graph G of order n with cardinality i, and let $d_r(G_n, i) = |G_n^i|$. The restrained domination polynomial (RDP) of G_n, $D_r(G_n, x)$ is defined as $D_r(G_n, x) = \sum_{i=\gamma_r(G_n)}^{n} d_r(G_n, i)x^i$. In this paper, we focus on the RDP of cycles and have, thus, introduced several novel ways to compute $d_r(C_n, i)$, where C_n is a cycle of order n. In the first approach, we use a recursive formula for $d_r(C_n, i)$; while in the other approach, we construct a generating function to compute $d_r(C_n, i)$.

Keywords: Domination number · Generating function · Restrained domination · Restrained domination polynomial

1 Introduction

Restrained domination was introduced by Telle et al. [5]. Finding the restrained domination number problem was initially viewed as a vertex partitioning problem. This problem is NP-hard for chordal graphs and bipartite graphs [3], however one of the uses of restrained domination problem is to solve the prisoner and guard problem [3]. Restrained domination problem is well studied and the details of this problem can be seen in [2]. Kayathri et al. [4] gave a recursive method to find the RDP of cycle of order n with the help of RDPs of paths of order $n - 2$ and of order n, which is $D_r(C_n, x) = D_r(P_n, x) + 3D_r(P_{n-2}, x)$, where P_n is a path of order n. The RDP of P_n, in terms of two variables P_n and x, is given by $D_r(P_n, x) = x^2[D_r(P_{n-2}, x) + 2D_r(P_{n-4}, x) + D_r(P_{n-6}, x)]$ for $n \geq 6$. However, they did not provide any bounds on $d_r(C_n, k)$. Moreover, in order to compute RDP of C_n, their approach forces computation of RDP of several paths of order $\leq n$.

The main contribution of this paper is a generating function to compute the total number of RDSs of cycle C_n with cardinality k, where $\gamma_r(C_n) \leq k \leq n$.

S.-Y. Hsieh et al. (Eds.): ICS 2022, CCIS 1723, pp. 135–144, 2022.
https://doi.org/10.1007/978-981-19-9582-8_12

We have also introduced a recursive method to compute the total number of restrained dominating sets of C_n, with cardinality i, using the number of restrained dominating sets of C_{n-1} and C_{n-3}, each with cardinality $i - 1$. We also report a few relations between the coefficients of restrained domination polynomial of cycles in Sect. 3 and conclude by providing some future directions in Sect. 4. Some of the results presented in this paper are immediate extensions of the results in [1], although the problems addressed are different. The results reported in this paper are plain sailing, but some of the proofs used are combinatorially interesting. Note that we assume $V(C_n) = \{1, 2, \cdots, n\}$.

2   Restrained Dominating Sets of Cycles

In this section, we discuss a few structural properties of the restrained dominating sets of cycles. We first list some existing facts on RDS of cycles. The restrained domination number of cycle counted by Domke et al. is given in Fact 1.

Fact 1. *[3]* $\gamma_r(C_n) = n - 2\lfloor \frac{n}{3} \rfloor$.

Corollary 1. *(i) For every odd $n \in \mathbb{N}$, $\gamma_r(C_n)$ is an odd number.*
(ii) For every even $n \in \mathbb{N}$, $\gamma_r(C_n)$ is an even number.

Proof. (i) We know $\gamma_r(C_n) = n - 2\lfloor \frac{n}{3} \rfloor$ by Fact 1, and n is an odd number, therefore, $\gamma_r(C_n)$ is an odd number.
(ii) Can be proved same as (i). ∎

Kayathri et al. characterized the cardinality of restrained dominating set given in Fact 2.

Fact 2. *[4] Let S be a restrained dominating set of C_n. Then $|S| \equiv n \pmod 2$.*

Let C_n^i be the set of restrained dominating sets of C_n with cardinality i.

Observation 1. $C_j^i = \phi$, *if and only if $i > j$ or $i < j - 2\lfloor \frac{j}{3} \rfloor$ or $(j - i)\%2 == 1$.*

We use Observation 1 to obtain a characterisation on the sets of restrained dominating sets of cycles.

Proposition 1. *For all $i \leq n$, the following properties holds*

(i) If $C_n^i \neq \phi$, then $C_n^{i-1} = C_n^{i+1} = C_{n-1}^i = C_{n+1}^i = \phi$.
(ii) If $C_{n-1}^{i-1} = C_{n-2}^{i-2} = \phi$, then $C_{n-3}^{i-3} = \phi$.
(iii) If $C_n^i = \phi$ and $C_{n+2}^{i-2} = \phi$, then $C_{n+1}^{i-1} = \phi$.
(iv) If $C_n^i \neq \phi$ and $C_{n-2}^i \neq \phi$, then $C_{n-1}^i = \phi$.

Proof. (i) Since $C_n^i \neq \phi$, by Observation 1, $(n - i)\%2 = 0$, therefore $(n - 1 - i)\%2 \neq 0 \Rightarrow C_{n-1}^i = \phi$ and $C_n^{i+1} = \phi$; also $(n + 1 - i)\%2 \neq 0 \Rightarrow C_{n+1}^i \neq \phi$ and $C_n^{i-1} \neq \phi$.

Similarly (ii), (iii) and (iv) can be proved. ∎

Lemma 1. *If $C_n^i \neq \phi$, then*

(i) $C_{n-1}^{i-1} = C_{n-2}^{i-1} = \phi$ and $C_{n-3}^{i-1} \neq \phi$ if and only if $n = 3k$ and $i = k$, for some $k \in \mathbb{N}$.

(ii) $C_{n-2}^{i-1} = C_{n-3}^{i-1} = \phi$ and $C_{n-1}^{i-1} \neq \phi$ if and only if $i = n$.

(iii) $C_{n-1}^{i-1} \neq \phi$, $C_{n-3}^{i-1} \neq \phi$ and $C_{n-2}^{i-2} = \phi$ if and only if $n = 3k+1$ and $i = k+1$.

(iv) $C_{n-1}^{i-1} \neq \phi$, $C_{n-3}^{i-1} \neq \phi$ and $C_{n-5}^{i-1} = \phi$ if and only if $i = n-2$.

(v) $C_{n-1}^{i-1} \neq \phi$ and $C_{n-3}^{i-1} \neq \phi$ if and only if $n - 2\lfloor \frac{n-1}{3} \rfloor \leq i \leq n-2$.

Proof. (i) $(\Rightarrow)$ Since $C_{n-1}^{i-1} = C_{n-2}^{i-1} = \phi$, by Observation 1, we have, $i-1 > n-1$ or, $i-1 < n-2 - 2\lfloor \frac{n-2}{3} \rfloor$ or, $n-1-i+1$ and $n-2-i+1$ are odd. However, the third case is not possible because two consecutive numbers cannot be odd. If $i-1 > n-1$, then $i > n$, then by Observation 1, $C_n^i = \phi$, a contradiction. So we have $i-1 < n-2 - 2\lfloor \frac{n-2}{3} \rfloor$, and $C_n^i \neq \phi$, which is $n - 2\lfloor \frac{n}{3} \rfloor \leq i < n-1 - 2\lfloor \frac{n-2}{3} \rfloor$ together, resulting in $n = 3k$ and $i = k$, for some $k \in \mathbb{N}$.

$(\Leftarrow)$ If $n = 3k$ and $i = k$ for some $k \in \mathbb{N}$, then by Observation 1, we have $C_{n-1}^{i-1} = C_{n-2}^{i-1} = \phi$ and $C_{n-3}^{i-1} \neq \phi$.

$(ii), (iii), (iv)$ and (v) can be proved in a similar way as of the proof of (i).

By using Observation 1, Proposition 1 and Lemma 1, we characterize the set of restrained dominating sets of C_n.

Theorem 1. *For every $n \geq 4$ and $i \geq n - 2\lfloor \frac{n}{3} \rfloor$,*

(i) If $C_{n-1}^{i-1} = C_{n-2}^{i-1} = \phi$ and $C_{n-3}^{i-1} \neq \phi$, then $C_n^i = C_n^{\frac{n}{3}} = \{\{1, 4, \ldots, n-2\}, \{2, 5, \ldots, n-1\}, \{3, 6, \ldots, n\}\}$.

(ii) If $C_{n-2}^{i-1} = C_{n-3}^{i-1} = \phi$ and $C_{n-1}^{i-1} \neq \phi$, then $C_n^i = C_n^n = \{\{1, 2, \ldots, n\}\}$.

(iii) If $C_{n-1}^{i-1} \neq \phi$, $C_{n-3}^{i-1} \neq \phi$ and $C_{n-5}^{i-1} = \phi$, then $C_n^i = C_n^{n-2} = \{\{1, 2, \ldots, n\} - \{x, y\}, \forall (x, y) \in E(C_n)\}$.

(iv) If $C_{n-1}^{i-1} \neq \phi$ and $C_{n-3}^{i-1} \neq \phi$, then for $X_1 \in C_{n-3}^{i-1}$ and $X_2 \in C_{n-1}^{i-1}$

$$C_n^i = \left\{ X_1 \cup \begin{cases} \{n-2\}, & \text{if } 1 \in X_1 \\ \{n\}, & \text{if } 1 \text{ and } 2 \notin X_1 \\ \{n-1\}, & \text{if } 1 \text{ and } n\text{-}3 \notin X_1 \end{cases} \right\} \cup$$

$$\left\{ X_2 \cup \begin{cases} \{n\}, & \text{if } 1 \in X_2 \text{ or } 1 \text{ and } 2 \notin X_2 \\ \{n-1\}, & \text{if } 1 \text{ and } n\text{-}1 \notin X_2, \text{ where } X_2 \end{cases} \right\}.$$

Proof. (i) Since $C_{n-1}^{i-1} = C_{n-2}^{i-1} = \phi$ and $C_{n-3}^{i-1} \neq \phi$, then by Lemma 1 (i), we have $n = 3k$ and $i = k$, for some $k \in \mathbb{N}$. Therefore $C_n^i = C_n^{\frac{n}{3}} = \{\{1, 4, 7, \ldots, n-2\}, \{2, 5, 8, \ldots, n-1\}, \{3, 6, 9, \ldots, n\}\}$.

(ii) Since $C_{n-2}^{i-1} = C_{n-3}^{i-1} = \phi$ and $C_{n-1}^{i-1} \neq \phi$, by Lemma 1(ii), we have $i = n$. Therefore $C_n^i = C_n^n = \{\{1, 2, \ldots, n\}\}$.

(iii) Since $C_{n-1}^{i-1} \neq \phi$, $C_{n-3}^{i-1} \neq \phi$ and $C_{n-5}^{i-1} = \phi$, by Lemma 1(iv), we have $i = n-2$. Therefore $C_n^i = C_n^{n-2} = \{\{1, 2, \ldots, n\} - \{x, y\}, \forall (x, y) \in E(C_n)\}$.

(iv) Since $C_{n-1}^{i-1} \neq \phi$ and $C_{n-3}^{i-1} \neq \phi$. Suppose that $C_{n-3}^{i-1} \neq \phi$, then there exists an RDS, $X_1 \in C_{n-3}^{i-1}$.

$$\text{Let } Y_1 = \left\{ X_1 \cup \begin{cases} \{n-2\}, & \text{if } 1 \in X_1 \\ \{n\}, & \text{if } 1 \text{ and } 2 \notin X_1 \\ \{n-1\}, & \text{if } 1 \text{ and n-3} \notin X_1 \end{cases} \right\}.$$

For vertices $1, 2, n-3$, by Fact 2, we have vertices 2 and $1 \notin X_1$, or vertices 1 and $n-3 \notin X_1$, or vertex $1 \in X_1$. If vertices 2 and $1 \notin X_1$, then $X_1 \cup \{n\} \in C_n^i$. If vertices 1 and $n-3 \notin X_1$, then $X_1 \cup \{n-1\} \in C_n^i$. If vertex $1 \in X_1$ then $X_1 \cup \{n-2\} \in C_n^i$. Thus $Y_1 \subseteq C_n^i$. Now suppose $C_{n-1}^{i-1} \neq \phi$, then there exists an RDS, $X_2 \in C_{n-1}^{i-1}$.

$$\text{Let } Y_2 = \left\{ X_2 \cup \begin{cases} \{n\}, & \text{if } 1 \in X_2 \text{ or } 1 \text{ and } 2 \notin X_2 \\ \{n-1\}, & \text{if } 1 \text{ and n-1} \notin X_2 \end{cases} \right\}.$$

If vertices 2 and $1 \notin X_2$, then $X_2 \cup \{n\} \in C_n^i$. If vertices 1 and $n-1 \notin X_2$, then $X_2 \cup \{1\} \in C_n^i$ but this case is covered when vertex $1 \in X_1$, for $X_1 \in C_{n-3}^{i-1}$, thus, $X_2 \cup \{n-1\} \in C_n^i$. If $1 \in X_2$ then $X_2 \cup \{n\} \in C_n^i$. Therefore we have proved that $Y_1 \cup Y_2 \subseteq C_n^i$.

Now let $Y \in C_n^i$. By Fact 2, among the vertices $n, n-1$, and $n-2$, either vertices n and $n-1 \notin Y$, or vertices $n-1$ and $n-2 \notin Y$, or the vertex $n-1 \in Y$. If the vertices n and $n-1 \notin Y$, then $Y = X \cup \{n-2\}$ for some $X \in C_{n-3}^{i-1}$, when vertex $1 \in X$, then $Y \in Y_1$, and for some $X \in C_{n-1}^{i-1}$ when vertices $n-1$ and $n-2 \notin X$, then $Y \in Y_2$. If vertices $n-1$ and $n-2 \notin Y$, then $Y = X \cup \{n\}$ for some $X \in C_{n-1}^{i-1}$ when vertex $1 \in X$, then $Y \in Y_2$, and for some $X \in C_{n-3}^{i-1}$ when vertex $n-3 \in X$, then $Y \in Y_1$. If vertex $n-1 \in Y$, then $Y = X \cup \{n-1\}$ for some $X \in C_{n-1}^{i-1}$ when vertices 1 and $n-1 \notin X$, then $Y \in Y_2$, and for some $X \in C_{n-3}^{i-1}$ when vertices 1 and $n-3 \notin X$, then $Y \in Y_1$. Now we have proved that $C_n^i \subseteq Y_1 \cup Y_2$. So $C_n^i = Y_1 \cup Y_2$.

Theorem 1 provides a characterization on the size of restrained dominating sets of cycles. We use Theorem 1 to obtain a recursion to compute restrained dominating sets of cycles.

Theorem 2. *For any cycle* C_n, $|C_n^i| = |C_{n-3}^{i-1}| + |C_{n-1}^{i-1}|$.

Proof. In order to prove this theorem, we consider the following cases:

(i) From Theorem 1(i), if $C_{n-1}^{i-1} = C_{n-2}^{i-1} = \phi$ and $C_{n-3}^{i-1} \neq \phi$, then $C_n^i = \{\{n\} \cup S_1, \{n-1\} \cup S_2, \{n-2\} \cup S_3 \mid$ vertices 1 and $2 \notin S_1$, vertices 1 and n-3 $\notin S_2, 1 \in S_3, S_1, S_2, S_3 \in C_{n-3}^{i-1}\}$.

(ii) From Theorem 1(ii), if $C_{n-2}^{i-1} = C_{n-3}^{i-1} = \phi$ and $C_{n-1}^{i-1} \neq \phi$, then $C_n^i = C_n^n = \{X \cup \{n\} \mid X \in C_{n-1}^{i-1}\}$.

(iii) From Theorem 1(iii), if $C_{n-1}^{i-1} \neq \phi$, $C_{n-3}^{i-1} \neq \phi$ and $C_{n-5}^{n-1} = \phi$, then

$$C_n^i = \left\{ X_1 \cup \left\{ \{n-2\}, \quad \text{where } X_1 \in C_{n-3}^{i-1} \right\} \cup \right.$$

$$\left. \left\{ X_2 \cup \begin{cases} \{n\}, & \text{if } 1 \in X_2 \text{ or } 1 \text{ and } 2 \notin X_2, \text{ where } X_2 \in C_{n-1}^{i-1} \\ \{n-1\}, & \text{if } 1 \text{ and n-1} \notin X_2, \text{ where } X_2 \in C_{n-1}^{i-1} \end{cases} \right\}.$$

(iv) From Theorem $1(iv)$, if $C_{n-1}^{i-1} \neq \phi$ and $C_{n-3}^{i-1} \neq \phi$ then

$$C_n^i = \left\{ X_1 \cup \begin{cases} \{n-2\}, & \text{if } 1 \in X_1, \text{ where } X_1 \in C_{n-3}^{i-1} \\ \{n\}, & \text{if } 1 \text{ and } 2 \notin X_1, \text{ where } X_1 \in C_{n-3}^{i-1} \\ \{n-1\}, & \text{if } 1 \text{ and } n\text{-}3 \notin X_1, \text{ where } X_1 in C_{n-3}^{i-1} \end{cases} \right\} \cup$$

$$\left\{ X_2 \cup \begin{cases} \{n\}, & \text{if } 1 \in X_2 \text{ or } 1 \text{ and } 2 \notin X_2, \text{ where } X_2 \in C_{n-1}^{i-1} \\ \{n-1\}, & \text{if } 1 \text{ and } n\text{-}1 \notin X_2, \text{ where } X_2 \in C_{n-1}^{i-1} \end{cases} \right\}. \text{ By}$$

above construction, in every case, we have $|C_n^i| = |C_{n-1}^{i-1}| + |C_{n-3}^{i-1}|$.

Since computing $|C_n^i|$ using recursion (without dynamic programming) is computationally exponential, therefore we developed a technique to find $|C_n^i|$, by constructing a generating function.

Theorem 3. *For every natural number $n \geq 4$, if $n - 2\lfloor \frac{n}{3} \rfloor \leq i \leq n$ then $|C_n^i|$ is coefficient of $x^n y^i$ in the series expansion of the function*

$$f(x, y) = \frac{x^4 y^2 (4 + y^2 + xy + 3x^2 + x^2 y^2)}{1 - xy - x^3 y} \tag{1}$$

The proof of Theorem 3 is straightforward, we leave it for the readers as an exercise.

Lemma 2. *For every $n, k \in \mathbb{N}$ and $k < n$, if $\gamma_r(C_n) < k$ and $(n - k)\%2 = 1$, then $d_r(C_n, k) = 0$.*

Proof. By Corollary 1(i), (ii), we know $i = \gamma_r(C_n)$ is either odd or even, if n is odd or even respectively. By Proposition 1(i), if $\gamma_r(C_n) < k$ and $(n - k)\%2 = 1$, then $d_r(C_n, k) = 0$.

Lemma 3. *Let the vertex set of C_n be V and S be an RDS of size k, then every component of $V - S$ is K_2. Moreover, the number of K_2 components is $\frac{n-k}{2}$.*

Proof. We will prove this by method of contradiction. On the contrary, let S be an RDS and $V - S$ have components that are not K_2. Then the components are of size 1 or greater than 2. In the former case, there are no neighbours in $V - S$, while in the latter case, there exists at least one vertex such that it has no neighbours in S, which are contradictions to the definition of RDS. Since every component of $V - S$ forms a K_2 and $|V - S| = n - k$, therefore, there are exactly $\frac{n-k}{2}$ numbers of K_2 components .

3   Restrained Domination Polynomial of a Cycle

In this section, we show how to compute the restrained domination polynomial of cycles using the recursion of Theorem 2. For completion purpose, we restate the definition of restrained domination polynomial of cycle.

The restrained domination polynomial of cycle C_n, $D_r(C_n, x)$ is defined as

$$D_r(C_n, x) = \sum_{i=n-2\lfloor \frac{n}{3} \rfloor}^{n} d_r(C_n, i)x^i$$

We now show the recursive computation of RDP of a cycle.

Theorem 4. *For every* $n \geq 4$,

$$D_r(C_n, x) = x[D_r(C_{n-3}, x) + D_r(C_{n-1}, x)],$$

with initial values $D_r(C_1, x) = x$, $D_r(C_2, x) = x^2$, $D_r(C_3, x) = 3x + x^3$.

Using Theorem 4, we obtain the coefficients of $D(C_n, x)$ for $1 \leq n \leq 23$ in Table 1 and verify it by Theorem 3. Let $d(C_n, j) = |C_n^j|$. We found a few relationships between the numbers $d(C_n, j)$ and $\gamma_r(C_n) \leq j \leq n$ which is shown in Table 1. The rows in Table 1 represent the orders of cycles and the columns represents the cardinality i of restrained dominating sets. The coefficient of x^i in the RDP of a cycle C_n is the (n, i)-th entry in Table 1.

Table 1. $d_r(C_n, i)$, the number of restrained dominating set of of cycle C_n with cardinality i.

n \ i	1	2	3	4	5	6	7	8	9	10	11	12	13	14	15	16	17	18	19	20	21	22	23
1	1																						
2	0	1																					
3	3	0	1																				
4	0	4	0	1																			
5	0	0	5	0	1																		
6	0	3	0	6	0	1																	
7	0	0	7	0	7	0	1																
8	0	0	0	12	0	8	0	1															
9	0	0	3	0	18	0	9	0	1														
10	0	0	0	10	0	25	0	10	0	1													
11	0	0	0	0	22	0	33	0	11	0	1												
12	0	0	0	3	0	40	0	42	0	12	0	1											
13	0	0	0	0	13	0	65	0	52	0	13	0	1										
14	0	0	0	0	0	35	0	98	0	63	0	14	0	1									
15	0	0	0	0	3	0	75	0	140	0	75	0	15	0	1								
16	0	0	0	0	0	16	0	140	0	192	0	88	0	16	0	1							
17	0	0	0	0	0	0	51	0	238	0	255	0	102	0	17	0	1						
18	0	0	0	0	0	3	0	126	0	378	0	330	0	117	0	18	0	1					
19	0	0	0	0	0	0	19	0	266	0	570	0	418	0	133	0	19	0	1				
20	0	0	0	0	0	0	0	70	0	504	0	825	0	520	0	150	0	20	0	1			
21	0	0	0	0	0	0	0	3	0	196	0	882	0	1155	0	637	0	168	0	21	0	1	
22	0	0	0	0	0	0	0	0	22	0	462	0	1452	0	1573	0	770	0	187	0	22	0	1
23	0	0	0	0	0	0	0	0	0	92	0	966	0	2277	0	2093	0	920	0	207	0	23	0	1

Next we characterize the coefficients of RDP of cycles and find a few relations between the coefficients of RDPs of cycles of different orders.

Observation 2. *The following properties holds for coefficients of $D_r(C_n, x)$, for every $n \in \mathbb{N}$:*

(i) $d_r(C_{3n}, n) = 3$.
(ii) *If $n \geq 3$, then $d_r(C_n, n) = 1$.*
(iii) *If $n \geq 3$, then $d_r(C_n, n-1) = 0$.*
(iv) *If $n \geq 3$, then $d_r(C_n, n-2) = n$.*

Theorem 5. *The following properties holds for the coefficients of $D_r(C_n, x)$, $\forall n \in \mathbb{N}$:*

(i) *If $n \geq 4$ and $i \geq n - 2\lfloor \frac{n}{3} \rfloor$, then $d_r(C_n, i) = d_r(C_{n-3}, i-1) + d_r(C_{n-1}, i-1)$.*
(ii) $d_r(C_{3n+1}, n+1) = 3n + 1$.
(iii) *If $n \geq 2$, then $d_r(C_{3n-1}, n+1) = \frac{n}{2}(3n - 1)$.*
(iv) *If $n \geq 5$, then $d_r(C_n, n-4) = \frac{n}{2}(n-5)$.*
(v) *If $n \geq 4$, then $\sum_{i=n}^{3n} d_r(C_i, n) = 2 \sum_{i=n-1}^{3(n-1)} d_r(C_i, n-1)$.*
(vi) *For $n \geq 3$,*
  – *if n is even, then*

$$\begin{cases} d_r(C_i, n) < d_r(C_{i+2}, n), & \text{for } n \leq i \leq 2n - 2 \\ d_r(C_i, n) > d_r(C_{i+2}, n), & \text{for } 2n \leq i \leq 3n - 2 \end{cases}$$

  – *if n is odd, then*

$$\begin{cases} d_r(C_i, n) < d_r(C_{i+2}, n), & \text{for } n \leq i \leq 2n - 1 \\ d_r(C_i, n) > d_r(C_{i+2}, n), & \text{for } 2n + 1 \leq i \leq 3n - 2 \end{cases}$$

(vii) *If $S_n = \sum_{i=\gamma_r(C_n)}^{n} d_r(C_n, i)$, then for every $n \geq 4$, $S_n = S_{n-1} + S_{n-3}$ with initial values $S_1 = 1, S_2 = 1, S_3 = 4$.*

Proof. (i) It follows from Theorem 2.
(ii) We prove it by induction on n. The result is true for $n = 1$, because $C_4^2 = \{\{1,2\}, \{2,3\}, \{3,4\}, \{4,1\}\}$. Therefore, $d_r(C_4, 2) = |C_4^2| = 4$. Now let us suppose the result is true for all natural numbers less than n, and we have to prove it for n. By $(i), (ii)$ and induction hypothesis, we have

$$\begin{aligned} d_r(C_{3n+1}, n+1) &= d_r(C_{3n}, n) + d_r(C_{3n-2}, n) \\ &= 3 + 3(n-1) + 1 \\ &= 3n + 1. \end{aligned}$$

Therefore, by method of induction $d_r(C_{3n+1}, n+1) = 3n + 1, \forall n \in \mathbb{N}$.

(iii) We prove it by induction on n. Since $C_5^3 = \{\{1,2,3\}, \{2,3,4\}, \{3,4,5\},$ $\{4,5,1\}, \{5,1,2\}\}$, so $d_r(C_5, 3) = 5$. The result is true for $n = 2$. Now let us suppose the result is true for all natural numbers less than n, and we have to prove it for n. By $(ii), (iii)$ and induction hypothesis, we have

$$d_r(C_{3n-1}, n+1)$$
$$= d_r(C_{3n-2}, n) + d_r(C_{3n-4}, n)$$
$$= 3(n-1) + 1 + \frac{n-1}{2}(3(n-1) - 1)$$
$$= \frac{n}{2}(3n - 1).$$

Therefore, by method of induction $d_r(C_{3n-1}, n+1) = \frac{n}{2}(3n-1)$, $\forall n \geq 2$.

(iv) We prove it by induction on n. The result is true for $n = 5$, because $C_5^1 = \phi$, so $d_r(C_5, 1) = 0$. Now let us suppose the result is true for all natural numbers less than n, and we have to prove it for n. By $(ii), (vii)$ and induction hypothesis, we have

$$d_r(C_n, n-4)$$
$$= d_r(C_{n-1}, n-5) + d_r(C_{n-3}, n-5)$$
$$= \frac{(n-1)}{2}(n-1-5) + n - 3$$
$$= \frac{n}{2}(n-5).$$

Therefore, by method of induction $d_r(C_n, n-4) = \frac{n}{2}(n-5)$, $\forall n \geq 5$.

(v) We prove it by induction on n. Firstly, let $n = 4$, then $\sum_{i=4}^{12} d_r(C_i, 4) = 32 = 2\sum_{i=3}^{9} d_r(C_i, 3)$. Now suppose the result is true for all natural numbers less than n, and we have to prove it for n. By $(ii), (vii)$ and induction hypothesis, we have

$$\sum_{i=n}^{3n} d_r(C_i, n)$$
$$= \sum_{i=n}^{3n} d_r(C_{i-1}, n-1) + \sum_{i=n}^{3n} d_r(C_{i-3}, n-1)$$
$$= 2 \sum_{i=n-1}^{3(n-1)} d_r(C_{i-1}, n-2) + 2 \sum_{i=n-1}^{3(n-1)} d_r(C_{i-3}, n-2)$$
$$= 2 \sum_{i=n-1}^{3(n-1)} d_r(C_i, n-1)$$

Therefore, by method of induction $\sum_{i=n}^{3n} d_r(C_i, n) = 2\sum_{i=n-1}^{3(n-1)} d_r(C_i, n-1)$, $\forall n \geq 4$.

(vi) We prove it by induction on n. The result holds for $n = 3$. Now suppose the result is true for all natural number less than n, and we have to prove it for n. To prove our claim, consider the following cases when n is even:

– Case 1:For $n \le i \le 2n - 2$:

By Theorem 2 and induction hypothesis, we have

$$
\begin{aligned}
d_r(C_i, n) &\\
&= d_r(C_{i-1}, n - 1) + d_r(C_{i-3}, n - 1) \\
&< d_r(C_{i+1}, n - 1) + d_r(C_{i-1}, n - 1) \\
&= d_r(C_{i+2}, n)
\end{aligned}
$$

– Case 2: For $2n \le i \le 3n - 2$:

By Theorem 2 and induction hypothesis, we have

$$
\begin{aligned}
d_r(C_i, n) &\\
&= d_r(C_{i-1}, n - 1) + d_r(C_{i-3}, n - 1) \\
&> d_r(C_{i+1}, n - 1) + d_r(C_{i-1}, n - 1) \\
&= d_r(C_{i+2}, n)
\end{aligned}
$$

Therefore, the statement holds when n is even.

Similarly, we can prove for odd n. Therefore, by method of induction the proposition holds for all $n \ge 3$.

(vii) By induction on n. Since we have $S_1 = 1, S_2 = 1, S_3 = 4$, so for $n = 4$, $S_4 = 4 = S_3 + S_1$. Now let us suppose the result is true for all natural number less than n, and we have to prove it for n. By Theorem 2 and induction hypothesis, we have

$$
\begin{aligned}
S_n &= \sum_{i=n-2\lfloor \frac{n}{3} \rfloor}^{n} d_r(C_n, i) \\
&= \sum_{i=n-2\lfloor \frac{n}{3} \rfloor}^{n} (d_r(C_{n-1}, i - 1) + d_r(C_{n-3}, i - 1)) \\
&= \sum_{i=n-1-2\lfloor \frac{n}{3} \rfloor}^{n-1} d_r(C_{n-1}, i) + \sum_{i=n-1-2\lfloor \frac{n}{3} \rfloor}^{n-3} d_r(C_{n-3}, i) \\
&= S_{n-1} + S_{n-3}.
\end{aligned}
$$

Therefore, by method of induction $S_n = S_{n-1} + S_{n-3}, \forall n \ge 4$.

Theorem 6. *Total number of terms in* $D_r(C_n, x) = 1 + \lfloor \frac{n}{3} \rfloor$.

Proof. Total number of terms in $D_r(C_n, x)$

$$
\begin{aligned}
&= (n - \gamma_r(C_n))/2 + 1 \\
&= \frac{n - (n - 2\lfloor \frac{n}{3} \rfloor)}{2} + 1 \\
&= \lfloor \frac{n}{3} \rfloor + 1
\end{aligned}
$$

4   Conclusion

In this paper, we introduced two novel methods for computing RDP and enumerating RDS of a cycle, namely, a recurrence on computing the restrained domination number and a generating function. We also presented a few characterizations on the restrained dominating sets of cycles. We listed several properties of the coefficients of RDP of cycles and reported empirical data on cycles with order up to 23 in Table 1. An immediate extension of this work is to find polynomial time algorithms to compute RDS, for subclasses of special classes of graphs, such as bipartite graphs and chordal graphs. Our approach maybe applied to graphs with fixed size cycles in it. In addition, another direction for this study is to find the complexity class of computing RDP of a graph.

References

1. Alikhani, S., Peng, Y:: Dominating sets and domination polynomials of cycles. arXiv preprint arXiv:0905.3268 (2009)
2. Chen, L., Zeng, W., Lub, C.: NP-completeness and APX-completeness of restrained domination in graphs. Theoret. Comput. Sci. **448**, 1–8 (2012)
3. Domke, G.S., Hattingh, J.H., Henning, M.A., Markus, L.R.: Restrained domination in graphs. Discret. Math. **203**, 61–69 (1999)
4. Kayathri, K., Kokilambal, G.: Restrained domination polynomial in graphs. J. Discrete Math. Sci. Cryptogr. **14**, 761–775 (2019)
5. Telle, J.A., Proskurowski. A.: Algorithms for vertex partitioning problems on partial k-trees. SIAM J. Discrete Math. **10**(4), 529–550 (1997)

Fault Diagnosability of Multigraph Matching Composition Networks

Xiao-Wen Qin[1,2], Rong-Xia Hao[1(✉)], and Sheng-Lung Peng[3]

[1] School of Mathematics and Statistics, Beijing Jiaotong University, Beijing, China
rxhao@bjtu.edu.cn
[2] College of Mathematics and Physics, Beijing University of Chemical Technology,
Beijing, China
xwqin@buct.edu.cn
[3] Department of Product Innovation and Entrepreneurship,
National Taipei University of Business, Taoyuan, Taiwan
slpeng@ntub.edu.tw

Abstract. A matching composition network (MCN) is a typical network structure which is obtained by adding a perfect matching between two connected graphs with a same order. To construct multiprocessor systems, we generalize matching composition networks (MCNs) to multigraph matching composition networks (MMCNs), which are connected graphs obtained by adding a perfect matching L between connected graphs $G_1, G_2, \cdots, G_m$ with a same order, where $m \geq 3$. In this paper, we propose a uniform method to determine the diagnosability of MMCNs under the PMC and MM* models.

Keywords: Diagnosability · Multigraph matching composition network · PMC model · MM* model

1 Introduction

An interconnection network can be modeled by a loopless undirected graph $G = (V(G), E(G))$, where $V(G)$ is the set of processors/vertices and $E(G)$ is the set of communication links/edges. In this paper, graphs and networks are used interchangeably. As networks increasing in size and complexity, the processor failure is inevitable. Therefore, the fault diagnosis, a process to discriminate between faulty processors and fault-free ones, plays an important role in keeping the network running normally. A network is t-*diagnosable* if all the faulty processors can be definitely identified given that the number of faulty processors is no more than t. The *diagnosability* of a network is the maximum value of t such that the network is t-diagnosable [2]. The diagnosability of the network G is usually denoted by $t(G)$.

Several models of diagnosis have been considered in relative literatures. One of the most classic models is the PMC model, which is proposed by Preparata, Metze and Chien in [12]. Under the PMC model, every processor is able to test

S.-Y. Hsieh et al. (Eds.): ICS 2022, CCIS 1723, pp. 145–155, 2022.
https://doi.org/10.1007/978-981-19-9582-8_13

the adjacent processor. The comparison model is proposed by Maeng and Malek in [11]. The diagnosis is carried out by sending the same testing task to a pair of processors and comparing their responses. The comparison is performed by a third processor, which is called a comparator. If the comparator is fault-free, a disagreement between the two responses is an indication of the existence of a faulty processor. To obtain more knowledge about the faulty status of the system, it was assumed that a comparison is performed by each processor for each pair of its distinct adjacent processors. This special case of the comparison model is called the MM* model, which is given by Sengupa and Dahbura in [15]. The diagnosability under the PMC and MM* models of several well-known inter-connection networks has been considered. For example, Kavianpour and Zheng et al. gave the diagnosability of star graphs under the PMC and MM* models respectively in [7] and [17]. Lin et al. determined the diagnosability of alternating group graphs under the PMC model in [10]. Ren et al. gave the diagnosability of bubble-sort graphs under the MM* model in [14]. Lai et al. showed the diagnos-ability of matching composition networks under the MM* model in [8]. There are some results according to other diagnostic strategies under the PMC and MM* models, we can refer to [3,5,6].

A common approach to scale up a network is to connect several small scale networks. Wang et al. considered the diagnosability of matching composition networks in [16]. In this paper, we generalize them to multigraph matching com-position networks (MMCNs). The detailed definition is given in Definition 1. In supporting cloud computing, many data center networks (DCNs) have been proposed in recent years. Most server-centric DCNs can be divided into blocks to realize parallel distributed computing. In order to realize information trans-fer and communication between blocks, servers in different blocks are connected according to some certain rules. To our knowledge, many DCNs with good per-formance are MMCNs, such as DCell [4], *L-HSDC* [13], *L-AQDC* [1].

In this paper, the diagnosability of each MMCN under the PMC and MM* models is determined just relying on their minimum degrees. Moreover, the min-imum degree condition above is sharp.

The remainder of this paper is organized as follows. In Sect. 2, main defi-nitions and lemmas are introduced. In Sect. 3, the diagnosability of MMCNs is given under the PMC and MM* models. In Sect. 4, we make a conclusion.

2 Preliminaries

For the graph $G = (V(G), E(G))$, the cardinality of $V(G)$ is called the *order* of G. Two vertices v_1 and v_2 in $V(G)$ are said to be *adjacent* if and only if $(v_1, v_2) \in E(G)$. If $(v_1, v_2) \in E(G)$, the vertices v_1 and v_2 are *incident* with the edge (v_1, v_2), and vise versa. In addition, the vertices v_1 and v_2 are called *ends* of the edge (v_1, v_2). The *neighbor* of a vertex u in $V(G)$ is a vertex adjacent to u in G and the *neighborhood* of a vertex u in G is a set of all neighbors of u, denoted by $N_G(u)$. The cardinality $|N_G(u)|$ represents the *degree* of u in G, denoted by $d_G(u)$ (or simply $d(u)$), and $\delta(G) = \min_{v \in V(G)} d_G(v)$ is the *minimum degree* of G. For a positive integer n, we use $[n]$ to represent the set $\{1, 2, \ldots, n\}$.

In the PMC model, let the ordered pair $(x; y)$ denote the vertex x testing its neighbor y. For the test result of $(x; y)$, if the vertex x is fault-free, then the test result is reliable. In the MM* model, let $(x; y)_w$ denote the vertex w testing its two neighbors x and y. For the test result of $(x; y)_w$, if w is fault-free, then the test result is reliable. Under the PMC or MM* model, the collection of all test results is called a *syndrome*, denoted as σ. Let F be a subset of $V(G)$. The set F is said to be *compatible* with a syndrome σ if σ can be obtained from the circumstance that all vertices in F are faulty and all vertices in $V(G) \setminus F$ are fault-free. Let $\sigma_F = \{\sigma : \sigma \text{ is compatible with } F\}$. Two distinct subsets F_1 and F_2 of $V(G)$ are said to be *indistinguishable* if and only if $\sigma_{F_1} \cap \sigma_{F_2} \neq \emptyset$; otherwise, F_1 and F_2 are said to be *distinguishable*. The symmetric difference of $F_1 \subseteq V(G)$ and $F_2 \subseteq V(G)$ is defined as the set $F_1 \vartriangle F_2 = (F_1 \setminus F_2) \cup (F_2 \setminus F_1)$.

The following two lemmas characterize the system which is t-diagnosable under the PMC and MM* models, respectively.

Lemma 1. (See [12].) *A system G is t-diagnosable under the PMC model if and only if any two distinct faulty subsets F_1 and F_2 of $V(G)$ with $\max\{|F_1|, |F_2|\} \leq t$ are distinguishable, that is, there is an edge $(u, v) \in E(G)$ with $u \in V(G) \setminus (F_1 \cup F_2)$ and $v \in F_1 \vartriangle F_2$.*

Lemma 2. (See [15].) *A system G is t-diagnosable under the MM* model if and only if any two distinct faulty subsets F_1 and F_2 of $V(G)$ with $\max\{|F_1|, |F_2|\} \leq t$ are distinguishable, that is, one of the following conditions holds:*

(1) *there are two vertices $u, w \in V(G) \setminus (F_1 \cup F_2)$ and there is a vertex $v \in F_1 \vartriangle F_2$ such that $(u, w) \in E(G)$ and $(v, w) \in E(G)$;*
(2) *there are two vertices $u, v \in F_1 \setminus F_2$ and there is a vertex $w \in V(G) \setminus (F_1 \cup F_2)$ such that $(u, w) \in E(G)$ and $(v, w) \in E(G)$;*
(3) *there are two vertices $u, v \in F_2 \setminus F_1$ and there is a vertex $w \in V(G) \setminus (F_1 \cup F_2)$ such that $(u, w) \in E(G)$ and $(v, w) \in E(G)$.*

The definition of multigraph matching composition networks is as follows.

Definition 1. *Let $G_1, G_2, \cdots, G_m$ be connected graphs with a same order n such that $n \geq 2$, $m \geq 3$, and $n \times m$ is even. A multigraph matching composition network, denoted by M_L, is a connected graph with $V(M_L) = \bigcup_{i \in [m]} V(G_i)$ and $E(M_L) = (\bigcup_{i \in [m]} E(G_i)) \cup L$, where L is a perfect matching of M_L and two ends of each edge in L are in different $G_j's$ for $j \in [m]$. Let $\mathbb{M}(G_1, \ldots, G_m)$ (M for short) be a family of M_L for all edge sets corresponding to L and graphs $G_1, \ldots, G_m$.*

Several known networks are MMCNs, such as star graphs, pancake graphs, bubble-sort graphs, alternating group networks, and so on.

3   Diagnosability of Multigraph Matching Composition Networks

First, the upper bound of the diagnosability of MMCNs under the PMC and MM* models will be discussed.

Theorem 1. *Let M_L be an MMCN in M. Then $t(M_L) \leq \delta(M_L)$ under the PMC and MM* models.*

Proof. Let x be a vertex of M_L with $d_{M_L}(x) = \delta(M_L)$. Assume $F_1 = N_{M_L}(x) \cup \{x\}$ and $F_2 = N_{M_L}(x)$. By Lemmas 1 and 2, the sets F_1 and F_2 are indistinguishable under the PMC and MM* models. Thus, $t(M_L) \leq \delta(M_L)$. □

3.1   Diagnosability of MMCNs Under the PMC Model

Lin et al. gave an extending star structure $T_G(v; t)$ to identify the state of a given vertex v by the algorithm $LDT_G(v; t)$ under the PMC model in [9]. The extending star structure $T_G(v; t) = (V(T), E(T))$ is a subgraph of the graph G, where $V(T) = \{v\} \cup \{x_j, y_j : j \in [t]\}$ and $E(T) = \{(v, x_j), (x_j, y_j) : j \in [t]\}$. See Fig. 1. We will use this structure to determine the lower bound of the diagnosability of MMCNs under the PMC model.

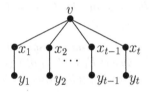

Fig. 1. An illustration for an extending star structure $T_G(v; t)$

Lemma 3. (See [9].) *Let $T_G(v; t)$ be an extending star rooted at the vertex v with a parameter t in a graph G. The algorithm $LDT_G(v; t)$ correctly identifies the state of the vertex v under the PMC model if the total number of faulty vertices in G does not exceed t.*

According to Lemma 3, a sufficient condition that a graph is t-diagnosable is obtained.

Theorem 2. *Let t be an positive integer. If the total number of faulty vertices in G does not exceed t, and there exists an extending star $T_G(v; t)$ rooted at the vertex v for any $v \in V(G)$, then G is t-diagnosable under the PMC model.*

Lemma 4. *Let M_L be an MMCN in M. Then $t(M_L) \geq \delta(M_L)$ under the PMC model.*

Proof. Let x be any vertex in $V(M_L)$. By Definition 1, we have that $V(M_L) = \bigcup_{i \in [m]} V(G_i)$ and $M_L = G_1 \cup G_2 \cup \cdots \cup G_m \cup L$, where L is a perfect matching of M_L and two ends of each edge in L are in different $G_j's$ for $j \in [m]$. Without loss of generality, assume that $x \in V(G_i)$ for some $i \in [m]$ and $(x', x) \in L$, where

$x' \in V(G_j)$ and $j \in [m]\backslash\{i\}$. By Theorem 2, we only need to construct an extending star $T_{M_L}(x; \delta(M_L))$ in M_L. We set $d_{G_i}(x) = t$ and $N_{G_i}(x) = \{x_1, x_2, \ldots, x_t\}$. For each $s \in [t]$, let $(x'_s, x_s) \in L$. Since $\delta(M_L) = \min_{k \in [m]} \delta(G_k) + 1 \leq \delta(G_i) + 1 \leq d_{G_i}(x) + 1$, it implies that $t \geq \delta(M_L) - 1$.

If $t \geq \delta(M_L)$, then $T_{M_L}(x; \delta(M_L)) = \bigcup_{j \in [\delta(M_L)]}\{(x, x_j), (x_j, x'_j)\}$ is a desired extending star in M_L. By Theorem 2, $t(M_L) \geq \delta(M_L)$ under the PMC model.

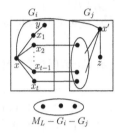

Fig. 2. $\{x\} \cup N_{G_i}(x) \subset V(G_i)$ in Lemma 4

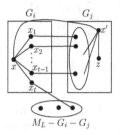

Fig. 3. $\{x\} \cup N_{G_i}(x) = V(G_i)$ in Lemma 4

If $t \leq \delta(M_L) - 1$, then $t = \delta(M_L) - 1$. Two situations are considered. If $\{x\} \cup N_{G_i}(x)$ is a proper subset of $V(G_i)$, since G_i is connected, there is a vertex $y \in V(G_i) \backslash (\{x\} \cup N_{G_i}(x))$ adjacent with some vertex in $\{x_1, x_2, \ldots, x_t\}$. Without loss of generality, assume $(x_1, y) \in E(G_i)$. Since $\delta(G_j) \geq t = \delta(M_L) - 1$, then $d_{G_j}(x') \geq \delta(M_L) - 1$, there is at least one vertex in $N_{G_j}(x') \backslash \{x'_2, x'_3, \ldots, x'_t\}$, denoted by z. Thus $T_{M_L}(x; \delta(M_L)) = (\bigcup_{s \in [t]}\{(x, x_s)\}) \cup (\bigcup_{2 \leq l \leq t}\{(x_l, x'_l)\}) \cup \{(x_1, y), (x, x'), (x', z)\}$ is a desired extending star in M_L. See Fig. 2. If $\{x\} \cup N_{G_i}(x) = V(G_i)$, at least one vertex in $\{x'_1, x'_2, \ldots, x'_t\}$ is not in $V(G_j)$. Otherwise, G_i, G_j and edges in L whose ends are in $V(G_i) \cup V(G_j)$ form a connected component of M_L, which contradicts to the connectedness of M_L. Without loss of generality, assume $x'_t \notin V(G_j)$. Since $\delta(G_j) \geq t = \delta(M_L) - 1$, then $d_{G_j}(x') \geq \delta(M_L) - 1$, there is at least one vertex in $N_{G_j}(x') \backslash \{x'_1, x'_2, \ldots, x'_{t-1}\}$, denoted by z. Thus $T_{M_L}(x; \delta(M_L)) = (\bigcup_{s \in [t]}\{(x, x_s), (x_s, x'_s)\}) \cup \{(x, x'), (x', z)\}$ is a desired extending star in M_L. See Fig. 3. By Theorem 2, $t(M_L) \geq \delta(M_L)$ under the PMC model. □

By Lemmas 1 and 4, we have the following Theorem 3.

Theorem 3. *Let M_L be an MMCN in $\mathbb{M}$. Then $t(M_L) = \delta(M_L)$ under the PMC model.*

Corollary 1. *Let F_1 and F_2 be two distinct vertex subsets in $M_L \in \mathbb{M}$ with $\max\{|F_1|, |F_2|\} \leq \delta(M_L)$. Then there is an edge between $F_1 \triangle F_2$ and $V(M_L) \backslash (F_1 \cup F_2)$.*

3.2 Diagnosability of MMCNs Under the MM* Model

Lemma 5. *Let F_1 and F_2 be two distinct vertex subsets in $M_L \in \mathbb{M}$ with $F_1 \cap F_2 = \emptyset$ and $\max\{|F_1|, |F_2|\} \leq \delta(M_L)$. If $\delta(M_L) \geq 4$, then (F_1, F_2) is a distinguishable pair under the MM* model.*

Proof. By Corollary 1, there is an edge $(x, y) \in E(M_L)$ between $F_1 \triangle F_2$ and $V(M_L) \setminus (F_1 \cup F_2)$. Without loss of generality, we set $x \in F_1 \triangle F_2$ and $y \in V(M_L) \setminus (F_1 \cup F_2)$. Since $\delta(M_L) \geq 4$ and $F_1 \cap F_2 = \emptyset$, at least one of the inequalities $|N_{M_L}(y) \cap (V(M_L) \setminus (F_1 \cup F_2))| \geq 1$, $|N_{M_L}(y) \cap (F_1 \setminus F_2)| \geq 2$ and $|N_{M_L}(y) \cap (F_2 \setminus F_1)| \geq 2$ holds. By Lemma 2, (F_1, F_2) is a distinguishable pair under the MM* model. $\qquad\square$

Lemma 6. *Let M_L be an MMCN in $\mathbb{M}$. If $\delta(M_L) \geq 4$, then $t(M_L) \geq \delta(M_L) - 1$ under the MM* model.*

Proof. By Definition 1, we have that $\min\{\delta(G_1), \ldots, \delta(G_m)\} \geq 3$. Let F_1 and F_2 be any two distinct vertex subsets of M_L with $\max\{|F_1|, |F_2|\} \leq \delta(M_L) - 1$. By Lemma 2, it needs to show that F_1 and F_2 are distinguishable. By Lemma 5, (F_1, F_2) is a distinguishable pair if $F_1 \cap F_2 = \emptyset$. Thus, we consider that $F_1 \cap F_2 \neq \emptyset$. Assume that (F_1, F_2) is an indistinguishable pair. By Corollary 1, there is an edge between $F_1 \triangle F_2$ and $V(M_L) \setminus (F_1 \cup F_2)$.

Case 1. There exists an edge between $F_1 \triangle F_2$ and $V(M_L) \setminus (F_1 \cup F_2)$ in L.

Select $(x, x') \in L$ such that $x \in F_1 \triangle F_2$ and $x' \in V(M_L) \setminus (F_1 \cup F_2)$. Without loss of generality, assume that $x \in F_1 \setminus F_2$, $x \in V(G_1)$ and $x' \in V(G_2)$. Since (F_1, F_2) is an indistinguishable pair and (x, x') is an edge between $F_1 \setminus F_2$ and $V(M_L) \setminus (F_1 \cup F_2)$, by Lemma 2, it implies that $|N_{M_L}(x') \cap (V(M_L) \setminus (F_1 \cup F_2))| = 0$, $|N_{M_L}(x') \cap (F_1 \setminus F_2)| = 1$ and $|N_{M_L}(x') \cap (F_2 \setminus F_1)| \leq 1$. Thus $N_{M_L}(x') \subseteq F_1 \cup F_2$ and $|N_{M_L}(x')| = |N_{M_L}(x') \cap (F_1 \setminus F_2)| + |N_{M_L}(x') \cap (F_2 \setminus F_1)| + |N_{M_L}(x') \cap (F_1 \cap F_2)|$. In addition, $|F_1 \cap F_2| \leq |F_1 \setminus \{x\}| \leq \delta(M_L) - 2$. Thus $\delta(M_L) \leq |N_{M_L}(x')| \leq 1 + 1 + \delta(M_L) - 2$, which derives that $|N_{M_L}(x') \cap (F_1 \cap F_2)| = \delta(M_L) - 2$, $|N_{M_L}(x') \cap (F_1 \setminus F_2)| = 1$ and $|N_{M_L}(x') \cap (F_2 \setminus F_1)| = 1$. That is $N_{M_L}(x') = F_1 \cup F_2$ and $(F_1 \cup F_2) \cap V(G_1) = \{x\}$. Since $N_{G_1}(x) \cap N_{M_L}(x') = \emptyset$ and $d_{G_1}(x) \geq 3$, there is a vertex $w \in N_{G_1}(x) \setminus (F_1 \cup F_2)$. Since $d_{G_1}(w) \geq 3$ and $(F_1 \cup F_2) \cap V(G_1) = \{x\}$, there is a vertex $z \in N_{G_1}(w) \setminus (F_1 \cup F_2)$. Then there exist two vertices $w, z \in V(M_L) \setminus (F_1 \cup F_2)$ and a vertex $x \in F_1 \setminus F_2$ such that $(x, w), (x, z) \in E(M_L)$. By Lemma 2, it contradicts with the assumption that F_1 and F_2 are indistinguishable.

Case 2. Any edge between $F_1 \triangle F_2$ and $V(M_L) \setminus (F_1 \cup F_2)$ is not in L.

Select a vertex $x \in F_1 \triangle F_2$ and a vertex $y \in V(M_L) \setminus (F_1 \cup F_2)$ such that $(x, y) \in E(M_L) \setminus L$. Since (F_1, F_2) is an indistinguishable pair, with a similar discussion in Case 1, we have that $|N_{M_L}(y) \cap (F_1 \cap F_2)| = \delta(M_L) - 2$, $|N_{M_L}(y) \cap (F_1 \setminus F_2)| = 1$ and $|N_{M_L}(y) \cap (F_2 \setminus F_1)| = 1$. That is $N_{M_L}(y) = F_1 \cup F_2$. Assume that $(x, x') \in L$. Since $(x, y) \notin L$, then x and y belong to a same G_i, where $i \in [m]$. By Definition 1, we have that $x' \notin N_{M_L}(y)$. Since $N_{M_L}(y) = F_1 \cup F_2$, then $x' \in V(M_L) \setminus (F_1 \cup F_2)$ and (x, x') is an edge between $F_1 \triangle F_2$ and

$V(M_L) \setminus (F_1 \cup F_2)$, which is a contradiction with that any edge between $F_1 \triangle F_2$ and $V(M_L) \setminus (F_1 \cup F_2)$ is not in L. □

Lemma 7. *Let M_L be an MMCN in $\mathbb{M}$. If $\delta(M_L) \geq 5$, then $t(M_L) \geq \delta(M_L)$ under the MM* model.*

Proof. By Definition 1, the edge set L is a perfect matching of M_L. For every vertex x in $V(M_L)$, let $(x', x) \in L$, where $x' \in V(M_L)$. The condition $\delta(M_L) \geq 5$ implies that $\min\{\delta(G_1), \ldots, \delta(G_m)\} \geq 4$. Let F_1 and F_2 be any two distinct vertex subsets of M_L with $\max\{|F_1|, |F_2|\} \leq \delta(M_L)$. By Lemma 2, it needs to show that F_1 and F_2 are distinguishable. By Lemma 5, (F_1, F_2) is a distinguishable pair if $F_1 \cap F_2 = \emptyset$. Thus, we consider that $F_1 \cap F_2 \neq \emptyset$. Assume that (F_1, F_2) is an indistinguishable pair. By Corollary 1, there is an edge between $F_1 \triangle F_2$ and $V(M_L) \setminus (F_1 \cup F_2)$. We have the following cases.

Case 1. There exists a vertex $x \in F_1 \triangle F_2$ such that $x' \in V(M_L) \setminus (F_1 \cup F_2)$, where $(x, x') \in L$.

Without loss of generality, assume that $x \in F_1 \setminus F_2$, $x \in V(G_1)$ and $x' \in V(G_2)$. By Definition 1, we have that $N_{M_L}(x) \cap N_{M_L}(x') = \emptyset$. Since $x \in F_1 \setminus F_2$ and $\max\{|F_1|, |F_2|\} \leq \delta(M_L)$, it implies that $|F_1 \cap F_2| \leq \delta(M_L) - 1$ and $|N_{M_L}(x') \cap (F_1 \cap F_2)| \leq \delta(M_L) - 1$. Since (F_1, F_2) is an indistinguishable pair, by Lemma 2, it implies that $|N_{M_L}(x') \cap (V(M_L) \setminus (F_1 \cup F_2))| = 0$, $|N_{M_L}(x') \cap (F_1 \setminus F_2)| = 1$ and $|N_{M_L}(x') \cap (F_2 \setminus F_1)| \leq 1$. Thus $N_{M_L}(x') \subseteq F_1 \cup F_2$ and $\delta(M_L) \leq |N_{M_L}(x')| = |N_{M_L}(x') \cap (F_1 \setminus F_2)| + |N_{M_L}(x') \cap (F_2 \setminus F_1)| + |N_{M_L}(x') \cap (F_1 \cap F_2)| \leq 1 + 1 + |N_{M_L}(x') \cap (F_1 \cap F_2)|$, which derives that $\delta(M_L) - 2 \leq |N_{M_L}(x') \cap (F_1 \cap F_2)|$. Moreover, if $|N_{M_L}(x') \cap (F_1 \cap F_2)| = \delta(M_L) - 2$, then $|N_{M_L}(x') \cap (F_1 \setminus F_2)| = 1$ and $|N_{M_L}(x') \cap (F_2 \setminus F_1)| = 1$. Since $d_{G_1}(x) \geq 4$ and $N_{M_L}(x) \cap N_{M_L}(x') = \emptyset$, there is a vertex in $N_{G_1}(x) \setminus (F_1 \cup F_2)$, denoted by w. Since $d_{G_1}(w) \geq 4$, there is a vertex in $N_{G_1}(w) \setminus (F_1 \cup F_2)$, denoted by z. Then there exist two vertices $w, z \in V(M_L) \setminus (F_1 \cup F_2)$ and a vertex $x \in F_1 \setminus F_2$ such that $(x, w), (x, z) \in E(M_L)$. By Lemma 2, it contradicts with the assumption that (F_1, F_2) is an indistinguishable pair. See Fig. 4.

Case 2. The vertex x' is in $F_1 \cup F_2$ for every vertex $x \in F_1 \triangle F_2$, where $(x, x') \in L$.

Since there is an edge between $F_1 \triangle F_2$ and $V(M_L) \setminus (F_1 \cup F_2)$, select a vertex $x \in F_1 \triangle F_2$ and a vertex $y \in V(M_L) \setminus (F_1 \cup F_2)$ such that $(x, y) \in E(M_L)$. Note that $y \neq x'$. Without loss of generality, assume that $x \in F_1 \setminus F_2$ and $x, y \in V(G_1)$. Since (F_1, F_2) is an indistinguishable pair, with a similar discussion in Case 1, we have that $\delta(M_L) - 2 \leq |N_{M_L}(y) \cap (F_1 \cap F_2)| \leq \delta(M_L) - 1$ and $N_{M_L}(y) \subseteq F_1 \cup F_2$. Moreover, if $|N_{M_L}(y) \cap (F_1 \cap F_2)| = \delta(M_L) - 2$, then $|N_{M_L}(y) \cap (F_1 \setminus F_2)| = 1$ and $|N_{M_L}(y) \cap (F_2 \setminus F_1)| = 1$. In the following, two subcases are considered according to the value of $|N_{M_L}(y) \cap (F_1 \cap F_2)|$.

Case 2.1. $|N_{M_L}(y) \cap (F_1 \cap F_2)| = \delta(M_L) - 1$.

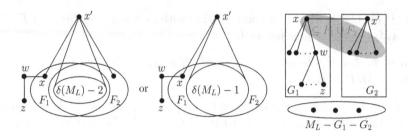

Fig. 4. An illustration for Case 1 in Lemma 7

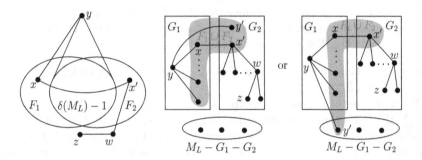

Fig. 5. An illustration for Case 2.1 in Lemma 7

Because $x' \in F_1 \cup F_2$ and $x' \notin N_{M_L}(y)$, we have $x' \in F_2 \setminus F_1$. Without loss of generality, assume that $x' \in V(G_2)$. Thus $N_{M_L}(y) \cup \{x'\} = F_1 \cup F_2$, which is shown by the shaded area in Fig. 5. Since $d_{G_2}(x') \geq 4$ and $|N_{G_2}(x') \cap (F_1 \cup F_2)| = |N_{G_2}(x') \cap N_{M_L}(y)| \leq 1$, there is a vertex in $N_{G_2}(x') \setminus (F_1 \cup F_2)$, denoted by w. Since $d_{G_2}(w) \geq 4$ and $|N_{G_2}(w) \cap (F_1 \cup F_2)| \leq 2$, we can find a vertex in $N_{G_2}(w) \setminus (F_1 \cup F_2)$, denoted by z. See Fig. 5. Then there exist two vertices $w, z \in V(M_L) \setminus (F_1 \cup F_2)$ and there is a vertex $x' \in F_2 \setminus F_1$ such that $(x, w), (x, z) \in E(M_L)$. By Lemma 2, it contradicts with the assumption that (F_1, F_2) is an indistinguishable pair.

Fig. 6. An illustration of F_1 and F_2 for Case 2.2 in Lemma 7

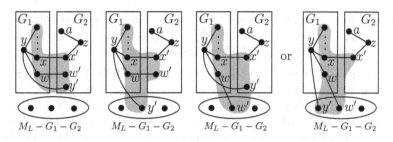

Fig. 7. An illustration of Case 2.2 in Lemma 7

Case 2.2. $|N_{M_L}(y) \cap (F_1 \cap F_2)| = \delta(M_L) - 2$.

It implies that $|N_{M_L}(y) \cap (F_2 \setminus F_1)| = 1$. Let $\{w\} = N_{M_L}(y) \cap (F_2 \setminus F_1)$. Note that $w \neq y'$. Thus $w \in V(G_1)$. Since $x, w \in F_1 \triangle F_2$, the vertices $x', w' \in F_1 \cup F_2$. Since $|N_{M_L}(y) \cap (F_1 \cap F_2)| = \delta(M_L) - 2$, $x' \neq w'$ and $x', w' \notin N_{M_L}(y)$, the vertices $x', w' \in F_1 \triangle F_2$, see Fig. 6. Thus $N_{M_L}(y) \cup \{x', w'\} = F_1 \cup F_2$, which is shown by the shaded area in Fig. 7. Without loss of generality, assume that $x' \in V(G_2)$. Since $d_{G_2}(x') \geq 4$ and $|N_{G_2}(x') \cap (F_1 \cup F_2)| = |N_{G_2}(x') \cap (N_{M_L}(y) \cup \{x', w'\})| \leq 2$, there is a vertex in $N_{G_2}(x') \setminus (F_1 \cup F_2)$, denoted by z. Since $d_{G_2}(z) \geq 4$ and $|N_{G_2}(z) \cap (F_1 \cup F_2)| \leq 3$, there is a vertex in $N_{G_2}(z) \setminus (F_1 \cup F_2)$, denoted by a, see Fig. 7. Then there exist two vertices $a, z \in V(M_L) \setminus (F_1 \cup F_2)$ and a vertex $x' \in F_1 \triangle F_2$ such that $(a, z), (z, x') \in E(M_L)$, which contradicts with the assumption that (F_1, F_2) is an indistinguishable pair. ☐

By Lemmas 1 and 7, we have the following Theorem 4.

Theorem 4. *Let M_L be an MMCN in* $\mathbb{M}$. *If $\delta(M_L) \geq 5$, then $t(M_L) = \delta(M_L)$ under the MM* model.*

By Theorem 4, we can determine that the diagnosibility of MMCNs under the MM* model is exactly equal to its minimum degree if it is at least 5. By Theorem 1 and Lemma 6, if M_L is an MMCN with $\delta(M_L) = 4$, one has that $\delta(M_L) - 1 \leq t(M_L) \leq \delta(M_L)$ under the MM* model. We will construct an infinite number of MMCNs such that the minimum degree of each of them is equal to 4, while the diagnosibility under the MM* model is not equal to its minimum degree. As a result, the condition of the minimal degree in Theorem 4 is tight.

Example 1. For any integer n with $n \geq 8$ and any even integer m with $m \geq 4$, let $V_i = \{(i-1) \cdot n + 1, (i-1) \cdot n + 2, \ldots, i \cdot n\} = [(i-1) \cdot n + 1, i \cdot n]$ with $i \in [m]$. For $3 \leq i \leq m$, let G_i be a complete graph with the vertex set V_i. For $j \in \{1, 2\}$, let G_j consist of a complete graph K_4 with the vertex set $[(j-1) \cdot n + 1, (j-1) \cdot n + 4]$ and a complete graph K_{n-4} with the vertex set $[(j-1) \cdot n + 5, j \cdot n]$. The two complete graphs in G_1 are connected by the edge $(4, 5)$ and the two complete graphs in G_2 are connected by the edge $(n+1, n+5)$. Let A and B

be the sets of all odd integers and even integers in $[m]$, respectively. Let $L = (\bigcup_{j\in[n-1],i\in A}\{((i-1)\cdot n+j, i\cdot n+j)\})\cup(\bigcup_{i'\in B\setminus\{m\}}\{(i'\cdot n, (i'+1)\cdot n)\})\cup\{(mn, n)\}$ and $G = G_1 \cup G_1 \cup \cdots \cup G_m \cup L$. The illustration of G is shown in Fig. 8.

By Definition 1, it can be checked that G is an MMCN. By the arbitrariness of the integer n satisfying $n \geq 8$ and the even integer m satisfying $m \geq 4$, there exists an infinite number of MMCNs. From Fig. 8, we can have that $\delta(G) = 4$. Let F_1 and F_2 be two different subsets of $V(G)$, where $F_1 = \{2, 4, n+1, n+2\}$ and $F_2 = \{3, 4, n+1, n+3\}$. Figure 9 gives an illustration of the set pair (F_1, F_2) and edges between $F_1 \cup F_2$ and $V(G) \setminus (F_1 \cup F_2)$. By Lemma 2, the set pair (F_1, F_2) is indistinguishable under the MM* model, that is, $t(G) \leq 3 = \delta(G) - 1$ under the MM* model. By Lemma 6, $t(G) = 3$ under the MM* model.

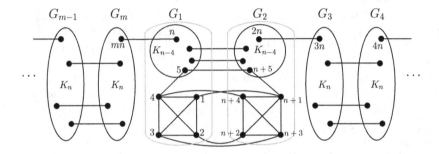

Fig. 8. An illustration of G in Example 1

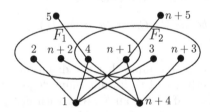

Fig. 9. The set pair (F_1, F_2) and edges between $F_1 \cup F_2$ and $V(G) \setminus (F_1 \cup F_2)$

4   Conclusion

In this paper, we give the definition of multigraph matching composition networks(MMCNs), and each of them is obtained by adding a perfect matching to connect several connected graphs with a same order. We determine the diagnosability of MMCNs under the PMC and MM* models just relying on their minimum degree. According to our main results, the diagnosability of several classical networks, including star graphs, bubble-sort graphs, alternating group networks, under these two models can be obtained directly. In addition, the results can also be applied to non-regular MMCNs. Furthermore, the diagnosability of MMCNs under other diagnostic strategies will be an interesting problem.

Acknowledgments. This research was supported by the National Natural Science Foundation of China (Nos. 11971054, 11731002 and 12161141005).

References

1. Chen, G., Cheng, B., Wang, D.: Constructing completely independent spanning trees in data center network based on augmented cube. IEEE Trans. Comput. **32**(3), 665–673 (2021)
2. Dahbura, A.T., Masson, G.M.: An $O(n^{2.5})$ fault identification algorithm for diagnosable systems. IEEE Trans. Comput. **33**(6), 486–492 (1984)
3. Gu, M.-M., Hao, R.-X., Zhou, S.: Fault diagnosability of data center networks. Theoret. Comput. Sci. **776**, 138–147 (2019)
4. Guo, C., Wu, H., Tan, K., Shi, L., Zhang, Y., Lu, S.: DCell: a scalable and fault-tolerant network structure for data centers. In: Proceedings of the ACM SIG-COMM (2008), pp. 75–86 (2008)
5. Guo, J., Lu, M.: Conditional diagnosability of the round matching composition networks. Theoret. Comput. Sci. **657**, 163–172 (2017)
6. Hsieh, S.-Y., Chen, Y.-S.: Strongly diagnosable systems under the comparison diagnosis model. IEEE Trans. Comput. **57**(12), 1720–1725 (2008)
7. Kavianpour, A.: Sequential diagnosability of star graphs. Comput. Electr. Eng. **22**(1), 37–44 (1996)
8. Lai, P.-L., Tan, J.J.M., Tsai, C.-H., Hsu, L.-H.: The diagnosability of the matching composition network under the comparison diagnosis model. IEEE Trans. Comput. **53**(8), 1064–1069 (2004)
9. Lin, C.-K., Kung, T.-L., Tan, J.J.M.: An algorithmic approach to conditional-fault local diagnosis of regular multiprocessor interconnected systems under the PMC model. IEEE Trans. Comput. **62**(3), 439–451 (2013)
10. Lin, L., Zhou, S., Xu, L., Wang, D.: The extra connectivity and conditional diagnosability of alternating group networks. IEEE Trans. Parallel Distrib. Syst. **26**(8), 2352–2362 (2015)
11. Maeng, J., Malek, M.: A comparison connection assignment for self-diagnosis of multiprocessors systems. In: Proceedings of the 11th International Symposium on Fault-Tolerant Computing (1981), pp. 173–175 (1981)
12. Preparata, F.P., Metze, G., Chien, R.T.: On the connection assignment problem of diagnosable systems, IEEE Trans. Electr. Comput. **EC-16**(6), 848–854 (1967)
13. Qin, X.-W., Hao, R.-X., Chang, J.-M.: The existence of completely independent spanning trees for some compound graphs. IEEE Trans. Parallel Distrib. Syst. **31**(2), 201–210 (2020)
14. Ren, Y., Wang, S.: Diagnosability of bubble-sort graph networks under the comparison diagnosis model. In: International Conference on Computational Intelligence and Communication Networks (2015), pp. 823–826 (2015)
15. Sengupta, A., Dahbura, A.T.: On self-diagnosable multiprocessor systems: diagnosis by the comparison approach. IEEE Trans. Comput. **41**(11), 1386–1396 (1992)
16. Wang, Y., Lin, C.-K., Li, X., Zhou, S.: Diagnosability for two families of composition networks. Theoret. Comput. Sci. **824–825**, 46–56 (2020)
17. Zheng, J., Latifi, S., Regentova, E., Luo, K., Wu, X.: Diagnosability of star graphs under the comparison diagnosis model. Inf. Process. Lett. **93**, 29–36 (2005)

Generating Scale-Free Outerplanar Networks

Md. Tahmidur Rafid, Rabeeb Ibrat[(✉)], and Md. Saidur Rahman[iD]

Graph Drawing and Information Visualization Laboratory, Department of Computer Science and Engineering, Bangladesh University of Engineering and Technology (BUET), Dhaka 1000, Bangladesh
0422052129@grad.cse.buet.ac.bd, 1605055@ugrad.cse.buet.ac.bd, saidurrahman@cse.buet.ac.bd

Abstract. Generating networks with desired degree distribution is an important topic of research in network science. Often network researchers need to perform empirical experiments on various types of networks and gain valuable observations. Synthetic network generators can help a lot by reducing loads on real world data. Among various degree distributions, the power-law degree distribution found in scale-free networks is the most common. Albert and Barabási have mentioned a number of models for generation of scale-free networks. However, these models do not impose any restriction on the planarity of generated networks. In this paper, we give an $O(n)$ time algorithm for generation of scale-free outerplanar networks. We also show that the degree distribution of a maximal outerplanar graph can not strictly fit power-law distribution for a scale-free network.

Keywords: Outerplanar graph · Scale free network · Degree sequence · Small world network

1 Introduction

Network Science aims to construct models that depict the properties of real systems. In recent years, it has been very popular to represent real-world networks as graphs having a large number of nodes and edges. Among the proposed models, Erdős and Rényi [8,9] introduced the idea to construct random networks where the vertices are associated with random edges. But the random network model barely characterizes the properties of real-world networks. Two special behaviors found in real networks are high clustering and small-world property [7]. The Erdős-Rényi model represents networks having small-world properties but low clustering. Another model proposed by Duncan Watts and Steven Strogatz [21] characterizes networks having high clustering but lacking in the small-world property. Later, Barabási and Réka Albert [1] proposed a new network structure following long-tailed power-law degree distribution and coined the term "scale-free network". They proposed a generative algorithm that

S.-Y. Hsieh et al. (Eds.): ICS 2022, CCIS 1723, pp. 156–166, 2022.
https://doi.org/10.1007/978-981-19-9582-8_14

is based on two important concepts: growth and preferential attachment. Preferential attachment refers to the likelihood of connecting a newly introduced node with large degree nodes.

A network is planar if it can be drawn on a 2D plane such that no two edges (links) cross each other except at their common end. A planar network is called an outerplanar network if it can be drawn on a 2D plane such that every vertex is drawn on the outer region. There are some algorithms those are NP-complete for other classes of graphs but can be solved in polynomial time for outerplanar graphs [4]. The study of outerplanar graphs is also interesting in the context of network science since RNA secondary structure is an outerplanar graph [22] and some complex networks are modeled using outerplanar graphs [6].

A natural question is whether there exists a scale-free outerplanar graph or not. The question can be answered trivially by setting the parameter $m = 1$ in the Barabasi-Albert model where a new node is connected with m existing nodes in the network. This indeed generates a scale-free tree taking $m = 1$, verified empirically by us, which is an outerplanar network. The question that remains then is: How many edges can we have in an outerplanar network of a given number of nodes, while still allowing it to be scale-free? To answer the question above, we develop an algorithm that generates a scale-free outerplanar network with more edges than found in a scale-free tree. This means that the outerplanar graph may indeed have cycles and may not be a tree.

We can generate a sequence of degrees from a given distribution but the question arises whether a graph can be constructed from a given degree sequence. This problem is known as the graph realization problem. Erdős & Gallai [10] provided us the answer to this question back in 1960. They proved that a non-increasing sequence, $S = (d_1, d_2, ..., d_n)$ can be the degree sequence of a simple graph if and only if the degree sum is even and

$$\sum_{i=1}^{k} d_i \leq k(k-1) + \sum_{i=k+1}^{n} min(d_i, k)$$

is true for every possible $1 \leq k \leq n$. Later, Havel [13] and Hakimi [11] showed a recursive algorithm for constructing a graph from a given degree sequence. Several works have been accomplished on the degree sequence of some special classes of graphs. For example, the characterization of Cacti graphs [13], split graphs [12,16], 2-trees [3], Halin graphs [2] are already known.

In this paper, our work is focused on generating scale-free outerplanar networks which obey the power-law degree distribution. Alongside Barabasi-Albert model, some other models are proposed for generating scale-free networks [14,20]. The models are focused on high clustering, power-law degree distribution, or keeping the diameter short. In our approach of generating the networks, we focus on obeying the power-law degree distribution while preserving outerplanarity. Much effort has gone into finding the complete characterization of the degree sequence of planar graphs [18], but the problem remains open. We show the characterization of the degree sequence of a special case of maximal outerplanars graphs. An outerplanar graph is maximal when no edge can be added without violating the outerplanar property. In this paper, we derive necessary and sufficient conditions for two special degree sequences which are realizable as maximal outerplanar graphs. Our derived sequences are the same as that found in a Master's thesis [15], but our proof is constructive and completely different from the proof of [15]. Our proof is useful in the generation of the scale-free outerplanar network in this paper. The rest of the paper is organized as follows. In Sect. 2, we define terminologies used throughout the paper. Section 3 deals with the degree sequence of maximal outerplanar graphs. In Sect. 4, we provide an algorithm for constructing a scale-free outerplanar graph. Finally, Sect. 5 is a conclusion.

2   Preliminaries

In this section, we define some terminologies. A graph is *planar* if it can be drawn on a 2D plane such that no two edges cross each other except at their common end. A planar graph is called an *outerplanar graph* if it can be drawn on a 2D plane such that every vertex is drawn on the outer region. A plane embedding of a planar graph divides the plane into some connected regions which are called *faces*. The *outer face* is the face with an infinite area. A graph is called *maximal outerplanar* if it has a planar drawing such that: (i) all vertices are on the outer face and (ii) all internal faces are triangulated. We call such a drawing a *maximal outerplane drawing*. The *outer cycle* of a maximal outerplanar graph is the cycle bounding the outer face (in maximal outerplane drawing) of the graph.

A sequence of integers is called a *maximal outerplanar graphic sequence* if it is the sequence of vertex degrees (in any order) of some maximal outerplanar graph. If we order the vertices along the outer cycle either clockwise or anti-clockwise, starting from any arbitrary vertex, then the maximal outerplanar graphic sequence obtained is an *ordered maximal outerplanar graphic sequence*. We consider the first element of an ordered maximal outerplanar graphic sequence to be at the right of the last element of that sequence, thus making an ordered maximal outerplanar graphic sequence a circular list.

We define a node having degree k as a *k-degree node*. We assume that a sequence, $S = (s_1, s_2, ..., s_n)$ is given and S is an ordered maximal outerplanar graphic sequence. We know, for every biconnected outerplanar graph, the number of 2-degree nodes is at least 2 [17]. So, in sequence S, there are at least two 2s. We now define the following operation as *2-elimination*:

(i) We choose an element s_k from the sequence S where $s_k = 2$
(ii) We remove s_k from the sequence and reduce the value of $s_{(k-1)\bmod n}$ and $s_{(k+1)\bmod n}$ by 1.

3   Degree Sequence of Maximal Outerplanar Graphs

In this section, we provide a characterization of the degree sequence of maximal outerplanar graphs having exactly two 2-degree nodes.

Lemma 1. *Let $S = (s_1, s_2, ..., s_n)$ be an ordered maximal outerplanar graphic sequence. Then a maximal outerplanar graph realizing S can be constructed in $O(n)$ time.*

Proof. If we remove a degree two vertex from a maximal outer plane graph, it is obvious that the resulting graph is also maximal outerplanar.

Now, we can find an element $s_k = 2$ from the sequence S. We apply 2-elimination operation on the element s_k. It can be easily observed that the operation is equivalent to removing a 2-degree vertex from the corresponding maximal outerplanar graph. Thus, the resulting sequence is the degree sequence of a maximal outerplanar graph. We continue performing the operation until the length of S is 3. We end up having a sequence like $(2, 2, 2)$. We draw a maximal outerplanar graph with 3 vertices. Now, we perform the reverse operation and add the removed elements from S one by one. Thus, a maximal outerplane graph can be constructed. Using a circular doubly linked list, one can construct the maximal outerplanar graph from a given ordered maximal outerplanar graphic sequence in $O(n)$ time. □

Lemma 2. *Let G be an outerplanar graph having exactly two 2-degree nodes. Then each 2-degree node has an adjacent 3-degree node on the outer cycle.*

Proof. If we remove a 2-degree node from a maximal outerplanar graph, the resulting graph is also maximal outerplanar. For contradiction, we assume that we have a 2-degree node whose adjacent node has a degree of at least 4. Now, if we remove the 2-degree node, the degree of its adjacent nodes is at least 3. The number of 2-degree nodes in the entire graph becomes one. But, every biconnected maximal outerplanar graph has at least two 2-degree nodes, a contradiction. □

Lemma 3. *For a maximal outerplanar graph having exactly two 2-degree nodes and the number of vertices greater than 4, if a 2-degree node has exactly x contiguous 3-degree nodes on one side of the outer cycle, then the node on the other side has degree $(3 + x)$.*

Proof. Let, an ordered maximal outerplanar graphic sequence, $S = (..., y, 2, \underbrace{3, \cdots, 3}_{x-times}, p, ...)$ is given. One side of the 2-degree node has x contiguous 3s and the degree of the node on the other side is y. If we apply 2-elimination on the 2, the 3 adjacent to 2 becomes 2 and the number of 3 is reduced by 1. After performing the operation x times, we have the sequence like $...(y - x), 2, p....$ Here p is greater than 3. So, from Lemma 2, we can say $y - x = 3$ or $y = x + 3$. □

Lemma 4. *Let $S = (s_1, s_2, ..., s_n)$ be a degree sequence such that exactly two elements in the sequence are 2, the rest of the elements are larger than 2 and the sum of the sequence is $4n - 6$. Then the number of 3s in S is $(\sum_{(s_i \geq 4)}(s_i - 4)) + 2$.*

Proof. We assume, the number of 3s in the sequence is f_3, the number of elements greater or equal to 4 is $f_{\geq 4}$. Thus, $n = f_3 + f_{\geq 4} + 2$. Here,

$$\sum_{i=1}^{n} s_i = \left(\sum_{s_i \geq 4} s_i \right) + 3 \times f_3 + 2 \times 2 \tag{1}$$

Again,

$$\sum_{i=1}^{n} s_i = 4n - 6$$

$$\Rightarrow \sum_{i=1}^{n} s_i = 4(f_3 + f_{\geq 4} + 2) - 6$$

$$\Rightarrow \sum_{i=1}^{n} s_i = 4\left(f_3 + f_{\geq 4}\right) + 2$$

$$\Rightarrow \left(\sum_{s_i \geq 4} s_i\right) + 3 \times f_3 + 2 \times 2 = 4\left(f_3 + f_{\geq 4}\right) + 2$$

$$\Rightarrow \left(\sum_{s_i \geq 4} s_i\right) + 3 \times f_3 + 2 - 4f_{\geq 4} = 4f_3$$

$$\Rightarrow \left(\sum_{s_i \geq 4} s_i\right) + 3 \times f_3 + 2 - 4f_{\geq 4} = 4f_3$$

$$\Rightarrow \left(\sum_{s_i \geq 4} s_i\right) - \left(\sum_{s_i \geq 4} 4\right) + 2 = f_3$$

$$\Rightarrow f_3 = \sum_{s_i \geq 4} (s_i - 4) + 2$$

$\square$

Theorem 1. *Let* $S = (s_1, s_2, ..., s_n)$ *be a degree sequence such that there are exactly two 2s and the rest of the elements are larger than 2. Then, we can construct a maximal outerplane graph if and only if the degree sum is* $4n - 6$.

Proof. We know, the total number of edges a maximal outerplanar graph is $2n - 3$ [19] and the degree sum of a maximal outerplanar graph is $4n - 6$. So the necessity is obvious.

For sufficiency, we assume that we are given a sequence $S = (s_1, s_2, \ldots s_n)$. A maximal outerplanar graph with $n \leq 3$ can not have exactly two 2-degree nodes. We thus show the sufficiency for $n \geq 4$. For $n = 4$, if we take the degree sequence following the order of the vertices on the outer cycle, the sequence becomes a cyclic rotation of the sequence $(2, 3, 2, 3)$. To prove the sufficiency, the sequence S should be rearranged to a sequence $S' = (s_1, s_2', \ldots s_n')$ such that S' becomes an ordered maximal outerplanar graphic sequence. From S', we can select an element $s_k' = 2$, apply 2-elimination on it and continue this process until the length of $|S'|$ is 4. If we end up getting a sequence like $(2, 3, 2, 3)$ or any cyclic rotation of it, then the proof is completed.

In S, there is exactly two 2 and at least two 3. We declare two sequences, $S_x = (2, 3)$, $S_y = (2, 3)$ and we remove two 2s and two 3s from S. Now, we remove an element $s_i > 4$ from S and prepend it before the 2 to the sequence S_x. From Lemma 4, it is obvious that, for each $s_i > 4$, S has $(s_i - 4)$ 3s. So, again we remove $(s_i - 4)$ 3s from the sequence S and append them to S_x. So, now $S_x = (s_i, 2, 3, \ldots, 3)$ where there are exactly $(s_i - 3)$ contiguous 3 in S_x. If we continue applying 2-elimination on S_x until the length of S_x is 2, we end up having S_x as $(3, 2)$. But reversing S_x, we get $(2, 3)$. We thus can call S_x as $(2, 3)$ equivalent. In this way, we can remove all the $s_i > 4$ and their corresponding 3s from the sequence S and add them to S_x. After all these operations, we can reduce S_x to $(2, 3)$ by applying 2-elimination. Now S has only some 4s remaining. We can remove one 4 from S and add to S_x such that the sequence becomes equivalents to $(4, 2, 3)$. Now if we apply 2-elimination on the 2, the sequence becomes $(3, 2)$ and reversing this, we get $(2, 3)$ equivalents. In this way, we can remove all the 4s and add them to S_x. Now S is empty. We can assume $S' = S_x S_y$ as the concatenation of S_x and S_y which is equivalent to $(2, 3, 2, 3)$. Thus, the proof is completed. □

4   Generating Scale-Free Outerplanar Graph

A graph is called scale-free if the degrees of the vertices obey the power-law distribution. Thus, the probability of a randomly chosen node having degree k is $p_k = \dfrac{k^{-\gamma}}{\sum_{K=k_{min}}^{\infty} K^{-\gamma}}$ where γ is between 2 and 3. In the previous section, we characterized the degree sequence of maximal outerplanar graph for a special case. The minimum degree of a maximal outerplanar graph is 2. So, setting $k_{min} = 2$, we get

$$p_k = \frac{k^{-\gamma}}{\sum_{K=2}^{\infty} K^{-\gamma}}.$$

Let $\langle k \rangle$ be the expected degree of a randomly chosen node. Then

$$\langle k \rangle = \sum_{k=2}^{\infty} k p_k.$$

We now prove the following theorem.

Theorem 2. *The degree distribution of a maximal outerplanar graph can not strictly fit power-law distribution.*

Proof. For the number of nodes n and expected degree $\langle k \rangle$, the expected degree sum is $n\langle k \rangle$. To satisfy the condition on the degree sum of maximal outerplanar graph, solving the equation $n\langle k \rangle = 4n - 6$ yields to $\gamma = 2.65$ where n is sufficiently large. Using the γ value, we can obtain $p_2 = 0.551n$ which indicates that a maximal outerplanar graph should have 55% 2-degree nodes. As it is very obvious, a maximal outerplanar graph can not have 2-degree nodes more than 50%, we can conclude that a maximal outerplanar graph can not fit power-law. □

Theorem 2 implies that it is unlikely to have a scale-free maximal outerplanar graph with strict power-law degree distribution. In the rest of this section, we show an approach to generate a outerplanar graph that strictly follows power-law. Our main idea is as follows. We first generate a list of degrees following the power-law for $\gamma = 2.878$. Assume that the list contains x number of 2s. We replace $(x - 2)$ number of 2s by 3s. We then adjust the degree of some nodes to make the degree sum exactly $4n - 6$ and a maximal outerplanar graph is constructed using the given degree sequence. From the constructed maximal outerplanar graph, we remove edges between adjacent 3-degree nodes to make those 2-degree nodes. We finally remove $\dfrac{(x - 2)}{2}$ edges so that the number of 2-degree nodes remains the same as before. The detailed algorithm and the supporting proofs are given below.

We can generate a sequence S of length n that follows power-law with an arbitrary γ value and assuming $k_{min} = 2$. Let the number of occurrences of 2s in the sequence S be f_2. Now, we select $(f_2 - 2)$ 2s and turn them into 3s to get a new sequence S', then the sequence S' is maximal outerplanar graphic if and only if the sum of the elements of S' is $4n - 6$. For S' being maximal outerplanar graphic sequence, the following condition should hold,

$$\langle k \rangle n + (p_2 n - 2) = 4n - 6$$

$$\Rightarrow \left(\sum_{k=2}^{\infty} \left(\frac{k^{-\gamma}}{\sum_{K=2}^{\infty} K^{-\gamma}} \right) k \right) n + \left(\left(\frac{2^{-\gamma}}{\sum_{K=2}^{\infty} K^{-\gamma}} \right) n - 2 \right) = 4n - 6$$

Solving the equation, we obtain $\gamma = 2.878$. So, we found a γ value that should be used while generating the sequence S following power-law degree distribution. The expected sum of all elements of the sequence S' should be $4n - 6$. But to construct an maximal outerplanar graph, we can adjust some large degree nodes so that the degree sum becomes exactly $4n - 6$. The sequence S' is a maximal outerplanar graphic sequence but it does not obey the power-law degree distribution. To prepare our constructed graph as scale-free, we should revert some 3-degree nodes into 2-degree. For obtaining the sequence S', almost $(p_2 n - 2)$ 2-degree nodes were converted to 3-degree. Removal of single incident edge from each pair of $(p_2 n - 2)$ 3-degree nodes result in the graph being scale-free. Now the question is whether it is possible to remove those edges from the constructed graph while preserving the outerplanar graphical property. A single edge can be removed between two adjacent 3-degree nodes to turn them into two 2-degree nodes. From the proof of Theorem 1, it is realizable that for every node having degree, $d \geq 5$, there are $(d - 4)$ contiguous 3-degree nodes on the outer cycle. If $(d - 4)$ is even, all those nodes can be turned into 2-degree nodes. On the contrary, for odd $(d - 4)$, one 3-degree node can be left unchanged. Here, the expected number of nodes having degree greater or equal to 5 is $\left(\sum_{k=5}^{\infty} \left(\frac{k^{-2.878}}{\sum_{K=2}^{\infty} K^{-2.878}} \right) k \right) n = 0.136n$ and expected number of 3-degree nodes $= 0.1856n$. We can turn enough 3-degree nodes into 2-degree and leave approximately $0.1856n$ nodes unchanged. The resulting graph should follow power-law and a scale-free outerplanar graph can be constructed.

For example, we assume that we have generated a sequence (2, 2, 2, 2, 2, 2, 2, 2, 2, 2, 2, 2, 2, 2, 3, 3, 3, 3, 4, 4, 5, 6, 9, 10) following the distribution $p_k = k^{-2.878}$. After turning 12 2s into 3s, the sequence is (2, 2, 3, 3, 3, 3, 3, 3, 3, 3, 3, 3, 3, 3, 3, 3, 3, 4, 4, 5, 6, 9, 10). Now, there are 24 elements in the sequence and their sum is $4 \times 24 - 6 = 90$. Therefore, we can construct a maximal outerplanar graph as shown in Fig. 1a. Now we remove 6 edges between adjacent 3-degree nodes to turn 12 3-degree nodes into 2-degree nodes. The resulting outerplanar graph shown in Fig. 1b should follow the power-law degree distribution.

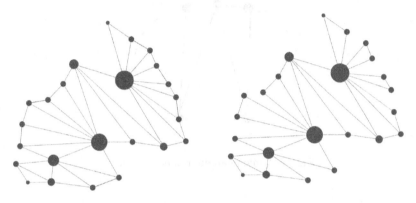

(a) A maximal outerplanar graph

(b) A scale-free outerplanar graph constructed from the graph in (a)

Fig. 1. Illustration for a scale-free outerplanar graph.

We call the algorithm described above *Algorithm Generate_Outerplanar*. We now have the following theorem.

Theorem 3. *Algorithm Generate_Outerplanar constructs a scale-free outerplanar graph in $O(n)$ time.*

Proof. We can generate a sequence of n integers following the distribution $p_k \sim k^{-2.878}$ in $O(n)$ time. We can turn necessary 2s into 3s in $O(n)$ time. The proof of Theorem 1 was the construction of ordered maximal outerplanar graphic sequence in $O(n)$ time. Lemma 1 helps us to construct maximal outerplanar graph from an order maximal outerplanar graphic sequence. Finally, the deletion of edges between consecutive 3-degree nodes to turn them into 2 degree nodes also takes $O(n)$ time. Therefore, the Algorithm Generate_Outerplanar takes $O(n)$ time to construct the graph.   □

We now present some observations on clustering coefficient and the diameters on graphs generated by our algorithm. The local clustering coefficient of a node refers to the probability that two of its neighbors are connected with an edge. We define C_k as the local clustering coefficient of a node having degree k. For a 2-degree node, $C_2 = 1$ otherwise the graph can not be maximal. A 3-degree node is connected with other three nodes and two of these should be connected with the third one otherwise the graph will not be maximal. Again, while removing edges, we only removed edges from the outer cycle between adjacent 3-degree nodes. But the neighbors of a 3-degree node can not be adjacent on the outer cycle for $n > 4$, which leads to $C_3 = \frac{2}{3}$. Before giving an observation on local clustering coefficient, we need the following lemma.

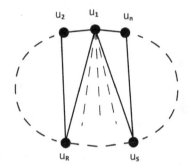

Fig. 2. A maximal outerplanar graph

Lemma 5. *Let G be a maximal outerplanar graph having exactly two 2-degree nodes. Then for any node u_1 with degree d_{u_1} four or more, $d_{u_2} - 2$ neighbors of u_1 are consecutive on the outer cycle and $d_{u_1} - 4$ consecutive neighbors have degree 3.*

Proof. We assume Fig. 2 as a maximal outerplanar graph with exactly two 2s where u_1 is a node having degree 4 or greater and $u_1, u_2, ..., u_R, ..., u_S, ...u_n$ are the nodes on the outer cycle taking in anti-clockwise order. We also assume that no node between $u_3, ..., u_{R-1}$ and $u_{S+1}, ..., u_{n-1}$ are adjacent to u_1. An induced subgraph of the nodes $u_1, u_2, ..., u_R$ is also a maximal outerplanar graph. So, among the nodes $u_2, u_3, ..., u_{R-1}$ there must be a 2-degree node. In the same manner, we can prove that there is a 2-degree node among $u_{S+1}, u_{S+2}, ..., u_n$. Here, all nodes between $u_R, ..., u_S$ should be adjacent to node u_1, otherwise a new 2-degree node will be introduced among $u_R, ...u_S$. From Fig. 2, it can be easily observed that all the nodes between $u_{R+1}, ..., u_{S-1}$ have degree 3. Thus, our claim is proved.   □

In Fig. 2, there exists a path $(u_2, u_R, u_{R+1}...u_{S-1}, u_S, u_n)$ containing the adjacent nodes of u_1. In generation of scale-free outerplanar network, we had to turn approximately $\left(\dfrac{2^{-2.878}}{2^{-2.878} + 3^{-2.878}} \times 100 \right) \% = 76.2\%$ 3-degree nodes into 2-degree from the constructed maximal outerplanar graph. From Lemma 5, we know that there are $(d_{u_1} - 5)$ edges in the path $(u_{R+1}, u_{R+2}, ..., u_S)$. If we assume the deletion of the edges from adjacent pair of 3-degree nodes is uniform, then from the path $(u_{R+1}, u_{R+2}, ..., u_S)$, approximately $0.381 \times (d_{u_1} - 5)$ links need to be removed. Thus, the clustering coefficient of any node having degree $k \geq 4$, $C_k \approx \frac{(k-1)-0.381\times(k-5)}{k(k-1)} \times 2 = \frac{1.238\times(k+1.46)}{k(k-1)}$. For large k, it behaves like, $C_k \sim \frac{1}{k}$. Thus, the local clustering coefficient in our generated networks is independent of the network size rather than dependent upon the degree of the node.

Cohen and Havlin [5] showed that any scale-free network following power-law with $2 < \gamma < 3$ has a very small diameter, behaving as $d \sim ln(n)$. We run two simulations taking the number of elements n as 10^4 and 10^6. We generate n number of integer numbers following the probability distribution $p_k \sim k^{-2.878}$. Then we generate scale-free outerplanar network following the algorithm we provided. A log-log plot of the degree distribution is shown in Fig. 3. Thus our generated networks also support the claim of Cohen and Havlin [5].

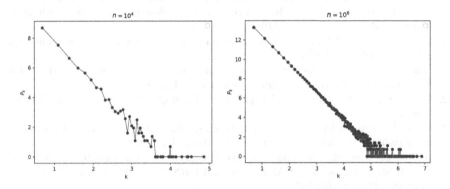

Fig. 3. log-log plot of the degree distribution based on our experiment

5   Conclusion

In this paper, we have characterized the degree sequence of maximal outerplanar graph for a special case that led us to generate a scale-free outerplanar network. Further research direction includes providing generative algorithms for some other special classes of graphs. In the generative model we developed, the network size is variable but the γ value is fixed. In future work, we may provide more flexibility so that γ, clustering coefficient, diameter, etc. become adjustable. Besides, we also aim to generate planar graphs with various target distributions, and we can also consider the case in which the nodes are actually fixed points on a 2D plane.

References

1. Barabási, A.L., Albert, R.: Emergence of scaling in random networks. Science **286**(5439), 509–512 (1999)

2. Bíyíkoglu, T.: Degree sequences of halin graphs, and forcibly cograph-graphic sequences. Ars Comb. **75** (2005)
3. Bose, P., et al.: A characterization of the degree sequences of 2-trees. J. Graph Theory **58**, 191–209 (2008). https://doi.org/10.1002/jgt.20302
4. Brandstädt, A., Le, V.B., Spinrad, J.P.: Graph Classes: A Survey. Society for Industrial and Applied Mathematics (1999). https://doi.org/10.1137/1.9780898719796, https://epubs.siam.org/doi/abs/10.1137/1.9780898719796
5. Cohen, R., Havlin, S.: Scale-free networks are ultrasmall. Phys. Rev. Lett. **90**, 058701 (2003). https://doi.org/10.1103/PhysRevLett.90.058701
6. Comellas, F., Miralles, A.: Modeling complex networks with self-similar outerplanar unclustered graphs. Phys. A. Stat. Mech. Appl. **388**(11), 2227–2233 (2009). https://doi.org/10.1016/j.physa.2009.02.004, https://www.sciencedirect.com/science/article/pii/S0378437109001149
7. Davidsen, J., Ebel, H., Bornholdt, S.: Emergence of a small world from local interactions: modeling acquaintance networks. Phys. Rev. Lett. **88**, 128701 (2002). https://doi.org/10.1103/PhysRevLett.88.128701
8. Erdös, P., Rényi, A.: On random graphs i. Publ. Math. Debrecen **6**, 290 (1959)
9. Erdos, P., Rényi, A., et al.: On the evolution of random graphs. Publ. Math. Inst. Hung. Acad. Sci. **5**(1), 17–60 (1960)
10. Erdős, P., Gallai, T.: Gráfok előírt fokszámú pontokkal. https://www.renyi.hu/~p_erdos/1961-05.pdf (1960)
11. Hakimi, S.L.: On realizability of a set of integers as degrees of the vertices of a linear Graph. I. J. Soc. Ind. Appl. Math. **10**(3), 496–506 (1962)
12. Hammer, P.L., Simeone, B.: The splittance of a graph. Combinatorica **1**, 275–284 (1981)
13. Havel, V.: Poznámka o existenci konečných grafů. Časopis pro pěstování matematiky **080**(4), 477–480 (1955). http://eudml.org/doc/19050
14. Holme, P., Kim, B.: Growing scale-free networks with tunable clustering. Phys. Rev. E Stat. Nonlinear soft Matter Phys. **65**, 026107 (2002). https://doi.org/10.1103/PhysRevE.65.026107
15. KÜGERL, M.: Degree sequences of triangulations of convex point sets. Master's thesis, Graz University of Technology (2010)
16. Merris, R.: Split graphs. Eur. J. Comb. **24**(4), 413–430 (2003)
17. Rahman, M.S.: Basic Graph Theory, 1st edn. Springer, Cham (2017). https://doi.org/10.1007/978-3-319-49475-3
18. Schmeichel, E., Hakimi, S.: On planar graphical degree sequences. SIAM J. Appl. Math. **32**(3), 598–609 (1977)
19. Syslo, M.: Characterizations of outerplanar graphs. Discrete Math. **26**, 47–53 (1979). https://doi.org/10.1016/0012-365X(79)90060-8
20. Vazquez, A.: Growing network with local rules: preferential attachment, clustering hierarchy, and degree correlations. Phys. Rev. E Stat. Nonlinear Soft Matter Phys. **67**, 056104 (2003). https://doi.org/10.1103/PhysRevE.67.056104
21. Watts, D.J., Strogatz, S.H.: Collective dynamics of 'small-world' networks. Nature **393**(6684), 440–442 (1998)
22. Wiegreffe, D., Alexander, D., Stadler, P.F., Zeckzer, D.: RNApuzzler: efficient outerplanar drawing of RNA-secondary structures. Bioinformatics **35**(8), 1342–1349 (2018). https://doi.org/10.1093/bioinformatics/bty817, https://doi.org/10.1093/bioinformatics/bty817

Hamiltonian Properties of the Dragonfly Network

Suying Wu, Baolei Cheng, Yan Wang, Yuejuan Han,
and Jianxi Fan(✉)

School of Computer Science and Technology, Soochow University, Suzhou, China
20205227094@stu.suda.edu.cn,
{chengbaolei,wangyanme,hyj,jxfan}@suda.edu.cn

Abstract. The dragonfly network is a hierarchical network with a low diameter and high throughput, which uses a set of high-cardinality routers to increase the effective cardinality of the network. The Hamiltonian property is instrumental in communication networks. In this paper, we study the Hamiltonian properties of the logical graph of the dragonfly network, denoted by $D(n, h, g)$, where n, h, and g represent the number of vertices in each group, the number of edges that each vertex connects to other groups, and the number of groups, respectively. Firstly, we show that there exists a Hamiltonian cycle and propose an $O(g)$ algorithm for constructing a Hamiltonian cycle in $D(n, h, g)$ when $n \geq 2$ and $h \geq 1$. Then, we prove that $D(n, h, g)$ is Hamiltonian-connected for $n \geq 4$ and $h \geq 2$.

Keywords: Dragonfly network · Interconnection network ·
Hamiltonian cycle · Hamiltonian-connected

1 Introduction

The rapid development of modern intelligent technologies such as 5G and super-computing has generated massive communication data, which has exceeded the scalability of traditional computers and architectures. High Performance Computing (HPC) systems play a significant role in computing power because of the high data tolerance and high computing speed. As a consequence, the interconnection network, as the core component of HPC systems, affects the overall performance of communication network in essence.

The dragonfly network introduced by Kim et al. [16] is an important interconnection network. The dragonfly network is hierarchical, with local links forming groups and global links joining the groups. It has many desirable properties, such as a small diameter and high scalability. The network design cost of dragonfly network is much lower than other network architectures such as flattened butterfly and folded Clos networks [28]. Furthermore, the dragonfly network provides rich path diversity by using high-cardinality routers, increasing the overall bandwidth of the network. These properties manifest that the dragonfly network has good communication performances and it has already been applied in production for some supercomputer manufacturers such as Cray Cascade architecture [5].

© The Author(s), under exclusive license to Springer Nature Singapore Pte Ltd. 2022
S.-Y. Hsieh et al. (Eds.): ICS 2022, CCIS 1723, pp. 167–179, 2022.
https://doi.org/10.1007/978-981-19-9582-8_15

1.1 Research on Dragonfly Networks

There were a lot of research results on the dragonfly network. In terms of the inter-group links (called global link arrangements), Salamah et al. [22] integrated per-router arrangement into existing schemes, and developed a large class of global link arrangements for practical dragonfly networks. The other aspect that gets a lot of attention is routing. It is mainly studied from fault-tolerant, deadlock-free, adaptive, traffic pattern and so on. Wu et al. [23] proposed a disjoint routing algorithm in dragonfly networks. Xiang and Liu [27] studied the deadlock-free broadcast routing algorithm in dragonfly networks. And successively, Xiang et al. [28] improved preceding algorithm and proposed a new deadlock-free adaptive fault-tolerant routing algorithm in dragonfly networks. In general, most of the existing routing algorithms use Virtual Channels (VCs) to prevent cycle dependencies. Maglione-Mathey et al. [19] overcame this limitation and presented a minimal-path routing for dragonfly networks that prevented deadlocks.

1.2 Research on Hamiltonian Property

Hamiltonian paths and Hamiltonian cycles can be used to solve the problem of deadlock and congestion in network communication. Lin and Ni [17] tackled the deadlock problem of dual-path and multi-path multi-cast based on Hamilton paths. Bahrebar and Stroobandt [1] presented a deadlock-free and highly adaptive minimal routing algorithm by using the Hamiltonian path. Fujita and Araki [10] improved the efficiency of the diagnostic algorithm by using the Hamiltonian cycle in binary n-cubes to complete the diagnosis in at most 3 test rounds. Then, a more general five-round adaptive diagnosis scheme for networks containing Hamiltonian cycle was proposed in [30]. Du et al. [4] put forward an efficient diagnosis algorithm based on Hamiltonian cycle to save system resources.

It is well-known that the problem of finding a Hamiltonian path or Hamiltonian cycle is NP-complete [11]. Thus, many works on Hamiltonian properties were conducted in specific networks. Fan [6] presented that the n-dimensional Möbius cube M_n is Hamiltonian-connected for $n \geq 3$. Wang et al. [24] proved that a k-level DCell built with n-port switches is Hamiltonian-connected for $k \geq 0$ and $n \geq 2$ aside from $(k, n) = (1, 2)$. A systematic method to construct a Hamiltonian path in honeycomb meshes was provided by Xu et al. [29]. Wang and Zhang [25] studied the problem of matchings extend to Hamiltonian cycles in k-ary n-cube. Moreover, fault-tolerant hamiltonicities of various networks were also studied [3,12,13,15]. Inspired by Hamiltonian cycles and Hamiltonian paths in networks, it is natural to investigate the existence of cycles and paths of various lengths in them. Such works can be referred to [2,7–9,18].

1.3 Organization of the Paper

This paper is organized as follows. Section 2 provides some basic terminologies and notations that will be used in this paper, and gives the definition and some properties of $D(n, h, g)$. In Sect. 3, firstly, we prove that there exists a Hamiltonian cycle in $D(n, h, g)$ and propose an algorithm for constructing a Hamiltonian cycle. Then, the problem about Hamiltonian connectivity of $D(n, h, g)$ is discussed in the remainder. Section 4 concludes this paper.

2   Preliminaries

This section first introduces some basic concepts of graph theory and symbolic representations used in this paper, and then introduces the logical structure of the dragonfly network.

2.1   Terminology and Notation

An interconnected network is usually represented as an undirected graph $G = (V(G), E(G))$, where $V(G)$ represents a set of vertices and $E(G)$ represents a set of edges. Each vertex $u \in V$ represents a processer, server or router etc., and a link between them is an edge $(u, v) \in E$ in the graph G. A graph G is called a simple graph when at most one edge exists between any two vertices and there is no loop in each vertex. A complete graph, denoted as K_n, is a graph in which every pair of different vertices is connected by exactly one edge. All graphs in this paper are simple and undirected graphs. Two simple graphs G and H are isomorphic, if there exists a bijection $\theta : V(G) \rightarrow V(H)$ such that $(u, v) \in E(G)$ if and only if $(\theta(u), \theta(v)) \in E(H)$, denoted by $G \cong H$. The set of vertices that are adjacent to vertex v is called the neighbors of v, denoted by $N_G(v)$, i.e., $N_G(v) = \{u \mid (u, v) \in E(G)\}$.

We call H to be a subgraph of G, denoted as $H \subseteq G$, if $V(H) \subseteq V(G)$ and $E(H) \subseteq E(G)$. If V' is a nonempty proper subset of V, then $G - V'$ is the subgraph obtained from G by deleting the vertices in V' together with their incident edges. If $V' = \{v\}$, $G - v$ is used to represent $G - \{v\}$. For any two distinct graphs G_1 and G_2, the union graph of G_1 and G_2, denoted by $G_1 \cup G_2$, is a new graph, with vertex set $V(G_1) \cup V(G_2)$ and edge set $E(G_1) \cup E(G_2)$. Similarly, the intersection graph of G_1 and G_2, is denoted by $G_1 \cap G_2$. Let S_1, S_2 denote two sets, the subtraction of them is denoted by $S_1 - S_2$. Especially, if $S_2 = \{x\}$, it can be denoted by $S_1 - x$ shortly.

We use a sequence of vertices $P = \langle u_0, u_1, ..., u_n \rangle$ to represent a path P where $u_i \in V(G)$ with $0 \leq i \leq n$ and $n \geq 1$. All vertices in P are distinct except u_0 and u_n, and we call u_0 and u_n the end-vertices of path P. For the sake of simplicity, we use (u_0, u_n)-path to represent a path P. Path can also be expressed as $P = \langle (u_0, u_1), (u_1, u_2), ..., (u_{n-1}, u_n) \rangle$, because there is an edge between two vertices u_i and u_{i+1} in the path P, where $i \in \{0, 1, ..., n-1\}$. We use $V(P)$ and $E(P)$ to denote the vertex set and edge set of P, respectively. Specially, a cycle C is a closed path, that is $C = \langle (u_0, u_1), (u_1, u_2), ..., (u_{n-1}, u_n) \rangle$ where $u_0 = u_n$. In addition, if $Q = \langle (u_0, u_1), (u_1, u_2), ..., (u_{n-1}, u_n), (u_n, u_{n+1}) \rangle$ is a path, we use $P + (u_n, u_{n+1})$ to express the path Q, where $(u_n, u_{n+1}) \in E(G)$ and $u_{n+1} \in V(G)$. Let H be a cycle, $u, v \in V(H)$ and $(u, v) \in E(H)$. Then, we use $H - (u, v)$

to represent the path R, where $V(R) = V(H)$ and $E(R) = E(H) - (u,v)$. That is, R is a (u,v)-path. If paths P_α and P_β satisfy $V(P_\alpha) \cap V(P_\beta) = \{v\}$, where v is the end-vertex of both P_α and P_β, then we define $P_\alpha + P_\beta$ to be the path with edge set $E(P_\alpha) \cup E(P_\beta)$ and vertex set $V(P_\alpha) \cup V(P_\beta)$.

In graph G, a path (cycle) including every vertex of G is called a Hamiltonian path (cycle). G is Hamiltonian if there exists a Hamiltonian cycle in G, and G is Hamiltonian-connected if there exists a Hamiltonian path between any two distinct vertices in G. If a (u,v)-path is a Hamiltonian path, then we use (u,v)-Hamiltonian path to represent it.

2.2   Logical Structure of the Dragonfly Network

The dragonfly network is a hierarchical network. It divides routers into g groups, each with an equal number of n routers while they are all connected to each other, and each router is connected to p terminals. Groups are connected through global links, and routers in a group are connected through local links. The basic topology structure (logical graph) of the dragonfly network can actually be represented by a graph $G = (V(G), E(G))$. $V(G)$ is the set of all routers in G and $E(G)$ is the set of all edges in G, that is, each element in $V(G)$ represents a vertex and each element in $E(G)$ represents a edge between two vertices in G. In the following, we give the definition of the logical structure of the dragonfly network, denoted as $DF(n, h, g)$. In fact, we can view $DF(n, h, g)$ as a compound graph [20] of g complete graphs.

Definition 1. *[23] For any integers n, h, and g with $n \geq 1$, $g \geq 1$, and $0 \leq h \leq g - 1$, the dragonfly network $DF(n, h, g)$ is a connected $(n - 1 + h)$-regular graph G that satisfies the following conditions:*

- *$V(G) = V(G_0) \cup V(G_1) \cup \cdots \cup V(G_{g-1})$, where $G_i \cong K_n$ with $V(G_i) = \{(i,k) \mid k \in \{0, 1, \ldots, n-1\}\}$ is the i-th group of $G = DF(n, h, g)$ and (i,k) represents router k in G_i with $V(G_i) \cap V(G_j) = \emptyset$, for any distinct integers i and j with $0 \leq i, j \leq g - 1$.*
- *For any vertex $(i, j) \in V(G)$ with $0 \leq i \leq g - 1$ and $0 \leq j \leq n - 1$, there are h vertices $(x_1, y_1), (x_2, y_2), \cdots, (x_h, y_h)$ with $|\{x_1, x_2, \cdots, x_h\}| = h$, such that $((i, j), (x_k, y_k)) \in E(G)$, with $\{x_1, x_2, \ldots, x_h\} \subseteq \{0, 1, \ldots, g - 1\} - \{i\}$ and $k \in \{1, 2, \ldots, h\}$.*

Next we give a formal definition of the dragonfly network, denoted by $D(n, h, g)$, with some conditions [23] in Definition 2. Figure 1 shows some simple examples. And the rest of the research is based on Definition 2.

Definition 2. *[23] For any integer n, h, and g with $n \geq 2$, $h \geq 1$, and $g = nh + 1$, $D(n, h, g)$ is defined as follows:*

- *$D(n, h, g) = (V, E)$, where the vertex set V is represented as $\{(x, y) \mid x \in \{0, 1, \ldots, g-1\}, y \in \{0, 1, \ldots, n-1\}\}$, and (x, y) represents router y in group x.*

– *For any two vertices $u = (x_1, y_1)$ and $v = (x_2, y_2) \in V, (u, v) \in E$ if and only if both of the following conditions are satisfied:*

- $y_2 = n - 1 - y_1$;
- $x_2 = (hy_1 + x_1 + k) \bmod g$ *for* $k = 1, 2, \ldots, h$.

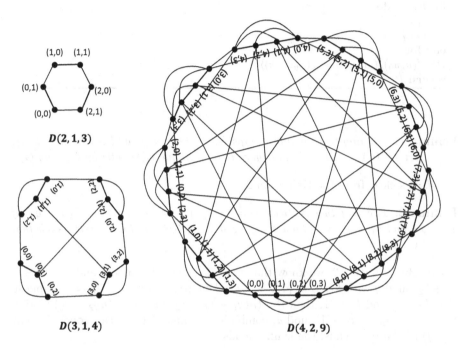

Fig. 1. $D(2, 1, 3)$, $D(3, 1, 4)$, and $D(4, 2, 9)$.

3   Hamiltonian Property of $D(n, h, g)$

In this section, we will first discuss the existence of the Hamiltonian cycle of $D(n, h, g)$ in Theorem 1 and give an algorithm with time complexity of $O(g)$ to find a Hamiltonian cycle in $D(n, h, g)$ when $n \geq 2$ and $h \geq 1$. Then, on the basis of the previous conclusion about the Hamiltonian cycle in $D(n, h, g)$, we prove that $D(n, h, g)$ is Hamiltonian-connected when $n \geq 4$ and $h \geq 2$.

Now we give some notations which will be used in this section and make no distinction between G and $D(n, h, g)$. Let I_g denote the set of ordinal numbers of groups, i.e., $I_g = \{i \mid i = 0, 1, \ldots, g - 1\}$. $D(n, h, g)$ contains g groups, and each group is a complete graph. Let $G_i \cong K_n$ denote a group with ordinal number i where $i \in I_g$, and a vertex $u = (x, y)$ means u are in group G_x. If $k \in \{1, 2, \ldots, h\}$ and $i = (hy + x + k) \bmod g$, then we call group i as an *external-group* of u, denoted by $EG(u^k)$. The set of all *external-groups* of u is denoted by GH_u, i.e., $GH_u = \{EG(u^k) \mid k = 1, 2, \ldots, h\}$.

Algorithm GHP $(D(n, h, g), G_i, u, v)$

Input: The dragonfly network, $D(n, h, g)$, two distinct vertices $u = (x, y_1)$ and $v = (x, y_2)$ in the same group G_i

Output: A (u, v)-Hamiltonian path in group G_i

$\quad I_r = \{0, 1, \cdots, n - 1\} - \{y_1, y_2\}$ and $j = 0$

$\quad$ **for** $k \in I_r$ **do**

$\quad\quad u_j = (x, k)$

$\quad\quad j = j + 1$

$\quad$ **end for**

$\quad P = \langle (u, u_0), (u_0, u_1), \cdots, (u_{n-3}, v) \rangle$

$\quad$ **return** P

Lemma 1. *For any two distinct groups G_μ in $D(n, h, g)$ and G_ν in $D(n, h, g)$, where $\mu, \nu \in \{0, 1, \ldots, g - 1\}$ and there is one unique edge between G_μ and G_ν.*

Proof. It's clear from the Definition 2.

Lemma 2. *For any two vertices $u = (x_1, y_1)$, $v = (x_2, y_2)$ in $D(n, h, g)$, if $x_1 = x_2$ and $y_1 - y_2 = 1$, then there exist $G_i \in GH_u$ and $G_j \in GH_v$ such that $(i - j) \bmod g = 1$.*

Proof. By Definition 2, we know that $i = (hy_1 + x_1 + k_1) \bmod g$ and $j = (hy_2 + x_2 + k_2) \bmod g$ with $k_1, k_2 = \{1, 2, \ldots, h\}$. Due to $x_1 = x_2$, $y_1 - y_2 = 1$, suppose that $k_1 = h$ and $k_2 = 1$, then $i = (h(y_1 + 1) + x_2) \bmod g = (hy_2 + x_2) \bmod g$. Since $j = (hy_2 + x_2 + 1) \bmod g$, combining Lemma 3.1, we can conclude that $(i - j) \bmod g = 1$. Thus, the lemma holds.

3.1 Hamiltonian Cycle of $D(n, h, g)$

In this section, we propose an algorithm *DFCycle* for constructing a Hamiltonian cycle in $D(n, h, g)$. Previously, a basic algorithm *GHP* which generates a (u, v)-Hamiltonian path in each group where u and v are any two distinct vertices of the group will be given for the main algorithm to be proposed. Algorithm *GHP* mainly makes use of the property that the complete graph is Hamiltonian connected, and finds the Hamiltonian path within a group by iterating through all vertices in the group. On this basis, algorithm *DFCycle* can obtain a Hamiltonian cycle by connecting the external-connected edge and the Hamiltonian path within each group.

Theorem 1. *For any integer n and h with $n \geq 2$ and $h \geq 1$, algorithm DFCycle can construct a Hamiltonian cycle in $D(n, h, g)$ with the $O(g)$ time complexity.*

Algorithm $DFCycle(D(n, h, g), u)$

Require: The dragonfly network, $D(n, h, g)$, a vertex $u = (x, y) \in G_i$ where G_i is a group in $D(n, h, g)$

Ensure: A Hamiltonian cycle in $(D(n, h, g))$

$\quad P = \langle \, \rangle$ and $j = 0$

$\quad$ **function** $DFCP(x, u, y, P)$

$\quad\quad$ **if** $y = 0$ **then**

$\quad\quad\quad x_i = (x + 1) \bmod g$

$\quad\quad\quad u_i = (x_i, n - 1)$ and $v_i = (x_i, 0)$

$\quad\quad$ **else if** $y = n - 1$ **then**

$\quad\quad\quad x_i = (x + h) \bmod g$

$\quad\quad\quad u_i = (x_i, 0)$ and $v_i = (x_i, n - 1)$

$\quad\quad$ **end if**

$\quad\quad P = P + (u, u_i) + GHP(D(n, h, g), G_i, u_i, v_i).$

$\quad\quad u = v_i$ and $x = x_i$

$\quad$ **end function**

$\quad$ **if** $y \neq 0$ and $y \neq n - 1$ **then**

$\quad\quad v = (x, n - 1)$ and $w = (x, 0)$

$\quad\quad P = GHP(D(n, h, g), G_i - v, u, w)$

$\quad\quad$ **while** $j < g - 1$ **do**

$\quad\quad\quad DFC(x, w, 0, P)$

$\quad\quad\quad j = j + 1$

$\quad\quad$ **end while**

$\quad\quad H = P + (u, v) + (v, (x, y))$

$\quad$ **else**

$\quad\quad$ **while** $j < g$ **do**

$\quad\quad\quad DFCP(x, u, y, P)$

$\quad\quad\quad j = j + 1$

$\quad\quad$ **end while**

$\quad\quad H = P$

$\quad$ **end if**

$\quad$ **return** H

Proof. Firstly, we prove the correctness of algorithm *DFCycle*. By Definition 2, we know for any integer $i \in I_g - \{g - 1\}$, if vertex $u = (i, 0) \in V(G_i)$, then there exists a vertex $v = (j, n - 1) \in G_j$ such that $i + 1 = j$ and $(u, v) \in E(D(n, h, g))$. Furthermore, if $i = g - 1$, we have $(h * 0 + g - 1 + k) \bmod g = 0$ when $k = 1$. Thus, $((g - 1, 0), (0, n - 1)) \in E(D(n, h, g))$. By Diestel [21], we know that complete graphs are Hamiltonian-connected. Therefore, there is a Hamiltonian path P_i in G_i for any $i \in I_g$. Let $I_m = \{((i, 0), (i, n - 1)) \mid i \in I_g\}$ and $P_m = \{P_i \mid i \in I_g\}$. Apparently, $I_m \cup P_m$ is a Hamiltonian cycle in $D(n, h, g)$. Hence, algorithm *DFCycle* can construct a Hamiltonian cycle in $D(n, h, g)$ for any integer n with $n \geq 2, h \geq 1$.

Then, we discuss the time complexity of algorithm *DFCycle*. For algorithm *GHP*, it includes a loop statement with $O(n)$ time complexity. As for algorithm *DFCycle*, it mainly contains a while loop with the $O(g)$ time complexity and calls the algorithm GHP with $O(n)$ time complexity. Therefore, the time complexity of algorithm $DFCycle$ is $O(g) + O(n) = O(g)$.

Hence, the theorem holds.

3.2 Hamiltonian Connectivity of $D(n, h, g)$

The Hamiltonian path problem is one of the most important problems in graph theory. Despite this fact, as we know there is no result on this problem for $D(n, h, g)$. In the following, we prove that $D(n, h, g)$ is Hamiltonian-connected when $n \geq 4$ and $h \geq 2$ on the basis of the previous conclusion about the Hamiltonian cycle. The main result is Theorem 2 and we will prove it by using a constructive method.

Theorem 2. *For any integers n and h with $n \geq 4$ and $h \geq 2$, $D(n, h, g)$ is Hamiltonian-connected.*

Proof. What we need to prove is that there exists a Hamiltonian path between any pair of distinct vertices u, v in $D(n, h, g)$. By Theorem 1, we know there exists a Hamiltonian cycle in $D(n, h, g)$. Then, in virtue of algorithm $DFCycle$, we will construct a Hamiltonian path between any two distinct vertices in $D(n, h, g)$. We consider the following two cases: either $u = (x_1, y_1)$ and $v = (x_2, y_2)$ are in the same group of $D(n, h, g)$, or else they are in distinct groups of $D(n, h, g)$.

Case 1. u and v are in the same group G_i. Because u and v are in the same group, we note $x_1 = x_2 = x$. Let $I_r = \{1, 2, \cdots, n-2\}$ and $S = \{(x, i) \mid i \in I_r\}$. We call vertices $(x, 0)$ and $(x, n-1)$ *end-vertices*. Obviously, all vertices in S are not *end-vertices*. Next, based on the classification of vertices u and v, we discuss the following three subcases.

Subcase 1.1. Either u or v is *end-vertices*. Without loss of generality, we assume that v is an *end-vertex*. Then, there are two subcases to consider.

Subcase 1.1.1. $v = (x_1, n-1)$. In this case, $u \in S$, let $t = (x_1, 0)$, then we can get a (u, t)-Hamiltonian path in $G_i - \{v\}$, denoted by P_i. By algorithm $DFCycle$, we can obtain a Hamiltonian cycle H in $D(n, h, g)$. Let $H_1 = H - \{S\}$, then, $H_1 + P_i$ is a (u, v)-Hamiltonian path in $D(n, h, g)$ what we required.

Subcase 1.1.2. $v = (x_1, 0)$. This case is similar to subcase 1.1.1, so the proof can be omitted.

Subcase 1.2. Neither u or v are *end-vertices*. For $n \geq 4$, each group has at least four vertices, so there exist two vertices $u_0 = (x, 0)$ and $u_{n-1} = (x, n-1)$ in G_i. We can get a (v, u_{n-1})-Hamiltonian path in $G_i - \{u, u_0\}$, denoted by P_i. By algorithm $DFCycle$, we can obtain a Hamiltonian cycle H in $D(n, h, g)$. Let $H_1 = H - \{S\}$, then, $(u, u_0) + H_1 + P_i$ is a (u, v)-Hamiltonian path in $D(n, h, g)$ what we required.

Subcase 1.3. Both u and v are *end-vertices*. Without loss of generality, we assume that $u = (x, 0)$ and $v = (x, n - 1)$. For $n \geq 4$, there are at least two vertices $u_i = (x, y_1)$ and $u_j = (x, y_2)$ in group G_i that are different from u and v with $y_1 - y_2 = 1$. Then we can get a (u_i, u_j)-Hamiltonian path in $G_i - \{u, v\}$, denoted by P_i. By Lemma 3.2, there are two distinct groups $G_\alpha \in GH_{u_i}$ and $G_\beta \in GH_{u_j}$ with $\alpha - \beta = 1$. Therefore, there are $u_\alpha \in G_\alpha$ and $u_\beta \in G_\beta$ such that $(u_i, u_\alpha), (u_j, u_\beta) \in E(D(n, h, g))$. Let $x_\alpha = (\alpha, 0), y_\beta = (\beta, n - 1), S_1 = V(G_\alpha) - \{x_\alpha\}$, and $S_2 = V(G_\beta) - \{y_\beta\}$. There is a (x_α, u_α)-Hamiltonian path in G_α, denoted by P_α and a (u_β, y_β)-Hamiltonian path in G_β, denoted by P_β. By algorithm *DFCycle*, we can obtain a Hamiltonian cycle H in $D(n, h, g)$. Let $H_1 = H - \{S, S_1, S_2\}$, then, $H_1 + P_\alpha + (u_i, u_\alpha) + P_i + (u_j, u_\beta) + P_\beta$ is a (u, v)-Hamiltonian path in $D(n, h, g)$ what we required.

Case 2. u and v are in the distinct groups. For any $i, j \in I_g$, let $u \in V(G_i)$ and $v \in V(G_j)$ with $i \neq j$. Let $I_r = \{1, 2, \cdots, n - 2\}$ and $S = \{(x_1, i) \mid i \in I_r\}$. Next, we discuss the following two subcases.

Subcase 2.1. $(u, v) \in E(D(n, h, g))$. Similar to Case 1, we classify the positions of u and v.

Subcase 2.1.1. v is not an *end-vertex*. Because $(u, v) \in E(D(n, h, g))$, $u \notin I_r$. By Definition 2 and $h \geq 2$, it is effortless to infer that there exists a group, denoted by G_k, which satisfies both $G_k \in GH_v$ and $|i - k| = 1$. Therefore, there exists a vertex $x_k \in V(G_k)$ such that $(x_k, v) \in E(D(n, h, g))$. Let $u_0 = (x_1, 0)$ and $x_0 = (k, 0)$, then we can get a (u_0, u)-Hamiltonian path in G_i, denoted by P_i, and a (x_0, x_k)-Hamiltonian path in G_k, denoted by P_k, respectively. Let $S_1 = V(G_k) - \{x_0\}$ and $S_2 = V(G_i) - \{u_0\}$. By algorithm *DFCycle*, we can obtain a Hamiltonian cycle H in $D(n, h, g)$. In like manner, we can get a Hamiltonian cycle H_v in $D(n, h, g) - \{v\}$ that not contain vertex v. Let $H_1 = H_v - \{S_1, S_2\}$, then, $P_i + H_1 + P_k + (x_k, v)$ is a (u, v)-Hamiltonian path in $D(n, h, g)$.

Subcase 2.1.2. v is an *end-vertex*.

Subcase 2.1.2.1. $v = (x_2, n - 1)$. Due to $(u, v) \in E(D(n, h, g))$, G_j is the *external-group* of u. Let v_m denote a vertex which is different from v in G_j. Then, we can conclude that there exists a group, denoted by G_m, which satisfies both $G_m \in GH_{v_m}$ and $m - i = 1$ by Definition 2. Let $m_t = (m, n - 1)$. Obviously, there exists a (v_m, v)-Hamiltonian path in G_j, denoted by P_j, a (u_i, u)-Hamiltonian path in G_i, denoted by P_i, and a (m_t, m_k)-Hamiltonian path in G_m, denoted by P_m, respectively. By Definition 2, we can infer that there exist two groups, denoted by G_t and G_k, which satisfies both $t - j = 1$ and $j - k = 1$, respectively. Therefore, if $x_t = (t, 0) \in V(G_t)$ and $x_k = (k, n - 1) \in V(G_k)$, then $(x_k, x_t) \in E(D(n, h, g))$. Consequently, following the idea of algorithm *DFCycle*, we can find a Hamiltonian cycle H_m in $D(n, h, g) - \{G_j\}$. Let $S_1 = V(G_m) - \{m_t\}$ and $H_1 = H_m - \{S, S_1\}$, then, $P_i + H_1 + P_m + (m_k, v_m) + P_j$ is a (u, v)-Hamiltonian path in $D(n, h, g)$.

Subcase 2.1.2.2. $v = (x_2, 0)$. This case is similar to subcase 2.1.2.1, so the proof can be omitted.

Subcase 2.2. $(u, v) \notin E(D(n, h, g))$. By Lemma 3.1, we know there is an external-connected edge between G_i and G_j, denoted by (u_α, v_β), where $u_\alpha \in V(G_i)$ and $v_\beta \in V(G_j)$. Let $x \in V(G_i)$ and $y \in V(G_j)$. The following three scenarios are discussed.

Subcase 2.2.1. $u \neq u_\alpha$ and $v \neq v_\beta$.

Subcase 2.2.1.1. $u \notin S$. Suppose that $u = (x_1, 0)$, $u_i = (x_1, n-1)$, then we can obtain a (u_i, u_α)-Hamiltonian path in $G_i - \{u\}$, denoted by P_i. Similarly, there exists a (v_β, v)-Hamiltonian path in G_j, denoted by P_j. By Definition 2, we can infer that there exist two groups, denoted by G_t and G_k, which satisfies both $t - j = 1$ and $j - k = 1$, respectively. Therefore, if $x_t = (t, 0) \in V(G_t)$ and $x_k = (k, n-1) \in V(G_k)$, then $(x_k, x_t) \in E(D(n, h, g))$. Consequently, following the idea of algorithm *DFCycle*, we can find a Hamiltonian cycle H_γ in $D(n, h, g) - \{G_j\}$. Let $H_1 = H_\gamma - \{S\}$, then, $H_1 + P_i + (u_\alpha, v_\beta) + P_j$ is a (u, v)-Hamiltonian path in $D(n, h, g)$.

Subcase 2.2.1.2. $u \in S$. Suppose that $x = (x_1, 0)$, $u_i = (x_1, n-1)$. If $x \neq u_\alpha$ ($x = u_\alpha$), then we can obtain a (u_i, u)-Hamiltonian path in $G_i - \{x, u_\alpha\}$ ($G_i - \{u_\alpha\}$), denoted by P_i. For convenience's sake, we assume that $x \neq u_\alpha$. There exists a (v_β, v)-Hamiltonian path in G_j, denoted by P_j. By Definition 2, we can infer that there exist two groups, denoted by G_t and G_k, which satisfies both $t - j = 1$ and $j - k = 1$, respectively. Therefore, if $x_t = (t, 0) \in V(G_t)$ and $x_k = (k, n-1) \in V(G_k)$, then $(x_k, x_t) \in E(D(n, h, g))$. Analogously, with the help of algorithm *DFCycle*, we can find a Hamiltonian cycle H_γ in $D(n, h, g) - \{G_j\}$ for this case. Let $H_1 = H_\gamma - \{S\}$, then, $P_j + (u_\alpha, v_\beta) + H_1 + P_i$ is a (u, v)-Hamiltonian path in $D(n, h, g)$.

Subcase 2.2.2. $u = u_\alpha$ and $v \neq v_\beta$. Let $u_i = (x_1, 0)$. Next, we discuss the following two subcases.

Subcase 2.2.2.1. $u \neq u_i$. For $h \geq 2$, u has at least two *external-groups*. Due to $(u, v_\beta) \in E(D(n, h, g))$, G_j is the *external-group* of u. Then, we can conclude that there exists a group, denoted by G_m, that satisfies both $G_m \in GH_{v_\beta}$ and $|i - m| = 1$ by Definition 2. Therefore, there must exist a vertex $x_m \in V(G_m)$ such that $(x_m, v_\beta) \in E(D(n, h, g))$. Obviously, there exists a (v_β, v)-Hamiltonian path in G_j, denoted by P_j, a (u_i, u)-Hamiltonian path in G_i, denoted by P_i and a (x_i, x_m)-Hamiltonian path in G_m, denoted by P_m, respectively. Similar to subcase 2.2.1.2, we can infer that there exist two groups, denoted by G_t and G_k, which satisfies both $t - j = 1$ and $j - k = 1$, respectively. Therefore, if $x_t = (t, 0) \in V(G_t)$ and $x_k = (k, n-1) \in V(G_k)$, then $(x_k, x_t) \in E(D(n, h, g))$. Analogously, with the help of algorithm *DFCycle*, we can get a Hamiltonian cycle H_γ in $D(n, h, g) - \{G_j\}$. Let $S_1 = V(G_m) - \{x_i\}$ and $H_1 = H_\gamma - \{S, S_1\}$, then, $P_i + H_1 + P_m + (x_m, v_\beta) + P_j$ is a (u, v)-Hamiltonian path in $D(n, h, g)$.

Subcase 2.2.2.2. $u = u_i$. This case is similar to subcase 2.2.2.1, and we can obtain a path $P_i + H_1 + P_k + (x_k, v_\beta) + P_j$, which is a (u, v)-Hamiltonian path in $D(n, h, g)$.

Subcase 2.2.3. $u \neq u_\alpha$ and $v = v_\beta$. This case is similar to subcase 2.2.2, so the proof can be omitted.

Hence, the theorem holds.

4 Conclusions

In this paper, we studied the hamiltonian properties of the logical graph $D(n, h, g)$ of the dragonfly network. Firstly, we show that there exists a Hamiltonian cycle and propose an $O(g)$ algorithm for constructing a Hamiltonian cycle in $D(n, h, g)$ for $n \geq 2$ and $h \geq 1$. Then, we prove that $D(n, h, g)$ is Hamiltonian-connected for $n \geq 4$ and $h \geq 2$. There are many other important properties in the network, such as restricted connectivity [14], and disjoint paths [26]. These properties are closely related to the fault-tolerance and communication of $D(n, h, g)$ and worthy to study in the future.

Acknowledgements. This work was supported by the National Natural Science Foundation of China (Nos. 62172291, 62272333, U1905211), and Jiangsu Province Department of Education Future Network Research Fund Project (FNSRFP-2021-YB-39).

References

1. Bahrebar, P., Stroobandt, D.: The Hamiltonian-based odd-even turn model for adaptive routing in interconnection networks. In: Proceedings of the 2013 International Conference on Reconfigurable Computing and FPGAs, pp. 1–6. IEEE, Cancun, Mexico (2013). https://doi.org/10.1109/ReConFig.2013.6732332
2. Chan, H.-C., Chang, J.-M., Wang, J.-M., Horng, S.-J.: Geodesic-pancyclicity and fault-tolerant panconnectivity of augmented cubes. Appl. Math. Comput. **207**(2), 333–339 (2009)
3. Chang, J.-M., Yang, J.-S., Wang, Y.-L., Cheng, Y.: Panconnectivity, fault-tolerant hamiltonicity and Hamiltonian-connectivity in alternating group graphs. Networks **44**(4), 302–310 (2004)
4. Du, X., Zhao, Z., Han, Z., Wang, B.: Data center network acquisition symptom algorithm based on Hamiltonian cycle. In: Proceedings of the 2020 International Conference on Cyberspace Innovation of Advanced Technologies, pp. 65–69. Association for Computing Machinery, Guangzhou, China (2020). https://doi.org/10.1145/3444370.3444549
5. Faanes, G., Bataineh, A., Roweth, D., Court, T., Froese, E., et al.: Cray cascade: a scalable HPC system based on a dragonfly network. In: Proceedings of the International Conference on High Performance Computing, Networking, Storage and Analysis, pp. 1–9. IEEE, Salt Lake City, UT, USA (2012). https://doi.org/10.1109/SC.2012.39

6. Fan, J.: Hamilton-connectivity and cycle-embedding of the Möobius cubes. Inf. Process. Lett. **82**(2), 113–117 (2002)
7. Fan, J., Lin, X., Jia, X., Lau, R.W.H.: Edge-pancyclicity of twisted cubes. In: Deng, X., Du, D.-Z. (eds.) ISAAC 2005. LNCS, vol. 3827, pp. 1090–1099. Springer, Heidelberg (2005). https://doi.org/10.1007/11602613_108
8. Fan, J., Jia, X., Li, X.: Complete path embeddings in crossed cubes. Inf. Sci. **176**(22), 3332–3346 (2006)
9. Fan, J., Jia, X.: Edge-pancyclicity and path-embeddability of bijective connection graphs. Inf. Sci. **178**(2), 340–351 (2008)
10. Fujita, S., Araki, T.: Three-round adaptive diagnosis in binary n-cubes. In: Deng, X., Du, D.-Z. (eds.) International Symposium on Algorithms and Computation (ISAAC 2004). LNCS, vol. 3341, pp. 442–451. Springer, Cham (2004). https://doi.org/10.1007/978-3-540-30551-4_39
11. Garey, M.-R., Johnson, D.-S., Tarjan, R.-E.: The planar Hamiltonian circuit problem is NP-complete. SIAM J. Comput. **5**(4), 704–714 (1976)
12. Qin, X.-W., Hao, R.-X.: Hamiltonian properties of some compound networks. Discret. Appl. Math. **239**, 174–182 (2018)
13. Qin, X.-W., Hao, R.-X.: Conditional edge-fault-tolerant Hamiltonicity of the data center network. Discret. Appl. Math. **247**, 165–179 (2018)
14. Hsieh, S.-Y., Huang, H.-W., Lee, C.-W.: 2,3-restricted connectivity of locally twisted cubes. Theor. Comput. Sci. **615**, 78–90 (2016)
15. Hsieh, S.-Y., Lee, C.-W., Huang, C.-H.: Conditional edge-fault Hamiltonian connectivity of restricted hypercube-like networks. Inf. Comput. **251**, 214–334 (2016)
16. Kim, J., Dally, W.-J., Scott, S., Abts, D.: Technology-driven, highly-scalable dragonfly topology. Comput. Archit. News **36**(3), 77–88 (2008)
17. Lin, X., Ni, L.-M.: Deadlock-free multicast wormhole routing in multicomputer networks. In: Proceedings of the 18th Annual International Symposium on Computer Architecture, pp. 116–25. IEEE, Montpellier, France, (1991). https://doi.org/10.1109/ISVLSI.2008.18
18. Lin, T.-J., Hsieh, S.-Y., Juan, J.S.-T.: Embedding cycles and paths in product networks and their applications to multiprocessor systems. IEEE Trans. Parallel Distrib. Syst. **23**(6), 1081–1089 (2012)
19. Maglione-Mathey, G., Yebenes, P., Escudero-Sahuquillo, J., Javier Garcia, P., Quiles, F.-J., Zahavi, E.: Scalable deadlock-free deterministic minimal-path routing engine for infiniBand-based Dragonfly networks. IEEE Trans. Parallel Distrib. Syst. **29**(1), 183–197 (2018)
20. Qin, X.-W., Hao, R.-X., Chang, J.-M.: The existence of completely independent spanning trees for some compound graphs. IEEE Trans. Dependable Secure Comput. **31**(1), 201–210 (2020)
21. Diestel, R.: Graph Theory. Springer, Cham (2012). https://doi.org/10.1007/978-3-662-53622-3
22. Salamah, Z., Alzaid, A., Saptarshi, B., Xin, Y., Michael, L.: Global link arrangement for practical Dragonfly. In: Proceedings of the 34th ACM International Conference on Supercomputing, p. 11. Association for Computing Machinery, New York, USA (2020). https://doi.org/10.1145/3392717.3392756
23. Wu, S., Fan, J., Cheng, B., Yu, J., Wang, Y.: Connectivity and constructive algorithms of disjoint paths in dragonfly networks. Theor. Comput. Sci. **922**, 257–270 (2022)
24. Wang, X., Erickson, A., Fan, J., Jia, X.: Hamiltonian properties of DCell networks. Comput. J. **58**(11), 2944–2955 (2015)

25. Wang, F., Zhang, H.: Matchings extend to Hamiltonian cycles in k-ary n-cubes. Inf. Sci. **305**, 1–13 (2015)
26. Wang, X., Fan, J., Lin, C.-K., Jia, X.: Vertex-disjoint paths in DCell networks. J. Parallel Distrib. Comput. **96**, 38–44 (2016)
27. Xiang, D., Liu, X.: Deadlock-free broadcast routing in dragonfly networks without virtual channels. IEEE Trans. Parallel Distrib. Syst. **27**(9), 2520–2532 (2016)
28. Xiang, D., Li, B., Fu, Y.: Fault-tolerant adaptive routing in dragonfly networks. IEEE Trans. Dependable Secure Comput. **16**(2), 259–271 (2019)
29. Xu, D., Fan, J., Jia, X., Zhang, S., Wang, X.: Hamiltonian properties of honeycomb meshes. Inf. Sci. **240**, 184–190 (2013)
30. Ye, L., Liang, J.: Five-round adaptive diagnosis in Hamiltonian networks. IEEE Trans. Parallel Distrib. Syst. **26**(9), 2459–2464 (2015)

Fine Grained Space Complexity and the Linear Space Hypothesis (Preliminary Report)

Tomoyuki Yamakami[✉]

Faculty of Engineering, University of Fukui, 3-9-1 Bunkyo, Fukui 910-8507, Japan
TomoyukiYamakami@gmail.com

Abstract. Theory of fine-grained time complexity has gained popularity in demonstrating tight bounds on the runtime required for solving target "tractable" problems under various complexity-theoretical hypotheses, including the strong exponential time hypothesis (SETH), the orthogonal vector problem (OVP), and the 3 sum problem (3SUM). Concerning space complexity limitations of tractable problems, as a natural analogy of SETH, the linear space hypothesis (LSH) was proposed in 2017 and it has been used to obtain better lower bounds on the space usage needed for solving several NL combinatorial problems. In further connection to LSH, we study the space complexity bounds of parameterized decision problems solvable in polylogarithmic time. In particular, we focus on a restricted OVP, which is called the 3-out-of-4 block orthogonal vector family problem (3/4-BOVF) parameterized by the number of matrix rows and, assuming LSH, we obtain a tight lower bound on the work space needed to solve 3/4-BOVF in polylogarithmic time. We also discuss space lower bounds of two more parameterized problems, called the 4 block matrix row majorization problem (4BMRM) parameterized by the number of matrix rows, and the 4 block vector summation problem (4BVSUM) parameterized by the number of set elements.

Keywords: Fine-grained complexity · Linear space hypothesis · 2SAT · Block orthogonal vector · Matrix row majorization · Block vector summation

1 Background and an Overview

Let us first give a motivational discussion on the subject of this paper and then briefly describe the main focal points of the paper.

1.1 From Fine-Grained Time Complexity to Fine-Grained Space Complexity

Traditionally, we have treated computational problems in P as "tractable" and a large effort has been made to efficiently solve "intractable" problems, mostly

© The Author(s), under exclusive license to Springer Nature Singapore Pte Ltd. 2022
S.-Y. Hsieh et al. (Eds.): ICS 2022, CCIS 1723, pp. 180–191, 2022.
https://doi.org/10.1007/978-981-19-9582-8_16

NP-complete problems. The difficulty in solving the 3CNF Boolean formula satisfiability problem (3SAT) in sub-exponential time motivated Impagliazzo, Paturi, and Zane [4,5] to propose two practical working hypotheses, known as the *exponential time hypothesis* (abbreviated as ETH) and the *strong exponential time hypothesis* (SETH), which are thought as stronger assumptions than the assumption P $\neq$ NP. Under the assumption of ETH or SETH, tight lower bounds on the time complexity of numerous well-known problems have been obtained. Such problems include: independent set, dominating set, clique cover, max cut, and hitting set (see, e.g., a survey [7]).

Lately, there have been also practical demands for an intensive study on computational resources necessary to solve even "tractable" problems. A collective effort has been made in determining the precise complexity of those problems. Williams [8] observed that the complexities of many tractable problems are in fact related to SETH or other similar hypotheses used in various fields of computer science. He initiated an intensive study on the computational complexity of tractable problems under the term of "fine grained (time) complexity" in a relevance to SETH.

Other than ETH and SETH, a collection of interesting hypotheses has been lately proposed to demonstrate tighter bounds on the runtime needed for algorithms to solve numerous tractable problems. A typical example of such hypothesis is the *orthogonal vector problem* (or OVP, for short), which has been spotlighted in close connection to SETH. This intriguing problem takes two sets S and T of n Boolean vectors of dimension d. We ask whether there are two special vectors $\alpha \in S$ and $\beta \in T$ such that α and β are orthogonal; that is, the inner product of α and β is zero (i.e., $\sum_{j=1}^{d} a_j b_j = 0$, provided that $\alpha = (a_1, a_2, \ldots, a_d)$ and $\beta = (b_1, b_2, \ldots, b_d)$). Williams [8] showed that, if SETH is true, then, for any constant $\varepsilon > 0$, there is no deterministic algorithm that solves OVP in time $O(n^{2-\varepsilon})$. The usefulness of OVP is demonstrated for obtaining better lower bounds on the amount of computational resources (mostly, runtime) needed to solve other combinatorial problems (see, e.g., [1,3,9]). Here, a key technical tool is the notion of *fine-grained (time) reductions*, which help us compare relative time complexities of various tractable problems.

In many real-life circumstances, small space computing of data processing of extremely large data sets has been spotlighted. To manage a large scale database on small-sized devices, we are more concerned about the memory space usage. Our primary target is a class of computational problems solvable in polynomial runtime using only "sub-linear" memory space. It is not known that all tractable problems fall into this complexity class. From an aspect of space-bounded computability, a working hypothesis analogous to SETH was proposed in 2017 under the name of the *linear space hypothesis* (or LSH, for short) [10], which is an assumption seemingly stronger than L $\neq$ NL and LOGDCFL $\neq$ LOGCFL. This hypothesis asserts that, for any constant $\varepsilon > 0$ and any polylogarithmic function $polylog(\cdot)$, no deterministic algorithm can solve a restricted form of 2SAT, called 2SAT$_3$, parameterized by the number $m_{vbl}(\phi)$ of variables in a given 2CNF formula ϕ, in time polynomial in $|x|$ using $O(m_{vbl}(x)^{\varepsilon} polylog(|x|))$ space on all instances x given to 2SAT$_3$. The linear space hypothesis has served as a useful assumption in cooperation with finding upper and lower bounds of space usage necessary to solve a certain type of NL-problems (together with reasonable "size" parameters). More examples of such "parameterized" decision problems were presented lately in [14]. As demonstrated in [10], for example, we obtain better lower bounds on the space usage needed to solve computational problems, such as restricted variants of the knapsack problem. Other relevant results were lately obtained in [11–13].

A series of recent studies on fine-grained time complexity of tractable problems suggests us to take a similar approach toward *fine-grained space complexity* of those problems.

1.2   New Challenges

Our intention of this paper is to provide a wider range of tractable problems, establish their mutual connections, and show tight lower bounds on the space usage of time efficient algorithms that correctly solve those problems. Our focal point lies on obtaining reasonable lower bounds on the space complexity of various tractable problems under the assumption of LSH. Among those problems, we are particularly interested in combinatorial problems parameterized by reasonable size parameters, which can be solvable in "polylogarithmic" time. We intend to establish a close connection between LSH and the space lower bounds of polylogarithmic-time computable parameterized problems.

Since we are interested in small space computation, the aforementioned relationship of OVP to SETH leads us to look into a similar tie between a "restricted" form of OVP and LSH. For this purpose, we first take a bold step toward an essential modification of OVP and introduce its variant, which we call the *3-out-of-4 block orthogonal vector family problem* (3/4-BOVF). This decision problem asks whether there exists a collection of "collectively" orthogonal vectors taken from each set of a given family of sets of d-dimensional vectors. In a similar spirit, we introduce the second problem, called the *4 block matrix row majorization problem* (4BMRM) asks whether, for a collectively "sparse" family of a rational matrices, the sum of some rows of the matrices majorizes a given vector. The third problem called the *4 block vector summation problem* (4BVSUM) asks whether, given a family of restricted sets of row vectors, the sum of some row vectors in the sets equals O (all-zero vector).

Together with "natural" size parameters, the above problems, 3/4-BOVFC, 4BMRMC, and 4BVSUM, are solvable in polylogarithmic time. We will present tight space bounds necessary to solve those problems in Sects. 3, 4 and 5 if LSH is true. We believe that an intensive study on the fine-grained space complexity is important and useful in determining better lower bounds on computational resources needed to solve many intriguing real-life combinatorial problems.

All the omitted proofs due to the page limit will be included in a forthcoming complete version of this paper.

2   Preparations: Notions and Notation

Let $\mathbb{N} = \{0, 1, 2, \ldots\}$, which is the set of all nonnegative integers. We set $\mathbb{N}^+ = \mathbb{N} - \{0\}$. For two integers m, n with $m \leq n$, $[m, n]_{\mathbb{Z}}$ denotes the integer interval $\{m, m+1, m+2, \ldots, n\}$. In particular, when $n \geq 1$, we abbreviate $[1, n]_{\mathbb{Z}}$ as $[n]$. For technical convenience, when $n < 1$, we automatically set $[n]$ to be $\varnothing$. Given an $m \times n$ matrix A and an index pair $(i, j) \in [m] \times [n]$, $A_{(i,j)}$ denotes the (i, j)-entry of A. Similarly, for a (column) vector $b = (b_1, b_2, \ldots, b_n)$ and any $i \in [n]$, $b_{(i)}$ denotes the ith entry b_i. The notation A^t denotes the *transpose* of a matrix A. Given an $m \times n$ matrix A, the l_∞-*norm* of A is $\|A\|_\infty = \max_{i \in [m], j \in [n]} |A_{(i,j)}|$. Given a vector b in $\mathbb{R}^n$, $\|b\|_\infty$ denotes the *max norm* (or the l_∞-*norm*) of b on $\mathbb{R}^n$, that is, $\max\{|b_{(1)}|, |b_{(2)}|, \ldots, |b_{(n)}|\}$. For convenience, the notation O is used to express the all-0 matrix or the all-0 vector of arbitrary dimension. For two functions f and g on $\mathbb{N}$ (i.e., from $\mathbb{N}$ to $\mathbb{N}$), we say that f *majorizes* g, denoted $f \geq g$, if $f(n) \geq g(n)$ holds for any number $n \in \mathbb{N}$.

An *alphabet* is a finite nonempty set of "symbols" or "letters." A *string* over alphabet Σ is a finite sequence of symbols in Σ. The *empty string* is denoted by λ. The notation Σ^* denotes the set of all strings over Σ, including λ. A *language* over Σ is a subset of Σ^*. We freely identify a decision problem with its associated language.

In our model of computation, we assume that each *integer* is expressed in binary with a sign bit that represents either negativeness (0) or non-negativeness (1). A *rational number* r is represented by (m, n) of integers satisfying that $r = \frac{m}{n}$, $n > 0$, and the greatest common divisor of m and n is 1.

2.1   Parameterized Decision Problems

In what follows, we discuss *parameterized decision problems*, which are simply pairs (L, m) of decision problems (freely identified with languages) L over alphabets Σ and size parameters m, where *size parameters* are functions from Σ^* to $\mathbb{N}$. For example, 2SAT$_3$ denotes the problem of determining whether a given 2CNF Boolean formula ϕ is satisfiable, provided that every variable in ϕ appears at most 3 times in the form of literals. As its size parameters, we set $m_{vbl}(\phi)$ and $m_{cls}(\phi)$ to be the number of variables and the number of clauses in ϕ, respectively.

To solve a parameterized problem, we use a mathematical model of *Turing machine* equipped with a read-only input tape and multiple rewritable work tapes together with a rewritable index tape, which is used to write the address of an input-tape cell for retrieving the information on the content of this cell. Any space bound of the machine is applicable only to the work tapes. Later, we will expand this model by adding an oracle query mechanism with (instance) oracles. A size parameter $m : \Sigma^* \to \mathbb{N}$ for an alphabet Σ is called a *log-space size parameter* if there exists a deterministic Turing machine M that takes an instance $x \in \Sigma^*$ and then produces $1^{m(x)}$ (in unary) on a write-once[1] output tape.

---

[1] A tape is *write-once* if its tape head always moves to the next blank cell as soon as the tape head writes down any non-blank symbol.

Let us recall from [10,12,14] the parameterized versions of L and NL, which are named respectively as para-L and para-NL. Formally, a parameterized decision problem (L, m) is in para-L (resp., para-NL) if there exists a deterministic (resp., nondeterministic) Turing machine such that, for any input x, M takes x as an input and then determines whether or not $x \in L$ within $(|x|m(x))^{O(1)}$ steps using $O(\log m(x))$ space. Similarly, we newly define para-PLOG^2 (parameterized polylog-time log-squared-space) by replacing the bounds $(|x|m(x))^{O(1)}$ and $O(\log m(x))$ in the above definition with $(\log |x|)^{O(1)}$ and $O(\log^2 m(x))$, respectively.

Given a parameterized problem (P, m), we say that a Turing machine M *solves* (P, m) *in polynomial time using sub-linear space* if M solves P within $p(|x|m(x))$ steps and $O(m(x)^\varepsilon \ell(|x|))$ tape cells on all instances x for a certain polynomial p, a certain constant $\varepsilon \in [0, 1)$, and a certain polylog function ℓ [10]. Notice that, when m is polynomially bounded (i.e., there exists a polynomial p satisfying $m(x) \leq p(|x|)$ for all x), we can replace $p(|x|m(x))$ by $p(|x|)$. The parameterized complexity class PsubLIN consists of all parameterized problems (L, m) such that there is a deterministic Turing machine solving (L, m) in polynomial time using sub-linear space [10]. Note that para-L $\subseteq$ para-NL $\cap$ PsubLIN.

Definition 1 [10]. *The* linear space hypothesis *(LSH) asserts that the parameterized decision problem* $(2SAT_3, m_{vbl})$ *is outside of* PsubLIN.

Notice that LSH is not known to be equivalent to the statement para-NL $\not\subseteq$ PsubLIN, because PsubLIN is not known to be closed under standard log-space reductions. If LSH is indeed true, then L $\neq$ NL and LOGDCFL $\neq$ LOGCFL follow.

2.2 How to Access Input: Oracle Query Model

To study polylogarithmic space computability, we need to modify our basic computational model because we cannot store a large amount of data to process it. We view a long input as a large-scale *database*, which is provided in the form of an oracle, and we access its entries by way of queries of the form "what is the data stored at this address?". This computational model is called an *oracle query model* or a *black-box model*, in which database information is retrieved from a given oracle by making oracle queries.

In this mode, an underlying Turing machine is equipped with a write-once query tape, on which a query word, say, i is produced and, when the machine enters a specific query state, the query word is transmitted to the oracle and, as a response from the oracle, the ith entry is instantly returned to the machine.

2.3 Fine Grained Space Reductions

To discuss the relative complexity of parameterized decision problems, Yamakami [10] introduced the notion of SLRF-T-reductions ($\leq_T^{SLRF}$), where "SLRF" stands for "polynomial-time sub-linear-space reduction family." This notion was further discussed in [11]. Such short reductions are useful in discussing the parameterized problems in direct connection to PsubLIN.

In order to discuss parameterized problems solvable using polylogarithmic space in connection to LSH, we need to refine the above-mentioned reductions.

Given an instance x indexed by an index set $I(x)$, the notation O_x denotes the function such that, for any index $z \in I(x)$, $O_x(z)$ equals the z-th element of x according to the indexing order. For example, if x is a binary string of length n and $I(x) = [n]$, then $O_x(i)$ equals the ith bit of x for any index $i \in I(x)$.

Definition 2. *Let (L_1, m_1) and (L_2, m_2) denote two arbitrary parameterized decision problems over alphabets Σ_1 and Σ_2, respectively. Let $a(n)$ and $b(n)$ be non-decreasing functions on $\mathbb{N}$. We say that (L_1, m_1) is (a, b)-space-reducible to (L_2, m_2), denoted $(L_1, m_1) \leq_{a,b}^{\text{space}} (L_2, m_2)$, if, for every fixed value $\varepsilon > 0$, there exist a number $\delta > 0$, constants $d, k > 0$, a function $h_\varepsilon : \Sigma_1^* \to \Sigma_2^*$, and an oracle (deterministic) Turing machine M_ε that satisfy the following two conditions. (1) For any instance $x \in \Sigma_1^*$, (i) $x \in L_1$ iff $h_\varepsilon(x) \in L_2$, (ii) $b(m_2(h(x)))^{1-\varepsilon} \leq d \cdot a(m_1(x))^{1-\delta}$, and (iii) $b(|h_\varepsilon(x)|m_2(h_\varepsilon(x))) \leq a(|x|m_1(x))^k$. (2) For any instance $x \in \Sigma_1^*$ and any index $z \in I(x)$, M_ε takes z as an input and computes the value $O_{h_\varepsilon(x)}(z)$ in time polynomial in $|x|m_1(x)$ using $O(m_1(x)^{1-\varepsilon})$ space with an access to the instance oracle O_x. In other words, M_ε computes the function $O_{h_\varepsilon(x)}$ with the help of O_x.*

Under certain conditions, the above reduction satisfies fundamental properties of reflexivity and transitivity. In the following lemmas, let (L, m), (L_1, m_1), (L_2, m_2), and (L_3, m_3) denote arbitrary parameterized decision problems.

Lemma 3. *Let a, b, c, d denote non-decreasing functions on $\mathbb{N}$.*

1. *Let $a(m(x)) \geq \lceil \log |x| \rceil$ for any x. If $a \geq b$, then $(L, m) \leq_{a,b}^{\text{space}} (L, m)$.*
2. *If $c \geq b$, $(L_1, m_1) \leq_{a,b}^{\text{space}} (L_2, m_2)$, and $(L_2, m_2) \leq_{c,d}^{\text{space}} (L_3, m_3)$, then $(L_1, m_1) \leq_{a,d}^{\text{space}} (L_3, m_3)$.*

Lemma 4. *Let a, b be two non-decreasing functions on $\mathbb{N}$. Assume that $(L_1, m_1) \leq_{a,b}^{\text{space}} (L_2, m_2)$. If (L_2, m_2) is solvable in $b(|z|m_2(z))^k$ time using $c \cdot b(m_2(z))^{1-\varepsilon}$ space for certain fixed constants $c, k > 0$ and $\varepsilon \in [0, 1)$, then (L_1, m_1) is also solvable in $O(|x|^e a(|x|m_1(x))^e)$ time using $O(a(m_1(x))^{1-\delta})$ space for certain constants $e > 0$ and $\delta \in [0, 1)$.*

3   3-Out-of-4 Block Orthogonal Vector Family Problem

As noted in Sect. 1.1, the *3-out-of-4 block orthogonal vector family problem* (3/4-BOVF) is a restricted form of the orthogonal vector problem (OVP). We formally introduce this problem and discuss its space complexity.

3.1   Introduction of 3/4-BOVF

Let us consider a $\{0, 1\}$-matrix $T = (\alpha_1, \alpha_2, \dots, \alpha_n)^t$ with (column) vectors $\alpha_1, \alpha_2, \dots, \alpha_n$ and $d = \omega(polylog(n))$. A partition $\{B_1, B_2, B_3, B_4\}$ of the index set $[n]$ is *4-sectioned* if there are two distinct numbers $e_1, e_2 \in [0, \lceil \log n \rceil]_{\mathbb{Z}}$ and a one-to-one function $f : \{0,1\}^2 \to \{1,2,3,4\}$ such that, for each pair $a, b \in \{0,1\}$, $B_{f(ab)}$ consists of all integers in $[n]$ whose binary representations hold a and b at their e_1th and e_2th bits, respectively. Each B_i in this partition is called a *block*. The above function f is "hidden" but it provides an algorithmic way to determine whether a given integer $l \in [n]$ belongs to a particular block B_i ($i \in [4]$). An $n \times d$ $\{0,1\}$-matrix T is said to have *3-out-of-4 block naughts* if, for each fixed index $j \in [d]$, (1) there is a 4-sectioned partition $\{B_{j1}, B_{j2}, B_{j3}, B_{j4}\}$ associated with the jth column, (2) every block B_{jl} ($l \in [4]$) has no distinct values, and (3) if there exists at least one 0 in the jth column, then either two or three blocks in $\{B_{j1}, B_{j2}, B_{j3}, B_{j4}\}$ contain 0s.

We say that a set $\{\beta_1, \beta_2, \ldots, \beta_k\}$ of d-dimensional $\{0,1\}$-valued row vectors is *collectively orthogonal* if $\sum_{j=1}^{d} (\prod_{i=1}^{k} (\beta_i)_{(j)}) = 0$. When $k = 2$, this collective-orthogonality notion coincides with the standard orthogonality notion. Despite the complexity of the description of 3/4-BOVF, this problem looks much easier to solve than OVP due to the condition of 3-out-of-4 block naughts.

3-OUT-OF-4   BLOCK   ORTHOGONAL   VECTOR   FAMILY   PROBLEM (3/4-BOVF):

○ INSTANCE: a family $\mathcal{T} = \{T_1, T_2, \ldots, T_k\}$ of $n \times d$ $\{0,1\}$-matrices, each of which has 3-out-of-4 block naughts and, for each index $j \in [d]$, there are at most two matrices T_{i_1} and T_{i_2} whose jth columns contain 0s, provided that $k = O(\log n)$ and $d = O(\log n)$.

○ QUESTION: is there any collectively orthogonal set $\{\beta_1, \beta_2, \ldots, \beta_k\}$ such that each β_i is a certain row of T_i for each index $i \in [k]$?

This problem 3/4-BOVF is not too far deviated from OVP, because, when k equals 2 and the condition of 3-out-of-4 block naughts is not required, 3/4-BOVF truly coincides with OVP, which is solvable in $O(n^{2-1/g(n)})$ time for a certain large value $g(n)$ [2].

For each instance x to 3/4-BOVF, we use the term "n" in the above definition as a size parameter $m_{set}(x) = n$. Solving the parameterized decision problem $(3/4\text{-BOVF}, m_{set})$ requires relatively small memory space. An appropriately designed polynomial-time deterministic algorithm can solve the problem using only polylogarithmic space.

Proposition 5. *There exists a deterministic algorithm that solves* $(3/4\text{-BOVF}, m_{set})$ *in time polylogarithmic in* $|x|m_{set}(x)$ *and using* $O(\log^2 m_{set}(x))$ *space, where* x *is "symbolic" input given to 3/4-BOVF. In other words,* $(3/4\text{-BOVF}, m_{set}) \in \text{para-PLOG}^2$.

3.2   Fine Grained Space Reductions and Space Complexity

One of the major contributions of this paper is to prove that, assuming that LSH is true, no polynomial-time algorithm can solve the problem $(3/4\text{-BOVF}, m_{set})$ using small space. More precisely:

Theorem 6. *Under LSH, it follows that, for any constant $\varepsilon > 0$, there is no deterministic algorithm that solves* $(3/4\text{-BOVF}, m_{set})$ *in time polylogarithmic in* $|x|m_{set}(x)$ *using* $O(\log^{2-\varepsilon} m_{set}(x))$ *space on all instances x to $3/4\text{-BOVF}$, where x denotes a "symbolic" input.*

The rest of this subsection is devoted to proving Theorem 6. The proof of the theorem exploits the fact that a Boolean formula given as an input to 2SAT_3 is in 2CNF and each variable appears at most three times in the form of literals. We note that every clause of a 2CNF formula can be assumed to be made up of two different variables. This can be done by, for any literal z, deleting $z \vee \bar{z}$, reducing $z \vee z$ to z, and finally changing z to $(z \vee x) \wedge (z \vee \bar{x})$ with a new variable x. Clearly, this modification does not alter the satisfiability of the original formula. We call such a modified formula an *exact* 2CNF formula.

Lemma 7. $(2\text{SAT}_3, m_{cls}) \leq^{\text{space}}_{n, \log^2 n} (3/4\text{-BOVF}, m_{set})$.

In the proof of Lemma 7, an underlying oracle Turing machine M_ε makes a query to an instance oracle, which, upon a query of the form (i, j, l) in $[k] \times [n] \times [d]$ in the aforementioned definition of $3/4\text{-BOVF}$, returns the Boolean value $(T_i)_{(j,l)}$.

Theorem 6 follows from Lemmas 4 and 7 as follows. Assuming that $(3/4\text{-BOVF}, m_{set})$ is solvable in $(\log |x|m_{set}(x))^{O(1)}$ time using $O(\log^{2-\varepsilon} m_{set}(x))$ space for an appropriate constant $\varepsilon > 0$. We set $a(n) = n$, $b(n) = \log^2 n$, and $\varepsilon' = \varepsilon/2$. Note that $b(m_{set}(x))^{1-\varepsilon'} = \log^{2-\varepsilon} m_{set}(x)$ and $b(|x|m_{set}(x)) = (\log |x|m_{set}(x))^2$. With the help of Lemma 4, we conclude from Lemma 7 that $(2\text{SAT}_3, m_{vbl})$ is solvable in $(|\phi|m_{cls}(\phi))^{O(1)}$ time using $O(m_{cls}(\phi)^{1-\delta})$ space for a certain fixed constant $\delta \in (0, 1]$. This yields the failure of LSH, and therefore, we obtain the theorem.

Proof Sketch of Lemma 7. Consider $(2\text{SAT}_3, m_{vbl})$. Take any instance ϕ to 2SAT_3 and let $V = \{x_1, x_2, \ldots, x_n\}$ denote the set of all variables in ϕ with $m_{vbl}(\phi) = n$. Let $d = m_{cls}(\phi)$. Since ϕ can be assumed to be *exact* 2CNF formula, for simplicity, we treat ϕ as a set $\{C_l\}_{l \in [d]}$ of d clauses, where each clause C_l is of the form $z_{l,k_l} \vee z_{l,k'_l}$ with $k_l, k'_l \in [n]$ and both z_{l,k_l} and z_{l,k'_l} are literals whose variables belong to V. We set $\tilde{n} = \lceil \sqrt{n} \rceil$ and add $\tilde{n}^2 - n$ extra dummy variables, say, $x_{n+1}, x_{n+2}, \ldots, x_{\tilde{n}^2}$. Abusing our notation, we use the same notation V to denote this expanded set. We then partition V into $\tilde{n}$ sets $V_1, V_2, \ldots, V_{\tilde{n}}$ of size $\tilde{n}$ each, where all the dummy variables are assumed to appear in the last set or the last two sets since $0 \leq \tilde{n}^2 - n \leq 2\sqrt{n}$. Notice that these dummy variables do not affect the satisfiability of ϕ. For each index $i \in [\tilde{n}]$, let $V_i = \{x_{i1}, \ldots, x_{i\tilde{n}}\}$ and treat it as a series $(x_{i1}, x_{i2}, \ldots, x_{i\tilde{n}})$. For simplicity, let $N = 2^{\tilde{n}}$. Note that $d = O(\log N)$.

For each index $i \in [\tilde{n}]$, let us define an $N \times d$ $\{0,1\}$-matrix T_i as follows. To the series $(x_{i1}, x_{i2}, \ldots, x_{i\tilde{n}})$ of variables in V_i, we assign a series $v = (v_1, v_2, \ldots, v_{\tilde{n}}) \in \{0,1\}^{\tilde{n}}$ of Boolean values. We write $v \models C_l$ if v forces C_l to be true. Notice that there are N such series v. Assuming a natural enumeration of all such series v, we identify each series with a number in $[N]$ and such a number is used as a row index of T_i. In what follows, we use the same notation v to denote both a series of Boolean values and a row index. For each index $v \in [N]$, we define the vth row $\alpha_{iv} = (a_{v1}, a_{v2}, \ldots, a_{vd})$ of T_i by setting, for any $l \in [d]$, $a_{vl} = 0$ if $v \models C_l$, and $a_{vl} = 1$ otherwise. Let w denote $\langle T_1, T_2, \ldots, T_{\tilde{n}} \rangle$, which is an appropriate encoding of $\{T_1, T_2, \ldots, T_{\tilde{n}}\}$. Note that $m_{set}(w) = N$.

We then claim that T_i has 3/4 block naughts. We first enumerate all elements in $\{0,1\}^d$ lexicographically and treat them as $\{0,1\}$-vectors of dimension d. For each index $l \in [d]$, recall that C_l has the form $z_{l,k} \vee z_{l,k'}$. Assume that the variables of $z_{l,k}$ and $z_{l,k'}$ are x_{e_1}, x_{e_2}, respectively. We then define e_1', e_2' as follows. Take an arbitrary index $i \in [\tilde{n}]$. If $x_{e_1}, x_{e_2} \in V_i$, then we set $e_1' = e_1 \bmod \tilde{n}$ and $e_2' = e_2 \bmod \tilde{n}$. If $x_{e_1} \in V_i$ but $x_{e_2} \notin V_i$, then we set $e_1' = e_1 \bmod \tilde{n}$ and $e_2' = (e_1' + 1) \bmod \tilde{n}$. If $x_{e_1}, x_{e_2} \notin V_i$, then we set $e_1' = 1$ and $e_2' = 2$. We then partition $\{0,1\}^d$ into four sets $B_{ab}^{(l,i)} = \{(v_1, v_2, \ldots, v_{\tilde{n}}) \mid v_{e_1'} = a, v_{e_2'} = b\}$ for any pair $a, b \in \{0,1\}$. There is either no ab or exactly one ab such that $(\alpha_{iv})_{(l)} = 0$ for all $v \in B_{ab}^{(l,i)}$. If $x_{e_1}, x_{e_2} \in V_i$ and C_l has the form $x_{e_1} \vee \overline{x_{e_2}}$, then, for any $ab \neq 01$ and for any $v \in B_{ab}^{(l,i)}$, $v \models C_l$; thus, we obtain $(\alpha_{iv})_{(l)} = 0$. The other cases are similarly handled.

It is also possible to prove that ϕ is satisfiable iff there is a set $\{\beta_1, \beta_2, \ldots, \beta_{\tilde{n}}\}$ of row vectors taken from $T_1, T_2, \ldots, T_{\tilde{n}}$, respectively, for which this set is collectively orthogonal.

Next, we consider the following deterministic algorithm M. Let ϕ be any instance to 3SAT$_3$ and let O_ϕ denote the corresponding instance oracle. Let T be the instance to 3/4-BOVF constructed above. Similarly to O_ϕ, we denote by O_T the corresponding instance oracle. Note that the above construction shows that $\phi \in$ 2SAT$_3$ iff $T \in$ 3/4-BOVF. We define $h(\phi) = \langle T \rangle$.

Note that we do not need to "construct" T entirely from ϕ in our case. It is actually impossible to do so in time polynomial in $\log N$. Instead, our goal is to "compute" O_T via an oracle access to O_ϕ using restricted resources. More precisely, for any given input z of the form (i, v, l) given to O_T, we want to design M to calculate the value $O_T(z)$ $(= (\alpha_{iv})_{(l)})$ by making queries to the instance oracle O_ϕ. Note that the size of the input z is $|z| = O(\tilde{n}) = O(\log N)$. The machine M first finds C_l and its literals and then determines whether $v \models C_l$ or not. Finally, M outputs the value $(\alpha_{iv})_{(l)}$. The run time of M is bounded by a polynomial in $|z|$ and the space usage is $O(|z|)$.

We define $a(s) = s$ and $b(s) = \log^2 s$ for any $s \in \mathbb{N}^+$. Since $\log^2 N \leq 2n$, we obtain $b(m_{set}(u)) = \log^2 N \leq 2n \leq 2a(m_{vbl}(\phi))$. Therefore, this algorithm (a, b)-space-reduces $(2\text{SAT}_3, m_{vbl})$ to $(3/4\text{-BOVF}, m_{set})$. $\square$

4   4 Block Matrix Row Majorization Problem

Let us introduce the second problem, called the *4 block matrix row majorization problem* (4BMRM), together with a reasonable log-space size parameter and discuss its space complexity under the assumption of LSH.

Given an $n \times d$ matrix, we append a row vector b of dimension d to A as the $(n+1)$th row and construct a new $(n+1) \times d$ matrix. We express the resulting matrix as (A, b). For any $i \in [n]$, $A[i]$ denotes the ith row of A. A row vector $v = (a_1, a_2, \ldots, a_d) \in \mathbb{R}^d$ is said to be *additively 4-sectioned* if, there exist two numbers $\alpha, \beta \in \mathbb{R}$ and a 4-sectioned partition $\{P_1, P_2, P_3, P_4\}$ of $[d]$ such that (i) $v_{(i)} = 0$ for all $i \in P_1$, (ii) $v_{(i)} = \alpha$ for all $i \in P_2$, (iii) $v_{(i)} = \beta$ for all $i \in P_3$, and $v_{(i)} = \alpha + \beta$ for all $i \in P_4$. Moreover, A is said to be *additively 4-sectioned* if every row of A is additively 4-sectioned. A family $\{A_1, A_2, \ldots, A_n\}$ of $n \times d$ matrices is called *collectively sparse* if, for each index $j \in [d]$, there are at most 2 indices i_1 and i_2 such that $A_i^t[j]$ has nonzero entries for every $i \in \{i_1, i_2\}$.

4 BLOCK MATRIX ROW MAJORIZATION PROBLEM (4BMRM):

- INSTANCE: a collectively sparse family $\{D_1, D_2, \ldots, D_k\}$ of $n \times d$ rational matrices and a row vector $b = (b_1, b_2, \ldots, b_d) \in \mathbb{Q}^d$ such that, for any index $i \in [k]$, D_i is additively 4-sectioned, provided that $\max_i \|D_i\|_\infty, \|b\|_\infty \leq n$, $d = O(\log n)$, and $k = O(\log n)$.
- QUESTION: is there any series $(j_1, j_2, \ldots, j_k)$ of indices in $[n]$ for which $\sum_{i=1}^{k} D_i[j_i] \geq b$?

It is possible to design a deterministic algorithm solving $(\text{4BMRM}, m_{row})$ in polylogarithmic time using $O(\log^2 m_{row}(x))$ space, where x is a "symbolic" input. Thus, we obtain the following proposition.

Proposition 8. $(\text{4BMRM}, m_{row})$ *is in* para-PLOG^2.

Assuming LSH, we can prove that the space usage $O(\log^2 m_{row}(x))$ in the above proposition cannot be made significantly smaller, such as $O(\log^{2-\varepsilon} m_{row}(x))$ for a certain constant $\varepsilon > 0$.

Theorem 9. *Under LSH, it follows that, for any constant $\varepsilon > 0$, there is no algorithm solving $(\text{4BMRM}, m_{row})$ in time polylogarithmic in $|x| m_{row}(x)$ using $O(\log^{2-\varepsilon} m_{row}(x))$ space, where x is a "symbolic" input.*

For the proof of Theorem 9, we utilize an NL-complete problem, called LP$_{2,3}$ [10]. This decision problem LP$_{2,3}$ asks whether, for a given $m \times n$ rational matrix A and a rational vector b, there exists a $\{0,1\}$-vector x satisfying $Ax \geq b$, provided that each row and each column of A respectively have at most 2 nonzero and at most 3 nonzero entries with $\|A\|_\infty, \|b\|_\infty \leq n$. This problem is further parameterized by the natural log-space size parameter $m_{col}(\langle A, b \rangle)$, which indicates the number n of columns of A. Theorem 9 is shown as follows. We start with assuming that $(\text{4BMRM}, m_{row})$ is solvable in time polynomial in $\log m_{rwo}(x)$ using $O(\log^{2-\varepsilon} m_{row}(x))$ space. We then claim that $(\text{LP}_{2,3}, m_{col}) \leq_{n,\log^2 n}^{\text{space}} (\text{4BMRM}, m_{row})$. Lemma 4 then implies that $(\text{LP}_{2,3}, m_{col})$ falls into PsubLIN. It is known in [12] that $(\text{LP}_{2,3}, m_{col}) \in$ PsubLIN iff LSH is true. From this equivalence, we conclude that LSH fails. Therefore, the theorem holds.

5   4 Block Vector Summation Problem

As the third problem, we introduce the *4 block vector summation problem* (4BVSUM). Recall that O denotes the all-0 vector of arbitrary dimension. Given a set B of n row vectors in $\mathbb{R}^m$, B is said to be *additively 4-sectioned* if, for each index $i \in [m]$, the vector $(a_{i,1}, a_{i,2}, \ldots, a_{i,n})$, where $a_{i,j}$ equals the value of the ith coordinate of the jth row vector of B, is additively 4-sectioned.

4 BLOCK VECTOR SUMMATION PROBLEM (4BVSUM):

- INSTANCE: a family $\{B_1, B_2, \ldots, B_k\}$ of sets of n row vectors in $\mathbb{Z}^m$ with $B_i = \{v_{i,1}, v_{i,2}, \ldots, v_{i,m}\}$ such that, for any index $i \in [k]$, B_i is additively 4-sectioned, provided that $\max_i \|B_i\|_\infty \le n$ and $k = O(\log n \cdot \text{polyloglog}(n))$.
- QUESTION: is there any series $(j_1, j_2, \ldots, j_k)$ of indices in $[n]$ satisfying $v_{i,j_i} \in B_i$ for all $i \in [k]$ and $\sum_{i=1}^k v_{i,j_i} = O$?

We define $m_{set}(\langle B_1, B_2, \ldots, B_k \rangle)$ to be the value n.

Proposition 10. *The problem* (4BVSUM, m_{set}) *can be solved in* $(\log|x|$ $m_{set}(x))^{O(1)}$ *time using* $O(\log^2 m_{set}(x) \cdot \text{polyloglog}(|x|))$ *space, where* x *is "symbolic" input.*

The hypothesis LSH helps us obtain the following tight lower bound on the space usage of polylogarithmic-time deterministic algorithm for (4BVSUM, m_{set}).

Theorem 11. *Under LSH, it follows that, for any constant* $\varepsilon > 0$, *there is no algorithm solving* (4BVSUM, m_{set}) *in time polylogarithmic in* $|x| m_{set}(x)$ *using* $O(\log^{2-\varepsilon} m_{set}(x))$ *space.*

Our final goal is to prove Theorem 11. For this purpose, we introduce another useful parameterized decision problem. Earlier, Jones, Lien, and Laaser [6] studied a computational problem of determining whether or not a given set of linear equations of special forms has a positive solution, and they showed that this problem is indeed NL-complete. We slightly modify this problem and introduce the $\{+1, 0, -1\}$-*entry positive solution linear equation problem* (PSLE$_{k,2}$). A real vector is said to be *positive-valued* if all of its entries are positive numbers. An input to PSLE$_{k,2}$ is an $n \times m$ $\{+1, 0, -1\}$-matrix A, each row of which has at most k nonzero entries and each column has at most 2 distinct nonzero entries, provided that there are no all-0 row and no all-0 column and $\|A\|_\infty, \|b\|_\infty \le n$. The problem PSLE$_{k,2}$ asks whether there exists a positive-valued column vector x in $\mathbb{Z}^n$ such that $\|x\|_\infty \le n$ and $Ax = O$. For any input $x = \langle A \rangle$ given to PSLE$_{k,2}$ we set $m_{row}(x) = n$ and $m_{col}(x) = m$.

It is not difficult to show that the parameterized problem (PSLE$_{k,2}$, m_{col}) is in para-PLOG^2. This problem is also closely related to 3DSTCON. The decision problem 3DSTCON asks whether there exists a path from vertex s to vertex t in a given directed graph G of degree at most 3. It is known in [10] that (2SAT$_3$, m_{ver}) $\in$ PsubLIN iff (3DSTCON, m_{ver}) $\in$ PsubLIN.

For the proof of Theorem 11, we first claim that $(3DSTCON, m_{ver}) \equiv_T^{sSLRF}$ $(PSLE_{4,2}, m_{col})$. From this claim, we can conclude that LSH is true iff $(PSLE_{4,2}, m_{col}) \notin PsubLIN$. Furthermore, we can prove that $(PSLE_{4,2}, m_{col})$ $\leq_{n,\log^2 n}^{space} (4BVSUM, m_{set})$. If $(4BVSUM, m_{set})$ is solvable in $(\log |x| m_{set}(x))^{O(1)}$ time using $O(\log^{2-\varepsilon} m_{set}(x))$ space, then $(PSLE_{4,2}, m_{col})$ must be in PsubLIN by Lemma 4. This leads to the conclusion that LSH is false. Therefore, Theorem 11 holds.

References

1. Abboud, A., Bringmann, K., Dell, H., Nederlof, J.: More consequences of falsifying SETH and the orthogonal vectors conjecture. In: The Proceedings of STOC 2018, pp. 253–266 (2018)
2. Abboud, A., Williams, R. R., Yu., H.: More applications of the polynomial method to algorithm design. In: The Proceedings of SODA 2015, pp. 218–230 (2015)
3. Damgård, I., Dupuis, F., Nielsen, J.B.: On the orthogonal vector problem and the feasibility of unconditionally secure leakage-resilient computation. In: Lehmann, A., Wolf, S. (eds.) ICITS 2015. LNCS, vol. 9063, pp. 87–104. Springer, Cham (2015). https://doi.org/10.1007/978-3-319-17470-9_6
4. Impagliazzo, R., Paturi, R.: On the complexity of k-SAT. J. Comput. System Sci. **62**, 367–375 (2001)
5. Impagliazzo, R., Paturi, R., Zane, F.: Which problems have strongly exponential complexity? J. Comput. System Sci. **63**, 512–530 (2001)
6. Jones, N.D., Lien, Y.E., Laaser, W.T.: New problems complete for nondeterministic log space. Math. Syst. Theory **10**, 1–17 (1976)
7. Lokshtanov, D., Marx, D., Saurabh, S.: Lower bounds based on the exponential time hypothesis. Bull. EATCS **105**, 41–71 (2011)
8. Williams, R.: A new algorithm for optimal 2-constraint satisfaction and its implications. Theor. Comput. Sci. **348**, 357–365 (2005)
9. Williams, V.V.: Hardness of easy problems: basing hardness on popular conjectures such as the strong exponential time hypothesis. In: The Proceedings of IPEC 2015, LIPIcs, vol. 43, pp. 16–29 (2015)
10. Yamakami, T.: The 2CNF Boolean formula satisfiability problem and the linear space hypothesis. In: The Proceedings of MFCS 2017, LIPIcs, vol. 83, pp. 62:1–62:14 (2017). A complete and corrected version is available at arXiv:1709.10453
11. Yamakami, T.: Parameterized graph connectivity and polynomial-time sub-linear-space short reductions. In: Hague, M., Potapov, I. (eds.) RP 2017. LNCS, vol. 10506, pp. 176–191. Springer, Cham (2017). https://doi.org/10.1007/978-3-319-67089-8_13
12. Yamakami, T.: State complexity characterizations of parameterized degree-bounded graph connectivity, sub-linear space computation, and the linear space hypothesis. Theor. Comput. Sci. **798**, 2–22 (2019)
13. Yamakami, T.: Supportive Oracles for parameterized polynomial-time sub-linear-space computations in relation to L, NL, and P. In: Gopal, T.V., Watada, J. (eds.) TAMC 2019. LNCS, vol. 11436, pp. 659–673. Springer, Cham (2019). https://doi.org/10.1007/978-3-030-14812-6_41, Available also at arXiv:1901.05854
14. Yamakami, T.: Parameterized-NL completeness of combinatorial problems by short logarithmic-space reductions and immediate consequences of the linear space hypothesis. In: The Proceedings of FTC 2022. LNNS, vol. 559, pp. 776–795. Springer, Cham (2022). https://doi.org/10.1007/978-3-031-18461-1_51

Partition-Edge Fault-Tolerant Hamiltonicity of Pancake Graphs

Kun Zhao[1], Hongbin Zhuang[1], Xiao-Yan Li[1(✉)], Fangying Song[2], and Lichao Su[1]

[1] College of Computer and Data Science, Fuzhou University, Fuzhou, China
xyli@fzu.edu.cn
[2] School of Mathematics and Statistics, Fuzhou University, Fuzhou, China

Abstract. The pancake graph is an interconnection network that plays a vital role in designing parallel and distributed systems. Due to the unavoidable occurrence of edge faults in large-scale networks and the wide application of path and cycle structures, it is essential and practical to explore the embedding of Hamiltonian paths and cycles in faulty networks. However, existing fault models ignore practical distributions of faulty edges so that only linear edge faults can be tolerated. This paper introduces a powerful fault model named the partitioned fault model. Based on this model, we study the existence of Hamiltonian paths and cycles on pancake graphs with large-scale faulty edges for the first time. We show that the n-dimensional pancake graph P_n admits a Hamiltonian path between any two vertices, avoiding $\sum_{i=4}^{n}((i-4)((i-2)!-2)-1)+1$ partition-edge faults for $4 \leq n \leq 7$, and avoiding $\sum_{i=8}^{n}(\frac{(i-1)!}{2}-1)+399$ faulty partition-edges for $n \geq 8$. Moreover, we prove that P_n admits a Hamiltonian cycle, avoiding $\sum_{i=4}^{n}((i-4)((i-2)!-2)-1)+2$ faulty partition-edges for $4 \leq n \leq 7$, and avoiding $\sum_{i=8}^{n}(\frac{(i-1)!}{2}-1)+400$ partition-edge faults for $n \geq 8$. The comparison results show that our results are a large-scale enhancement of existing results.

Keywords: Edge-fault-tolerant · Hamiltonicity · Interconnection networks · Pancake graphs · Partitioned fault model

1 Introduction

The *interconnection network* plays a vital role as the underlying topology in parallel and distributed computer systems. It usually can be deemed a graph $G = (V(G), E(G))$, where the vertex set $V(G)$ represents the set of processors, and the edge set $E(G)$ represents the set of links connecting the processors. Hereafter, we do not distinguish between interconnection networks, parallel and distributed computer systems, and graphs. Due to the rapid expansion of network size, the

This work was supported by the Natural Science Foundation of Fujian Province (2022J05029) and the National Natural Science Foundation of China (62002062 and 61902071). (K. Zhao and H. Zhuang—Contributed equally to this work).

S.-Y. Hsieh et al. (Eds.): ICS 2022, CCIS 1723, pp. 192–204, 2022.
https://doi.org/10.1007/978-981-19-9582-8_17

occurrence of processor or link faults is inevitable, which places a challenge for networks to maintain reliable operation in the event of faults [1].

The n-dimensional pancake graph P_n, proposed by Akers *et al.* [2], is an attractive topology for designing massively parallel and distributed systems owing to its attractive properties such as regularity, strong hierarchies, symmetry, and maximal fault tolerance [2,3]. This graph was introduced from the famous combinatorial problem "pancake problem", whose answer is exactly the diameter of the corresponding pancake graph [4]. *Pancake-like graphs* are a general term for a class of graphs similar to pancake graphs. Many properties of pancake-like graphs have been investigated extensively, such as diagnosability [5–8], connectivity [9–12], path and cycle embedding [13–16], tree embedding [17–19].

Paths and *cycles* are two fundamental network structures in parallel and distributed systems [20]. Many efficient algorithms for solving algebraic and graph problems were designed based on path and cycle structures [21]. The *Hamiltonian path* is a special path that traverses all the vertices in a network exactly once. A *cycle* is a path with the same begin and end vertices. The *Hamiltonian cycle* is a cycle that includes all the vertices in a network. Specifically, Hamiltonian paths can be used in designing deadlock-free routing algorithms [22,23], and Hamiltonian cycles can be applied to design fault diagnostic algorithms [24]. Let G be an interconnection network. Then G is *Hamiltonian* (resp. *Hamiltonian connected*) if it contains a Hamiltonian cycle (resp. a Hamiltonian path between arbitrary two distinct vertices of G).

In large-scale interconnection networks, failures of components are inevitable. It is important and practical to embed Hamiltonian paths and cycles in large-scale networks [25], avoiding faulty edges (or vertices). Therefore, the concept of fault-tolerant Hamiltonian paths and cycles embedding has been proposed. Hsieh *et al.* [26] proposed that a graph is k-*edge fault-tolerant Hamiltonian* if $G - F$ is Hamiltonian for any faulty edge set $F \subseteq E(G)$ with $|F| \leq k$. Then Huang *et al.* [27] proposed that a graph is k-*edge fault-tolerant Hamiltonian connected* if $G - F$ is Hamiltonian connected for any faulty edge set $F \subseteq E(G)$ with $|F| \leq k$. The above concepts are under the *random fault model*. This model assumes that the distribution of faulty edges is not restricted. Some recent literature has paid attention to Hamiltonian paths and cycles embedding under the random fault model. Zhou *et al.* [28] proved that n-dimensional balanced hypercubes with $n \geq 2$ admit a Hamiltonian path between two vertices from different partite sets when $2n-2$ faulty edges occur. Fan *et al.* [29] showed that $(s+t+1)$-dimensional locally exchanged twisted cubes is $(s-1)$-edge fault-tolerant Hamiltonian and $(s-2)$-edge fault-tolerant Hamiltonian connected with $s \geq 2$, $t \geq 3$, and $s \leq t$. In fact, under the random fault model, the worst case tends to happen when all the faulty edges are concentrated at some vertex. However, this edge distribution case rarely occurs in the realistic scenario. The *conditional fault model* is proposed to overcome this flaw, which assumes that each vertex must be incident to at least two fault-free edges. This model attracted numerous researchers to study Hamiltonian paths and cycles embedding under the conditional fault model. Hsieh *et al.* [30] embedded a Hamiltonian path into the n-dimensional restricted hypercube-like network with at most $2n - 7$ conditional faulty edges for $n \geq 5$.

Kuo and Cheng [31] proposed that an n-dimensional folded hypercube is $(3n-7)$-edge fault-tolerant Hamiltonian under the conditional fault model for $n \geq 3$.

This paper introduces a novel fault model, called *partitioned fault model*, to explore the existence of Hamiltonian paths and cycles in the n-dimensional pancake graph P_n with large-scale faulty edges. This model allows restricting the number of faulty edges in each dimension so that stronger fault-tolerant Hamiltonian properties of networks can be achieved. On the basis of this model, we evaluate the edge fault tolerance of P_n with $n \geq 4$ when embedding Hamiltonian paths and cycles. Our contributions are presented as follows:

(1) Under the partitioned fault model, we prove that $P_n - F$ admits a Hamiltonian path between any two distinct vertices, where F is a faulty partition-edge set (defined in Sect. 2) with $|F| \leq \sum_{i=4}^{n}((i-4)((i-2)!-2)-1)+1$ for $4 \leq n \leq 7$ and $|F| \leq \sum_{i=8}^{n}(\frac{(i-1)!}{2}-1)+399$ for $n \geq 8$.
(2) Based on result (1), we further explore the existence of a Hamiltonian cycle in $P_n - F$ where F is a faulty partition-edge set with $|F| \leq \sum_{i=4}^{n}((i-4)((i-2)!-2)-1)+2$ for $4 \leq n \leq 7$ and $|F| \leq \sum_{i=8}^{n}(\frac{(i-1)!}{2}-1)+400$ for $n \geq 8$.
(3) We make a comparison of our results with existing results. The comparison shows that our results are a large-scale improvement from $n-4$ in [15] to $\sum_{i=4}^{n}((i-4)((i-2)!-2)-1)+1$, $n-3$ in [15] and $2n-7$ in [16] to $\sum_{i=4}^{n}((i-4)((i-2)!-2)-1)+2$ for $4 \leq n \leq 7$, and $n-4$ in [15] to $\sum_{i=8}^{n}(\frac{(i-1)!}{2}-1)+399$, $n-3$ in [15] and $2n-7$ in [16] to $\sum_{i=8}^{n}(\frac{(i-1)!}{2}-1)+400$ for $n \geq 8$.

The rest of this paper is organized as follows. Section 2 introduces necessary notations and the proposed fault model, and provides the definition and several important properties of pancake graphs. In Sect. 3, we study the fault-tolerant Hamiltonicity of the pancake graph under the partitioned fault model. Then, we compare our results with the existing results in Sect. 4. Finally, Sect. 5 concludes this paper.

2   Preliminaries

2.1   Notations and Definitions

The interconnection network can be represented as an undirected graph $G = (V(G), E(G))$, where $V(G)$ and $E(G)$ are its vertex set and edge set, respectively. Then $|V(G)|$ and $|E(G)|$ denote the size of $V(G)$ and $E(G)$, respectively. Given a graph H, if $V(H) \subseteq V(G)$ and $E(H) \subseteq E(G)$, then H is a *subgraph* of G. Let F be a faulty edge set of G, and let $G - F$ represent a graph by deleting all edges of F from G. Given a positive integer n, we denote the set $\{n, n-1, \ldots, 1\}$ as $\langle n \rangle$. To distinguish between sets and multisets, we use $\{[a, a, b]\}$ to denote the multiset $\{a, a, b\}$. We denote a complete graph with n vertices by K_n. A *path* Q is represented by $Q = \langle v_1, v_2, \ldots, v_k \rangle$, where $v_0, v_1, \ldots, v_k$ is a sequence of distinct vertices and (v_i, v_{i+1}) is an edge of Q with $i \in \langle k-1 \rangle$. A *cycle* C is the path such that $v_1 = v_k$. The *length* of Q (resp. C) is the number of edges in Q (resp. C). A path Q (resp. cycle C) is a *Hamiltonian path* (resp. *Hamiltonian cycle*) of G when $V(Q) = V(G)$ (resp. $V(C) = V(G)$). If for any two distinct vertices u, v in G, there exists a Hamiltonian path of G from u to v, then we say G is *Hamiltonian connected*, and G is a *Hamiltonian connected graph*. If there exists a *Hamiltonian cycle* in G, then G is *Hamiltonian*, and G is a *Hamiltonian graph*.

Definition 1 [26,27]. *Given a graph G and a faulty edge set F with $|F| \leq t$, if $G - F$ is still a Hamiltonian (resp. Hamiltonian connected) graph, then G is t-edge fault-tolerant Hamiltonian (resp. Hamiltonian connected).*

Next, we introduce the definition of partitioned fault model. Let G be a graph such that $E(G)$ can be partitioned into n subsets, denoted by E_i for $i \in \langle n \rangle$. Let F be a faulty edge set with $F \subseteq E(G)$, and $F_i = F \cap E_i$ with $i \in \langle n \rangle$ and $\{[|F_i| \mid i \in \langle n \rangle]\} = \{[e_1, e_2, \ldots, e_n]\}$ such that $e_n \geq e_{n-1} \geq \cdots \geq e_1$. A faulty edge set F is a *faulty partition-edge set* if $e_i \leq f(i)$ for each $i \in \langle n \rangle$, where $f(i)$ is a function of i. Next, we give the main definitions used in this paper based on partitioned fault model.

Definition 2. *Given a graph G and a faulty partition-edge set F with $|F| = \sum_{i=1}^{n} e_i \leq t$, if $G - F$ is still a Hamiltonian connected graph, then G is t-partition-edge fault-tolerant Hamiltonian connected.*

Definition 3. *Given a graph G and a faulty partition-edge set F with $|F| = \sum_{i=1}^{n} e_i \leq t$, if $G - F$ is still a Hamiltonian graph, then G is t-partition-edge fault-tolerant Hamiltonian.*

2.2 The Pancake Graph

An n-dimensional pancake graph $P_n = (V(P_n), E(P_n))$ can be defined as follows:

Definition 4 [2]. *$P_n = (V(P_n), E(P_n))$, where $V(P_n) = \{a_1 a_2 \cdots a_n | a_i \in \langle n \rangle$ and $a_i \neq a_j$ for $i \neq j\}$ and $E(P_n) = \{(a_1 a_2 \cdots a_{i-1} a_i \cdots a_n, a_i a_{i-1} \cdots a_2 a_1 \cdots a_n) | a_1 a_2 \cdots a_n \in V(P_n)$ and $2 \leq i \leq n\}$.*

Let $u = a_1 a_2 \cdots a_{i-1} a_i \cdots a_n$ be a vertex of P_n. We use u^i to denote the vertex $a_i a_{i-1} \cdots a_2 a_1 \cdots a_n$ with $2 \leq i \leq n$. Then edge (u, u^i) is called i-dimensional edge and the set of all i-dimensional edges is denoted by E_i with $2 \leq i \leq n$. For $2 \leq i \leq n$, by removing all i-dimensional edges from P_n, we obtain n disjoint subgraphs $P_n^1, P_n^2, \ldots, P_n^n$, and each subgraph is isomorphic to P_{n-1}. For $1 \leq i, j \leq n$ and $i \neq j$, we use $E^{i,j}(P_n)$ ($E^{i,j}$ for short) to denote the set of edges between P_n^i and P_n^j. The structure of pancake graph P_4 is illustrated in Fig. 1, where each edge is colored according to its dimension.

Some properties of n-dimensional pancake graph P_n are as follows [5].

(1) P_n is regular with degree $n - 1$, $|V(P_n)| = n!$, and $|E(P_n)| = n!(n-1)/2$.
(2) P_n is vertex symmetric and edge symmetric.

Definition 5. *Given an integer* $n \geq 5$, *let* $V \subseteq \langle n \rangle$ *and* F *be a faulty edge set of* P_n. $PT_n(V, F)$ *is the graph* $G = (V(G), E(G))$, *where* $V(G) = V$ *and* $E(G) = \{(i,j) | i, j \in V$ *and* $|E^{i,j}(P_n) \cap F| \leq (n-2)! - 3\}$.

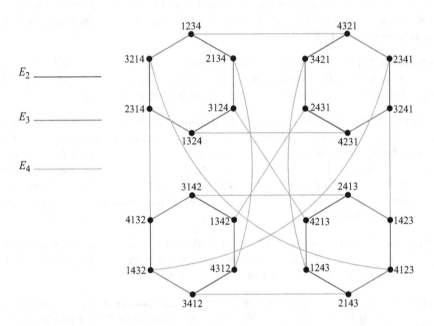

Fig. 1. The structures of P_4, where E_2 represents 2-dimensional edge, E_3 represents 3-dimensional edge, and E_4 represents 4-dimensional edge.

It is easy to see that $PT_n(V, F)$ maps the subgraphs P_n^i in $P_n - F$ into a vertex i in G for all $i \in V$. In fact, G is obtained from $K_{|V|}$ by removing the edge between i and j if $|E^{i,j}(P_n) \cap F| \geq (n-2)! - 2$. And for $i \neq j \in V$, if i and j are adjacent in G, then there exists at least three fault-free edges between P_n^i and P_n^j.

Lemma 1. *Let* $G = PT_n(V, F)$ *for* $V \subseteq \langle n \rangle$ *with* $|V| \geq 2$ *and* F *be a faulty edge set of* P_n. *Let* $x \in V(P_n^{j_1})$ *and* $y \in V(P_n^{j_2})$ *with* $j_1, j_2 \in V$. *Assume that* $P_n^i - F$ *is Hamiltonian connected for each* $i \in V$. *Then there is a path crossing all vertices in all* P_n^i *with* $i \in V$ *from* x *to* y *without crossing edges in* F *if there is a Hamiltonian path from* j_1 *to* j_2 *in* G.

Proof. Let $|V| = m$ and $\langle j_1, j_3, j_4, \ldots, j_m, j_2 \rangle$ be a Hamiltonian path in G between j_1 and j_2. When $m \geq 3$, since j_1 and j_3 are adjacent in G, there exists an edge (u_1, v_3) between $P_n^{j_1}$ and $P_n^{j_3}$ such that $u_1 \neq x \in V(P_n^{j_1})$ and $v_3 \in V(P_n^{j_3})$. Then since each $P_n^i - F$ are Hamiltonian connected, there exists a Hamiltonian path in $P_n^{j_1} - F$ from x to u_1. Repeating this process, we can obtain a Hamiltonian path between x and y, crossing all vertices in all P_n^i for

$i \in V$. When $m = 2$, since $|E^{j_1,j_2}(P_n)| - |E^{j_1,j_2}(P_n) \cap F| \geq 3$, there exists at least one fault-free edge (u,v) between $P_n^{j_1}$ and $P_n^{j_2}$ such that $u \neq x \in P_n^{j_1}$ and $v \neq y \in P_n^{j_2}$. Moreover, since $P_n^{j_1} - F$ and $P_n^{j_2} - F$ are Hamiltonian connected, there exists a Hamiltonian path Q_1 in $P_n^{j_1} - F$ from x to u, and a Hamiltonian path Q_2 in $P_n^{j_2} - F$ from v to y. Thus, $Q_1 \cup Q_2 \cup \{(u,v)\}$ froms the required Hamiltonian path (see Fig. 2). Then this lemma holds. □

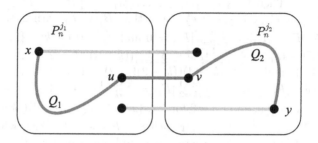

Fig. 2. Illustration of Lemma 1.

3 Partition-Edge Fault-Tolerant Hamiltonicity of Pancake Graphs

This section studies the edge fault-tolerant Hamiltonicity of the pancake graph under the partitioned fault model. First, we give some related lemmas.

Lemma 2 [32]. K_n is $(n-4)$-edge fault-tolerant Hamiltonian connected for $n \geq 4$.

Lemma 3 [15]. P_n is $(n-4)$-edge fault-tolerant Hamiltonian connected and $(n-3)$-edge fault-tolerant Hamiltonian for $n \geq 4$.

Note that $E(P_n)$ can be partitioned into $n-1$ subsets, denoted by E_i for $2 \leq i \leq n$. Let $F_i = F \cap E_i$ for $2 \leq i \leq n$ and $f(i)$ be a function of i. Then the faulty partition-edge set F of P_n is a faulty edge set such that $\{[\|F_i\| \mid 2 \leq i \leq n]\} = \{[e_2, e_3, \ldots, e_n]\}$, $e_n \geq \cdots \geq e_3 \geq e_2$, and $e_i \leq f(i)$ for each $2 \leq i \leq n$.

Theorem 1. For $n \geq 4$, let $F \subseteq E(P_n)$ be a faulty partition-edge set, then $P_n - F$ is Hamiltonian connected if

(1) $|F| \leq \sum_{i=4}^{n}((i-4)((i-2)! - 2) - 1) + 1$ for $4 \leq n \leq 7$;
(2) $|F| \leq \sum_{i=8}^{n}(\frac{(i-1)!}{2} - 1) + 399$ for $n \geq 8$;
(3) $e_i \leq \frac{(i-1)!}{2} - 1$ for each $i \in \langle n \rangle \setminus \langle 7 \rangle$;
(4) $e_i \leq (i-4)((i-2)! - 2) - 1$ for each $i \in \{5,6,7\}$;
(5) $e_i = 0$ for $i \in \{2,3,4\}$.

Proof. We will prove this theorem by induction on n. By Lemma 3, this theorem holds on P_4. For $n \geq 5$, assume that this theorem holds for P_m with $m < n$. Next we need to prove this theorem holds for P_n. Since P_n is edge symmetric, without loss of generality, let $|F_n| = \max\{[|F_n|, |F_{n-1}|, \ldots, |F_2|]\}$. That is, $|F_n| = e_n$. Then we divide P_n into n disjoint subgraphs $P_n^1, P_n^2, \ldots, P_n^n$ by deleting E_n, all of which are isomorphic to P_{n-1}.

Let x and y be arbitrary two vertices of P_n. Let $B_j^i = E(P_n^i) \cap F_j$ with $i \in \langle n \rangle$ and $2 \leq j \leq n$. Then let $\{[e_{n-1}^i, e_{n-2}^i, \ldots, e_2^i]\} = \{[|B_{n-1}^i|, |B_{n-2}^i|, \ldots, |B_2^i|]\}$ such that $e_{n-1}^i \geq e_{n-2}^i \geq \cdots \geq e_2^i$. Note that $B_j^i \subseteq F_j$ with $2 \leq j \leq n-1$. When $n = 5$, $|F| - |F_n| = \sum_{k=2}^4 |F_k| = 0$ and $e_k^i = 0$ for $k \in \{2,3,4\}$. When $6 \leq n \leq 8$, $|F| - |F_n| = \sum_{k=2}^{n-1} |F_k| \leq \sum_{k=5}^{n-1}((k-4)((k-2)!-2)-1)$, $e_k^i = 0$ for $k \in \{2,3,4\}$, and $e_k^i \leq (k-4)((k-2)!-2)-1$ for $k \in \{5,6,7\}$. When $n \geq 9$, we have $|F| - |F_n| = \sum_{k=2}^{n-1} |F_k| = \sum_{k=8}^{n-1} e_k + \sum_{k=5}^7 e_k + \sum_{k=2}^4 e_k \leq \sum_{k=8}^{n-1}(\frac{(k-1)!}{2}-1) + 399$, and $e_k^i = 0$ for $k \in \{2,3,4\}$, $e_k^i \leq (k-4)((k-2)!-2)-1$ for $k \in \{5,6,7\}$, $e_k^i \leq \frac{(k-1)!}{2} - 1$ for each $8 \leq k \leq n-1$. Thus, when x and y are in same $V(P_n^j)$ for $j \in \langle n \rangle$, there is a Hamiltonian path in $P_n^j - F$ between x and y. Next, we have the following cases.

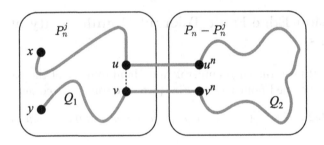

Fig. 3. The constructions in Case 1 of Theorem 1.

Case 1. Both x and y are in $V(P_n^j)$ with $j \in \langle n \rangle$.

By the induction hypothesis, there is a Hamiltonian path Q_1 in $P_n^j - F$ between x and y. Since $|V(P_n^j)| = (n-1)!$, the length of Q_1 is $(n-1)! - 1$. Thus there are $\lceil \frac{(n-1)!-1}{2} \rceil = \frac{(n-1)!}{2}$ mutually disjoint edges on Q_1. Since $\frac{(n-1)!}{2} - |F_n| \geq 1$ for $n \geq 5$, there exists at least one edge (u,v) of Q_1 such that $(u, u^n), (v, v^n) \notin F_n$. Assume that $u^n \in P_n^{j_1}$ and $v^n \in P_n^{j_2}$. Let $V = \langle n \rangle \setminus \{j\}$. Since $|F_n| \leq (n-4)((n-2)!-2)-1 = (n-5)((n-2)!-2)+(n-2)!-3$, $G = PT_n(V, F)$ is isomorphic to $K_{n-1} - L$ in the worst case, where L is a faulty edge set of K_{n-1} with $|L| = n-5$. By Lemma 2, there is a Hamiltonian path in G between j_1 and j_2. By Lemma 1, there is a path Q_2 crossing all vertices of all P_n^i for $i \in V$ between u^n and v^n. Thus, $Q_1 \cup Q_2 \cup \{(u, u^n), (v, v^n)\} \setminus \{(u,v)\}$ forms the required Hamiltonian path between x and y in $P_n - F$ (see Fig. 3).

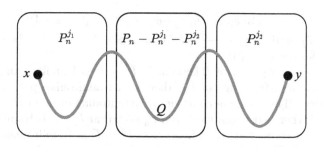

Fig. 4. The constructions in Case 2 of Theorem 1.

Case 2. $x \in V(P_n^{j_1})$ and $y \in V(P_n^{j_2})$ with $j_1, j_2 \in \langle n \rangle$ and $j_1 \neq j_2$.

Let $V = \langle n \rangle$. Since $|F_n| \leq (n-4)((n-2)! - 2) - 1 = (n-5)((n-2)! - 2) + (n-2)! - 3$, $G = PT_n(V, F)$ is isomorphic to $K_n - L$ in the worst case, where L is a faulty edge set of K_n and $|L| = n-5$. By Lemma 2, there exists a Hamiltonian path of G between j_1 and j_2. Thus, by Lemma 1, there is a Hamiltonian path Q in $P_n - F$ between x and y (see Fig. 4). □

Based on the Theorem 1 and Definition 2, we can obtain Theorem 2.

Theorem 2. *The n-dimensional pancake graph P_n is $(\sum_{i=4}^{n}((i-4)((i-2)! - 2) - 1) + 1)$-partition-edge fault-tolerant Hamiltonian connected for $4 \leq n \leq 7$ and $(\sum_{i=8}^{n}(\frac{(i-1)!}{2} - 1) + 399)$-partition-edge fault-tolerant Hamiltonian connected for $n \geq 8$.*

Theorem 3. *For $n \geq 4$, let $F \subseteq E(P_n)$ be a faulty partition-edge set, then $P_n - F$ is Hamiltonian if*

(1) $|F| \leq \sum_{i=4}^{n}((i-4)((i-2)! - 2) - 1) + 2$ *for* $4 \leq n \leq 7$;
(2) $|F| \leq \sum_{i=8}^{n}(\frac{(i-1)!}{2} - 1) + 400$ *for* $n \geq 8$;
(3) $e_i \leq \frac{(i-1)!}{2} - 1$ *for each* $i \in \langle n \rangle \setminus \langle 7 \rangle$;
(4) $e_i \leq (i-4)((i-2)! - 2) - 1$ *for each* $i \in \{5, 6, 7\}$;
(5) $e_2 + e_3 + e_4 \leq 1$.

Proof. We will prove this theorem by induction on n. By Lemma 3, this theorem holds on P_4 obviously. For $n \geq 5$, assume that this theorem holds for P_m with $m < n$. Next we need to prove this theorem holds for P_n. Since P_n is edge symmetric, without loss of generality, let $|F_n| = \max\{[|F_n|, |F_{n-1}|, \dots, |F_2|]\}$. That is, $|F_n| = e_n$. Then we divide P_n into n disjoint subgraphs $P_n^1, P_n^2, \dots, P_n^n$ by deleting all n-dimensional edges, all of which are isomorphic to P_{n-1}. Let $B_j^i = E(P_n^i) \cap F_j$ with $i \in \langle n \rangle$ and $2 \leq j \leq n$. Moreover, let $\{[e_{n-1}^i, e_{n-2}^i, \dots, e_2^i]\} = \{[|B_{n-1}^i|, |B_{n-2}^i|, \dots, |B_2^i|]\}$ such that $e_{n-1}^i \geq e_{n-2}^i \geq \cdots \geq e_2^i$. Note that $B_j^i \subseteq F_j$ with $2 \leq j \leq n-1$. When $n = 5$, $|F| - |F_n| = \sum_{k=2}^{4} |F_k| = 1$. When $6 \leq n \leq 8$, $|F| - |F_n| = \sum_{k=2}^{n-1} |F_k| \leq \sum_{k=5}^{n-1}((k-4)((k-2)! - 2) - 1) + 1$, $e_2^i + e_3^i + e_4^i \leq 1$, and $e_k^i \leq (k-4)((k-2)! - 2) - 1$ for $k \in \{5, 6, 7\}$. When $n \geq 9$, we have $|F| - |F_n| = \sum_{k=2}^{n-1} |F_k| = \sum_{k=8}^{n-1} e_k + \sum_{k=5}^{7} e_k + \sum_{k=2}^{4} e_k \leq$

$\sum_{k=8}^{n-1}(\frac{(k-1)!}{2}-1)+400$. In addition, $e_2^i+e_3^i+e_4^i \le 1$, $e_k^i \le (k-4)((k-2)!-2)-1$ for $k \in \{5,6,7\}$, and $e_k^i \le \frac{(k-1)!}{2}-1$ for each $8 \le k \le n-1$. Then $P_n^j - F$ is Hamiltonian for each $j \in \langle n \rangle$.

When $e_2 + e_3 + e_4 = 0$, by Theorem 1, $P_n - F$ is Hamiltonian connected. Then for every fault-free edge in P_n, there is a Hamiltonian path between its two end vertices. Thus, we can construct a Hamiltonian cycle in $P_n - F$. When $e_2+e_3+e_4 = 1$, there exists one subgraph P_n^j such that $P_n^j - F$ is Hamiltonian but not Hamiltonian connected. By Theorem 1, $P_n^l - F$ is Hamiltonian connected for $l \in \langle n \rangle \setminus \{j\}$. Then there exists a Hamiltonian cycle C in $P_n^j - F$. Since $|V(P_n^j)| = (n-1)!$, the length of C is $(n-1)!$. Then there are $\frac{(n-1)!}{2}$ mutually disjoint edges on C. Since $\frac{(n-1)!}{2} - |F_n| \ge 1$ for $n \ge 5$, there exists at least one edge (u,v) in C such that (u,u^n) and (v,v^n) is fault-free. Similar with Case 1 in Theorem 1, there is a Hamiltonian path Q of $P_n - P_n^j - F$ from u^n and v^n. Thus, $C \cup Q \cup \{(u,u^n),(v,v^n)\} \setminus \{(u,v)\}$ forms the required Hamiltonian cycle in $P_n - F$ (see Fig. 5). $\qquad\square$

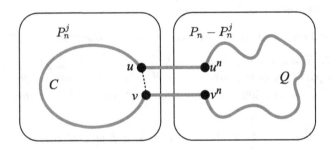

Fig. 5. Hamiltonian cycle of $P_n - F$.

Based on the Theorem 3 and Definition 3, we can obtain Theorem 4.

Theorem 4. *The n-dimensional pancake graph P_n is $(\sum_{i=4}^{n}((i-4)((i-2)! - 2) - 1) + 2)$-partition-edge fault-tolerant Hamiltonian for $4 \le n \le 7$ and $(\sum_{i=8}^{n}(\frac{(i-1)!}{2} - 1) + 400)$-partition-edge fault-tolerant Hamiltonian for $n \ge 8$.*

4   Comparison Results

In this section, we compare the edge fault-tolerant Hamiltonicity of the pancake graphs P_n under the partitioned fault model with other known results. Hung et al. [15] proved that P_n is $(n-3)$-edge fault-tolerant Hamiltonian and $(n-4)$-edge fault-tolerant Hamiltonian connected for $n \ge 4$. Tsai et al. [16] showed that P_n is $(2n-7)$-edge fault-tolerant Hamiltonian under the conditional fault model for $n \ge 4$. We proved that P_n is $(\sum_{i=4}^{n}((i-4)((i-2)! - 2) - 1) + 2)$-partition-edge fault-tolerant Hamiltonian for $4 \le n \le 7$, $(\sum_{i=8}^{n}(\frac{(i-1)!}{2} - 1) + 400)$-partition-edge fault-tolerant Hamiltonian for $n \geq 8$, $(\sum_{i=4}^{n}((i-4)((i-2)!-2)-1)+1)$-partition-edge fault-tolerant Hamiltonian connected for $4 \leq n \leq 7$, and $(\sum_{i=8}^{n}(\frac{(i-1)!}{2} - 1) + 399)$-partition-edge fault-tolerant Hamiltonian connected for $n \geq 8$. We show all results mentioned above in Table 1. For the simplicity of comparison, the fault tolerance of P_n when embedding Hamiltonian paths under the random fault model is denoted as $RTQ(P_n)$, the fault tolerance of P_n when embedding Hamiltonian cycles under the random fault model is denoted as $RTC(P_n)$, the fault tolerance of P_n when embedding Hamiltonian cycles under the conditional fault model is denoted as $CTC(P_n)$, the fault tolerance of P_n when embedding Hamiltonian paths under the partitioned fault model is denoted as $PTQ(P_n)$, and the fault tolerance of P_n when embedding Hamiltonian cycles under the partitioned fault model is denoted as $PTC(P_n)$. That is, $RTQ(P_n) = n - 4$, $RTC(P_n) = n - 3$, $CTC(P_n) = 2n - 7$ for $n \geq 4$, $PTQ(P_n) = \sum_{i=4}^{n}((i-4)((i-2)! - 2) - 1) + 1$ for $4 \leq n \leq 7$, $PTQ(P_n) = \sum_{i=8}^{n}(\frac{(i-1)!}{2} - 1) + 399$ for $n \geq 8$, $PTC(P_n) = \sum_{i=4}^{n}((i-4)((i-2)! - 2) - 1) + 2$ for $4 \leq n \leq 7$, and $PTC(P_n) = \sum_{i=8}^{n}(\frac{(i-1)!}{2} - 1) + 400$ for $n \geq 8$.

Table 1. The upper bounds of edge faults that P_n can tolerate under different fault models when embedding Hamiltonian paths and cycles.

	Random fault model	Conditional fault model	Partitioned fault model
Hamiltonian paths embedding	$n - 4$ for $n \geq 4$ [15]	Unknown	$\sum_{i=4}^{n}((i-4)((i-2)!-2)-1)+1$ for $4 \leq n \leq 7$ $\sum_{i=8}^{n}(\frac{(i-1)!}{2} - 1) + 399$ for $n \geq 8$ (Theorem 1)
Hamiltonian cycles embedding	$n - 3$ for $n \geq 4$ [15]	$2n - 7$ for $n \geq 4$ [16]	$\sum_{i=4}^{n}((i-4)((i-2)!-2)-1)+2$ for $4 \leq n \leq 7$ $\sum_{i=8}^{n}(\frac{(i-1)!}{2} - 1) + 400$ for $n \geq 8$ (Theorem 3)

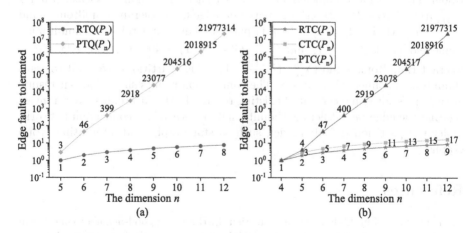

Fig. 6. The comparisons among (a) the results in [15] and Theorem 1; (b) the results in [15,16] and Theorem 3.

We show the values of RTQ(P_n), RTC(P_n), CTC(P_n), PTQ(P_n), PTC(P_n) variety with n in Fig. 6. Figure 6(a) shows the variation of RTQ(P_n) and PTQ(P_n) with the dimension n. It can be seen that PTQ(P_n) = 3 and RTQ(P_n) = 1 when n = 5. However, with the growth of n, the gap between PTQ(P_n) and RTQ(P_n) increases rapidly. When n = 12, PTQ(P_n) = 21977314 and RTQ(P_n) = 8, which implies that the number of faulty edges tolerated in our method is more than 2747K (K is thousand) times higher than that of the random fault model. Figure 6(b) shows the variation of RTC(P_n), CTC(P_n), and PTC(P_n) with the dimension n. When n = 4, RTC(P_n) = CTC(P_n) = PTC(P_n) = 1 since the basis of our induction is [15]. When n = 12, RTC(P_n) = 9 and CTC(P_n) = 17. However, PTC(P_n) = 21977315, which means that the upper bound of edge faults tolerance in our method is 2442K times higher than that of [15] and 1293K times higher than that of [16].

Based on the above comparison, it can be shown that the number of faulty edges tolerated under the partitioned fault method grows explosively with n advances. Compared to our proposed model, the fault tolerance obtained through the random fault model and conditional fault model is limited to the linear scope of n. Therefore, as the value of n grows, the partitioned fault model can better evaluate the fault tolerance of the pancake graph.

5   Conclusion

Fault tolerance is an important research topic in interconnection networks. In this paper, we study the Hamiltonicity of pancake graphs under a powerful fault model called partitioned fault model. This fault model achieves better fault tolerance by restricting the distribution of faulty edges in each dimension. Under the partitioned fault model, we show that n-dimensional pancake graph is $(\sum_{i=4}^{n}((i-4)((i-2)!-2)-1)+2)$-partition-edge fault-tolerant Hamiltonian and $(\sum_{i=4}^{n}((i-4)((i-2)!-2)-1)+1)$-partition-edge fault-tolerant Hamiltonian connected for $4 \leq n \leq 7$, and $(\sum_{i=8}^{n}(\frac{(i-1)!}{2}-1)+400)$-partition-edge fault-tolerant Hamiltonian and $(\sum_{i=8}^{n}(\frac{(i-1)!}{2}-1)+399)$-partition-edge fault-tolerant Hamiltonian connected for $n \geq 8$. The comparison results show that our results are a large-scale enhancement of existing results. In the future, it is worth investigating the edge fault-tolerant Hamiltonicity of other interconnection networks under the partitioned fault model, such as star graphs and alternating group graphs.

References

1. Peng, S.-L., Lin, C.-K., Tan, J.J.M., Hsu, L.-H.: The g-good-neighbor conditional diagnosability of hypercube under PMC model. Appl. Math. Comput. **218**(21), 10406–10412 (2012)
2. Akers, S.B., Krishnamurthy, B.: A group-theoretic model for symmetric interconnection networks. IEEE Trans. Comput. **38**(4), 555–565 (1989)

3. Kanevsky, A., Feng, C.: On the embedding of cycles in pancake graphs. Parallel Comput. **21**(6), 923–936 (1995)
4. Gates, W.H., Papadimitriou, C.H.: Bounds for sorting by prefix reversal. Discret. Math. **27**(1), 47–57 (1979)
5. Liu, W., Lin, C.-K.: Diagnosability and diagnostic algorithm for pancake graph under the comparison model. J. Interconnect. Netw. **15**(1–2), 1550005:1–1550005:15 (2015)
6. Song, S., Zhou, S., Li, X.-Y.: Conditional diagnosability of burnt pancake networks under the PMC model. Comput. J. **59**(1), 91–105 (2015)
7. Song, S., Li, X.-Y., Zhou, S., Chen, M.: Fault tolerance and diagnosability of burnt pancake networks under the comparison model. Theor. Comput. Sci. **582**, 48–59 (2015)
8. Chang, N.-W., Wu, H.-J., Hsieh, S.-Y.: Pancake graphs: structural properties and conditional diagnosability. J. Comb. Optim. (2022). https://doi.org/10.1007/s10878-022-00877-8
9. Wang, N., Meng, J., Tian, Y.: Neighbor-connectivity of pancake networks and burnt pancake networks. Theor. Comput. Sci. **916**, 31–39 (2022)
10. Gu, M.-M., Chang, J.-M.: Neighbor connectivity of pancake graphs and burnt pancake graphs. Discret. Appl. Math. **324**, 46–57 (2023)
11. Gu, M.-M., Hao, R.-X., Tang, S.-M., Chang, J.-M.: Analysis on component connectivity of bubble-sort star graphs and burnt pancake graphs. Discret. Appl. Math. **279**, 80–91 (2020)
12. Lin, C.-K., Huang, H.-M., Hsu, L.-H.: The super connectivity of the pancake graphs and the super laceability of the star graphs. Theor. Comput. Sci. **339**(2), 257–271 (2005)
13. Konstantinova, E., Medvedev, A.: Independent even cycles in the pancake graph and greedy prefix-reversal gray codes. Graphs Comb. **32**(5), 1965–1978 (2016)
14. Lin, C.-K., Tan, J.J.M., Huang, H.-M., Hsu, D.F., Hsu, L.-H.: Mutually independent Hamiltonian cycles for the pancake graphs and the star graphs. Discret. Math. **309**(17), 5474–5483 (2009)
15. Hung, C.-N., Hsu, H.-C., Liang, K.-Y., Hsu, L.-H.: Ring embedding in faulty pancake graphs. Inf. Process. Lett. **86**(5), 271–275 (2003)
16. Tsai, P.-Y., Fu, J.-S., Chen, G.-H.: Edge-fault-tolerant Hamiltonicity of pancake graphs under the conditional fault model. Theor. Comput. Sci. **409**(3), 450–460 (2008)
17. Pai, K.-J., Chang, R.-S., Chang, J.-M.: Constructing dual-CISTs of pancake graphs and performance assessment of protection routings on some Cayley networks. J. Supercomput. **77**(1), 990–1014 (2021)
18. Yang, Y.-C., Kao, S.-S., Klasing, R., Hsieh, S.-Y., Chou, H.-H., Chang, J.-M.: The construction of multiple independent spanning trees on burnt pancake networks. IEEE Access **9**, 16679–16691 (2021)
19. Cheng, D.-W., Chan, C.-T., Hsieh, S.-Y.: Constructing independent spanning trees on pancake networks. IEEE Access **8**, 3427–3433 (2020)
20. Fan, J., Jia, X.: Edge-pancyclicity and path-embeddability of bijective connection graphs. Inf. Sci. **178**(2), 340–351 (2008)
21. Akl, S.G.: Parallel Computation: Models and Methods. Prentice Hall, Upper Saddle River (1997)
22. Ebrahimi, M., Daneshtalab, M., Liljeberg, P., Plosila, J., Flich, J., Tenhunen, H.: Path-based partitioning methods for 3D networks-on-chip with minimal adaptive routing. IEEE Trans. Comput. **63**(3), 718–733 (2014)

23. Fan, J.: Hamilton-connectivity and cycle-embedding of the Möbius cubes. Inf. Process. Lett. **82**(2), 113–117 (2002)
24. Ye, L.-C., Liang, J.-R.: Five-round adaptive diagnosis in Hamiltonian networks. IEEE Trans. Parallel Distrib. Syst. **26**(9), 2459–2464 (2015)
25. Wang, X., Erickson, A., Fan, J., Jia, X.: Hamiltonian properties of DCell networks. Comput. J. **58**(11), 2944–2955 (2015)
26. Hsieh, S.-Y., Chen, G.-H., Ho, C.-W.: Fault-free Hamiltonian cycles in faulty arrangement graphs. IEEE Trans. Parallel Distrib. Syst. **10**(3), 223–237 (1999)
27. Huang, W.-T., Tan, J.J.M., Hung, C.-N., Hsu, L.-H.: Fault-tolerant Hamiltonicity of twisted cubes. J. Parallel Distrib. Comput. **62**(4), 591–604 (2002)
28. Zhou, Q., Chen, D., Lü, H.: Fault-tolerant Hamiltonian laceability of balanced hypercubes. Inf. Sci. **300**, 20–27 (2015)
29. Fan, W., Fan, J., Han, Z., Li, P., Zhang, Y., Wang, R.: Fault-tolerant Hamiltonian cycles and paths embedding into locally exchanged twisted cubes. Front. Comput. Sci. **15**(3), 1–16 (2021)
30. Hsieh, S.-Y., Lee, C.-W., Huang, C.-H.: Conditional edge-fault Hamiltonian-connectivity of restricted hypercube-like networks. Inf. Comput. **251**, 314–334 (2016)
31. Kuo, C.-N., Cheng, Y.-H.: Hamiltonian cycle in folded hypercubes with highly conditional edge faults. IEEE Access **8**, 80908–80913 (2020)
32. Ho, T.-Y., Shih, Y.-K., Tan, J.J.M., Hsu, L.-H.: Conditional fault Hamiltonian connectivity of the complete graph. Inf. Process. Lett. **109**(12), 585–588 (2009)

Cloud Computing and Big Data

Query Regrouping Problem on Tree Structure for GPUs Accelerated Platform

Che-Wei Chang[1]([⊠]), Xinyu Zhang[2], and Hung-Chang Hsiao[3]

[1] Longwe University of Science and Technology, Taoyuan, Taiwan
AlfredChang@mail.lhu.edu.tw
[2] Chinese Culture University, Taipei, Taiwan
A9107048@ulive.pccu.edu.tw
[3] National Cheng Kung University, Tainan, Taiwan
hchsiao@csie.ncku.edu.tw

Abstract. The paper presents an ongoing study to maximize query performance for tree-like structures on the GPUs platform. We formalized the problem with an assignment problem for minimizing the number of global memory accesses. We also conduct experiments to identify the benefits of query performance optimization.

Keywords: GPUs · Tree · Query

1 Introduction

GPUs are cost-efficient to accelerate processing on large data sets due to high on-chip memory bandwidth and instruction throughput with thousands of processing cores. In GPUs, cores are managed by Streaming Processors (SMs), and tasks are divided into blocks and scheduled to SMs to be executed in parallel. In Fig. 1, we have 9 SMs in a GPU, each including 12 Cores, and twelve tasks are scheduled and assigned to the SM for execution.

Before execution, each task transfers data between global and local memory when executed. In Fig. 1, the green arrow indicates two memory accesses: local and global. Note that global memory latency can be dozens of times that of local memory [1] and reducing access to global memory is recommended.

The memory access pattern can be significant in execution performance. It is suggested to coalesce memory access to promote memory performance. In Fig. 2, for the non-coalesced memory access, three memory accesses are needed; however, it only requires one memory access since data are re-arranged and stored with a continuous memory address.

In addition, tasks in a block execute one instruction at a time; the tasks in different branch paths need to wait for another. In Fig. 3, we can see that the tasks are divided into *it* and *else* branches and executed in two consecutive stages so that the latency of the execution time will be extended. Therefore, it is necessary to avoid branch divergence to utilize computation resources [1].

S.-Y. Hsieh et al. (Eds.): ICS 2022, CCIS 1723, pp. 207–211, 2022.
https://doi.org/10.1007/978-981-19-9582-8_18

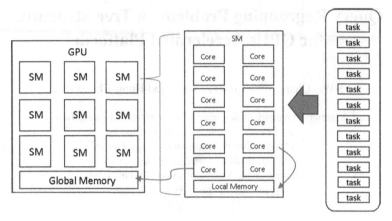

Fig. 1. An example of GPU architecture and execution model.

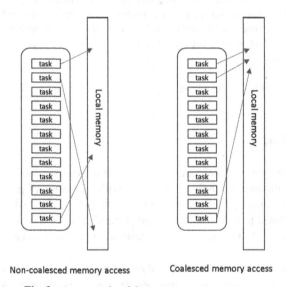

Fig. 2. An example of the memory access pattern.

Recently, several studies have been proposed using GPUs to accelerate queries on tree-like structures [3–5] and tend to conquer the challenges mentioned above but require a system model for the optimal solution. In this paper, we proposed a formal model to transform the performance optimization problem into an assignment problem. We also show the benefit of the optimal solution to the assignment problem can significantly improve the query performance.

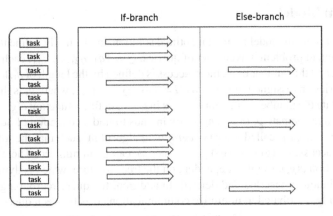

Fig. 3. An example of branch divergence.

2 Query Acceleration on Tree Structure

Tree structures are essential in modern applications. However, accelerated queries in the tree structure are challenging since queries traverse different paths, causing branching divergence issues. Each path step also needs multiple global memory access whose bandwidth is lower than local memory access. Recent work [2] suggested arranging tasks into blocks can improve query performance.

For example, in Fig. 4, there are four queries with targeted id 2, 30, 35, and 1, denoted as q (2), $q(30)$, $q(35)$, and $q(1)$. Assume that we have four query tasks initially assigned into two query groups, say $g_1 = \{q(2), q(30)\}$ and $g_2 = \{q(35), q(1)\}$. The number of global memory access is 4 for each group since queries in g_1 and g_2 have different branch paths. Suppose that we regroup the query to $g'_1 = \{q (2), q(1)\}$ and $g'_2 = \{q(35), q(30)\}$. In that case, the number of global memory access can be reduced to 3 for both g'_1 and g'_2 since the first step of the query path for $q(1)$ and $q(2)$ (or for $q(35)$ and $q(30)$) are both in the same branch path and only need one global memory access. Note that the second step of q (1) and $q(2)$ cannot be coalesced by one global memory access since the nodes are not stored in a continuous memory address, the same as g'_2.

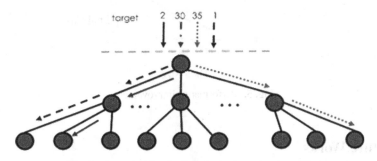

Fig. 4. An example of queries on a tree structure [2].

3   System Model

We propose a system model to find an optimal solution and formally define the problem as an assignment problem. Given a set of queries, $Q = \{q_1, q_2, ..., a_n\}$, each q_i traverse on a path p_i, and the number of memory access is defined by the length of p_i, $|p_i|$. Assume that the queries are assigned into groups $G = \{g_1, g_2, ..., g_m\}$, where g_i is the subset of Q. To calculate the number of memory access in g_i, we define a function $c(g_i)$ as the total number of edges on path p_i in g_i. Our study intends to find a collection of query groups $G = \{g_1, g_2, ..., g_m\}$, called a query *regrouping* algorithm, such that the total number of memory accesses, $c(g_1) + c(g_2) + ... + c(g_m)$, can be minimized. The challenge is that the function $c(g_i)$ is highly dependent on the tree structure, which is dynamic when data is continuously inserted and deleted. In addition, the query regrouping algorithm should be fully distributed to minimize communication costs between query tasks.

4   Experimental Result

We evaluate the improvement gap between average and optimized query performance to understand our system model better. We test the total query time (Latency) for data sizes ranging from 2^{16} to 2^{21}. Since a tree structure dominates the query performance, we create a perfect binary tree to find an optimal case. We then simulate the average case with a randomly shuffled set of keys (Average Case) and a sorted set of keys (Optimal Case). Each query group is divided into equal sizes. We measure the latency of queries, and the experimental results show that the latency of the average case increases dramatically with a large data size compared to the optimal case and leads to low utilization. The results also show that an average case can be improved significantly (Fig. 5).

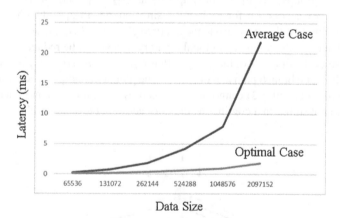

Fig. 5.   Performance improvement.

5   Future Works

Previous research on GPU acceleration lacks a formal problem definition [7–12]. In this short paper, we argue that query performance can be optimized by regrouping queries and demonstrate the low computation utilization for queries on a tree structure. For future work, we seek a distributed, fine-grained mechanism for the regrouping queries with close to optimal performance applied on a dynamic tree structure.

Acknowledgment. Che-Wei Chang and Hung-Chang Hsiao were partially supported by the Intelligent Manufacturing Research Center (iMRC) from The Featured Areas Research Center Program within the framework of the Higher Education Sprout Project by the Ministry of Education (MOE) and Ministry of Science and Technology (MOST) under Grant NSTC 111-2222-E-034-002 - in Taiwan.

References

1. CUDA C++ Programming Guide. https://docs.nvidia.com/cuda/cuda-c-programming-guide/index.html. Accessed 7 Oct 2022
2. Zhang, W., Yan, Z., Lin, Y., Zhao, C., Peng, L.: A high throughput B+tree for SIMD architectures. IEEE Trans. Parallel Distrib. Syst. **31**, 707–720 (2020)
3. Awad, M.A., Ashkiani, S., Johnson, R., Farach-Colton, M., Owens, J.D.: Engineering a high-performance GPU B-tree. In: Proceedings of the 24th Symposium on Principles and Practice of Parallel Programming (2019)
4. Xie, Z., Cai, Q., Jagadish, H.V., Ooi, B.C., Wong, W.: PI: a parallel in-memory skip list based index (2016)
5. Zhang, J., et al.: S3: a scalable in-memory skip-list index for key-value store. Proc. VLDB Endow. **12**, 2183–2194 (2019)
6. Gregg, C., Hazelwood, K.M.: Where is the data? Why you cannot debate CPU vs. GPU performance without the answer. In: (IEEE ISPASS) IEEE International Symposium on Performance Analysis of Systems and Software, pp. 134–144 (2011)
7. Bakkum, P., Skadron, K.: Accelerating SQL database operations on a GPU with CUDA. GPGPU-3 (2010)
8. Kim, C., et al.: FAST: fast architecture sensitive tree search on modern CPUs and GPUs. In: Proceedings of the 2010 ACM SIGMOD International Conference on Management of Data (2010)
9. Kaczmarski, K.: Experimental B+-tree for GPU. ADBIS (2011)
10. Jin, G., Endo, T., Matsuoka, S.: A multi-level optimization method for stencil computation on the domain that is bigger than memory capacity of GPU. In: 2013 IEEE International Symposium on Parallel & Distributed Processing, Workshops and PHD Forum, pp. 1080–1087 (2013)
11. Rawat, P.S., Rastello, F., Sukumaran-Rajam, A., Pouchet, L., Rountev, A., Sadayappan, P.: Register optimizations for stencils on GPUs. In: Proceedings of the 23rd ACM SIGPLAN Symposium on Principles and Practice of Parallel Programming (2018)
12. Jin, G., Endo, T., Matsuoka, S.: A parallel optimization method for stencil computation on the domain that is bigger than memory capacity of GPUs. In: 2013 IEEE International Conference on Cluster Computing (CLUSTER), pp. 1–8 (2013)

The Enhancement of Classification of Imbalanced Dataset for Edge Computing

Chih-Ming Huang[1]([✉]), Ming-Ya Hsu[1], Chuan-Sheng Hung[1],
Chun-Hung Richard Lin[1], and Shi-Huang Chen[2]

[1] National Sun Yat-Sen University, Kaohsiung 804, Taiwan
andrewh232@gmail.com, cshung@g-mail.nsysu.edu.tw,
lin@cse.nsysu.edu.tw
[2] Shu-Te University, Kaohsiung 824, Taiwan
shchen@stu.edu.tw

Abstract. The applications of imbalanced datasets are very common in real life around the world, such as patients with rare disease, detection of mechanical abnormalities, etc. Those types of datasets require the better construction of a classification model in order to get better predictions of which group the data belongs to. Therefore, how the classification models been constructed and how to improve the accuracy of the imbalanced data is more and more crucial.

This paper uses Convex Hull and Hyperplane algorithms to improve the original prediction method, which based on the Location-based Nearest Neighbor (LBNN), proposed for one-class classification problems. With this prediction model, we found this method can also benefit for edge computing with limited CPU processing power and memory as the unclassified data can be judged if it belongs to target class on the edge node.

From our experimental result shows that the improved method has better performance in most imbalanced datasets. Besides, in terms of data storage we don't need to keep historical data by retained only the model of calculation matrix, which can determine whether the unknown data belongs to the target class or not. This would significantly reduce the computing and storage effort.

Keywords: Imbalance data · Location-Based Nearest Neighbor (LBNN) · Convex hull · Hyperplane

1 Introduction

Imbalanced data learning is one of the important areas of machine learning. It mainly focuses on how to learn data patterns from imbalanced data. Taking a two-classes data set as an example, while the amount of data in one class is much larger than the amount of data in the other class, we usually call the data set "Imbalanced Data". Imbalanced datasets are very common in reality. One of the examples is fraudulent transaction detection in Fintech and eCommerce. Fraudulent transaction dataset is account for a very small portion of the total number of transactions. Another example is the detection

© The Author(s), under exclusive license to Springer Nature Singapore Pte Ltd. 2022
S.-Y. Hsieh et al. (Eds.): ICS 2022, CCIS 1723, pp. 212–222, 2022.
https://doi.org/10.1007/978-981-19-9582-8_19

of product quality in the factory. The number of qualified products is much larger than the number of unqualified products.

The minority data commonly has much lower probability of occurrence and also requiring a long time for collection. For instance, in one of medical area, bacteremia is a kind of serious disease caused by blood infection of bacteria. The diagnosis of this disease requires about one week of blood culture. However, only less than one percent of those blood culture reports are positive of those patients who are suspected with bacteremia. It doesn't make sense for patients to wait for the report for such long time and then starting the treatment. So, if we could take the blood test reports that can come out within a few hours to predict the results of blood culture, the earlier of the treatment been implied on patient, and the fewer medical resources been wasted.

For such kind of imbalanced datasets, we are more concerned about the minority data. Therefore, how to make a better classifier to find out the minority data is our concern.

The One-Class Classification (OCC) problem is a unique case in machine learning. In the process of collecting data, we can easily obtain the target class data. However, the non-target class data is very rare or even absent. Nevertheless, it is great importance to capture the data of those non-target class. For example, if a severely traumatized patient can be marked within the stroke data set, the Visiting Staff (VS) can take more active treatment for this patient.

In practice, such problems as machine misdiagnosis and rare disease identification, the target class of data (standard operation of the machine, judgment of non-rare disease patients) often account for almost the entire data set, and the non-target class of data are difficult to obtain due to the limit budget or physiological characteristics, etc. If we take traditional classification methods to classify imbalanced data, the prediction results of the classification model are usually more biased towards majority samples, resulting in getting poor results. Therefore, for imbalanced classification problems, we take the OCC method for improvement.

For One-Class Classification problem, commonly only the data of the target class can be obtained, but the data of the non-target class may not exist. [1] One-Class Nearest Neighbor (OCNN) is taken for distinguishing whether the data is the target class. A set of theoretical analyses are proposed to show the relationship between different parameters and been taken to identify invisible examples for non-target class. However, those methods just compare the data locally and do not consider the distribution characteristics of the overall data. Therefore, a Location-Based Nearest Neighbor (LBNN) based on clustering is derived [2]. Nonetheless, both the two nearest neighbor search strategies require storing all historical data points to determine the type of undetermined data. Considering the hardware with limited computing resources, such algorithms consume large memory and time, which doesn't suitable for local edge computing system.

In this paper, we try to improve the Location-Based Nearest Neighbor (LBNN) method by taking convex hulls and hyperplanes to replace the Nearest Neighbor mechanism. We substituted the model with edge computing so that the process for predicting unknown data can be calculated on the edge nodes, while also effectively improving the accuracy rate of the model. Concerning the experimental part, we take the KEEL data sets to verify the performance improvement of the algorithm.

2 Related Work

2.1 Imbalanced Data

In the real world, there are many types of imbalanced data. Imbalanced data make traditional machine learning methods tend to distinguish all samples as the majority class in classification. Moreover, it would result in bad prediction accuracy for minority class data samples. This problem is called "Class Imbalance Problem". Such problem has caused new challenges for research in the field of data mining.

The so-called "imbalanced data" means that the number of one class in the data is much larger than the other class, and class with minority data are usually much more important. For example, in the medical diagnosis data of rare diseases, the diseased data samples are hard to access compares with common diseases. While we take classifiers to classify imbalanced data sets, the classification performance usually gets poor result. It's mainly because the classifiers would generate learning biases (towards most categories) and result in poor classification [3].

In practice, class imbalance problems already exist in many fields, such as medical diagnosis [4, 5], customer churn detection [6], etc. Those classes with minority data are often the part that experts would focus to. Take bankruptcy prediction as an example. Only a small number of companies will get bankruptcy. Fail to catch these bankrupt companies would result in significant losses for the bank. Therefore, the problem of imbalanced class requires more attentions from experts.

The class imbalance problem often has the following two characteristics:

- Category overlap: As shown in Fig. 1(a), when different classes overlap, it would be difficult for the classifier to distinguish. The common situation is that the minority class is classified as the main class.
- Small separation: As shown in Fig. 1(b), a small number of samples are scattered in different feature spaces in small groups, which would make the process of training and classification more complicated.

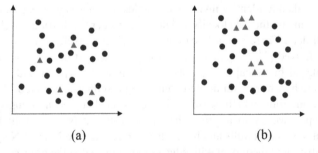

(a)   (b)

Fig. 1. Category overlap and small separation

2.2   One-Class Classification Problem

The hypothesis of the one-class classification problem [7] is that only one class can be used in the training process. We call this class "target class", and the rest are "non-target class". The one-class classifier uses the characteristics of the target class to try to find a boundary to include all the target class data. In practice, personal ECG wearable devices in delicate medical care as one typical example (using ECG to predict hyperglycemia, hyperkalemia, etc.). In the initial stage of using the devices, only healthy data can be collected, and it's not making sense that if we let the patient put on the wearable device for collecting target data until it collected enough data for a long time then start the prediction. Another way for above case is to take big data for predicting personal illness. However, it has proven ineffective because the physiological characteristics of individuals are apart from others. For example, the electrocardiogram wavelength, the position, and height of the peak are all different. In order to overcome the dilemma of traditional classification algorithms situation, one-class classification algorithms have played an important role.

A suitable one-class classifier must have good generalization ability. In addition to having a high recognition rate for non-target classes, it cannot overuse the information of the target class, causing overfitting and losing the ability to recognize the target class. At the same time, it must properly handle the target class and outliers to get a good decision boundary. A one-class classification problem is shown in Fig. 2. The blue crosses belong to the target class, the red points belong to the non-target class, and the black dashed line is the decision boundary. We can use the following mathematical formula (2) to express one-class classification problems:

$$f(z) = (d(z) < \theta_z) \tag{2}$$

$d(z)$ is an unknown data z the measured value of the target class group (such as distance, density, etc.), θ_z is the threshold of $d(z)$, $f(z)$ is a categorical, used to decide whether to accept z as the target class.

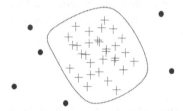

Fig. 2. One-class classification diagram

2.3 Location-Based Nearest Neighbor (LBNN)

According to One-Class Nearest Neighbor (OCNN), whether it is 11NN or JKNN, when an unknown data comes in, they must perform two rounds of nearest neighbor searches for the entire training data sets. The first-round searches for J nearest neighbors, and the second-round search for J. K nearest neighbors, the time complexity is $O(2dn + J \times 2dn) \rightarrow O((J + 1) \times 2dn)$, which searches for the nearest neighbors of the nearest neighbors. We can expect that these nearest neighbors are mostly located in neighboring blocks. The unknown data and these nearest neighbors are mostly compared locally, without considering the distribution characteristics of the overall data sets, which may affect the final performance of the model. So, [2] propose the nearest neighbor search strategy LBNN based on clustering is compared with 11NN and JKNN (Fig. 3).

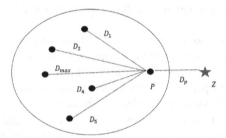

Fig. 3. JKNN search diagram

LBNN first classifies the training data by KMOR and sets a percentile $Q, 0 \leq Q \leq 1$. For an unknown data $u_i, i \in \{1, 2, ...n\}$, find a nearest neighbor $P_{i,c}, c \in \{1, 2, ...k\}$ from each group. Treat these nearest neighbors as the reference point of the group it belongs to and finally calculate the distance table $L_{i,c}$ between the reference point $P_{i,c}$ and other data in the group. If the distance from the unknown data to the reference point of any group $d_{i,c}$ is less than the percentile Q of the distance table $L_{i,c}$. We differentiate the unknown data as the target class, and the search time complexity of LBNN strategy is $O(kdn + kdn) \rightarrow O(2kdn)$.

3   Research Method

The data sets that we leveraged in this paper are all bases two classes. First, we use the Isolation Forest algorithm to detect outliers. Then delete them and perform principal component analysis (PCA) on all data to reduce the dimensionality. In the training process, we set the majority of data as the target class. Second, split the data into training data set and test data set using K-fold cross-validation. Third, training data set with K-means clustering then each group of data we find convex hull and get hyperplane matrix equation. Fourth, the test data set is taken to verify this model. Ultimately, various validation indexes will be retrieved by the machine (Fig. 4).

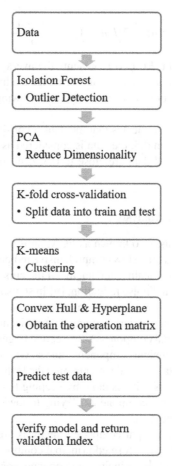

Fig. 4. Research method flowchart

3.1 Isolation Forest

General anomaly detection algorithms commonly take distance or density calculations to try to divide the boundary between target data and outliers. Isolation Forest [8] randomly selects feature spaces in a tree structure then split them. Storing each piece of data in leaf nodes and forming a completed binary tree, so-call itree. To overcome the problem of result deviation caused by random cutting, it is necessary to establish multiple itrees at the same time, that is, iforest. Isolation Forest has excellent computing speed and is suitable for processing enormous amounts of data. The basic concept is that the closer the data to the root node, the more likely it is an outlier.

In order to evaluate the degree of abnormality of each piece of data, we use formulas (3) and (4) to calculate the anomaly score of each piece of data:

$$S(x, n) = 2^{-\frac{E(h(x))}{c(n)}} \tag{3}$$

$$c(n) = 2H(n-1) - \frac{2(n-1)}{n} \tag{4}$$

n is the total number of data, $E(h(x))$ represents the average height of data x in each itree, $c(n)$ mainly uses harmonic numbers to normalize the height of the tree, according to the calculated anomaly score, we can discuss the following three situations:

- If anomaly score close to 1 indicates that the data is considered as anomalous data.
- If anomaly score is less than 0.5, the data is considered as a normal data.
- If the anomaly scores of all data are close to 0.5, it means that the data set has no obvious outlier.

3.2 Principal Component Analysis

Principal component analysis, also known as PCA, aims to adapt the idea of dropping transform multiple indicators into a few comprehensive indicators. It's taken for machine learning to reduce the dimensionality of data, avoid the curse of dimensionality, and be taken for feature extraction and noise reduction. [9] In statistics, it is a typical technique to simplify data sets. It takes linear transformation to transform the data into a new coordinate system, so the first large variance of any data projection is at the first coordinate (called the first on the principal component), the second largest variance is on the second coordinate (called second principal component), and so on. Component analysis reduces the dimensionality of the data sets while maintaining the feature that contributes the most to the variance of the data sets. This is done by keeping the low principal components and ignoring the high principal components. Trying to lower content and retaining the most important aspects of the data.

The important goal of principal component analysis are representativeness, independence and simplicity. The transformed principal components retain the information of the original variables, and the principal components cannot be overlapped. A few principal components replace the original multiple variables.

3.3 Convex Hull and Hyperplane

In geometric space, a hyperplane is a subspace with a co-dimension of 1 in n-dimensional Euclidean space. Simply put, it is a subspace with one dimension less than the space in which it is located. In general, it's of a straight line in a plane or a plane in space. For example, a one-dimensional line can divide a two-dimensional surface into two parts, and a two-dimensional surface can divide a three-dimensional body into two parts. That is, hyperplane is (n − 1)-dimensional subspace can be used to divide the n-dimensional space. When there are enough hyperplanes, a closed space can be formed. The convex polygon P can be enclosed by five hyperplanes. Through this concept, we can use the hyperplane equation to define the space enclosed by convex hull.

4 Experimental Results

4.1 Experimental Environment

(See Table 1).

Table 1. Execution environment

OS	Ubuntu 20.04
CPU	AMD Ryzen 7 2700X
Graphics card	Nvidia GeForce RTX 2080
RAM	32 GB
Programming language	Python

4.2 Experimental Data Set

We selected 10 standard imbalanced data sets from the KEEL-dataset repository. These data sets are all with two categories and collected from different fields. The "glass2" and "glass4" are the data sets for glass classification. The "2" in "glass2" means that the second category is taken as positive, and the other categories are taken as negative, forming a "one-versus-rest" two-category data set. "glass4", "Yeast4" and "ecoli4" are all having the similar concepts.

Table 2. KEEL data set

KEEL dataset	Feature	Samples	Minority samples	Majority samples	Imbalance ratio
segment0	19	2308	329	1979	6.02
Yeast4	8	1484	51	1433	28.09
Yeast5	8	1484	44	1440	32.72
Yeast6	8	1484	35	1449	41.4
ecoli4	7	336	20	316	15.8
glass2	9	214	17	197	11.58
glass4	9	214	15	199	15.47
pageblocks0	10	5472	559	4913	8.79
abalone9-18	8	731	42	689	16.4
pima	8	768	268	500	1.86

The data sets of "Yeast" series and "ecoli4" are applications of biological sciences (classification of proteins). "segment0" is the image classification of outdoor objects, where the characters are various pixel information in the image. "pageblocks0" is the classification of the document, and the character is the layout information of the document. "pima" is the diabetes diagnosis data of Indians, characterized by basic physiological information. (Age, BMI, etc…) Finally, "abalone9-18" is the age classification of abalone (Table 2).

4.3   Experimental Results and Analysis

After the algorithm model has been trained, k matrices of size $p*(n+1)$ will be obtained. k is the number of clusters. p is the number of points required to enclose the convex hull in the clusters. n represents the data dimension. When an unknown data inputs, it will be multiplied with matrix, and plus the offset. That is, the time complexity is $O(kpn+kp)$.

The purpose of running with KEEL dataset is to observe the applicability of each method to imbalanced data set. The results show that the improved method has better performance in most data sets. In the AUC part, most data set results are higher than 0.7, indicating that the model has the value to predict. The few data set results that do not exceed 0.7 might be due to the data set has a high degree of overlapping or the number of clusters are not enough to present the characteristics of the class. At the same time, the accuracy looks good. The results indicate that the improved method has better stability in general cases (Tables 3 and 4).

Table 3. AUC

Algorithm dataset	One-class SVM	11NN	JKNN	LBNN	Advanced method
segment0	0.652	0.726	0.803	0.861	**0.869**
yeast4	0.473	0.511	0.503	0.534	**0.848**
yeast5	0.502	0.589	0.599	0.605	**0.841**
yeast6	0.467	0.640	0.584	0.626	**0.873**
ecoli4	0.494	0.668	0.699	**0.753**	0.737
glass2	0.481	0.717	0.789	**0.813**	0.701
glass4	0.555	0.623	0.689	0.764	**0.781**
pageblocks0	0.521	0.771	0.807	0.855	**0.890**
abalone9–18	0.424	0.596	**0.639**	0.622	0.619
pima	0.466	0.501	0.506	0.508	**0.581**

Table 4. Accuracy

Algorithm dataset	One-class SVM	11NN	JKNN	LBNN	Advanced method
segment0	0.808	0.965	**0.976**	0.869	0.874
yeast4	0.501	0.574	0.427	0.681	**0.793**
yeast5	0.577	0.706	0.517	0.701	**0.781**
yeast6	0.497	0.675	0.525	0.777	**0.813**
ecoli4	0.620	0.576	0.591	**0.741**	0.735
glass2	0.635	0.632	0.735	**0.855**	0.756
glass4	0.736	0.552	0.669	**0.773**	0.735
pageblocks0	0.542	0.960	**0.979**	0.883	0.879
abalone9–18	0.467	0.516	0.569	0.618	**0.684**
pima	0.449	0.545	0.398	0.429	**0.583**

5 Conclusion

In practical applications, the collection of industrial or medical data commonly gets the One-Class or data imbalanced problem. Traditional algorithms commonly required to sample data sets or taking specific methods such as weight adjustment and cost-sensitive learning to adapt for those situations then get logical results. However, those specific methods usually include some disadvantages. Sampling methods reduce the number of majority class and would cause the loss of information. Increasing the number of minority class may lead to overfitting. The generation of synthetic samples makes the interpretability of the model problematic. Weight adjustment and cost-sensitive methods are focusing on the algorithms which must correctly classify minority class data that would reduce the recognition rate of majority class data.

For imbalanced data, we take one-class classification. We took the class with majority data for training and alternately mix the remaining majority data and all the class of the minority data as the test data. The results indicated that the improved method can effectively improve accuracy rate.

References

1. Khan, S.S., Ahmad, A.: Relationship between variants of one-class nearest neighbors and creating their accurate ensembles. IEEE Trans. Knowl. Data Eng. **30**(9), 1796–1809 (2018)
2. Wun-Hui, Z.: The Study of Enhancement of One-Class Nearest Neighbor for Imbalanced Dataset. National Sun Yat-sen University, Taiwan (2021)
3. Padmaja, T.M., Dhulipalla, N., Bapi, R.S., Krishna, P.R.: Unbalanced data classification using extreme outlier elimination and sampling techniques for fraud detection. In: International Conference on Machine Learning and Cybernetics on Advanced Computing and Communications, pp. 511–516 (2007)

4. Su, C.-T., Chen, L.-S., Yih, Y.: Knowledge acquisition through information granulation for imbalanced data. Expert Syst. Appl. **31**(3), 531–541 (2006)
5. Cohen, G., Hilario, M., Sax, H., Hugonnet, S., Geissbuhler, A.: Learning from imbalanced data in surveillance of nosocomial infection. Artif. Intell. Med. **37**, 7–18 (2006)
6. Xie, Y., Lia, X., Ngai, E.W.T., Ying, W.: Customer churn prediction using improved balanced random forests. Expert Syst. Appl. **36**, 5445–5449 (2009)
7. Wenzhu, S., Wenting, H., Zufeng, X., Jianping, C.: Overview of one-class classification. In: 2019 IEEE 4th International Conference on Signal and Image Processing, pp. 6–10 (2019)
8. Liu, F.T., Ting, K.M., Zhou, Z.: Isolation forest. In: 2008 Eighth IEEE International Conference on Data Mining, pp. 413–422 (2008)
9. Hoyle, D.C., Rattray, M.: PCA learning for sparse high-dimensional data. Europhys. Lett. **62**(1), 117–123 (2003)

Development of Personnel Epidemic Prevention Monitoring Access Control System

Shih-Wen Jiang[1], Syuan-You Chen[2], Whai-En Chen[2], and Hsin-Te Wu[3]([⊠])

[1] National Lo-Tung Commercial Vocational High School, Yilan, Taiwan
[2] Asia University, Taichung, Taiwan
[3] National Ilan University, Yilan, Taiwan
hsinte@niu.edu.tw

Abstract. Because of coronavirus variants, it is necessary to pay attention to epidemic prevention measures in the cultivation or product packaging processes. In addition to giving customers more peace of mind when using the products, it also ensures that operators wear masks, work clothes and gloves in the work area. This paper constructs an access control system for personnel epidemic prevention monitoring, which uses IoTtalk [1] to connect IoT devices (such as magnetic reed switches, intelligent switches, RFID readers, and RFID wristbands), utilizes RFID for personnel identification, and employs real-time streaming protocol [2] to take the image of IP Cam for YOLOv4 [3] identification program. The identification program detects whether the personnel is indeed wearing the required equipment. If the personnel is not wearing the required device, the detector will trigger a push broadcast system constructed by LINE Notify to inform the operator for processing. Moreover, we developed an emergency entry mechanism; if an emergency happens, the personnel can trigger the emergency door opening by swiping the card multiple times within a specified time. This function allows the person to enter without wearing the required equipment.

Keywords: IoTtalk · RFID · Real time streaming protocol · YOLOv4 · LINE notify

1 Introduction

The 2020 novel coronavirus outbreak (COVID-19) has caused a global pandemic that has upended economies worldwide; to stop the spread of the virus, governments around the world have adopted a series of strict preventive measures, including lockdowns, quarantines, remote work, travel bans and more. The constant mutation of the new coronavirus makes it impossible to relax the epidemic prevention policies. Therefore, the breeding industry must also focus on epidemic prevention and give customers (consumers) more peace of mind when using products. However, as far as self-prevention procedures are concerned, they cannot be verified and confirmed, and there may be loopholes in epidemic prevention. According to the literature survey, there are many kinds of door lock systems. In [4], the author proposes an intelligent door lock system architecture to analyze the possible threats and corresponding solutions. The main architectural process is

© The Author(s), under exclusive license to Springer Nature Singapore Pte Ltd. 2022
S.-Y. Hsieh et al. (Eds.): ICS 2022, CCIS 1723, pp. 223–229, 2022.
https://doi.org/10.1007/978-981-19-9582-8_20

that the user logs in to the system through the application for registration and credential verification, the server will return the authentication response to the user, and provide unlockable resources to the user who has successfully logged in. Then, after the user makes an unlock request, the request will be verified by the server. The server will verify the authorization scope of the user. If it is within the authorized range, forward the user's unlock request message to the corresponding ESP8266, and finally unlocked door. There is another document [5] similar to the architecture of the above-mentioned document [4], the operation of which is that users can use tablet computers, smart phones, laptops and other devices to install the application developed by the author to control unlocking or locking. The unlocking method is controlled by providing login credentials, such as username and password, which will be verified in the database through the Internet of Things. If the credentials are invalid, a buzzer will sound and an SMS alert will be sent to the building owner. In the architecture of document [5], we also found several short-comings. (1) If the user is in a WIFI environment, the bluetooth in the architecture will easily interfere with the WIFI and become unstable. The system in this paper uses WIFI to transmit or receive messages throughout the process. (2) Arduino UNO is a develop-ment version and needs to be connected to a Bluetooth module, which is not practical in practice. In contrast, the system in this paper uses a microcomputer device. The micro-computer itself has strong computing power, and has USB and display interface. It also has a network connection function. After the setting is completed, the internal program can be modified and executed through remote access. (3) The structure design of open-ing the door with a servo motor is not practical, and there is no practical experience to prove it. The system in this paper has been deployed and applied in the actual field, and the practicality is high. (4) Because the system needs to perform user login verification before opening the door, and the database is on the external network, if the network is unstable, it is easy to cause abnormal data verification. In contrast, because the system in this paper is deployed under the local network, it is less likely that the internal network system will be paralyzed due to problems with the external network. If the notification function of this paper fails to send out the message due to the unstable network, warn-ing lights can also be deployed on the site to notify the on-site management personnel. Another system related to PPE detection and unlocking, the author of the literature [6] uses the Convolutional Neural Network (CNN) method to train pre-collected images of workers wearing PPE (including safety helmets, safety glasses, safety masks and safety earmuffs). After training, it is divided into 12 categories, and then the red and green lights are triggered according to the classification results. A red light means no full wear, and a green light means full wear. The system has two activation mechanisms, and workers need to wear safety shoes before PPE identification. The first mechanism is to activate the RFID reader if the safety shoes are detected, and the second mechanism is to activate the PPE identification if the RFID reader is triggered. However, in the case of its PPE classification, the identification results of PPE classification will cause the system classi-fication error due to workers wearing safety glasses, which will reduce the identification rate. As far as the method of identifying equipment in this article is concerned, it is to use a single photo to detect multiple objects and add a voting mechanism to improve the accuracy. In addition, in terms of wearing reminders, the literature [6] uses green lights and red lights as reminders, and can only know whether the wearing is complete or not.

This paper further considers what the staff is wearing and what they are not wearing, in other words, it is used to remind the staff whether there is a lack of equipment, and if there is a lack of equipment, it can indicate what is missing. The epidemic in recent years has prompted governments around the world to implement a policy of wearing masks when going out to reduce the risk of virus infection. Among them, the author of the literature [7] proposed a method for identifying face masks. It mainly captures faces through OpenCV. The main step is to first identify whether there is a face on the scene. If there is a face, then continue to identify whether the face is wearing a mask. If there is a mask, it will output the words "wearing a mask" and frame it. If it is identified that someone is not wearing a mask, it will be further identified who (name) is not wearing a mask. If the face is a person in the database, an email notification will be sent to remind the person that the person is not wearing a mask. However, as for the method used, there is no actual data to prove the recognition stability of the system, and the comparison of face identity data requires pre-training of a large number of human face data, and it should be based on the premise that the data is easy to obtain. It is necessary to pay attention to relevant epidemic prevention measures during the breeding or the product packaging processes. If there is a system that can detect whether the epidemic prevention regulations are implemented, it is possible to check and assist monitoring personnel in completing the self-epidemic prevention process before they enter the aquaculture farm. First, the operator will be asked to wear the required equipment, such as masks, work clothes and gloves, and then swipe a security card to enter the testing area to wait for the system to check whether the equipment is complete. Finally, swiping the card again will unlock the system. Moreover, we have planned the equipment and traffic flow required for the onsite installation system based on the experimental site, as shown in Fig. 1.

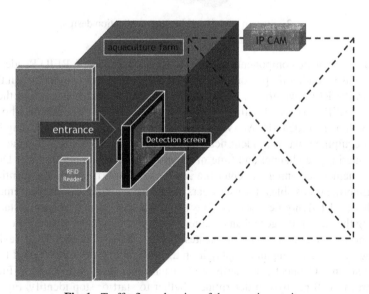

Fig. 1. Traffic flow planning of the experiment site.

2 Experiment Environment Architecture

This paper is to implement a set of "personnel epidemic prevention monitoring access control system" to solve the problems discussed in this paper. Through IoTtalk, this thesis integrates the two major modules of this system, the personnel detection module and the access control module, as shown in Fig. 2.

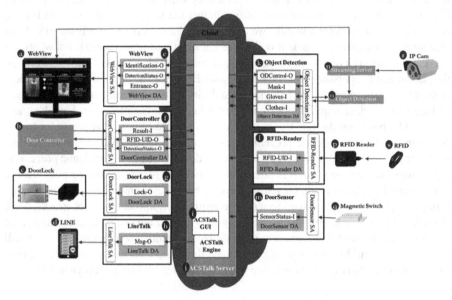

Fig. 2. System overall architecture application design.

Its main hardware components include (a) RFID wristband & RFID Reader, which are mainly used to identify personnel, and bind personnel information through the card number in the RFID wristband, when the person puts the bracelet close to the RFID Reader, the RFID wristband will be swiped, and the identity of the person who swipes the card will be recorded. (b) WebView is used to display real-time monitoring images, specified equipment wearing identification status, personnel photos, personnel names, time of entering the channel and time of entering the aquaculture farm. (c) Doorlock controls whether personnel can enter the aquaculture farm based on the identification results. Entering is possible if the user wears the device as required or triggers emergency entry rules. (d) LINE notifies the user if any abnormal state occurs. Abnormal state refers to swiping the card or triggering an emergency entry state without wearing the required equipment. (e)A magnetic switch indicates that the door is opened. Then device will return the time of entering and display it on the webpage. (f) IP Cam is used to obtain video streaming. Connect each hardware to each other through IoTtalk, in Fig. 2(k), ODControl-O will be used to determine whether to start or stop identify, Fig. 2(n) is used to capture the video stream and divide the stream into two parts, the first is used to display the real-time picture in Fig. 2(a), the second is to use Fig. 2(o) to identify whether there are equipment (masks, gloves and work clothes) worn according to regulations, and the identification result will be passed to IoTtalk through Fig. 2(k), in addition, Fig. 2(e) records the RFID card number, recognition result and door opening state respectively. Figure 2(f) will receive the card number and the identification result and pass it to Fig. 2(b), and will return three different results according to rules, (1) Emergency entry state, (2) Unequipped state, (3) Normal entry state, and finally forwarded by IoTtalk to Fig. 2(h) for message push broadcast, and forwarded to Fig. 2(g) to perform the action of whether to open the door.

3 Experiment Results

In this paper, the screen of the personnel epidemic prevention monitoring access control system is shown in Fig. 3, and information such as equipment identification results, personnel identities, and the time of entering the detection channel are recorded. In addition, in addition to evaluating the reliability of the model, this paper also tested 1767 photos, of which only 20 were not recognized, and the recognition accuracy was about 98.86%. In addition, this research introduces AIoT technology for development, and also uses IoTtalk to integrate software and hardware modules, so that each module can perform its own duties, thereby reducing the difficulty of subsequent maintenance. In the process of system development, a number of mechanisms have been added one after another. After repeated testing and improvement, they are more and more in line with humanized development. In addition, this paper also sorts out the differences between other related literatures and this paper (see Table 1).

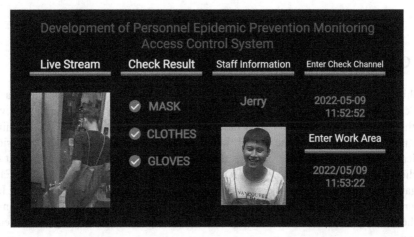

Fig. 3. Screen of the personnel epidemic prevention monitoring access control system.

Finally, this paper will combine OnePose technology in the future to detect whether masks, gloves and work clothes are in relative positions, so as to avoid the system from detecting the above three objects, but not actually wearing them.

Table 1. Feature comparison table of related literature.

Function / Literature	Object recognition	Control unlock	Immediacy	Power saving	Live image
ACSTalk	✓	✓	✓	✓	✓
[4]		✓	✓		
[5]		✓	✓		
[6]	✓		✓	✓	
[7]	✓		✓		✓

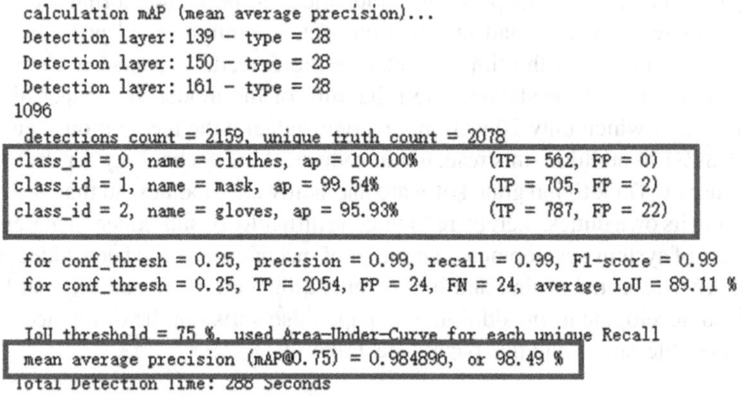

```
calculation mAP (mean average precision)...
Detection layer: 139 - type = 28
Detection layer: 150 - type = 28
Detection layer: 161 - type = 28
1096
detections count = 2159, unique truth count = 2078
class_id = 0, name = clothes, ap = 100.00%      (TP = 562, FP = 0)
class_id = 1, name = mask, ap = 99.54%          (TP = 705, FP = 2)
class_id = 2, name = gloves, ap = 95.93%        (TP = 787, FP = 22)

for conf_thresh = 0.25, precision = 0.99, recall = 0.99, F1-score = 0.99
for conf_thresh = 0.25, TP = 2054, FP = 24, FN = 24, average IoU = 89.11 %

IoU threshold = 75 %, used Area-Under-Curve for each unique Recall
mean average precision (mAP@0.75) = 0.984896, or 98.49 %
Total Detection Time: 288 Seconds
```

Fig. 4. Model evaluation.

4   Conclusion

In this paper, YOLOv4 is used for 6000 times of training, the labels include masks, work clothes, and gloves. After the AI model is learned from the training set, it will go through the test set for so-called model evaluation (as shown in Fig. 4). It mainly evaluates the reliability of the model, which mainly includes AP (average precision) indicates the evaluation index of target detection; TP (True Positive) indicates that the prediction is correct; FP (False Positive) indicates that the prediction is wrong; FN (False Negative) indicates that the object actually exists, but the object is not recognized; IoU (intersection over union)) represents the overlap of two objects divided by the union of the two objects; mAP (mean average precision) represents the average AP of each object.

References

1. Lin, Y.B., Lin, Y.W., Huang, C.M., Chih, C.Y., Lin, P.: IoTtalk: a management platform for reconfigurable sensor devices. IEEE Internet Things J. 4(5), 1552–1562 (2017)
2. Schulzrinne, H., Rao, A., Lanphier, R.: RFC2326: real time streaming protocol (RTSP) (1998)

3. Bochkovskiy, A., Wang, C.Y., Liao, H.Y.M.: Yolov4: optimal speed and accuracy of object detection. arXiv preprint arXiv:2004.10934 (2020)
4. Pavelić, M., Lončarić, Z., Vuković, M., Kušek, M.: Internet of Things cyber security: smart door lock system. In: 2018 International Conference on Smart Systems and Technologies (SST) (2018)
5. Shanthini, M., Vidya, G., Arun, R.: IoT enhanced smart door locking system. In: 2020 Third International Conference on Smart Systems and Inventive Technology (ICSSIT) (2020)
6. Pradana, R.D.W., et al.: MIdentification system of personal protective equipment using Convolutional Neural Network (CNN) method. In: 2019 International Symposium on Electronics and Smart Devices (ISESD) (2019)
7. Adusumalli, H., Kalyani, D., Krishna Sri, R., Pratapteja, M., Prasada Rao, P.V.R.D.: Face mask detection using OpenCV. In: 2021 Third International Conference on Intelligent Communication Technologies and Virtual Mobile Networks (ICICV) (2021)

The Use of Serverless Processing in Web Application Development

Robert Banaszak and Anna Kobusinska[(✉)]

Faculty of Computing and Telecommunications, Poznan University of Technology,
ul. Piotrowo 3, 60-965 Poznan, Poland
{Robert.Banaszak,Anna.Kobusinska}@cs.put.poznan.pl

Abstract. This paper analyses the applicability of serverless processing in the web application field. We discuss whether the serverless approach fulfils the web applications' requirements, and provide the hands-on implementation of a serverless-based web application to illustrate the new possibilities offered by the serverless environment and provide a deeper understanding and practical experience of the researched domain.

Keywords: Serverless processing · FaaS · Web applications

1 Introduction

Serverless approach is gaining increased popularity as an approach to develop and manage applications and services [4]. It changes the perspective of the application architecture, basing it on the stateless and short-lived functions executed on-demand [1]. The serverless approach is an attractive solution for many companies, due to the benefits it brings in terms of cost reduction, increased agile development and a focus on business logic alone [2].

At the same time, the field of web applications expanded significantly, making them an appealing medium for various companies to modernise their businesses or to introduce new products [3]. The widespread availability of the Internet, as well as computers and mobile devices, contributed to the significant growth of available web applications, covering many areas of human life. The development of web applications is related to the requirement of their increased availability, but also their efficiency and scaleability according to the number of active users while at the same time ensuring security, along with a rich and intuitive interface [5].

Given the popularity and wide applicability of both of the above-mentioned approaches, the key objective of this paper is to research whether the serverless processing and Function as a Service model could be beneficial in web application development. To answer this question, we discuss the requirements currently imposed on web applications and analyse whether the application of the serverless paradigm in web application development will meet them. Moreover, we analyze the serverless processing model concerning an interesting example implementation covering the web application responsible for generating interactive presentations based on the LaTeX files. The chosen example of a web

S.-Y. Hsieh et al. (Eds.): ICS 2022, CCIS 1723, pp. 230–242, 2022.
https://doi.org/10.1007/978-981-19-9582-8_21

application is distinguished by its complexity, so the considered application in a serverless approach has to meet different requirements and is difficult to apply. In the paper, we show that utilizing the instant scalability of the serverless architecture with a pay-as-you-go billing model could be beneficial to meet the variable demand of the presentation processing requests and solve the above-mentioned problems.

The paper is structured as follows. Section 2 characterises the requirements of web applications and discusses the applicability of the serverless paradigm in the web application domain. Section 3 describes the proposed implementation of serverless-based web application. Section 4 discusses the optimisation process and experimental results. Section 5 presents the final remarks on serverless processing in web applications. Finally, Sect. 6 concludes the paper.

2 Fulfilment of the Web Application Requirements by Serverless Processing

Despite the diversity of web applications, some of the defined requirements can be shared by the majority of them [6]. It is desired that web applications scale according to the workload demands without noticeable performance degradation, preserving availability and characterising with resilience and fault-tolerance. Moreover, with the increase in the data volumes processed, the web applications should remain safe and compliant with various confidentiality regulations. Finally, the maintainability of the web application is important, covering the monitoring, observability, and deployment processes from the operational point of view, along with the ease of development and preserving good modularity to ensure a satisfying agility level when developing new features.

Below we discuss how the serverless paradigm meets the requirements of web applications in terms of solution scalability, performance, cost reduction, reliability and development flexibility.

Performance and Scalability. The stateless and short-lived design of the serverless function facilitates horizontal scaling. However, performance from a single request point of view is still debatable, given the cold start phenomenon. In addition, the ephemeral nature of processing and lack of addressability requires the use of external components to maintain state and communicate with other services. The time required to allocate resources and load the function execution environment, along with the communication load between the components that make up the load processing, can significantly affect the overall processing time. However, architects and developers by carefully designing application architecture can partially alleviate the undesired latency to make it acceptable for the web application. Cloud providers tend to make further improvements to mitigate the unpredictability of the serverless platform and provide dedicated functionality to ensure predictable execution and response times. As a result, the performance of serverless implementations is comparable to more traditional architectures, with more stable characteristics and lower degradation rates, especially when the application is experiencing traffic growth and needs to scale appropriately to meet the load demand, as well as maintain satisfactory response time [7]. Moreover, the serverless components are characterized by fine-grained scaling capabilities, enabling instant horizontal scaling to meet the demand. Scaling is handled automatically by the cloud platform in response to events coming into the system, affecting only the components required to process them. The serverless architecture is therefore designed to track and respond to workloads with greater fidelity compared to scaling a solution based on containers or virtual machines.

Reliability. According to the characteristics of the serverless components, services are designed with implicit high availability. Multiple serverless components provide various retry mechanics in case of errors occurring during the processing related to issues with the application logic or hardware faults. For example, by default AWS, Lambda invoked asynchronously retries the event processing 2 times upon processing failure. If the processing is not completed successfully after retries, based on the configuration, the event can be placed in Dead Letter Queue (DLQ), which is a dedicated Amazon SQS instance for handling failed messages.

Along with programmatic solutions, establishing processes including proper monitoring, observability, and triggering alarms in case of undesired component behaviour could be beneficial, mitigating further administrator intervention or even restoring the system automatically to the appropriate state. For production running application, the solutions considering the microservices architecture as well as all efforts required to ensure proper monitoring and observability could be applied. The automated tests running as part of the deployment pipeline in the environment mirroring the one available in production, along with the load tests, can indicate various discrepancies.

The serverless solution reliability can further benefit from the higher level deployment techniques and instant rollback capability in case of observing issues after release. Lastly, the serverless function can utilise the services providing dynamic configuration, enabling them to alter their behaviour by toggling certain features or implementing a solution similar to a circuit breaker pattern, preventing the whole system degradation in case of bugs introduced into the implementation.

Maintainability. The serverless paradigm shifts the need to maintain, share and manage resources and run applications to a cloud platform. It significantly reduces the operational costs of running the application. It also simplifies the deployment process, where developers must provide the artefact with appropriate configuration and the platform is responsible for running the application. The granularity of the components and the distributed nature of serverless processing requires that appropriate monitoring is configured and that an adequate level of observability is provided to ensure that the application is running correctly. The use of tools capable of distributed tracking along with alerting when certain metrics exceed predefined limits can give better insight into the behaviour of the application. Moreover, leveraging automation allows configuring multiple checks and performing automation tests in the deployment pipeline to give confidence when deploying the serverless solution. Due to the ephemeral nature of serverless computing taking place in the cloud, end-to-end testing on a mirrored test environment running in the cloud is required to validate the software. Finally, the serverless architecture makes it easy to make changes and adapt architectures to current needs with little effort and facilitates the evolution of applications and encourages experimentation and the introduction of new features in a convenient way.

3 Hands-on Insight into the Implementation of the Serverless-Based Web Application

Further research concerns an example web service implemented in a serverless architecture. The example provided is used to discuss some of the features of the serverless architecture together with the implemented patterns in order to analyse in more detail the implications of the serverless paradigm in the developed solution.

3.1 Presentation Processing—Web Application

The web application under consideration is a virtual mathematics tutor service for students, which provides a large collection of exercises that users can further customise by changing the values of the exercise parameters. Based on the data entered by the user, the service generates an interactive slideshow showing the steps required to solve the exercises and an audio commentary explaining the mathematical operations performed. In order to allow the creator of the presentation to easily define mathematical calculations, present graphics, show geometric tasks, provide conditional logic, etc., the web application used the LaTeX composition language and its processor.

The processing flow of a user request is as follows: (1) initial step—used to validate the user input. The values entered can be compared with the exercise constraints. (2) Exercise variables from the input data are injected into a LaTeX file. The presentation is then generated into a PDF file, which is further subdivided into separate slides as SVG files. (3) Along with the generation of the slideshow, the initial presentation file can contain additional annotated directives, which are taken and supplemented with user input variables. The processed text can be further transformed into audio commentary using voice synthesis software. (4) Some metadata about the presentation can be downloaded, including the duration of the slideshow or when to play the audio commentary, which will be sent and used later by the client application. Steps 2–4 can be performed in parallel. Once completed, the result can then be sent to the client to preview the slideshow with user exercises.

In a traditional web application architecture, presentation processing can be separated into a service that runs one of the workers based on user requests. With limited traffic, an approach with a separate service communicating with a set of workers would be appropriate, but when a larger group of users would make requests to be processed in a short period of time, the scalability of such a system should require scaling the number of available workers accordingly, thus reducing the cost of the application. Moreover, due to the large number of user-definable parameters and their value domains, generating slides and comments for all possible input values may take up a lot of memory and be uneconomical.

3.2   Presentation Processing—Serverless Approach

The serverless processing of the presentation, together with the communication with the client application responsible for displaying the slideshow based on the generated data, is shown in Fig. 1.

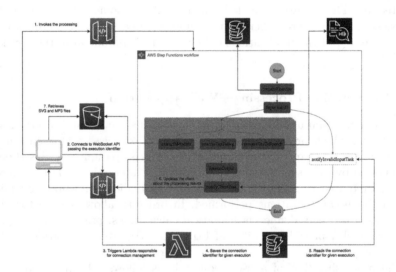

Fig. 1. Architecture of presentation processing

Function Orchestration Using the AWS Step Function —The presentation processing flow relies on several AWS Lambda instances, and an AWS Step Function coordinates the entire process. AWS Lambda performs the initial task, retrieving the details of the exercise, validating the user input against the constraints of the exercise and defining tasks for subsequent serverless function calls if the provided input meets the constraints. Based on the output of the first task, further processing is performed or the user is notified of an invalid request. The presentation processing task is further divided into two parts. The first generates a slideshow of a few initial slides, which is sent to the client as soon as possible after processing and displays a preview to the user. In contrast, the second portion, including the remainder of the presentation, is delivered to the client later when the user is busy viewing the initial portion of the slideshow. For each portion, three AWS Lambda instances are executed concurrently. They are responsible for processing the LaTeX file and extracting the slides as SVG files, which are then uploaded to Amazon S3, generating voice comments using Amazon Polly, which are further stored in Amazon S3, and extracting some metadata about the generated slideshow. Once all three tasks are completed, the function output is formatted and another serverless function is called to push the processing results to the client using the WebSocket API.

Pushing the Update to the Client —AWS Step Function coordinates processing asynchronously, which requires notification to the client when processing is complete. The client application calls the AWS Step Function and retrieves its execution ID. It then connects to the WebSocket API and sends a message with the received ID, calling AWS Lambda, which stores the execution ID and associated connection ID in DynamoDB. When a presentation snippet is generated, the serverless function retrieves the data based on the execution ID and sends a message with the processing results to the associated client application. Finally, the slides and audio files stored in the Amazon S3 under a predefined path are downloaded.

3.3   Discussion

The proposed solution is based on processing orchestration, involving serverless function calls performing different tasks at different processing stages. AWS Step Function enables processing to maintain a state between function execution and flow orchestration, which can include some branching tasks executed in parallel, subtask list mapping and task group result collection. The solution provides flexibility when defining the processing pattern and provides visualisation of the workflow, giving a better insight into the processing being performed. However, the size of the cumulative state in AWS Step Function is strictly limited, which is insufficient for storing the results of processing LaTeX files in it, and requires the use of Amazon S3. Furthermore, as the processing is done asynchronously, an additional solution is required to update the client when the results are ready. The proposed solution calls the AWS Step Function via the REST API and then connects via the WebSocket API to get a notification when the slideshow is available. Another challenge of the proposed processing flow is related to the processing of LaTeX files. The use of the Lambda layer, allows custom tasks to be performed and enriches the Lambda execution environment with numerous capabilities. Finally, the use of AWS Polly provided a development opportunity, allowing the slideshow to be easily enhanced with audio commentary without having to host a similar service or incorporate another third-party service running outside the cloud platform.

4   Optimisation Process

In the presented research, the Step Function was used to coordinate the processing of AWS Lambda instances performing step processing throughout the flow. Tests and measurements are carried out on the basis of two sample presentations prepared using the LaTeX composition system. Both sample presentations resemble exercises that could be used in a web-based application and are characterised by varying degrees of complexity. The first exercise involves a 71-page presentation containing the derivation of the solution of a trigonometric equation. The second exercise is more challenging and is a 103-page presentation, the first part of which contains graphics and describes the required steps to solve a geometry task, while the second part contains additional calculations. Based on initial research and experimentation, the process of exporting the presentation to PDF has been identified as a bottleneck in the overall processing, which takes significantly longer than other steps performed in parallel. The performance tests conducted mainly take into account the processing time from the client's point of view, which is calculated as the time from the request for the Step Function call, to the client receiving the processing results, once the slideshow generation is complete and the resources are available in S3. Along with the processing time measurement, several other metrics have been collected to give more insight into the performance of the various processing steps.

Initially, the infrastructure was re-deployed after each execution to ensure a cold start. However, due to the horizontal scalability of the serverless components, the same processing time was obtained when the client application executed 10 requests simultaneously. Each of the concurrent functions included a cold start. This behaviour confirms the scalability of an application based on a serverless architecture. In addition, LaTeX files associated with the presentation generation are removed from the temporal storage space of the function execution container after processing is completed. The operation is performed to avoid the situation where a subsequent function execution uses the same serverless function instance and may benefit from intermediate processing results from the previous call, which could affect the results of a warm start execution.

4.1   Custom Lambda Container Image and Lambda Layer

Generating a presentation from a LaTeX file can be classified as a non-standard type of processing for the serverless runtime environment beyond its standard set of tasks. Possible approaches of the serverless platform to perform such non-standard tasks include the following: (1) Container image—uses the official Amazon container image for the Node.js runtime environment with additional LaTeX distribution and other libraries required for processing; (2) Lambda layer—contains the LaTeX distribution extracted from the container image into a separate container.

Both approaches execute the same function code running in the Node.js runtime environment, using the provided LaTeX distribution to generate the presentation. One of the key elements of the container and Lambda layer image processing is related to cold and warm start times, which differ significantly. The cold start time can be divided into two parts—the first part takes into account the overhead associated with allocating resources from a large resource pool hosted by the cloud provider, downloading the function code and running a new, ephemeral container to execute the function. The second part concerns the loading of the function runtime environment and the initialisation of the dependencies required to execute the function procedure. The detailed results of the cold start analysis are shown in Tables 1 and 2.

The initialisation time for the Lambda layer solution is comparable for both exercises, averaging 273 ms and 279 ms for exercise 1 and exercise 2, respectively. For processing using the container-based solution, the initialisation time of the execution environment is on average 1108 ms and 810 ms, which has a noticeable impact on the total processing time. Furthermore, the initialisation time of the container image-based solution is additionally billed according to the AWS Lambda price list, in contrast to the Lambda layer approach, where the cold start time is not included. The orchestration overhead, calculated as the total processing time of the step function minus the time of the individual tasks defined in the step function flow, ranges from 400 ms to 450 ms for both cold and warm start. Based on the results of the comparison, which are shown in Fig. 2, the Lambda layer was selected as the more suitable solution for further workflow optimisation.

Table 1. Impact of the cold start on the presentation processing task for approach using Lambda layer

Exercise	Execution	Function [ms]	Environment [ms]	Runtime [ms]	Execution [ms]
Exercise 1	Cold start	3609	914	273	2422
	Warm start	1614	34	0	1580
Exercise 2	Cold start	7802	468	279	7055
	Warm start	4661	52	0	4609

Table 2. Impact of the cold start on the presentation processing task for an approach using custom container image for Lambda

Exercise	Execution	Function [ms]	Environment [ms]	Runtime [ms]	Execution [ms]
Exercise 1	Cold start	6548	637	1108	4803
	Warm start	1638	45	0	1593
Exercise 2	Cold start	8945	316	810	7819
	Warm start	4614	35	0	4579

4.2   Function Chain Length

The flow proposed in Sect. 3.1 describes the additional step of extracting the individual slides of the presentation into SVG files. To achieve this, the lightweight *pdf2svg* library is used. The following scenario tests the processing performance in two configurations (1) Single function—the conversion is a single function that generates the presentation and extracts the slides, which are stored further in the S3 bucket. (2) Function chain—the processing is performed in separate functions, storing the intermediate PDF file in the S3 bucket. When combining several functions to perform a certain workflow, the overhead associated with communication and cold start is complex. Additionally, intermediate results have to be stored in some external components, introducing additional work and delays that can be noticeable, especially when working with large volumes of data. On the other hand, the small size of the *pdf2svg* library makes it suitable to be added with dependencies to a Lambda layer that already contains a LaTeX distribution. However, the limitations of the Lambda layer approach must be taken into account, as at some point it may not be possible to extend the functionality further. A comparison of solutions using a single function and a chain of functions to process a presentation in terms of response time is shown in Fig. 3.

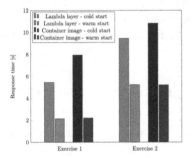

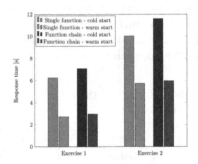

Fig. 2. Custom container image for AWS Lambda

Fig. 3. Single function and function chain to process the presentation

4.3 Parallel Processing

Serverless architectures are characterised by the ability to automatically scale instantly to meet processing demand. Certain types of computation can be redesigned to take advantage of such architectural features and improve overall processing time through load parallelization. Generating presentations from LaTeX files to PDF can be parallelized to some extent under certain circumstances. A predefined range of slides from a presentation prepared with the Beamer package can be selected using the *textbackslash includeonlyframes* directive. However, processing LaTeX files requires some initial and common parts of the processing to be repeated regardless of the selected subset of slides, resulting in some parts of the processing being repeated for each section of the presentation. The proposed optimisation splits LaTeX processing into several parallel executions of serverless functions. Each function is assigned to generate slides for predefined presentation fragments containing five consecutive slides. Once all serverless functions have completed processing, including commenting, transcription and metadata extraction, the user is notified of the processing results.

The processing graph of the Step Function is shown in Fig. 4. A presentation generation is split into parts, which are mapped to independent function calls and executed in parallel. As expected, the complexity of the selected examples has a significant impact on the total processing time. Measuring and comparing the processing time on the local machine, the independent generation of fragments for exercise 1 reduced the total processing time by 32%, while for exercise 2 it reached about 74%, confirming that although the processing of presentation generation cannot be effectively parallelized, the total processing time during parallel processing of LaTeX files is reduced for both examples given. The results obtained show that it is important to take into account the additional overhead associated with the orchestration of several serverless functions processing sections of the presentation in parallel. In the following example, the overhead associated with the orchestration is calculated as the duration of the step function minus the average task duration. This is equal to 873 ms (cold start) and 890 ms (warm start) for exercise 1 and 1765 ms (cold start) and 1745 ms (warm start) for exercise 2.

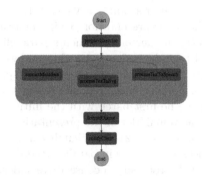 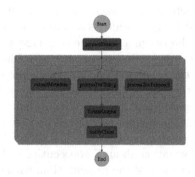

Fig. 4. Generating the presentation chunks in parallel

Fig. 5. Independently processed presentation chunks

In addition to the overhead associated with processing, parallel execution also involves additional costs for each serverless function executed and the execution time. In addition, in the example under consideration, the processing cannot be effectively parallelized and part of the processing and retrieval of the file is repeated for each function called, which affects the total cost of computation (Fig. 6).

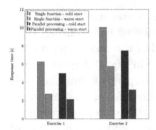 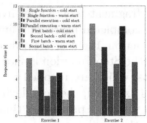 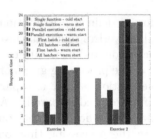

Fig. 6. Single function and parallel processing of separate fragments

Fig. 7. Update to the client in 1st batch (5 slides) and 2nd batch (remaining data)

Fig. 8. Update to the client in separate batches

4.4 Updating the Client with Processed Batches

The approach outlined in the previous section makes it possible to parallelize processing and effectively reduce the overall processing time. Nonetheless, it is limited because all parts of the presentation must be processed in order to communicate the update to the client. When considering how to prepare a presentation, most often the first few slides contain an introduction to the exercise, which usually takes longer than 10 s. From the user's point of view, only the first batch of slides is required to start the slideshow presentation, while the rest of the resources can be delivered later. Hence, further enhancements paralleliise presentation processing at a higher level to independently provide updates to the processed portions of the presentation. A step-function processing graph of the suggested approach is shown in Fig. 5. Further measurements reflect the response time for two flow configurations: (1) The first batch with the initial 5 slides processed and the second batch with the remainder of the presentation—processing is effectively parallelized in two branches. (2) Each batch contains information about 5 consecutive slides—processing is done in parallel according to the size of the presentation, with each branch processing 5 consecutive slides.

The processing results are compared with the processing time of the entire presentation by a single serverless function and with the situation when processing is done in parallel. The results are shown in Figs. 7 and 8. For the first of the configurations considered, the results of which are shown in Fig. 7, the response time for the first batch, including the first slides, is shorter. Once it is received by the client, the user can start previewing the slideshow, while the second batch, containing the remaining data, can be processed and received by the client later. This solution allows the user to start previewing the exercise more quickly, while the processing time of the entire presentation is hidden from the user's perspective. Meanwhile, in the second configuration, which evenly divides the presentation fragments and processes in parallel, the overhead of the Step Function responsible for orchestration significantly prolongs the processing. In addition, a batch containing the initial five slides is often provided as one of the most recent, significantly pushing back the time at which the user can start previewing the exercise, as shown in the Fig. 8.

5   Serverless-Based Web Applications—Final Remarks

The serverless processing model relies heavily on asynchronous and event-driven processing, valuing the loose coupling of its components, making it similar to a microservices architecture. However, it pushes boundaries further, splitting service implementation into multiple functions and other serverless components configured to work together within a single application domain. Asynchronous workflows are more suitable for stateless and short-lived serverless functions, containing a variety of components, including publish-and-subscribe services, queues and event buses to exchange messages and coordinate processing between successive function executions. These components can be configured to provide additional functionality including event containment and persistent caching, reliable distribution of events to multiple providers, aggregation of the data stream sent to multiple consumers and much more, depending on the requirements of the serverless workflow.

Services such as Amazon SNS, Amazon SQS and Amazon EventBridge are used to choreograph asynchronous event-driven workflows, creating a loosely coupled chain of components responsible for processing application logic. However, certain types of tasks require more precise coordination of processing. AWS Step Function is suitable for orchestrating more complex workloads that require reliable collaboration between different services, capturing the entire business flow and handling more complex branching logic, errors, and transactional logic across multiple services.

6   Conclusions

Serverless architecture appears to be an attractive technology for web application development. The benefits include development capabilities with significant cost reductions, precise scaling of the infrastructure to meet unpredictable workloads at a proportionate cost, more affordable web application evolution with increased team agility and decoupling of processing along with scaling according to high throughput processing tasks. Compared to traditional monolithic or microservices architectures, the serverless approach is more flexible in terms of scaling. In contrast, for larger workloads, the performance of serverless solutions is comparable to the above approaches, with the additional distinction of having more stable performance characteristics. However, the cost-effectiveness of a serverless solution requires an accurate cost estimate, including all serverless components used and additional costs, including, for example, other services and data transfer. The future direction of our work will be related to gathering metrics from production-grade applications and providing more in-depth analysis of the impact of user behaviours that are most often less regular, especially in the context of an entire day, such as, for example, as well as providing detailed reports covering the costs of realised workloads.

References

1. Aslanpour, M.S., et al.: Serverless edge computing: vision and challenges. In: ACSW 2021: 2021 Australasian Computer Science Week Multiconference, Dunedin, New Zealand, 1–5 February 2021, pp. 1–10. ACM (2021)
2. Carver, J.C., Penzenstadler, B., Scheuner, J., Staron, M.: (Research) insights for serverless application engineering. IEEE Softw. **38**(1), 123–125 (2021)
3. Chang, V., et al.: A survey on intrusion detection systems for fog and cloud computing. Future Internet **14**(3), 89 (2022)
4. Eismann, S., et al.: Serverless applications: why, when, and how? IEEE Softw. **38**(1), 32–39 (2021)
5. Holík, F., Neradova, S.: Vulnerabilities of modern web applications. In: 40th International Convention on Information and Communication Technology, Electronics and Microelectronics, MIPRO 2017, Opatija, Croatia, 22–26 May 2017, pp. 1256–1261. IEEE (2017)
6. Lichtenthäler, R., Prechtl, M., Schwille, C., Schwartz, T., Cezanne, P., Wirtz, G.: Requirements for a model-driven cloud-native migration of monolithic web-based applications. SICS Softw.-Intensive Cyber Phys. Syst. **35**(1), 89–100 (2020)
7. Lin, C., Khazaei, H.: Modeling and optimization of performance and cost of serverless applications. IEEE Trans. Parallel Distributed Syst. **32**(3), 615–632 (2021)

Scaling Model for vIMS on the Cloud

Ming-Huang Tsai, Yun-He Wang, and Wu-Chun Chung[(✉)]

Department of Information and Computer Engineering, Chung Yuan Christian University,
Taoyuan, Taiwan
{g10877019,g11077040,wcchung}@cycu.edu.tw

Abstract. European Telecommunications Standards Institute (ETSI) releases a
white paper to illustrate the reference framework for Network Function Virtualization (NFV). This new architecture brings a new challenge for cloud computing
to allocate resources with a time-varying workload while maintaining a certain
level of quality. In the literature, fewer studies simultaneously consider horizontal and vertical scaling policies with a system-wide validation. This paper takes
the virtual IP multimedia subsystem (vIMS) as an NFV application to model the
scaling prediction in a practical cloud system. A generalized additive model is
adopted as the modeling tool and the R^2 value of the model after training can
approach 0.8. When the cloud system has to scale the resources, the proposed
model predicts the combination of resources and the scaling strategy for a better
successful call rate. Experimental results show that the model provides scaling
recommendations to achieve an optimal successful call rate with the given information about the expected loading and the resource combinations at present. The
error value between the predicted and actual successful call rates is less than 1.8%,
and the proposed scaling strategy is consistent with a practical scenario.

Keywords: Cloud computing · Network function virtualization · Scaling
model · Virtual IP multimedia subsystem

1 Introduction

Recently, the 5G mobile network service has become a hot topic on autonomous driving, augmented reality, smart internet of things, etc. Deploying the network service
requires dedicated hardware to perform network functions. Consequently, telecom operators spend a large capital expenditure (CAPEX) to purchase proprietary hardware. In
2012, European Telecommunications Standards Institute (ETSI) illustrates the concept
of Network Function Virtualization (NFV) [1]. NFV technology aims at decoupling network functions from dedicated hardware. Therefore, network functions can be run on
a cloud system as software. With this approach, network service providers can significantly reduce CAPEX and maintenance costs [2, 3]. Furthermore, the network service
provider also takes advantage of cloud computing features such as high availability and
scalability to provide better services.

© The Author(s), under exclusive license to Springer Nature Singapore Pte Ltd. 2022
S.-Y. Hsieh et al. (Eds.): ICS 2022, CCIS 1723, pp. 243–254, 2022.
https://doi.org/10.1007/978-981-19-9582-8_22

Although NFV brings benefits to service providers, NFV also poses many challenges. Resource allocation [4, 5] is one of the critical topics. Because the network traffic is not static, dynamically allocating resources to meet the time-varying demands is an important issue. Most discussions [6–9] focus on how to place or embed VNFs. However, the scaling strategy for elastic resource management is not discussed in their works. The literature on resource placement generalizes NFV systems to a demand and supply model [10–12]. However, the model simplifies the actual system and is not fully suitable for the production environment.

Another problem is how to compute the performance of vCPU. For example, in [13], the authors assume that one vCPU provides 10,000 MIPS. However, in practical systems, the assumption of a linear relationship between computing power and vCPUs does not apply to all scenarios. In general, most systems cannot operate correctly with heavy workloads, but the literature does not mention this limitation. Most dynamic scaling policies use CPU utilization as a metric [13–15]. In a traditional web application architecture, each Virtual Machine (VM) is independent. However, in the case of a Service Function Chain (SFC), VNFs are highly dependent on each other. The scaling should adjust the VNF resources with respect to available resources. This consideration is ignored in the literature. In addition, most literature works only discuss the horizontal scaling. However, in a production environment, performance improvement brought by scaling up may be better than scaling out. Meanwhile, the application should be balanced between performance and availability. With this consideration, horizontal scaling may result in low utilization. Zhou et al. [16] illustrate that vertical scaling has a shorter boot time than newly deployed VMs and maximizes potential resource utilization.

Since the discussion of NFV scaling problem in the literature is insufficient, this paper conducts the impacts of workload and resource allocation on performance metrics. In addition, this paper deploys the virtual IP Multimedia Subsystem (vIMS) as an application. The experiments use call rate and Successful Call Rate (SCR) to represent the workload and the performance metric, respectively. After obtaining the data, the Generalized Additive Model (GAM) [17] is applied to derive a regression model to present the true behavior of the system. This model determines the optimal scaling strategy to maximize SCR with respect to resource allocation and the call rate. Empirical results show that the R^2 of the model can reach about 0.8 which means the predictive capability of the model is acceptable. The results also show that the error between the predicted and actual success rate is less than 1.8%, and the proposed scaling direction is consistent with the actual situation.

The rest of this paper is organized as follows. Section 2 discusses our method with related works. Section 3 firstly introduces the background of vIMS architecture and then presents the scaling modeling, training, and evaluation of the proposed model. Section 4 describes the experimental design and the results. Finally, Sect. 5 concludes this paper with future remarks.

2 Related Works

Most research works on resource allocation mainly focus on the placement issue because of the high complexity. Accordingly, the placement problem has no deterministic solution. Some works solve the problem of resource placement with multiple objectives including low-cost or low-energy usage. Since the placement problem is a non-deterministic polynomial hard (NP-hard), the literature tends to solve this problem with a heuristic method. This paper summarizes the differences between our approach and the previous works in Table 1.

Table 1. Summary of related work

Works	SFC	vIMS as scenario	Scale up and out	Balance metric	Balance scaling
Toosi et al. [13]	V	-	V	-	-
Duan et al. [14]	V	V	-	-	-
Mauro et al. [15]	V	V	-	-	-
Mechtri et al. [18]	V	-	-	-	-
Chen et al. [19]	V	-	-	-	-
Tang et al. [20]	V	-	-	-	-
Fei et al. [21]	V	-	-	-	-
Arteaga et al. [22]	-	V	-	-	-
Alawe et al. [23]	-	V	-	-	-
This Paper	V	V	V	V	V

Marouen Mechtri et al. [18] try to solve the placement problem and propose an eigendecomposition-based approach to speed up the computational process using the properties of linear algebra. Jing Chen et al. [19] invent the QMORA algorithm based on Q-learning to accelerate finding the solution to multi-objective placement problems. This algorithm uses the feedback and memory function to find the optimal solution. Lun Tang et al. [20] use markov decision process with actor-critic learning to allow the machine to correct the decisions and eventually meet the low latency and high utilization. In addition to resource allocation, some works investigate service quality degradation due to traffic changes. Xincai Fei et al. [21] use traffic predictions to determine whether the existing resources are sufficient for the next round. If the resources are inadequate, the system allocates more resources in advance to avoid the degradation in service quality. Because the real system takes time to complete the resource allocation, the time cost is included in the problem model. The previous works have provided well-sounded methods, but their experiments are not conducted in a practical system.

Arteaga et al. [22] adopt Q-learning to find the relationship between the performance and the number of VMs. This method allows the machine to adaptively choose the number of VMs. With performance feedback, the machine learns how to make better decisions. However, the experiment only focuses on a major VNF of MME instead of all VNFs in an SFC. Imad Alawe et al. [23] propose an LSTM to construct a flow prediction model and plan for resource deployment accordingly. The results show that using a flow prediction model is better than the traditional threshold model. The threshold model only responds to the flow passively. Based on the predicted flow, the prediction model takes more effective strategies in advance. However, the experiment also considers only a VNF of AMF instead of all the VNFs in an SFC. These works only consider a major VNF and ignore the other VNFs in the SFC. Therefore, the discussion of SFC characteristics is incomplete.

On the other hand, many works also adopt the vIMS architecture in the literature. For example, Jingpu Duan et al. [14] use a demand prediction model to determine whether the system needs more or less VM. When VM is insufficient, VM can be deployed in advance to meet the service demand. Mario Di Mauro et al. [15] try to minimize the IMS waiting time by using the waiting network model and propose a split flow architecture for single/multi-class before the VNF of HSS. This method considers the trade-off between cost and performance. ElasticSFC [13] considers horizontal and vertical scaling to dynamically adjusts the VNF number or bandwidth with respect to the cost requirements when the utilization is too high. However, the experiment only applies a CloudSIM simulation, not conducted in a practical environment.

To sum up, most previous works are not verified in an actual system and only focus on a single VNF. The literature also ignores the interaction characteristic between multiple VNFs of an SFC. In addition, the previous works only discuss horizontal scaling when the resources are insufficient and do not consider horizontal and vertical scaling simultaneously in a real cloud system.

3   Scaling Model for NFV on the Cloud

In this section, the vIMS architecture is first introduced and then the scaling problem is defined. Afterward, the training of a scaling model is presented on a practical cloud.

3.1   Overview of vIMS Architecture

This paper uses the open-source Clearwater vIMS [24] which is provisioning with cloud features such as high scalability and high availability. Clearwater consists of six main components as shown in Fig. 1. Each component is deployed in a VM and cooperates with the other to provide telecom services.

i)   **Bono** is an edgy proxy. This component provides access points for users to connect their devices to the Clearwater system. In addition to the standard SIP/UDP and SIP/TCP protocols [25], Bono also supports the WebRTC protocol.

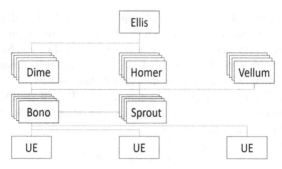

Fig. 1. vIMS architecture

ii) **Sprout** acts as a SIP router. This component is responsible for SIP registration, authorized routing server, and user authentication. Moreover, to fulfill the scalability feature, Sprout does not store long-lived association data. The data is placed in an independent component, named Vellum.

iii) **Dime** is a Diameter gateway to store subscriber registration information and authentication credentials. This component also provides billing functions. The I-CSCF function is integrated and split among the Sprout and Vellum services in the Clearwater implementation.

iv) **Vellum** stores permanent data for vIMS in the backend. This component adopts a distributed storage architecture in cloud computing, named Cassandra.

v) **Homer** is used as an XML Document Management Server (XDMS) to store the configuration files of the application server.

vi) **Ellis** provides a web interface for administrators to register users and easy-to-use features for the vIMS service.

The vIMS is composed of an application layer and a control layer. For the application layer, Mobile Telephony Application Server (MMTel-AS) processes the multimedia stream from Sprout and generates multimedia services for the user. A call flow typically consists of three phases: session initiation, establishment, and termination. In the control layer, the system will complete a SIP REGISTRATION transaction when a user enters the vIMS system. Then the user obtains the IP address of the vIMS system and is bound to a specific P-CSCF. Besides, the system records binding information in the S-CSCF. Later, when another party calls the user, vIMS can find out the location of the user for routing purposes. The discovery mechanism is that the S-CSCF stores the P-CSCF bound by the user at the time of registration. When a user tries to communicate with a party, the user sends a SIP INVITE transaction with a callee ID to the system. The system queries the P-CSCF which binds the callee and forwards the call to the callee. Finally, the SIP BYE transaction is sent out when the communication is completed so that the conversation is finished.

3.2 Scaling Problem

This paper uses the actual NVF system, vIMS, as the application scenario. An NFV system has various SFCs. The customers choose a specific SFC according to their needs.

Each SFC contains several VNFs in a fixed sequence. Each VNF is deployed in a VM. The VNFs require resources to handle requests. Each server hosts multiple VMs at the same time to provide services. Let S denote a set of SFCs and s be an SFC, in which $s \in S$. Let f_i^s denote the ith VNF of SFC s, $i = 1, 2,..., |s|$, in which $|s|$ denotes the length of SFC s. This paper focuses on the SFC of the control plane in the vIMS, including Bono, Sprout, and Dime. The model acquires the number of vCPUs of each VNF, the number of Sprout VMs, and the call rates as input factors. The output is SCR. Accordingly, the NFV scaling problem is presented below:

$$\sum_{i=1}^{s} \alpha_{c,b,r}^s \mu_{f_i^s} \approx \text{SCR} \tag{1}$$

$$\text{s.t.} \quad b, r, \ \mu_{f_i^s} > 0 \tag{2}$$

$$b \leq \text{total number of Sprout VMs in a host} \tag{3}$$

$$\mu_{f_i^s} \leq \text{total number of vCPUs in VNFs} \tag{4}$$

$$\text{SCR} = \text{all successful calls/total number of calls} \tag{5}$$

The α in Eq. (1) is the coefficient of f_i^s vCPUs, which is varied with specific conditions. The symbol c of the $\alpha_{c,b,r}$ represents the resource combination of vCPU allocation for all VNFs. The symbol b represents the number of Sprout instances. The symbol r represents the total calls per second. Take $\alpha_{212,2,80}^s$ as an example, the tuple of (212, 2, 80) means that this coefficient belongs to an SFC s with three kinds of VNFs. The number of vCPUs of these three VNFs are 2, 1, and 2, respectively. Furthermore, the SFC has two Sprout instances and the call rate is 80. The $\mu_{f_i^s}$ represents the number of vCPUs of ith VNF in the SFC s.

Since the Sprout is a bottleneck, this paper mainly considers the number of Sprout instances. In addition, the model requires the number of vCPUs because the Sprout is CPU-bounded component [26]. Therefore, Eqs. (2) – (4) are the constraints. Equation (2) limits the vCPU number, Sprout VMs, and call rate by at least one. Equation (3) marks that the maximum number of Sprout instances is lower than the system limitation. Equation (4) limits the maximum number of vCPUs with respect to the capacity of VNFs. Equation (5) explains that the SCR is calculated with total successful calls and the total number of calls.

To acquire a solution from Eq. (1) is difficult. The coefficient cannot be obtained due to the relationship among the vCPU of VNFs, the number of Sprout instances, and the call rate on SCR being unknown. Therefore, this paper applies the regression approach based on empirical results to construct the scaling model. The regression approach is based on GAM to obtain the correlation between the resource allocation and the SCR. The variables used in this model are the number of vCPUs for each major VNF, the number of Sprout instances, and the call rate. The NFV scaling regression model is shown in Eq. (6).

$$\begin{aligned} g(E(\text{SCR})) = {} & \text{B0} + \text{f1(bono cpus)} + \text{f2(sprout cpus)} + \text{f3(dime cpus)} \\ & + \text{f4(sprout vms)} + \text{f5(call rate)} \end{aligned} \tag{6}$$

3.3 Scaling Model Construction

Figure 2 illustrates the methodology of model construction. First, OpenStack [27] is deployed as Network Function Virtualization Infrastructure (NFVI), followed by the deployment of the vIMS system. After the testing environment is established, the tests are started according to the test sets and conditions. The test environment will be adjusted according to different test combinations.

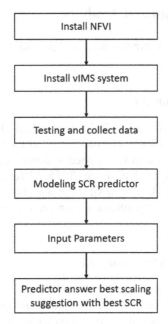

Fig. 2. Methodology of model construction

After the scaling model is built, the model provides the best scaling suggestion according to the SCR under the current condition. In other words, the model can predict the successful call rate based on the current resource combination. After setting up and running the vIMS, the system is tested by each test combination and corresponding conditions. This paper applies SIP stress to test the whole system and collect the results. The collected data and the SCR values are used to build the regression model and evaluate the R^2 for different model parameters. Afterward, this paper chooses the set of parameters with the best R^2 to construct the model and assesses the training results.

For the test combination, the number of vCPUs for Bono, Sprout, and Dime is ranging from 1, 2, 4, and 8. The number of Sprout instances is 1, 2, and 3. The VM has 3 GB RAM and a 20 GB virtual hard disk. For test parameters, the call rate per second starts from 40 to 140, in which each step is 10, and each stage continues for 5 min. This paper repeats five cycles and takes the results on average.

When finishing data collection, the scaling model is trained by the Python suite, pyGAM [28] with version 0.8. This paper also has a lambda parameter to control the overfitting for each dimension during the GAM training. The program automatically selects the group with the lowest Generalized Cross-Validation (GCV) score. The model parameters that will be evaluated are the prediction factor, the resource allocation, the number of spline functions, and the number of the lambda function. This paper takes all 5 prediction factors. The number of b-spline is set to 20 and the value of lambda is one. Results show that the maximum R^2 under this condition is 0.7969, which is closer to 0.8 and within an acceptable degree.

4 Experimental Design and Analysis

This section first introduces the experimental configurations and then presents the results and discussions of findings.

4.1 Experimental Environment

The experimental environment is aligned with the standard NFV architecture. The underlying NFVI is based on OpenStack. The paper deploys the Clearwater vIMS on OpenStack via Cloudify [29]. The server is equipped with two Intel Xeon Silver 4210 CPUs, 160 GB RAM, and XXV710 10G NIC. Each CPU has 10 cores. The VMs are connected via VxLAN, and the OpenStack neutron ML2 driver is OVS [30]. The versions of OpenStack, host OS, and Cloudify OpenStack plugin are Ussuri, 18.04 LTS, and v2.14.7, respectively.

4.2 VCPU Ratios Between Different VNFs

In this experiment, the call rates are 80, 100, 120, and 140. The number of Sprout instances is one. vCPU ratios between Bono, Sprout, and Dime are 111, 121, 112, and 211, respectively. The experimental results are shown in Fig. 3. The vCPU ratio of 111 with a call rate of 100 is a baseline. When the call rate is lower than 100, the SCR of each ratio is similar, except in the case of 112. The SCR of ratio 112 is the worst with a value of 87%.

When the call rate is 120, the SCR of ratio 121 is up to 90%, followed by the SCR of ratio 211 is 86%, and the worst SCR of ratio 112 is 72%. When the call rate is up to 140, the SCR of ratio 121 is also the best performance with a value of 75%. According to the previous analysis, the SCR of ratio 121 is better than that of ratios 111, 211, and 112 in any case. Even in call rate 140, the SCR of ratio 121 is at least 15% higher than that of other ratios. That is because ratio 121 has more resources on the Sprout. The Sprout interacts with the database and handles both callers and callees. When Sprout has a heavy workload, the SCR of ratio 121 performs the best. Therefore, allocating more computing resources to Sprout is able to improve the SCR in vIMS.

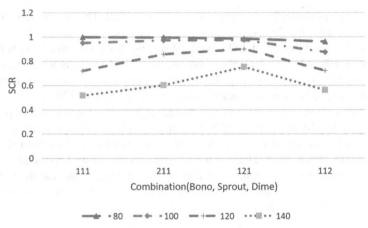

Fig. 3. Impact of different call rates and VNF ratios on SCR

4.3 Effectiveness of the Scaling Model

This paper conducts an experiment to examine the capability of the proposed scaling model. The test conditions include the vCPU number of Bono, Sprout, and Dime are 2, 3, and 2, respectively. The call rate is set to 100 in this experiment. The model has to figure out which combination has the best SCR.

Empirical results are shown in Table 2. The combination with the lowest predicted SCR is 233 because its SCR is 0.93237. The highest SCR of combination is 242 (vertical scaling) because its SCR is 1.00256. Meanwhile, the SCR of combination 242 (horizontal scaling) is 0.99809 which is lower than that of vertical scaling. Therefore, the scaling model suggests the current system for vertical scaling with the combination of 242 to get the best SCR. Moreover, the difference between the actual and predicted values is also examined. The actual SCR of combination 242 with a vertical scaling is 0.99337. The SCR is lower than the predicted value and the difference ratio is 0.9%. If the system applies the combination of 242 with horizontal scaling, the actual SCR is 0.98085. The SCR is 0.01724 lower than the predicted value and the difference ratio is 1.8%. Therefore, the scaling model can provide better decision-making and a low difference ratio for system scaling.

Table 2. Prediction results of combination 232 at call rate 100

Combination	Predicted value	Actual value	Difference	Difference %
332	0.94649	-	-	-
242(scale up)	1.00256	0.99337	0.00919	0.9%
242(scale out)	0.99809	0.98085	0.01724	1.8%
233	0.93237	-	-	-

Table 3 shows the SCR when the call rate is up to 120. The combination with the lowest predicted SCR is 233 with a value of 0.87491. The maximum predicted SCR is 0.94452 with a combination of 242 in vertical scaling. If the system adopts horizontal scaling, the predicted SCR of combination 242 is 0.93753 which is lower than that of combination 242 in vertical scaling. Based on the prediction, the model recommends a combination of 242 for a vertical scaling strategy at a call rate of 120.

Furthermore, this paper reviews the difference between the actual and predicted values. The actual SCR for the combination of 242 with a vertical scaling is 0.96063. This value is higher than that of the predicted value, so the difference ratio is -1.7%. In contrast, the actual SCR value for the combination 242 with horizontal scaling is 0.94645. This value is also higher than that of the predicted value and the difference ratio is -0.9%. Therefore, the scaling model can provide better decision-making with an acceptable difference ratio for system scaling.

Table 3. Prediction results of combination 232 at call rate 120

Combination	Predicted value	Actual value	Difference	Difference %
332	0.90000	-	-	-
242(scale up)	0.94452	0.96063	−0.0161	−1.7%
242(scale out)	0.93753	0.94645	−0.0089	−0.9%
233	0.87491			

5 Conclusion

To investigate the scaling problem of vIMS, this paper proposes a scaling prediction model for a better SCR. The proposed model is built on a regression method with considerations of resource combinations and call rates. This model constructs the correlation between all factors and the SCR. Furthermore, this paper analyzes the empirical results and finds that the SCR is higher when the vCPU ratio of Bono and Sprout is 1 to 2. Finally, experimental results also show that the predicted error is less than 1.8%. Based on the information, the service provider can determine the necessary placement prior to the system overloading.

In this paper, the vIMS is experienced without any performance tuning. For the NFV on a cloud system, the performance of the existing OVS is not affordable for heavy loading. Accordingly, the current vIMS performance is not fully optimized. The system performance can be further enhanced by adopting network improvement techniques such as DPDK [31]. How to leverage enhanced network techniques to improve prediction accuracy is an interesting topic for future work.

Acknowledgment. This work was supported by the National Science and Technology Council (NSTC) of Taiwan under Grants 108-2218-E-033-008-MY3 and 111-2221-E-033–033.

References

1. ETSI NFV: https://www.etsi.org/technologies/nfv. Accessed 11 Dec 2022
2. Vladislavic, D., Huljenic, D., Ozegovic, J.: Enhancing VNF's performance using DPDK driven OVS user-space forwarding. In: 25th International Conference on Software, Telecommunications and Computer Networks, pp. 1–5., SoftCOM, Split (2017)
3. Bonafiglia, R., Cerrato, I., Ciaccia, F., Nemirovsky, M., Risso, F.: Assessing the performance of virtualization technologies for NFV: a preliminary benchmarking. In: 4th European Workshop on Software Defined Networks, pp. 67–72. EWSDN, Bilbao (2015)
4. Laghrissi, A., Taleb, T.: A survey on the placement of virtual resources and virtual network functions. IEEE Commun. Surv. Tutor. **21**(2), 1409–1434 (2018)
5. Kaur, K., Mangat, V., Kumar, K.: A comprehensive survey of service function chain provisioning approaches in SDN and NFV architecture. Comput. Sci. Rev. **38**, 100298 (2020)
6. Harutyunyan, D., Shahriar, N., Boutaba, R., Riggio, R.: Latency-aware service function chain placement in 5G mobile networks. In: IEEE Conference on Network Softwarization, pp. 133–141. NetSoft, Paris (2019)
7. Pei, J., Hong, P., Xue, K., Li, D.: Efficiently embedding service function chains with dynamic virtual network function placement in geo-distributed cloud system. Trans. Parallel Distrib. Syst. **30**(10), 2179–2192 (2019)
8. Beck, M.T., Botero, J.F., Samelin, K.: Resilient allocation of service function chains. In: IEEE Conference on Network Function Virtualization and Software Defined Networks, pp. 128–133. NFV-SDN, Palo Alto (2016)
9. Wang, S., Zhao, Y., Xu, J., Yuan, J., Hsu, C.H.: Edge server placement in mobile edge computing. J. Parallel Distrib. Comput. **127**, 160–168 (2019)
10. Sun, G., Zhu, G., Liao, D., Yu, H., Du, X., Guizani, M.: Cost-efficient service function chain orchestration for low-latency applications in nfv networks. IEEE Syst. J. **13**(4), 3877–3888 (2019)
11. Mishra, P., Moustafa, A.: Reinforcement learning based monotonic policy for online resource allocation. Futur. Gener. Comput. Syst. **138**, 313–327 (2023)
12. Liu, J., Lu, W., Zhou, F., Lu, P., Zhu, Z.: On dynamic service function chain deployment and readjustment. IEEE Trans. Netw. Serv. Manage. **14**(3), 543–553 (2017)
13. Toosi, A.N., Son, J., Chi, Q., Buyya, R.: ElasticSFC: auto-scaling techniques for elastic service function chaining in network functions virtualization-based clouds. J. Syst. Softw. **152**, 108–119 (2019)
14. Duan, J., Wu, C., Le, F., Liu, A.X., Peng, Y.: Dynamic scaling of virtualized, distributed service chains: a case study of IMS. IEEE J. Sel. Areas Commun. **35**(11), 2501–2511 (2017)
15. Di Mauro, M., Liotta, A.: Statistical Assessment of IP multimedia subsystem in a softwarized environment: a queueing networks approach. IEEE Trans. Netw. Serv. Manage. **16**(4), 1493–1506 (2019)
16. Zhou, W., Yang, Y., Xu, M., Chen, H.: Accommodating dynamic traffic immediately: a VNF placement approach. In: IEEE International Conference on Communications, pp. 1–6. ICC, Shanghai (2019)
17. Hastie, T., Tibshirani, R.: Generalized additive models: some applications. J. Am. Stat. Assoc. **82**(398), 371–386 (1987)
18. Mechtri, M., Ghribi, C., Zeghlache, D.: A scalable algorithm for the placement of service function chains. IEEE Trans. Netw. Serv. Manage. **13**(3), 533–546 (2016)
19. Chen, J., Chen, J., Hu, R., Zhang, H.: QMORA: a Q-learning based multi-objective resource allocation scheme for NFV orchestration. In: IEEE 91st Vehicular Technology Conference, pp. 1–6. VTC-Spring, Antwerp (2020)

20. Tang, L., Yang, H., Ma, R., Hu, L., Wang, W., Chen, Q.: Queue-aware dynamic placement of virtual network functions in 5g access network. IEEE Access **6**, 44291–44305 (2018)
21. Fei, X., Liu, F., Zhang, Q., Jin, H., Hu, H.: Paving the way for NFV acceleration: a taxonomy, survey and future directions. ACM Comput. Surv. **53**(4), 1–42 (2020)
22. Arteaga, C.H.T., Risso, F., Rendon, O.M.C.: An adaptive scaling mechanism for managing performance variations in network functions virtualization: a case study in An NFV-based EPC. In: 13th International Conference on Network and Service Management, pp. 1–7. CNSM, Tokyo (2017)
23. Alawe, I., Ksentini, A., Hadjadj-Aoul, Y., Bertin, P.: Improving traffic forecasting for 5g core network scalability: a machine learning approach. IEEE Netw. **32**(6), 42–49 (2018)
24. Clearwater Architecture: https://clearwater.readthedocs.io/en/stable/Clearwater_Architecture.html. Accessed 11 Dec 2022
25. SIP: Session Initiation Protocol: https://www.ietf.org/rfc/rfc3261.txt. Accessed 11 Dec 2022
26. Cao, L., Sharma, P., Fahmy, S., Saxena, V.: NFV-VITAL: a framework for characterizing the performance of virtual network functions. In: IEEE Conference on Network Function Virtualization and Software Defined Network, pp. 93–99. NFV-SDN, San Francisco (2015)
27. OpenStack: https://www.openstack.org/. Accessed 11 Dec 2022
28. pyGAM: https://pygam.readthedocs.io/en/latest/. Accessed 11 Dec 2022
29. Cloudify: https://cloudify.co/. Accessed 11 Dec 2022
30. Open vSwitch: https://www.openvswitch.org/. Accessed 11 Dec 2022
31. DPDK, https://doc.dpdk.org/guides/linux_gsg/intro.html. Accessed 11 Dec 2022

Using Classification Algorithms to Predict Taiwan Stock Market - A Case Study of Taiwan Index Futures

Chen-Shu Wang and Yean-Lin Lee[✉]

National Taipei University of Technology, New Taipe, Taiwan
wangcs@ntut.edu.tw, lili.0955425877@gmail.com

Abstract. Due to the interaction of different factors, the characteristics of the market are constantly complex and volatile. Roughly speaking, it is somewhat difficult to accurately predict stock prices. Hence this study regards price trend prediction as a classification problem.

The research purposes are to compare the effectiveness of different classification models forecast for Taiwan stock market and explore whether the use of American stock market data as features can improve the accuracy of Taiwan stock market.

We use Random Forest, Logistic regression and Support Vector Machine, which is frequently used in stock price classification as models. Use closing price and trading volume of NASDAQ index, the Net Buy/Sell of Three Institutional Investors, and the trading volume of Taiwan index futures as the features. In addition to OOB Error Rate, we focused more on the measurement of model performance, and introduced six ratios extended by the confusion matrix for evaluation.

The empirical results show that the nine models in this study predict the decline of Taiwan stocks more frequently than rise. But all of the models do a better job of sorting the upside than the downside. So we suggest it probably can combined with SVM III to predict the Taiwan stock market, so as to improve the prediction rate of the rise data. Through the analysis of the above model, the prediction accuracy of using the data of the US stock market combined with Taiwan stock market data is better than only using Taiwan stock market or the US stock market data.

Keywords: Taiwan stock market · Random Forest · Logistic regression · SVM

1 Introduction

Investors are usually attracted by the steep returns and put off by the elevated risk of investing in stocks or futures. In order to reduce investment risk, investors combine different financial tools, such as technical analysis indicators, machine learning, media framing and so on to predict stock prices. But predicting prices has consistently been highly challenging, both from an economic and investor perspective. Vulnerability to economic uncertainty makes it tough to predict price movements. On the individual level

© The Author(s), under exclusive license to Springer Nature Singapore Pte Ltd. 2022
S.-Y. Hsieh et al. (Eds.): ICS 2022, CCIS 1723, pp. 255–266, 2022.
https://doi.org/10.1007/978-981-19-9582-8_23

of investors, although the academic community has countless references and put forward pricing theories of financial commodities, the actual value is still difficult to measure, so investors will rely on subjective judgment, and everyone has his own idea, and everyone has different predicted value of the stock market, resulting in the stock market volatility.

From the above description, we can understand that financial commodity prices are subject to rapid changes due to various factors. The price is a series of dynamic, chaotic time series data and contains a lot of noise in the data, therefore the short-term trend is usually seen as a stochastic process. However, as with the rate of return in stock price dynamics, if the time is extended over the long-term, the price movement will not be random, but will be traceable.

With the development of hardware and algorithms, and machine learning is suitable for processing huge amounts of data and multidimensional data, therefore this research hopes to find market trends more efficiently through machine learning and want to through this method, with significant features, to predict the future stock index futures prices.

In the past, quite a number of models used time series or multivariate analysis to predict the price of financial commodities. In these methods, the price trend of financial commodities would be expressed in the form of time series functions, so the final prediction result would be a certain value. In practice, however, the financial commodity prices is the nature of the chaos and high volatility, there are too many factors and interference exists, thus to accurately predict the price of a certain value for future is very difficult, in order to solve this problem if the judgment is the price up or down allows investors to have data to support this, there are rules to follow, Therefore, if the goal of price prediction is changed to the classification problem of predicting the future rise or fall, the purpose of price prediction can be achieved more efficiently.

The objectives of this study are:

1. Compare the model effectiveness of different classification models on the forecasting ability of Taiwan stock market.
2. Explore whether the use of Taiwan stock market data and American stock market data as features can improve the prediction ability of classification model for Taiwan stock market.

2   Preliminaries

2.1   Literature on Machine Learning Prediction of Stock Prices

In the secondary market, thousands of investors are trying to find profitable trading strategies, hoping to predict the future price trend through historical data. There are various methods to establish trading strategies in the past literature. [1] uses Logistic regression to find out the financial ratio factors that could affect stock return, and expected to build a model that could accurately predict stock return. The model is based on the Indian market, and the authors use data on the top 30 companies by market capitalization in India from 2005 to 2008. If the annual stock return (which is calculated in a certain month each year) exceeds the NIFTY, the annual return is marked as Good, and if it is not, it is marked as Poor. Eight financial ratios with normal distribution were selected as explanatory variables to construct Logistic stock decision, which finally obtained an average accuracy of 74.6%.

[6] use a variety of models, including Support Vector Machine, Back-Propagation Neural Network, Nearest Neighbor method, Decision tree and Logistic Regression. The feasibility of machine learning method to predict stock price trend is verified. At the same time, the concept of majority decision is used to improve the prediction ability of the model. Different from the general majority decision learning, they add the Wrapper Feature Selection Method proposed by [5] to find the most suitable features for each model. These models were then used to determine the result, using 23 technical indicators as explanatory variables and labeling the next day's rise or falls as reactive variables. Finally, they used the stock indexes of Taiwan and South Korea from June 1990 to May 1991 to model the first 80% and verify the last 20%, and obtained the prediction results of 76.06% and 80.28% respectively.

[3] took the United States, China, Hong Kong, Taiwan, Singapore, Malaysia, South Korea, New Zealand and Australia as the research objects. Sample time from February 2000 to June 2010 stock market weekly return data. Using the time series method, this paper discusses the dynamic correlation of Asian stock markets. The empirical results show that: 1. The US stock market has a significant impact on the stock markets of countries in the Asia-Pacific region. 2. During the 2008 financial crisis in the United States, there was a significant correlation between stock markets.

[2] investigated the predictability of financial movement direction with SVM by forecasting the weekly movement direction of NIKKEI 225 index. They compared SVM with Linear Discriminant Analysis, Quadratic Discriminant Analysis and Elman Backpropagation Neural Networks. The experiment results showed the SVM outperformed the other classification methods.

In the literature in recent years, more and more various machine learning model has been applied to the study of trading strategies, and cheered, repeated numerous of the empirical results support the possibility of the application on machine learning in trading strategies, let's exploration of trading strategy have a deeper thought, among them, the majority validation study did in the past papers, it shows that it is better than a single classifier. Therefore, many literatures have begun to discuss the choice of the underlying model, that is, which one should be used to construct the majority decision model.

The United States as the world's largest and highest level of development of the economy, and therefore is one of the many investors focus on goals, in addition, the movements of the United States government and reserve is not only about the U.S. stock market, more will affect the stock market return rate in many countries around the world, by the literature shows that, the U.S. stock market has a significant influence on stock markets in the Asia-pacific region, among them, For Taiwan, the NASDAQ index has the most significant impact on the Taiwan stock market. Therefore, this study is expected to use US stock market data to forecast the Taiwan stock market, in addition to the Net Buy/Sell of Three Institutional Investors in Taiwan, and evaluate the effectiveness of various models to find the most suitable data and models for Taiwan stock prediction.

3   Methodology

3.1   Overview

This study first collects historical data of Taiwan index futures, Net Buy/Sell of Taiwan's institutional investors and NASDAQ index of the United State, processes and merges the data, then applies the model calculation, and finally analyzes the model fit through the future rise and fall prediction (Fig. 1).

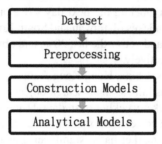

Fig. 1.   Flow chart of study

3.2   Dataset

The data used in this study are all from the data database of CMoney Investment Support System. The data period is from January 1, 2018 to July 30, 2022. A total of three pieces of data are collected. First, a total of 1116 Taiwan index futures data include date, opening price, high price, low price, closing price and volume (Table 1). Second, the data of 1116 transactions of the three Institutional Investors in Taiwan listed counters, including the date and the Net Buy/Sell of Three Institutional Investors in Taiwan listed company (Table 2). Third, there are 1152 data of NASDAQ index in the United States, including date, opening price, highest price, lowest price, closing price and trading volume (Table 3). These data constitute the original data set of the whole study.

Table 1.   Taiwan index futures dataset

Date	Open	High	Low	Close	Volume
2018/01/02	10629	10710	10621	10709	108602
2018/01/03	10748	10797	10729	10789	120998
...					
2000 /07/29	14936	14990	14870	14938	94106

Table 2. The Net Buy/Sell of three institutional investors

Date	Net Buy/Sell (NT$/million)
2018/01/02	3309.98
2018/01/03	4650.96
...	
2022/07/28	−781.97
2022/07/29	−566.55

Table 3. NASDAQ index in the United States

Date	Open	High	Low	Close	Volume
2018/01/02	6938	7007	6924	7007	1914930000
2018/01/03	7017	7069	7017	7066	2166780000
2018/01/04	7090	7098	7072	7078	1820000000
...					
2022/07/27	11775	12082	11718	12032	4559800000
2022/07/28	12036	12179	11887	12163	4892770000
2022/07/29	12240	12426	12181	12391	4893090000

Visual Studio Code is the tool used in the experimental environment of this study. Python language and machine learning suite sklearn are used to conduct data analysis experiments and.

3.3 Preprocessing

Firstly, check whether there are missing values or invalid values to fill the data, and finish data cleaning. Due to the discrepancy between the trading days of Taiwan and other data sets, Taiwan stock market is mainly used, and the trading days with the excess of US stocks are deleted to complete the data integration: In addition, the closing price of the Taiwan stock market, the trading volume of the Taiwan stock market, the Net Buy/Sell of Three Institutional Investors, the closing price of the NASDAQ index and the trading volume of the NASDAQ index are converted into 1 and 0 values. If the data value of today is greater than the previous day, it is marked as 1, and if it is less than or equal to the previous day, it is marked as 0. Finally, the samples were cut, with 70% of the data used as the training set and 30% as the prediction set.

3.4 Construction Models

In this study, three classification algorithms including Random Forest, Logistic Regression and Support Vector Machine were used to construct prediction models, and four features were input into different models, namely, the trading volume label of Taiwan stocks, the Net Buy/Sell of Three Institutional Investors label, the closing price label of NASDAQ INDEX and the trading volume of NASDAQ index. Additional detailed definitions, descriptions, and methods are described in the following sections.

Random Forest

Random Forest is composed of multiple decision tree classifier aggregation, and the data sample set is randomly sampled by repeated action of extracting and putting back. The main difference between the decision tree model and other statistical classification models is that the classification of decision tree is a logical classification mode, while the general statistical classification model is a non-logical classification mode.

The measure of fit and prediction ability is called the out-of-bag error rate (OOB error rate), which is calculated using the data obtained by the bootstrap method. Calculation will be the first step in using the method of drawing boots to extract the information construction of the first K tree, and have not been to, the information is known as the first K tree outside the bag samples (OOB sample), therefore, not involved in each training data will be constructed tree (roughly a third of the tree), namely each data point is likely to be as a few trees outside the bag samples, The ratio of the misclassified data to the total data is the OOB error rate of the Random Forest model. And it can directly generate an unbiased estimate of the error in the process of generating the model without the need for time-consuming Cross Validation to estimate the error rate of the model. In this study, the number of trees in the forest (N_estimators) of the Random Forest model parameter will be set according to the OOB error rate to strike a balance between training difficulty and model effect.

As can be seen from the results below (Fig. 2 and 3), when the number of decision tree model I and II increases to 19, the OOB Error Rate of the model will converge to a stable sufficient degree. Therefore, if the number parameter of the above decision tree is set to 19, the constructed random forest trading strategy will be stable sufficiently. However, the OOB of the random forest III model fluctuates after about 10 and reaches the highest point at 87. Therefore, 87 is adopted for N_estimators in this model (Fig. 4).

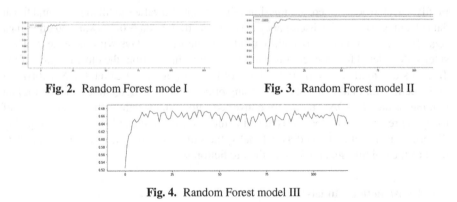

Fig. 2. Random Forest mode I   **Fig. 3.** Random Forest model II

Fig. 4. Random Forest model III

Logistic Regression
Logistic Regression analysis can be used when the dependent variables are dummy variables of a binary decision, and when the dependent variables are categorical data. The model is a nonlinear model, which is a retransformation model of probability density function of cumulative logistic logic.

Logistic Regression analysis for the problem of the data processing category utilization rate is high, but because the category information belongs to the discrete data, so data needs to be in early treatment, namely must transform the discrete data of continuous shape data type between numerical value between 0 and 1, after to the continuous data for return after the transformation.

Use the Linear model from the Python sklearn suite for the Logistic Regression function, where no additional parameters are required to set.

Support Vector Machine
Support Vector machine (SVM) is a method that can be used as a classification method. It can simultaneously minimize the empirical error and maximize the geometric edge region. This is because it is based on the VC dimension theory and the minimum principle of structural risk in statistical theory, so it has a excellent ability to solve tiny samples, nonlinearity, steep dimensions and local minimum points to achieve the purpose of classification [4].

The kernel function of the model is set as rbf, which is a classification method of polynomial type. Compared with Linear, it has a better classification effect. The penalty coefficient C represents the tolerance degree for errors. On the contrary, setting too narrow will cause the problem of low degree fitting. The value of C is set to three in all three models.

Select Features
The label combination of four data was used as the input value of three models, and nine model combinations were produced. The first is to take the trading volume label of Taiwan stocks and the Net Buy/Sell of Three Institutional Investors label as the input values of the I models. The second is to take the trading volume label of Taiwan stocks, the closing price label of NASDAQ index and the trading volume label of NASDAQ index as the input values of the II models. The third is to use the trading volume label of Taiwan stocks, the Net Buy/Sell of Three Institutional Investors label, the closing price label of NASDAQ index, and the trading volume label of NASDAQ index as the input values of the III models. The following table shows the integrated model and feature selection in this study (Table 4).odel to predict the rise is slightly better th

Table 4. Integration table of model features

	X1	X2	X3	X4	The number of features
R.F. I	V	V			2
R.F. II	V		V	V	3
R.F. III	V	V	V	V	4
L.R. I	V	V			2
L.R. II	V		V	V	3
L.R. III	V	V	V	V	4
SVM I	V	V			2
SVM II	V		V	V	3
SVM III	V	V	V	V	4

Note: X1: trading volume label of Taiwan stocks, X2: net Buy/Sell of Three Institutional Investors label, X3: closing price label of NASDAQ index, X4: trading volume label of NASDAQ index.

Analytical Models

In addition to the most basic OOB Error Rate, the Confusion Matrix generated by the OOB data can produce further ratios that are helpful for measuring the quality of the model, as shown in the following table (Table 5):

Table 5. Confusion matrix

	Ture Positive	Ture Negative
Predicted Positive	True Positive (TP)	False Positive (FP)
Predicted Negative	False Negative (FN)	True Negative (TN)

Precision: Also known as the Positive predictive Value (PPV), it is used to show the percentage of Predicted Positive results that are actually Positive. The formula is as follows (1):

$$\text{Precision} = \frac{TP}{TP + FP} \tag{1}$$

Negative Predictive Value (NPV): The number of Predicted Negative results will be Negative. The formula is as follows (2):

$$\text{NPV} = \frac{TN}{TN + FN} \tag{2}$$

Recall: also known as Sensitivity or True Positive Rate (TPR), it represents the percentage of the True Positive data that has been correctly predicted. The formula is as follows (3):

$$\text{Recall} = \frac{TP}{TP + FN} \tag{3}$$

Specificity: Also known as True Negative Rate (TNR), represents how many of the truly Negative data have been correctly predicted, and the formula is as follows (4):

$$\text{Specificity} = \frac{TN}{TN + FP} \tag{4}$$

Prevalence rate stands for the proportion of true positivity among all data. The formula is as follows (5):

$$\text{Prevalence} = \frac{TP + FN}{TP + FP + TN + FN} \tag{5}$$

Accuracy: represents how many ratios of all data are correctly predicted. The formula is as follows (6):

$$\text{Accuracy} = \frac{TP + TN}{TP + FP + TN + FN} \tag{6}$$

4 Empirical Result

4.1 Descriptive Statistics

This study takes Taiwan index futures as the research object, whose underlying asset is the TAIEX Index. The sample period is from January 1, 2018 to July 30, 2022, with a total of 1116 daily data excluding non-trading days. Taiwan index futures have risen 611 days and declined 505 days. The sample period covers a period of price turbulence, as you can see from the chart that the Taiwan index futures price initially fell from about 11,000 points to about 8,300 points in 2020 and then rebounded to about 18,000 points (Fig. 5).

Fig. 5. Taiwan stock price index futures closing price

There is a total of one prediction target - Taiwan stock futures rise and fall label, and four features, respectively, Taiwan stock trading volume label, three major corporate labels, NASDAQ closing price label, Nasdaq trading volume label, the data source is CMoney investment support system database.

4.2   Performance Evaluation

Different algorithms will have different effects on the model performance. The following table shows the ratios calculated from the confusion matrix obtained by inputting different features into the Random Forest model, Logistic Regression and SVM model. What's remarkable is that all three models with the same features get the same results. After our double confirmation, there are no errors in the program. When predicting, each model predicts different results, but they happen to be the same when calculating into the following six evaluation indicators (Table 6).

Table 6. Performance of Random Forest model

	Precision	NPV	Recall	Specificity	Prevalence	Accuracy
R.F. I	79.78%	63.41%	44.10%	89.66%	21.19%	67.76%
R.F. II	63.93%	61.69%	50.32%	73.81%	24.15%	62.54%
R.F. III	71.67%	66.01%	55.48%	79.76%	26.63%	68.11%
L.R. I	79.78%	63.41%	44.10%	89.66%	21.19%	67.76%
L.R. II	63.93%	61.69%	50.32%	73.81%	24.15%	62.54%
L.R. III	73.04%	65.87%	54.19%	81.55%	26.01%	68.42%
SVM I	79.78%	63.41%	44.10%	89.66%	21.19%	67.76%
SVM II	63.93%	61.69%	50.32%	73.81%	24.15%	62.54%
SVM III	80.95%	63.60%	43.87%	90.48%	21.05%	68.11%

First of all, for the R.F.I, L.R.I and SVM I prevalence is 21.19% and accuracy is 67.76%. From these two ratios, we can see that the prediction ability of all signals has improved by about 46%, and the reason for this 46% improvement must be judged by the remaining ratios. Precision, NPV, recall and specificity is 79.78%, 63.41%, 44.10% and 89.66%, respectively. The above results indicate that the model has a high accuracy in predicting a rise, but it is easy to predict a fall for the data, because specificity is higher than recall. That is to say, the prediction signal of these three models are more likely to predict a fall, and when the prediction is a fall, there is about 63.41% chance of a fall in the future.

The accuracy of for the R.F.II, L.R.II and SVM II is 62.54%, precision, NPV, recall, specificity at 63.93%, 61.69%, 50.32%, and 73.81%, respectively. The above results indicate that the accuracy of the model to predict the rise and fall is similar, but it is easy to predict the data to fall because specificity is higher than recall. That is to say, the probability of the rise and fall predicted by these three models are almost the same, and when the forecast is a rise, about 2% of the probability will rise in the future.

The accuracy of R.F. III is 68.11%, precision is 71.67%, NPV is 66.01%, recall is 55.48%, and specificity is 79.76%. The above results indicate that the accuracy of the model to predict the rise is slightly better than that to predict the fall of 6%, but it is easy to predict the data to fall because of the high specificity. That is to say, the probability of the rise and fall predicted by the R.F. III is about the same, but when the forecast is the fall, about 66.01% of the probability will fall in the future.

L.R. III, the accuracy, precision, NPV, recall and specificity is 68.42%, 73.04%, 65.87%, 54.19% and 81.55%, respectively. The above results indicate that the accuracy of the model to predict an increase is slightly better than that to predict a decline of 7%. However, for the L.R. III, it is easier to predict a decline because specificity is higher than recall. In other words, the L.R. III model is slightly easier to predict an increase, but when the forecast is a decline, there is about 81.55% chance of future decline.

The accuracy of SVM III is 68.11%, precision, NPV, recall and specificity are 80.95%, 63.6%, 43.87% and 90.48%, respectively. The above results represent that the accuracy of the model to predict an increase is much better than that to predict a decline of 17%, but for the data, it is easy to predict a decline, because of the high specificity, that is to say, the SVM III is easier to predict a decrease, but when the forecast is an increase, there are 80.95% of the probability will rise in the future.

5   Conclusion

This study aims to explore the prediction status of classification models in machine learning for the Taiwan stock market. Using three machine learning models (Random Forest, Logistic Regression and Support Vector Machine), four characteristics (trading volume label, the Net Buy/Sell of Three Institutional Investors label, the NASDAQ index closing price label, the NASQAQ index volume label), six evaluation indexes (Precision, NPV, recall, specificity, prevalence, accuracy) to construct the model of performance assessment.

Firstly, the number of decision trees of Random Forest is evaluated by the OOB rate, and then the Random Forest model is constructed by inputting different features into each model. Finally, the advantages and disadvantages of the model are evaluated by the six-item ratio derived from the confusion matrix.

The precision of SVM III is 80.95%, which is the highest among all models, indicating that it predicts the rise is better than others. The NPV of R.F. III was 66.01%, which was the highest among all models, indicating that it predicts the fall is better than others.

The recall of R.F. III was 55.48%, which was the highest among all the models, indicating that R.F. III more likely to predict rise than the other models. The specificity of SVM III was 90.48%, which was the highest among all models that more likely to predict fall than the other models.

Finally, the accuracy of L.R. III is 68.42%, which is the highest among all models, but the difference with the lowest accuracy model is only 6%.

It can be found from the empirical results that the specificity of the nine models in this study is all higher than recall, but the number of fall day in this study only accounts for 45% of the total data, indicating that the model is easy to predict as a relatively small number of down data. But all of the models predict rise are more accuracy than down. So, we suggest that multiple models may be combined in the future to increase the weight of SVM III to improve the prediction rate of rise data. The accuracy of model III using the data of US stock market and Taiwan stock market is higher than that of I and II, which proves that using the data of US stock market and Taiwan stock market at the same time has higher prediction accuracy.

References

1. Dutta, A.: Prediction of stock performance in the Indian stock market using logistic regression. Int. J. Bus. Inf. **7**(1), 105 (2012)
2. Huang, W., Nakamori, Y., Wang, S.Y.: Forecasting stock market movement direction with support vector machine. Comput. Oper. Res. **32**(10), 2513–2522 (2005)
3. Hwang, C-L., Md. Masud, A.S.: Multiple Objective Decision Making—Methods And Applications: A State-of-the-Art Survey, vol. 164. Springer, Berlin (2012). https://doi.org/10.1007/978-3-642-45511-7
4. Jin, D., Liu, Z., He, D., Gabrys, B., Musial, K.: Robust detection of communities with multi-semantics in large attributed networks. In: Liu, W., Giunchiglia, F., Yang, B. (eds.) KSEM 2018. LNCS (LNAI), vol. 11061, pp. 362–376. Springer, Cham (2018). https://doi.org/10.1007/978-3-319-99365-2_32
5. Kohavi, R., John, G.H.: Automatic parameter selection by minimizing estimated error. In: Machine Learning Proceedings, pp. 304–312. Morgan Kaufmann (1995)
6. Yu, M.-L., et al.: Rapid virological response and treatment duration for chronic hepatitis C genotype 1 patients: a randomized trial. Hepatology **47**(6), 1884–1893 (2008)

Semi-automatic Chatbot Generation for Web APIs

Sheng-Kai Wang, Wan-Lin You, and Shang-Pin Ma[✉]

Department of Computer Science and Engineering, National Taiwan Ocean University, Keelung, Taiwan
{11057052,10857036}@mail.ntou.edu.tw, albert@ntou.edu.tw

Abstract. The Chatbot is a new and popular technology in recent years. With Web API technology becoming increasingly mature, how to integrate Web APIs and Chatbots has become an issue of great interest. Based on the concept of Model-Driven Engineering, this research proposes a semi-automatic generation method and its associated tool, called BOTEN, to allow application developers to build Chatbot interfaces with specified Web APIs quickly. To ensure that the Chatbot has sufficient NLU (natural language understanding) capability, we also propose a method, called SCASG (sentence coupling analysis and sentence generation), to evaluate the training sentences written by the developer based on TF-IDF, Word-Net, and SpaCy techniques. SCASG provides the "coupling" analysis for sentences and warns the developer to modify the poor-quality training sentences. SCASG can also automatically increase the number of training sentences to improve the NLU capability of a Chatbot.

Keywords: Web API · Chatbot · Rasa · Swagger · TF-IDF · WordNet · SpaCy · NLU

1 Introduction

Chatbots use computer programs to simulate real people to interact with users. They allow users to chat with them via text or voice through interfaces such as communication platforms; its applications include e-commerce, customer service, content promotion, push notifications, personal assistants, etc. [1]. Many companies have begun to use conversational bots in actual operations. Typical cases include Chatbots that assist in handling customer problems in restaurants [2], Chatbots that can help in team management [3], and Chatbots that serve as recommendation experts in specific fields [4], etc.; it is pretty applicable diversely in various domains.

On the other hand, with Web API technology becoming increasingly mature, more and more companies expose their own services as Web API to provide in-organization or third-party developers for application development and service integration. Based on the technology trend, how to combine Web APIs and Chatbot technologies is also starting to gain more and more attraction. According to a research survey [5], developers pay the most attention to the integration issues for integrating Chatbots and Web APIs. Vaziri

© The Author(s), under exclusive license to Springer Nature Singapore Pte Ltd. 2022
S.-Y. Hsieh et al. (Eds.): ICS 2022, CCIS 1723, pp. 267–278, 2022.
https://doi.org/10.1007/978-981-19-9582-8_24

et al. developed a great approach, SwaggerBot [6], to solve the issues mentioned earlier. SwaggerBot is a Chatbot generated by the compiler after the OpenAPI-related elements are added to the extended specification. By providing a Swagger (also known as OAS: OpenAPI Specification [7]) document with a complete specification, SwaggerBot could compile as a Chatbot that can access the RESTful API. However, SwaggerBot uses the name of each API endpoint as a unique training sentence to cause Intent recognition problems/constraints on the generated Chatbot. It needs to manually create shortcuts and shortcut synonyms for accessing existing functions by power users to enhance its NLU capability. In addition, there is no story flow between various endpoints; thus, composite services cannot be provided to end users.

We further analyze the integration of Web APIs and Chatbots then find that its complexity falls into three parts: (1) Developers need to have detailed knowledges of the Chatbot development framework, and they need to be familiar with the configuration settings and operation steps required for the Chabot development. (2) It is necessary to write various adapters between Chatbots and Web APIs to appropriately set up the Chatbot components, such as Intent, Entity, Slot, etc., and write code to convert the received data to invoke the target APIs. In addition, it is also needed to properly parse the service responses to extract required information for the conversation. (3) It is essential to write training sentences of sufficient quality and quantity to train a Chatbot with able NLU capabilities to correctly determine the Intents of the end user. Therefore, to reduce the complexity of Chatbot development, our strategy is based on the concept of Model-Driven Engineering [8], hoping to enable developers to focus on the conceptual integration of Web APIs and Chatbots, rather than underlying implementation details and adapters/converters. Swagger is the most widely used description language for Web APIs. Many Web API developers have provided Swagger description documents. Thus, we propose a semi-automatic Chatbot generation approach based on Swagger, called BOTEN. We defined an extended format, called BotSwagger, to add the configuration for the core elements of Chatbot to the Swagger. We also devised an execution engine, called the BOTEN engine, to parse the BotSwagger documents and generate the Chatbots.

Meanwhile, the typical Chatbot NLU model identifies the Intents behind the sentence input by the user, and uses it as the basis for executing subsequent actions. Confidence is a common metric to represent the degree of precision for the Intent identification. If the confidence is too low, recognition errors may occur. Therefore, to improve confidence and enhance the NLU capability of Chatbot, we provide a method, called SCASG (sentence coupling analysis and sentence generation), to perform "coupling" analysis and automatically generate training sentences based on the sentences provided by the developer. If the meanings of training sentences with different intents are too similar, SCASG will warn the developer to make modifications to enhance the quality of the sentences. The developer can also choose whether to automatically generate more training sentences by SCASG to enhance the NLU capabilities of the Chatbot.

The expected operation mode is that the Chatbot developer supplements the Chabot's relevant settings on the Web API's Swagger file, fills in the training statement, and then uploads the file to the BOTEN system. The executable Chatbot can be automatically generated, and the training sentences can be further naturally added. Afterward, end users can use the Chatbot system to access the functions of the Web API in a conversational manner. They can directly view the aggregated service response results, reducing the complexity and development cost of integrating Web APIs and Chatbots.

2 Background and Related Work

2.1 Cohesion and Coupling

In the field of software engineering, cohesion refers to the degree of interdependence of functions or data within a program module/component, and coupling is the degree of independence between program modules/components [9]. Generally, developers would like to increase the cohesion to make the program easier to maintain and reuse, and reduce the coupling to improve the independence between modules and curtail the possibility of system communication errors, also known as "high cohesion, low coupling."

When writing Swagger, we also hope that developers can pay attention to the coupling between training sentences, reduce the similarity of training sentences between different intents, and avoid the training sentences of different intents being too similar, causes intent recognition errors in the trained NLU model. In addition, it can improve confidence in model identification and make the trained model more accurate. As for the cohesion of the training sentences under the same Intent, developers should try to write various training sentence patterns to avoid overfitting the trained Chatbot model, so this research does not explicitly require users to pay attention to cohesion. After the developer has finished writing the BotSwagger, before converting it into Chatbot, it will go through a series of BotSwagger pre-processing to check whether the format is correct and whether the information provided is complete. It calculates the similarity between training sentences with TF-IDF, WordNet and SpaCy technologies, warns the sentences with too high coupling, and recommends developers modify them.

2.2 TF-IDF, WordNet and SpaCy

To improve the natural language understanding ability of the Chatbot model, TF-IDF (Term Frequency-Inverse Document Frequency), WordNet, and SpaCy technologies are used to calculate the similarity between training sentences in the pre-processing stage of the BotSwagger, and warnings are issued for sentences that are too similar in meaning between different intents. After that, you can choose whether to use WordNet further to expand the training sentences input by the user, then use SpaCy to filter out the sentences that have a significant difference in meaning from the original sentence, and then train a model with better quality.

TF-IDF [10] is a commonly used weighting technique for information retrieval and text mining. It is a statistical method used to evaluate the importance of words to a document in a collection or a corpus. It consists of two parts: term frequency (TF) and inverse document frequency (IDF). TF refers to the number of times a given word appears in a document, and IDF refers to the inverse of the number of the document which the term appears in a total of several documents. By multiplying TF and IDF, the weight of a given word in a document can be calculated.

WordNet [11] is an English dictionary built and maintained under the direction of George A. Miller, professor of psychology at Princeton University's Cognitive Science

Laboratory. WordNet groups words according to their meanings, each group of words with the same meaning is called a synset (synonym set), and various relationships also connect these sets. By consulting WordNet, the system can find out the synonyms of each word in the training sentence, and then arrange and combine multiple synonyms of the original sentence.

SpaCy [12] is an open-source library for natural language processing. The word vector is generated through the pre-trained model in its corpus, and the Cosine Similarity between the vectors can be used to compare the similarity of the two sentences directly.

2.3 Related Work

Telang et al. [13] proposed a conceptual framework for Chatbots, which consists of five related responsibilities: Dialog Manager (manage natural language dialog), Inference Engine (extract user intentions), Knowledge Base (Reasoning and planning), Planner (generate execution plans), External Services (combined with external functions actually to perform dialog interactions).

Soler et al. [14] proposed a model-driven engineering method to develop Chatbots. They designed the meta-model of Chabot and Domain Specific Language (DSL): Conga, which can be used with multiple Chatbot platforms such as (Dialogflow or Rasa's code parser and code generator to generate Chatbot. This method also provides a platform recommender that suggests suitable target Chatbot platforms based on the DSL.

Pietro et al. [15] proposed a method for generating Chatbots through annotations in HTML of web pages, and it can set intentions, dialogue sentences, keywords, and categories. This method hopes to achieve conversational website browsing based on natural language dialogue, allowing users to access the content and functions. They need through "talking to the website" instead of operating the graphical UI through the keyboard and mouse. This method uses Selenium to automate the operation of the browser, and parses HTML to generate intents and perform machine learning.

Daniel et al. [16] proposed an open-sourced Xatkit platform. They designed two domain-specific languages (DSL) to model Chatbots: (1) Intent Package uses training sentences, contextual information, and matching conditions to describe user intent. And (2) Execution Package connects the user's intention and response actions as a part of the definition of Chatbot behavior, and the execution component usually involves to back-end services, which is then implemented by the definition of Platform Package. In addition to providing domain-specific languages to define Chatbot, Xatkit also provides a modular execution engine that can automatically deploy Chatbot applications and manage the defined dialog logic on the selected platform.

3 Approach Descriptions

3.1 Operating Concepts and Requirement Analysis for BOTEN

To elicit the requirements of the proposed BotSwagger file format and the goals of the BOTEN platform, we analyze the operating concepts through two practical application scenarios: The first part is that the developers design and deploy the Chatbot process. The second part is that the end-users operate the Chatbot via a conversational user interface. Note that multiple functionalities of BOTEN are based on Rasa[1], an open source machine learning framework to automate conversations in text or voice.

A developer plans to develop a Chatbot that integrates the APIs (e.g., the API of sights recommendation). The overall process is shown in Fig. 1. The developer first writes the BotSwagger file and uses BOTEN to generate the configuration files for the Chatbot. The API provider is supposed to write the first version of BotSwagger, and subsequent application developers can follow this BotSwagger to obtain a prototype of Chatbot, which can be modified after receiving the prototype. They can also write a customized BotSwagger file according to their own requirements for conversations. After the developer inputs the BotSwagger file, it will be validated. Following passing the validation, a temporary configuration file in JSON (JavaScript Object Notation) will be generated, where the developer can modify the settings. After confirming the settings, BOTEN converts the JSON to the Rasa profiles, and push them to GitHub for version control in the meantime. Then the developer can decide whether to expand the training sentences of Rasa automatically. The developer can deploy the dialogue Chatbot whether the expansion step is performed. After the deployment is finished, end-users can operate the produced Chatbot via a conversational user interface, and get the API execution responses in the form of human readable table.

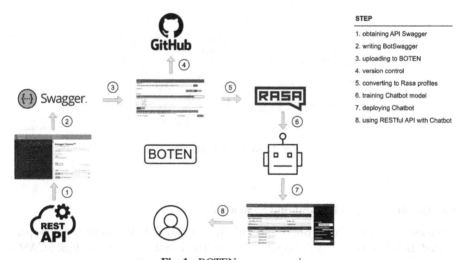

Fig. 1. BOTEN usage scenario

3.2 Architecture Design for BOTEN

Based on the mentioned requirement analysis, we then designed the system architecture, as shown in Fig. 2, to realize the requirements and goals of this research. This research mainly focuses on four phases: the conversion phase, the version control phase, the

---

[1] https://rasa.com/.

expansion sentence phase, and the execution phase. (1) The conversion phase converts the BotSwagger into Chatbot profiles according to the pipeline sequence. (2) We use the GitHub API in the version control phase to download Rasa's universal configuration files for user. The user can also push the Rasa profiles or revised ones to the repository by BOTEN for version control. (3) In the expansion sentence phase, BOTEN will further analyze and process the generated Rasa profiles to improve the capability of recognizing the intent. (4) In the execution phase, developers can build and deploy Chatbot. The built Chatbot is a conversational application with the Rasa framework as the bottom layer, and it can be used with the front-end web interface to allow end users to chat with the Chatbot.

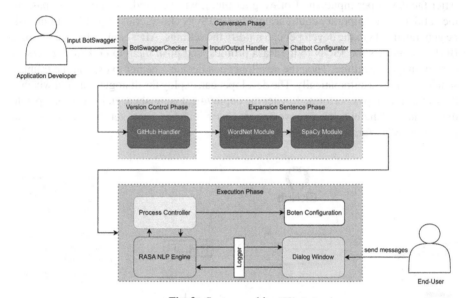

Fig. 2. System architecture

3.3 Quality Analysis for Training Sentences

When the developer inputs a BotSwagger file, the proposed SCASG method will be performed. BOTEN will verify the input document based on the SCASG method. SCASG first converts all the text to lowercase, removes the stopwords that are not important, performs lemmatization on the remaining words, and then calculates the weights of all words in individual sentences to establish a corpus index by TF-IDF technology. The weight value represents the constituent words of each training sentence and the sentence can be converted into a one-dimensional vector. Finally, the Cosine Similarity between the sentence vectors can be calculated to obtain the similarity value of the two sentences.

Since the length of the training sentences of Chatbot is usually short, it may happen that although the two sentences have similar meanings, the calculated Cosine Similarity is still low because the same words do not appear in these two sentences. Therefore, SCASG also supports the following features:

(1) SCASG finds out the synonyms of all words used in the training sentences by consulting the dictionary of WordNet, add these synonyms to the corpus index, and use SpaCy to calculate the similarity between the synonyms and the original words. Multiply the weight value of the original word by the similarity between the synonym and the original word as the weight value of the synonym in the corpus index, as shown in Fig. 3. These synonyms are also regarded as the words of the sentence to which the original word belongs, and the similarity between all training sentences is recalculated.

(2) In addition to calculating the Cosine Similarity between sentences through the weight value obtained by TF-IDF, SpaCy is also used in SCASG to calculate the similarity between sentences. Therefore, two different similarity values between the two sentences are obtained, since SpaCy has a bigger corpus. Then these two values are calculated at a specific ratio as the weighted similarity between the two sentences (coupling).

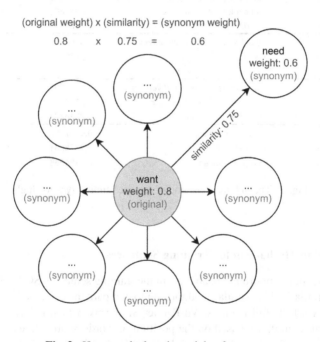

Fig. 3. How to calculate the weight of synonyms

Using the above two similarity calculation methods simultaneously, SCASG can now accurately evaluate the similarity between training sentences (coupling), and issue warnings for sentences that are too similar but belong to different intents. As for the judgment method of too high similarity shown in Fig. 4, all sentences are taken as a reference sentence in turn (sentence 2-1 is used as the reference sentence in Fig. 4), all of the sentences are compared with the reference sentence, and the similarity is calculated. The similarity between the sentence and itself is "1.0". After obtaining all the similarity values, we calculate the sum of the similarity of sentences with the same intent, and compare these values. If the sum of the sentence similarities for one intent is greater than the sum of the sentence similarities for the intent which reference sentence belongs, the sentence with the largest similarity for the intent will be regarded as too coupled. This algorithm can not only preserve the diversity of sentences for the same Intent, but also find out the sentences that are too similar. Regarding the verification of the effectiveness of this method, will be explained in the subsequent experiment section.

reference sentence: 2-1	1-3 is too similar to 2-1		
intent - sentence number	sentence	similarity	sum
1-1	I want to get information about venues	0.5266195	
1-2	Get attractions explore	0.6880899 step.3	2.0041394
1-3	I want to get the venues	0.7894299	
2-1	**I want to get explore about venues**	1.0000000	step.2
2-2	Get explore of attractions	0.6942862 step.1	1.9072807
2-3	Search for attractions	0.2129945	
3-1	I want to get tips about venues	0.5754928	
3-2	Get tips of attractions	0.2672742	1.6865370
3-3	get explore about venues	0.8437699	
4-1	I want to get hours about venues	0.5734294	
4-2	Get opening time of attractions	0.2750190	1.0502737
4-3	Attraction opening hours	0.2018253	
5-1	I want to get next venues	0.6137682	
5-2	Get next attractions	0.2778281	1.2050529
5-3	see next venues	0.3134566	

Fig. 4. The judgment method of sentence similarity is too high

3.4 Expansion Mechanism for Training Sentences

To expand the more important vocabulary in the training sentence, SCASG uses Word-Net's wup_similarity [17] similarity algorithm to compare the expanded new word with the original word. Its full name is Wu-Palmer Similarity, which is based on equation (1). It calculates similarity based on the position of words relative to each other in the hypernym tree. LCS (Least Common Subsumer) [18] is the deepest common ancestor in the classification tree, and the depth refers to the depth in the classification tree. The calculation equation is as follows:

$$Wup_{similarity}(w1, w2) = 2 * \frac{depth(lcs(w1, w2))}{(depth(w1) + depth(w2))} \tag{1}$$

The usage can be divided into the following steps: (1) First, SCASG segments all the training sentences, and splits the sentence into tokens. (2) SCASG lemmatizes each token and removes the stopwords. (3) SCASG uses WordNet to obtain the synonyms of each meaningful token. (4) Through the wup_similarity algorithm, SCASG evaluates the similarity between the synonym and the original token, cross-compare the similarity of the two sets of synonyms by Cartesian product, and obtains the average. (5) As long as the average value is higher than "0.3", it is regarded as a synonym of this token. (6) These synonyms and the previously removed stopwords are combined according to their relative position in the original sentence. The words other than stopwords are replaced in turn with the newly generated synonym to combine multiple sentences with the same meaning as the original sentence. The reason for the average parameter being "0.3" will be discussed in the subsequent experiment section.

After WordNet expansion, a little part of the newly generated sentences is too different from the original sentence, which may cause Rasa to train an inaccurate model. Therefore, we further filter the newly generated sentences through SpaCy, which will use the similarity algorithm of SpaCy. The calculation mechanism is as follows: (1) Create a collection of multiple tokens after segmenting each sentence. (2) Through the algorithm of word embedding, the token vector is calculated by the pre-trained model of the SpaCy's corpus. (3) Calculating the average of the sentence's token vectors as its sentence vector. And (4) comparing the cosine similarity between sentence vectors, the calculation equation is as follows:

$$SpaCy_{similarity}(s1, s2) = \frac{\vec{s1} \cdot \vec{s2}}{\|s1\| \times \|s2\|} \tag{2}$$

In usage, it can be divided into the following steps: (1) comparing all newly generated sentences with the original sentences one by one for similarity, and (2) keeping the sentences with a similarity greater than "0.7" and writing them back to Rasa profiles as training sentences to complete the expansion. The reason for the similarity parameter being "0.7" will be also discussed in the subsequent experiment section.

4 Evaluation Experiments

The designed experiment is to find the most suitable similarity parameter and evaluate the effectiveness of the process of expanding Rasa training sentences. A Confidence experiment is performed to judge whether the Rasa training model's determination is consistent with the intent classification judgment by human testers after the sentence expansion.

We prepared three Web APIs to be the test cases: A1: the scenic spot recommendation service, "Foursquare", A2: the movie recommendation service, "The Movie Database", and A3: the Route Planning service, "Graph Hopper Direction".

We adjusted the similarity parameters, compared the confidence of the training model after the sentence expansion, and tried to find the best parameters and achieve the highest confidence. The experiment steps include:

- Experiment#C1: The purpose of this step is to find the best solution for the parameters of the similarity algorithm for WordNet.
- Experiment#C2: The purpose of this step is to test whether the confidence can be improved by removing the stopwords and performing the lemmatization.

- Experiment#C3: The purpose of this step is to find the best solution for the parameters of the similarity algorithm of SpaCy.

We invited three users who have the experiences of using Chatbots to assist in this experiment, and asked them to decide what is the correct intent corresponding to the testing sentence, and take the majority vote as the correct answer to evaluate whether the judgment of the Rasa model is correct.

The experiment's results are shown in Table 1 (based on cases A1 and A2) and Table 2 (based on cases A1, A2, and A3). The experiments with parameters "0.1", "0.2", and "N/A" are the experiments that cannot be completed due to the expansion of sentences or the training time of the model being too long. "c" (correct) means the intent is judged correctly and confidence is higher than "0.9", "a" (acceptable) means the intent is judged correctly, but the confidence is lower than "0.9", and as for the case which the intent is judged incorrectly, we use "i" (incorrect) to represent. And we put the best results in bold.

According to the results of experiment C1, we found that the wup_similarity algorithm of WordNet has the best results when the similarity is set to "0.4", so we compared this result with the experiment C2. We also found that in the case of removing stopwords and performing lemmatization, if the degree is set to "0.3", the confidence value is best. Then in the experiment C3, if the SpaCy similarity parameter is set to "0.7", then confidence can have the best performance, and all of the intents are judged correctly. Thus it is known that the WordNet wup_similarity's parameter is set to "0.3", and the SpaCy parameter is set to "0.7"; it is the best solution.

Table 1. Confidence experiement

Experiment	Original	0.3	0.4	0.5	0.6	0.7	0.8	0.9
#C1 (WordNet)	4c	N/A	**6c**	5c	4c	5c	4c	4c
	1a		**1a**	1a	0a	0a	2a	1a
	5i		**3i**	4i	6i	5i	4i	5i
#C2 (Stopwords and Lemmatization)	4c	**9c**	7c	7c	7c	3c	6c	5c
	1a	**0a**	1a	1a	1a	4a	2a	3a
	5i	**1i**	2i	2i	2i	3i	2i	2i
#C3 (SpaCy)	4c	8c	8c	8c	7c	**10c**	7c	9c
	1a	0a	0a	0a	2a	**0a**	1a	0a
	5i	2i	2i	2i	1i	**0i**	2i	1i

The results of the experiment for expansion sentences are shown in Table 2. In both cases, it can be found that the sentences improved by SCASG can effectively improve the accuracy of training model (too high coupling), and it can be further improved by expanding sentences. Now a Chatbot with the better NLU capability can be established.

Table 2. Experiment for sentences expansion

Cases	Bad quality and no sentences expansion	Bad quality and sentences expansion	Good quality and no sentences expansion	Good quality and sentences expansion
Case A1	2c 0a 3i	2c 0a 3i	4c 1a 0i	4c 1a 0i
Case A2	0c 3a 2i	3c 0a 2i	4c 0a 1i	5c 0a 0i
Case A3	2c 0a 2i	3c 0a 1i	3c 0a 1i	4c 0a 0i

5   Conclusions

This research proposes a semi-automatic Chatbot generation mechanism for Web APIs. The experiments also demonstrate the successful implementation of the system features and its natural language understanding capabilities. In the future, we plan to provide a mechanism that allows users to ask what parameters have been filled in previously to improve the convenience. This mechanism will be provided by the system automatically without the developers to specifically write the training sentences for this intent.

Acknowledgement. This research was sponsored by the National Science and Technology Council (NSTC) in Taiwan under the grant 110-2221-E-019-039-MY3.

References

1. Brandtzaeg, P.B., Følstad, A.: Why people use chatbots. In: Kompatsiaris, I., et al. (eds.) INSCI 2017. LNCS, vol. 10673, pp. 377–392. Springer, Cham (2017). https://doi.org/10.1007/978-3-319-70284-1_30
2. Michaud, L.N.: Observations of a new Chatbot: drawing conclusions from early interactions with users. IT Prof. **20**(5), 40–47 (2018)
3. Toxtli, C., Monroy-Hernández, A., Cranshaw, J.: Understanding Chatbot-mediated task management. In: Proceedings of the 2018 CHI Conference on Human Factors in Computing Systems, pp. 1–6 (2018)
4. Cerezo, J., Kubelka, J., Robbes, R., Bergel, A.: Building an expert recommender Chatbot. In: 2019 IEEE/ACM 1st International Workshop on Bots in Software Engineering (BotSE), pp. 59–63. IEEE (2019)
5. Abdellatif, A., Costa, D., Badran, K., Abdalkareem, R., Shihab, E.: Challenges in Chatbot development: a study of stack overflow posts. In: Proceedings of the 17th International Conference on Mining Software Repositories, pp. 174–185 (2020)
6. Vaziri, M., Mandel, L., Shinnar, A., Siméon, J., Hirzel, M.: Generating chat bots from web API specifications. In: Proceedings of the 2017 ACM SIGPLAN International Symposium on New Ideas, New Paradigms, and Reflections on Programming and Software, pp. 44–57 (2017)
7. OpenAPI Specification. https://github.com/OAI/OpenAPI-Specification/blob/main/versions/3.1.0.md
8. Schmidt, D.C.: Model-driven engineering. IEEE Comput. **39**(2), 25 (2006)

9. Josikakar. Software Engineering I Coupling and Cohesion (2021). https://www.geeksforg eeks.org/software-engineering-coupling-and-cohesion/
10. Understanding TF-IDF (Term Frequency-Inverse Document Frequency). https://www.geeksf orgeeks.org/understanding-tf-idf-term-frequency-inverse-document- frequency/
11. What is WordNet? https://wordnet.princeton.edu/
12. Word vectors and semantic similarity. https://spacy.io/usage/linguistic-features#vectors-sim ilarity
13. Telang, P.R., Kalia, A.K., Vukovic, M., Pandita, R., Singh, M.P.: A conceptual framework for engineering Chatbots. IEEE Internet Comput. **22**(6), 54–59 (2018)
14. Pérez-Soler, S., Guerra, E., de Lara, J.: Model-driven Chatbot development. In: Dobbie, G., Frank, U., Kappel, G., Liddle, S.W., Mayr, H.C. (eds.) ER 2020. LNCS, vol. 12400, pp. 207–222. Springer, Cham (2020). https://doi.org/10.1007/978-3-030-62522-1_15
15. Chittò, P., Baez, M., Daniel, F., Benatallah, B.: Automatic generation of Chatbots for con- versational web browsing. In: Dobbie, G., Frank, U., Kappel, G., Liddle, S.W., Mayr, H.C. (eds.) ER 2020. LNCS, vol. 12400, pp. 239–249. Springer, Cham (2020). https://doi.org/10. 1007/978-3-030-62522-1_17
16. Daniel, G., Cabot, J., Deruelle, L., Derras, M.: Xatkit: a multimodal low-code Chatbot development framework. IEEE Access **8**, 15332–15346 (2020)
17. NLP I WuPalmer – WordNet Similarity (2022). https://www.geeksforgeeks.org/nlp-wup almer-wordnet-similarity/
18. Sample usage for wordnet. https://www.nltk.org/howto/wordnet.html

Prediction of Middle-Aged Unhealthy Facial Skin Using VGG19 and Support Vector Machine Models

Rita Wiryasaputra[1,2], Chin-Yin Huang[1], Rio Williyanto[2], and Chao-Tung Yang[3,4(✉)]

[1] Department of Industrial Engineering and Enterprise Information,
Tunghai University, Taichung 407224, Taiwan
`huangcy@go.thu.edu.tw`
[2] Department of Informatics, Krida Wacana Christian University,
Jakarta 11470, Indonesia
`rita.wiryasaputra@ukrida.ac.id`
[3] Department of Computer Science, Tunghai University, Taichung 407224, Taiwan
`ctyang@thu.edu.tw`
[4] Research Center for Smart Sustainable Circular Economy, Tunghai University,
Taichung 407224, Taiwan

Abstract. In human communication, the resource of primary information can be read from a human's face. Health problems occur in line with age, and one way to detect health issues is through changes in facial skin. People typically pay less attention to initial facial skin changes, even though the changes might be linked to a particular disease, such as Lupus. Treatment for Lupus takes time and is costly. Cutting-edge technology and Artificial Intelligence (AI) bring a new horizon to the medical field where a disease can be detected or predicted early. This paper presents the classification of training images for the early detection of middle-aged unhealthy facial skin. The Multi-Task Cascaded Convolutional Neural Networks (MTCNN) technique provides the face boundary box and the performance of face detection uses VGG19 architecture. The images dataset was divided into data training and data testing with a ratio of 80%: 20%, respectively, and the healthy or unhealthy face image was determined with a machine learning approach. The experimental results showed that the accuracy of the proposed Support Vector Machine classifier model was 92.2%.

Keywords: Face detection · Machine learning · MTCNN · SVM · VGG19

1 Introduction

It is undeniable that a person's first impression is reflected in the face. In human communication, the resource of primary information can be read from a human's face. Based on the World Health Organization (WHO), the age classification is

S.-Y. Hsieh et al. (Eds.): ICS 2022, CCIS 1723, pp. 279–289, 2022.
https://doi.org/10.1007/978-981-19-9582-8_25

as follows: young age (25–44 years old), middle age (44–66 years old), elderly age (60–75 years old), senile age (75–90 years old), elderly (above 60 years old) and long-livers who have more than 90 years old [6]. Many diseases merge in line with age, and one way to detect health problems is via facial skin. Most people typically do not notice the initial changes in their facial skin early on, even though some of the changes may be linked to diseases such as lupus, rosacea, herpes, erysipelas, and eczema. The cause of those skin disorders is ranging from viruses, bacteria, environment, or autoimmune problems. If a certain skin disorder is not detected early, the treatment cost could be high. For example, lupus is an autoimmune disease, and its symptoms often mimic another disease thus it is not easy to diagnose. Lupus also causes inflammation of particular body areas including the skin, joints, blood cells, kidneys, brain, heart, and lungs. The most distinctive sign of lupus is a facial rash that resembles the wings of a butterfly unfolding across both cheeks. There is no cure for lupus, but symptoms can be controlled through treatments. Advancements in technology and Artificial Intelligence (AI) particularly in the medical field offer new horizons to the healthcare world. Machine learning, as a subset of AI, has many models for classification and prediction purposes making early detection and screening of diseases possible. Convolutional Neural Network (CNN) is a machine learning unit algorithm. Based on a CNN, Multi-Task Cascaded Convolutional Neural Networks (MTCNN) enable the definition of the face into a boundary box as the first step of verification. MTCNN as a face detector is more accurate than DLIB. MTCNN can find faces at unfavorable angles whereas DLIB enables identification of the faces from the front [2]. The selection boundary box crop and extract with the VGG19 model to gain its feature. Previous studies have used VGG19 approach across various domains [1,7,8,10,11,13,14]. Moreover, underfitting issues are possible to experience with model. Underfitting is a phenomenon that occurs when the model cannot generate a low error value in the training set [18] To address the best result of classification, the Support Vector Machine (SVM) as the powerful machine learning classifier deals with complex datasets to recognize subtle and nondistinctive class [11]. The SVM classifier is also the most widely used in classification problem [3,9]. The study objectives used ML methods to identify healthy and unhealthy middle-aged facial skin. The structure of this paper is as follows: the first section reviews the background, previous research is explained in Sect. 2, and Sect. 3 presents the research methodology. To deepen the understanding of the study's objective, Sect. 4 features an experiment section. The conclusion is outlined in Sect. 5 along with future research directions.

2   Related Works

This section describes the literature study stage in which the papers assessed were from Google Scholar, Science Direct, and the IEEEXplore repositories. The research conducted by Taeb shows that augmented real and fake faces could be determined by conducting Custom CNN, DenseNet121, VGG19 approaches; the highest accuracy was achieved through the VGG19's performance [13]. Ahmed [1] found that the VGG19 had the best accuracy compared with other face recognition models. Goel [7] examined several models such as FaceNet, VGGFace, VGG16, and VGG19 in face recognition for sibling identification cases. Assessments on discrimination used cosine similarity, Euclidean distance, structured similarity, Manhattan distance, and Minkowski distance as the standard measures. The VGG16 and VGG19 models provided favorable results for foreheads. The accuracy of VGGFace classification reached more than 95% for the full-frontal face and eyes, but not for the nose. However, the FaceNet approach generated the best result for nose classification. Table 1 gives the related work of image classification.

Table 1. The related work of image classification

Reference	Model	Objective
[1]	AlexNet, MobileNet, VGG16, VGG19	A comparative study of several model Convolution Neural Network for face recognition
[7]	FaceNet, VGGFace, VGG16, VGG19	Classification with VGG19 in forehead
[14]	DenseNet, VGG16, VGG19	Classification with fruits images
[13]	DenseNet, VGG19	Comparing the common face detection classifiers
[8]	VGG16, VGG19, DenseNet	Classification using the limited size of the sample data sets from publicity data on modest hardware
[10]	VGG16, VGG19, DenseNet	Adjust densely-connected classifier with VGG19 pretrained model
[11]	VGG16, VGG19, DenseNet	A method for multi-label classification with confusion matrices

3 Methodology

This section presents the research stages, encompassing the dataset collection process, the stage of feature extraction, and the image classification stage. The overall approach is illustrated in Fig. 1.

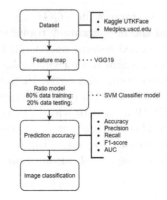

Fig. 1. Research methodology

3.1   MTCNN

The MTCNN architecture has three serial layers - P-Net, R-Net, and O-net - as shown in Fig. 2. This architecture facilitates and accelerates the fastest form of computation. The P-Net module was the most time-consuming in processing the full CNN to generate three outcomes [16] MTCNN applies Non-Maximum Suppression (NMS) to unite similar squares. The outcome from the P-Net module becomes the R-Net input module to improve decisions regarding the possibility of face segmentation, meanwhile, the NMS is applied to the output of the R-Net module. The main difference between P-Net and R-Net module is in the final layer in which the R-Net module features a fully connected layer for its last two layers [5].

3.2   VGG19

VGG19 is the variant of Visual Geometry Group (VGG) based on the CNN architectures which have 19 layers that consist of 16 convolution layers and 3 fully connected layers [8]. The feature extraction with the VGG19 algorithm has been widely used [13] and this is shown in Fig. 3.

3.3   Support Vector Machine

Support Vector Machine (SVM) is used in regression tasks or classification tasks [17]. To avoid misclassification, SVM uses the concept of maximum margin so the model can be generalized [4,12]. It has the following characteristics: the first is SVM's cut line has the largest margin. The second characteristic is the easiness to make non-linear lines (non-linear decision boundaries) by replacing the kernel function. Finding an optimal classifier for data with two different classes, yet separated by complex multidimensional boundaries [15].

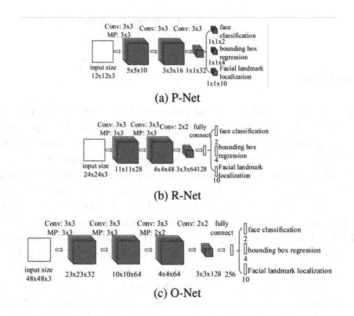

Fig. 2. MTCNN architecture

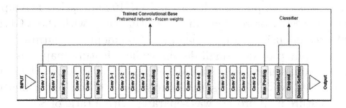

Fig. 3. VGG19 architecture

3.4 Model Evaluation

The model was evaluated with confusion matrices in the simplest form of a table with two rows and two columns, which represents four possibilities of a classification outcome: True Positive (TP), False Positive, True Negative (TN) and False Negative (FN) [11]. The model evaluated the confusion matrices form as well as, measured the model in terms of accuracy, precision, recall, and the F1-score. The equations refer to Eqs. 1, 2, 3, 4 respectively.

$$Accuracy = \frac{TP + TN}{TP + TN + FP + FN} \tag{1}$$

$$Recall = Sensitivity = \frac{TP}{TP + FP} \tag{2}$$

$$Precision = \frac{TP}{TP + FN} \tag{3}$$

$$F1 - score = \frac{2 * Precision * Recall}{Precision + Recall} \qquad (4)$$

4   Experiment

This section covers the efficacy of the proposed model which was tested by carrying out experiments as described in the previous section. All experiments were generated using Google collaboration tools. The experiment used two resources of image datasets. The first dataset was Kaggle's UTKFace which consists of over 20,000 face images, and the other was images from the medpics.uscd.edu website. The unhealthy images are images of faces with skin disorders due to a disease. To ensure the outcome of a good result, the image collection was screened. The chosen images were classified as non-blurred images, with a clear tone, and no redundant image in one frame. The images were labeled as one of the three classes (healthy, unhealthy, non_middle- aged). The labeling images are depicted in Fig. 4. Every class had various sizes of images. The total images consist of 629 images with 223 non_middle-aged images, 179 images of middle age healthy images, and 227 images of adult unhealthy images. Examples of unhealthy facial skin are shown in Fig. 5. Detector MTCNN cropped and resized the images. The purpose of resizing is to adjust the image size so they have the same pixel (224 as the input default for the VGG19 approach). The input image features were detected or retained in the feature map with the VGG19 model pre-trained without using its own classifier. Commonly, a feature map that is closest to the input provided small details while a feature map most similar to the model output captures more general features. Figure 6 shows the feature map that was processed by VGG19. Using this approach, the amount of images resulting from the feature map process was separated with a ratio of 80% accounts for the training set and the remaining accounts for the testing set. The SVM model

Fig. 4. Labelling images

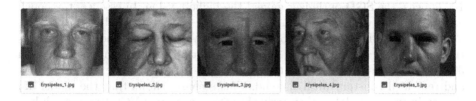

Fig. 5. Unhealthy

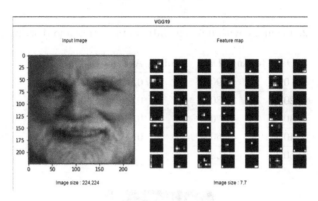

Fig. 6. Feature map

was given sets of data training and data testing, so the classifier can distinguish the images. Receiver Operating Characteristic (ROC) is the probability curve and Area Under Curve (AUC) represents the degree or measure of separateness. The higher the AUC value, the better the model prediction. To assess whether a machine learning algorithm can distinguish between the classes, in the confusion matrices, the precision value is obtained from the right guess. True Positive (TP) means an actual object of interest was identified correctly. The high precision value is affected when there is no false positive (FP). Meanwhile, a high recall value is affected when there is no false negative (FN). F1-score is the accuracy value of each existing class. The combinations of value data training and data testing with interval 10 were explored to gain more insight. Table 2 shows the higher value of the training data or the smaller value of the testing data in getting accurate results and the AUC came close to number 1. Due to a 92.2% accuracy result, the dataset used can be studied by the model. Several SVM kernel parameters such as Linear, RBF, Poly, and Sigmoid were evaluated in different ratio data testing and data training, shown in Table 3. The best accuracy was achieved by linear kernel. Table 4 shows the comparison optimizer in different epoch. The comparison optimizers that were namely used, the: Adam, Adamax, Adadelta, SGD optimizers began with 15 epochs until 1000 epochs. The result of the validation accuracy value generated by each optimizer was similar or did not change significantly. The Adadelta optimizer had the smallest accuracy during an experiment with several epochs. Running the VGG19 model in 50 epochs and

100 epochs, the SGD optimizer gained the highest value. In essence, the epoch value correlates with the accuracy value; more epochs means better accuracy. Without an SVM classifier, the performance of VGG19 experienced an underfitting circumstance. The graph in Fig. 12 demonstrates the Adam optimizer with 30 epochs. During the VGG19 training process, the loss value decreased to 1 and remained constant until the end. This scenario shows that the model did not study the given dataset properly thus the accuracy of VGG19 approach had a lower value (Figs. 7, 8, 9, 10 and 11).

Table 2. Accuracy with different ratio data testing and data training

Data testing	Data training	Accuracy	Train AUC
10%	90%	0.965	0.999
20%	80%	0.922	0.997
30%	70%	0.907	0.991
40%	60%	0.908	0.990
50%	50%	0.895	0.930

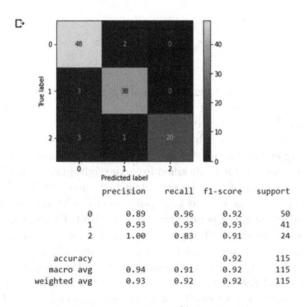

Fig. 7. Accuracy with 20% data testing

Table 3. Evaluation of Different SVM Kernel

Data testing	Data training	Linear	RBF	Poly	Sigmoid
10%	90%	0.928	0.920	0.856	0.900
20%	80%	0.930	0.921	0.835	0.916
30%	70%	0.920	0.912	0.815	0.902
40%	60%	0.912	0.898	0.810	0.898
50%	50%	0.916	0.891	0.786	0.881

Table 4. Comparison between optimizer in different Epoch

Epoch	Adam	Adamax	Adadelta	SGD
15	0.461	0.417	0.426	0.400
30	0.435	0.417	0.409	0.357
50	0.409	0.400	0.365	0.417
100	0.400	0.426	0.391	0.439

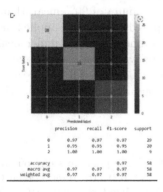

Fig. 8. Accuracy with 10% data testing

Fig. 9. Accuracy with 30% data testing

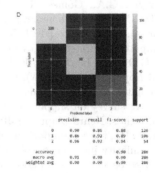

Fig. 10. Accuracy with 40% data testing

Fig. 11. Accuracy with 50% data testing

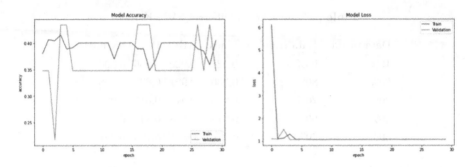

Fig. 12. Epoch30

5 Conclusion

Technological advancements have introduced new paradigms to the field of medicine. Based on the results and discussion, the proposed model's accuracy reached 92.2% with the ratio of data training and data testing as 80% and 20% respectively. The high accuracy results with a minimum of 90% mean that the dataset which is used can be studied by the proposed model. The applied model may possibly detect a middle-aged person's face and classify it under healthy or unhealthy facial skin because there is a process where the model used is not classified as an underfitting model. Further research efforts will be necessary to compare and integrate with another model for conducting in edge computing.

References

1. Ahmed, T., Das, P., Ali, M.F., Mahmud, M.-F.: A comparative study on convolutional neural network based face recognition. In: 2020 11th International Conference on Computing, Communication and Networking Technologies (ICCCNT), pp. 1–5 (2020)
2. Bezerra, G.A., Gomes, R.B.: Recognition of occluded and lateral faces using MTCNN, Dlib and homographies (2018)
3. Carvalho, T., De Rezende, E.R., Alves, M.T., Balieiro, F.K., Sovat, R.B.: Exposing computer generated images by eye's region classification via transfer learning of VGG19 CNN. In: 2017 16th IEEE International Conference on Machine Learning and Applications (ICMLA), pp. 866–870 (2017)
4. Cervantes, J., Garcia-Lamont, F., Rodríguez-Mazahua, L., Lopez, A.: A comprehensive survey on support vector machine classification: applications, challenges and trends. Neurocomputing **408**, 189–215 (2020)
5. Du, J.: High-precision portrait classification based on MTCNN and its application on similarity judgement, vol. 1518. Institute of Physics Publishing (2020)
6. Dyussenbayev, A.: Age periods of human life. Adv. Soc. Sci. Res. J. **4**, 3 (2017)
7. Goel, R., Mehmood, I., Ugail, H.: A study of deep learning-based face recognition models for sibling identification. Sensors **21**, 8 (2021)
8. Horry, M.J., et al.: COVID-19 detection through transfer learning using multimodal imaging data. IEEE Access **8**, 149808–149824 (2020)

9. Huang, S., Cai, N., Pacheco, P.P., Narrandes, S., Wang, Y., Xu, W.: Applications of support vector machine (SVM) learning in cancer genomics. Cancer Genomics Proteomics **15**(1), 41–51 (2018)
10. Jaworek-Korjakowska, J., Kleczek, P., Gorgon, M.: Melanoma thickness prediction based on convolutional neural network with VGG-19 model transfer learning, pp. 2748–2756. IEEE Computer Society (2019)
11. Krstinić, D., Braović, M., Šerić, L., Božić-Štulić, D.: Multi-label classifier performance evaluation with confusion matrix, pp. 1–14. Academy and Industry Research Collaboration Center (AIRCC) (2020)
12. Senekane, M.: Differentially private image classification using support vector machine and differential privacy. Mach. Learn. Knowl. Extr. **1**, 483–491 (2019)
13. Taeb, M., Chi, H.: Comparison of deepfake detection techniques through deep learning. J. Cybersecur. Privacy **2**, 89–106 (2022)
14. Tripathi, M.: Analysis of convolutional neural network based image classification techniques. J. Innovative Image Process. **3**, 100–117 (2021)
15. Vos, K., Peng, Z., Jenkins, C., Shahriar, M.R., Borghesani, P., Wang, W.: Vibration-based anomaly detection using LSTM/SVM approaches. Mech. Syst. Signal Process. **169**, 108752 (2022)
16. Xie, Y.G., Wang, H., Guo, S.H.: Research on MTCNN face recognition system in low computing power scenarios. J. Internet Technol. **21**, 1463–1475 (2020)
17. Yang, C., Oh, S.K., Yang, B., Pedrycz, W., Fu, Z.W.: Fuzzy quasi-linear SVM classifier: design and analysis. Fuzzy Sets Syst. **413**, 42–63 (2021)
18. Zhang, H., Zhang, L., Jiang, Y.: Overfitting and underfitting analysis for deep learning based end-to-end communication systems (2019)

Computer Vision and Image Processing

Real-Time Intentional Eye Blink Detection Using Rhombus Identification

Alan Shu-Luen Chang[(⊠)]

National Taiwan University, Taipei 10617, Taiwan
almondchang0629@gmail.com

Abstract. Eye blinking is an indicator for various applications such as face recognition, drowsiness detection, phone unlocking, etc. Existing work on blink recognition typically considers the normal expressions that the two eyes are unintentionally opened and closed simultaneously. There is no literature on detecting intentional eye blink with simultaneous one eye open and one eye closed. Such intentional eye blinks can serve as a customized signal for various applications, such as activating an intelligent security system by a member in danger. Further, the existing work uses the outline of an eye (called the *Eye Aspect Ratio (EAR)* method) to judge whether to blink or not. However, the sizes of people's eyes could be different, and this method is thus prone to misjudgment. To remedy these loopholes, we propose the following two methods: (1) An intentional eye blinking mechanism with simultaneous one eye open and one eye closed as a signal to activate an intelligent security system; (2) A novel, fast, and accurate *Rhombus Identification Method (RIM)*, considering the eye contour and *normalized area*, which can accurately identify expressions with eyes open and closed simultaneously, as a signal to activate security alarms. Compared with the EAR method, our RIM has significantly higher accuracy rates under different situations. Based on machine learning, we incorporate our RIM into an intelligent security system and justify the practicability of our RIM.

Keywords: Face recognition · Eye blink detection · Machine learning · Intelligent security system

1 Introduction

Eye blinking is typically an unintentional/involuntary rapid closing and opening of an eye. Blinking is a popular indicator for various applications such as face recognition, drowsiness detection, anti-cheating recognition, phone unlocking, etc. Current blink detection is often performed by computer vision and machine learning to determine whether an eye is opened and closed in a short time.

In particular, existing literature on blink recognition typically consider the normal expressions that the two eyes are unintentionally opened and closed at the

This Projet is Partially Sponsored by the MediaTek Foundation.

S.-Y. Hsieh et al. (Eds.): ICS 2022, CCIS 1723, pp. 293–304, 2022.
https://doi.org/10.1007/978-981-19-9582-8_26

same time. To our best knowledge, there is no literature on detecting intentional eye blink with simultaneous one eye open and one eye closed.

For many applications, such as an intelligent security system with face/eye recognition, an intruder may hold a family member or even deceive the security system with a family member's photo to break into the home. With normal face and eye blinking detection, the security system may make false alarms and thus reduce the practicability of the system. Therefore, a better scenario would be when a family member makes a special code (e.g., intentional eye blink) that only family members know, the system can judge that the family member is in danger and activate the hostage information to the security system.

Moreover, the existing literature uses the outline of an eye (called the *Eye Aspect Ratio (EAR)* method) [10] to judge whether to blink or not. However, the sizes of people's eyes could be different, and this method is thus prone to misjudgment.

To remedy these loopholes, we propose the following two methods: (1) An intentional eye blinking mechanism with simultaneous one eye open and one eye closed as a signal to activate an intelligent security system with automatic alarms to prevent hostages and camouflage photos; (2) A novel, fast, and accurate *Rhombus Identification Method (RIM)*, considering the eye contour and *normalized area*, which can accurately identify expressions with eyes open and closed simultaneously as a signal to activate security alarms.

Compared with the EAR method, our RIM has significantly higher accuracy rates under different situations. For the situation where the left and right eyes are not closed, the average accuracy of our RIM is 98.0%, while the EAR method has an average accuracy of only 88.8%. For the situation where the left eye is closed and the right is opened, the average accuracy of our RIM is 91.7%, while the EAR method is only 11.7% because it is intended for only the blink detection of both eyes.

Based on machine learning, we incorporate our RIM into an intelligent security system and justify the practicability of our RIM. With our RIM, the probability of correctly activating the system is extremely high and that of wrongly activating the system is extremely low.

The remainder of this paper is organized as follows. Section 2 introduces some background image detection techniques. Section 3 presents our proposed algorithm. Section 4 reports and analyzes the experimental results. Finally, Sect. 5 concludes this paper.

2   Preliminaries

Existing eye blink detection is mainly based on machine learning. We shall first survey some machine learning basics.

2.1   Machine Learning Basics

Neural networks are used to imitate the operation mechanism of a biological neural network (human brain), use neurons to connect and transmit information, and apply mathematical models to estimate functions. Our adopted convolutional neural network consists of multiple perception layers: input layer, convolution layer, pooling layer, flatten layer, hidden layer, and output layer. Each layer consists of neurons to receive signals.

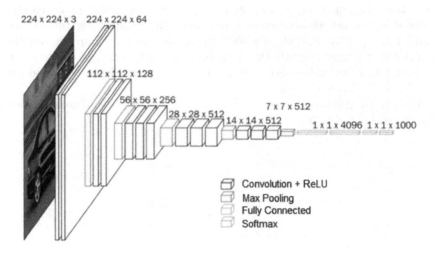

Fig. 1. The VGG16 convolutional neural network model [1,9].

The convolutional layer is to extract the features (say, in an image). For VGG16, a filter matrix of the kernel size is first used to scan each pixel of the image and perform calculations to extract features, and these features will become the input of the next layer [2].

Pooling is similar to convolution and also preserves the features of an image. In this work, we adopt Maximum Pooling [8], which will take the largest value in a 2×2 pixel matrix of an image and save it to a new one. This pooling reduces the number of training parameters and avoids the possibility of over-learning.

The flattened layer is usually used after the convolutional layer to convert the matrix into a one-dimensional array, which is a necessary step before the model enters the hidden layer.

From one layer to the next, neuron conversion might be required. The conversion formula for each neuron is given by $y = xw + b$, where w is the weight, and b is the bias. The values of w and b are random numbers in each epoch, and the optimal parameters are stored during training. Machine learning also needs to add a nonlinear activation function to make the input and output nonlinear such as the nonsigmoidal rectified linear unit *ReLU activation function* [7].

2.2 Detection Models

We employ the Python programming language to train and validate the VGG16 convolutional neural network model [1,9] built in Keras (visualized in Fig. 1), execute and store the best parameters, and use the built-in camera of the computer for testing.

In the VGG16 model, the first large layer in the figure has two layers of `convolution+ReLU` (convolutional layer plus the ReLU activation function), the second largest layer has one layer of `max pooling` (pooling layer), plus two layers of `convolution+ReLU`, and so on. `Fully Connected` (fully connected layer) is placed at the end, whose purpose is to convert the results of the previous convolution and pooling into classification results so that the computer can make predictions. `softmax` converts the value input by Fully Connected into a number from 0 to 1 (the value output by the Fully Connected layer can be positive, negative, or 0) for prediction.

The eye blink detection uses the built-in 68-point facial landmarks model of Dlib [3], shown in Fig. 2 [6].

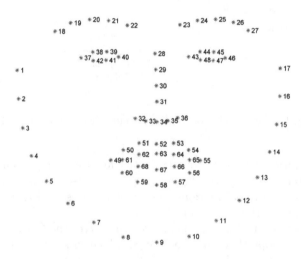

Fig. 2. The 68 facial landmark coordinates [6].

3   Detection Algorithm

Our intentional eye blinking detection algorithm consists of three major stages: face detection, facial landmark detection, and rhombus eye blink detection, as shown in Fig. 3. We use computer vision and machine learning libraries to capture faces from an image and determine the eyes of each face in the images in real-time. We employ the haar-cascade classifier algorithm [4] to detect faces, and the facial landmark detection algorithm in the Dlib library [3] to extract the coordinates of the 68 points (and the eyes) from a detected face.

After that, we perform intentional eye blink detection based on our proposed *Rhombus Identification Method*, which is more accurate, efficient, and robust

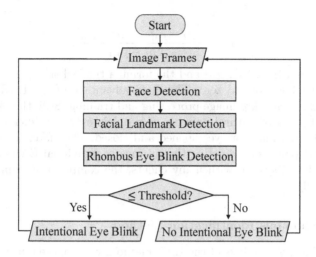

Fig. 3. The intentional eye blink detection flow.

than the existing Eye Aspect Ratio (EAR) method [10]. We shall first review the EAR method which captures the eye contour to determine whether an eye is opened or closed.

3.1   The EAR Eye Contour Detection

The EAR method uses facial landmarks to detect human eyes first, and the six points $p_1, p_2, \ldots$, and p_6 on the outline of the eyes are identified, as shown in Fig. 4(a).

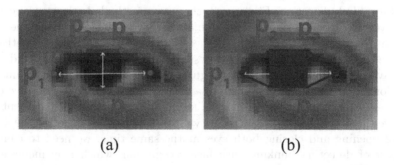

(a)   (b)

Fig. 4. The six points of an eye contour. (a) The six points in the EAR method [10]. (b) The proposed RIM method uses two triangles and a rectangle to approximate the area of the open eye part.

Using the six points, the work [10] defines the EAR as follows:

$$EAR = \frac{||p_2 - p_6|| + ||p_3 - p_5||}{2||p_1 - p_4||}. \tag{1}$$

It can be seen from Fig. 4(a) and the formula that when a person's eyes are closed, the EAR is close to zero. The main advantage of the EAR method is that the machine can skip image processing and training. Still, the disadvantage is that the degrees of natural opening of people's eyes are different, resulting in different EAR values for eyes opened and closed. Therefore, the accuracy of this method depends on adjusting the settings of individual EARs and is thus not general. For a system with many clients, the computation complexity will increase rapidly.

3.2   Our Rhombus Identification Method

To remedy the shortcomings of the EAR method, we propose a new area detection method. Area detection is similar to contour detection, but the judgment method is completely different. Area detection is to calculate the area enclosed by the outline of the eyes and uses the *Eye Open Ratio (EOR)* to make judgments. The EOR is defined as follows:

$$EOR = Detected\ Eye\ Area/Normal\ Eye\ Opening\ Area \tag{2}$$

In this method, the area of the detected eye-opening is divided by that of the normal eye-opening to determine whether there is blinking. Different from the contour method, the advantage of this method is that there is no need to adjust parameters according to individual eye characteristics. Thus the generality of applications is obviously better. But the disadvantage is that the calculation of the overall judgment will be more complicated and time-consuming.

We observe that the EAR and EOR methods alone are not suitable for intentional eye blink detection. First of all, these two methods both open and close both eyes at the same time to determine whether to blink. Suppose the blink of both eyes opened or closed simultaneously is used to determine whether to activate the security system under duress. In that case, the system could often be activated by mistake because of regular facial expressions. As a result, the intentional non-normal action of simultaneous one eye closed and one eye open must be used as the security activation mechanism to reduce misjudgment and improve the practicability of the security system. Moreover, if we use the detection of opening and closing both eyes at the same time, we need to combine the part of detecting blinking with face recognition, which may increase the detection time.

Because of this, we propose a hybrid detection method of eye contour and area, which is fast and sufficient for accurate intentional eye blink detection. Based on the six feature points, two triangles and one rectangle are used to approximate the area of the open eye part; see Fig. 4(b).

However, the calculation of this method is complicated, and we can simplify the method as follows: Assuming a rhombus, take the average of the two straight line segments $\| p2 - p6 \|$ and $\| p3 - p5 \|$ as a diagonal of the corresponding rhombus, as follows:

$$\frac{\| p_2 - p_6 \| + \| p_3 - p_5 \|}{2}. \tag{3}$$

The area of a rhombus is the multiplication of the lengths of the two diagonals divided by 2, so the area of the rhombus can be approximated by the following formula:

$$\frac{(\| p_2 - p_6 \| + \| p_3 - p_5 \|) \times \| p_1 - p_4 \|}{4}. \tag{4}$$

However, using this formula has the same problem as using the EAR: people's eye areas could be different. Because the proposed custom code is to close one eye and open one eye at the same time, in fact, the area of the left eye and the right eye can be normalized, i.e., the area of the left eye is divided by that of the right eye. The above rhombus is calculated and combined with the normalization of the area of the left eye and the right eye to obtain the following *Rhombus Identification Method (RIM)* formula:

$$RIM = \frac{(\| p_{l2} - p_{l6} \| + \| p_{l3} - p_{l5} \|) \times \| p_{l1} - p_{l4} \|}{(\| p_{r2} - p_{r6} \| + \| p_{r3} - p_{r5} \|) \times \| p_{r1} - p_{r4} \|}, \tag{5}$$

where p_{li} is the p_i of the left eye, and p_{ri} is the p_i of the right eye, $i = 1, 2, \ldots, 6$.

The normalization criteria for left and right eye areas are calculated as follows: The area where the left eye is detected is divided by that where the right eye is detected. For the security system application, for example, we can evaluate when a family member tries her best to close her left eye while opening her right eye at the same time, and the ratio of the closed left eye area and opened right eye area is selected as the *threshold* Θ. If a detected ratio is smaller than or equal to Θ, intentional eye blinking is detected (and the alarm should be activated); otherwise, no intentional eye blinking occurs. See Fig. 5.

4   Experimental Results

The experimental platform used a Macbook Air with a 1.6 GHz CPU, 8 GB RAM and 256 GB storage space. We conducted experiments to compare the EAR method and our RIM for eye blink recognition. In our experiment, the RIM threshold Θ was set as 0.83.

We began with a simple comparative study to see the effects of the two eye blink detection methods. As shown in Fig. 6, the family member squinted her eyes slightly instead of closing her left eye. The RIM gives the value of 0.86 (the ratio of the left and right eye areas), which is greater than 0.83, so it is judged that there is no simultaneous left eye closed and right eye opened, which is a correct detection result. As shown in Fig. 7, the value calculated by the EAR method is 0.07. According to the EAR model, if the value is less than 0.18, it is

Fig. 5. Evaluating a family member's RIM threshold Θ by trying her best to close her left eye while opening her right eye simultaneously.

judged that the eyes are closed; otherwise, the eyes are judged to be opened. As a result, the EAR method incurs an incorrect detection for this case. Because the EAR method is to detect double eye blinks, it is difficult to judge the squinting condition of the left eye, while our proposed RIM can correctly identify this case.

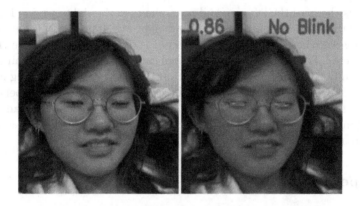

Fig. 6. The family member squinted her eyes slightly instead of closing her left eye. The RIM gives the value of 0.86, which is greater than 0.83, so it is judged that there is no simultaneous left eye closed and right eye opened, a correct detection result.

To conduct more detailed comparisons, we expanded the amount of data to 400 photos for each of the three family members, including photos of non-left-closed and right-opened photos, of which 300 photos were non-left-closed and right-opened photos, and 100 were left-closed and right-open photos. The non-left-closed and right-open photos here include 100 photos for each of three situations: left-open and right-open, left-closed and right-closed, and left-open

Fig. 7. The family member squinted her eyes slightly instead of closing her left eye. The EAR method gives the value of 0.07. According to the EAR model, if the value is less than 0.18, it is judged that the eyes are closed, incurring a wrong detection.

and right-closed. The accuracy comparisons between the EAR method and our RIM are reported in Table 1.

As shown in Table 1, the detection accuracy of our RIM is much higher than that of the EAR method. Under the condition that the security system is not activated when the left and right eyes are not closed, the average accuracies of the RIM are 99.0%, 97.3%, and 97.7% (the total average is 98.0%) for the three family members, while the EAR method has an average accuracy of only 93.7%, 85.0% and 87.7%, respectively (the total average is 88.8%). The average accuracy of the RIM is significantly higher than that of EAR. The difference is more significant when the left eye is closed and the right is opened (where the security system is activated). For this situation, the average accuracies of the RIM for the three family members are 90.0%, 95.0%, and 90.0% (the total average is 91.7%), while the EAR method are only 10.0%, 10.0%, and 15.0% (the overall average is only 11.7%).

The EAR method is intended for only the blink detection of both eyes. This method calculates the EAR value of the two eyes and then averages them to obtain the final EAR value. However, the sizes of people's eyes and the degrees of eye opening are different, so the EAR detection in this situation is not accurate.

The above comparison is based on the average accuracy of a single photo. At first glance, the average accuracy of each photo of the RIM is significantly higher than that of the EAR method, under the condition that the left eye is closed and the right is opened (the security system is activated), but the accuracy of the RIM is only 90.0% for Family Members 1 and 3, which seems to be far from practical accuracy. However, the operation of the security system is to capture a specific number of photos according to the system operation speed within a given real-time for comprehensive judgment; for example, the duration of a specific action of closing the left eye and opening the right for 0.5 s. The following two scenarios elaborate on the accuracy and practicability

Table 1. Accuracy comparison between the EAR method and our RIM (FPS = 20).

Condition	Non-left-eye-closed and Right-eye-open (Non-Activation)		
Data Amount	300 photos		
Family Member	1	2	3
EAR Correct Detection	282 photos	255 photos	263 photos
EAR Average Accuracy	93.7%	85.0%	87.7%
RIM Correct Detection	297 photos	292 photos	293 photos
RIM Average Accuracy	99.0%	97.3%	97.7%
RIM Accuracy ($r = 3$)	99.999999%	99.999832%	99.999987%
Condition	Left-eye-closed and Right-eye-open (Activation)		
Data Amount	100 photos		
Family Member	1	2	3
EAR Correct Detection	10 photos	10 photos	15 photos
EAR Average Accuracy	10.0%	10.0%	15.0%
RIM Correct Detection	90 photos	95 photos	90 photos
RIM Average Accuracy	90.0%	95.0%	90.0%
RIM Accuracy (0.5 sec)	99.99999999% $(1 - 0.1^{10})$	99.999999999999% $(1 - 0.05^{10})$	99.99999999% $(1 - 0.1^{10})$

of the security system constructed based on the RIM: (1) the accuracy of the security system is correctly activated when the left eye is closed and right eye opened, and (2) the probability of the security system is wrongly activated when it is not left eye closed and right eye open, that is, the false alarm rate:

- **Scenario 1:** The security system was implemented with OpenCV and executed on Macbook Air with the aforementioned hardware specifications, and the number of frames per second (FPS) is about 20. The family member activates the security system with intentional eye blinking that closes the left eye and opens the right eye. Assuming this eye blink lasts for 0.5 s, it is set to activate the security system when an intentional eye blink that closes the left eye and opens the right eye is detected. Under this setting, the system takes a total of 10 photos when the blink lasts for 0.5 s, and the average accuracy of each photo of the RIM is over 90%. As a result, the system constructed by the RIM has an accuracy of $1 - 0.1^{10} = 99.99999999\%$ (i.e., ten 9's). To prevent the system from activating the security system due to false detection of the left-eye-closed and right-eye-open expressions, the system can be set to detect the customization of left-eye-closed and right-eye-open as long as any q out of ten photos (for example, $q = 2$) are detected to activate the system to achieve a balance between the accuracy of correctly activating the security system with left eye closed and right eye open and the false activation of the security system due to false detection of the left eye closed and right eye open. In fact, because the left-eye-closed and right-eye-open expressions are extremely special, the chance that a family member will not be able to activate the security system with this expression is very small.

– **Scenario 2:** To reduce the probability of false activation of the security system (false alarm probability), within $0.5\,\mathrm{s}$, if there are r ($r < 0.5 \times FPS$) detections that are judged to be a normal state other than left eye closed and right eye open, the system will not be activated to prevent false alarms. If $r = 1, 2, 3$, and 4, for Family Member 2 with the highest probability of false alarm, the true probability of error of this system is only $2.7\%(1 - 97.3\%), 0.0729\%((1 - 97.3\%)^2 = 0.000729)$, $0.001677\%((1 - 97.3\%)^3 = 0.00001677)$ and $0.000045\%((1 - 97.3\%)^4 = 0.00000045)$, respectively. In other words, when $r = 3$ and 4, this system is 99.9998323% and 99.9999955% accurate not to be falsely activated, respectively. Therefore, the probability that the security system will be activated by mistake is very small.

Based on the above discussions, the accuracy of activating this security system with the intentional eye blink of left eye closed and right eye open is extremely high, and the probability of incorrectly activating this system is extremely low, so the system is practical and feasible.

5   Conclusions

This paper has presented the first work on detecting intentional eye blink with simultaneous one eye open and one eye closed, which can serve as a customized signal for various applications such as activating an intelligent security system by a member in danger. We have also presented a novel, fast, and accurate RIM, considering the eye contour and normalized area, which can accurately identify expressions with eyes open and closed simultaneously, as a signal to activate security alarms. Compared with the EAR method, our RIM has significantly higher accuracy rates under different situations. For the situation where the left and right eyes are not closed, the average accuracy of our RIM is 98.0%, while the EAR method has an average accuracy of only 88.8%. For the situation where the left eye is closed and the right is opened, the average accuracy of our RIM is 91.7%, while the EAR method is only 11.7% because it is intended for only the blink detection of both eyes. Based on machine learning, we have incorporated our RIM into an intelligent security system and justified the practicability of our RIM. With our RIM, the probability of correctly activating the system is extremely high, and that of wrongly activating the system is extremely low.

Acknowledgements. The author would like to thank Professor Hung-Yun Hsieh of Department of Electrical Engineering, National Taiwan University for his valuable suggestions.

References

1. Aung, H., Bobkov, A.V., Tun, N.L.: Face detection in real time live video using yolo algorithm based on Vgg16 convolutional neural network. In: Proceedings of International Conference on Industrial Engineering, Applications and Manufacturing (ICIEAM), Sochi, Russia, May 2021
2. Baskin, C.: Image Convolution with an input Image of Size 7 × 7 and a Filter Kernel of Size 3 × 3, October 2020
3. Boyko, N., Basystiuk, O., Shakhovska, N.: Performance evaluation and comparison of software for face recognition, based on Dlib and Opencv library. In: Proceedings of the IEEE 2nd International Conference on Data Stream Mining & Processing (DSMP), Lviv, Ukraine (2018)
4. Dalal, N., Triggs, B.: Histograms of oriented gradients for human detection. In: Proceedings of the IEEE Conference on Computer Vision and Pattern Recognition (CVPR), vol. 1, pp. 886–893 (2005)
5. Neurohive: VGG16-Convolutional Network for Classification and Detection, November 2018. https://neurohive.io/en/popular-networks/vgg16/
6. Rosebrock, A.: Facial Landmarks with dlib, OpenCV, and Python, 3 July 2021
7. Schmidt-Hieber, J.: Nonparametric regression using deep neural networks with ReLU activation function. Ann. Stat. **48**(4), 1875–1897 (2020)
8. Javed Mehedi Shamrat, F.M.: A deep learning approach for face detection using max pooling. In: Proceedings of the International Conference on Trends in Electronics and Informatics (2021)
9. Simonyan, K., Zisserman, A: Very Deep Convolutional Networks for Large-scale Image Recognition arXiv:1409.1556 (2014)
10. Soukupova, T., Cech, J.: Real-time eye blink detection using facial landmarks. In: Proceedings of the 21st Computer Vision Winter Workshop, Rimske Toplice, Slovenia, February 2016

Difficulty-Aware Mixup for Replay-based Continual Learning

Yu-Kai Ling, Ren Chieh Yang, and Sheng-De Wang[⊠]

Department of Electrical Engineering, National Taiwan University,
New Taipei, Taiwan
{r09921054,r10921098,sdwang}@ntu.edu.tw

Abstract. Deep neural networks suffer from the issue of catastrophic forgetting in the scenario of continual learning, causing a sudden deterioration in performance when training on new tasks. Replay-based methods, which are one of the most effective solutions, alleviate catastrophic forgetting by replaying the subset of past data stored in memory buffer. However, due to the limited storage space, a small amount of past data can be stored, and will lead to a data imbalance situation between old and new tasks. Hence, in this work, we tried to increase the diversity of past samples by mixup. In addition, we propose a difficulty-aware mixup approach that modifies the mixing coefficient according to the distance between output logits and ground truth labels to reduce the ambiguity of hard examples. We implement our method on ER, DER, and DER++, and test it on split-CIFAR10, split-CIFAR100, and split-miniImagenet. The experimental result shows that the proposed method can effectively improve the average accuracy and reduce the forgetting without adding too many computing resources.

Keywords: Continual learning · Deep learning · Data augmentation

1 Introduction

Deep neural networks have achieved the state of the art performance in many different tasks, especially classification problems. Those models are designed to solve an individual task or learn offline with a fixed-size dataset. As more and more tasks occur in the real world, we can't store all the models eventually. Moreover, there is a computation issue if we use all the data of different tasks to train a model. Therefore, the application should learn continually without forgetting when a new task or new data emerges. However, the performance of previous tasks dramatically deteriorates after trained on a new task, referred to as catastrophic forgetting [8].

To address this issue, continual learning aims to train a model from the stream of non i.i.d samples and avoid catastrophic forgetting at the same time. In recent years, many continual learning methods have been proposed. Among these methods, the replay-based method is one of the most effective solutions. By storing part of old data and replaying it when receiving a batch of new data, the model can preserve past knowledge well. The main problem of the replay-based method is data

S.-Y. Hsieh et al. (Eds.): ICS 2022, CCIS 1723, pp. 305–316, 2022.
https://doi.org/10.1007/978-981-19-9582-8_27

imbalance between new tasks and old tasks. Bias Correction [15] was proposed to deal with this issue. They add an additional layer to correct the task bias. Another work like Separated Softmax [1] computes softmax probability of each task separately to prevent the old class output from being overly penalized.

Nevertheless, data augmentation of replay samples can be an important part of this problem. There are few papers focused on which kind of data augmentation can reduce the impact of data imbalance. In our work, we try to use mixup [18] to increase the diversity of replay samples. The result shows that the original mixup can lead to better performance with a large replay buffer size but poor performance with a small buffer size. And we believe this is because the merging coefficient randomly sampled from beta distribution makes the hard examples ambiguous and difficult to train. Hence, we modify the merging coefficient according to cross entropy loss between stored target and output logits, which we call difficulty-aware mixup, and obtain a remarkable improvement in the average accuracy and the forgetting measure. Figure 1 is a comparison between the baseline method and our method.

In summary, our contributions are as followed:

- We introduced mixup replay samples into three different types of replay methods, which increased the diversity of replay samples and got better performance with a large replay buffer.
- We proposed the novel difficulty-aware mixup approach modifying the merging coefficient between two images according to the degree of difficulty, which made the model more effectively alleviate catastrophic forgetting than the original mixup and improved the performance.

2   Related Works

2.1   Continual Learning

Recently, a lot of papers have been proposed to mitigate forgetting in continual learning. We can classify those methods into two categories: regularization-based and rehearsal-based.

The idea of regularization-based methods is to add a regularization term to penalize the updates of all parameters so that the past information can be kept after learning the new task. The algorithm will estimate how important the parameters are for the past tasks. The more important parameter changes less, the less one changes more. The loss function can be formulated as Eq. 1. θ_i is the current parameter i, θ_i^b is the past parameter i, and b_i is the importance of the parameter i. The larger the value, the more important this parameter is for the previous task. And $(\theta_i - \theta_i^b)^2$ needs to be smaller to reduce the loss function, that is, this parameter cannot be changed too much, and vice versa. Related researches include EWC [6], SI [17], etc.

$$L'(\theta) = L(\theta) + \lambda \sum_i b_i \left(\theta_i - \theta_i^b\right)^2 \tag{1}$$

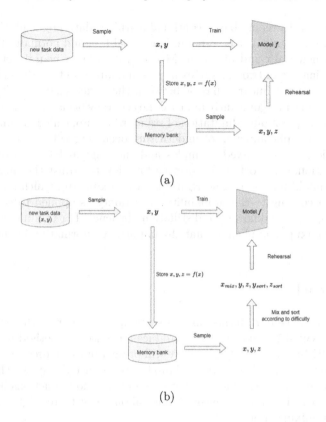

Fig. 1. Comparison between baseline method (a) and our method (b)

The rehearsal-based method can be illustrated in Fig. 1a. These methods store a subset of past data in a limited size of the memory buffer and replay it to prevent catastrophic forgetting. ER (Experience Replay) [9,12] combines old samples with current samples into a training batch. MER (Meta experience replay) [11] view the rehearsal-base method as a meta-learning problem maximizing knowledge transfer between tasks and minimizing the interference caused by current tasks. iCaRL [10] uses a nearest-mean-of-exemplars classifier to against changes in data representation. DGR (Deep generative replay) [13] trains a generative adversarial network to reconstruct past data. DER [2] shows that replaying the network's logits instead of ground truth labels performs the better result. DER++ [2], which use both logits and labels for rehearsal, mitigates the shortcoming that weakens DER caused by the logits that are highly biased when a sudden distribution shift occurs.

2.2   Data Augmentation

Data augmentation is a common technique in machine learning which is used to increase the size and diversity of training samples so that the trained model can be more general. In replay-based continual learning, data augmentation mainly includes full-size random crop, random horizontal flip, and normalization applying to both new data and old data. Mixup [18] trains a neural network on a convex combination of two pairs of examples and labels so that the model is regularized to learn the linear behavior between the mixed examples. This simple training method can significantly improve the accuracy of classification problems. H. Guo et al. [3] point out a limitation of standard mixup, called "manifold intrusion", which is a phenomenon of underfitting occurring with conflicts between the synthetic labels of mixed examples and the original labels. AdaMixup [3] uses an additional network and objective function to adjust the mixing policy to avoid manifold intrusion. Uncertainty-aware mixup [16], which adopts adaptive mixup according to the probability uncertainty, is applied to compact the knowledge to improve knowledge distillation efficiency. For the uncertain examples, a mild mixup is applied so that the important information in them can be reserved.

3   Approach

Before we introduce our method in this section, we'll describe the problem formulation in Sect. 3.1. Next, we will introduce our baseline method includes ER, DER, and DER++ in Sect. 3.2. Last, we will present our proposed method which contains two parts. The first part is Mixup for experience replay, which describes how to apply mixup to the baseline method and their loss functions in Sect. 3.3. The second part is difficulty-aware Mixup about how to reweight the mixing coefficient in mixup in Sect. 3.4.

3.1   Problem Formulation

We consider class-incremental continual learning classification problem that we have to train a classifier model f with parameters θ over continual data of each task in sequence. We can formulate the data of each task $\tau \in \{1, ..., T\}$ as $\mathcal{D}_\tau = \{x_\tau^i, y_\tau^i\}_{i=0}^{n^\tau}$, where x_τ^i is the input data, y_τ^i is corresponding ground truth label, and n^τ is the number of data for the task. In addition, the data of the same class will appear in the same task. The goal of class-incremental learning is to learn the new categories while maintaining the performance of the old categories. The objective function can be formulated as:

$$\underset{\theta}{\operatorname{argmin}} \sum_{\tau=0}^{T} \underset{(x,y)\sim\mathcal{D}_\tau}{\mathbb{E}} [\mathcal{L}(f(x;\theta),y)] \tag{2}$$

where $\mathcal{L}(f(x;\theta),y)$ is cross-entropy loss for classification problem. Hence, the Eq. 2 can be rewrited as:

$$\underset{\theta}{\operatorname{argmin}} \sum_{\tau=0}^{T} \underset{(x,y)\sim\mathcal{D}_\tau}{\mathbb{E}} [\text{CE}(\text{softmax}(f(x;\theta)),y)] \tag{3}$$

Our method is based on the replay-based method. We allocate the memory buffer $\mathcal{M}$ with fixed size $|\mathcal{M}|$ to store part of past data for old classes during training. Each sample in the memory buffer contains $\{x, y, z\}$ pairs, in which x is the input data, y is the corresponding label, and z is the model output logits $f(x, \theta)$ at the time of inserting to the memory buffer. When training on a batch of new data, we sample a batch of old data from $\mathcal{M}$ and replay it to reserve the past information. The loss function when training on task τ can be defined as:

$$\mathcal{L}_{\mathrm{CL}} = \underset{(x,y)\sim\mathcal{D}_\tau}{\mathbb{E}} \left[\mathrm{CE}\left(\mathrm{softmax}\left(f\left(x;\theta\right)\right), y\right)\right] + \mathcal{L}_R \tag{4}$$

where $\mathcal{L}_R$ is replaying loss which keeps the model from forgetting the old experiences.

3.2   Baseline Method

To compare the effectiveness of our proposed method implemented on different replay-based methods, we choose ER, DER, and DER++ as our baseline methods and implement our method on them. In this section, we briefly introduce these methods and their loss functions.

ER [9,12] ER is a simple replay-based method that just replays the past data with ground truth labels. It concatenates a batch of old and new data and minimizes cross-entropy loss for both. The replaying loss function of ER can be formulated as:

$$\mathcal{L}_R = \mathcal{L}_{\mathrm{ER}} = \underset{(x,y,z)\sim\mathcal{M}}{\mathbb{E}}\left[\mathrm{CE}\left(\mathrm{softmax}\left(f\left(x;\theta\right)\right), y\right)\right] \tag{5}$$

DER [2] DER uses knowledge distillation [5] to encourage the model to imitate the past output response for continual learning. The objective is to minimize:

$$\mathcal{L}_R = \alpha \cdot \underset{(x,y,z)\sim\mathcal{M}}{\mathbb{E}}\left[KL\left(\mathrm{softmax}\left(z\right), \mathrm{softmax}\left(f(x;\theta)\right)\right)\right] \tag{6}$$

where KL denotes KL divergence loss, and α is a scale factor balancing the terms. Furthermore, the author in [5] assumes that the optimization of KL divergence loss is equivalent to minimizing the Euclidean distance between the output logits. Thus, we can rewrite the Eq. 6 and obtain the replaying loss function of DER:

$$\mathcal{L}_R = \mathcal{L}_{\mathrm{DER}} = \alpha \cdot \underset{(x,y,z)\sim\mathcal{M}}{\mathbb{E}}\left[\|z - f(x;\theta)\|_2^2\right] \tag{7}$$

DER++ [2] When a sudden distribution shift happens, the logits that are highly biased will weaken DER. DER++ is proposed to solve this defect by replaying both logits and ground labels. The replaying loss function of DER++ can be defined as

$$\mathcal{L}_R = \mathcal{L}_{\mathrm{DER++}} = \mathcal{L}_{\mathrm{DER}} + \beta \cdot \underset{(x,y,z)\sim\mathcal{M}}{\mathbb{E}}\left[\mathrm{CE}\left(\mathrm{softmax}\left(f\left(x;\theta\right)\right), y\right)\right] \tag{8}$$

where β is a hyper-parameter balancing the term.

3.3   Mixup for Experience Replay

The standard mixup trains the model on convex combination of a pair of input images and labels:

$$\widetilde{x} = (1 - \lambda) \cdot x_i + \lambda \cdot x_j$$
$$\widetilde{y} = (1 - \lambda) \cdot y_i + \lambda \cdot y_j$$

where (x_i, y_i), (x_j, y_j) are two input-target pair data sampled from training data, and λ is mixing coefficient sampled from Beta distribution. The objective function can be formulated as:

$$
\begin{aligned}
\mathcal{L}(\widetilde{x}, \widetilde{y}) &= \text{CE}\left(\text{softmax}\left(f\left(\widetilde{x}; \theta\right)\right), \widetilde{y}\right) \\
&= (1 - \lambda) \cdot \text{CE}\left(\text{softmax}\left(f\left(\widetilde{x}; \theta\right)\right), y_i\right) \\
&\quad + \lambda \cdot \text{CE}\left(\text{softmax}\left(f\left(\widetilde{x}; \theta\right)\right), y_j\right)
\end{aligned}
\tag{9}
$$

In our work, we apply mixup to a batch of old data. When observing new data, we first sample a batch of old data (x, y, z) from the memory buffer $\mathcal{M}$. Then, we shuffle the data and denote it as $(x_{\text{shuffle}}, y_{\text{shuffle}}, z_{\text{shuffle}})$. The mixed image can be created from:

$$\widetilde{x} = (1 - \lambda) \cdot x_{\text{shuffle}} + \lambda \cdot x \tag{10}$$

The loss function can be formulated same as the Eq. 9. Therefore, we can simply rewrite the Eq. 5, 7, and 13 as:

$$
\begin{aligned}
\mathcal{L}_R = \mathcal{L}_{\text{ER,mixup}} = \mathop{\mathbb{E}}_{(x,y,z)\sim\mathcal{M}} & \left[(1 - \lambda) \cdot \text{CE}\left(\text{softmax}\left(f\left(\widetilde{x}; \theta\right)\right), y_{\text{shuffle}}\right) \right. \\
& \left. + \lambda \cdot \text{CE}\left(\text{softmax}\left(f\left(\widetilde{x}; \theta\right)\right), y\right)\right]
\end{aligned}
\tag{11}
$$

$$
\begin{aligned}
\mathcal{L}_R = \mathcal{L}_{\text{DER,Mixup}} = \alpha \cdot \mathop{\mathbb{E}}_{(x,y,z)\sim\mathcal{M}} & \left[(1 - \lambda) \cdot \left\|z_{\text{shuffle}} - f(\widetilde{x}; \theta)\right\|_2^2 \right. \\
& \left. + \lambda \cdot \left\|z - f(\widetilde{x}; \theta)\right\|_2^2\right]
\end{aligned}
\tag{12}
$$

$$
\begin{aligned}
\mathcal{L}_R = \mathcal{L}_{\text{DER++,Mixup}} = & \mathcal{L}_{\text{DER,Mixup}} \\
& + \beta \cdot \mathop{\mathbb{E}}_{(x,y,z)\sim\mathcal{M}} \left[(1 - \lambda) \cdot \text{CE}\left(\text{softmax}\left(f\left(\widetilde{x}; \theta\right)\right), y_{\text{shuffle}}\right) \right. \\
& \left. + \lambda \cdot \text{CE}\left(\text{softmax}\left(f\left(\widetilde{x}; \theta\right)\right), y\right)\right]
\end{aligned}
\tag{13}
$$

3.4   Difficulty-Aware Mixup

The mixing coefficient in original mixup is randomly sampled from the beta distribution. However, since old tasks are mostly underperforming especially when the size of memory buffer is small, and the random mixup may blur the hard examples, the model is hard to be trained on these ambiguous images. To solve this issue, we proposed to reweight the mixing coefficients according to the degree of difficulty. Before we mix a batch of input data x, we feed them into the model and calculate the difficulty of each data. Because we store the ground truth labels in memory buffer, we can simply use cross-entropy loss to evaluate the difficulty of input samples:

$$D(x, y) = \text{CE} \left(\text{softmax} \left(f \left(x; \theta \right) \right), y \right) \tag{14}$$

Then, we sort the input x in descending order according to their difficulty and denote it as x_{sort}. The alternated mixup can be designed as:

$$\widetilde{x} = (1 - \lambda') \cdot x_{sort} + \lambda' \cdot x \tag{15}$$

where λ' is the mixing coefficients modified by reweighted factor $c \in [0, 0.5]$, the modified mixing coefficients can be formulated as:

$$\lambda' = c \cdot \lambda$$

The value of c is associated with the degree of difficulty defined as the Eq. 14. For the hard samples like past tasks' images, c is set to a small value, and $(1 - \lambda')$ is close to 1, so that the mixed images look like the original image. For the simple samples like currant task's images, c is set to a large value, and $(1 - \lambda')$ is close to 0.5, so that the mixed images look like a mix of two images. Since we sort the input data before and define the mixup function with x_{sort}, c can be a monotonically increasing function of the difficulty ranking. In our work, we select the sigmoid function same as [16]:

$$c = 0.5 \cdot \text{sigmoid} \left(w \cdot \frac{ranking - batchsize/2}{batchsize} \right)$$

where w controls the range of the sigmoid function. In addition, we select top k images from all the mixing images to remove a large number of ambiguous samples caused by the sigmoid function. In our experiments, we set w to 10, batch size to 48, and k to 32, Fig. 2 shows the value of c according to difficulty ranking.

4 Experiments

4.1 Experiment Setup

Dataset. To verify the effectiveness of our method for problems of varying complexity, we use CIFAR10, CIFAR100, and miniImageNet datasets. Moreover, following the setting of class-incremental learning, we split dataset into different tasks to evaluate our method. The detailed information of the three datasets we evaluate is as follow:

- split CIFAR-10 [7]: 10 classes with 32×32 images, and 2 classes per task.
- split CIFAR-100 [7]: 100 classes with 32×32 images, and 10 classes per task.
- split mini-ImageNet [14]: 100 classes with 84×84 images, and 5 classes per task.

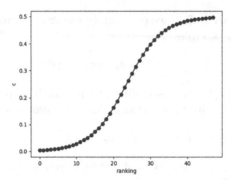

Fig. 2. The value of c according to difficulty ranking in our experiment

Training. We consider ER, DER, and DER++ as our baseline algorithms, and we implement mixup and difficulty-aware mixup on them. We choose ResNet18 [4] as our backbone. All models are trained from scratch. We adopt the SGD optimizer. the learning rate is set to 0.1 and 0.03 for ER and DER/DER++, respectively. We set batch size to 32 for all datasets and train each task for 50 epochs. For CIFAR100 and miniImagenet, the learning rate is divided by 10 at 35th and 45th epoch. For each experiment, we run 5 times and average the results.

4.2   Evaluation Metrics

First, we compute the test accuracy of each previous task until learning the last task T. And we use the average accuracy (ACC), and the forgetting measure (FM) to evaluate our method. The definitions of ACC and FM are as follows:

$$ACC = \frac{1}{T} \sum_{i=0}^{T} a_{T,i}$$

$$FM = \frac{1}{T} \sum_{i=0}^{T} max_j(a_{j,i} - a_{T,i})$$

where $a_{j,i}$ is the accuracy of task i after learning task j.

4.3   Results

We compare the result of our method against the selective baseline methods on split-CIFAR10, split-CIFAR100, and split-miniImageNet. The results on split-CIFAR10, split-CIFAR100, and split-miniImageNet are shown in Table 1, Table 2 and Table 3, respectively.

Comparing the results of baseline methods w/ and w/o mixup, the original mixup on methods that replay the ground truth labels (ER and DER++) perform worsen when the memory buffer size is small (buffer size 200 and 500 on S-CIFAR10, and buffer size 500 on S-CIFAR100, buffer size 5000 on S-minImageNet) but better when the buffer size is enough (buffer size 2000 on S-CIFAR100). Hence, we can briefly conclude that mixup for label-based replay methods is sensitive to the size of the memory buffer that stored past data.

Comparing the results of baseline methods w/ and w/o difficulty-aware mixup, difficulty-aware mixup can improve average accuracy and reduce forgetting significantly, especially ER and DER. In addition, the forgetting measure of DER with difficulty-aware mixup in a large buffer size setting is better than DER++ with difficulty-aware mixup.

Table 1. Results on split CIFAR10

Dataset	S-CIFAR10			
Buffer size	200		500	
	ACC ($\uparrow$)	Forgetting ($\downarrow$)	ACC ($\uparrow$)	Forgetting ($\downarrow$)
ER	49.63 $\pm$ 1.08	58.85 $\pm$ 1.26	60.66 $\pm$ 4.01	39.70 $\pm$ 5.54
+mixup	45.52 $\pm$ 6.50	58.10 $\pm$ 9.32	55.88 $\pm$ 4.21	49.16 $\pm$ 5.48
+DAmixup	52.36 $\pm$ 2.99	49.42 $\pm$ 3.39	62.84 $\pm$ 3.34	38.78 $\pm$ 3.96
DER	61.26 $\pm$ 1.78	40.82 $\pm$ 2.52	71.08 $\pm$ 1.06	28.62 $\pm$ 1.48
+mixup	61.18 $\pm$ 0.97	40.14 $\pm$ 1.04	70.26 $\pm$ 2.19	29.06 $\pm$ 3.20
+DAmixup	65.08 $\pm$ 1.14	32.64 $\pm$ 1.51	73.84 $\pm$ 1.19	20.90 $\pm$ 2.01
DER++	64.86 $\pm$ 0.79	33.74 $\pm$ 0.72	72.94 $\pm$ 1.05	23.90 $\pm$ 1.56
+mixup	60.92 $\pm$ 1.32	37.98 $\pm$ 2.11	71.26 $\pm$ 0.79	26.14 $\pm$ 1.36
+DAmixup	65.92 $\pm$ 1.22	30.60 $\pm$ 1.44	74.46 $\pm$ 0.78	21.06 $\pm$ 1.55

4.4 Analysis

Trend of Average Accuracy. As mentioned in the previous section, there is a significant improvement when applying difficulty-aware mixup to baseline methods. To discuss the result after learning the new task further, we visualize the trend of average accuracy on split-CIFAR100 experiments with 500 memory size in Fig. 3. It can be seen that difficulty-aware mixup can retain the performance well after being trained on the new task. Besides, we find that original mixup can get better results on ER experiments at the early stages, but drop in the late period. We thought it is because the replay method with cross-entropy loss is hard to be optimized with the ambiguous mixed image of hard samples.

Table 2. Results on split CIFAR100

Dataset	S-CIFAR100			
Buffer size	500		2000	
	ACC (↑)	Forgetting (↓)	ACC (↑)	Forgetting (↓)
ER	21.42 ± 0.89	72.46 ± 0.55	33.54 ± 2.14	58.34 ± 2.09
+mixup	20.46 ± 0.85	75.12 ± 1.06	34.90 ± 1.91	57.86 ± 2.11
+DAmixup	24.46 ± 1.92	67.40 ± 1.72	40.00 ± 1.68	50.78 ± 1.82
DER	35.14 ± 0.94	55.06 ± 1.21	50.42 ± 0.56	34.44 ± 1.06
+mixup	36.16 ± 1.11	53.66 ± 1.12	50.84 ± 0.41	32.20 ± 0.86
+DAmixup	37.94 ± 1.62	48.70 ± 1.75	51.88 ± 0.73	27.76 ± 1.71
DER++	36.23 ± 0.92	52.55 ± 1.75	51.09 ± 0.57	34.44 ± 1.15
+mixup	36.05 ± 0.97	52.06 ± 1.51	51.41 ± 0.42	34.89 ± 0.65
+DAmixup	38.08 ± 0.51	47.92 ± 1.26	53.00 ± 0.49	32.68 ± 0.54

Table 3. Results on split miniImageNet

Dataset	S-miniImageNet	
Buffer size	5000	
	ACC (↑)	Forgetting (↓)
ER	30.44 ± 1.99	49.78 ± 4.62
+mixup	27.34 ± 1.77	61.04 ± 1.58
+DAmixup	32.66 ± 2.24	49.60 ± 2.61
DER	40.00 ± 1.28	33.36 ± 1.36
+mixup	38.62 ± 1.35	35.46 ± 2.71
+DAmixup	43.02 ± 0.63	25.66 ± 1.09
DER++	41.72 ± 3.02	35.64 ± 3.75
+mixup	43.40 ± 0.72	37.64 ± 1.30
+DAmixup	42.78 ± 1.14	34.48 ± 1.30

New Task Bias. Because of the data imbalance between old and new tasks, the model is biased toward the new task. In Fig. 4, we show the visualization of the final accuracy of each task after learning the last task. We observe that difficulty-aware mixup makes the accuracy of each task more uniform, especially in DER experiments. It implies that our method can effectively reduce bias caused by data imbalance.

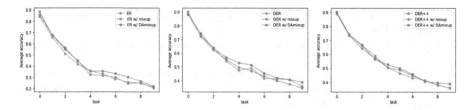

Fig. 3. Trend of average accuracy on S-CIFAR100 experiments with 500 memory size

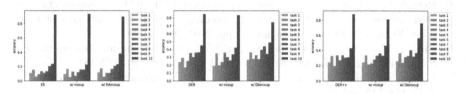

Fig. 4. Final task accuracy on S-CIFAR100 experiments with 500 buffer size

5   Conclusion

In this paper, we implement mixup on ER, DER, DER++ and present a novel difficulty-aware mixup approach to tackle the problem caused by the ambiguous mixed images of some examples that make the model hard to be trained. We evaluate our proposed method on split-CIFAR10, split-CIFAR100, and split-miniImageNet datasets, and the experimental result shows that our method can improve the average accuracy and mitigate forgetting effectively. Meanwhile, our method can reduce the bias of probability between current and past tasks. In the future, we plan to implement our method in other continual learning settings, like general continual learning. Furthermore, mixup with current and old data is also a research direction in the future.

References

1. Ahn, H., Kwak, J., Lim, S., Bang, H., Kim, H., Moon, T.: SS-IL: separated softmax for incremental learning. In: Proceedings of the IEEE/CVF International Conference on Computer Vision, pp. 844–853 (2021)
2. Buzzega, P., Boschini, M., Porrello, A., Abati, D., Calderara, S.: Dark experience for general continual learning: a strong, simple baseline. Adv. Neural. Inf. Process. Syst. **33**, 15920–15930 (2020)
3. Guo, H., Mao, Y., Zhang, R.: Mixup as locally linear out-of-manifold regularization. In: Proceedings of the AAAI Conference on Artificial Intelligence, vol. 33, pp. 3714–3722 (2019)
4. He, K., Zhang, X., Ren, S., Sun, J.: Deep residual learning for image recognition. In: Proceedings of the IEEE Conference on Computer Vision and Pattern Recognition, pp. 770–778 (2016)
5. Hinton, G., Vinyals, O., Dean, J., et al.: Distilling the knowledge in a neural network. arXiv preprint arXiv:1503.02531, vol. 2, no. 7 (2015)

6. Kirkpatrick, J., et al.: Overcoming catastrophic forgetting in neural networks. Proc. Natl. Acad. Sci. **114**(13), 3521–3526 (2017)
7. Krizhevsky, A.: Learning multiple layers of features from tiny images. Technical report (2009)
8. McCloskey, M., Cohen, N.J.: Catastrophic interference in connectionist networks: the sequential learning problem. In: Psychology of Learning and Motivation, vol. 24, pp. 109–165. Elsevier (1989)
9. Ratcliff, R.: Connectionist models of recognition memory: constraints imposed by learning and forgetting functions. Psychol. Rev. **97**(2), 285 (1990)
10. Rebuffi, S.A., Kolesnikov, A., Sperl, G., Lampert, C.H.: ICARL: incremental classifier and representation learning. In: Proceedings of the IEEE Conference on Computer Vision and Pattern Recognition, pp. 2001–2010 (2017)
11. Riemer, M., et al.: Learning to learn without forgetting by maximizing transfer and minimizing interference. arXiv preprint arXiv:1810.11910 (2018)
12. Robins, A.: Catastrophic forgetting, rehearsal and pseudorehearsal. Connect. Sci. **7**(2), 123–146 (1995)
13. Shin, H., Lee, J.K., Kim, J., Kim, J.: Continual learning with deep generative replay. In: Advances in Neural Information Processing Systems, vol. 30 (2017)
14. Vinyals, O., Blundell, C., Lillicrap, T., Wierstra, D., et al.: Matching networks for one shot learning. In: Advances in Neural Information Processing Systems, vol. 29 (2016)
15. Wu, Y., et al.: Large scale incremental learning. In: Proceedings of the IEEE/CVF Conference on Computer Vision and Pattern Recognition, pp. 374–382 (2019)
16. Xu, G., Liu, Z., Loy, C.C.: Computation-efficient knowledge distillation via uncertainty-aware mixup. arXiv preprint arXiv:2012.09413 (2020)
17. Zenke, F., Poole, B., Ganguli, S.: Continual learning through synaptic intelligence. In: International Conference on Machine Learning, pp. 3987–3995. PMLR (2017)
18. Zhang, H., Cisse, M., Dauphin, Y.N., Lopez-Paz, D.: mixup: beyond empirical risk minimization. arXiv preprint arXiv:1710.09412 (2017)

Vision-Based Lightweight Facial Respiration and Heart Rate Measurement Technology

Kai-Xiang Liu[1], Chuan-Yu Chang[1(✉)], and Huei-Ming Ma[2]

[1] Department of Computer Science and Information Engineering, National Yunlin University of Science and Technology, Yunlin, Taiwan
chuanyu@yuntech.edu.tw
[2] Emergency Medicine, Cardiology, National Taiwan University Hospital Yunlin Branch, Yunlin, Taiwan

Abstract. Heart rate and respiratory rate are important information reflecting human vital signs. Many studies have used face detection and feature point tracking to find ROI (region of interesting) for non-contact analysis and measurement. However, these methods all convert the features into a single signal for processing, and when there is noise interference in the ROI area, it is easy to cause measurement errors. This paper adopts multiple ROIs to select multiple features. Significant signals are selected by correlation and integrated by principal component analysis to reduce the impact on measurements when individual signals are disturbed. Considering that the real-time measurement is affected by the computational performance, this paper uses optical flow tracking to replace the face detection of each frame which makes the tracking features more stable. This paper measures the RPPG (remote photoplethysmography) signal to estimate the heart rate, and then measures the respiration according to the facial micro-vibration generated by the breathing movement. Experimental results show that for heart rate measurement, the proposed method achieves a MAE of 6.53 and an RMSE of 8.684 in the Ostankovich's dataset. Furthermore, the proposed method is combined with the ensemble empirical mode decomposition, and the MAE and RMSE are further reduced to 4.124 and 6.897. The respiration rate detection results of the proposed method have a MAE of 2.017 and an RMSE of 2.676. Furthermore, the proposed method can actually run on a Raspberry Pi 4 platform with less computing power, proving the real-time processing capability of the system.

Keywords: Non-contact analysis · ROI · RPPG · Optical flow · Ensemble empirical mode decomposition · Raspberry pi4

1 Introduction

Heart rate and respiration rate are the most instant information that reflects the human vital signs and can be used to observe human health [1, 2]. Currently, many methods of measuring heart rate and respiration rate have been developed. Electrocardiogram (ECG) is commonly used in medicine, which mainly measures signals by inducing human cardiac current [3]. The photoplethysmography (PPG) method used on the oximeter or

© The Author(s), under exclusive license to Springer Nature Singapore Pte Ltd. 2022
S.-Y. Hsieh et al. (Eds.): ICS 2022, CCIS 1723, pp. 317–328, 2022.
https://doi.org/10.1007/978-981-19-9582-8_28

wearable device optically measures the change in the amount of light absorbed by the skin, which reflects the detection of blood flow through the dermis and subcutaneous tissue for the calculation of physical signals [4, 5].Because the change of respiratory motion is more obviously accompanied by the breathing signal, it can be detected directly by breathing-induced thoracic undulation or by airflow through the mouth and nose [3]. This paper mainly uses remote photoplethysmography (RPPG) technology. It analyzes the light reflection caused by the blood flowing through the skin collected by the camera to obtain the PPG-related signals to achieve long-distance measurement [6]. In respiration rate detection, this paper uses facial vibration information as the measurement signal because of obvious breathing movement.

There have been many studies have been using RPPG for heart rate measurement. It was first introduced by Verkruysse *et al.* [7] in 2008 to analyze the RGB of the image. In 2011, Poh *et al.* [8] used face position as ROI for analysis. However, the measurement of the whole face will be affected by the inclusion of non-physiological information such as background, human hair, glasses, etc. In subsequent studies, many people chose the forehead and cheeks as ROIs for analysis. Rouast *et al.* [9] selected the forehead position to collect the signal features by a specific scale selection during the signal acquisition process. Li *et al.* [10] in 2014, Lee *et al.* [11] in 2018 and Mehta *et al.* [12] in 2021 used face feature points to make the collected signal more stable. However. These studies used many methods to select better ROI, the information collected by ROI selection is obtained by averaging a single value. This method encounters the interference of non-measurement data in some ROI selection areas on the image, which will affect the overall value. In this paper, multiple range ROIs are selected with the combing of box and feature points. Using correlation coefficient score and principle component analysis (PCA) to effectively integrate signals from different ROIs to reduce measurement results with extreme values. Because of the high accuracy of the measurement with Empirical Mode Decomposition (EEMD) [11], this paper designed the process with EEMD to discuss the accuracy and performance.

In addition to use of RPPG signal for heart rate measurement, many studies also use this signal to detect respiration rate. Addison *et al.* [13] shown that the autonomic nerve will cause periodic changes in the pulse during breathing, which in turn affects the PPG. Considering that breathing signals are closely related to thoracic rise and fall, some studies have used micro-vibration information caused by changes in the thoracic cavity to measure respiration rate. Wiede *et al.* [14] used optical flow tracking to observe the visual changes caused by thoracic ups and downs for measurement.

In this paper, the system design can perform real-time measurement without complete video recording. The real-time detection is different from video recording, which has a fixed number of frames per second (FPS). The processing time of each frame should be considered and it should not be too long. In this paper, the optical flow method is used for feature point tracking. The principle of optical flow is the value calculated by comparing the frames before and after. In addition to stabilizing the effect of feature point tracking, the time spend is reduced by using optical flow method to replace the face detection and feature point regression calculation every frame.

The videos collected by Ostankovich [15] were used to test the measurement capability. Three evaluation metrics including mean absolute error (MAE), root mean square error (RMSE), and Pearson correlation coefficient (PCC) were adopted. Comparisons with other methods and different ROIs selection demonstrate that the analysis and ROI selection of this paper are better. In the performance evaluation, Comparisons with the costs caused by different ROI tracking methods described the performance improved with optical flow tracking. With the performance, the feasibility of system running on the embedded computing device of Raspberry Pi 4 is demonstrated.

2 Method

Visual-based respiratory rate and heart rate measurements are mainly composed of signal collection and signal processing. During signal collection, appropriate ROIs are selected from each frame in the video and processed to obtain representative features. Signal processing is mainly based on the collected signals to obtain the final respiration and heart rate results.

2.1 Signal Collection

The signal collection process starts with image input, perform face detection to locate the subject's face position, and set a limit box to reduce the scope of subsequent image processing. The process uses regression tree technology to extract feature points from the detected face, also uses the optical flow method to continuously track the face feature points to increase the stability of feature point tracking. According to the different characteristics of breathing rate and heart rate, the different signals are used as the feature collection. The collected features are accessed with queue method, and processing are performed when a sufficient number is collected. In this paper, in order to improve the performance of image processing, optical flow tracking is used for each frame to replace face detection and feature point matching to directly track feature points continuously, which improves the operating efficiency of the system. The signal collection process is shown in Fig. 1.

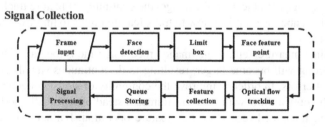

Fig. 1. Signal collection process.

Face Detection. This paper uses a lightweight face detection convolution network Yunet [16] to find the face position of the measurement target from the image. This network architecture was introduced by OpenCV in 2020. It has high detection speed and high accuracy in face detection.

Limit Box. The image processing is calculated according to different targets and the background information is also under consideration. Except the target and some surrounding areas need to be calculated, calculation on the rest area will cause waste of computing resources. In this paper, the limit box is set according to the outward extension of the face bounding box. Operations performed with limit box reduce the large number of operations that would result from processing the whole image.

Face Feature Point. In this paper, the ensemble of regression trees (ERT) proposed by Kazemi *et al.* [17] is used to extract face features based on a cascaded regression tree composed of regression trees. This algorithm iteratively corrects and returns the average face shape to match the real face, then obtains the positioning closest to the face feature points. Considering that blood is mainly transported by arteries, refer to the distribution of arterial blood vessels in human facial skin [18]. This paper uses seven feature points to collect information as shown in Fig. 2.

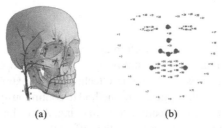

(a)   (b)

Fig. 2. (a) Arterial vascular on the skin surface distributed by Arx et al. [18] (b) 68 face feature points and selected tracking points in this paper.

Optical Flow Tracking. The feature calculation based on the regression tree algorithm is easily affected by the position and size of the face detection frame, resulting in discontinuous feature points in adjacent frames. Considering that optical flow is calculated through the changes of objects in the image, the continuity of feature tracking is better. Therefore, this paper uses optical flow to track feature points to improve the stability of collected signals.

In real-time measurement, if the image processing time is too large, the time interval of collecting will become larger, resulting in discontinuous signals and increased measurement errors. In order to improve the continuity of signal collection, this paper calculates the optical flow with adjacent frames instead of repeatedly performing face detection and integrated regression tree feature operation. Further, the setting of the limit box reduces the range of optical flow calculation and improves the processing performance of each frame.

Feature Collection. The heart rate signal adopts the method of RPPG. The green-light signal is combined with the red-light signal, and the ROI is set according to the tracking feature points for average operation to obtain the signals of seven positions for feature collection as Fig. 3 (a).

The respiration rate considers the breath movement, the lungs relaxation causes the significant fluctuate and reflects the respiration situation stably. In this paper, the signal is collected based on the body micro-vibration information, and the y-coordinate of the optical flow tracking is used as the signal source of the respiration rate as Fig. 3(b).

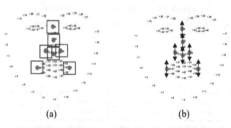

(a)   (b)

Fig. 3. (a) The ROI of RPPG measurement. (b) The micro-variation information of y-coordinate.

Queue Storing. The measurement of heart rate and respiration rate is to analyze and calculate the signals for a period. This paper adopts the concept of queuing to add new processed data while removing the oldest recorded data. The number of records required for signal processing is set to 250 and the time spent in feature collection is recorded to provide time-related counts during signal processing. Considering that the system performs continuous measurement, it will update and measure data according to the number of 100 signals and use time queue to record the time to be removed when updating. The queue process is shown in Fig. 4.

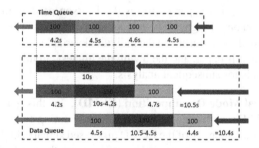

Fig. 4. Queue storing of signal and using time.

2.2 Signal Processing

In signal processing, a large amount of noise is filtered from the input signal through the bandpass filter. The signals collected by multiple features are subjected to Pearson correlation calculation to select stable signals. The principal component analysis is applied for integrated analysis. The peak counting is used to extract the number in the time segment. Finally, the measurement result is counted considering the time factor.

In this paper, considering the different characteristics of the heart rate and respiration rate signals, different processing methods are used, such as band-pass filter frequency band selection, peak detection and counting methods. In addition, considering the performance of EEMD in signal analysis, it is discussed whether to add EEMD processing in the process design. Figure 5 is the flow chart of the signal processing in this paper. The red block indicates that different processing is performed according to the respiratory rate and heart rate. The dotted line indicates that it is added to the process according to the design requirements.

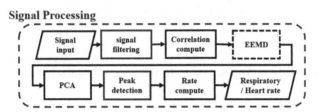

Fig. 5. Signal processing process.

Bandpass Filter. The average heart rate is about 45–180 beats per minute and the breathing rate is about 9–30 beats per minute. The corresponding frequencies are 0.75–3 Hz (heart rate) and 0.15–0.5 Hz (respiration rate) respectively. In this paper, the order 3 Butterworth filter is used for signal filtering.

Correlation Computing. Considering that the signal with high correlation has less noise or extreme value, this paper performs the Pearson product-moment correlation coefficient calculation on the signal. The correlation between the two sets of signals was analyzed by the ratio of the covariate to the individual variable. There are 7 multi-feature point signals input in this paper, and the 3 with the highest cumulative correlation value are used as the signals for subsequent analysis.

Ensemble Empirical Mode Decomposition (EEMD). In this paper, the signal is decomposed by EEMD, and selected the signal by counting the correlation with the filtered value. The peak integrity of the EEMD processed signal is higher than that of the signal processed by filtering, as shown in Fig. 6. However, this method needs to perform EMD calculation with multiple sets of signals mixed with white noise, resulting in a significant increase in the amount of computation. If the number of mixed white noise is to large, the system may not work for continuous measurement.

Principal Component Analysis (PCA). PCA is used to find the maximum covariance between the signals through projection, and then extract the principal components among the signals. In this paper, the original signal is selected for numerical comparison with different principal component signals.

Peak Detection. This paper adopts the peak counting method as counting method and uses topographic prominence and peak interval limit to emit the signal noise peak. The topographic prominence is mainly used to measure the independence of the mountain. This paper calculates the topographic prominence of the peak and sets a threshold to filter out the low-independence peaks. In addition, the heart rate signal will maintain a certain frequency. The interval distance is calculated by the peaks and the distance limit is set to remove abnormal peak. The peak detection result of heart rate is obtained by removing the noise peak through the threshold limit, as shown in Fig. 7(a).

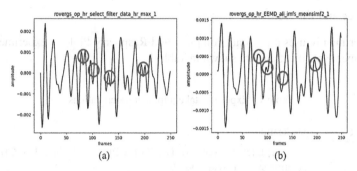

Fig. 6. Signal comparison (a) without EEMD (b) selected signal after EEMD

Compared with the heart rate signal, the number of signal peaks after the respiration signal is processed is less, and the signal complexity is also smaller. Therefore, this paper does not use a threshold for peak filtering in the peak count of the respiration signal. The detection results are shown in Fig. 7(b).

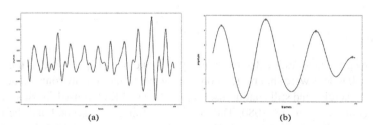

Fig. 7. Peak detection result. (a) heart rate signal (b) respiratory rate signal.

Result Counting. Due to the boundary problem at the beginning and end of the signal, the peak count has an error of 0–2. In order to avoid such problems, this study selects the peak value from the initial to the last peak interval, and counts the results by the actual time spent in analyzing the data. The calculation is as shown in Eq. (1) and Eq. (2).

$$Heartrate = \frac{N_{heart} - 1}{T_{finalpeak} - T_{firstpeak}} \times 60 \tag{1}$$

$$Respiratoryrate = \frac{N_{respiratory} - 1}{T_{finalpeak} - T_{firstpeak}} \times 60 \tag{2}$$

where N_{heart} and N_{breath} are the number of peaks of heart and breath signal after signal processing. $T_{finalpeak}$ is the time point of the last peak, and $T_{firstpeak}$ is the time point of the first peak.

3   Experimental Results

3.1   Device and Environment

This paper mainly uses a personal computer and Raspberry Pi 4 for experiments, and the equipment specifications are shown in Table 1.

Table 1. Experimental equipment specifications

Equipment	Specification
PC	Processor: Intel(R) Core(TM) i7-8700K CPU @ 3.70 GHz 3.70 GHz Operating system: Windows 10
Raspberry Pi 4	Processor: Broadcom BCM2711, Quad core Cortex-A72 (ARM v8) 64-bit SoC @ 1.5 GHz Operating system: Ubuntu20.04 LTS
Camera	Logitech BRIO 4KHD 1920 * 1080, 30FPS
Breathing belt	Go Direct Breath Monitoring Chest Strap

3.2   Dataset

In this paper, the heart rate video recorded by Ostankovich [15] are used as the dataset. A total of 30 videos were shot by 15 people in a general lighting environment according to the post-exercise and still conditions. Canon Legria HFR 66 is used for shooting. The image resolution is 1920 * 1080. The video is 25 frames per second and the time of video is about 20 s. In the dataset, ECG signal is collected through ECG Lite while the video is being shot.

The respiration rate is recorded with real-time measured. A total of 112 record by 14 people under the illumination of fluorescent lamps with an illumination intensity of 600–750lx. Recorded with Logitech BRIO 4HD and measured the actual value of respiration rate with Go Direct Breathing belt. The video is 30 frames per second, the image resolution is 1920 * 1080, and the length of the video is about 40 s for the blood pressure measurement time.

3.3   Evaluation Metrics

In order to evaluate the measurement accuracy of different methods, this paper uses the mean absolute error (MAE), the Root Mean Square Error (RMSE) and the Pearson correlation coefficient (PCC). The formulas are shown in (3), (4) and (5).

$$MAE = \frac{1}{n} \sum\nolimits_{i=1}^{n} |y_i - x_i| \tag{3}$$

$$RMSE = \sqrt{\frac{1}{n} \sum\nolimits_{i=1}^{n} (y_i - x_i)^2} \tag{4}$$

$$PCC = \frac{\sum_i (x_i - \overline{x})(y_i - \overline{y})}{\sqrt{\sum_i (x_i - \overline{x})^2} \sqrt{\sum_i (y_i - \overline{y})^2}} \tag{5}$$

where x_i and y_i represents the i-th measurement result and its corresponding actual value, n is the number of measurements, and $\overline{x}, \overline{y}$ represent the means of the x and y.

3.4 Heart Rate Detection

To demonstrate the efficiency of the proposed method, four methods based on different ROIs selection and feature tracking were compared [9–12]. Table 2 shows the comparison results based on the Ostankovich's dataset.

Table 2. Comparison of heart rate detection with Ostankovich's dataset

	MAE	RMSE	PCC
Li's [10]	12.033	19.639	0.2454
Rouast's [9]	15.924	20.958	0.4383
Lee's [11] (EEMD)	5.004	9.767	0.7907
Mehta's [12]	8.048	14.772	0.5764
The proposed	**6.530**	**8.684**	0.7827
The proposed - EEMD	**4.124**	**6.897**	0.9164

In the measurement results of the Ostankovich's dataset, the accuracy and correlation of the proposed method are higher than those of other papers. Although Lee et al. [11] mainly used EEMD for signal analysis, the evaluation of MAE is better than the analysis without EEMD process in this paper, but the method of this paper has better performance in the evaluation of RMSE. The main reason is that the method of this paper adopts multi-feature signal collection to reduce the extreme values caused by the instability of single-signal signal collection. Considering that the EEMD method has a good performance in signal analysis, this paper combines the EEMD method to analyze the results. Both MAE and RMSE are obviously better than other methods. However, EEMD is caused by multiple white noise processing, the performance cost of the system may affect be continuously detected with the same process as the original process. Figure 8 shows the comparison between the measured signals and Ostankovich's ECG signal. After the comparison, it is obvious that the peaks accurately correspond to the ECG heart rate related signals, and it can be observed from the red circle that the EEMD processing effectively removes the noise peaks.

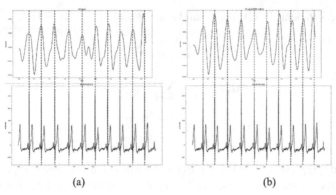

(a)   (b)

Fig. 8. Comparison of the measured signal with Ostankovich's ECG signal (a) without EEMD (b) with EEMD processing

3.5 Respiratory Rate Detection

This paper uses the collected data to measure the respiratory rate, and to compare it with the method of Wiede *et al.* [14]. In addition to the tracking of the positional changes of the face feature points based on vibration caused by thoracic undulation, the RPPG method is used according to the variation of the blood vessel wall due to thoracic respiration. The results are shown in Table 3.

Table 3. Comparison of respiratory rate detection

	MAE	RMSE	PCC
Wiede's [14]	1.244	1.427	0.968
The proposed	2.017	2.676	0.930
The proposed - RPPG	3.631	5.423	0.438

According to the measurement results, the result of the method in this paper is similar to the result of Wiede's method. However, the vibration through the face is indirectly generated by the thoracic undulation. The signal is small and the vibration signal is prone to be affected by the movement of the head. The result is hard to have high accuracy. Since the measurement of RPPG relies on the change of blood vessel oxygen supply, the measurement result cannot correspond to the actual result because there is no obvious change in the blood vessel. Figure 9 is a comparison of the waveforms of different respiration rate measurement methods and respiration belt measurement. It can be observed that the method of measuring through the thoracic cavity has obvious waveforms. The micro-vibration method used in this paper has similar results. However, the signal measured by RPPG is not obvious because the waveform signal is weak.

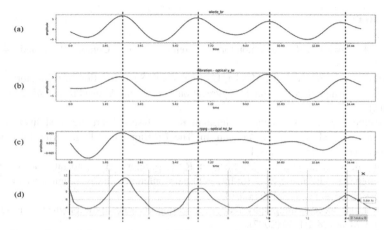

Fig. 9. Comparison of the waveforms of different respiration rate measurement methods and respiration belt measurement.

4 Conclusions

In this paper, the optical flow tracking multi-feature method is used to collect the signal, and then the signal is analyzed by filtering, correlation coefficient, EEMD and PCA processing methods. Finally, the values of heart rate and respiration rate are calculated through the peak count and threshold limit. In terms of accuracy, according to the experimental results using the Ostankovich's dataset, it is confirmed that the multi-feature signal selection is used in this paper to exclude the affected signals, which has better stability than the signals collected by a single ROI. The MAE and RMSE are 6.53 and 8.684, respectively, which are better than other methods, and the measurement extreme value of the proposed method is also lower than other measurement methods. In addition, the processing method combined with EEMD has a significant improvement in accuracy, and the MAE and RMSE are reduced to 4.124 and 6.897, respectively. In the respiration rate part, we can see that the MAE and RMSE of the facial micro-vibration information used in this paper are 2.017 and 2.676 respectively, which is close to the method of observing the chest cavity measurement, and the measurement signal is also displayed through the signal comparison. The correlation with the actual breathing motion confirms the feasibility of this facial micro-vibration detection of breathing rate.

In order to effectively reduce the computational complexity of the proposed method, this paper uses (1) optical flow tracking to replace face detection for each frame of image, which greatly reduces the processing time for collecting features in each frame. (2) The calculation of the entire image is replaced by the design of the limit box, which further reduces the calculation time of the optical flow. Considering that real-time processing is different from the fixed number of frames per second of recorded images, this paper makes the time basis of real-time measurement more flexible and reliable through the characteristics and time recording of the queuing method. Take instant measurements on the Raspberry Pi.

References

1. Jain, P.K., Tiwari, A.K.: Heart monitoring systems—a review. Comput. Biol. Med. **54**, 1–13 (2014)
2. Prathosh, A.P., Praveena, P., Mestha, L., Bharadwaj, S.: Estimation of respiratory pattern from video using selective ensemble aggregation. IEEE Trans. Signal Process. **65**, 2902–2916 (2016)
3. Sengthipphany, T., Tretriluxana, S., Chitsakul, K.: Analysis of heart rate variability and breath to breath interval in frequency domain. In: The 7th Biomedical Engineering International Conference 2014, pp. 1–4 (2014)
4. Daimiwal, N., Sundhararajan, M., Shriram, R.: Respiratory rate, heart rate and continuous measurement of BP using PPG. In: International Conference on Communication and Signal Processing 2014, pp. 999–1002 (2014)
5. Allen, J.: Photoplethysmography and its application in clinical physiological measurement. Physiol. Meas. **28**, R1-39 (2007)
6. Chen, X., Cheng, J., Song, R., Liu, Y., Ward, R., Wang, Z.J.: Video-based heart rate measurement: recent advances and future prospects. IEEE Trans. Instrum. Meas. **68**(10), 3600–3615 (2019)
7. Verkruysse, W., Svaasand, L.O., Nelson, J.S.: Remote plethysmographic imaging using ambient light (in eng). Opt. Express **16**(26), 21434–21445 (2008)
8. Poh, M., McDuff, D.J., Picard, R.W.: Advancements in noncontact, multiparameter physiological measurements using a webcam. IEEE Trans. Biomed. Eng. **58**(1), 7–11 (2011)
9. Rouast, P., Adam, M., Dorner, V., Lux, E.: Remote Photoplethysmography: Evaluation of Contactless Heart Rate Measurement in an Information Systems Setting (2016)
10. Li, X., Chen, J., Zhao, G., Pietikäinen, M.: Remote heart rate measurement from face videos under realistic situations. In: IEEE Conference on Computer Vision and Pattern Recognition, pp. 4264–4271 (2014)
11. Lee, K., Han, D.K., Ko, H.: Video analytic based health monitoring for driver in moving vehicle by extracting effective heart rate inducing features. J. Adv. Transp. **2018**, 8513487 (2018)
12. Mehta, A.D., Sharma, H.: Heart rate estimation from RGB facial videos using robust face demarcation and VMD. In: National Conference on Communications (NCC) 2021, pp. 1–6 (2021)
13. Addison, P.S., Watson, J.N., Mestek, M.L., Mecca, R.S.: Developing an algorithm for pulse oximetry derived respiratory rate (RR(oxi)): a healthy volunteer study (in eng). J. Clin. Monit. Comput. **26**(1), 45–51 (2012)
14. Wiede, C., Richter, J., Manuel, M., Hirtz, G.: Remote respiration rate determination in video data - vital parameter extraction based on optical flow and principal component analysis. In: VISIGRAPP (2017)
15. Ostankovich, V., Prathap, G., Afanasyev, I.: Towards human pulse rate estimation from face video: automatic component selection and comparison of blind source separation methods. In: International Conference on Intelligent Systems (IS) 2018, pp. 183–189 (2018)
16. S. Yu. "Libfacedetection." https://github.com/ShiqiYu/libfacedetection
17. Kazemi, V., Sullivan, J.: One millisecond face alignment with an ensemble of regression trees. In: IEEE Conference on Computer Vision and Pattern Recognition 2014, pp. 1867–1874 (2014)
18. von Arx, T., Tamura, K., Yukiya, O., Lozanoff, S.: The face – a vascular perspective. a literature review. Swiss. Dent. J. **128**(5), 382–392 (2018)

GAN-Based Criminal Suspect Face Generator

Sophia Yang[1]([✉]), Jun-Teng Zhang[1], Chia-Wen Lin[2], and Chih-Chung Hsu[3]

[1] National Tsing Hua University, Hsinchu, Taiwan
sophias94171@gmail.com
[2] Department of Electrical Engineering and the Institute of Communications Engineering,
National Tsing Hua University, Hsinchu, Taiwan
[3] Institute of Data Science, National Cheng Kung University, Tainan, Taiwan

Abstract. We propose a criminal suspect face generator based on GANs to replace the problematic process of traditional criminal investigation. The proposed method consists of two crucial components: DCGAN for feature-based face generation, and StyleGAN for feature-guided face manipulation. The proposed framework addresses several practical problems of criminal investigation by first generating a face based on a feature and then transferring the face to different features or expressions for unlimited times in an objective and efficient way. Preliminary experimental results are promising to address the problems of crime investigations in real scenarios.

Keywords: Generative adversarial networks · Text to image · Human face generation

1 Introduction

To reconstruct the face of a criminal suspect is an important but troublesome task. Suppose polices are trying to reconstruct a suspect's face to help them solve a case, the typical method adopted by polices is to hire a painter to create a portrait according to the descriptions provided by eyewitnesses. Then the polices rely on this portrait to search for anyone who looks like it. However, this method is usually problematic in real scenarios. There exist four main problems that need to be addressed:

- The portrait largely depends on the painter's art style, so the same person may not look the same in different art styles.
- Art is well-known to be subjective, so it's difficult to distinguish the similarities between the portrait and the original face.
- Facial expressions also affect the result significantly, so we need a facial generator which can deal with a variety of facial expressions.
- The sketching process is too time-consuming without enough interaction. All these four problems usually lead to difficulties to find the real criminals.

Therefore, we propose a new suspect face generating framework which is not only fast and objective but also user-friendly so as to create interactive atmosphere to reconstruct suspect faces.

© The Author(s), under exclusive license to Springer Nature Singapore Pte Ltd. 2022
S.-Y. Hsieh et al. (Eds.): ICS 2022, CCIS 1723, pp. 329–340, 2022.
https://doi.org/10.1007/978-981-19-9582-8_29

To address the problems in practical criminal investigation, the proposed framework not only acts as a general face generator, but also has some special attributes designed for real crime investigation scenarios. As compared to the traditional way, we transfer the facial features provided by eyewitnesses to generate a suspect's face with a lot of variety. To be more specific, the proposed method consists of two parts, DCGAN [1] for feature-based face generation, and StyleGAN [2] for feature-guided face manipulation. We first generate a face based on a feature and then transfer the face to different features or expressions for unlimited times so eyewitnesses can continually revise the generated image to fit the suspect face better. Figure 1 shows the framework of the proposed method.

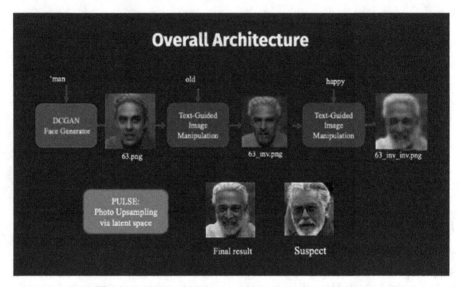

Fig. 1. Framework of the proposed suspect face generator

The proposed framework has the following contributions:

- The art style problem in real investigation scenario is resolved because our model generates photo-like results instead of artistic portraits.
- The proposed system outputs relatively objective results because they are generated by a machine instead of an artist.
- A style-based Generative Adversarial Network, called StyleGAN [2], is applied to generate pictures with several facial expressions; hence it increases the diversity of the same face.
- In addition to the application of criminal investigation, the proposed model can also be utilized to generate fictional characters or to customize game characters.

2 Methods

2.1 Deep Convolutional GAN

The first step of the proposed method is to use DCGAN [1] to generate some models for StyleGAN in the next step for further usage. DCGAN focuses on improving GAN in the network architecture, replacing the generator and discriminator with CNN. Figure 2 shows the details of the constructure and capabilities of DCGAN.

Constructure. The constructure contains the following features:

- Remove pooling, use strided convolution in discriminator and transpose convolution in generator.
- Use batch normalization on generator and discriminator.
- Remove fully connected layers.
- In the generator, the output layer uses tanh, and all other layers use Rectified Linear Unit (ReLU).

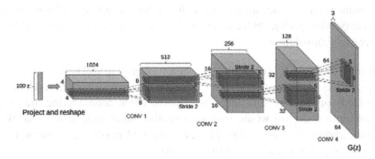

Fig. 2. Generator network constructure [1]

Training Details. The training details of our DCGAN are composed of deconvolution and batch normalization:

Deconvolution (Transposed Convolution). The normal convolution maps a 4×4 image to a 2×2 image. The deconvolution does the reverse.

Batch Normalization. The batch normalization can speed up the training process and prevent gradient vanishing. It can also reduce the influences produced by data initialization of tanh or sigmoid, and eventually improve the accuracy of training.

Capabilities. To verify capabilities, we put features into L2-SVM and compare the result with other unsupervised-learning.

2.2 Style-Based Generator

The second step of the proposed method is to construct a neural network which can translate the work into corresponding latent code. Then we use the latent code to modify the original image with different looks. Compared to the traditional GAN, we use StyleGAN [2] as our basic model. Figure 3 shows the overall architecture of StyleGAN and how it works with evaluation methods.

AdaIN. The AdaIN operation is defined in Eq. (1).

$$AdaIN(x_i, y) = y_{s,i} \frac{x_i - \mu(x_i)}{\sigma(x_i)} + y_{b,i} \tag{1}$$

Each feature map x_i is normalized separately, and then scaled and biased using the corresponding scalar components from style y. Thus, the dimensionality of y is twice the number of feature maps on that layer.

Stochastic Variation. The generator generates stochastic details by introducing explicit noise inputs. They feed a dedicated noise image to each layer of the synthesis network. The noise image is broadcasted to all feature maps using learned per-feature scaling factors and then added to the output of the corresponding convolution. Traditional generator implements stochastic variation by adding noise through input latent code, which consumes network capacity. On the other hand, StyleGAN architecture can add per-pixel noise after each convolution.

Style Mixing. StyleGAN uses latent code at each layer of neural networks, which leads to learning process to be more relevant. To reduce the correlation, our model randomly uses two kinds of input vectors and generates the latent code. During the process of training an input code, we would switch to another input code at random. By doing so, we could reduce the correlation. However, it could not increase the performance. Instead, it could generate the images in coherence.

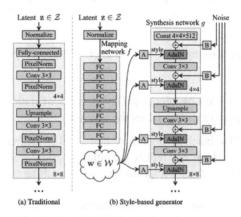

(a) Traditional   (b) Style-based generator

Fig. 3. StyleGAN [2]: style-based generator

Perceptual Path Length. A perceptually based pairwise image distance is a weighted difference between two VGG16 embeddings. If they subdivide a latent space interpolation path into linear segments, they can define the total perceptual length of this segmented path as the sum of perceptual differences over each segment. We use Perceptual Path Length to measure how smooth the latent code can be. In other words, if two images have similar image quality, they should have similarity in latent space. In general, the bad quality of image would be restricted to a small region. The difference between good from bad is the perceptual distance. A long perceptual distance means bad quality in latent space which prevents it from generating nice one.

Linear Separability. Linear separability is an important concept in neural networks. The idea is to check if you can separate points in an n-dimensional space using only $n-1$ dimensions. We start by generating 200 K images with $z \sim P(z)$ and classify them using an auxiliary classification network with label Y. We keep 50% of samples with the highest confidence score. This result in 100k high-score auto-labeled (Y) latent-space vectors z for progressive GAN and w for the Style-GAN. We fit a linear SVM to predict the label X based only on the latent-space point (z and w for the Style-GAN) and classify the points by this plane. Next, we compute the conditional entropy $H(Y \mid X)$ where X represents the classes predicted by the SVM and Y are the classes determined by the classifier. We calculate the separability score as $exp(\Sigma (H(Y \mid X)))$, summing for all the given attributes of the dataset. We basically fit a model for each attribute. Note that the CelebA dataset contains 40 attributes such as gender information.

3 Experiment

3.1 Dataset

In our implementation, we choose CelebA dataset for training. CelebA, as known as CelebFaces Attribute, collects lots of images of celebrities and their face attributes. The data set contains 10,177 distinct celebrities and 202,599 images in total, each image has 40 attribute annotations. It is provided by the Chinese University of Hong Kong and is widely used in some tasks, including face attribute recognition, face recognition, face detection, landmark localization, etc. For our task, we use it to train a model, which can generate fake images according to the input features. We use the aligned and cropped images it provided as our training data and extract 20,000 images for each attribute. By doing this, we can train different model to generate specific image.

3.2 Generation

In the first part, we use DCGAN to generate a fake image. After we extract images for each attribute, we get 40 corresponding folders. In our implementation, it creates a data loader to load the dataset for the specified feature. As for our DCGAN training setting, we use batch_size 128, image_size 64, num_epoch 100, learning_rate 0.0002, beta1 for Adamoptimizer 0.05 and weight initialization from N(0,0.02). Each model takes about 3 ~ 4 h to train, and we can use the trained model to generate fake images as shown in Fig. 4.

Fig. 4. Image generated by our DCGAN

3.3 Style Transfer

In the second part, the images produced in previous stage are transform based on any designated feature. We use an open-source method called TediGAN [3] to achieve our goal. The TediGAN contains three parts: StyleGAN inversion module, visual-linguistic similarity learning, and instance-level optimization. It uses StyleGAN as a method to transfer facial features of an image, and an inversed model as an image encoder, which can map the input image into the latent space of the pretrained StyleGAN. To learn text-to-image matching, it uses a pretrained text encoder, which is called CLIP (Contrastive Language-Image Pre-Training), and the encoder maps the image and text into a common embedding space. The overall flow is to give an input image, subsequently get an encoding result by inversion process, then perform the StyleGAN and CLIP model to get the final images as shown in Fig. 5.

Fig. 5. The result of style transferring. The left image is generated by our DCGAN, after performing two inversions, we can get middle and right images with different facial expressions.

3.4 Demo

Our program can be divided to several steps. First, we need to select a certain feature, which is contained in the CelebA. Then our DCGAN model generates a fake image as shown in Fig. 6. After we get the image, we can select any feature to transfer the image to whatever we expect. The styleGAN can transfer the image based on the input, and we can get the edited image. The process can be repeated until the ideal image is produced as shown in Fig. 7.

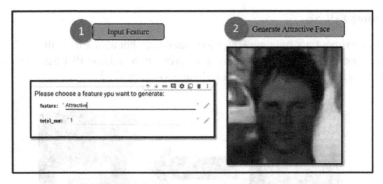

Fig. 6. The process of DCGAN

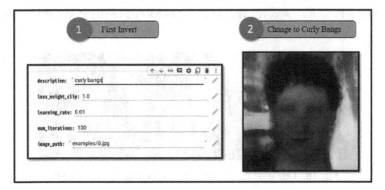

Fig. 7. The process of StyleGAN

3.5 Comparison

For comparison purpose, our generated image is compared with outputted images generated by other GAN including CGAN, attrGAN and progressive GAN as shown in Fig. 8. We can notice that the quality of the images we generated is not very good, compared to the three images generated by other GANs. Nevertheless, further improvements is possible if images can be upgraded with higher resolution.

Fig. 8. The comparison of images generated by DCGAN, cDCGAN, attrGAN and progressive GAN (from left to right)

3.6 Adding PULSE

The last experiment not only generates low resolution but also affects the performance of transferring of style. We try to address the problem by adding PULSE [6] which can generate a high-resolution image by a self-supervised method.

Fig. 9. Adding PULSE to improve quality of image, then we trained the model with higher epoch.

Fig. 10. Our style transferring process before adding PULSE.

Fig. 11. Our style transferring process after adding PULSE

As you can see in Figs. 9, 10 and 11, the quality of images gets much better. In conclusion, out model is highly dependent on input images. By adding PULSE, the quality of our images is successfully improved after the transfer of each layer. It indicates our approach is working properly.

We also observe that the distortion of generated pictures is greater when the times of inversion increases. To address this problem, we add PULSE right after DCGAN and let the resolution increases from 64×64 to 256×256. As shown in Figs. 9, 10 and 11, the distortion becomes insignificant.

3.7 Evaluation

Although we can use GAN to generate a fake image, there is not a perfect criterion to evaluate the model. Because training GAN does not need an objective function, it is hard to measure the difference between real and fake images. Nonetheless, there are still some methods which can judge the quality or diversities of GAN. We plan to conduct the evaluation accordingly in the future.

Inception Score (IS). Inception Score [4] is calculated based on the InceptionNet, it considers the quality and diversities of the generated images. For the quality purpose, it puts a generated image into an InceptionNet to perform classification. If the quality of the image is high, then there would be high probability to be labelled a certain class. On the other hand, the measure of diversity is to generate an enough number of images by the model. Ideally, the number of each category should be similar, or it would be lack of diversity. The formula of Inception Score is in Eq. (2).

$$IS(G) = \exp(E_{\{x \sim p_g\}} D_{KL}(p(y|x)||p(x))) \tag{2}$$

The actual meaning is the difference between the entropy of the distribution function of all generated samples in each category and the entropy of the probability distribution of each sample in each category. Nevertheless, the Inception Score has some limitations. First, high quality images can get a high IS value, but high IS value doesn't assure high quality images. Second, the original calculation needs lots of images to achieve high precision. Third, the InceptionNet is trained on the ImageNet, so the GAN should also use ImageNet to train, or the score has no meaning. Last, Inception Score would not tell us whether the GAN has the overfitting problem.

Frechet Inception Distance Score (FID). FID [7] is a new method proposed as an improvement of IS, it calculates the mean and covariance of the images based on the comparison of the statistics of a set of generated images with the statistics of real images from the target domain. The output of the function is generalized to a multivariate Gaussian distribution. These statistics are then used to calculate the activation functions on the real and generated image sets, and the distance between these two distributions is calculated using the Frechet distance (as known as Wasserstein-2 distance). The formula of FID is in Eq. (3).

$$FID(x, g) = \left|\left|u_x - u_g\right|\right|_2^2 + Tr(\Sigma_x + \Sigma_g - 2(\Sigma_x \Sigma_g)^{\frac{1}{2}}) \tag{3}$$

The smaller the FID, the closer the generated distribution is to the real image.

4 Discussion

We present some advantages and disadvantages regarding the proposed framework.

4.1 Advantages

First, we use DCGAN to train the model. Compared with traditional GAN, DCGAN has the following characteristics [5]:

- model instead of pooling layers; In the generator model, fractional convolutions are used to complete the generation process from random noise to images.
- In addition to the output layer of the generator and the input layer of the corresponding discriminator, the batch normalization is used on other layers in the network structure. In this way, we can fix weak initializations and resolve gradient propagation. In each layer, it also prevents the generator from converging all samples to the same point.
- DCGAN uses various activation functions, such as Adam optimization, ReLU, and Leaky ReLU.

Second, we use StyleGAN for image style transferring. StyleGAN has the following characteristics:

- StyleGAN generates artificial images step-by-step, starting from very low resolutions and going all the way up to high resolutions. By modifying the input at each level in the network separately, it can control the visual features represented at that level, from coarse features such as face pose and shape to fine details such as hair color, without affecting other levels.
- StyleGAN can not only generate high-quality and realistic images, but also enable better control and understanding of the generated images; hence making it easier than ever to generate high-confidence fake images.

4.2 Disadvantages

First, DCGAN has some shortcomings:

- By removing the fully connected layer, and directly using the convolution layer to connect the input and output layers of the generator and discriminator, DCGAN increases the stability of the model but slows down the convergence speed.
- The generator produces a limited variety of samples and is highly sensitive to the selection of hyperparameters.
- Occasionally, the parameters of the model can destabilize and never converge.

Next, StyleGAN also has some disadvantages that can be improved:

- Images generated by StyleGAN contain speckle-like artifacts.
- Many facial details such as teeth, eyes, and other parts are not clear enough.

4.3 Discussion of Our Work

There are some shortcomings and difficulties encountered by the proposed method used in our implementation:

- Instead of generating corresponding images through a full sentence of text description, the current implementation can only accept inputs of a single feature at a time.
- The DCGAN has no way to generate fake pictures of the corresponding features, so we choose to separate the datasets according to the features to train the model and generate fake images.
- The underlying environment is Colab that has some hardware limitations. Hence, there is no way to train too much data, and the effects of the outputs are relatively limited.

On the other hand, the proposed work has some advantages in the real application of crime investigation.

- The criminal investigation process is often highly interactive in the process of describing the face characteristics of a criminal suspect. Therefore, the proposed framework can first propose the most critical characteristics of the criminal suspect, and properly generate a fake image. Then, according to the detailed descriptions of eyewitnesses, the facial features of the suspect are continuously corrected step-by-step to achieve an efficient investigation process.

The proposed work not only can be applied to criminal investigation, but also to games, animations, and novels. The same framework can be used to generate several potential faces as a reference to design the facial appearances of virtual characters.

5 Conclusion

We propose a novel method for criminal suspect face synthesis based on facial attributes. The proposed method unifies two kinds of GANs into a new framework and achieves high controlability and user-friendliness. The DCGAN is applied to effectively synthesize images with selectable features, and the following face-guided manipulation is performed by utilizing StyleGAN. Preliminary experimental results are promising to address the problems of crime investigations in real scenarios.

In the future, we plan to generate images of higher quality and resolution by adopting a high-quality dataset such as CelebA HQ. By doing this, we expect to generate 1028×1028 images with little distortion. Moreover, we will try to extend our current framework by utilizing the NLP method. Instead of using a single feature as input, a long sentence or description can be inputted to reveal more clues of the suspect face and the system can be even more helpful in real scenarios of criminal investigation.

References

1. Radford, A., Metz, L., Chintala, S.: Unsupervised representation learning with deep convolutional generative adversarial networks. arXiv preprint arXiv:1511.06434 (2015)
2. Karras, T., Laine, S., Aila, T.: A style-based generator architecture for generative adversarial networks. In: Proceedings of the IEEE Conference on Computer Vision and Pattern Recognition (2019)

3. Xia, W., Yang, Y., Xue, J., Wu, B.: TediGAN: text-guided diverse face image generation and manipulation. In: Proceedings of the IEEE Conference on Computer Vision and Pattern Recognition (2021)
4. Barratt, S., Sharma, R.: A note on the inception score. arXiv preprint arXiv:1801.01973 (2018)
5. Dewi, C., Chen, R.-C., Liu, Y.-T., Yu, H.: Various generative adversarial networks model for synthetic prohibitory sign image generation. Appl. Sci. **11**(7), 2913 (2021). https://doi.org/10. 3390/app11072913
6. Menon, S., Damian, A., Hu, S., Ravi, N., Rudin, C.: Pulse: self-supervised photo upsampling via latent space exploration of generative models. In: Proceedings of the IEEE conference on computer vision and pattern recognition (2020)
7. Heusel, M., Ramsauer, H., Unterthiner, T., Nessler, B., Hochreiter, S.: GANs trained by a two time-scale update rule converge to a local Nash equilibrium. In: Advances in Neural Information Processing Systems (2017)

Cryptography and Information Security

Automatic Summarization of Critical Threat Intelligence Using Transfer Learning

Chia-Mei Chen[1]([⊠]), Yu-Xuan Wang[1], Zheng- Xun Cai[1], Boyi Lee[1], and Gu- Hsin Lai[2]

[1] National Sun Yat-Sen University, Kaohsiung 804, Taiwan
cmchen@mis.nsysu.edu.tw
[2] Taiwan Police College, Taipei 116, Taiwan

Abstract. The advancement of hacking techniques has extended the sophistication of cyberattacks. Facing evolving cyberattacks, security officers need to acquire information about cyberattacks to gain visibility into the fast-evolving threat landscape. This research proposes a novel threat intelligence summarization system that extracts critical information and produces a summary report. This study combines BERT and BiLSTM and proposes a hybrid word embedding model to capture the critical information in the corpus. The evaluation results show that the proposed system could summarize reports effectively.

Keywords: Cyber threat intelligence · Advanced persistent threat · Natural language processing

1 Introduction

Businesses apply modern information technologies to expand services and improve customer satisfaction; people utilize computers and networks to perform their jobs and daily activities, such as shopping, gaming, news reading, or information searching. In the meantime, they are facing potential cyberattacks. With the growing number of data breaches, businesses are becoming increasingly concerned about cyberattacks that have become one of the most impactful and concerning risks for running businesses globally.

Cyberattacks are becoming more aggressive and widespread in the latest decades. Cyberattacks have been rated the fifth top risk in 2020 and continue growing in recent years [1]. The COVID-19 pandemic is moving the world toward increased remote work and technology innovation, in the meantime, cybercrimes are also on the rise, with a 600% increase [2]. Cyberattacks cause tremendous financial losses every year. The annual loss is approximately over 30 million U.S. dollars for large companies, and about 96,000 for small-to-medium companies [3]. Accompanying the surge of cyberattacks, the number of vulnerabilities has reached another record-high, over 22 thousand discovered last year, and half of application vulnerabilities are high-risk [4].

Cyberattacks have increased in frequency and sophistication, presenting significant challenges for organizations that must defend their data and systems from capable threat attackers. They utilize a variety of tactics, techniques, and procedures (TTPs) to compromise systems, disrupt services, commit financial fraud, and expose or steal intellectual property and other sensitive information. Given the risks these threats present, organizations seek solutions to improve information security and reduce cyberattack risks.

According to a guide to cyber threat information sharing published by the National Institute of Standards and Technology (NIST) [5], cyber threat information or cyber threat intelligence (CTI) is any information that can help an organization identify, assess, monitor, and respond to cyber threats. It covers a wide range of information including indicators of compromise (IoCs), TTPs, suggested actions to detect, contain, or prevent attacks, and the findings from the analyses of incidents. Many organizations focus on specific areas of knowledge. For example, a unit focuses on collecting malicious domains and IPs and another focuses on identifying malware signatures.

TTPs are the patterns of activities or methods associated with a specific threat actor or group of threat actors [6], which help to identify common attack vectors and possible vulnerable systems likely compromised. The CTI data can come from many sources, ranging from threat feeds to external data sources, while external data sources such as cybersecurity news and incident reports contribute over 77% of threat data sources [7].

A summary should contain critical CTI information. Cybersecurity staff needs to acquire a wide range of articles in order to comprehend the information and produce a summary. Such a task is labor-intensive and desires an efficient and automatic threat entity retrieval and summarization method. Therefore, this study proposes a summarization method that provides summarization of a security document.

2 Literature Review

From the perspective of data collection, data can be divided into two categories: indicator-based and document-based. The first is indicator-based data feeds (Indicator Feeds). Indicator-based data feeds mainly share indicators of compromise (IoC) to achieve attack prevention in a short time, including the blacklist IP address, malicious domains, and malware hashes. The document-based data may contain rich and comprehensive threat information than the former one, which requires to apply NLP techniques and analysis models to retrieve them.

MITRE ATT&CK framework [8] is popularly adapted for cybersecurity community to identify attacks and exchange CTI, which is a comprehensive matrix of tactics, techniques, and procedures (TTPs) for classifying attacks and assessing security risk. The ATT&CK Matrix for enterprise consists of 14 tactics defining the "why" part of the framework and including reconnaissance, resource development, initial access, execution, persistence, privilege escalation, defense evasion, credential access, discovery, lateral movement, collection, command and control, exfiltration, and impact, where each tactic contains an array of techniques used by malware or threat actors and a procedure describes the way adversaries or malware implements a technique. The framework has been commonly used by threat hunters, defenders, and CTI sharing to analyze and detect adversaries for illustrating the threat actions that attackers may perform.

Liao et al. [9] presented an automatic IoC extraction method based on the observation that the IoCs are described in a predictable way: being connected to a set of tokens like "download". It generated 900K IoC items with a precision of 95% and a coverage of over 90%. Kurogome et al. [10] proposed an automatic malware signature generation system from given malware samples, and the evaluation demonstrated that the produced IOCs are as interpretable as manually-generated ones.

Benjamin and Chen [11] utilized recurrent neural network language models (RNNLMs) coupled with methodology from lexical semantics for learning hacker language. They demonstrated that RNNLMs can be used to develop the capability for understanding hacker language and different embedding models may impact the performance of the machine learning model.

Deliu et al. [12] explored the potential of Machine Learning methods to retrieve relevant threat information from hacker forums and compared the text classification performance of a modern ML approach, CNN (Convolutional Neural Network), against a traditional ML approach, SVM (Support Vector Machines). They concluded that SVM performs equally well as CNN.

3   The Proposed Method

In order to make sure that the generated summarization contains the most critical CTI information, this study proposes a summarization method. Figure 1 overviews the major components of the proposed summarization method.

As mentioned in the introduction, the critical CTI information considered in this study includes attack tactics, technologies, procedures, threat actions (attack behaviors), threat actors (hacker groups), attack targets (victims), attack time and location, explored vulnerabilities, and vulnerable platforms or applications. To extract critical CTI information, this study adopts TAminer [13] to extract threat actions and develops a BERT-BiLSTM model to extract threat entities.

The past research on NER mainly adopted text annotation with BIO scheme labeling self-defined entity classes and built a text classification model with the labeled data. In the NER model building, a set of training data is collected and threat entities are annotated in BIO tagging. This study adopts a transformer model, BERT, to perform word embedding and BiLSTM to extract threat entities.

The collected data is used for training and evaluation, where it is achieved by developing a web crawler to gather security-related documents from cybersecurity news websites. Common NLP techniques are adopted to reduce the feature dimension, including tokenization, stop word removal, stemming, and lemmatization. This study adopts the stop word list provided by the NLTK (Natural Language Toolkit) [15] and the NLTK Tokenize package. This study defines the named entity classes (threat entity classes) and labels data in BIO tagging. For feature embedding, a pre-trained model, BERT is added to the BiLSTM model as the feature representation layer and is used to generate word vectors.

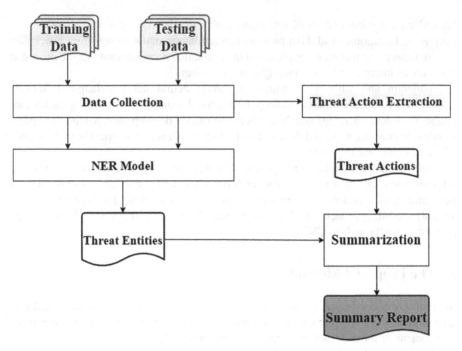

Fig. 1. The proposed system architecture.

4 System Evaluation

The study designs an experiment that evaluates the quality of the proposed summarization method with human-generated summary. Exp 5 adopts ROUGE to evaluate summarization performance.

The past research on summarization applied ROUGE (Recall-Oriented Understudy for Gisting Evaluation) [16] metrics to assess the quality of automatically produced summary by comparing it against the reference summaries created by humans.

The training datasets are categorized into two types: cybersecurity reports and cybersecurity news, where the former is sourced from APTNotes [14] and the latter is collected from the popular cybersecurity vendor's websites. APTNotes have acquired comprehensive APT attack investigation reports published by cybersecurity companies, which explain attack chains and threat actions in detail. This study selected and annotated 10 representative reports from APTNotes that were divided into 8:2 for training and testing.

This study developed a web crawler to collect cybersecurity news articles published from January 2020 to March 2021. This study randomly selected 50 articles and labelled them. The annotated data was further divided in 8:2 for training and testing.

This experiment investigates the performance of the proposed summarization method. To evaluate the summarization quality, three cybersecurity analysts provided reference summaries and verified the automatically generated summaries manually. The produced summarization obtained ROUGE score of 88%.

5   Conclusion

Acquiring cyber threat knowledge is essential for organizations to gain visibility into the fast-evolving threat landscape. Identifying key threat entities and threat actions play an important role in disseminating threat information and correlate significantly with the number of cyber-attacks observed in the real world. Furthermore, text summarization skeletons important CTI information. The case study of the produced summary report demonstrates the usefulness and novelty of the proposed solution.

The past research on CTI exploring word vector language models was limited, and that on summarization most provide textual summarization. The novelty of this study includes applying a pre-trained model, BERT, to automatically extract critical CTI information and producing a summary report. The evaluation demonstrates that the produced summarization is valid.

As this research focuses on retrieving threat actions, other pieces of CTI information might be useful for attack prevention. Exploring the relationships among adversaries, victims, and threat actions is another possible research direction for understanding the correlations of these parties.

References

1. Embroker Team. 2022 Must-Know Cyber Attack Statistics and Trends. https://www.emb roker.com/blog/cyber-attack-statistics/. Accessed 4 July 2022
2. The Associated Press: The Latest: UN warns cybercrime on rise during pandemic. https://abcnews.go.com/Health/wireStory/latest-india-reports-largest-single-day-virus-spike-708 26542. Accessed 5 July 2022
3. Microsoft: Cybersecurity threats to cost organizations in Asia Pacific US$1.75 trillion in economic losses (2018). https://news.microsoft.com/apac/2018/05/18/cybersecurity-threats-to-cost-organizations-in-asia-pacific-us1-75-trillion-in-economic-losses/. Accessed 20 June 2022
4. O'Driscoll, A.: 25+ cyber security vulnerability statistics and facts of 2022. https://www.com paritech.com/blog/information-security/cybersecurity-vulnerability-statistics/. Accessed 5 July 2022
5. Johnson, C., Badger, M., Waltermire, D., Snyder, J., Skorupka, C.: Guide to cyber threat information sharing. National Institute of Standards and Technology (2016)
6. Friedman, J., Bouchard, M.: Definitive Guide to Cyber Threat Intelligence. https://cryptome.org/2015/09/cti-guide.pdf. Accessed 11 Nov 2022
7. Brown, R., Lee, R.M.: SANS Cyber Threat Intelligence (CTI) Survey (2021). https://www.cybersixgill.com/wp-content/uploads/2021/02/SANS_CTI_Survey_2021_Sixgill.pdf
8. Saremi, A., Jula, P., ElMekkawy, T., Wang, G.G.: Appointment scheduling of outpatient surgical services in a multistage operating room department. Int. J. Prod. Econ. **141**(2), 646–658 (2013)
9. Liao, X., Yuan, K., Wang, X., Li, Z., Xing, L., Beyah, R.: Acing the ioc game: toward automatic discovery and analysis of open-source cyber threat intelligence. In: Proceedings of the 2016 ACM SIGSAC Conference on Computer and Communications Security, pp. 755–766 (2016)
10. Kurogome, Y., et al.: EIGER: automated IOC generation for accurate and interpretable endpoint malware detection. In: Proceedings of the 35th Annual Computer Security Applications Conference, pp. 687–701 (2019)

11. Benjamin, V., Chen, H.: Developing understanding of hacker language through the use of lexical semantics. In: 2015 IEEE International Conference on Intelligence and Security Informatics (ISI) , pp. 79–84. IEEE (2015)
12. Deliu, I., Leichter, C., Franke, K.: Extracting cyber threat intelligence from hacker forums: support vector machines versus convolutional neural networks. In: 2017 IEEE International Conference on Big Data (Big Data) , pp. 3648–3656. IEEE (2017)
13. Chen, C.-M., Kan, J.-Y., Ou, Y.-H., Cai, Z.-X., Guan, A.: Threat Action Extraction using Information Retrieval, pp. 13–19 (2021)
14. kbandla: Aptnotes. https://github.com/aptnotes/data. Accessed 11 Nov 2020
15. Natural Language Toolkit. https://www.nltk.org/. Accessed 1 May 2020
16. Lin, C.-Y.: Rouge: A package for automatic evaluation of summaries. In: Text summarization branches out, pp. 74–81 (2004)

Anti-screenshot Watermarking Algorithm About Archives Image Based on Deep Learning Model

Wei Gu[1], Ching-Chun Chang[2], Yu Bai[3], Yunyuan Fan[3], Liang Tao[1], and Li Li[3(✉)]

[1] Anhui University, Hefei 230039, China
[2] University of Warwick, Coventry CV47AL, UK
[3] Hangzhou Dianzi University, Hangzhou 310018, China
`lili2008@hdu.edu.cn`

Abstract. In recent years, there are an increasing number of incidents in which archives images have been ripped. Leak tracking is possible by adding an anti-screenshot digital watermark to an archive image. However, because an archives image's texture is single, there is a problem of low detection rate of watermark with the existing algorithm. So in order to improve the robustness of archives image anti-screenshot, we propose an anti-screenshot deep learning model (DLM): ScreenNet. It aims to enhance the background and enrich the texture with style transfer. Firstly, a preprocessing process based on style transfer is added before the archives image is input into the encoder. Secondly, the ripped images usually have moiré, so we generate a database of ripped archives images with moiré by means of a moiré network. Lastly, by improving the Stagstamp model, the watermark information is encoded/decoded through the improved ScreenNet model using the ripped archives image database as the noise layer. The experiment proves that the algorithm is able to resist anti-screenshot attacks and achieve the ability to detect watermark information to leak trace of ripped images.

Keywords: Anti-Screenshot · Deep Learning Model · Archives image · Watermarking

1 Introduction

An image watermarking algorithm should have strong robustness because the watermarked image may be attacked in the transmission process. Common attacks include cropping, compression, Gaussian noise and so on, all of which may change the pixel value of the watermarked image, and then the watermark information cannot be extracted smoothly. Screenshot attack is a very complex image attack that includes perspective deformation and moiré pattern. In this paper, the noise between the screen and the camera exists commonly. However, the traditional robust watermarking algorithm shows poor robustness, so it is necessary to introduce a DLM to improve the performance of the algorithm.

In recent years, DLM has been widely applied in computer vision, natural language processing and other fields. Researchers also explore image watermarking algorithm based on DLM. Zhu et al. [1] that initiated the HiDDeN model in 2018. The model introduces a variety of noises between the encoder and decoder to improve the robustness of the auto-encoder. However, it cannot effectively resist the problems of moiré attack, perspective deformation and color transformation. In order to simulate screenshot attacks in real scenes, Wengwowski et al. [2] proposed the light field messaging (LFM) system in 2019. LFM specially trains a network to simulate the effect of cover image to screenshot process. Although LFM has a good effect on screenshot attacks, it has limitations for print attacks. In 2020, Matthew et al. [3] proposed the Stegastamp model. It was applied to simulate the distortion caused by print attack and screenshot attack. But it does not add the cropping noise layer. Therefore, the image cropping attack has limitations, which leads to the poor quality of dense image.

Above all, with this paper we propose a robust archives image watermarking algorithm based on the Stegastamp model. The algorithm structure includes five parts: the preprocessing network is mainly applied to add color and texture to the archives image. The encoder is mainly applied to embed the watermark information into the cover image successfully. It also minimizes the difference between the watermark image and the cover image, and finally generates the watermark image with good visual quality. The Stegastamp noise layer is designed to distribute the watermark image generated by the encoder to simulate the effect of a screenshot attack. The purpose of the moiré network is to further add real moiré to the disturbed watermarked image. The decoder is to extract watermark information from the moiré-watermarked image. The main innovations of this paper are as follows:

1. A style transfer network is applied to improve the richness of background texture about archives image, and then improve the robustness of the image watermarking algorithm.
2. A moiré network is constructed to produce the moiré archives image dataset. In addition, moiré images taken in realistic environments were added to build a rich database of screenshot images.
3. The anti-screenshot capability of the Stegastamp model is improved by placing these datasets in the noise layer. It solves the problem of lack of standard moiré dataset in digital watermarking field.

2 Stegastamp Model

Recently, plenty of learning-based algorithms leverage encoder and decoder to embed different kinds of watermark in images. Among these algorithms is the Stegastamp. Stegastamp is a DLM for screenshot watermarking. This model applies DLM to the screenshot watermarking algorithm by modeling more realistic distortions of water-marked image. Firstly, the cover image and the expanded watermarked sequence are fed to the encoder. Then, the watermarked image output from the encoder goes through the printing and screenshot process. To improve the robustness of the algorithm, during the model training, watermarked image is added with some attacks by the noise layer, examples of which include: Perspective warp, Motion/defocus blur, Color manipulation, Noise and JPEG compression. The noise layer makes the watermarked image closer to the real application scenario. Therefore, the decoder can robustly decode the watermarked image even during the screenshot process. The decoder locates, corrects and extracts the watermarked image in the captured image to form the corrected image. Finally, the decoder extracts the watermark information from the corrected image.

However, the StegaStamp model is vulnerable for having visible noise on the watermarked image during the encoding process, which very unfavorable for archives images with a single color background, so that it reduces the robustness and imperceptibility of the watermarking algorithm. Therefore, the algorithmic performance of the StegaStamp model for archives images needs to be improved.

3 Proposed Algorithm

The algorithmic flow chart is shown in Fig. 1. The first stage is preprocessing of cover image. The input 100 bit watermark information is fully connected to get the tensor. And then the tensor is upsampled to make the size consistent with the image size after preprocessing. After a series of convolution operations, the watermark is embedded into watermarked image. Then the noise layer simulates the screenshot attack in the real scene with watermarked image. After the watermarked image with noise is attacked by real moiré, the decoder extracts the watermark information through a series of convolution operations and fully connects.

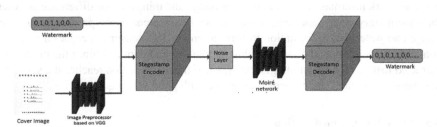

Fig. 1. Overall flow chart of algorithm

3.1 Archives Image Preprocessing

An archives image has a large range of single background. This is very disadvantageous for watermarking because the watermarking in a single background will be very conspicuous, which makes the algorithmic imperceptibility terrible. Therefore, the archives image needs to be preprocessed before being input into the model. In this work, we apply the style transfer algorithm to preprocess the archives image. This makes the archives image to add different colors and textures, which is more conducive to embed image watermark, improving both the imperceptibility and robustness of the algorithm. The structure of the algorithm is shown in Fig. 2.

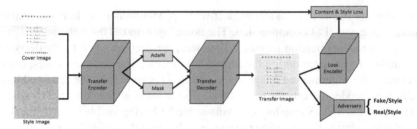

Fig. 2. The flowchart of archives image preprocessing

The preprocessing model applies the trained VGG network [4] as the encoder to extract features. The structure of the transfer encoder and loss encoder are identical. They cover and output the features of different levels of convolution layer by jumping connection. Then adaptive instance normalization (AdaIN) is applied to adjust the first-order and second-order statistics of features. And the spatial mask automatically adjusts the level of stylization. The structure of the decoder is basically symmetrical to the encoder, and it needs to be trained from the beginning. The discriminator is used to predict the style types of the image and distinguish the authenticity of the transfer image at the same time.

3.2 Encoder Construction

Encoder's architecture is similar to the U-net [5]. The encoder is mainly applied to embed the watermark information into the transfer image and minimize the difference between the watermarked image and the transfer image. It concatenates the preprocessed cover image and watermark information to form a tensor. This tensor undergoes a series of convolution, pooling, and downsampling operations, and then combines the previously extracted features for upsampling. Finally, when the loss function reaches the standard, the encoder generates the watermarked image with good visual quality.

3.3 Noise Layer Construction

The noise layer is consistent with the Stegastamp cover noise layer. Different from the design of Stegastamp model noise layer, the noise layer of Stegastamp model mainly contains six different types of noise attacks, such as cropping, Gaussian noise, JPEG compression and so on. No suitable differentiable function has been designed to simulate the attack types generated in the screenshot process. Stegastamp's noise layer is designed to resist the attacks generated in the screenshot process and printing process. In this work we regard these attacks as the superposition of a series of attacks, including perspective deformation, motion and defocusing blur, color transformation, Gaussian noise and JPEG compression.

3.4 Moiré Network Construction

In this work we first apply the standard dataset in the field of Moiré removal, which was proposed by Sun et al. [6] in 2015. This dataset contains 100,000 pairs of cover images and moiré images. We select 6,000 pairs of images as the training set. On this basis, in order to improve the robustness of the watermarking algorithm in the archives image, we add some archival images into the dataset. The dataset image is shown in Fig. 3.

Fig. 3. Example of our dataset image

In this paper, we propose a novel moiré network to improve the robustness of the algorithm by adding realistic moiré disturbance to the watermarked image. Unlike the cover Stegastamp noise layer using differentiable functions to simulate screenshot attacks, the moiré network does not apply the established functions to learn attacks, but applies the learning characteristics of convolutional neural network (CNN) to learn the moiré attacks in realistic scenes.

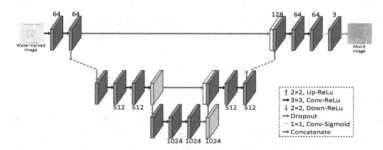

Fig. 4. Structure of moiré network

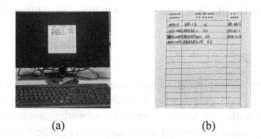

(a)   (b)

Fig. 5. Collection and correction of moiré image (a) Screen image (b) Correct image

Figure 4 shows the network structure of the moiré network, which applies U-net for reference. The network architecture consists of three parts: the encoding stage on the left, the decoding stage on the right and the hop connection. The encoding stage is used to down sample the cover image and extract high-level semantic information. The decoding stage is used to decode high-level semantic features and generate the final moiré image after moiré attack. Jump join is used to fuse the features of the two stages to make the result more accurate. Because of the weak moiré in this dataset, we used iPhone 8, Hongmi K30 and Huawei hi nova9 mobile phones to collect the moiré image dataset. Five hundred images were randomly selected from Div2k dataset [7] and displayed on the screen for camera shooting. The display monitor is HP N246v. The distance and angle of the mobile phone shooting are shown in Fig. 5. The distance between the mobile phone and the monitor is about 20 ~ 30cm. An example of the image pair of the self-built moire dataset is shown in Fig. 6. In order to improve the generalization ability of moiré network, the collected 2,000 pairs of images are augmented [8].

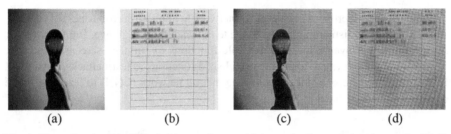

(a)   (b)   (c)   (d)

Fig. 6. Example of self-built moiré image dataset. (a) is a color image belonging to the Div2k dataset. (b)is a archives image. (c) and (d) are the corrected images after screenshot, respectively.

3.5 Decoder Construction

The decoder is applied to extract the watermark from the moiré image. Some geometric attacks may be encountered in the transmission of moiré images. In order to increase the robustness of geometric attacks and improve the accuracy of watermark extraction, some preprocessing is needed before watermark from the moiré image is extracted. Therefore, a spatial transformation network (STN) is used in the decoder, which can learn in an end-to-end manner without changing the loss function and improve the performance of the model.

3.6 Model Training

DLM needs to select the appropriate loss function to guide network training. The loss function carries on the back propagation through the error between the predicted sample and the real sample. It also guides the learning of network parameters. In this paper, we choose different loss functions for different sub-networks. The MSE mean square error loss function and LPIPS sensing loss function [9] are applied in the encoder, which are recorded as L_{R1} and L_P. MSE loss function and LPIPS perceived loss function are shown in Eqs. (1) and (2), respectively.

$$L_{R1}\left(I_{\text{Cover}}, I_{\text{Stego}}\right) = \frac{1}{C \times H \times W}\left\|I_{\text{Cover}} - I_{\text{Stego}}\right\|_2^2 \qquad (1)$$

$$L_P(I_{\text{Cover}}, I_{\text{Stego}}) = \sum_l \frac{1}{H_l W_l} \sum_{h,w} \left\| w_l \times \left(\hat{y}^l - \hat{y}_0^l \right) \right\|_2^2 \tag{2}$$

where I_{Cover} is the cover image, and I_{Stego} is the image with watermark. l feature maps are extracted from the layer and normalized in channel dimension $\hat{y}^l \in R^{H_l \times W_l \times C_l}$ and $\hat{y}_0^l \in R^{H_l \times W_l \times C_l}$. Compute distance L_2 by scaling activations in the channel dimension by $W_l \in R^{C_l}$. Finally, average the distance in space and sum in channel dimension.

The loss function L_{R2} of moiré network applies MSE, which is shown in Eq. (3).

$$L_{R2}(I_{\text{Cover}}, I_{\text{Screen}}) = \frac{1}{C \times H \times W} \| I_{\text{Cover}} - I_{\text{Screen}} \|_2^2 \tag{3}$$

where I_{Screen} is the watermarked image after moiré attack.

The decoder uses the cross entropy loss function L_M[10], which is widely applied in classification tasks. The formula for L_M is shown in Eq. (4).

$$L_M(M, M') = -\frac{1}{N} \sum_{i=1}^{N} \left[M_i \log(M_i') + (1 - M_i) \log(1 - M_i') \right] \tag{4}$$

where M is the cover watermark information, and M' is the extracted watermark information. N is the capacity of image watermark. The total loss function L of the model is shown in Eq. (5)

$$L = \lambda_{R1} L_{R1} + \lambda_P L_P + \lambda_{R2} L_{R2} + \lambda_M L_M \tag{5}$$

where $\lambda_{R1}, \lambda_P, \lambda_{R2}, \lambda_M$ are the parameters of corresponding loss function.

Finally, the encoder, moiré network and decoder are trained against each other, which make the model iterate continuously until convergence [11].

4 Experimental Results

4.1 Experimental Environment and Settings

ScreenNet is the robust watermarking algorithm based on standard moiré dataset and custom moiré dataset. The dataset of confrontation training is MIRFLICKR [12]. In this work, 20,000 images are selected for training, and the image size is adjusted to 400 × 400. From the MIRFLICKR dataset, 1,000 images that do not intersect with the training set are selected to form the verification set to evaluate the robustness under common noise attacks.

Watermark bit is a random sequence composed of 0 and 1. As shown in Table 1, an increase in watermark information bits will lead to the decline of PSNR and SSIM. Based on the comprehensive consideration of watermark capacity and image quality, 100 bit watermark information is selected to embed into the cover image.

Table 1. PSNR and SSIM of watermarked image with different watermark capacity

Evaluation standards	50 bits	100 bits	150 bits	200 bits
PSNR	30.43	30.02	28.87	23.48
SSIM	0.923	0.919	0.845	0.808

In this work, the accuracy of extracting watermark information is used to evaluate the robustness of the algorithm against screen shot attack. The formula of accuracy is shown in Eq. (6)

$$Accuracy = 1 - BER \tag{6}$$

4.2 Performance Comparison Before and After Preprocessing

This section compares the performance before and after the archives image preprocessing. Figure 7 shows the cover archives image and the preprocessed archives image. We can observe that the preprocessed archives image can still identify the text and color of the archives image. After preprocessing, the archives image is closer to the archives image stored in real life.

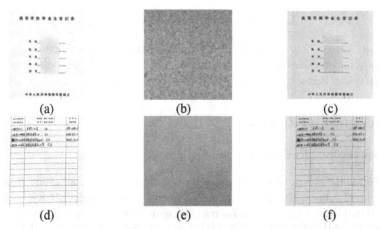

Fig.7. Archives images before and after preprocessing. (a) and (d) are archives images. (b) and (e) are two style images. (c) and (f) are their corresponding transfer images.

4.3 Network Training Speed Comparison

Inspired by the CDTF network in LFM, with this paper we propose a novel moiré network. Based on this, the ScreenNet algorithm is proposed. Due to the addition of the

Table 2. Network performance comparison

Method	Iteration time	Per iteration time (s)	Total time (min)
Stegastamp	140000	0.185	432
ScreenNet	140000	0.244	569

moiré network in Stegastamp model, the overall network architecture is more complex such that ScreenNet algorithm has slower convergence speed compared to Stegastamp model.

Table 2 shows the training speed comparison between Stegastamp and ScreenNet. Compared with Stegastamp model, the training time of ScreenNet is 2.5 h longer. In the follow-up work, we need to standardize the data and select the appropriate learning rate to improve the training speed.

4.4 Noise Robustness Comparison

In this section, five common noise attacks are applied to evaluate the robustness of ScreenNet model. As shown in Fig. 8, the five images in the first line are watermark images output by ScreenNet model. The five images in the second line are the noisy images after the watermarked image is attacked. The five images in the last row are difference images between the watermarked image and the noisy image. The watermarked image is marked as I_{en}. The noise graph after the attack is marked as I_{no}. The residual diagram is I_{re}. Their relationship is shown in Eq. (7)

$$I_{re} = |I_{en} - I_{no}| \tag{7}$$

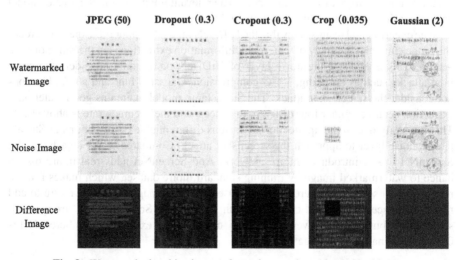

Fig. 8. Watermarked archive image after noise attack and its residual image

As shown in Table 3, five common noise attacks used in hidden are selected as the basis for evaluating robustness, including JPEG Compression (50), Dropout (0.3), Cropout (0.3), Crop (0.035) and Gaussian (2). The numbers in brackets represent the noise intensity. It can be observed from Table 3 that the accuracy of the ScreenNet model is robust of cropout, dropout, Gaussian and JPEG compression. And this table shows excellent robustness of the algorithm. But for crop attacks, accuracy is only about 60%. The main reason is that the cover noise layer of Stegastamp does not consider the situation of crop attack in the training process, so the differentiable function is not applied to simulate this process. As a result, the watermark information is almost covered in the whole cover image, and a large amount of watermark information will be lost when the cropping attack is carried out.

Table 3. Comparison of accuracy under different noise attacks

Attack	Attack range	Stegastamp	ScreenNet
JPEG compression	20	0.9988	0.9931
Dropout	0.3	0.9594	0.9963
Cropout	0.3	0.8244	0.8673
Crop	0.05	0.6048	0.6405
Gaussian	2	0.9974	0.9823

4.5 Robustness Comparison of Screenshot at Different Distances

In this section, experiments are conducted on the robustness of HiDDeN, Stegastamp, ScreenNet model from different distances. The relevant images of the ScreenNet model anti-screenshot experiment are shown in Table 4.

The experimental results show that the HiDDeN model has poor robustness to screenshot attack, and the accuracy of watermark information extraction is in the range of 69% ~ 83%. This is because the noise layer of HiDDeN model only considers the common attacks such as cropping, JPEG compression, Gaussian blur and so on, but does not consider the screen shot attack. The Stegastamp model maintains good watermark extraction accuracy under four different distances, and the accuracy rate is above 92%. This is mainly due to the application of various differentiable perturbations in Stegastamp's noise layer to approach the screenshot attack. Compared with Stegastamp, the ScreenNet model introduces moiré network. And ScreenNet adds real moiré disturbance to watermarked image by training standard moiré dataset, which makes it more robust against screenshot. ScreenNet also uses archives image dataset of moiré to add real disturbances. Therefore, compared with Stegastamp, ScreenNet has stronger anti screenshot robustness. The average accuracy of watermark extraction with ScreenNet is 0.9% higher than that of Stegastamp.

Table 4. Accuracy comparison of screenshot attack at different distances

Distance	20cm	30cm	40cm	50cm
Water-marked Image				
Corrected Image				
HiDDeN	0.8274	0.7966	0.7576	0.6978
Stegastamp	0.9658	0.9508	0.9267	0.9286
ScreenNet	0.9739	0.9763	0.9969	0.9790

4.6 Robustness Comparison of Screen Shots at Different Angles

In this experiment, we selected different perspective angles to take screenshots for water-marked images. The relevant experimental result are shown in Table 5. The experimental results show that the HiDDeN model has poor robustness to screenshot attack under different perspective angles. The accuracy rate of watermark information extraction is less than 60%. The Stegastamp model also maintains good watermark extraction accuracy under different perspective angles, and its extraction accuracy of watermark information

Table 5. Accuracy comparison of screen shot attack under different angle

Angle	30 ° down	45 ° down	30 ° up	45 ° up
Water-marked Image				
Corrected Image				
HiDDeN	0.5964	0.5634	0.5830	0.5591
Stegastamp	0.7857	0.9831	0.8197	0.7906
ScreenNet	0.9713	0.9883	0.9794	0.9873

reaches about 85% of ScreenNet. Under different perspective angles, the accuracy of watermark extraction in ScreenNet network is slightly higher than that of Stegastamp. Because ScreenNet applies the self-built moiré dataset with more obvious moiré traces, the accuracy of watermark information extraction is improved. It can be observed that the ScreenNet algorithm is more robust to screenshoot.

5 Conclusion

In this paper, a robust screenshot watermarking auto-encoder ScreenNet based on Stegastamp model is proposed. It is mainly composed of the encoder, noise layer, moiré network and decoder. Different from the previous anti-screenshot robust watermarking algorithms based on CNN, we no longer use differentiable functions to simulate the moiré noise in real scenes. Instead, we train the constructed moiré network by removing the standard moiré dataset and the self-built moiré dataset, so as to add real moiré noise to the cover image. The experimental results show that the watermark image generated by the model has strong robustness against screeshot attacks at different distances and perspective angles, and has high watermark information extraction accuracy, which can effectively solve some practical problems.

Acknowledgments. This work was partially supported by National Natural Science Foundation of China (No. 62172132) and Science and Technology Projects of National Archives Administration of China (No. 2020-X-058).

References

1. Zhu, J., Kaplan, R., Johnson, J., Li, F.-F.: HiDDeN: hiding data with deep networks. In: Ferrari, V., Hebert, M., Sminchisescu, C., Weiss, Y. (eds.) Computer Vision – ECCV 2018: 15th European Conference, Munich, Germany, September 8-14, 2018, Proceedings, Part XV, pp. 682–697. Springer International Publishing, Cham (2018). https://doi.org/10.1007/978-3-030-01267-0_40
2. Wengrowski, E., Dana, K.: Light field messaging with deep photographic steganography. In: IEEE Conference on Computer Vision and Pattern Recognition, pp.1515–1524 (2019)
3. Tancik, M., Mildenhall, B., Ng, R.: Stegastamp: invisible hyperlinks in physical photographs. In: IEEE Conference on Computer Vision and Pattern Recognition, pp. 2117–2126 (2020)
4. Simonyan, K., Zisserman, A.: Very deep convolutional networks for large-scale image recognition. arXiv preprint arXiv:1409.1556 (2014)
5. Ronneberger, O., Fischer, P., Brox, T.: U-net: convolutional networks for biomedical image segmentation. In: Navab, N., Hornegger, J., Wells, W.M., Frangi, A.F. (eds.) Medical Image Computing and Computer-Assisted Intervention — MICCAI 2015. LNCS, vol. 9351, pp. 234–241. Springer, Cham (2015). https://doi.org/10.1007/978-3-319-24574-4_28
6. Sun, Y., Yu, Y., Wang, W.: Moiré photo restoration using multiresolution convolutional neural networks. IEEE Trans. Image Process. **23**(2), 4160–4172 (2018)
7. Agustsson, E., Timofte, R.: NTIRE 2017 challenge on single image super-resolution: dataset and study. In: IEEE Conference on Computer Vision and Pattern Recognition Workshops, pp.1122–1131 (2017)

8. Cubuk, E.D., Zoph, B., Mane, D., Vasudevan, V., Le, Q.V.: AutoAugment: Learning augmentation policies from data. In: IEEE Conference on Computer Vision and Pattern Recognition, pp.113–123 (2019)

9. Zhang, R., Isola, P., Efros, A.A., Shechtman, E., Wang, O.: The unreasonable effectiveness of deep features as a perceptual metric. In: IEEE Conference on Computer Vision and Pattern Recognition, pp. 586–595 (2018)

10. Li, L., Doroslovacki, M., Loew, M.H.: Approximating the gradient of cross-entropy loss function. IEEE Access **8**(1), 111626–111635 (2020)

11. Li, X.-W., et al.: Area-Preserving hierarchical NURBS surfaces computed by the optimal freeform transformation. Comput. Aided Des. **143**, 103134 (2022). https://doi.org/10.1016/j.cad.2021.103134

12. Huiskes, M.J., Lew, M.S.: The MIR flickr retrieval evaluation. In: ACM International Conference on Multimedia Information Retrieval, pp.39–46 (2008)

Detecting Android Malware by Combining System Call Sequence Relationships with Local Feature Calculation

Chien-Hui Hung$^{(\boxtimes)}$, Yi-ming Chen, and Chao-Ching Wu

Department of Information Management, National Central University, Taoyuan City, Taiwan
u2020050@gmail.com, {cym,109423077}@cc.ncu.edu.tw

Abstract. Android, the most popular operating system in the mobile market, is the main target of hackers. The dynamic analysis in malware analysis is not affected by obfuscation and dynamic loading attacks. Therefore, this study uses a dynamic detection approach and uses system calls as a feature to represent the behaviour of an application. The TF-IDF feature processing method can assign different weights to the system call features according to the number of occurrences and the overall relationship, but this method uses one system call as a unit and therefore does not calculate the pre- and post- sequence relationships, which are important in system call sequences. This study uses the concept of n-grams to form system call groups combined with local TF-IDF to allow sequence-based data to be characterised by the pre-post relationship and importance of the sequences, and to analyse Android applications on a deep learning model that has shown excellent classification results in the field of malware detection. In this study, it is shown that this method improves the accuracy of multiple classification of apps by more than 3% and 11% for the unknown 2019 dataset.

Keywords: Android malware analysis · Dynamic analysis · System call sequences · Sequence relationships · Deep learning

1 Introduction

In the information age, mobile devices have become inseparable from life, from recording personal information to connecting with the world through mobile devices. According to Kaspersky [1], more than 670,000 malware APKs were detected in the third quarter of 2021, and malware detection is particularly important as it threatens users' privacy. Its open source nature and ease of download and installation on third-party platforms make it a target for hackers.

In the field of malware detection, the analysis methods are mainly divided into static analysis and dynamic analysis.

Static analysis: The method uses various anti- compilation tools to obtain relevant features, such as permissions, API calls, etc., and then uses the features to classify the malware.

© The Author(s), under exclusive license to Springer Nature Singapore Pte Ltd. 2022
S.-Y. Hsieh et al. (Eds.): ICS 2022, CCIS 1723, pp. 362–373, 2022.
https://doi.org/10.1007/978-981-19-9582-8_32

Dynamic analysis: In order to avoid endangering the real mobile device through actual execution, a common method is to install the application in a sandbox to simulate the user's behaviour by triggering events, and then obtain the records generated during execution. The relevant features, such as system calls,network traffic activities…, are later processed and classified as described in MADAM [3], where system calls describe the lowest level of behaviour in the device, making it difficult to hide malicious behaviour through encryption or obfuscation.

Although static analysis is faster, as mentioned in [4], many malicious applications use techniques such as bytecode encryption, reflection and native code execution to avoid static analysis, so this study uses dynamic analysis and features common System calls.

In recent years, deep learning has excelled in various fields due to the advancement of computing power. Therefore, the advantage of analyzing through deep learning methods is that it only requires a lot of hardware resources and algorithms to automatically learn the important relationships of features through neurons in neural networks, learn different sample key features by themselves and assign weights to them, thus reducing the time spent on processing features manually.

In this study, System calls in dynamic analysis are used as extracted features to detect Android applications, while this paper combines the sequence relationship of system calls with local feature calculation method [5] and then combines with deep learning to analyze the application, the contribution of this study is as follows.

- A method is proposed to enhance the information presentation of sequence-based data using a combination of pre- and post-sequence sequential relationships and local features to allow the model to learn more information about sequence-based data, and to experimentally validate the effectiveness of the method to demonstrate that it can improve the accuracy of detection applications.
- The proposed approach to detect datasets of unknown vintage and to demonstrate that models that learn more characteristic relationships can more accurately classify classes of applications when detecting unknown datasets compared to features that do not consider serial relationship.

2 Related Work

2.1 Related Studies on Extraction of Features

Android is Linux-based, and system calls are connected to the kernel. In order to prevent harming the real device, there are ways to use emulators to do this, such as AndroPyTool [6], which proposes an extraction tool that integrates dynamic and static analysis. In the dynamic analysis part, DroidBox [7] is used to simulate the user's behaviour, and during the execution process, the system calls generated by the application are recorded by Strace and subsequently exported in csv format.

2.2 Related Studies on Long Series Features

As mentioned in [8], when the length of a sequence exceeds 120, it is called a long sequence. Long sequence features can cause problems, such as the disappearance of gradients in RNN-based models. Feature selection [9]: Feature selection algorithms such as Correlation-based Feature Selection, Chi Square, Information Gain, etc. are used to select the key features that have a greater impact. The truncation approach [10]: setting all sequences to a fixed length uniformly, and deleting more than one, also loses many features, so how to effectively process the original raw sequence while retaining important feature information is an important study in using sequence-based features for analysis. The subsequence method [5] is a method that retains all sequence information and is divided into two types, the Fixed Length Subsequence (FLS) method and the Evenly Partition Subsequence (EPS) method.

- Fixed Length Subsequence (FLS) method: the original system call sequence is sliced by a fixed length L_F so that the number of subsequences to be cut varies according to the L_F The number of subsequences will vary according to the length.
- Evenly Partition Subsequence (EPS) method: divides the original sequence into S_N into subsequences, where S_N is a custom variable, so that the number of subsequences can be controlled.

As mentioned in [5], EPS is independent of the length of the original sequence and can be used as a feature computation method by formulating the number of variables in the subsequence on demand. S_N Unlike [11] where only the number of uses is counted, the system calls in each subsequence are also taken into account to present the differences in features, as shown in Fig. 1, allowing the model to learn more effectively.

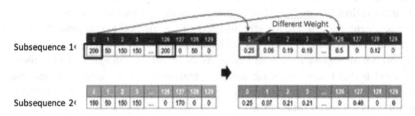

Fig. 1. Schematic diagram of the difference in weighting values (Image source: [5])

However, this approach neglects the information brought by the order relationship within the subsequence, which is mentioned in Xie et al. (Fig. 2).

Xie et al. [12] mention that the sequence of system calls contains many behavioural messages. However, if the setuid and kexec_load are before the reboot, this is suspicious, as both require root privileges, and therefore may have been done illegally before the reboot. Therefore, if we only consider whether a system call is used or not, we will lose the relationship between sequential behaviour, which is why we consider sequential relationships in this study.

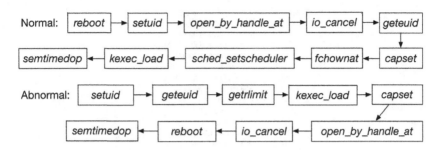

Fig. 2. Normal and abnormal differences (Image source: [12])

3 Proposed Methods

3.1 System Architecture

The system architecture of this study is illustrated in Fig. 3 and is divided into four modules.

The first module is the System Call Extraction Module, the function of which is to install the APK file into a sandbox environment to record the system call sequence generated during execution, so as to obtain the original system call characteristics of the analyzed application. The second module is the System Call Conversion Module (SCCM), which converts the recorded system call sequences into coded sequences according to the corresponding codes of the system call. The last module is the Classification Module, which determines whether the APK is a malicious program or not, and the binary classification and multiple classification of malicious programs are carried out according to different tasks.

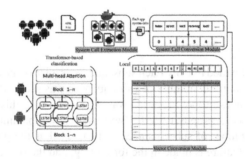

Fig. 3. System architecture

3.2 System Call Extraction Module

To avoid endangering the real device, the APK file was installed in the Droidbox [7] sandbox in the dynamic analysis module of the Andropytool [6] framework, and the MonkeyRunner was used to simulate the user's trigger behaviour for 300 s, and the system calls generated by the execution were recorded and exported as shown in Fig. 4.

呼叫時間	PID	System call
23:08.0	1016	futex(0xb68d557c
23:08.0	1016	munmap(0xaf3c8000
23:08.0	1016	sigprocmask(SIG_SETMASK
23:08.0	1016	munmap(0xaf2c8000
23:08.0	1016	exit(0) = ?
23:08.0	59	<... futex resumed>) = 1
23:08.0	59	open("/proc/self/task"
23:08.0	59	getdents64(24
23:08.0	59	getdents64(24
23:08.0	59	close(24) = 0
23:08.0	59	sigaction(SIGCHLD
23:08.0	59	fork(<unfinished ...>

Fig. 4. Extracted system calls

3.3 System Call Switching Module

A csv file is the result of an application recording. In this module, the system call fields are removed from each csv file, and the parameters are removed in chronological order to form a sequence that represents the behaviour of each application as it is executed, as shown in Fig. 5.

```
[0, 0, 0, 1, 4, 5, 4, 0, 0, 0, 0, 0, 0, 6, ...    383724   benign
[0, 0, 0, 1, 2, 2, 3, 1, 4, 5, 4, 0, 0, 0, 0, ...  190420   benign
[0, 0, 0, 1, 2, 2, 3, 1, 4, 5, 4, 0, 0, 0, 0, ...  157390   benign
[0, 0, 0, 1, 2, 2, 3, 1, 4, 5, 4, 0, 0, 0, 0, ...  177629   benign
[0, 0, 0, 1, 2, 2, 3, 1, 4, 5, 4, 0, 0, 0, 0, ...     953   benign
                                                      ...
[0, 0, 0, 1, 2, 2, 3, 1, 4, 5, 4, 0, 0, 0, 0, ...    5932   malware
[0, 0, 0, 1, 4, 5, 4, 0, 0, 0, 0, 0, 0, 6, ...       1799   malware
[0, 0, 0, 1, 4, 5, 4, 0, 0, 0, 0, 0, 0, 6, ...     220088   malware
```

Fig. 5. Conversion of system calls into numerical codes

3.4 Vector Conversion Modules

The sequence is first divided into SN Each subsequence is a 1/8 of the complete sequence. SN In this study, the optimal number of subsequences was set by [5]. SN The optimal number of subsequences proposed by [5] was set as $SN =$ In this study, the optimal number of subsequences proposed by [5] was used as the parameter setting. In this study, the optimal number of subsequences $= 10$ is used as the parameter setting. In each subsequence, a feature is made in the form of 3g, and the sequence relationship of the feature is strengthened by the concept of pre- and post-sequence relationship of n-grams (hereinafter referred to as the system call group), 1,3), (1,3,9), (3,9,1) as the system call group for this subsequence, and this method is useful when faced with sequences that use similar system calls but in different order, e.g. subsequence 1: 0,1,3,9,1 with (0,1,3), (1,3,9), (3,9,1) as the system call group for this subsequence and subsequence 2: 1,3,0,1,9 with (1, (3,0), (3,0,1), (0,1,9) as the systematic callsets of this subsequence. If only a single system call is used as a feature, these two similar subsequences would produce the same result, but processing by the method of this study produces different systematic callsets, which further reveals the difference in sequence relationships.

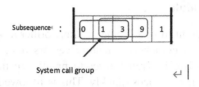

Fig. 6. Schematic diagram of the system call group

The TF-IDF of the local subsequence from [5] is then used to calculate the weights. The schematic diagram is shown in Fig. 6, so that in the TF-IDF of system call groups combined with local subsequences *tfSCG, Subseq* is the number of times the system call group is used in each sub-sequence, where SCG represents a certain system call group, Subseq represents a certain sub-sequence, and n*SCG, Subseq* represents the number of times a system call group is used in a subsequence.idf SCG To calculate whether a system call group appears frequently in a subseq, a lower weight is given to more frequent occurrences so that the model can focus on the more rare system call groups, where lAppl represents the total number of subseqs for this application and I {Subseq: t SCG ∈ dS/0123}l lAppl represents the total number of sub-sequences of this application,

And t SCG represents the total number of subsequences of the application, while lAppl represents the number of subsequences in which the system call group appears, and *tfSCG, Subsequence* and *idfSCG*. The multiplication oflAppl represents the total number of subsequences in this application, and lAppl represents the number of subsequences in which this system call group occurs. $SN \times NSCG$ vector, where *NSCG* represents the number of total system call groups and is given by (Fig. 7):

$$fSCG, \, Subseq = nSCG, \, Subseq \tag{1}$$

$$idf_{SCG} = \log[(1 + |Appl|)/(1 + |\{ \, Subseq{:}t_{SCG} \in d_{s/0123}\}|) + 1 \tag{2}$$

$$tfidf_{SCG}, \, Subsequence = tf_{SCG}, \, Subsequence \; idf_{SCG} \tag{3}$$

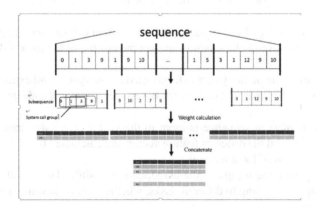

Fig. 7. Schematic diagram of the combined system call group and local TF-IDF

3.5 Classification Module

This framework is different from the general Transformer model, which uses Bi-LSTM to learn the semantics of compressed feature vectors first, and then uses the Multi-head Attention mechanism in Transformer to parallelize the computation and learn the relationship between sequences quickly. This is followed by using the Multi-head Attention mechanism in Transformer to parallelize the computation and learn the inter-sequence relationships quickly, and finally incorporating the Pooling layer to extract the key features.

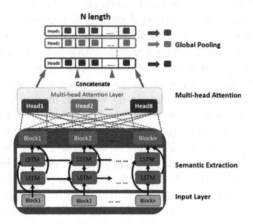

Fig. 8. Transformer architecture proposed by Chen et al. (Image source: [17])

3.6 System Flow

In this study, we propose a method to characterize the sequence relationship and combine it with a local weight calculation method, which is applied to a malware detection system as shown in Fig. 8, providing users to detect whether an application is a malware.

1. Send the collected application samples to the system call extraction module to run the application through the sandbox and get the csv file of the recorded system call from it.
2. Transfer the csv file of the system call extracted by the system call extraction module to the system call conversion module to convert the system call code into a numerical sequence.
3. The coded numerical sequence is input to the vector conversion module as a 3 g system call set, and the different feature vectors are calculated by TF- IDF using the sub-serial method of local features.
4. Input the system call weight to the classification module. The classification result will be output according to different tasks, whether it is a malware or what type of malware it is.

4   Experimentation and Discussion

This chapter categorises applications, which feature system calls, to evaluate model detection performance. The experiment was conducted under Windows 10 with an Intel Core i5-9400F CPU, 48 GB DDR4 memory, NVIDIA RTX 2080ti graphics card and Tensorflow and Keras deep learning packages. The experimental design was divided into three main parts; the first part was a comparison of the parameters of the system call group, the second part was the validity of the methodology for this study, and the third part was the adaptation of the model with the dataset CICMalDroid2020 [18], as shown in Table 1, and a ten- fold cross-validation was used for the follow-up experiments.

Table 1. CICMalDroid2020 dataset

Category	Quantity
Adware	1,378
Banking	1,717
SMS	1,901
Benign	3,612
Total	8,608

4.1   Comparison of the Parameters of the System Call Groups

4.1.1   Comparison of the Parameters of the Experimental One- and Binary Classification of the n-gram

This experiment used the data set data for binary classification (to determine whether it was a malicious program), and investigated the Accuracy and the effect of different parameters on the classification results for 2g and 3g. $F7 - score$ The results of the experiment are shown in Table 2.

Table 2. Comparison of binary classification parameters

Parameters	Accuracy	$F1 - score$
n = 2	96.13%	96.13%
n = 3	96.51%	96.50%

n = 1 means that the sequence of system calls is not taken into account for feature vector transformation and the weighting is calculated for a single system call, while n = 2 and n = 3 means that the system calls are bundled in a subsequence with the preceding and following sequences and a group of system calls is formed for subsequent weighting. This is a higher accuracy rate than the 96.13% achieved in 2 g.

4.1.2 Comparison of Parameters of n-grams for Experiment 2, Multivariate Classification

The experiment was conducted using data set data for multivariate classification, and a ten-fold cross- validation was carried out on 2 g and 3 g to investigate the Accuracy and the impact of different parameters on the classification results. $F7 - score$ The results of the experiment are shown in Table 3.

Table 3. Comparison of multiple classification parameters

Parameters	Accuracy	$F7 - score$
N = 1	88.02%	87.92%
N = 2	89.97%	89.88%
N = 3	91.06%	91.02%

The results showed that the average Accuracy of 3g was 91.06%, which was higher than the 89.97% accuracy of 2 g.

4.2 Validity of the Methodology of This Study

The different feature vector conversions for the comparison are as follows.

- Statistics: takes the original complete system call sequence, without cutting, and directly calculates the number of its system calls in use (vector dimension: 1×130).
- Subsequence statistics: subsequences were counted using a preprocessing method proposed by Chen et al. [11], which divides the original complete system call sequence equally into S_N subsequences. $S_N = $ The number of uses of each system call in each subsequence is then counted (vector dimension: 10×130).
- Global: The original complete system call sequence is taken directly, without cutting, and the weight value of its system calls to the overall data set is calculated directly using TF-IDF (vector dimension: 1×130).
- Local weights: the original complete system call sequence was divided equally into S_N a subsequence with $S_N = 10$ and calculate the weight value (vector dimension: 10×130) of its system calls to the single application call sequence using the local TF-IDF proposed in [5]

4.2.1 Experiment 3, Binary Classification

This experiment was conducted to investigate the Accuracy and impact of this study's method and different eigenvector transformation methods on the binary classification of classification models.

The binary classification results in the CICMalDroid2020 dataset, as shown in Table 4, achieved 96.51% for Accuracy in this study, and 96.50% for $F7 - score$ achieved 96.50%.

Table 4. Binary classification results

Methods	Accuracy	$F1 - score$
Statistics	87.98%	87.87%
Subseries&Statistics	92.73%	92.69%
Global	93.08%	93.06%
Local weighting	94.93%	94.93%
This study	**96.51%**	**96.50%**

4.2.2 Experiment 4, Multiple Classification

This experiment was conducted to investigate the impact of the present study and different eigenvector transformation methods on the Accuracy and $F7 - score$.

Table 5. Multiple classification results

Methods	Accuracy	$F1 - score$
Statistics	71.60%	70.87%
Subseries&Statistics	83.24%	83.11%
Global	84.21%	84.06%
Local weighting	88.02%	87.92%
This study	**91.06%**	**91.02%**

The experimental results are shown in Table 5, where the Accuracy of multivariate classification reached 91.06% and $F7 - score$ Therefore, it can be found that the proposed local weighting method, which combines the system call order with the system call group and local feature calculation, is more effective for model learning and classification applications than using only local weights.

4.3 Adaptation of the Model

4.3.1 Experiment 5: Unknown Data Set Test

This experiment used the Androzoo dataset, for a total of 500 samples, each malicious sample had to be judged as malicious by VirusTotal. The test was conducted using the CICMalDroid2020 dataset as training and 500 samples from 2019.

The experimental results for the unknown malicious sample in 2019 are shown in Table 6, where it can be seen that the average Accuracy of this study reached 81.74%, which is an 11.64% improvement compared to the locally calculated comparator, and $F1 - score$ The average Accuracy for this study was 81.35%, an increase of 13.86% compared to compartor.

Table 6. Unknown data set test

	Accuracy	$F_1 - score$
Local Weighting	70.10%	67.49%
This study	81.74%	81.35%

5 Conclusion and Future Works

This study is a systematic call study with dynamic analysis and proposes a method that combines serial relationships with local weights TF-IDF. This study achieves 96.51% Accuracy and 96.50% F_1-score for the CICMalDroid2020 dataset in binary classification, and 91.06% Accuracy and 91.02% F_1-score in multivariate classification, to demonstrate that the proposed system call set combined with local TF-IDF can effectively This demonstrates the importance of sequence relationships and the ability of this experiment to learn more characteristic relationships to improve accuracy. The parameters used in this study, such as the number of subsequences and n-grams, were set using the best settings from relevant studies. In the future, experiments can be conducted with different combinations to investigate the differences in results, or the best parameters can be adjusted using a dynamic approach on a rolling basis. The dataset used in this study is relatively balanced. Although a large number of malware emerge every year in the real world, there is still a gap in the number of malware compared to the average application, or there may be families with a smaller sample size. So future works can be conducted to investigate whether this research method can be effective in classifying malware with an unbalanced sample size.

References

1. Kaspersky: IT threat evolution Q3 2021. Mobile statistics (2021). https://securelist.com/it-threat-evolution-in-q3-2021-mobile-statistics/105020/
2. StatCounter: Mobile Operating System Market Share Worldwide (2022). https://gs.statcounter.com/os-market-share/mobile/worlwide/#monthly-202101-202203-bar
3. Saracino, A., Sgandurra, D., Dini, G., Martinelli, F.: MADAM: Effective and Efficient Behavior-based Android Malware Detection and Prevention (2016)
4. Feng, P., Ma, J., Sun, C., Xu, X., Ma, Y.: A novel dynamic android malware detection system with ensemble learning. IEEE Trans. Depend. Secur. Comput. **20**, 1–10 (2018)
5. Liu, Y.-C.: A call sequence compression method for local weighting system using mobile malware detection. Master's thesis, Institute of Information Management, National Central University (2021)
6. Martín, A., Lara-Cabrera, R., Camacho, D.: Android malware detection through hybrid features fusion and ensemble classifiers: the AndroPyTool framework and the OmniDroid dataset. Inf. Fusion **52**, 128–142 (2019). https://doi.org/10.1016/j.inffus.2018.12.006
7. pjlantz. Github-pjlantz/Droidbox: Dynamic analysis of Android apps. https://github.com/pjlantz/droidbox
8. Yan, J., Qi, Y., Rao, Q.: LSTM-based hierarchical denoising network for android malware detection. Secur. Commun. Netw. **2018**, 1–18 (2018). https://doi.org/10.1155/2018/5249190

9. Mas'ud, M.Z.: A comparative study on feature selection method for N-gram mobile malware detection. Int. J. Netw. Secur. **19**(5), 727–733 (2017)
10. Jahromi, A.N., Hashemi, S., Dehghantanha, A., Parizi, R.M., Choo, K.-K.-R.: An enhanced stacked LSTM method with no random initialization for malware threat hunting in safety and time-critical systems. IEEE Trans. Emerg. Topics Comput. Intell. **4**(5), 630–640 (2020)
11. Chen, Y.M., Hsu, C.H., Chung, K.C.K.: A novel preprocessing method for solving long sequence problem in android malware detection. In: 2019 Twelfth International Conference on Ubi-Media Computing (Ubi- Media), pp. 12–17. IEEE, August 2019
12. Xie, W., Xu, S., Zou, S., Xi, J.: A system-call behavior language system for malware detection using a sensitivity-based LSTM model. In: Proceedings of the 2020 3rd International Conference on Computer Science and Software Engineering, pp. 112–118 (2020)
13. Vaswani, A., et al.: Attention is all you need. In: Advances in Neural Information Processing Systems, pp. 5998–6008 (2017)
14. Graves, A.: Supervised sequence labelling with recurrent neural networks, pp. 37–45 (2012)
15. Yong, Y., Si, X., Hu, C., Zhang, J.: A review of recurrent neural networks: LSTM cells and network architectures. Neural Comput. **31**(7), 1235–1270 (2019). https://doi.org/10.1162/neco_a_01199
16. Xiao, X., Zhang, S., Mercaldo, F., Hu, G., Sangaiah, A.K.: Android malware detection based on system call sequences and LSTM. Multimed. Tools App. **78**(4), 3979–3999 (2017). https://doi.org/10.1007/s11042-017-5104-0
17. Chen, Y.M., He, A.C., Chen, G.C., Liu, Y.C.: Android malware detection system integrating block feature extraction and multi- head attention mechanism, pp. 408–413. IEEE (2020)
18. Mahdavifar, S., Kadir, A.F.A., Fatemi, R., Alhadidi, D., Ghorbani, A.A.: dynamic android malware category classification using semi-supervised deep learning. In: 2020 IEEE International Conference on Dependable, Autonomic and Secure Computing, International Conference on Pervasive Intelligence and Computing, International Conference on Cloud and Big Data Computing, International Conference on Cyber Science and Technology Congress (DASC/PiCom/CBDCom/CyberSciTech), pp. 515–522. IEEE (2020)

A Detector Using Variant Stacked Denoising Autoencoders with Logistic Regression for Malicious JavaScript with Obfuscations

Shin-Jia Hwang[✉] and Tzu-Ping Chen

Department of Computer Science and Information Engineering, Tamkang University, Tamsui Dist, 251301 New Taipei City, Taiwan (R.O.C.)
sjhwang@mail.tku.edu.tw

Abstract. JavaScript malware often contains obfuscation to evade malware detection. The contents of these obfuscated JavaScript malwares are often changed so that the lexical features of the JavaScript malwares with similar function become distinct. However, their semantic features may remain similar. In this paper, the deobfuscation preprocessing and our variant of Stacked denoising Autoencoder-Logistic Regression (SdA-LR, for short) are proposed to enhance the detection. To extract features with similarity between obfuscated malwares and original one, the process of adding noises is replaced with randomly obfuscation on the original JavaScript and train our variant of SdA model in unsupervised way. The SdA is then combined with Logistic Regression layer to form our variant of Stacked denoising Autoencoder-Logistic Regression (SdA-LR, for short) model to detect whether the JavaScript is benign or malicious. As a result, our variant of SdA-LR has high accuracy against obfuscations. Our variant of SdA is useful to extract the features with similarities then enhance the performance of detection. Our model also resists unknown obfuscations due to our variant of SdA.

Keywords: Malware detection · Stacked denoised autoencoder · Feature learning · JavaScript

1 Introduction

Malicious web applications become damages since the raise of web applications. Among these web applications, over 90% of them are using JavaScript [1]. JavaScript (JS, for short) provides an ability for dynamic programming, which allows users to generate necessary codes during the application execution [2]. This characteristic also allows attackers to easily embed malicious programs inside web applications using JavaScript. So many research are proposed to detect malicious JS web applications [3].

JS malware detection using machine learning/deep learning has become popular in recent research [4, 5]. Be compared with traditional malware detection approach, the machine learning approach and deep learning reduce the hardness of feature selection and automatically detect malicious programs. They can also detect malicious zero-day programs, even though their signatures are unknown [6]. Moreover, machine leaning

© The Author(s), under exclusive license to Springer Nature Singapore Pte Ltd. 2022
S.-Y. Hsieh et al. (Eds.): ICS 2022, CCIS 1723, pp. 374–386, 2022.
https://doi.org/10.1007/978-981-19-9582-8_33

needs more human effect than deep learning to choose the features. Therefore, the deep learning is the most suitable and efficient one to design JS malware detection.

Obfuscation techniques are often used by attackers to evade the malware detection. These obfuscations often change the malicious codes in human unreadable forms or insert redundant codes. Due to these techniques, obfuscated malicious programs may successfully avoid the malware detection of traditional approach based on fingerprints or signatures [7]. Moreover, some benign programs might use obfuscation technique for protecting their privacy and authorization. This leads to a raise of the difficulty to classify malicious and benign programs.

To resist the impact of obfuscations, some research performs the preprocess analysis and feature extraction to improve the detection performance [8]. Those features can be classified into two types: Lexical and semantic features. The lexical features usually are keywords or tokens in the programs. For example, the detections [8–10] extract keyworks or tokens from the JS source codes as features to classify malicious JS codes.

Though these detections using lexical features achieve a good performance, lexical features are weak against obfuscations. For program languages, the functions and variables are easily renamed and some specific statements are contained [4]. Therefore, the obfuscations have great impact on the detections using lexical features than the ones using semantic features. Semantic features is more robust against obfuscations than the lexical features [11]. Researches in [9, 12, 13] showed that Abstract Syntax Trees (ASTs, for short) is able to improve the detection against random obfuscation, data obfuscation, and encoding obfuscation. In [11, 12], Control Flow Graph (CFG for short) and Data Flow Graph (DFG for short) are used for further analysis against obfuscations. CFP and DFG are both generated from the program's AST. Though they provide more features to distinguish benign from malicious JS codes, some JS codes may not have their CFG or DFG. Furthermore, it requires extra computation cost to generate CFG and DFG. To reduce the computational load, only ASTs are used as the features to mitigate the impact of obfuscations.

In addition, some semantic similarity still exists among the original program and its obfuscated ones. Figure 1 shows an example of a program and its obfuscated result using random obfuscation. The function and variable names are replaced with some no-meaning names, and dead codes are injected. Although these two programs look different, they have the similar semantic structures. Therefore, the obfuscated program is more similar to the original program than to the other distinct programs.

```
1  function functionA(name){          1  function _0xa57(_0x94e9){
2      alert("Hello "+ name);          2      alert("Hellow " + _0x94e9)
3  }                                    3  }///some random comment
4  myName = "world";                    4  var _865k = "world", _un=1;
5  functionA(myName);                   5  _0xa57(_865k); var tt="x2";
       (a) The original program.               (b) The obfuscated program.
```

Fig. 1. An example of an obfuscated program using random obfuscation techniques.

Stacked denoised Autoencoder (SdA, for short) is one of feature learning models used to extract representative features to enhance detection, which can provide more representative features than human selected features [14]. In the original SdA, the noises are added in random to against the natural noises. However, the most of obfuscation are artificial, so it is better to use the obfuscated version of the JS codes to generate the noised features for the SdA model, instead of the randomly added noises.

Based on the observation, our variant of SdA is proposed to extract robust features against obfuscation. In our variant of SdA, the features adding random noises is replaced with the features generated from the randomly obfuscated version of the original JS. Then our variant of SdA can extract the similarity among the original JS codes and its obfuscated ones. The final feature vectors generated by our variant of SdA is more robust than the ones generated by original SdA against obfuscations and improve the detection accuracy. This is our major contribution.

This paper is organized as below. Section 2 gives a brief overview of related knowledge and some recent work. Section 3 presents our model for malicious JS detection against obfuscation. Section 4 shows the hyperparameter and performance of our model. The last section is our conclusions.

2   Related Work: Autoencoders and the Variants

An autoencoder (AE, for short) is a kind of neural network which is widely used in dimension reduction tasks and feature learning. The training of autoencoder is unsupervised, so it does not require the labels of data. Instead, the AE model is trained to generate low-dimension output which is used to almost recover the input data. During the training, the reconstruction error is used to adjust the weights of the model to minimize the reconstruction error.

The autoencoder consist of an encoder and a decoder being illustrated in Fig. 2. The middle layer at the end of encoder usually call the hidden/bottleneck layer, whose output is the latent feature of the input data. The input layer though the hidden layer to the bottleneck layer is the encoder, while the bottleneck layer though the hidden layer to the output layer is the decoder. The neuron number of output layer is equal to the input layer in order to reconstruct the input data. The neuron number of hidden layers is usually less than the input layer, but also could be equal or larger in sparse autoencoder, for example. When the neuron number of the bottleneck is less than the one of the input layer, the autoencoder could generate lower-dimensional representation for features.

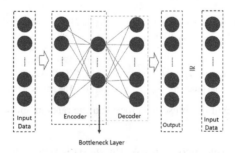

Fig. 2. The structure of an autoencoder.

A stacked autoencoder is an autoencoders with multiple-layers for encoders/decoders. A single AE may not generate sufficiently low-dimension vector to maintain robust original information. Hence stacked multiple autoencoders are proposed to generate robust features to keep most information about the original data.

A denoising Autoencoder (dA, for short) is a variant one of autoencoder to against the noised data. The dA can be trained to recover the input data from the noised input data. Because dA is robust against noised input data, the generated feature of dA more robust than AE. Figure 3 illustrates the structure of dA. The encoder/decoder in dA can contain multiple layers to generate robust features. This structure is called the Stacked denoising Autoencoder (SdA, for short).

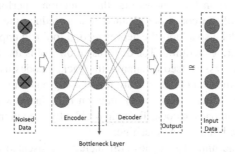

Fig. 3. The structure of a stacked denoising autoencoder.

3   Our Detection Model

3.1   Our Architectures

Our detection model against obfuscation consists of four phases: Data preprocessing, feature generation, feature extraction, and model detection. This architecture is illustrated by Fig. 4. In data pre-processing phase, the obfuscation of JS codes is roughly removed using a deobfuscation tool and unpacking codes to obtain the cleaned JS codes. The cleaned JS codes are then parsed into a 1d array of its Abstract Syntax Trees (ASTs, for short). The 1d array of an AST is randomly projected into a one-dimension (1d for short) feature vector. On this 1d feature vector, our new variant of SdA is used to generate feature vectors against obfuscation. Finally, the Logistic Regression (LR, for short) with softmax function is adopted to classify whether the JS code is benign or malicious.

3.2   Data Preprocessing

In this phase, the JS source codes are cleaned using a deobfuscation tool and unpacked the packed codes. Malicious codes may contain obfuscated codes adopting the pack and four different obfuscation techniques to evade the malware detection. Meanwhile, benign codes may also contain obfuscated or packed codes for protection from illegal copy. To mitigate the impact of obfuscation, the codes are cleaned before parsing to

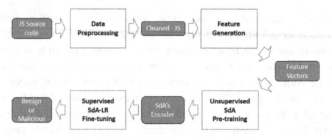

Fig. 4. The Architecture of Our Model

ASTs. The experiments in [15] shows that the detection's performance is improved if some obfuscation of the codes are cleaned first to reduce the impact of encoding obfuscation. Our model also adopts the deobfuscation tool and unpack method to clean the codes before feature generation. The deobfuscation tool is the JS-Beautifier [17].

The unpacking process is used to unpack the packed codes using eval () function. The packed codes by the eval () function are found using regular expression in NodeJS. When a packed code is found, the eval () function is replaced with the Console.log() function to extract the unpacked code. To avoid accidently execution during this process, this process is executed in a virtual machine.

To prevent that the unpacked codes still include obfuscated codes, JS-Beautifier cleans all unpacked codes again. As a result, assume that the codes may be clean and recovered to the original codes. These processed JS codes are called the cleaned JS codes.

3.3   AST Feature Vectors Generation

To gain the semantic information, the cleaned JS codes are parsed into 1d array of their ASTs by Esprima [18], which is a common JS parser for static code analysis to produce the AST of JS code. The AST is represented in a 1d array by traversing the AST in post order. Since there are 69 different node types in ASTs, all node types are numbered from 1 to 69, and 0 is used for padding usage to extend the length to the fixed length of an array.

The length of the 1d array of an AST may be longer than 100,000 dimensions in general in the experiments. Due to our hardware limitation, only the ASTs with the length being less than 60,000 are selected. Meanwhile, the array being shorter than 60,000 are padded 0 such that all the AST arrays have the same length.

To reduce the training load, the very sparse random projection [19] is used to generate the short projected feature vectors for the 1d array of ASTs. In [19], a random very spare matrix E is used. Let d be the length of the 1d arrays of AST and $s = \sqrt{d}$. To generate the matrix E, the value of the elements E_{ij} is obtained by

$$E_{ij} = \sqrt{s} \begin{cases} 1, & with probability \frac{1}{2s} \\ 0, & with probability\ p = 1 - \frac{1}{s} \\ -1, & with probability\ p = \frac{1}{2s} \end{cases} \tag{1}$$

The product of E and the 1d array is the projected vector. The projected vector is then normalized by rescaling the value into the range between 0 to 1. This normalized feature vectors of the cleaned ASTs are used to train our SdA model in the next phase.

3.4 Unsupervised Pre-training SdA

To against the known/unknown obfuscation coding techniques, our variant of SdA model is proposed to extract the similarity feature of JS codes. The extraction of features with similarity is the major advantage of our SdA. The SdA generates the latent feature and then the latent feature is used to recover the (similar) input using the decoder. Since the decoder almost recover the input, the latent feature of the input is more similar to the one of the noised inputs than the one of the other distinct inputs. The SdA is a dA with more than one hidden layer in the autoencoders.

Being inspired of the adding noise concept, the (unpacked) obfuscated JS codes are more similar to the (unpacked) original code than the other distinct codes. In our variant of SdA model, the randomly noised projected vector are replaced with the projected vector generated from obfuscated JS codes, to train our variant SdA. Then our SdA model generates the latent features. Those latent features should be grouped into many clusters, containing the original code and its obfuscated codes. Those clusters are useful for the further detection of malicious codes against the known/unknown obfuscation. The structure of the stacked denoising autoencoder is shown in Fig. 5.

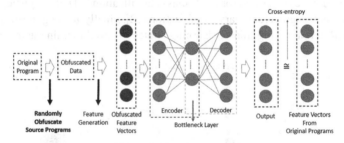

Fig. 5. The structure of our SdA.

In order to train our SdA to resist the known/unknown obfuscation techniques, the original JS codes are randomly obfuscated as noised input vectors. In original SdA, the input data is added Gaussian noise or randomly set a fixed percent of data to be zero to corrupt the input data. Generally, these random added noises can enhance the extendibility of the model. However, they may also bring some meaningless impact on the model then reduce the accuracy. Hence, the noises in our approach are added by randomly obfuscating the original JS codes. Attackers can generate multiple versions of a same program by obfuscation techniques. The contents of these obfuscated codes may look very different, but they still contain similar semantic information. Due to this, obfuscating the original code to simulate the attacker's method is more artificial and meaningful as the semantic noises to enhance the performance of SdA.

In our approach, JavaScript-Obfuscator (JS-Obfuscator for short) [20] is used to obfuscate some JS codes. In fact, JS-Obfuscator is used to protects programs by obfuscation techniques, including variables renaming, strings encryption, dead code injection, etc. Then the obfuscated code is preprocessed, generated the 1d array of ASTs, and then randomly projected into a lower 1d feature vector as the noised input vector. In other words, the noised vector of cleaned AST features is the cleaned obfuscated projected features.

When training the SdA, the model is trained to reconstruct cleaned projected AST features from cleaned obfuscated projected features. Our SdA uses the ReLU activation function in all hidden layers. For the decoder, all hidden layers adopt ReLU activation function, and the output layer use the sigmoid function.

To minimize the reconstruction error of the autoencoder, the binary cross-entropy is used as the loss function in our model. Since the sigmoid function is used at the output layer of the model, the output value will lie between 0 to 1. Hence, binary cross-entropy can be adopted as the loss function (BCE).

3.5   Supervised Fine-Tuning SdA-LR Detectors

After pretraining the SdA model, the SdA-LR model is proposed for malicious/benign classification. The structure of SdA-LR is shown in Fig. 6. The encoder in SdA is the feature extractor for similarity while the LR layer using softmax function adopts those similarity features as the malicious/benign classifier. Though the softmax regression is an extension of logistic regression for multi-class classification [21], the logistic regression with softmax is also good for binary classification [22]. Finally, to integrate the pretrained SdA with LR, a fine-tuning transfer learning strategy is used to train the integration.

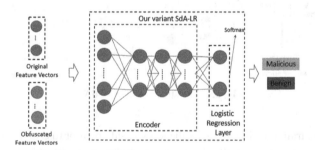

Fig. 6. The structure of our SdA-LR.

4   Our Experiments

4.1   Experiment Setup

Our dataset consists of 29,602 malicious JS codes and 49,796 benign JS codes. The malicious JS are obtained from the Hynek Petrak's dataset on Github, which collects approximately 40,000 malicious JS codes from 2016 to 2019. The JS benign codes are collected from SRILAB [23]. To obtain better evaluation performance, 5-fold cross-validation is adopted. The dataset is split into 80% for the training data set, and 20% for the testing data set. Meanwhile, 5-fold cross-validation is adopted to train our model using the training dataset. The performance is evaluated by statistical measures: Accuracy, precision, recall, and F1-score.

4.2 The Size of Randomly Projected Vectors

To decide the size of projected vectors, our experiment is designed to compare the performance of our model on different sizes of projected vectors, with the fixed parameters of SdA and then SdA-LR models. The average of validation results is used in the comparisons.

In our experiment, the sizes of projected features are 200, 300, 400, 500, 600, 700, 800, 900, and 1000. The SdA has 3 hidden layers including the bottleneck layer and each layer has 200 neurons. The learning rate is 10^{-4}, batch size is 128, and the model is trained in 500 epochs. To fine-tune the SdA-LR, all parameters in SdA are adjusted during the training of SdA-LR. The learning rate is 10^{-5}, batch size is 64, and the model is trained in 500 epochs. In both models, the optimizer is Adam as and the loss function is the cross-entropy function.

Table 1 shows the results of our model with different projected vector sizes. The most suitable accuracy, precision and F1 score appeared at the size of 500 with suitably short training time. However, the highest recall rate is found for the size 600, but the recall rate for 600 size is slightly lower than the recall rate for the size 500. The training time of both SdA and SdA-LR both grows longer as the feature size become larger. Due to the balance of consideration between accuracy and the consuming time, the size 500 is chosen as the suitable size of projected feature.

Table 1. The performance of different randomly projected vector sizes

Vector sizes	Accuracy	Precision	Recall	F1	SdA training time (in seconds)	SdA-LR training time (in seconds)
200	96.39%	96.31%	93.93%	95.11%	1944	6889
300	96.59%	96.28%	95.49%	95.42%	1946	7109
400	97.04%	96.37%	95.68%	96.02%	1985	7125
500	97.41%	97.17%	95.85%	96.51%	2027	7151
600	97.34%	96.66%	96.19%	96.42%	2076	7203
700	97.36%	96.98%	95.93%	96.45%	2106	7253
800	97.08%	96.23%	96.12%	96.17%	2122	7312
900	97.27%	96.69%	96.55%	96.62%	2158	7389
1000	97.14%	96.22%	96.12%	96.17%	2195	7592

4.3 The Number of Neurons of Hidden Layer

The second experiment is used to compare the performance of the different number of neurons of hidden layers. Five different number of neurons of hidden layers, 200, 250, 300, 350, and 400, are compared. The number of hidden layers of SdA is 3. All hidden layers have the same number of neurons. To train SdA, the learning rate is 10^{-4} and the batch size is 128. The fine-tuning train of SdA-SR, the learning rate is 10^{-5} and the batch size is 64. Both models are trained by 500 epoch and uses the cross-entropy as the loss function for SdA and Adam for optimizer. Table 2 shows the comparison in which the accuracy is the average of 5-fold cross-validation.

As long as the neuron number grows larger, all the accuracy, precision and F1 score grow higher. The highest performance appears at 400 neurons, which are 98.26% accuracy, 97.74% precision, 97.60% recall rate, and 97.67% F1-score. However, all the lines of accuracy, precision and F1 score become flat after the size 250. To balance the accuracy and training time, the 250 neurons are used as the size of all hidden layers.

Table 2. The performance of different hidden layer sizes.

Sizes of hidden layers	Accuracy	Precision	Recall	F1
200	96.39%	96.31%	93.93%	96.11%
250	97.89%	97.20%	97.15%	97.17%
300	98.15%	97.67%	97.10%	97.51%
350	98.17%	97.71%	97.17%	97.44%
400	98.26%	97.74%	97.60%	97.67%

4.4 The Numbers of Hidden Layers

The number of hidden layers between 1 to 5 are evaluated in the experiment. Each hidden layer in SdA contains 250 neurons. To train SdA, the learning rate is 10^{-4} and batch size is 128. To train SdA-SR with fine-tuning all whole model, the learning rate is 10^{-5} and batch size is 64. All trainings use 500 epochs while the loss function is cross-entropy, and the optimizer is Adam. Table 3 illustrates the results being the average of 5-fold cross-validation.

Table 3 shows that all the performance raised when the model become deep but become smooth after 3 hidden layers. The peak of all accuracy, precision, and F1 score is at the model with 3 hidden layers, at which they are 97.89%, 97.20% and 97.17%, respectively. Only the recall rate becomes slightly low when 4 and 5 hidden layers are used. As a result, 3 hidden layers is recommended.

4.5 The Epochs to Train SdA

In this experiment, the performance of training epochs of SdA are compared. The compared epochs are 100, 200, 300, ..., and1000. The training parameters are fixed to 3

Table 3. The performance of different numbers of hidden layer

Number of hidden layers	Accuracy	Precision	Recall	F1
1	92.97%	94.99%	86.27%	90.09%
2	96.56%	95.84%	94.93%	95.37%
3	97.89%	97.20%	97.15%	97.17%
4	97.67%	96.34%	97.47%	96.90%
5	97.75%	96.50%	97.51%	97.00%

hidden layers, and each layer contain 250 neurons. The learning rate is 10^{-4} and batch size is 128. To train SdA-SR with fine-tuning all whole model, the learning rate is 10^{-5} and batch size is 64. All trainings use 500 epochs while the loss function is cross-entropy, and the optimizer is Adam. The average of 5-fold cross-validation are shown in Table 4.

Table 4 shows that the highest performance appears at 700 training epochs. The model has 97.91% accuracy, 96.69% precision, 97.74% recall and 97.18% F1-score. The performance of the trained epochs less than 700 are all lower than 700 epochs. Meanwhile, when the trained epochs more than 700, the performance start decrease. The possible reason is that the model may be trained overfitting. Therefore, 700 training epochs may be a suitable chose for the SdA.

Table 4. The performance of different SdA training epochs of hidden layer

Trained epochs	Accuracy	Precision	Recall	F1
100	96.55%	95.43%	96.455%	96.06%
200	96.81%	94.79%	97.07%	95.77%
300	97.30%	95.66%	97.18%	96.41%
400	97.11%	95.17%	97.17%	95.94%
500	97.67%	96.28%	97.54%	96.90%
600	97.69%	96.22%	97.64%	96.93%
700	97.91%	96.69%	97.74%	97.18%
800	97.36%	95.72%	97.26%	96.23%
900	97.47%	96.06%	97.20%	96.63%
1000	97.39%	95.55%	97.36%	96.54%

4.6   The Epochs for Fine-Tune SdA-LR

The fine-tuning process is the last step of training the SdA-LR model. The performance of the model trained different epochs from 100 to 1000 are compared. The encoder from pre-trained phase is trained for 700 epochs, which has 3 hidden layers and contain 250 neurons in each layer in SdA. During fine-tuning the SdA-LR model, the learning rate is 10^{-5} and the batch size is 64. The results are the average of 5-fold cross-validation in Table 5. The performance is smoothly growing after training 800 epochs. However, to continuing train the model may cost unnecessary burdens and negative impact such as overfitting. As a result, 800 epochs are the recommended for fine-tuning model.

Table 5. The performance of different fine-tuning epochs of SdA-LR.

Trained epochs	Accuracy	Precision	Recall	F1
100	93.64%	92.98%	89.96%	91.34%
200	96.12%	95.13%	94.44%	94.78%
300	96.89%	95.78%	95.89%	95.84%
400	97.35%	96.48%	96.42%	96.45%
500	97.60%	96.88%	96.68%	96.94%
600	97.80%	97.23%	96.85%	97.04%
700	97.88%	97.31%	96.98%	97.25%
800	98.04%	97.46%	97.02%	97.36%
900	98.07%	97.90%	96.91%	97.40%
1000	98.08%	97.87%	97.19%	97.42%

4.7 Comparison with Wang et al.'s Model [16]

Table 6 shows the comparison between our model and the approach in [16] using our data set. In [16], the JS code characters are transformed into ASCII byte representation in binary form as the features. The ASCII byte representation in binary form is then reduced the dimensionality of these features. [16] also adopts SdA-LR model for the feature extraction and malware classification. According to Table 6, our variant of SdA-LR is better than Wnag et al.'s model [16] with higher accuracy. Additionally, our model requires less pre-train epochs and fine-tuning epochs where they required 1000 epochs to pre-train their SdA and 6000 epochs to fine-tune their SdA-LR model.

Table 6. A comparison with Wang et al.'s model [16]

	Accuracy	Precision	Recall	F1
Our Variant of SdA-LR	98.04%	97.46%	97.02%	97.36%
Wang et al.'s [16]	93.73%	85.94%	43.08%	57.39%

5   Our Conclusion

Obfuscations hide the malicious JS source codes from the JS malware detection. However, some semantic similarities of similar codes may constrain after obfuscation. In this paper, our variant of SdA-LR with deobfuscation pre-processing is proposed enhance the detection. To train our model to extract similarity features among similar programs, the noised input vectors is replaced with randomly obfuscate the original codes. Furthermore, these noised vectors may contain more artificial features comparing to random added noised. As demonstrated in our experiment, our variant of SdA extracts representative features against obfuscation and enhance the accuracy of detections. Our model achieves higher performance than Wang et al.'s Model [16].

References

1. Global Data at Risk: State of the Web Report (2020). https://go.talasecurity.io/hubfs/Content/White%20Papers%20and%20Reports/_Global%20Data%20at%20Risk_2020%20State%20of%20the%20Web%20Report_.pdf
2. JavaScript. Accessed Nov 2021. https://developer.mozilla.org/en-US/docs/Web/JavaScript
3. Sohan, M.F., Basalamah, A.: A systematic literature review and quality analysis of JavaScript malware detection. IEEE Access **8**, 190539–190552 (2020)
4. Fang, Y., Huang, C., Su, Y., Qiu, Y.: Detecting malicious JavaScript code based on semantic analysis. Comput. Secur. **93**, 101764 (2020)
5. Skolka, P., Staicu, C.-A., Pradel, M.: Anything to hide? Studying minified and obfuscated code in the web. In: The World Wide Web Conference, pp. 1735–1746 (2019)
6. Yousefi-Azar, M., Varadharajan, V., Hamey, L., Tupakula, U.: Autoencoder-based feature learning for cyber security applications. In: 2017 International joint conference on neural networks (IJCNN), pp. 3854–3861 (2017)
7. Xu, W., Zhang, F., Zhu, S.: Jstill: mostly static detection of obfuscated malicious javascript code. In: Proceedings of the third ACM Conference on Data and Application Security and Privacy, pp. 117–128 (2013)
8. Patil, D.R., Patil, J.: Detection of malicious javascript code in web pages. Indian J. Sci. Technol. **10**, 1–12 (2017)
9. Ndichu, S., Ozawa, S., Misu, T., Okada, K.: A machine learning approach to malicious JavaScript detection using fixed length vector representation. in 2018 International Joint Conference on Neural Networks (IJCNN), pp. 1–8, (2018)
10. Stokes, J.W., Agrawal, R., McDonald, G., Hausknecht, M.: Scriptnet: neural static analysis for malicious javascript detection. In: MILCOM 2019–2019 IEEE Military Communications Conference (MILCOM), pp. 1–8 (2019)
11. Song, X., Chen, C., Cui, B., Fu, J.: Malicious JavaScript detection based on bidirectional LSTM model. Appl. Sci. **10**, 3440 (2020)
12. Fass, A., Backes, M., Stock, B.: JSTAP: a static pre-filter for malicious javascript detection. In: Proceedings of the 35th Annual Computer Security Applications Conference, pp. 257–269 (2019)
13. Ndichu, S., Kim, S., Ozawa, S., Misu, T., Makishima, K.: A machine learning approach to detection of JavaScript-based attacks using AST features and paragraph vectors. In: Applied Soft Computing, vol. 84, p. 105721 (2019)
14. Xu, W., Zhang, F., Zhu, S.: The power of obfuscation techniques in malicious JavaScript code: a measurement study. In: 2012 7th International Conference on Malicious and Unwanted Software, pp. 9–16 (2012)

15. Ndichu, S., Kim, S., Ozaw, S.: Deobfuscation, unpacking, and decoding of obfuscated malicious JavaScript for machine learning models detection performance improvement. CAAI Trans. Intell. Technol. **5**, 184–192 (2020)
16. Wang, Y., Cai, W., Wei, P.: A deep learning approach for detecting malicious JavaScript code. Secur. Commun. Netw. **9**, 1520–1534 (2016)
17. js-beautifier. Accessed Nov 2021. https://github.com/beautify-web/js-beautify
18. Esprima. Accessed Nov 2021. https://esprima.org/
19. Li, P., Hastie, T.J., Church, K.W.: Very sparse random projections. In: Proceedings of the 12th ACM SIGKDD International Conference on Knowledge Discovery and Data Mining, pp. 287–296 (2006)
20. JavaScript   obfuscator.   https://github.com/javascript-obfuscator/javascript-obfuscator. Accessed 11 Jan 2021
21. Kayabol, K.: Approximate sparse multinomial logistic regression for classification. IEEE Trans. Pattern Anal. Mach. Intell. **42**, 490–493 (2019)
22. Herrera, J.L.L., Figueroa, H.V.R., Ramírez, E.J.R.: Deep fraud. A fraud intention recognition framework in public transport context using a deep-learning approach. In: 2018 International Conference on Electronics, Communications and Computers (CONIELECOMP), pp. 118–125 (2018)
23. Raychev, V., Bielik, P., Vechev, M., Krause, A.: Learning programs from noisy data. ACM SIGPLAN Notices **51**, 761–774 (2016)

A Lightweight and Robust Authentication and Key Agreements with Physically Unclonable Function in Manufacturing Environments

Bo-An Lai[1], Yi-Hsiu Yeh[1], Guan-Yu Chen[2], Jheng-Jia Huang[2(✉)], and Nai-Wei Lo[2]

[1] Department of Computer Science and Information Engineering, National Taiwan University of Science and Technology, Taipei, Taiwan
[2] Department of Information Management, National Taiwan University of Science and Technology, Taipei, Taiwan
jhengjia.huang@mail.ntust.edu.tw
https://aclab.cs.ntust.edu.tw

Abstract. With the growth of networks and semi-conduction, the Internet of things (IoT) is undergoing a golden year nowadays. At the same time, the Internet of Things (IoT) in the manufacturing environment has faced a critical problem with information security. As the network technology flourish, the way of attack is richer and richer. The traditional defense solution no longer fits with manufacturing environments. Therefore, the industry is willing to get a lighter weight and stronger security mechanism to confront security challenges in the future. In order to achieve the state above, the new mechanism needs to have the ability to generate the truly random value to avoid the collision that the algorithm used now may face, although it seldom happens. Simultaneously, it needs to reduce power consumption as much as possible. Thus, Physically Unclonable Function (PUF) is a solution. Because it has the property which can generate truly random values to avoid collision and save power when executing, our proposed scheme aims to improve the performance and reliability of Physically Unclonable Functions (PUF) to authentication to create a secure channel. When devices in the manufacturing environment transmit a message, it will be bypassed by a secure channel to the destination safely.

Keywords: Lightweight authentication · Internet of Things · Manufacturing environments · Physically unclonable function

1 Introduction

In recent years, with the explosive growth of network technology, whole manufacturing environments have introduced the "Internet of Things" in succession. However, the existing solutions for information security cannot deal with manufacturing environments completely. Although information security solutions spring

S.-Y. Hsieh et al. (Eds.): ICS 2022, CCIS 1723, pp. 387–397, 2022.
https://doi.org/10.1007/978-981-19-9582-8_34

up all over the information industry, solutions for manufacturing environments are still restricted by their hardware limits and the properties of the field [1].

Due to the characteristic of manufacturing environments, industries usually use the embedded system to provide the network-connection service to machines. Nevertheless, the embedded system is designed to save power and the extreme climate. Hardware performance is not its highest priority. So, our information security solutions are too "heavy" for the embedded system. It leads the industry to have no answer that can handle the information security problem [2]. In the past, this situation may not make a fatal weakness for the manufacturing system. However, nowadays, many devices are connected to the internet, and this weakness will be acute and make the system vulnerable.

Therefore, this research takes advantage of the Physically Unclonable Function (PUF) to design a solution for the information security problem of manufacturing environments. The Physically Unclonable Function (PUF) is a device that exploits inherent randomness introduced during manufacturing to give a physical entity a unique "fingerprint" or trust anchor. In addition, it is characteristic of low-performance cost and "true" randomness. As stated above, the Physically Unclonable Function (PUF) provides an almost ideal answer for the information security problem of manufacturing environments [4]. However, the Physically Unclonable Function (PUF) has extremely high requirements for the environment it stays. Any climate factors will affect the value generated by the Physically Unclonable Function (PUF) [3].

Thus, using algorithms to overcome climate factors is the method that this research takes. It uses a mechanism that manages and verifies the key generated by the Physically Unclonable Function (PUF) to ensure the quality of keys. This mechanism is elastic to implement and can be deployed by software and hardware. This research uses the software method to evaluate the performance because of the cross-platform flexibility.

In our proposed scheme, our scheme uses the Physically Unclonable Function (PUF) property to provide the "true" random value, which can avoid collision during the key generated absolutely under an unstable climate. At the same time, the scheme can create the key with a lightweight and low-performance cost, ensuring node-to-node or machine-to-machine communication's reliability, confidentiality, and integrity without high resource consumption.

2   Preliminaries

The Internet of Things (IoT) opens opportunities for manufacturing environments to integrate all devices into the internet. On the other hand, all devices connected to the internet present all data flow transmitted by the internet, which may make the classified materials leak. Nowadays, businesses attach more and more importance to copyrights, and the protection of the design and product information is non-negligible. In the past, an enterprise may deploy some policy to protect their classified materials in their office side, which have many internets connection. And the manufacturing environments usually be ignored because there is seldom an internet connection.

For a complete manufacturing enterprise network environment, the encryption of classified materials is crucial. In the manufacturing climate, the main focus is ensuring the product's design does not leak with low-performance consumption. The study of data encryption in the manufacturing environment is significant; similarly, for the government, it is vital to protect some military industry designs that the opponent country may breach. Therefore, good protection of manufacturing environments is not only protecting the profit of a business but also protecting the safety of a nation.

Our proposed scheme will be based on the confidentiality and integrity of essential transmit service based on encryption mechanisms and improve its verification, randomness, and non-repudiation by using Physically Unclonable Function (PUF) and its related technologies.

2.1 Physically Unclonable Function

Physically Unclonable Function (PUF) is a property in which a device's characteristic exploits randomness introduced during manufacturing to give a physical entity a unique trust anchor or digital fingerprint [5]. For example, when an SRAM chip has been initiated, its internal electric potential will be distributed randomly and seen as a Physically Unclonable Function (PUF) [6]. Because the value we get from the Physically Unclonable Function (PUF) will be unique, this property can be an identifiable entity in an authentication protocol. In addition, the Physically Unclonable Function (PUF) can generate the "true" random value compared to the existing method of generating random value. The way by which a computer generates a random number now uses a function related to time which we call "pseudo" random [7]. By using SRAM to implement the Physically Unclonable Function (PUF), we can introduce a function that almost shows the property of "true" random.

2.2 Diffie Hellman

Diffie-Hellman is a key exchange system that is wildly used by many industries. Diffie-Hellman key exchange system not directly used for encryption and digital signature. It is only used for key exchange. Diffie Hellman uses the character of the RSA encoding algorithm, which uses congruence modulo dividing and exponentiation. Although it is hard to compute the private key from the public key with the Diffie-Hellman algorithm, this algorithm may get thread from Man-in-the-middle Attack. To solve this situation, the common method is using the Pre-shared Secret. The Pre-shared Secret can ensure security when Diffie-Hellman exchange information in authentication phase, which is called Two-step information exchange.

2.3 IPsec

IP Security protocol (IPsec) is a widely used Virtual Private Network (VPN) protocol to create a secure channel. Because most transmit protocols use IP packets to send the information, users cannot expect which route the packet will use. The packet has a high risk of approaching a node that is unsafe. Thus, users need a secure mechanism to protect the information they send. The IP Security protocol (IPsec) is a complete solution for this situation, which contain Internet Key Exchange (IKE), Public Key Infrastructure (PKI), Authentication Header (AH), Security Association (SA), and Encapsulation Security Payload (ESP). For instance, Authentication Header (AH) can provide the source authentication and ensure integrity. Furthermore, it can prevent replay attacks efficiently. In summary, the IP Security protocol (IPsec) can provide a reliable, confidential, and complete solution to establish a secure channel quickly.

3   Our Scheme

This paper aims to integrate the Physically Unclonable Function (PUF) into the existing key generate method. Therefore, this paper combines authentication, P2P encryption, and key management into the solution. In addition, we also use solutions designed to be lightweight and saving-performance, i.e., the controller just needs to initial the PUF module once. Also, we use hashing to improve the stability of values generated by the Physically Unclonable Function (PUF). The notations used in our scheme are listed in Table 1, and this paper uses SHA-256 hashing mechanisms for data encryption and authentication. For the key agreement, we use Diffie-Hallman to create a joint key to replace the existing pre-sharing key. After nodes create a secure channel, the node-to-node communication, and the key re-authentication will use the joint key to encrypt, which is no longer needed to initiate the Physically Unclonable Function (PUF).

Table 1. Notation

Notations	Descriptions
C	The key controller
N_i	The ith encryption node
id_{all}	The list of id for all encryption node
id_i	The id of ith encrytion node
V_{PUF}	The value generated by PUF module
V_{random}	The value generated by the controller randomly
V_{hash}	The value returned by PUF module in initialization phase
K_{ps}	The pre-sharing key
VN_i	The value generated by ith node
$E_{ps}(\cdot)$	Encryption with the key K_{ps}
$D_{ps}(\cdot)$	Decryption with the key K_{ps}
HN_i	The hash value generated from VN_i
T	The timestamp
$H_{SHA-256}(\cdot)$	SHA-256 hashing
K_{common}	The joint key
$E_{common}(\cdot)$	Encryption with the key K_{common}
$D_{common}(\cdot)$	Decryption with the key K_{common}

3.1 Initialization Phase

The first step is initialing the controller to generate the pre-sharing key and pair encryption nodes. At first, the controller sets id_{all}, which contains id of all nodes in the pairing group. After that, the controller randomly chooses a value V_{random} and gets a value V_{PUF} from the PUF module.

3.2 Registration Phase

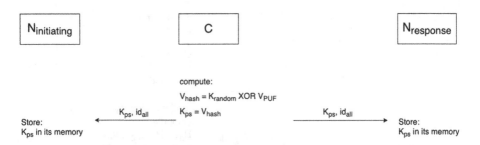

Fig. 1. The registration phase

During the registration phase, all encryption nodes must get the pre-sharing key and list of pairing nodes.First, the controller computes $V_{hash} = K_{random} \oplus V_{PUF}$ in order to generate the pre-sharing key. Next, the controller hash V_{hash} with SHA-256 to get the pre-sharing key $K_{ps} = H_{SHA-256}(V_{hsah})$. Consequently, the controller uses the security channel to send K_{ps} and id_{all} to all nodes, and all nodes store K_{ps} and id_{all} in their memory (Fig. 1).

3.3 Authentication Phase

In order to establish a secure channel between all nodes, the initiating node N_{init} will generate a value VN_{init} randomly. After that the initiating node will generate the timestamps T and encrypt the VN_{init}, id_{init}, and T with K_{ps}. Then, the node will send the request containing id_{init} and $E_{ps}(VN_{init}, id_{init}, T)$ to the response node $N_{response}$ (Fig. 2).

After the response node $N_{response}$ receives the request, the node will decrypt the encrypted part of request $E_{ps}(VN_{init}, id_{init}, T)$ to get the id_{init} and check if the T is in the acceptable time range, and the id id_{init} is in the list id_{all} to verify that the source node is from a node in the pairing group. If the id id_{init} is in the list id_{all}, the response node will randomly choose a value $VN_{response}$ and hash VN_{init} to get the hash value $HN_{init} = H_{SHA-256}(VN_{init})$. At last, the response node generate a timestamp T and encrypts HN_{init}, $VN_{response}$, $id_{response}$, and T with K_{PS} and sends the response containing $id_{response}$ and $E_{ps}(HN_{init}, VN_{response}, id_{response}, T)$ back to the initiating node N_{init}.

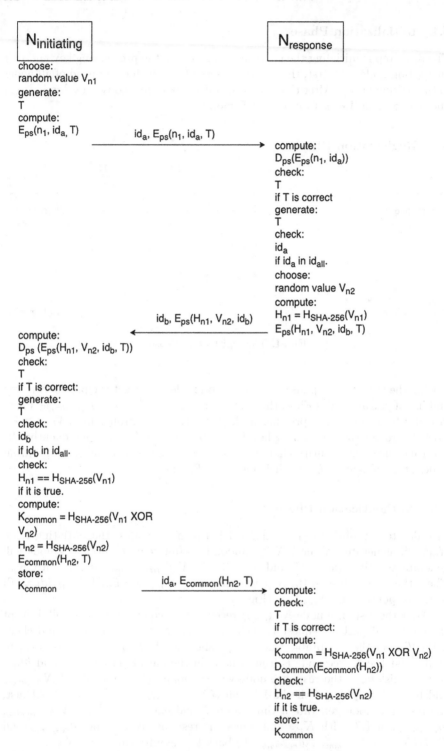

Fig. 2. The authentication phase

When the initiate node N_{init} receives the response, the node will decrypt the encrypted part $E_{ps}(HN_{init}, VN_{response}, id_{response}, T)$ of what it recives. Next, the node check whether the T is in the acceptable time range, and the $id_{response}$ is in the list id_{all} to verify that the response is from a node in the pairing group. Then, the node will hash N_{init} to get the hash value HN_{init} and confirm HN_{init} is equal to $H_{SHA-256}(VN_{init})$ to affirm that the response node $N_{response}$ has received the request it sent. After acknowledging it, the initiating node computes $K_{common} = H_{SHA-256}(VN_{init} \oplus VN_{response})$ to get the joint key. Afterward, the node generate the timestamp T and hash the value $VN_{response}$ to get the hash value $HN_{response}$. At last, the node encrypts $HN_{response}$ and T with the joint key K_{common}, and the node will send the response containing id_{init} and $E_{common}(HN_{response}, T)$ to the response node $N_{response}$ and store the joint key K_{common} in its memory.

When the response node $N_{response}$ has sent the response, it also simultaneously computes the joint key K_{common} to decrypt the response it will receive. When the node gets the response from initiating node N_{init}, the response node will decrypt it to get the hash value $HN_{response}$ and verify that the timestamp T is in acceptable range and $HN_{response}$ is equal to $H_{SHA-256}(VN_{response})$ to check whether the response's origin can be trusted. If the response's origin can be trusted, the node will store the joint key K_{common} in its memory. After all, the initiating and response node create a secure channel successfully.

4   Security Analysis

We claim that our solution is resistant to Man-in-the-middle attacks and replay attacks and also has features such as mutual authentication. The security analysis of these features is described in detail as follows.

4.1   Man-in-the-middle Attack

To prevent the Man-in-the-middle attack, a mechanism to exchange keys and verify authentication safety is needed. Therefore, a method to avoid the Man-in-the-middle is essential. In the proposed scheme, we use the pre-sharing key K_{ps} and node id list id_{all} to ensure the information does not leak during the authentication phase. The crucial information which the Diffie-Hellman algorithm need will be encrypted by the pre-sharing key K_{ps}, which is pre-deployed. Furthermore, when a node receives any initiating information, the node will confirm that the source node id, represented by this id, is from the same group of nodes id_{all}. In addition, we set a value HN_i to confirm that the peer node will acknowledge the message we send yet to ensure the data integrity.

4.2   Replay Attack

To prevent the replay attack, the most common cyberattack method on the internet, we need to find an efficient mechanism to ensure the data received. In this kind of attack, the adversary eavesdrops on the transmission process in the authentication phase and captures packets, messages, or data segments. Then the adversary will resend the information captured to the recipient once intact. Cause the original sender sent the information at the beginning, the recipient will have difficulty identifying and accepting the data without hesitation. When a replay attack happens, the recipient cannot effectively verify who sends the message. It may be a critical loophole. The disadvantage of a replay attack is that an adversary does not even have to use advanced skills to decrypt a message after capturing it during the transmission process. Just by resending the whole thing, the attack could succeed. Therefore, our proposed scheme adds a timestamp to the encryption message during the transmission process in the authentication phase to prevent a replay attack. When any nodes send the message, it will generate a timestamp and encrypt it to the message it will send. After that, when the receiving node gets this message, the node will decrypt it and check whether the timestamp is within an acceptable range. If the timestamp it got is expired, a replay attack may happen. In summary, the node can ideally prevent the replay attack with the timestamp.

4.3   Mutual Authentication

In our application context, mutual authentication between nodes is indispensable because an attacker may pose as a node to obtain information. To verify whether a node is in a node group, the controller will share all node's id in id_{all} belonging group. When the node establishes a communication channel in the authentication phase, the response node will verify whether the source node id_{init} in the trusted id list id_{all}. After that, when the response node replies to the message to initiating node, the initiating node will also check whether this response is from a trusted node $id_{response}$ in the group id_{all}. Therefore, in our proposed scheme, the nodes have met the requirement of mutual authentication.

5   Performance Evaluation

In this section, we will measure the computation cost at each phase in order to provide informed data for the efficiency of our scheme.

5.1   Computation Cost

In our proposed scheme, we simulate the cryptography module to calculate the computation cost with the SHA-256 [9] and the AES [8] ctx mode. Our simulation environment are showed in the Tables 2 and 3. Also, we calculate simulation result with different cryptography module. The simulation result are show at the Table 4.

Table 2. The virtual machine set up

Hardware type	Hardware specification
CPU	2 cores
Memory	1 GB
SWAP	1 GB

Table 3. The calculation cost

Function	Calculation cost
$E_{ps}(\cdot)$	0.039962 s
$D_{ps}(E_{ps}(\cdot))$	0.040181 s
$H_{SHA-256}$	0.000005 s

Table 4. The testing platform information

Hardware type	Hardware specification
CPU	R9 3900×
GPU	RX 6600
Memory	64 G DDR4 3200 MHz
File size	257 KB

At the initialize phase, we only generate some value and keys. Nothing calculation exist. So the calculation cast is ignored. At the registration phase, the controller do a 256 bit XOR and a SHA-256 calculation. The bits operation can be ignored, and the SHA-256 costs about 0.000005 s, so the calculation cost in registration phase is about 0.000005 s. At the authentication phase, first, the initial node N_{init} needs to calculate the encryption function, the calculation costs of first section is about 0.039962 s. Second, the response node $N_{response}$ needs to calculate a decryption function, a hash function, and a encrypt function. The cost of second section is about 0.080148 s. $E_{ps}(\cdot)\times1+H_{SHA-256}\times1+D_{ps}(E_{ps}(\cdot))\times1 \approx 0.080148$. Third, the initial node N_{init} needs to calculate a decrypt function, three hash function, and a encrypt function. The total time at the third section is about 0.080158 s. $E_{ps}(\cdot) \times 1 + H_{SHA-256} \times 3 + D_{ps}(E_{ps}(\cdot)) \times 1 \approx 0.080158$ Forth, the response node $N_{response}$ needs to compute two hash function and a decryption function. The total time at the forth section is about 0.040191 s $H_{SHA-256} \times 2 + D_{ps}(E_{ps}(\cdot)) \times 1 \approx 0.040191$. The total calculation cost in the authentication phase is about 0.240459 s (Table 5).

Table 5. Time cost of each stage.

Phase	Controller	$node_i$	$node_{i+1}$
Registration	$H_{SHA-256}$		
Authentication		$E_{ps}(\cdot)$	
Authentication			$D_{ps}(E_{ps}(\cdot)) + H_{SHA-256}(\cdot) + E_{ps}(\cdot)$
Authentication		$D_{ps}(E_{ps}(\cdot)) + H_{SHA-256}(\cdot) \times 3 + E_{ps}(\cdot)$	
Authentication			$H_{SHA_2 56}(\cdot) \times 2 + D_{ps}(E_{ps}(\cdot))$

6 Conclusion

The scheme of this paper is structured by Physically Unclonable Function (PUF), Diffie Hellman, and protocol design, which aim to reduce power consumption and generate truly random values to improve security reliability. Therefore, there are three phases in our scheme, including the initialization phase, the registration phase, and the authentication phase. In addition to authentication, the main goal of this paper is to create a secure channel between nodes by using a Physically Unclonable Function (PUF) to generate value, verify identity, and revoke it efficiently. This paper also ensures that power consumption fits manufacturing environments by queuing the value. In the security analysis, this paper analyzed Man-in-the-middle attacks, replay attacks, and mutual authentication, which means that our scheme proves to be secure in use and more importantly, also protects transmission security, making it possible to achieve both authentication and save performance consumption in manufacturing environments (Table 6).

Table 6. The contribution comparison.

	RSA	OurScheme
Memory usage(KB)	25,891	15,679
Time cost(ms)	16,270	70
Truly random	Doesn't used	Pseudo

Acknowledgement. This work was partially supported by the Ministry of Science and Technology of Taiwan under grant MOST 111-2218-E-011-016- and MOST 111-2221-E-011-112.

References

1. Gurunath, R., et al.: An overview: security issue in IoT network. In: 2018 2nd International Conference on I-SMAC (IoT in Social, Mobile, Analytics and Cloud)(I-SMAC) I-SMAC (IoT in Social, Mobile, Analytics and Cloud)(I-SMAC). IEEE (2018)
2. Lo'ai, T., et al.: IoT privacy and security: challenges and solutions. Appl. Sci. **10**(12), 4102 (2020)

3. Charles, H., et al.: Physical unclonable functions and applications: a tutorial. Proc. IEEE **102**(8), 1126–1141 (2014)
4. Shamsoshoara, A., Korenda, A., Afghah, F., Zeadally, S.: A survey on physical unclonable function (PUF)-based security solutions for Internet of Things. Comput. Netw. **183**, 107593 (2020)
5. Babaei, A., Schiele, G.: Physical unclonable functions in the internet of things: state of the art and open challenges. Sensors **19**(14), 3208 (2019)
6. John, R.A., et al.: Halide perovskite memristors as flexible and reconfigurable physical unclonable functions. Nat. Commun. **12**(1), 1–11 (2021)
7. Gao, Y., Al-Sarawi, S.F., Abbott, D.: Physical unclonable functions. Nat. Electron. **3**(2), 81–91 (2020)
8. tiny-AES-c. https://github.com/kokke/tiny-AES-c. Accessed 22 Dec 2021
9. sha256. https://github.com/LekKit/sha256. Accessed 9 Aug 2020

Image Compression and Meaningful Ciphertext Encryption Based on Histogram Shift Embedding

Zheng Tang[1], Shiwei Jing[2], Jianjun Li[2(✉)], Guobao Hui[1], and Wanyong Tian[1]

[1] Key Laboratory of Data Link, CETC 21th Institute, China Electronics Technology Group Corporation, XiAn 710071, Shanxi, China

[2] School of Computer Science and Technology, Hangzhou Dianzi University, Hangzhou 310018, China

Jianjun.li@hdu.edu.cn

Abstract. In this paper, a meaningful ciphertext compression and encryption method is proposed. Firstly, the image is sparsely transformed based on wavelet transform, scrambled and compressed to get the Gaussian noise-like ciphertext. Then, the distribution of noise-like ciphertext is changed by a histogram shift, and the meaningful ciphertext is obtained by the least significant bit (LSB) XOR. Finally, the ciphertext is modified by 2^K correction, and the ciphertext with better quality is obtained. In order to ensure the plaintext sensitivity and the ability to resist the attack of selecting plain ciphertext, the plaintext of SHA-256 is used to generate dynamic keys so that the whole process can achieve the effect of one-image-one-key. Experimental results show that this meaningful ciphertext encryption method has excellent quality of ciphertext and ensures visual security as well as. At the same time, the algorithm has a good ability to resist conventional attacks and has certain practicability.

Keywords: Image encryption · Meaningful ciphertext · Histogram shift

1 Introduction

Image encryption is one of the main ways to protect image security, and the conventional encryption process of digital images mainly includes scrambling, diffusion and so on [1, 2]. These encryption algorithms encrypt the plaintext image into a noise image, which is easy to be detected and attacked by attackers in the transmission process. Therefore, Bao and Zhou [4] proposed a meaningful ciphertext encryption method. They embed the noise-like ciphertext into the carrier image so that the ciphertext is visually the same as the carrier image, which greatly reduces the possibility of the ciphertext being discovered. So far, many meaningful ciphertext encryption methods have been mainly divided into the transform domain and space domain according to the embedded domain. [4] first proposed the embedding method of meaningful ciphertext in the embedding method of the wavelet transform, which is also the most common modified method. The main

S.-Y. Hsieh et al. (Eds.): ICS 2022, CCIS 1723, pp. 398–406, 2022.
https://doi.org/10.1007/978-981-19-9582-8_35

process is to directly replace the two high-frequency information after the wavelet transform of the carrier image with hundreds and ten's digit and the one's digit of the noise-like ciphertext. [5–7] proposed the method of modifying both the noise-like ciphertext encryption and the embedding method. Even though the ciphertext obtained by this intrusion method has robust texture features, the quality of the ciphertext is not high. Therefore, a large number of modification schemes have been proposed successively [8–13]. Among them, the PSNR of ciphertext in [12,13] reach more than 45, which is the highest level in the transformation domain embedding method. [14–16] improve the quality of ciphertext by learning weight parameters of noise-like ciphertext and the carrier high-level information. The quality of the ciphertext can be optimized by adjusting the weight parameters, but there is information loss in the subsequent quantization of the ciphertext. The spatial domain mainly includes the LSB embedding method [17,18] and matrix encoding [19]. [18] added 2^K correction after the LSB embedding, which made the relative change smaller and the ciphertext quality improved, and the PSNR of the ciphertext reached 46.3. The carrier image in the above meaningful ciphertext encryption methods needs to be four times or even more than the noisy ciphertext [5,16,19], which leads to a large volume of ciphertext and is not convenient for the transmission of ciphertext. Therefore, compressed sensing (CS) has been introduced into many meaningful ciphertext encryptions. CS can not only compress the image volume but also change the pixel value, which is also in line with the encryption characteristics, making CS very suitable for image encryption. But they do not take into account the distribution of measured values well and set better embeddings based on their distribution.

Based on the above analysis, this paper designs a new meaningful ciphertext encryption method with the following innovations.

1 After fully considering the distribution of measured values, using the idea of cyclic shift of histogram, the distribution of measured values is close to both sides and combined with LSB XOR embedding and 2^K correction, the ciphertext quality has reached a very high level. When the plaintext is the same size as the carrier, the peak signal-to-noise ratio of the ciphertext and the carrier can reach about 48, which is much better than other algorithms.

2 In order to resist selected plaintext and ciphertext attacks and improve the sensitivity of plaintext, this paper uses SHA-256 of plaintext to generate dynamic keys to control the generation of chaotic sequences so that the whole process forms a one-image-one-key encryption effect and the security is greatly enhanced.

2 The Meaningful Ciphertext Generation of Histogram Shift

2.1 2^K Correction Method

The 2^K correction method [18] is a mathematical adjustment method to optimize the quality of the ciphertext. This method adjusts the first k bits of the ciphertext through the difference between the ciphertext and the carrier, which can be expressed by Equation (1).

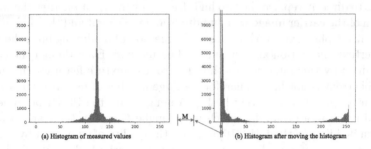

Fig. 1. The comparison histogram of the compressed value histogram of plaintext woman before and after cyclic shift

$$I_1(i,j) = \begin{cases} I(i,j) - 2^K & I(i,j) - C(i,j) > 2^{K-1} and I(i,j) - 2^K \geq \text{LB} \\ I(i,j) + 2^K & I(i,j) - C(i,j) < -2^{K-1} and I(i,j) + 2^K \leq \text{UB} \\ I(i,j) & other \end{cases} \quad (1)$$

LB and UB are the upper and lower bounds of the data type, which are 0 and 255, respectively, in this paper, and K is set to 2 in this method.

2.2 Histogram Shift Embedding

In this paper, bits of noise-like ciphertext are embedded in the lowest two bits of the cover image in the form of XOR. When the noise-like ciphertext is uniformly distributed and the cover image is 4 times of the noise-like ciphertext. The theoretical value of this PSNR is 44.1514, and the theoretical value is 46.3699 after 2^K correction. If the proportion of 00 bits of noise-like ciphertext increases, the PSNR will be higher. Therefore, this paper adopts the histogram rotation shift method to improve its proportion. Equations (2) and (3) explain the histogram cyclic shift process. Figure 1 shows the histogram change of woman's measured value before and after moving. After moving in this way, the proportion of 00 bits is around 1/2, and then the PSNR can reach about 48.

$$TT = \text{argmax}((\text{hist}(y))) + M \quad (2)$$

$$y_{new(i)} = \begin{cases} y_{(i)} - TT + 256 & y_{(i)} \leq TT \\ y_{(i)} - TT & y_{(i)} > TT \end{cases} \quad (3)$$

3 Encryption and Decryption Process

3.1 Encryption Process

The encryption process in this paper is mainly divided into pseudo-random sequence generation, compression encryption and meaningful ciphertext embedding. The main process is shown in Fig. 2.

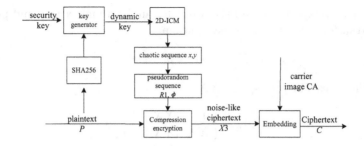

Fig. 2. Encryption process

Step1 pseudo-random sequence generation. Calculating the SHA-256 hash function value of the plain image p, divide it into 8-bit blocks, and obtain a decimal sequence of length 32, denoted as $h_1, h_2, \cdots, h_{32}$. This process is represented by (4).

$$h_1, h_2, \cdots, h_{32} = \text{sha256}(p) \tag{4}$$

The dynamic key is generated according to the following formula.

$$h = \frac{h_1 + h_2 + \cdots + h_{32}}{256 \times 32} \tag{5}$$

$$x_0 = \left(\frac{h_1 \oplus h_2 \cdots \oplus h_8 - 127.5}{127.5} + x_0'\right) \times \frac{h}{2} \tag{6}$$

$$y_0 = \left(\frac{h_9 \oplus h_{10} \cdots \oplus h_{16} - 127.5}{127.5} + y_0'\right) \times \frac{h}{2} \tag{7}$$

$$a = \frac{h_{17} \oplus h_{18} \cdots \oplus h_{24}}{25.5} \times \frac{h}{2} + a' \tag{8}$$

$$b = \frac{h_{25} \oplus h_{26} \cdots \oplus h_{32}}{255} \times \frac{h}{2} + b' \tag{9}$$

where x_0', y_0', a' and b' are security keys for manual control parameters. x_0, y_0, a and b are dynamic keys. Take x_0, y_0, a, b into Equation (10) 2D-ICM chaos [3], iterate $1000 + m \times n$ times, remove the first 1000 times to get the sequence x, y, and then substituted into the following equation to generate a pseudo-random sequence R for control scrambling and a measurement matrix ϕ for sampling.

$$\begin{cases} x_{n+1} = \sin(a/y_n)\sin(b/x_n) \\ y_{n+1} = \sin(a/x_n)\sin(b/y_n) \end{cases} \tag{10}$$

$$R = \text{sort}(x) \tag{11}$$

$$\phi = \text{reshape}(y[1 : cr \times m \times m], (cr \times m, m)) \tag{12}$$

$$\phi_i = \begin{cases} -1 & \phi_i \leq 0 \\ 1 & \phi_i > 0 \end{cases} \tag{13}$$

compression encryption Obtain the wavelet transform matrix ww, and perform wavelet transform according to the equation

$$XX = ww \times p \times ww^*$$ (14)

Use the threshold T to sparse XX.

$$X1_i = \begin{cases} 0 & |XX_i| \leq T \\ XX_i & |XX_i| > T \end{cases}$$ (15)

$X1$ is changed into one dimension, and $X2$ is obtained by scrambling with the R sequence under Formula (16). Finally, it is quantized and its shape is changed into two dimensions to obtain a noise-like ciphertext $X3$.

$$X2_i = X1_{R_i}$$ (16)

$$X3 = \text{round}\left(\frac{255 \times (X2 - X2_{\min})}{X2_{\max} - X2_{\min}}\right)$$ (17)

Embedding $X4$ is obtained by histogram shifting the noise-like ciphertext $X3$ according to Eqs. (2) and (3). The bit-separated sequence $X4_{bit}$ is obtained as the following formula.

$$\begin{cases} CA = \text{floor}(X4, 2^6) \\ CH = \text{floor}(\text{mod}(X4, 2^6), 2^4) \\ CV = \text{floor}(\text{mod}(X4, 2^4), 2^2) \\ CD = \text{mod}(X4, 2^2) \end{cases}$$ (18)

$$X4_{bit} = [CA, CH; CV, CD]$$ (19)

$X4_{bit}$ is XORed with the carrier image CA to obtain $X5$, which is brought into formula (1) for 2^K correction to obtain the final ciphertext C.

3.2   Decryption Process

The decryption process is the inverse of the encryption process. In addition to passing the dynamic key to the user, $X2_{min}$, $X2_{max}$ and histogram movement parameter TT need to be transmitted to the user. These keys can be encrypted by the conventional asymmetric RSA algorithm and transmitted over the public network or directly transmitted over the private network. The specific decryption process here will not be described again.

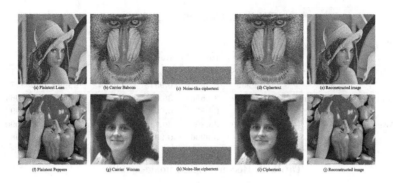

(a) Plaintext Lean   (b) Carrier Baboon   (c) Noise-like ciphertext   (d) Ciphertext   (e) Reconstructed image

(f) Plaintext Peppers   (g) Carrier Woman   (h) Noise-like ciphertext   (i) Ciphertext   (j) Reconstructed image

Fig. 3. Encryption process

4 Experiment Analysis

The computer used is running memory 16G, i7 processor, Windows 10 system, and the simulation software is pycharm2021. Set sec_{key}=[$x'_0 = 0.55$, $y'_0 = 0.55$, $a' = 21$, $b' = 21$], and generate the corresponding dynamic key according to different plaintext, the histogram shift parameter $M = -3$. The sampling rate CR of the image is set to 0.25; the "Sym8" wavelet is used to decompose the image by DWT, the sparse threshold $T = 20$, and NSL0 is used for reconstruction ($deta = 0.98$, sigma $= 0.1$, $ksai = 0.1$). All experimental codes are published at: https://github.com/jsw1995/MCE-HSE.

4.1 Encryption and Decryption Results

In order to verify the feasibility and advanced nature of this paper, this paper uses images of standard test images, datasets for performance analysis. Figure 3 presents the simulation results.

It can be seen from Fig. 3, the plaintext information can not be recognized in the noise-like ciphertext at all, and both the ciphertext and the carrier image are not seen visually, which shows that the algorithm has a good encryption effect. The reconstructed image also clearly reflects the plaintext information, indicating that the decryption effect is good.

4.2 Comparison of Ciphertext and Reconstruction Quality

In order to prove the progressiveness of this paper, PSNR and SSIM are used to quantify and compare the ciphertext and decryption quality. Among them, document [4,12] does not have a specific noise-like encryption method, so the noise-like encryption method in this paper is used for comparison.Table 1 and Table 2 show the PSNR and MSSIM of the ciphertext and decrypted image of different algorithms, respectively.

It can be seen from Table 1 that the PSNR of the ciphertext of this algorithm can reach 48, which is much larger than other algorithms, and the MSSIM has

Table 1. Ciphertext quality

Plain image	Carrier image	PSNR/MSSIM					
		Ref. [16]	Ref. [17]	Ref. [20]	Ref. [12]	Ref. [4]	Our
Lena	Baboon	32.4068	35.1636	35.4068	45.3526	28.2244	48.1115
		0.9955	0.9941	0.9973	0.9994	0.9694	0.9997
Peppers	Woman	31.1572	36.5561	38.0258	45.2558	31.2116	48.1064
		0.9913	0.9870	0.9933	0.9997	0.9935	0.9999
Average		31.7820	35.8599	36.7163	45.3042	29.718	48.1090
		0.9934	0.9906	0.9953	0.9996	0.9815	0.9998

Table 2. Reconstructed image quality

Plain image	Carrier image	PSNR			
		Ref. [16]	Ref. [17]	Ref. [20]	Our
Lena	Baboon	31.0864	33.0984	32.9538	33.9760
Peppers	Woman	31.1202	32.6477	33.6672	32.3988
Average		31.1033	32.8731	33.3105	33.1874

(a) Plaintext   (b) Attack image   (c) Cracked image

Fig. 4. Select plaintext attack analysis

been very close to 1, which indicates that the ciphertext is very similar to the carrier image. The PSNR of the reconstructed image in Table 2 can also reach more than 33, which shows that the decrypted image has no impact on extracting the image information and can be used in practice.

4.3   Select Plaintext and Ciphertext Attacks

Choosing plaintext and ciphertext attacks is the most threatening to the encryption system. As long as it can resist such attacks, it can basically resist other common attacks [1]. Therefore, this paper selects the first pixel of the plaintext plus 1 as the attack image when the plaintext is Lean to obtain the cracked image, as shown in Fig. 4.

It can be seen from Fig. 4 that when the attack image is only one pixel away from the original image, the original image cannot be cracked even if the human eye cannot distinguish it, and it is more difficult in other cases. This is mainly because this paper uses SHA-256 in plain text to generate dynamic keys, which makes the whole process achieve the encryption effect of one-image-one-key.

5   Conclusion

In this paper, the PSNR of ciphertext is about 48 by using the LSB XOR embedding method of histogram shift and 2^K correction, which is much higher than other existing meaningful ciphertext encryption methods. Also, its visual security of ciphertext is higher. The use of CS makes the volume of ciphertext smaller and facilitates the transmission of ciphertext. The 2D-ICM hyperchaos is used to ensure the randomness of the pseudo-random sequence and the security of the entire encryption system. Finally, this paper uses SHA-256 of plaintext to generate dynamic keys to control chaos to generate pseudo-random sequences so that the entire encryption system can have good plaintext sensitivity and anti-chosen-ciphertext attack ability.

Acknowledgements. This work was supported in part by the national Natural Science Fund of China no.61871170; Key Research and Development Plan of Zhejiang: No. 2021C03131. Open Fund of Key Laboratory of Data Link Technology of CETC 20th Institute: No.CLDL-20202207.

References

1. Guo, Y., Jing, S., Zhou, Y., Xu, X., Wei, L.: An image encryption algorithm based on logistic-fibonacci cascade chaos and 3D bit scrambling. IEEE Access. **8**, 9896–9912 (2020). https://doi.org/10.1109/ACCESS.2019.2963717
2. Liu, L., Wang, J.: A cluster of 1D quadratic chaotic map and its applications in image encryption. Math. Comput. Simul. **204**, 89–114 (2022). https://doi.org/10.1016/j.matcom.2022.07.030
3. Cao, W., Mao, Y., Zhou, Y.: Designing a 2D infinite collapse map for image encryption. Signal Process. **171**, 107457 (2020). https://doi.org/10.1016/j.sigpro.2020.107457
4. Bao, L., Zhou, Y.: Image encryption: generating visually meaningful encrypted images. Inf. Sci. **324**, 197–207 (2015). https://doi.org/10.1016/j.ins.2015.06.049
5. Chai, X., Gan, Z., Chen, Y., Zhang, Y.: A visually secure image encryption scheme based on compressive sensing. Signal Process. **134**, 35–51 (2017). https://doi.org/10.1016/j.sigpro.2016.11.016
6. Chai, X., Wu, H., Gan, Z., Zhang, Y., Chen, Y.: Hiding cipher-images generated by 2-D compressive sensing with a multi-embedding strategy. Signal Process. **171**, 107525 (2020). https://doi.org/10.1016/j.sigpro.2020.107525
7. Chai, X., Wu, H., Gan, Z., Han, D., Zhang, Y., Chen, Y.: An efficient approach for encrypting double color images into a visually meaningful cipher image using 2D compressive sensing. Inf. Sci. **556**, 305–340 (2021). https://doi.org/10.1016/j.ins.2020.10.007
8. Yang, Y.G., Zhang, Y.C., Chen, X., Zhou, Y.H., Shi, W.M.: Eliminating the texture features in visually meaningful cipher images. Inf. Sci. **429**, 102–119 (2018). https://doi.org/10.1016/j.ins.2017.11.009
9. Kanso, A., Ghebleh, M.: An algorithm for encryption of secret images into meaningful images. Opt. Lasers Eng. **90**, 196–208 (2017). https://doi.org/10.1016/j.optlaseng.2016.10.009

10. Wang, H., Xiao, D., Li, M., Xiang, Y., Li, X.: A visually secure image encryption scheme based on parallel compressive sensing. Signal Process. **155**, 218–232 (2019). https://doi.org/10.1016/j.sigpro.2018.10.001

11. Armijo-Correa, J.O., Murguía, J.S., Mejía-Carlos, M., Arce-Guevara, V.E., Aboytes-González, J.A.: An improved visually meaningful encrypted image scheme. Opt. Laser Technol. **127**, 106165 (2020). https://doi.org/10.1016/j.optlastec.2020.106165

12. Yang, Y.-G., Wang, B.-P., Yang, Y.-L., Zhou, Y.-H., Shi, W.-M., Liao, X.: Visually meaningful image encryption based on universal embedding model. Inf. Sci. **562**, 304–324 (2021). https://doi.org/10.1016/j.ins.2021.01.041

13. Yang, Y.-G., Wang, B.-P., Pei, S.-K. Zhou, Y.-H., Shi, W.-M., Liao, X.: Using M-ary decomposition and virtual bits for visually meaningful image encryption. Inf. Sci. **580**, 174–201 (2021). https://doi.org/10.1016/j.ins.2021.08.073

14. Wang, X., Ren, Q., Jiang, D.: An adjustable visual image cryptosystem based on 6D hyperchaotic system and compressive sensing. Nonlinear Dyn. **104**, 4543–4567 (2021). https://doi.org/10.1007/s11071-021-06488-y

15. Huang, X., Dong, Y., Guodong, Y.E., Shi, Y.: Meaningful image encryption algorithm based on compressive sensing and integer wavelet transform. Front. Comput. Sci. **104**, 1–20 (2022). https://doi.org/10.1007/s11704-022-1419-8

16. Zhu, L., et al.: A robust meaningful image encryption scheme based on block compressive sensing and SVD embedding. Signal Process. **175**, 107629 (2020). https://doi.org/10.1016/j.sigpro.2020.107629

17. Chai, X., Wu, H., Gan, Z., Zhang, Y., Chen, Y., Nixon, K.W.: An efficient visually meaningful image compression and encryption scheme based on compressive sensing and dynamic LSB embedding. Opt. Lasers. Eng. **124**, 105837 (2020). https://doi.org/10.1016/j.optlaseng.2019.105837

18. Yang, Y.-G., Wang, B.-P., Yang, Y.-L., Zhou, Y.-H., Shi, W.-M., Liao, X.: A visually meaningful image encryption algorithm based on adaptive 2D compressive sensing and chaotic system. Multimed. Tools App. 1–30 (2022). https://doi.org/10.1007/s11042-021-11656-8

19. Hua, Z., Zhang, K., Li, Y., Zhou, Y.: Visually secure image encryption using adaptive-thresholding sparsification and parallel compressive sensing. Signal Process. **183**, 107998 (2021). https://doi.org/10.1016/j.sigpro.2021.107998

20. Jiang, D., Liu, L., Zhu, L., Wang, X., Rong, X., Chai, H.: Adaptive embedding: a novel meaningful image encryption scheme based on parallel compressive sensing and slant transform. Signal Process. **188**, 108220 (2021). https://doi.org/10.1016/j.sigpro.2021.108220

A Robust Two Factor Authentication Scheme with Fine Grained Biometrics Verification

Fang-Ting Wu, Shao-Wei Tung, and Jheng-Jia Huang(✉)®

Department of Information Management, National Taiwan University of Science
and Technology, Taipei, Taiwan
jhengjia.huang@mail.ntust.edu.tw
https://aclab.cs.ntust.edu.tw

Abstract. The traditional account and password verification method
has not only been inconducive to user experience but also security
threats. Although biometrics improves the user experience, biometric
data can be stolen. FIDO is a rapid authentication mechanism however
it does neither pass user biometrics through the server nor performs biometric identification on the user devices. This study develops a robust
two factors authentication scheme with fine-grained biometrics verification for preserving privacy that seamlessly processes users' authentication identities. Results of the simulation showed the proposed protocol
had more properties in user authentication than the existing authentication schemes.

Keywords: Biometric-based · Two-factor · User authentication
protocol

1 Introduction

As cloud computing services scale up, many companies have stored their information on cloud-based platforms, user authentication has become a vital gateway to
access cloud services [6]. Taking the financial industry as an example, majority
digital financial services have used the account number and text password as an
identification method to login. Considering the text password authentication is
not secure enough to protect users' access to personal information, many financial service providers have adopted a one-time password (OTP) SMS approach to
strengthen user authentication. The National Institute of Standards and Technology (NIST) alerted this two-stage authentication has risks such as man-in-
the-middle attack (MITM) and other threats and recommended that enterprises
should avoid using SMS or voice to conduct user authentication [10]. To prevent
users' passwords from being threatened by attacks such as Dictionary File, Brute
Forcing Attack, Rule-Based Attack, and Password Guessing, service providers
impose various restrictions on passwords to improve password security [4]. However, this authentication method is not conducive to user experience including

S.-Y. Hsieh et al. (Eds.): ICS 2022, CCIS 1723, pp. 407–418, 2022.
https://doi.org/10.1007/978-981-19-9582-8_36

passwords must be changed frequently, password types are becoming increasingly complex, and users are prone to forgetting or losing their passwords [2,11,14]. Physiological characteristics are the characteristics of individuals who remain unchanged over their lifetime, biometric identification technology may replace the entry of complex password, but it also has safety problems [8]. An example of 1.1 million fingerprint data leakage incidents of the US Bureau of Personnel in 2015, the user's biometrics were stored in the bureau's server by scrambled and compared for identification. The user's biometrics are shared by every service which increases the threat of attacks. Once personal data has stolen or leaked, it causes significant damage. To improve problems of identity verification, FIDO Alliance (Fast Identity Online Alliance) developed technical standards for fast online identity verification. According to FIDO, both authentication mechanism and user's biometrics are executed at local devices [1]. This method prevents the user and the server from being attacked during data transmission of authentication. However, the identification in users' devices have different quality which may cause the accuracy of a biometric identification to be different, and the verification at the local end cannot ensure absolute security. Facing the above issues of user authentication, it is necessary to develop a reliable and agile way for a two-factor user authentication scheme by integrating biometrics and passwords.

1.1   Contributions

This study aims to develop a two-factor user authentication scheme to improve the problems in biometrics and FIDO. The main contributions of the proposed scheme include:

1. True two-factor authentication: using password and biometrics, where passwords represent what you know, and biometrics mean what you are, and they are all verified at the end device.
2. Reliable biometrics privacy: in the proposed scheme, each user's biometric model and biometrics samples are protected while the server performs the matching algorithm. The server is unable to recognize biometrics during the authentication process. Therefore, the server itself or any opponent that has corrupted the server cannot get the actual biometrics from the users.
3. Security analysis: the proposed protocol meets the requirements of comprehensiveness and validity that are consistent the two-factor authentication security definition.

1.2   Organization

In Sect. 2, we review some background knowledge, including RSA (Rivest-Shamir-Adleman) encryption and fuzzy extractor. In Sect. 3, we show some related works for a two-factor scheme with biometric-based. The security analysis is given in Sect. 4. The comparisons and simulations between our scheme and existing protocols are given in Sect. 5. Finally, we conclude our work and future directions in Sect. 6.

2 Preliminaries

2.1 RSA

The RSA (Rivest-Shamir-Adleman) encryption is an asymmetric cryptography algorithm in which the private key needs to encrypt the message and uses the public key to decrypt it [19]. The definition of RSA algorithm is defined as below:

1. Randomly select two large prime numbers of about the same size p and q, and compute the composite $N = pq$.
2. To calculate the Euler's function and count the number of integers less than n that are relatively prime to N.
3. Randomly select an integer $e \in [1, N]$, so that e and N are relative prime. $gcd(e, \phi(N)) = 1$ So, the public key is (e, N).
4. Resolved d satisfactorily $1 = ed(mod\ \phi(N))$, i.e. e and d are the inverse of each other modulo $\phi(N)$. So, the private key is d.

For instance, user Alice uses user Bob's public key $PK = (e, N)$ for encrypting the message, and only Bob can use the corresponding private key $SK = d$ to retrieve the message. The formal statements are listed below.

$$Q = M^e(mod\ N)\ and\ M = Q^d(mod\ N)$$

However, noting that $M = Q^d(mod\ N) = M^{ed} = M(mod\ N)$ since $ed = 1(mod\ \phi(N))$

2.2 Fuzzy Extractor

The fuzzy extractor is an algorithm that generates constant information from biometric data including noise. It is a cryptographical primitive designed to reliably get a key from a noise source. A fuzzy extractor [9] is made up of a generate(Gen) probability production procedure and a reproduce(Rep) deterministic reproduction procedure. The probability production procedure Gen on input of user biometric BIO ($\omega \in M$), which M is a metric space outputs an extracted string $R \in \{0, 1\}^{\ell}$ and a helper string $P \in \{0, 1\}^{\ell}$. The fuzzy extractor reliably extracts almost consistently random R from its input. The extraction is defect tolerant in the same direction as R changes even though it remains reasonably close to the initial value. The deterministic reproduction procedure Rep takes an element $BIO^* \in M$ and a bit string $P \in \{0, 1\}^{\ell}$ as inputs. At the same time, it will check the correctness property of fuzzy extractors guarantees whether in the legal defect tolerant value. The formal statements are listed below.

1. $BIO \rightarrow Gen(P, R)$
2. $Rep(BIO^*, P) \rightarrow R$

3   The Proposed Scheme

To improve the current FIDO's biometric problems, a two-factor, revocable, and privacy biometric authentication scheme is proposed, as shown in Fig. 1. Considering a user and a server both has been asked to join an authentication, the proposed scheme consists of four phases: the initialization phase, registration phase, login and authentication phase, and biometric update phase. The RSA algorithm is used to protect the message in the transaction flow. Assuming the server is a semi-trusted third party, the notations used in the proposed scheme are illustrated as the following phases (Table 1).

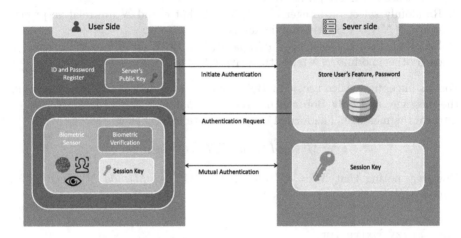

Fig. 1. System model of the proposed scheme

3.1   Initialization Phase

In the initialization phase, the server randomly chooses two large prime numbers p and q and calculates $N = p \times q$. Randomly select an integer $e \in [1, N]$, so that $gcd(e, \phi(N)) = 1$. Further, to resolved d satisfactorily $1 = ed(mod\ \phi(N))$. Finally, the server will produce the public key $PK = (N, e)$ and private key $SK = d$. Then, it was published secure one-way hash function $h(\cdot)$ and public key PK by the server.

3.2   Registration Phase

U_i complete the following steps with S via a secure channel to be a legal user in the registration phase, as shown in Fig. 2.

Table 1. Notations of the proposed scheme

Notation	Meaning
S	The server
U_i	The ith user
$Gen(\cdot)$	An fuzzy extractor algorithm
$Rep(\cdot)$	An fuzzy extractor algorithm
p, q	Two sufficiently large prime number
PK	The server's public key
SK	The server's private key
T	Time stamp
ID_i	The identity of U_i
PW_i	The password of U_i
B_1	The biometric sample which U_i store in server
B_i	The user's biometric
B_i^{new}	A new biometric system is used for the update phase
sk_s	The session key produced by the server
sk_u	The session key computed by the user
$E_{sk}(\cdot)$	Using a symmetric encryption function to encrypt the message by the session key

1. Consider a user U_i with an identity ID_i who wishes to register with the server S. The user U_i randomly chooses a nonce $\alpha \in \mathbb{Z}_p$, selects a password PW_i and imprints B_i and obtains $(R_{bi}, P_{bi}) = Gen(B_i)$.
2. To protect user's biometric, computing the $B_1 = R_{bi} \oplus \alpha$.
3. U_i sends $\{ID_i, B_1, h(PW_i||ID_i)\}$ to the server through a secure channel where $h(\cdot)$ is a public one-way hash function.
4. Once the application for registration has been received, S checks whether ID_i corresponds to any existing entry in the identity information table. If it is invalid, S rejects the request.
5. Differently, S computes $X = h(B_1||h(PW_i||ID_i))$ and stores the B_1, X, ID_i into the server.
6. While U_i receives the response by S, the U_i computes $C_1 = \alpha \oplus PW_i$. When calculating C_1, it is possible to check whether the user is legal in the login and authentication phase. U_i then stores C_1, P_{bi} into the device.

3.3   Login and Authentication Phase

In this phase, the user and the server are mutually authenticated whenever the user wishes to request services. The following steps are performed, as shown in Fig. 3.

1. U_i inputs a ID_i^* and PW_i^* on the terminal and randomly chooses $r_1 \in \mathbb{Z}_p$. The user then computes $C_3 = (ID_i^*||r_1||T||h(PW_i^*||ID_i^*))^{PK}$ using the asymmetric encryption feature key, which is the server's public key PK.

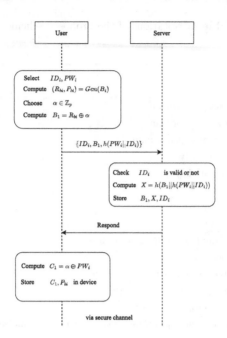

Fig. 2. Registration phase

2. U_i sends $\{C_3, T\}$ to the server.
3. The server decrypts C_3 via the private key SK and checks the time stamp $|T' - T| \leq \Delta T$. It checks if ID_i^* is valid according to the ID table.
4. After that, the server checks $h(h(PW_i^* || ID_i^*) || B_1) \overset{?}{=} X$. If it is false, S rejects the request. Otherwise, S proceeds to the next step.
5. S randomly selects a number $r_2 \in \mathbb{Z}_p$, and generates a set of session key $sk_s = r_1 \oplus r_2$ to compute $C_4 = r_1 \oplus h(PW_i^* || ID_i^*) \oplus r_2$ and $C_5 = E_{sk_s}(B_1 || T)$ encrypting the user's biometrics with its session key. Then, S sends $\{C_4, C_5, T\}$ to U_i.
6. Upon receiving messages, U_i computes $r_2 = C_4 \oplus r_1 \oplus h(PW_i^* || ID_i^*)$ and $sk_u = r_1 \oplus r_2$.
7. The user uses the session key to decrypt C_5 and checks the time stamp $|T' - T| \leq \Delta T$.
8. Otherwise, it continues to compute $\alpha = C_1 \oplus PW_i^*$, $R'_{bi} = B'_1 \oplus \alpha$ and $R_{bi}^* = Rep(B_i^*, P_{bi})$. Finally, the user checks whether $R_{bi}^* \overset{?}{=} R'_{bi}$ is a predefined threshold value or not. If true, the user will accept the login request of S. Otherwise, the user will terminate the session.

3.4   Biometric Update Phase

In this phase, U_i updates the biometrics through the following steps, as shown in Fig. 4.

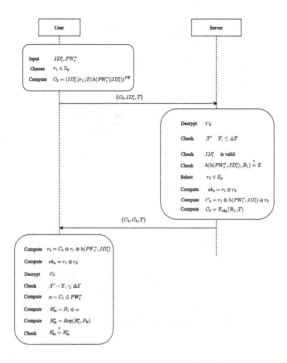

Fig. 3. Login and Authentication phase

1. U_i executes the login phase, and sends additional biometrics change request to S.
2. S executes the first step of the authentication phase. If it is legal, S computes $S_a = h(r_1 || h(PW_i^* || ID_i^*))$. Then, the S computes $C_6 = (S_a || T)^{SK}$ using the asymmetric encryption feature key, which is the server's private key SK. Finally, S sends $\{C_6, T\}$ to the user.
3. The user uses the server's public key PK to decrypt C_6 and check the time stamp $|T' - T| \leq \Delta T$.
4. After decrypt C_6 to get S_a and the permission, U_i first checks $S_a \overset{?}{=} h(r_1 || h(PW_i || ID_i))$. If it keeps, U_i inputs a new biometric information to compute $(R_{bi}^{new}, P_{bi}^{new}) = Gen(B_i)$ at the same time in the terminal.
5. The user randomly chooses a new $\alpha^{new} \in \mathbb{Z}_p$ to compute $B_1^{new} = R_{bi}^{new} \oplus \alpha^{new}$ and $C_7 = (B_1^{new} || T)^{PK}$. Then, the user update P_{bi}^{new} and send $\{C_7, T\}$ to the server.

4 Security Analysis

To perform security analysis of the proposed schema, an asymmetric encryption with a one-way hash function to test the schema against most attacks including dictionary attacks, etc. Details of safety analysis are described as the follows.

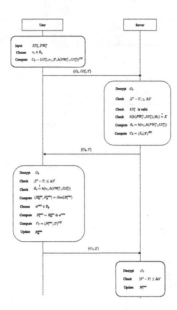

Fig. 4. Biometric update phase

4.1 Mutual Authentication

Mutual authentication is one of the most important properties in group authentication. In our scheme, the goal of the mutual authentication property is to verify the legal user and create a robust group session key sk for all group members. When S receives the user login message, it authenticates C_3 using the asymmetric encryption feature key, which is the server's public key PK. Only the legal user can decrypt C_3 using the asymmetric encryption feature key to get the r_1. In this way, each user can protect the transmission data with asymmetric encryption after the group authentication phase. After that, S generates a set of the session key $sk_s = r_1 \oplus r_2$ to compute $C_4 = r_1 \oplus h(PW_i^*\|ID_i^*) \oplus r_2$ for the user. If it is legal, user can compute the correct r_2 and sk_u to decrypt C_5. If both are equal, U_i authenticates S. Consequently, the proposed scheme completes the mutual authentication.

4.2 Dictionary Attack

The dictionary attack, considered to be one of the most efficient means of obtaining the password, uses well-known words or phrases that would have been used in the password [12,20]. However, according to Feldmeier and Karn [8] methods studied the only way to improved password safety is that users increase the entropy of the passwords they create. The goal of these protocols [3,17] is to overcome offline dictionary attacks on protocols in which participants share a low entropy secret. Thus, the proposed scheme is capable to resist dictionary attacks while the RSA and AES algorithms are used. Moreover, a session key is adopted to protect the plaintext for each transaction flow in the login and authentication phase.

4.3 Replay Attack

When the user U_i transmits message to the server S, an adversary may try to intercept message C_3 and C_5 in the login and authentication phase and use it to perform replay attack. To withstand such attack, a time stamp T incorporated. If the time stamp T is not within reasonable limits $|T' - T| \leq \Delta T$, it will not be accepted by the user and the server. As a result, the messages are different within the respective communication sessions. The proposed scheme is completely resistant to replay attacks.

4.4 Modification Attack

In the login and authentication phase, every transmitted message is encrypted. First, the user executes the login request that the transmits message C_3 is encrypted by the server's public key PK via the secure asymmetric encryption. Then, the server uses random numbers r_1, r_2 to compute $C_4 = r_1 \oplus h(PW_i^*\|ID_i^*) \oplus r_2$. Finally, the sever generates a set of session key to encrypt $C_5 = E_{sk_s}(B_1\|T)$. Thus, only the legal user can decrypt this message. Therefore, the attacker cannot modify the message without the encryption key.

4.5 Man-in-the-Middle Attack

In this attack, an attacker $\mathcal{A}$ may try to pretend to be a valid user U or server S by intercepting messages. This type of attack can be prevented because a mutual authentication is achieved. Hence, the proposed scheme is secure against from the man-in-the-middle attack.

4.6 Biometrics Protection

In the proposed scheme, a nonce $\alpha \in \mathbb{Z}_p$ to unconstraint R_{bi} from the fuzzy extractor produced $Gen(B_i)$ is randomly chosen and computed the $B_1 = R_{bi} \oplus \alpha$. A one-way hash function $h(\cdot)$ is used to protect biometrics B_1, password PW_i and other values stored at the server S. Finally, the proposed scheme of biometrics protection is established.

5 Performance Comparison

5.1 Property Comparison

In this section, the properties and performance of the proposed scheme are compared with the traditional biometrics [15] and FIDO. Five properties are compared among the three schemes, as shown in Table 2. The mutual authentication

Table 2. Properties comparison

Properties	Traditional [15]	FIDO	Ours
Mutual authentication	Yes	Yes	Yes
Session key agreement	No	None	Yes
Reliable biometrics privacy	No	Yes	Yes
Device extractor independent	No	No	Yes
Time synchronization	Yes	Yes	Yes

Table 3. Communication cost of login and authentication phase

Properties	The user side	The server side	The total cost
Ours	1120 bits	384 bits	1504 bits

property offers the user and the server the possibility of identifying themselves. The session key agreement property allows group members to obtain the same session key once authentication processes are completed. Reliable biometrics privacy protects each user's biometric model and biometrics samples while the server performs the matching algorithm. Not only does our scheme match biometrics on the user's device, but it also considers biometrics' privacy. The proposed scheme uses the user biometrics stored on the server for authentication, it is unnecessary to rely on the device extractor for biometric mapping. Because timestamp-based authentication has been used, clocks in the server and local devices must be synchronized and the time of the connection message transmission must also be limited. Apart from the same properties as traditional and FIDO schemes, such as mutual authentication, biometrics privacy, and time synchronization, results show the proposed scheme has embedded other properties including session key agreement absent in traditional scheme and device extractor unseen in FIDO.

5.2   Communication Simulation

Assuming that the output size of the secure one-way hashing function [5] is 256 bits, the key size for an asymmetric cryptosystem is 1024 bits, the key size for a symmetric encryption key is 128 bits, the size for a public-key cryptosystem of RSA is 1024 bits, the size of identification is 32 bits, the size of a random value is 64 bits, and the output size of an asymmetric cryptocurrency [7,18] is based on the content of the ciphertext. Results of the simulation showed 1120 bits communication cost for the user side, 384 bits communication cost for the server side, and 1504 bits in total communication cost, as shown in Table 3.

5.3   Computation Simulation

Results showed the computational costs in the login and authentication phase. T_h be the time to perform a secure unidirectional hash operation, T_e be the cost

Table 4. Computation cost of login and authentication phase

	The user side	The server side	The total cost
Ours	$2T_h + T_e + 5T_{xor} + T_{aes}$ $\approx 243.2T_m$	$T_h + T_e + 3T_{xor} + T_{aes}$ $\approx 242T_m$	$3T_h + 2T_e + 8T_{xor}$ $+2T_{aes} \approx 485.2T_m$

of a modular exponentiation, T_m be the cost of a modular multiplication, T_{aes} be the performing time of a symmetric encryption key, and T_{xor} be the cost of an exclusive-or computation. We assume that $T_h \approx T_{aes} \approx T_{xor} \approx 0.4\ T_m$ which based on [16] and $T_e \approx 240\ T_m$ which based on [13]. The computational costs required during the login and authentication phase of our scheme for the user U_i and server S are $2T_h + T_e + 5T_{xor} + T_{aes}$, and $T_h + T_e + 3T_{xor} + T_{aes}$, respectively. The total computational cost is then $3T_h + 2T_e + 8T_{xor} + 2T_{aes}$, as shown in Table 4.

6   Conclusion

This study develops a robust two factors authentication scheme with fine-grained biometrics verification between the server and end devices. The proposed protocol is practically novel in three aspects. First, user's biometrics are verified on the server, biometrics are not dependent on the extractor's threshold values. Second, FIDO's biometrics are verified on the user devices, the user's biometrics cannot be leaked on the server side. Third, a key agreement based on asymmetric cryptography is adopted in this scheme. This scheme can be applied to any kind of biometric authentication because it is able to protect biometrics privacy on the user's device without the device extractor for biometric mapping. However, even though the proposed scheme provides more protections, it is not cost-effective in terms of computation and communication performances. Future directions is suggested to refine the algorithms for this scheme.

Acknowledgements. This work was partially supported by the Ministry of Science and Technology of Taiwan under grant MOST 111-2218-E-011-016- and MOST 111-2813-C-011-021-H.

References

1. Fido alliance (2018). https://fidoalliance.org/. Accessed 12 Aug 2022
2. Why the password isn't dead quite yet (2021). https://arstechnica.com/information-technology/2021/07/why-the-password-isnt-dead-quite-yet/. Accessed 7 Aug 2022
3. Bellovin, S.M., Merritt, M.: Encrypted key exchange: Password-based protocols secure against dictionary attacks (1992)
4. Chertoff, M., Grant, J.: 8 ways governments can improve their cybersecurity. Harvard Business Review (2017)

5. Dang, Q.H., et al.: Secure hash standard (2015)
6. Dillon, T., Wu, C., Chang, E.: Cloud computing: issues and challenges. In: 2010 24th IEEE International Conference on Advanced Information Networking and Applications, pp. 27–33. IEEE (2010)
7. Dworkin, M.J., et al.: Advanced encryption standard (AES) (2001)
8. Feldmeier, D.C., Karn, P.R.: UNIX password security - ten years later. In: Brassard, G. (ed.) CRYPTO 1989. LNCS, vol. 435, pp. 44–63. Springer, New York (1990). https://doi.org/10.1007/0-387-34805-0_6
9. Huang, X., Xiang, Y., Chonka, A., Zhou, J., Deng, R.H.: A generic framework for three-factor authentication: preserving security and privacy in distributed systems. IEEE Trans. Parallel Distrib. Syst. **22**(8), 1390–1397 (2010)
10. Hwang, M.S., Li, L.H.: A new remote user authentication scheme using smart cards. IEEE Trans. Consum. Electron. **46**(1), 28–30 (2000)
11. Kim, H.S., Lee, S.W., Yoo, K.Y.: ID-based password authentication scheme using smart cards and fingerprints. ACM SIGOPS Oper. Syst. Rev. **37**(4), 32–41 (2003)
12. Kyaw, A.K., Sioquim, F., Joseph, J.: Dictionary attack on wordpress: security and forensic analysis. In: 2015 Second International Conference on Information Security and Cyber Forensics (InfoSec), pp. 158–164. IEEE (2015)
13. Lauter, K.: The advantages of elliptic curve cryptography for wireless security. IEEE Wirel. Commun. **11**(1), 62–67 (2004)
14. Lee, S.-W., Kim, W.-H., Kim, H.-S., Yoo, K.-Y.: Efficient password-based authenticated key agreement protocol. In: Laganá, A., Gavrilova, M.L., Kumar, V., Mun, Y., Tan, C.J.K., Gervasi, O. (eds.) ICCSA 2004. LNCS, vol. 3046, pp. 617–626. Springer, Heidelberg (2004). https://doi.org/10.1007/978-3-540-24768-5_66
15. Li, C.T., Hwang, M.S.: An efficient biometrics-based remote user authentication scheme using smart cards. J. Netw. Comput. Appl. **33**(1), 1–5 (2010)
16. Li, Z., Higgins, J., Clement, M.: Performance of finite field arithmetic in an elliptic curve cryptosystem. In: MASCOTS 2001, Proceedings Ninth International Symposium on Modeling, Analysis and Simulation of Computer and Telecommunication Systems, pp. 249–256. IEEE (2001)
17. Lucks, S.: Open key exchange: how to defeat dictionary attacks without encrypting public keys. In: Christianson, B., Crispo, B., Lomas, M., Roe, M. (eds.) Security Protocols 1997. LNCS, vol. 1361, pp. 79–90. Springer, Heidelberg (1998). https://doi.org/10.1007/BFb0028161
18. Rivest, R.L.: The RC5 encryption algorithm. In: Preneel, B. (ed.) FSE 1994. LNCS, vol. 1008, pp. 86–96. Springer, Heidelberg (1995). https://doi.org/10.1007/3-540-60590-8_7
19. Rivest, R.L., Shamir, A., Adleman, L.: A method for obtaining digital signatures and public-key cryptosystems. Commun. ACM **21**(2), 120–126 (1978)
20. Wang, D., Wang, P.: Offline dictionary attack on password authentication schemes using smart cards. In: Desmedt, Y. (ed.) ISC 2013. LNCS, vol. 7807, pp. 221–237. Springer, Cham (2015). https://doi.org/10.1007/978-3-319-27659-5_16

Electronics and Information Technology

Applying an IoT Analytics Framework in East Asia Area

Chih-Che Chang[1]([✉]), Chia-Mei Chen[1], and Han-Wei Hsiao[2]

[1] National Sun Yat-Sen University, No.70 Lien-Hai Road, Kaohsiung, Taiwan
d104020003@nsysu.edu.tw, cmchen@mail.nsysu.edu.tw
[2] National University of Kaohsiung, No. 700 Kaohsiung University Road, Kaohsiung, Taiwan
hanwei@nuk.edu.tw

Abstract. IoT devices are universal in people's life, and are deployed in many fields. MQTT is one of the most commonly-used communication protocols in IoT. Many IoT have been released on the market without sufficient cyber security protection, it causes many security risks, even causing destruction events. In this study, a new MQTT analytics framework is proposed. The aim of this framework merges reconnaissance, broker exploitation, and risk labeling to label 4 risk severity and 10 common applied fields. The framework makes profiles of MQTT brokers finally, and those profiles help security analysts to filter potential risk MQTT brokers rapidly. This study applies this framework to the East Asia area in order to analyze the brokers distribution and to compare it with the neighboring economic entities with similar backgrounds. In advanced analysis, three interesting application instances were found, and those instances can inspire us how is fragile those services may cause.

Keywords: IoT analytics framework · Large-scale analysis methodology · MQTT brokers

1 Introduction

Internet of Things (IoTs) have become popular and have been deployed in many applications. They are usually small embedded controllers/sensors with communication capability and limited computing resources. IoTs connect sensors, machines, databases, and business information systems into a whole network and collect data for business operations. With limited computing resources, they usually transmit in plain text. Therefore, it's become an attractive target for cyber adversaries as they are usually not facilitated with a proper defensive mechanism. The Statista report pointed out that the number of IoT devices had reached 13.8 billion in 2021 [1], while the Garner research predicted that the amount will grow to 20 billion by 2025 [2]. Therefore, Businesses need to know the usage status of the deployed devices in order to assess the underlying cyber security risk.

Message Queuing Telemetry Transport (MQTT) is a simple and lightweight messaging protocol designed for constrained devices and low-bandwidth networks, frequently

© The Author(s), under exclusive license to Springer Nature Singapore Pte Ltd. 2022
S.-Y. Hsieh et al. (Eds.): ICS 2022, CCIS 1723, pp. 421–433, 2022.
https://doi.org/10.1007/978-981-19-9582-8_37

used in IoTs. It follows a client-server publish/subscribe messaging model. The protocol defines two types of network entities: a broker and a number of clients, where clients can be a publisher or subscriber. Figure 1 illustrates the MQTT communication architecture, where the entire communication is managed by the broker establishing a point-to-point connection between two clients. The broker is a server that receives all messages from the publishers and then routes the messages of the subscribed topics to the destination subscribers, where the messages are organized in topics, a publisher publishes messages on a topic, and a subscriber can subscribe one or multiple topics.

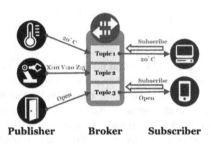

Fig. 1. MQTT communication architecture.

There are a number of security issues due to the design of the MQTT protocol itself, such as identity spoofing, information disclosure, elevation of privileges and data tampering. Most past research developed an improved version or a new one to address these security issues. However, those solutions are not applicable for public use. Some cloud service providers develop their own solution. For example, Azure Active Directory (AAD) and AWS Identity and Access Management (AWS IAM) apply the X509 certificate and OAuth mechanism to enhance identify authentication and access control. However, the aforementioned mechanisms requires comprehensive configuration and are served limited for their customers only. These limitations drive users to deploying a genuine MQTT architecture.

Even though the MQTT protocol is intended for IoT communication over internal networks, it has been misused by many applications. Many brokers can be accessed from public networks without any authentication mechanism and become an entry point for adversaries compromising the network. To address the above issues, this study proposes an IoT analysis framework that explores the accessible brokers from the public networks and classifies their risk levels and the application fields. Such information is useful for understanding the security risk imposed by IoT devices.

The proposed framework consists of three phases: reconnaissance, broker exploitation, and risk labeling. To save computing resources, the reconnaissance phase collects publicly accessible brokers from open-source intelligence (OSINT) and security organizations. In the broker exploitation phase, this study develops an efficient active scanning technique gathering detailed information about the potentially risky brokers. The last phase classifies risk level and application field by expert-defined rules.

The aim of this study is to develop a framework that identifies efficiently the vulnerable brokers that are accessible publicly and to serve as an initial step of identifying and assessing IoT risks in a large-scale network environment. The contributions of this study are stated below.

1. A large-scale analysis methodology identifies vulnerable brokers that are accessible from public networks without any protection.
2. The proposed approach for collecting the potentially risky brokers is efficient by integrating OSINT intelligence and cloud computing.
3. The expert-defined rules of risk labeling are efficient and flexible.

Our preliminary study indicates that Korea possesses the most brokers than her neighboring economic entities. Therefore, this study applies this framework to the East Asia area in order to analyze her broker distribution and to compare it with the neighboring economic entities with similar backgrounds, such as population, economic, technology.

This paper is organized in the following way. Section 2 briefs the background knowledge and overviews the past research; Sect. 3 explains the proposed IoT risk analysis framework; Sect. 4 presents the analysis results, followed by the conclusions and future work in Sect. 5.

2 Literature Review

IoTSE (Internet of Thing Search Engine) is a type of tools identifying the accessible devices in the Internet, such as Shodan, Censys, BinaryEdge, FOFA, ZoomEye, etc. Shodan and Censys are the most commonly used. Shodan was released as a commercial service in 2009, providing real-time IoT intelligence; Censys searches for devices as well as websites exposed in the Internet [3].

IoTSEs are a promising resource for researchers to gather public accessible information (open-source intelligence; OSINT) to produce actionable intelligence. The past studies have adopted the OSINT from IoTSEs to analyze cyber security threats. Daskevics and Nikiforova applied Shodan and BinaryEdge to inspect the publicly accessible databases [4]. Marnerides et al. gathered the industrial control systems from Censys and identified the compromised energy systems [5]. Kant et al. utilized the information from Shodan and discussed the security issues of the publicly accessible IoT devices [6].

Organizations adopt MQTT for device to device communication in their IoT environments but often ignored the potential risks imposed by misconfiguration or the deficiency of security control. Dizdarević et al. analyzed cyberattacks on smart devices facilitating with multiple IoT communication protocols and shed light on the security issues of MQTT [7].

MQTT protocol has been employed in various environments and application fields. Some past research categorized the IoT applications in different application fields. Mishra and Kertesz classified them into the following five fields: healthcare, agriculture, logistics, smart city services, and disaster management [8]; Patel and Doshi categorized them into the similar five fields: smart industry, smart parking, smart home, smart healthcare, and smart weather monitoring [9]; Soni and Makwana divided them into the following three broad fields: social networking, energy, and utilities [10]. Many IoTs are deployed for control purpose, but the past research rarely considered such purpose.

To fill up the research gap, this study acquires and analyzes the IoTs accessible on the Internet, and, to better understanding the areas of the IoT networks, this study defines application fields in finer coarse as listed in Table 1 and summarizes which are covered by the past research.

To address the MQTT's security issues, some past research suggested an improved version, such as AugMQTT [11], MQTT-Auth [12], and MQTT-PRESENT [13], and some proposed a new security architecture [9, 14, 15]. However, these solutions were not applied generally for the public. Such limitation drives people to deploy a genuine MQTT architecture.

Based on our best knowledge, the past researches rarely proposed a security analysis framework to inspect MQTT brokers in large scale. To fill up the above research gaps, this study proposes an MQTT analytics framework to examine and profile the potential security risks of the MQTT brokers and demonstrates its applicability by analyzing IoT networks in the East Asia area.

Table 1. The proposed IoT fields.

		Past research MQTT taxonomy of applications		
Field ID	Field of IoT applications	Mishra and Kertesz 2020 [8]	Patel and Doshi 2020 [9]	Soni and Makwana 2017 [10]
1	Environment Detection	-	Smart Weather Monitoring	-
2	Industrial Control	-	Smart Industry	Energy and Utilities
3	Agriculture	Agriculture	-	-
4	Transportation	Smart City Services	Smart Parking	-
5	Financial	-	-	-
6	Home and Office	-	Smart Home	-
7	Academic Research	-	-	-
8	Medical and Healthcare	Healthcare Disaster Management	Smart Healthcare	Healthcare
9	Commercial Service	Logistics	-	Social Networking
10	Device Control	-	-	-

3   Proposed Analytics Framework

The proposed IoT analytics framework consists of three phases: reconnaissance, broker exploitation, and risk labeling, as illustrated in Fig. 2. Phase 1, reconnaissance, collects the IoT information from IoTSEs and security organizations, preprocesses the data to remove noises and unify the format, and identifies the available MQTT brokers; phase 2, broker exploitation, verifies the availability of the MQTT brokers and collects more detailed information in order to evaluate their security risk; phase 3, risk labeling, labels their risk level and the category of the Application field by expert-defined rules.

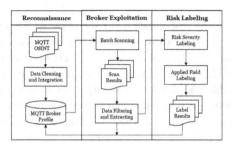

Fig. 2. MQTT analysis framework.

3.1 Reconnaissance

To collect IoT information in large scale, it is time-consuming and computation-intensive to perform thorough scan without any a priori knowledge. OSINT is the collection of data gathered from open sources and could save lots of recon efforts that this study intends to. This study collects information from the following frequently-used IoTSEs: Shodan, Censys, and FOFA. Beside the public available sources, this research collaborates with some other security organizations to retrieve more East Asia information, including Shadow server Foundation and Taiwan National Computer Emergency Response Team (TWNCERT). In order to receive information from IoT devices, the available brokers must be found. Therefore, the first phase utilizes the aforementioned data sources to identify and profile MQTT servers for the preparation of the next phase: analyzing these servers in large scale. This phase profiles an MQTT server by collecting the following information: MQTT server's IP address, TCP/UDP port number, broker software brand, broker software version, autonomous system number, geographic information, and access timestamp.

3.2 Broker Exploitation

To reduce false positives, this phase performs active scan to verify the availability of the brokers and to obtain their detailed information. Comparing with the census method, the proposed active scan by IP addresses improves detection performance as well as mitigates the cost of probing and service identification.

Large-scale scanning faces some challenges, as most organizations deploy a defense mechanism against it. To overcome this barrier, this study utilizes cloud computing to perform the scan and develops a fuzzy scan technique to evade the defense mechanism.

Cloud computing partitions the active scan into multiple scanning tasks; each task randomly selects an IP to be scanned from different countries. For profiling the public accessible brokers, this phase collects detailed information including the broker status, MQTT protocol version, and topic content.

3.3 Risk Labeling

This study assess the security risk of the MQTT servers as well as recognizes their application fields. Our preliminary study has gathered the domain knowledge from security experts who inspect the IoT devices and classify their security risks and application fields. Based on the preliminary study, this study defines four levels of security risk and ten application fields and develops labeling rules to automate risk labeling and application categorization. As different application fields might have different security requirements, the proposed labeling provides a summarized risk assessment of a broker in its application field, which support the organization for decision making on further improvement.

Risk Severity. This study defines four risk levels based on the following three common threats:

1. Internet Exposure—A broker exposed in the Internet would be an entry point for cyber adversaries to attack the organizational network.
2. Broken Authentication—A broker with broken authentication or no authentication might allow cyber attackers to intrude the network without authentication and compromise data confidentiality.
3. Plaintext Transmission—A broker transmits data in plaintext might suffer from man-in-the-middle attack and compromise data integrity and confidentiality.

Table 2 outlines the threats faced by each risk level. Even though low-risk brokers are exposed in the Internet, they have deployed access control and data encryption mechanisms to against cyberattacks. Medium-risk brokers use the default port (1883) to transfer data in plaintext but have installed access control for attack prevention. Brokers in high or critical risk level have broken authentication, which can be accessed either by default/weak credentials or without any authentication. Critical-risk brokers are the most vulnerable as they possess all the above mentioned threats.

Application Field. By integrating the expert knowledge collected from our preliminary study and the categorizations of the past research, this study defines ten application fields as shown in Table 3. Three extra application fields, academic research, financial, and device control, are proposed in this study in order to classify the IoT applications in fine-coarse. To avoid misclassification, brokers not providing enough information 7 will be classified as the following categories: default system information, or unrecognized, depending on the received topic content.

Table 2. The proposed risk metric. (Key: "O" indicates match and "-" mismatch.)

Risk level	Risk severity	Internet exposure	Broken authentication	Plaintext transmission
1 (Low)	Low	O	-	-
2 (Medium)		O	-	O
3 (High)		O	O	-
4 (Critical)	High	O	O	O

Table 3. The categories of the applications.

No.	Application field	Description
1	Environmental detection	It transmits environment-related data, such as temperature, humidity, and wind speed
2	Industrial control	It is applied in an industrial control system environment, such as programmable logic controller or human machine interface
3	Agriculture	It is applied for agriculture or fishing activities, such as illuminance detection, water quality detection, and green house lifter control
4	Transportation	It is applied for traffic transportation tasks, such as smart traffic light, vehicle status detection, and logistics monitoring
5	Financial	It is applied on financial-related activities, such as transmitting transaction data, stock information, and options information
6	Home and office	It is applied in a home or office environment, such as smart home appliances, network printers, and surveillance cameras
7	Academic research	It is deployed in an academic institute for research or lab device monitoring
8	Medical and healthcare	It monitors a healthcare related environment, such as Using patient vital status, smart long-term care, or disaster management
9	Commercial Service	It is deployed for a commercial service, such as smart parking, instance messenger service, or point of sale payment
10	Device control	The information received from topic content is not enough to classify its Application field
11	Default sys Info	Only default system information of the broker is obtained
12	Unrecognized	No system information is provided by the broker

4   Discussion

This study has implemented the proposed research framework and analyzed the brokers in the East Asia area including Taiwan, Japan, and Korea. In phase 1, a total of 171,827 brokers has been collected from the IoTSEs and the security organizations in Aug. 2021.

In phase 2, active scan identified 3,461 brokers that expose sensitive system information. All of them adopt open-source software solution, where Eclipse Mosquitto is the most applied open-source solution, 89.6%, and the rest of open-source solutions only occupy a small share: Apache ActiveMQ (3.5%), EMQ X (0.7%), and VerenMQ (0.2%).

4.1 Risk Level

Table 4 presents the analysis results of the proposed framework applied in the East Asia area. Low-risk brokers applied encryption in data transfer; Medium-risk brokers use the default port (1883) to transfer data in plaintext but install access control for attack prevention. Critical-risk brokers have no protective mechanisms.

Korea owns over 97% of the brokers, which implies that it applies IoT technologies intensively. Furthermore, almost all the brokers in Korea (98.2%) are medium risk and only a small portion (1.3%) are critical risk. It has the most secure IoT networks, which may imply that their IoT technologies are the most mature comparing with the nearby areas. Another interesting finding is that the medium-risk brokers in Korea are administrated by the same internet service provider (ISP) that operate them well for its subscribers. A half of the brokers in Taiwan and Japan are medium risk, but Japan has a lower portion of critical-risk brokers. Over one third of the brokers in Taiwan are at critical risk, which indicates that they do not deploy any defense mechanism against cyberattacks. In general, Japan's IoT networks are more secure than Taiwan's.

Table 4. Distribution of MQTT broker risk level.

Risk Level	The number of brokers (ratio)			Total
	Taiwan (TW)	Japan (JP)	Korea (KR)	
1 (Low)	259 (12.9%)	958 (32.0%)	768 (0.5%)	1,985
2 (Medium)	1,012 (50.6%)	1,499 (50.1%)	163,870 (98.2%)	166,381
3 (High)	15 (0.8%)	25 (0.8%)	27 (0.0%)	67
4 (Critical)	715 (35.7%)	512 (17.1%)	2,167 (1.3%)	3,394
Total	2,001 (1.2%)	2,994 (1.7%)	166,832 (97.1%)	171,827

4.2 Application Field

To address the security risks imposed by high- and critical-risk (risk levels 3 and 4) brokers. This study further investigates their application fields. Among the total of 3461 high- and critical risk brokers, 61.5% only transmit default system information, lacking enough information to determine the application field. However, some sensitive information may be revealed, such as the number of connected clients, the amount of received message, and the version of the broker, which is valuable for adversaries preparing a target attack. There are 11.1% "Unrecognized" brokers, indicating that the received topic content is not enough to determine the application field. Some unrecognized brokers are at the testing phase of the service development.

About 27.4% of the high- and critical- risks brokers provide enough information for categorization, where Fig. 3 outlines their application fields. Most of them serve in smart home or smart office environments, which implies that those users most likely install them with default setting and lack security knowledge to configure them. Securely.

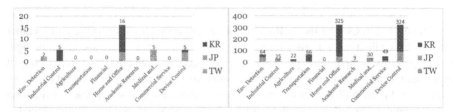

Fig. 3. The application fields of the risk levels 3 and 4 brokers.

Among the applied fields, 36% serve in the top most "Home and Office" environments, followed by "Device Control" (34.7%), "Transportation" (7%), "Environmental Detection" (7%), "Commercial Service" (5.2%), "Medical and Healthcare" (3.7%), "Industrial Control" (3.2%), "Agriculture" (2.3%), "Academic Research" (1%), and "Financial" (0.1%). The distribution results show that IoT networks have been applied in many fields and that they impact our daily life and work intensively.

Korea possesses the most (70.8%) of the IoT networks in the 10 application fields, followed by Taiwan (18.4%) and Japan (10.9%). Among the "Transportation" (6.2%) applications, many Korea's install the same third-party software for monitoring Tesla electric vehicles; for "Medical and Healthcare" (2.8%) applications, most Taiwan's use the same pharmaceutical detection software that detects medicine preservation.

4.3 Lessons Learned

Our further investigation has discovered some interesting instances helping us learn how a vulnerable IoT network could be compromised in the security CIA triad model: Confidentiality, Integrity, and Availability. The first two IoT networks serve as a part of a nation's critical infrastructure and the third one is a popular app for car owners. The findings are explained below.

AIoT Smart Traffic Control System. The traffic control system monitors traffic amount and adjusts traffic light timing dynamically to improve traffic congestion. It connects to the regional critical infrastructure for traffic network management. Figure 4 outlines the deployed IoT architecture, where the surveillance cameras are responsible for measuring traffic volume at street blocks by identifying transportation objects 10 and measuring their speeds, and the MQTT server sends the traffic adjustment commands based on the received traffic data from the surveillance cameras.

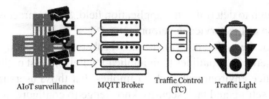

AIoT surveillance   MQTT Broker   Traffic Control   Traffic Light
                                        (TC)

Fig. 4. AIoT smart traffic light control system processes.

The MQTT broker of the traffic control system keeps track of traffic and weather data including the type of transportation object, object count, average speed, traffic light timing patterns, temperature, perception, wind speed, etc., where transportation object types include all types of moving objects: trailer, truck, automobile, scooter, bicycle, or pedestrian. Figure 5 illustrates the broker's topic information about an object containing object count and speed, where there are 3 bikes on the street and the average speed is 8.26 kph.

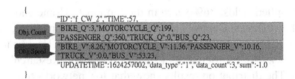

Fig. 5. An illustration of topic content of the traffic control broker.

The high-risk (level 3) traffic control system is vulnerable for its weak CIA triad protection. Its potential cybersecurity threats are summarized below.

- **Internet Exposure.** The system is exposed on the Internet so that adversaries can launch DoS attacks to impact its availability.
- **Broken Authentication.** Adversaries can access the broker without credentials, which compromises its confidentiality. Furthermore, an adversary can disguise as a subscriber and injects fake topic data to interfere traffic plans, which impacts data integrity and worse personal safety.

Water Supply System. An IoT-based water supply system monitors water capacity of a dam, serving as a part of critical infrastructure for a water supply company. The MQTT broker keeps track of water supply information including water level, flow speed, and water gate open status. Figure 6 illustrates a sample topic information collected by the broker.

Compromising critical infrastructure may cause catastrophic for the nation. A critical-risk (risk level 4) IoT network connecting to critical infrastructure largely increases the severity of its threats. This instance implies that IoT networks in CI should be examined to ensure CI is well-protected. The potential threats of this instance are stated as follows.

Gate status	nantou/no9/DataTime: 2021/06/08 11:18:00
Gate electric	nantou/no9/door: 0
Input Speed	nantou/no9/electric: 0
Output speed	nantou/no9/gate_dr: 0.44887
Gate open high	nantou/no9/gate_in: 0.03949
Flow rate (CMS)	nantou/no9/no9_level: 0.06987
Water level high	nantou/no9/no9_level_cms: 0.02673
	nantou/no9/river_level: 0.73954

Fig. 6. The MQTT broker's topic of the smart water supply system.

- **Internet Exposure and Broken Authentication.** Like the previous instance, this IoT network is exposed on the Internet so that adversaries launch DoS at-tacks to compromise its availability. Furthermore, its risk of broken authentication allows adversaries access the system and then attack by remote code execution (RCE).
- **Plaintext Transmission.** This system transmits data in plaintext, which may suffer from man-in-the-middle (MITM) attacks. Adversaries can temper the topic content, or worse control the water supply command. Such vulnerability compromises data integrity and confidentiality.

Electric Vehicle Monitor System. A third-party app for Tesla, TeslaMate, used by Tesla car owners to connect to their vehicles and access the vehicle information such as energy consumption, location history, driving statistics, and data for troubleshooting and diagnosing problems. It serves as a data logger, which can be installed on the owner's mobile phone and usually connects to his/her home network. This app is classified as risk level 4, critical-risk. Because of the security flaws in its user interface, it allows anonymous access or accesses with default passwords if not changed. Therefore, attackers might expose the above sensitive data or remotely control the vehicles. Figure 7 illustrates a real attack case that compromises data confidentiality and obtains driving routes [16].

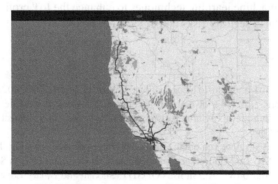

Fig. 7. The user interface of TeslaMate [16].

5 Conclusion and Future Work

About 18 billion IoT devices connect to different network infrastructures for achieving extensive functionality, bringing a new challenge of how to secure all the data. Data breach, remote execution, or DoS attacks might impact the network, if the IoT connection is not properly secure. Furthermore, catastrophic incidents might happen if the IoT networks connect to critical infrastructure.

This study presents a novel a framework for large-scale IoT network analysis and profiles IoT networks with the risk level and application field. The analysis results assist security analysts to screen out the risky brokers efficiently. To demonstrate the applicability of the proposed framework, this study implemented it and analyzed IoT networks in the East Asia areas.

This research has collected and studied a total of 171,827 MQTT brokers, where the applied broker software includes Eclipse Mosquitto (89.6%), Apache ActiveMQ (3.5%), EMQ X (0.7%), and VerenMQ (0.2%). Most of the IoT networks (96.8%) are medium risk (risk level 2); 3,461 are in high or critical risk. Most IoT networks are deployed in "Home and Office" (36%) environments, followed by "Device Control" (34.7%), "Transportation" (7%), "Environmental Detection" (7%), and "Commercial Service" (5.2%).

Korea applies IoT technologies intensively as it the most (70.8%) IoT applications followed by Taiwan (18.4%) and Japan (10.9%). It has the highest medium risk (risk level 2) brokers as well, implying that their IoT security is better than the neighboring economic entities. Furthermore, 6.2% of the total "Transportation" applications use the same third-party app for Tesla vehicles in Korea; 2.8% "Medical and Healthcare" applications use the same pharmaceutical detection software that detects medicine preservation in Taiwan.

Three vulnerable IoT networks were investigated further to better understand the potential attacks imposed by the threats. Our analysis results indicate that a vulnerable IoT network connecting with critical infrastructure may cause serious damages and one connecting to home network may put personal life in danger as well. An extension of this study may apply machine learning techniques to enhance the IoT profiling capability or to automatically label security risks and application fields.

References

1. Vailshery, L.S.: IoT and non-IoT connections worldwide 2010–2025. 2021. https://www.sta tista.com/statistics/1101442/iot-number-of-connected-devices-worldwide/
2. Hung, M.: Leading the IoT, Gartner insights on how to lead in a connected world. Gartner Res. 1, 1–5 (2017)
3. Durumeric, Z., et al.: A search engine backed by Internet-wide scanning. In: Proceedings of the 22nd ACM SIGSAC Conference on Computer and Communications Security (2015)
4. Daskevics, A., Nikiforova. A.: ShoBeVODSDT: Shodan and Binary Edge based vulnerable open data sources detection tool or what Internet of Things Search Engines know about you. In: 2021 Second International Conference on Intelligent Data Science Technologies and Applications (IDSTA). 2021. IEEE (2021)
5. Marnerides, A.K., Giotsas, V., Mursch, T.: Identifying infected energy systems in the wild. In: Proceedings of the Tenth ACM International Conference on Future Energy Systems (2019)

6. Kant, D., Johannsen, A., Creutzburg, R.: Analysis of IoT security risks based on the exposure of the MQTT protocol. Electr. Imag. **2021**(3), 961–968 (2021)
7. Dizdarević, J., et al.: A survey of communication protocols for internet of things and related challenges of fog and cloud computing integration. ACM Comput. Surv. **51**(6), 1–29 (2019)
8. Mishra, B., Kertesz, A.: The use of MQTT in M2M and IoT systems: a survey. IEEE Access **8**, 201071–201086 (2020)
9. Patel, C., Doshi, N.: A novel MQTT security framework in generic IoT model. Procedia Comput. Sci. **171**, 1399–1408 (2020)
10. Soni, D., Makwana. A.: A survey on MQTT: a protocol of internet of things (IoT). In International Conference on Telecommunication, Power Analysis and Computing Techniques (ICTPACT-2017) (2017)
11. Shin, S., et al.: A security framework for MQTT. IEEE Conference on Communications and Network Security (CNS) **2016**, 432–436 (2016)
12. Calabretta, M., et al.: MQTT-Auth: a token-based solution to endow MQTT with authentication and authorization capabilities. J. Commun. Softw. Syst. **14** (2018)
13. Sahmi, I., et al.: MQTT-PRESENT: approach to secure internet of things applications using MQTT protocol. Int. J. Electr. Comput. Eng. **11**(5), 4577–4586 (2021)
14. Longo, E., et al.: BORDER: a benchmarking framework for distributed MQTT brokers. IEEE Internet of Things J. **9**, 17728–17740 (2022)
15. Lohachab, A., Karambir, E.C.C.: based inter-device authentication and authorization scheme using MQTT for IoT networks. J. Inf. Secur. Appl. **46**, 1–12 (2019)
16. Colombo, D.: How I got access to 25+ Tesla's around the world. By accident. And curiosity. Medium (2022)

Android Malware Classifier Combining Permissions and API Features to Face Model Drifting

Wen-Ting Chang, Yi-Ming Chen, and Hui-Hsuan Yang[✉]

Department of Management, National Central University, Taoyuan City, Taiwan
{cym,110423001}@cc.ncu.edu.tw

Abstract. Machine learning is widely used in Android malware detection research, and it has been proven that machine learning models can achieve good results. However, detection models trained by old samples are hard to identify new malware with the changes in the Android development environment and the evolution of Android applications. That is, the models' detection ability is not sustainable. This phenomenon is called model aging. A common solution to this problem is to retrain models. But if the model ages quickly, it will make retraining more difficult. More importantly, the detection system has low protection against new malware before the retrained model is released. Using AUT and F_1-Score at each time slot to evaluate the degree of aging. This research establishes asn Android malware detection system with higher sustainability. Specifically, this research combines APKs' permissions and APIs by the weights learned by linear models and will build two detection models using soft voting to decide whether the application is malware or not. Evaluating the detection system on the same period and overtime performance on the dataset of years 2012 to 2019. Compared to other Android malware detection research, the AUT increased by 3% –23%.

Keywords: Model aging · Machine learning · Android malware detection · Static analysis

1 Introduction

The high market share and openness of Android applications cause them become target of many attackers. Numerous malicious programs bring various threats to users [1], forcing defenders to provide effective detection methods. Malware detection system nowadays using machine learning [2]. However the changes in the Android development environment and the continuous improvement of malware by attackers make such detectors unable to maintain effective detection power for a long time [3]. According to Kaspersky's 2020 report [4], its machine learning-based malware detector dropped from nearly 100% recall to 60% within three months. This phenomenon in which the detection ability of a model decreases over time is called Model Aging, and the reason can be explained by Concept Drift.

© The Author(s), under exclusive license to Springer Nature Singapore Pte Ltd. 2022
S.-Y. Hsieh et al. (Eds.): ICS 2022, CCIS 1723, pp. 434–446, 2022.
https://doi.org/10.1007/978-981-19-9582-8_38

To Concept drift means that the feature of training data and test data distribute different, so a model that only learns the features of training data and cannot effectively detect test data. In the field of Android malware detection, there are two main reasons for conceptual drift [5]: (1) attackers continue to improve malware to avoid detection through obfuscation and other methods; (2) changes in the Android development environment, such as new or deprecated APIs, etc. Other factors include changes in attack types and changes in software development methods, etc., which will make the characteristics of Android App change over time, and thus reduce the model detection effect over time.

A common solution to model aging is adding old data with new data to retrain the model, so that the model can also learn the characteristics of new samples. Although retrain is an effective way to model aging, it still facing some problem. For example, if the model ages quickly, frequent retraining will consume more computing and storage resources, and it is difficult to obtain new labeled data with good quality [6]. More importantly, compared to models with a slow aging rate, even if there is a retraining mechanism, a model with a fast aging rate is more likely to have a window period, which in turn makes users more vulnerable to malicious programs. Therefore, simply retraining the model at predefined intervals still cannot effectively protect users.

According to previous studies [7, 8], though the same type of malware will continuity update the code, the core malicious behavior is roughly the same. APIGraph [7] takes an Android malware named Xloader as an example. In the three versions of the malware, nevertheless its malicious behavior is to transmit user information to the attacker's server, the implementation method different. For example, in terms of data transmission, the first version uses "HttpURLConnection", the second version uses "SocketFactory", and the third version uses "SSLSocketFactory". Therefore, if there is no special treatment when using APIs as features, the machine learning model will regard these semantically similar APIs as different features, and will also think that the three versions of the malware behave differently, and such detectors are vulnerable to Implementation changes affect detection capabilities. Through the observation of previous research, this research further observed that the APIs can all correspond to the permission "android.permission.INTERNET" because of their similar functions, so it is inferred that the permission is implemented by the Android application. Changes in methods may cause less changes than APIs. Therefore, one of the characteristics used by the Android malware detection system established in our study is permissions, and in the follow-up experiments, we will explore the sustainability difference between permissions and API's data set detection capabilities from 2012 to 2019. Since a previous study [9] pointed out that the Android permissions commonly used by malicious and benign software are similar, it is difficult to distinguish malicious software. The experimental results of another study [10] also show that the effect of using permissions to detect malware is worse than that of API. To improve the detection system's ability to judge malware, our study also uses API as a feature.

In summary, the Android malware detection system in our study is characterized by combining permissions and APIs. Through the corresponding relationship between API and permission, the two are combined in the same feature, and the weight of each API and permission combination is automatically learned with a linear model. This research will build two models with the same machine learning classification algorithm, and use Soft Voting to determine whether the APK is malware.

In conclusion, our major contributions include the following (1) Develop an Android malware detection system, use permissions and API as features, combine the two through the relationship between the two features, and use a linear model to learn the weight of the combination.; (2) The original API, permissions and the sustainability of the detection capability of our study were tested with samples from 2012 to 2019. The experimental results show in generally, our study has a higher F1-Score and AUT compared with only API, only permissions or other related studies.

The structure of the follow-up article, the second chapter is related research, which discusses the related research that the detection model effect decreases with time; the third chapter is the research method, which explains the overall structure of the Android malware detection system in this study; the fourth chapter is the evaluation, which introduce the dataset and metrics we use; the fifth chapter is the experiment; The sixth chapter is the research limitation and the seventh is conclusion.

2   Related-Work

2.1   MamaDroid

Since the changes of API Family and API Package are smaller than that of API Call, MaMaDroid [11] reduces the change between the features of old and new samples by abstracting the API. MaMaDroid has two modes of operation with two different degrees of abstraction. Family Mode abstracts API to API Family, for example "java.lang.Throwable: String getMessage()" will become "java". Another mode is Package Mode, which abstracts the API to the Package level. For example, "java.lang.Throwable: String getMessage()" will become "java.lang". In feature processing, MaMaDroid first obtains the Function Call Graph (FCG) from the APK file, then abstracts the API in the FCG into Family or Package, and then uses the Markov Chain to calculate each abstraction The probability of an API transitioning to another abstracted API, this probability is the eigenvalue. The author subsequently uses the K-nearest neighbor algorithm (KNN) and random forest (Random Forest) for classification, and the performance of random forest is better.

2.2   APIGraph

APIGraph [7] observes that the evolution of Android malware often retains the same semantics, but changes the way it is implemented. APIGraph takes an Android malware named Xloader as an example. The malicious behavior of the three versions before and after the malware is to send the user's mobile phone information to the attacker's server. For example, in a certain version, the International Mobile Equipment Identity (IMEI) may be obtained and sent using HTTP. In another version, it may be changed to obtain the International Mobile Subscriber Identity (IMSI) and send it via Socket. From the above example, it can be found that both "HttpURLConnection" and "SocketFactory" are related to the connection of the remote host. If they are regarded as different characteristics, they are easily affected by malicious program changes. APIGraph uses crawler technology to capture the introduction of each API in Android official documents, and defines 10 relationships, such as "refers_to", "inheritance" and "uses_permission". After sorting out the relationship between the API and the API, the author uses the TransE algorithm in the graph theory to convert the API into a vector. Then use the k-Means algorithm to divide the API vector into 2,000 groups, and use the center point of the group to represent API in the group.

3 Methodology

This chapter describes the establishment method of the Android malware detection system in this study.

3.1 System Architecture

The system architecture of this study is shown in Fig. 1, which is divided into four modules. The first is Feature Database, which pre-sorts permissions and APIs appeared in the specific year; the second is Feature Extraction, which extracts permissions and APIs from original APK file; the third is Feature Combination, this module combine permission and API by their corresponding relationship, using a linear model to learn the weight of the combination; the fourth is malware classification, it will build two models with the same classification algorithm, using Soft Voting to synthesize the final judgment.

3.2 Feature Database

The feature database contains two kinds of data, which is the annual permission/API list and the corresponding relationship between the annual permissions and APIs.

Annual Permission/API List. According to the permissions listed in current Android official website [15] and the API level (API Level) of the permissions, our study sorts the annual permission list. Therefore, in the permission list, this permission will be listed in 2018 and later years. This permission will not be used when the model is trained with 2017 APK, when testing 2018 APK. API features are based on the official APIs collated by [7], and the annual API list is collated in the same way.

Relationship Between Annual Permissions and APIs. Since the official Android document does not provide a complete correspondence between APIs and permissions, this study uses the data provided by the previous research APIGraph [7] and Androguard [16] to sort the corresponding relationship every year. However, because the years of these data are relatively old, the corresponding relationship between permissions and APIs used in this study is only up to 2016, and most of the relationships are before 2013. The storage form of the correspondence between API and permissions is shown in Fig. 2.

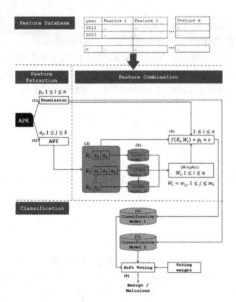

Fig. 1. System architecture

$permission_1$	API_1	API_3	API_5	X	X
$permission_2$	API_1	API_3	X	X	X
$permission_3$	API_2	API_4	X	X	X
$permission_4$	API_6	API_7	API_8	API_9	API_{10}

Fig. 2. Feature correspondence form

3.3 Feature Extraction

This module uses the reverse analysis tools Androguard [16] and apktool [17] to analyze the AndroidManifest.xml and Dex files of the APK to extract permissions and API features.

3.4 Feature Combination

This module uses the corresponding relationship between permissions and APIs to combine the two, and the length of the final feature vector is the same as the length of the feature vector of permissions. The features of each sample in the dataset are represented by p and Rel (Eq. 1). The subsequent malware classification module will build two models based on these two features.

First, corresponding to the numbers (1) and (2) in Fig. 1, the permission feature is represented by p, and the API feature is represented by a. The feature value is 0 or 1, 0 means the APK does not use this feature, and 1 means it does. Then, according to the aforementioned feature database, APIs are divided into n groups, one group corresponds to one permission, and the corresponding relationship is represented by R. R contains n arrays of different lengths $(R_1, R_2, \cdots, R_n)$. R_i contains m_i APIs, which means there are m_i APIs related to the ith permission (No. (3) in Fig. 1).

Then each set of permissions and the API $(R_1, R_2, \cdots, R_n)$ will be trained using a Logistic Regression Model. If there are n permissions, this step will create n logistic regression models and extract the model's coefficients which is the highest weights of feature combinations, so n groups of weights can be obtained, as shown in No. (4) in Fig. 1. Each set of weights W_i is an array of length m_i, and a value in the array corresponds to the weight of an API.

Each set of weights W_i and R_i is multiplied item by item (Entry-Wise Product) to obtain a scalar, this value plus p_i is the value of the ith element in the final output feature vector Rel, as shown in Eq. 1. In Eq. 1, W_i is the characteristic coefficient in a linear model, and m_i is the number of APIs in the ith group of correspondences. For example, $m_i=3$, which means that the ith group of relations contains 3 APIs, so the ith linear model has 3 features and there are three elements in W_i.

$$ith\ element\ in\ Rel = f(R_i, W_i) + p_i \times s$$
$$= \sum_{j=1}^{m_i} a_{ij} w_{ij} + p_i \times s$$
$$\begin{cases} s = 1, & if\ f(R_i, W_i) \geq 0 \\ s = -1, & otherwise \end{cases} where\ \ 1 \leq i \leq n \tag{1}$$

3.5 Malware Classification

The malware classification module uses the p and Rel features produced by the feature combination module to establish two classification models with same classification algorithm, and then uses Soft Voting to synthesize the judgment of the APK samples by the two models. The calculation method is shown in Eq. 2, where $Model_{(p, benign)}$ is the probability that the output sample of the model established using the p feature is benign, and the rest are analogous. If $Score_{malware} \geq Score_{benign}$, the sample will be classified as malicious. V in Eq. 2 is an adjustable voting weight, and subsequent experiments will compare the results of different weight values (v).

$$\begin{cases} Score_{benign} = Model_{(p, benign)} \times v \times diff + Model_{(Rel, benign)} \\ Score_{malware} = Model_{(p, malware)} \times v \times diff + Model_{(Rel, malware)} \end{cases} where$$
$$\begin{cases} diff = 0, & if\ training\ year\ equals\ to\ testing\ year \\ diff = 1, & otherwise \end{cases} \tag{2}$$

In terms of classification algorithm, in the experiments in Sect. 4, this research uses Random Forest, K-Nearest Neighbor (KNN), Support Vector Machine (SVM), Multilayer Perception The five classification algorithms of Multilayer Perceptron (MLP) and Convolutional Neural Network (CNN) were used to evaluate the malware detection ability of the feature representation in this study when used in the above algorithms, as well as different classification algorithms. The extent to which it is affected by time.

4 Evaluation

4.1 Dataset

The APK used in this study was collected from AndroZoo, and the files were randomly downloaded from AndroZoo based on the last modification time of the Dex file and the score (vt_scan) of VirusTotal [18]. In this study, the samples whose vt_scan is 0 are labeled "Benign", and the samples whose vt_scan is greater than or equal to 15 are labeled "Malware". The division method is the same as [6. 7, 12].

Table 1. Dataset of our experiment

Year	Benign	Malware
2012	2,347	2,342
2013	2,433	1,933
2014	2,035	2.091
2015	2,282	2,425
2016	2,512	1,963
2017	2,094	1,756
2018	1,535	1,630
2019	554	538
Count	15,792	14,678
Total: 30,470		

Since the detectors on VirusTotal will be updated, samples that have not been judged as malware by any detector in the past may have different judgments today. Therefore, the benign APK files downloaded from AndroZoo in this study will be re-checked by VirusTotal for detection. As a result, if any of the detectors considered the sample to be malware, it was excluded from the dataset. In addition, this study removes duplicate samples based on the calculation results of the SHA1 hash value. The sample sizes for each year are listed in Table 1.

4.2 Metrics

In the following experiments, this study compares detection capability and sustainability with other methods. The detection ability is the detection effect of the model on samples of the same year, measured by F1-Score. F1-Score is a commonly used indicator in research related to Android malware detection. In terms of sustainability, in addition to measuring the degree of impact of the model by the F1-Score of each test year, this study also uses AUT to synthesize the F1-Score of each test year to give a convenient comparison result.

The sustainability of this study means how much detection ability the model can maintain. It means that even if the F1-Score declines greatly, there is still a higher F1-Score for the model with higher sustainability. Aspects are measured in AUT. AUT only considers the level of the evaluation index when calculating, but does not consider how much the evaluation index has dropped compared to the training year, see Eq. 3 for details. Therefore, this study uses AUT to measure the sustainability of the model.

$$\text{AUT(f, N)} = \frac{1}{N-1} \sum_{k=1}^{N-1} \frac{[f(x_{k+1}) + f(x_k)]}{2} \tag{3}$$

5 Evaluation

The following experiments are all conducted with 10-fold cross-validation, and the experimental data are the average of 10 experiments. F1-Score and AUT (Area Under Time) [19] were used in the evaluation methods of experiments 5.1 to 5.3.

5.1 Compare to Only Permissions or Only APIs

Sample in the Same Year. Table 2 shows the performance when the training sample and the test sample have the same year. From the table, it can be seen that the F1-Score of the API is the same as that of the permission in 2015, and all others are greater than the permission, and can be up to 7% higher. When compared with permissions in this study, the F1-Score was improved by 2% to 8%. When compared with the API in this study, except for the F1-Score in 2019, which was 2% lower, all other performances were greater than or equal to the API, and could be higher by up to 2%.

Table 2. Performance regardless of time (metrics: F1-score)

	Only API	Only permission	Our study
2012	0.97	0.93	0.97
2013	0.95	0.89	0.95
2014	0.95	0.91	0.96
2015	0.94	0.94	0.96
2016	0.93	0.92	0.95
2017	0.94	0.87	0.95
2018	0.94	0.90	0.96
2019	0.95	0.88	0.93

Sample in Different Years. Table 3 shows the performance of API, permissions, and our study when comparing the sustainable performance of the three detection capabilities. The first year of the x-axis in Table 3 is the year of the training sample. It can be seen from the figure that compared with API and permissions, this study generally maintains a better F1-Score in the test year. Judging from the AUT indicator, the difference between this study and the permissions is small in the early stage, and the difference with the API in the later stage is small. The AUT for this study was higher than permissions and APIs in all years. Another notable point in Table 3 is that permissions are more sustainable than API on early samples, but API is better on late samples. In terms of AUT, the two were tied in the 2015 training year, and after the 2016 training year, the API was higher than the permissions. Because this study combines both, the performance of the other two characteristics can still be greater than or equal to in this experimental data set.

Table 3. Performance when considering the time (metrics: AUT)

Train data year	Test data year	Only API	Only permission	Our study
2012	2013– 2016	0.61	0.85	0.86
2013	2014 – 2017	0.63	0.86	0.89
2014	2015 – 2018	0.81	0.86	0.89
2015	2016 – 2019	0.84	0.85	0.88
2016	2017– 2019	0.89	0.85	0.90
2017	2018 – 2019	0.92	0.87	0.93
2018	2019	0.92	0.87	0.93

5.2 Compare the Detection Performance and Aging Degree to MaMaDroid

Sample in the Same Year. Table 4 shows the performance of this study and related studies under the same sample training and testing years. It can be seen from the table that the F1-Score of this study is 0% –5% higher than that of MaMaDroid. Except for the same year as MaMaDroid in 2017, the rest All performed well.

Table 4. The performance of this study and related studies regardless of sample time (evaluation indicator: F1-score)

	MamaDroid	Our study
2012	0.93	0.97
2013	0.92	0.95
2014	0.91	0.96
2015	0.92	0.96
2016	0.94	0.95
2017	0.95	0.95
2018	0.93	0.96
2019	0.93	0.96

Sample in Different Years. Figure 3 shows the performance of this study and related studies when time is considered. The first year on the x-axis in Fig. 3 is the year of the training samples. In our study, AUT was 3%–23% higher than MaMaDroid. MaMaDroid only use API as feature, so the performance of the original API improves with the years, and the performance of MaMaDroid also improves.

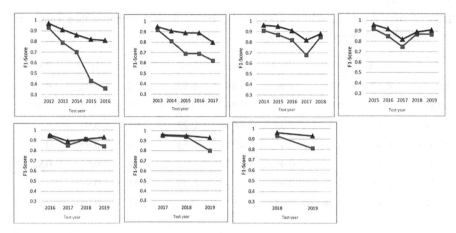

Fig. 3. Compare MaMaDroid with our study in different year (metrics: AUT)

5.3   Evaluate on Various Classification Models

In this chapter we choose Random Forest (RF), K-Nearest Neighbor (KNN), Support Vector Machine (SVM), Multilayer Perceptron (MLP) and convolution Neural network (Convolutional Neural Network, CNN) as classification algorithms, including three traditional machine learning algorithms, two neural network architectures. The model architectures are listed in Table 5.

Table 5. Classifier architecture

Model		Description
Random Forest (RF)		Using scikit-learn 1.0.2 as default parameters
SVM		
KNN		
MLP	More neural (MLP 1)	3 hidden layers (256, 128, 64)
	Less neural (MLP 2)	3 hidden layers (64, 32, 16)
CNN	More layers (CNN 1)	1 batch normalization layer, 2 convolution layers, 2 mean pooling layers, 3 hidden layers
	Less later (CNN 2)	1 batch normalization layer, 1 convolution layer, 1 mean pooling layer, 2 hidden layers

Sample in the Same Year. Table 6 shows F1-Score performance of five classification algorithms using the method of this study when the training year is the same as the testing year. It can be seen from the table that the performance of random forest (RF) is the best in each year. Overall, the seven models have little difference in the detection performance of malware.

Table 6. The performance of this study on various classification algorithms without considering the time (evaluation index: F1-Score)

	2012	2013	2014	2015	2016	2017	2018	2019
RF	**0.97**	**0.95**	**0.96**	**0.96**	**0.95**	**0.95**	**0.96**	**0.93**
SVM	0.96	0.93	0.94	0.94	0.92	0.91	0.92	0.91
KNN	0.95	0.93	0.93	0.94	0.92	0.93	0.93	0.91
MLP 1	0.96	0.94	0.95	0.95	0.93	0.94	0.95	0.92
MLP 2	0.96	0.94	0.95	0.95	0.93	0.94	0.94	0.92
CNN 1	0.95	0.92	0.93	0.95	0.93	0.91	0.92	0.91
CNN 2	0.96	0.94	0.94	0.95	0.93	0.93	0.94	0.92

Sample in Different Years. Table 7 shows the performance of the seven classification models in this study when the sample time is considered, that is, the performance of the sustainability of the detection ability of each model. All seven models have AUT above 0.8, with random forest having the highest AUT.

Table 7. Performance of our study on various classifier (evaluation indicator: AUT calculated using F1-score)

Train year	2012	2013	2014	2015	2016	2017	2018
Test year	2012 ~ 2016	2013 ~ 2017	2014 ~ 2018	2015 ~ 2019	2016 ~ 2019	2017 ~ 2019	2017 ~ 2019
RF	0.86	**0.89**	**0.89**	**0.88**	**0.90**	**0.93**	**0.93**
SVM	0.82	0.86	**0.89**	0.87	0.87	0.91	0.91
KNN	0.82	0.86	0.87	0.87	0.88	0.92	0.92
MLP 1	**0.87**	0.87	0.87	0.87	0.89	0.92	0.92
MLP 2	**0.87**	0.86	0.88	0.87	0.88	0.92	0.92
CNN 1	**0.87**	0.86	0.88	0.87	0.88	0.91	0.91
CNN 2	**0.87**	0.87	0.88	0.87	0.89	0.92	0.92

5.4 Discussion

Based on the above experiments, the experimental data set in this study from 2012 to 2019 generally has higher F1-Score and higher F1-Score compared to other related researches using only API, only using permissions, or other Android malware detection. AUT (5-1, 5-2). And the method of this study is not limited to a single classification algorithm, and can be applied to other traditional machine learning and deep learning (5-3). The F1 of each model is greater than 0.9, and the AUT is also greater than 0.8. Another point of the above experiment is that permissions are more sustainable than APIs before 2015, but as the years go by, the original official API is gradually less affected by time than permissions (5-2). The reasons for the reversal of the sustainability of APIs and permissions require additional experiments and analysis.

6 Conclusion

Machine learning is widely used in Android malware detection research, although it can achieve impressive detection results. However, due to changes in Android applications, model checking capabilities tend to degrade over time. This study combines two features, permission and API, and uses a linear model to learn the weight of feature combination. At the same time, use the permission feature and the feature combined with the permission and API to build two classification models with the same classification algorithm, and then use Soft Voting to synthesize the judgment of the two models. This research experiment is based on the data set from 2012 to 2019. Compared with only using API, only using permissions, or compared with other two related researches on Android malware detection, the overall detection ability and sustainability are better.

References

1. Huang, H., et al.: A large-scale study of android malware development phenomenon on public malware submission and scanning platform. IEEE Trans. Big Data **7**(2), 255–270 (2021). https://doi.org/10.1109/TBDATA.2018.2790439
2. Kumar, K.A., Raman, A., Gupta, C., Pillai, R.R.: The recent trends in malware evolution, detection and analysis for android devices. J. Eng. Sci. Techol. Rev. **13**(4), 240–248 (2020). https://doi.org/10.25103/jestr.134.25
3. Allix, K., Bissyandé, T.F., Klein, J., Le Traon, Y.: Are your training datasets yet relevant? In: Piessens, F., Caballero, J., Bielova, N. (eds.) ESSoS 2015. LNCS, vol. 8978, pp. 51–67. Springer, Cham (2015). https://doi.org/10.1007/978-3-319-15618-7_5
4. Machine Learning Methods for Malware Detection [Kaspersky]: SecureReading. https://securereading.com/downloads/machine-learning-methods-for-malware-detection-kaspersky/. Accessed 26 Aug 2022
5. Kan, Z., Pendlebury, F., Pierazzi, F., Cavallaro, L.: Investigating Labelless drift adaptation for malware detection. In: Proceedings of the 14th ACM Workshop on Artificial Intelligence and Security, Virtual Event Republic of Korea, November 2021, pp. 123–134. https://doi.org/10.1145/3474369.3486873
6. Xu, J., Li, Y., Deng, R.H., Xu, K.: SDAC: a slow-aging solution for android malware detection using semantic distance based API clustering. IEEE Trans. Depend. Secur. Comput. **19**(2), 1149–1163 (2022). https://doi.org/10.1109/TDSC.2020.3005088
7. "Enhancing State-of-the-art Classifiers with API Semantics to Detect Evolved Android Malware. In: Proceedings of the 2020 ACM SIGSAC Conference on Computer and Communications Security (2020). https://dl.acm.org/doi/https://doi.org/10.1145/3372297.3417291. Accessed 26 Aug 2022
8. Park, S., Gondal, I., Kamruzzaman, J., Zhang, L.: One-shot malware outbreak detection using spatio-temporal isomorphic dynamic features. August 2019, pp. 751–756 (2019). https://doi.org/10.1109/TrustCom/BigDataSE.2019.00108

9. Sanz, B., Santos, I., Laorden, C., Ugarte-Pedrero, X., Bringas, P.G., Álvarez, G.: PUMA: permission usage to detect malware in android. In: International Joint Conference CISIS 2012-ICEUTE´12-SOCO 2012 Special Sessions, Berlin, Heidelberg, 2013, pp. 289–298 (2012). https://doi.org/10.1007/978-3-642-33018-6_30

10. Peiravian, N., Zhu, X.: Machine learning for android malware detection using permission and API Calls. In: 2013 IEEE 25th International Conference on Tools with Artificial Intelligence, November 2013, pp. 300–305 (2013). https://doi.org/10.1109/ICTAI.2013.53

11. Onwuzurike, L., Mariconti, E., Andriotis, P., Cristofaro, E.D., Ross, G., Stringhini, G.: MaMaDroid: detecting android malware by building markov chains of behavioral models (extended version). ACM Trans. Priv. Secur. **22**(2), 14:1–14:34 (2019). https://doi.org/10.1145/3313391

12. Xu, K., Li, Y., Deng, R., Chen, K., Xu, J.: DroidEvolver: self-evolving android malware detection system. In: 2019 IEEE European Symposium on Security and Privacy (EuroS&P), June 2019, pp. 47–62 (2019). https://doi.org/10.1109/EuroSP.2019.00014

Design and Implementation of the Optimized Computing Architecture for Matrix Decomposition Algorithms

Jih-Ching Chiu, Yu-Quen Chen, Yi-Xiang Wang[✉], and Yung-Chi Liu

Department of Electrical Engineering, National Sun Yat-Sen University, 70 Lien-Hai Road, Kaohsiung 804, Taiwan
xiang102987@gmail.com

Abstract. This paper will take the recursive CORDIC computing unit developed in our laboratory as the main computing core. The computing data is arranged in parallel by the method of adaptive data arrangement, and an expandable core group is proposed with multiple CORDIC operation cores. Shift operation is realized by using lookup table. When the matrix size is 16 × 16, eigenvalue operation efficiency is increased by 10.54 times, and the iteration speed is increased by 25.5 times. This paper uses software to simulate the speed of eigenvalue decom-position of a 16 × 16 matrix in 200 MHz environment. Compared with the architecture proposed in this lab, when the number of cores is 16 cores, there is a 2.08 times increase in speed.

Keywords: CORDIC · Matrix factorization · QR algorithm · Golub-Reinsch algorithm

1 Introduction

Matrix decomposition is an important operation in current technological applications. In advanced communication 5G and 6G systems, encryption algorithms for information security, and conversion operations for positioning space, etc. the latest technologies can be applied to. With the increasing demand for real-time operations and computation, the chip-based design of operations for large-scale matrices has become a trend. One of the most important issues in large-scale matrix operations is data access. Using register array to store data would be a waste of area. In paper [2], the matrix data is accessed using DDR3 memory, which greatly reduces the number of registers in the circuit. However, due to the need to frequently exchange data with the memory, the operating efficiency will be limited by the data access time.

CORDIC (COordinate Rotation DIgital Computer) is a way to use recursive opera-tions to complete trigonometric functions. Due to its simple architecture, it is often used

This paper presents partial results of a long-term research project financed by both NSTC of R.O.C. under contract no. MOST 111-2218-E-110-004 and the industry.

© The Author(s), under exclusive license to Springer Nature Singapore Pte Ltd. 2022
S.-Y. Hsieh et al. (Eds.): ICS 2022, CCIS 1723, pp. 447–459, 2022.
https://doi.org/10.1007/978-981-19-9582-8_39

in matrix decomposition operations. When computing matrix decomposition, multiple CORDIC operation units are often used for parallel operations [4].

This paper presents partial results of a long-term research project financed by both NSTC of R.O.C. under contract no. MOST 111-2218-E-110-004 and the industry.

However, because the size of the matrix has been fixed at the beginning, only the matrix of the specified size can be operated. At the same time, it also leads to the need to do additional design when the operation is to be expanded in the future.

This paper hopes to design the computing architecture for matrix decomposition algorithm. Highly parallelized data using the same architecture and adaptive data arrangement. Based on the component operation, a vector operation method suitable for different situations is constructed to simplify the design of the control circuit. Matrix data is stored in block arrangement, and multiple matrix data is accessed at one time to reduce the number of times of data exchange with external memory. By optimizing algorithm of matrix decomposition, the efficiency of data usage is further improved. Use deflation and shift operations to reduce the iteration times of matrix decomposition and speed up the performance of matrix operations. In order to improve the expandability of the CORDIC operation core and the achievability of the hardware, a CORDIC 4 module composed of the CORDIC computing core is pro-posed. Using the CPU to connect multiple CORDIC 4 in parallel, the design of more computing cores has been achieved in parallel.

2   General Overview

2.1   CORDIC Operation Unit

CORDIC is a method used to simplify the matrix rotation operation. The matrix rotation operation that originally needed to be completed by trigonometric functions is simplified into the repeated recursive operation of shift and addition. For hardware, only shifter, adder and look-up-table are needed.

In the operation of CORDIC, there are three inputs and three outputs, the input is x y θ, and the output is x' y' θ'. They will operate according to different modes. Rotation mode is to rotates x y with the input θ, and the output x' y' is the rotated vector. The second mode is Vectoring mode, which rotates the vector to the x-axis and outputs the angle between the vector and the x-axis.

The paper [2] in this laboratory proposes a recursive CORDIC operation unit, which uses bypass operation and skips large-angle operations. When doing matrix iterative operations of eigenvalue decomposition or singular value decomposition. The rotation angle will gradually decrease with the convergence of the matrix elements. By discarding the large-angle rotation operation, the operation will be accelerated.

2.2   Row and Column Operations

This paper will define two formulas for basic vector rotation operations, and use vector rotation to combine different matrix decomposition algorithms. The operation of vector rotation can be combined using the rotation of the two basic components. One of the component rotations is the component rotate operation and the component vector operation. The formulas are as follows.

$$rotate(a_x, a_y, \theta) := \begin{bmatrix} \cos\theta & -\sin\theta \\ \sin\theta & \cos\theta \end{bmatrix} \begin{bmatrix} a_x \\ a_y \end{bmatrix}$$

$$vector(a_x, a_y, \theta) := \begin{bmatrix} \cos\theta & -\sin\theta \\ \sin\theta & \cos\theta \end{bmatrix} \begin{bmatrix} a_x \\ a_y \end{bmatrix},$$

$$\theta = -\tan^{-1}\frac{a_y}{a_x}$$

Combining the component rotation into different vector rotation operations, the vector rotation operation is to rotate two vectors at the same angle, there are vector rotation operation and vector vectoring operation. The vector rotation operation is to perform the component rotate operation on the components in the two vectors one-to-one. The vector vectoring operation is to perform the component rotate operation on the components in the two vectors, and the rotation angle is the angle at which the specified component is used for the component vector operation. The two rotation operations using the component rotation operation formula are expressed as follows

$$rotateV\left(\mathbf{A_x}, \mathbf{A_y}, \theta\right) = rotate\left(a_{xi}, a_{yi}, \theta\right)\Big|_{i=0}^{n-1}$$

$$rotateV\left(\mathbf{A_x}, \mathbf{A_y}, \theta\right), \theta = -\tan^{-1}\frac{a_{x,0}}{a_{y,0}}$$

$$= rotate\left(a_{xi}, a_{yi}, \theta\right)\Big|_{i=0}^{n-1}, \theta = -\tan^{-1}\frac{a_{x,0}}{a_{y,0}}$$

3   Optimized Computing Design

When performing the eigenvalue decomposition operation, there may be situations in which row operation and column operation need to be performed on the same angle. For example, when performing Hessenberg reduction, in addition to using the left-multiplying Householder matrix to eliminate elements, it is also necessary to right-multiply the same Householder matrix to have a similar matrix relationship with the original matrix. There are two ways to handle this situation. One of them is that row operation and column operation are performed at the same time, which is called mix operation in this paper. Another way is to do the column operation first, and then do the row operation, which is called Row Major Operation.

Mix Operation: First use the row operation to obtain the rotation angle θ, and then immediately perform the column operation at the same angle. As shown, use the row operation on the matrix to be reduced, perform the row operation on the A_1 row vector and the A_2 row vector, and use the CORDIC vector to calculate the rotation angle θ.

After the row operation is completed, the column operation is performed on the column vector A^1 and the column vector A^2 using the same angle.

$$\begin{bmatrix} a_{0,0} & a_{0,1} & a_{0,2} & a_{0,3} & a_{0,4} \\ a_{1,0} & a_{1,1} & a_{1,2} & a_{1,3} & a_{1,4} \\ a_{2,0} & a_{2,1} & a_{2,2} & a_{2,3} & a_{2,4} \\ a_{3,0} & a_{3,1} & a_{3,2} & a_{3,3} & a_{3,4} \\ a_{4,0} & a_{4,1} & a_{4,2} & a_{4,3} & a_{4,4} \end{bmatrix}$$

$$rotateV\,(A_1, A_2, \theta),\ \theta = -\tan^{-1}\frac{a_{2,0}}{a_{1,0}}$$

$$\begin{bmatrix} a_{0,0} & a_{0,1} & a_{0,2} & a_{0,3} & a_{0,4} \\ a_{1,0}' & a_{1,1}' & a_{1,2}' & a_{1,3}' & a_{1,4}' \\ 0 & a_{2,1}' & a_{2,2}' & a_{2,3}' & a_{2,4}' \\ a_{3,0} & a_{3,1} & a_{3,2} & a_{3,3} & a_{3,4} \\ a_{4,0} & a_{4,1} & a_{4,2} & a_{4,3} & a_{4,4} \end{bmatrix}$$

$$rotateV\left(A^1, A^2, \theta\right),\ \theta = -\tan^{-1}\frac{a_{2,0}}{a_{1,0}}$$

In this way, the angle θ obtained by the row operation is directly used for the column operation, and it is not necessary to use the register to store the angle. However, in this operation, there will be data dependencies between row operations and column operations. Although after using the CORDIC vector to obtain the rotation angle, the remaining components can be processed in parallel, but the data dependencies between row operations and column operations still need to wait for the overlapped part.

Row Major Operation: After all row operations are completed, column operations are performed. As shown, use the A_1 column vector to eliminate $a_{2,0}$ to $a_{4,0}$, and then use the angle obtained by the row operation to rotate the vector against the corresponding column vector.

$$\begin{bmatrix} a_{0,0} & a_{0,1} & a_{0,2} & a_{0,3} & a_{0,4} \\ a_{1,0} & a_{1,1} & a_{1,2} & a_{1,3} & a_{1,4} \\ a_{2,0} & a_{2,1} & a_{2,2} & a_{2,3} & a_{2,4} \\ a_{3,0} & a_{3,1} & a_{3,2} & a_{3,3} & a_{3,4} \\ a_{4,0} & a_{4,1} & a_{4,2} & a_{4,3} & a_{4,4} \end{bmatrix}$$

$$rotateV\,(A_1, A_i, \theta),\ \theta = -\tan^{-1}\frac{a_{i,0}}{a_{1,0}}\Bigg|_{i=2}^{4}$$

$$\begin{bmatrix} a_{0,0} & a_{0,1} & a_{0,2} & a_{0,3} & a_{0,4} \\ a_{1,0}' & a_{1,1}' & a_{1,2}' & a_{1,3}' & a_{1,4}' \\ 0 & a_{2,1}' & a_{2,2}' & a_{2,3}' & a_{2,4}' \\ 0 & a_{3,1}' & a_{3,2}' & a_{3,3}' & a_{3,4}' \\ 0 & a_{4,1}' & a_{4,2}' & a_{4,3}' & a_{4,4}' \end{bmatrix}$$

$$rotateV\left(A^{1}, A^{i}, \theta\right), \theta = -\tan^{-1}\frac{a_{i,0}}{a_{1,0}}\Big|_{i=2}^{4}$$

Unlike the mix operation, this method processes the row operations together, and then processes the column operations together. There is no dependency between each operation data. As long as the CORDIC vector calculates the angle in the row operation, the rest of the components can be calculated in parallel (Fig. 1).

4 Circuit Architecture Design

4.1 Overall System Architecture

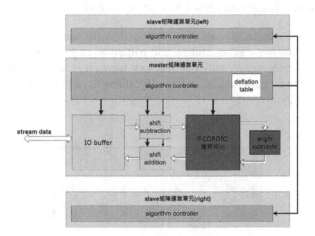

Fig. 1. Overall system architecture diagram

IO Buffer is responsible for exchanging matrix data with external, and storing matrix data. According to the current operation mode, determine the storage mode of the matrix to reduce the number of times of data exchange with the outside. And take the vector as the unit, send the data to the multi-CORDIC operation core.

Shift subtraction and shift addition are shift operation circuits, which perform shift operation when the IO buffer exchanges vector data with multi-CORDIC operation core. The shift value will be given by the algorithm controller.

Multi-CORDIC operation core, which contain multiple CORDIC operation cores. It will design basic component operations, and then combine component operations into vector operations to calculate the rotation of row and column vectors. Angle calculate is used to calculate the special angle that the algorithm needs to use.

The algorithm controller contains the state machines of various algorithms, and determines the control of each row and column operation according to different algorithms, and sends control signals to each circuit. The algorithm controller contains a deflation table, which is used to record the convergence of the matrix and the value of the shift operation.

The master matrix operation unit and the slave matrix operation unit have the same structure. The master matrix operation unit is responsible for computing the original matrix, and the two slave matrix operation units remove the eigenvectors and singular vectors respectively.

4.2 IO Buffer Design

In the design of the IO Buffer, the matrix data is stored in an appropriate way, and the number of times of reading the memory is reduced by reading multiple matrix data at one time. Firstly, discuss the storage format of the matrix in memory, analyze the data locality in operation, and define the data storage format of this paper. Design the data buffer circuit and the corresponding way of matrix vector according to the data format, and record the data in the buffer block by creating an IO Buffer table.

Row Major: The data in the same row is stored in the same memory location, and this storage method has a good arrangement pattern when performing row operations. When fetching a row vector, only one memory location is accessed. However, when per-forming column operations, all memory locations must be accessed to fully access vector data (Fig. 2).

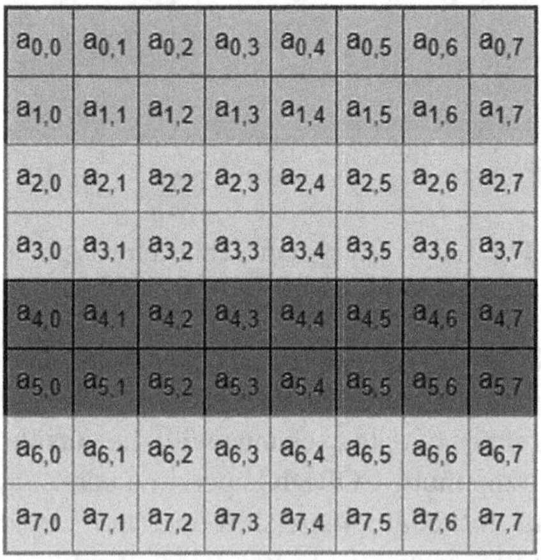

$a_{0,0}$	$a_{0,1}$	$a_{0,2}$	$a_{0,3}$	$a_{0,4}$	$a_{0,5}$	$a_{0,6}$	$a_{0,7}$
$a_{1,0}$	$a_{1,1}$	$a_{1,2}$	$a_{1,3}$	$a_{1,4}$	$a_{1,5}$	$a_{1,6}$	$a_{1,7}$
$a_{2,0}$	$a_{2,1}$	$a_{2,2}$	$a_{2,3}$	$a_{2,4}$	$a_{2,5}$	$a_{2,6}$	$a_{2,7}$
$a_{3,0}$	$a_{3,1}$	$a_{3,2}$	$a_{3,3}$	$a_{3,4}$	$a_{3,5}$	$a_{3,6}$	$a_{3,7}$
$a_{4,0}$	$a_{4,1}$	$a_{4,2}$	$a_{4,3}$	$a_{4,4}$	$a_{4,5}$	$a_{4,6}$	$a_{4,7}$
$a_{5,0}$	$a_{5,1}$	$a_{5,2}$	$a_{5,3}$	$a_{5,4}$	$a_{5,5}$	$a_{5,6}$	$a_{5,7}$
$a_{6,0}$	$a_{6,1}$	$a_{6,2}$	$a_{6,3}$	$a_{6,4}$	$a_{6,5}$	$a_{6,6}$	$a_{6,7}$
$a_{7,0}$	$a_{7,1}$	$a_{7,2}$	$a_{7,3}$	$a_{7,4}$	$a_{7,5}$	$a_{7,6}$	$a_{7,7}$

Fig. 2. Row major storage format

Column Major: The data in the same column is stored in the same memory location, and this storage method has a good arrangement pattern when performing column oper-ations. When fetching a column vector, only one memory location is accessed. However, when performing row operations, all memory locations must be accessed to fully access vector data (Fig. 3).

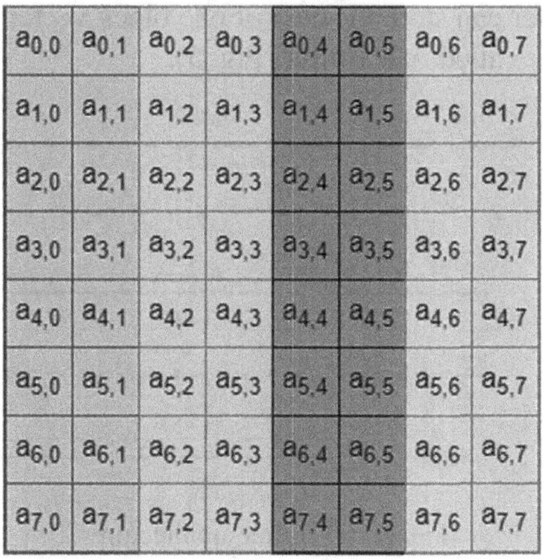

$a_{0,0}$	$a_{0,1}$	$a_{0,2}$	$a_{0,3}$	$a_{0,4}$	$a_{0,5}$	$a_{0,6}$	$a_{0,7}$
$a_{1,0}$	$a_{1,1}$	$a_{1,2}$	$a_{1,3}$	$a_{1,4}$	$a_{1,5}$	$a_{1,6}$	$a_{1,7}$
$a_{2,0}$	$a_{2,1}$	$a_{2,2}$	$a_{2,3}$	$a_{2,4}$	$a_{2,5}$	$a_{2,6}$	$a_{2,7}$
$a_{3,0}$	$a_{3,1}$	$a_{3,2}$	$a_{3,3}$	$a_{3,4}$	$a_{3,5}$	$a_{3,6}$	$a_{3,7}$
$a_{4,0}$	$a_{4,1}$	$a_{4,2}$	$a_{4,3}$	$a_{4,4}$	$a_{4,5}$	$a_{4,6}$	$a_{4,7}$
$a_{5,0}$	$a_{5,1}$	$a_{5,2}$	$a_{5,3}$	$a_{5,4}$	$a_{5,5}$	$a_{5,6}$	$a_{5,7}$
$a_{6,0}$	$a_{6,1}$	$a_{6,2}$	$a_{6,3}$	$a_{6,4}$	$a_{6,5}$	$a_{6,6}$	$a_{6,7}$
$a_{7,0}$	$a_{7,1}$	$a_{7,2}$	$a_{7,3}$	$a_{7,4}$	$a_{7,5}$	$a_{7,6}$	$a_{7,7}$

Fig. 3. Column major storage format

Block: The matrix is stored in the memory location in block units. Divide the original matrix into multiple sub-matrices, each of which is stored in a memory location. Since the memory size can store 16 matrix elements, the size of each sub- matrix is 4*4. For example, whether you want to get a row vector or a column vector, you only need to access two memory locations to get the complete vector data (Fig. 4).

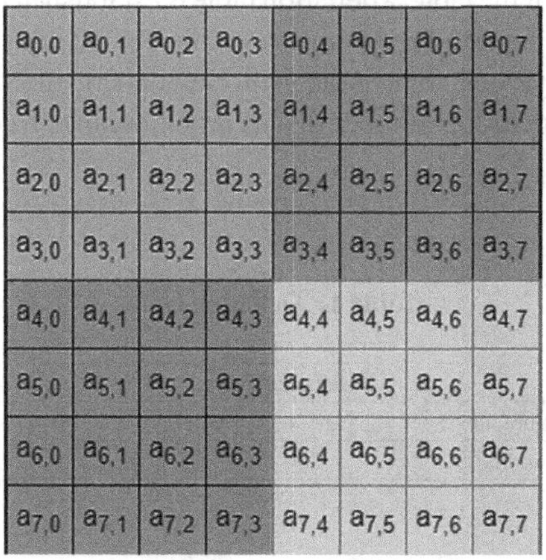

$a_{0,0}$	$a_{0,1}$	$a_{0,2}$	$a_{0,3}$	$a_{0,4}$	$a_{0,5}$	$a_{0,6}$	$a_{0,7}$
$a_{1,0}$	$a_{1,1}$	$a_{1,2}$	$a_{1,3}$	$a_{1,4}$	$a_{1,5}$	$a_{1,6}$	$a_{1,7}$
$a_{2,0}$	$a_{2,1}$	$a_{2,2}$	$a_{2,3}$	$a_{2,4}$	$a_{2,5}$	$a_{2,6}$	$a_{2,7}$
$a_{3,0}$	$a_{3,1}$	$a_{3,2}$	$a_{3,3}$	$a_{3,4}$	$a_{3,5}$	$a_{3,6}$	$a_{3,7}$
$a_{4,0}$	$a_{4,1}$	$a_{4,2}$	$a_{4,3}$	$a_{4,4}$	$a_{4,5}$	$a_{4,6}$	$a_{4,7}$
$a_{5,0}$	$a_{5,1}$	$a_{5,2}$	$a_{5,3}$	$a_{5,4}$	$a_{5,5}$	$a_{5,6}$	$a_{5,7}$
$a_{6,0}$	$a_{6,1}$	$a_{6,2}$	$a_{6,3}$	$a_{6,4}$	$a_{6,5}$	$a_{6,6}$	$a_{6,7}$
$a_{7,0}$	$a_{7,1}$	$a_{7,2}$	$a_{7,3}$	$a_{7,4}$	$a_{7,5}$	$a_{7,6}$	$a_{7,7}$

Fig. 4. Block storage format

It consists of IO buffer controller and two data buffers, A Buffer and B buffer. The IO buffer controller exchanges matrix data with the external memory. When receiving the command to send the matrix vector, it will query which buffer the matrix vector is stored in by look-up table, and send the matrix vector to the multi-CORDIC operation core. To receive new matrix data, it will determine whether the received block data should be stored in A buffer or B buffer according to the operation mode of the current algorithm.

A buffer and B buffer can store the data of one block vector at a time. A buffer and B buffer are collectively called A/B Buffer (Fig. 5).

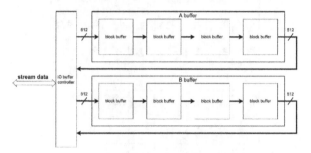

Fig. 5. IO Buffer architecture

5   Deflation and Shift Operation Circuit Design

Deflation: When the elements to be converged in the matrix have converged to the tolerance value, the original matrix can be divided into two small matrices. In terms of hardware implementation, this paper adopts the method of building tables and skipping operations to achieve deflation.

In the construction of the table, a deflation table is established to store the convergence situation of the current matrix. The operation number in the table will be compared with the element to be converged. If it is an 8*8 Hessenberg matrix, the matrix element corresponding to the operation number 0 is $a_{1,0}$, the number 1 corresponds to $a_{2,1}$, and so on (Table 1).

Table 1. Deflation table

deflation table															
operation number	0	1	2	3	4	5	6	7	8	9	10	11	12	13	14
convergence(1bit)															

Shift Operation: The shift operation can speed up the number of matrix convergence operations. The value of shift μ is divided into three types, namely zero shift, Rayleigh quotient shift, and Wilkinson shift. Wilkinson shift uses the eigenvalue of the bottom right 2*2 matrix as μ. If this method is used, an additional circuit for calculating the eigenvalue will be required. Rayleigh quotient shift is to use the element in the lower right corner as μ, without adding additional calculation circuits, just record the diagonal elements in the matrix and find the value in the lower right corner.

The deflation is to divide the original large matrix into multiple small matrices to operate separately, and the elements in the lower right corner of each small matrix are different, and the shift value to be done will also be different. When looking up the table, you must first go through some operations to find the bottom right element of the matrix (Table 2).

Table 2. Deflation table with shift

deflation table															
operation number	0	1	2	3	4	5	6	7	8	9	10	11	12	13	14
convergence(1bit)															
shift(32bit)															

6 Deflation and Shift Operation Circuit Design

6.1 Synthesis

Using TSMC's 130 nm process for CORDIC 4, the synthesis area is about 232891, and the fastest operating frequency is about 200 MHz (Tables 3 and 4).

Table 3. Area result table

Area (um^2)	
Combinational area	162213.727264
Buf/Inv area:	26666.153576
Noncombinational area:	70678.037659
Macro/Black Box area:	0
Total cell area:	232891.764923

Table 4. Timing results table

Critical path (ns)	
Clock clk (rise edge)	5.00
Library setup time	−0.21
Data required time	4.79
Data arrival time	4.79
Slack (MET)	0.0000

6.2 Matrix Operations and the Number of Operation Cores

Use software to simulate the cycle number of the circuit, analyze the operating speed efficiency between 4 operation cores and 16 operation cores by eigenvalue decomposition and singular value decomposition. Use a random number generator to generate a matrix of real numbers with elements between −1 and 1, and input the matrix into the circuit. Average the results of 1000 runs to estimate the average number of cycles in the actual operation of the circuit.

Under the 16 × 16 matrix, the operation speed of 16 operation cores is 2.15 times faster than that of 4 operation cores. Under the 8 × 8 matrix, the operation speed of 16 operation cores is 1.4 times faster than that of 4 operation cores (Fig. 6).

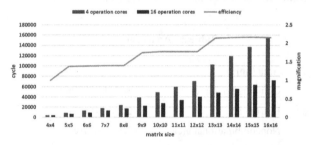

Fig. 6. Comparison diagram of the operation core of eigenvalue decomposition

Because the singular value decomposition will convert the matrix into the form of upper bidiagonal matrix before starting the iteration, so that in the iterative operation, only three groups of components need to be calculated in each row and column operation. Therefore, compared with eigenvalue decomposition, the efficiency improvement of multiple operation cores will be less. In the case of matrix size 16 × 16, 16 operation cores will be 1.5 times faster than 4 operation cores. In the case of a matrix size of 8 × 8, 16 operation cores will be 1.22 times faster than 4 operation cores (Fig. 7).

6.3 Comparison with Computer Environment

In the computer computing environment, use the Intel Core i7-8700@ 3.2 GHz CPU, and use the C++ programming language with higher execution efficiency, with the linear

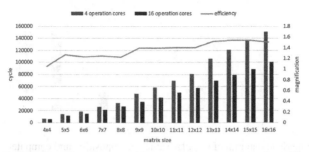

Fig. 7. Singular value decomposition operation core comparison diagram

algebra function library Eigen, to analyze the running speed of matrix de-composition operations in the computer environment. Use Eigen's built-in matrix de-composition function to perform matrix decomposition on matrices of different sizes. The calculation of the circuit running time is to use the software to simulate the number of clocks running by the circuit. Based on the speed of 200 MHz, which can be achieved by the TSMC 130 (nm) process, the total number of clocks is multiplied by 5ns to calculate the running time of the circuit.

Under the small matrix size of 8×8, the operation time of this paper is 0.085 ms, and the running time of the computer environment is 1.58 ms, which is about 18.6 times faster. In the case of a large matrix with a matrix size of 128×128, the operation time of this paper is 26.523 ms, and the running time of the computer environment is 1148.68 ms, which is about 43.3 times faster (Fig. 8).

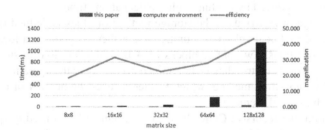

Fig. 8. Comparison diagram of eigenvalue decomposition and computer environment

Use the same method to analyze singular value decomposition. Under the small matrix size of 8×8, the operation time of this paper is 0.134 ms, and the running time of the computer environment is 0.323 ms, which is about 2.41 times faster. In the case of a large matrix with a matrix size of 128×128, the operation time of this paper is 18.099 ms, and the running time of the computer environment is 325.353 ms, which is about 8.46 times faster (Fig. 9).

It can be seen in the computer environment that the speed of computing singular value decomposition will be about 3.2 times faster than that of eigenvalue decomposition. In the architecture of this paper, singular value decomposition is only about 1.465 times faster than eigenvalue decomposition. The difference between them is that the singular value decomposition algorithm cannot be optimized in the way of Row Major. This makes

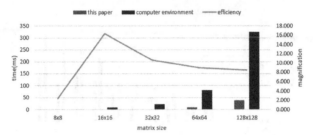

Fig. 9. Comparison diagram of singular value decomposition and computer environment

singular value decomposition less optimized than eigenvalue decomposition compared to software.

7 Conclusions

This paper defines the basic row-column operations of matrices by observing various matrix decomposition algorithms. And use the CORDIC operation circuit to explain how the row and column operations are done using CORDIC. And the operation behavior of each matrix decomposition method is divided into sweep mode and diagonal mode, and the circuit is designed based on the above basis.

In the optimization calculus, the design of the Row Major operation is proposed to reduce the complexity of the data in the row and column operations. The matrix data can be stored in an adaptive arrangement, and the number of times of reading the memory can be effectively reduced by reading multiple data at one time.

In the storage of matrix data, the storage method of block is defined first, and the matrix is stored in 4×4 sub-matrix units, so that there is good data locality in row and column operations. Two buffer blocks of A/B Buffer are used to store data, and the storage location of matrix data is determined according to the operation behavior of the matrix decomposition method, which further reduces the number of times of data exchange with external memory.

In operation, the recursive CORDIC operation unit of [2] is used to speed up the CORDIC operation by skipping large-angle rotation by bypass. With the same operation core architecture and adaptive data allocation, an operation mode with multiple computing cores is designed, so that the operation cores can be flexibly expanded. In addition, through the shift operation, the number of iterations of the matrix operation is greatly reduced. Using software to simulate the operation of the entire architecture, in addition to evaluating the performance, it also uses the simulation results to verify the correctness of the multiple CORDIC operation cores through the testbench. Finally, by modularizing the four computing cores into CORDIC 4, the overall architecture can be controlled by the CPU to achieve more flexible expansion.

The operation method of Row-Major operation proposed in this paper can optimize the operation of eigenvalue decomposition. However, when doing singular value decomposition, due to the limitation of the algorithm, it is impossible to use the Row-Major operation method to optimize the operation. In the future, it is hoped that there will be a more efficient way to calculate the singular value decomposition.

When the number of CORDIC 4 modules increases, although the parallelism of the operation will increase, the CPU will need more time to put the data into the module. In the future, a memory controller will be used, allowing the controller to allocate vector data into the module.

References

1. Watkins, D.S.: Understanding the QR algorithm. SIAM Rev. **24**(4), 427–440. JSTOR (1982)
2. Tsai, C.-Y., et al.: Design, optimization and Implementation of Matrix decomposition applied to advanced communication systems by HW/SW co-design platform. Master thesis, National Sun Yat-sen University, Kaohsiung (2021)
3. Parlett, B.N.: The QR algorithm. Comput. Sci. Eng. **2**, 38–42 (2000)
4. Wu, Y.-C., Tsai, P.-Y.: A generalized matrix-decomposition processor for joint MIMO transceiver design. In: IEEE International Conference on Acoustics, Speech and Signal Processing (ICASSP) (2017)
5. Hsiao, Y.L., et al.: Design and Implement of software and hardware co-design architecture by integrating FPGA and memory modules. Master thesis, National Sun Yat-sen University , Kaohsiung (2019)
6. Wu, C.-H., Tsai, P.Y.: An SVD processor based on Golub-Reinsch algorithm for MIMO precoding with adjustable precision. IEEE Trans. Circ. Syst. I: Regular Papers (2019)
7. Hsiao, S.F.: Parallel singular value decomposition of complex matrices using multidimensional CORDIC algorithms. IEEE Trans. Signal Process. **44**, 685–697 (1996)
8. Maharatna, K., Troya, A., Banerjee, S., Grass, E.: Virtually scaling-free adaptive CORDIC rotator. Comput. Digit. Tech. IEE Proc. **151**, 448–456 (2004). https://doi.org/10.1049/ip-cdt: 20041107
9. Shiri, A.: An FPGA implementation of singular value decomposition. In: 27th Iranian Conference on Electrical Engineering (ICEE) (2019)
10. Chao-Chuan, H., et al.: CORDIC-based signed-bit predictable SIN-COS generator and It's FPGA implementation. Master thesis, National Sun Yat-sen University , Kaohsiung (2000)
11. Masram, B.Y., Karule, P.T.: Design and Implementation of 111 MHz frequency compression efficient CORDIC based 2D-DCT using FPGA and its power performance. IEEE Bombay Section Signature Conference (IBSSC) **2021**, 1–6 (2021)
12. Mohindroo, P.B., Suneja, K.: Hardware Design of image encryption and decryption using CORDIC based chaotic generator. In: 2020 5th IEEE International Conference on Recent Advances and Innovations in Engineering (ICRAIE), pp. 1–5 (2020)
13. Singh, N., Joshi, S., Birla, S.: Suitability of singular value decomposition for image watermarking. In: 2019 6th International Conference on Signal Processing and Integrated Networks (SPIN), pp. 983–986 (2019)

Design and Implementation of the CNN Accelator Based on Multi-streaming SIMD Mechanisms

Jih-Ching Chiu, Zhe-You Yan, and Yung-Chi Liu$^{(\boxtimes)}$

Department of Electrical Engineering, National Sun Yat-sen University, Kaohsiung, Taiwan
ms066452@gmail.com, chiujihc@ee.nsysu.edu.tw

Abstract. In this paper, we propose a SIMD architecture for CNN model computing based on multi-streaming SIMD concepts. The proposed processor is called the Basic Multiple CNN Operation Cell (BMCOC). With BMCOC, we can expand as the many BMCOC architecture to achieve massive parallelism for execution of CNN models. Some designed philosophies are following such as 1) building fixed-point operation flow with adaptive quantization for the lossless CNN computing, 2) constructing the double local buffer to provide the overlapped computing model, 3) taking scalability mechanisms to design BMCOC module to suitable module scaling distribution to get high data parallel performance through the adaptive data set arrangement. In the simulation and verification results, Under the TSMC 90 nm process, the operating frequency can reach 100 MHz, the area is about 305,613 μm^2, and the power consumption is about 2.98 mW. Based on this operating frequency, the performance in comparison, using MobileNet designed for embedded environments as the operating model, under the Multi-Streaming SIMD architecture with 32 BMCOC cores, the computing speed is about 30.6 times higher than that of Cortex-M55, and 4.15 times higher than that of PC. Compared with the GPU, the speed is about 3.12 times faster.

Keywords: CNN parallel processor · Multi-streaming SIMD architecture · Weight data arrangement · CNN model computing

1 Introduction

In recent years, as science and technology have evolved and numerous businesses have received investment, image recognition technology has also advanced and been used in a variety of industrial applications [1–3].

Convolutional Neural Network (CNN) based methods have achieved great success in a large number of applications and have been among the most powerful and widely used techniques. However, CNN requires a high amount of computation and a large amount of weight data in operation. Therefore, CNN-based methods are computational-intensive and resource-consuming, and thus are hard to be integrated into embedded

This paper presents partial results of a long-term research project financed by both NSTC of R.O.C. under contract no. MOST 111-2218-E-110-004 and the industry.

systems such as smart phones, smart glasses, and robots. To fit the needs of CNN's real-time computing, many methods to accelerate CNN computing have been proposed, such as graphics processor, FPGA or ASIC. However, to achieve high performance with low power, sufficient computing parallelism is necessary, and this also means that the computing unit must have enough data bandwidth and scalable parallel processing mechanism.

For the properties of CNN computing models, such as flexible kernel size, uncertain convolution operation layer, and diverse classification quantum, some studies [7, 8] used the SIMD instruction set architectures for embedded applications to support changeable and high performance computing to accelerate CNN computing in lower power processing environments. With the data parallel computing methods provided by SIMD instructions, these processors can solve a little for the repetitive computing requirements of CNN models in the embedded systems. But, the data processing bandwidth is the key factor to effect the CNN computing efficiency. How to expand the factor is the main goal of this paper.

The data processing parallelism of the traditional SIMD processor architecture is limited by the data bandwidth of the SIMD vector register. The SIMD architecture for parallel processing of multiple data streams is proposed by Chiu etc. [11], which enabled simultaneously manipulate multiple data streams for SIMD instructions to provide high data bandwidth and high parallel computing.

Based on the multi-streaming SIMD concepts, we designs a processor, called the Basic Multiple CNN Operation Cell (BMCOC), to adapt to the CNN algorithm. For supporting the quantized operations to speedup computing efficiency, we build the fixed-point operation flow with adaptive quantization for the lossless CNN computing. For reducing data loading and process executing latency, we construct the double local buffer to provide the overlapped computing model. For achieving higher expansion performance, we take scalability mechanisms to design BMCOC module to suitable module scaling distribution to get high data parallel performance through the adaptive data set arrangement.

Finally, we builds a BMCOC simulation verification platform through System Verilog to verify the correctness of the BMCOC functions with CNN models. By the results, the computing speedup is about 30.6 times higher than Cortex-M55, and 4.15 times higher than PC.

2 Basic Multiple CNN Operation Cell (BMCOC)

2.1 Architecture Overview

As shown in Fig. 1, BMCOC is a SIMD processor designed for CNN operations, In the computing unit architecture, a SIMD Processing Unit is composed of multiple MOSU (Multimedia Operation Storage Unit) with SIMD computing capability and a hardware acceleration circuit DAQU (Data Adaptive Quantification Unit) designed for the elastic quantization method of CNN algorithm [10] and can provide a high degree of data parallel computing capability through Multi-Streaming SIMD operation. In this architecture, the operation data and instruction data will be captured through DMA and put into the Instruction Pool and Data Pool respectively for temporary storage, the SIMD Processing

Unit obtains operation data by sharing the Data Pool with the DMA, and read the Instruction from Pool instructions to perform operations.

1) *SIMD Processing Unit*

The vector operation register MOSU integrated with bit operation storage has four 64-bit vector registers, each time an operation is performed, eight 8-bit, four 16-bit, two 32-bit and one 64-bit data parallel operations can be provided through subword parallelism, And with the register group mode to reconfigure the computing resources of 4 MOSUs, the computing unit can increase the SIMD computing efficiency by up to 4 times in the way of Multi-Streaming SIMD. The quantization acceleration circuit DAQU designed for the flexible quantization method of the CNN algorithm can perform up to 16 quantization operations in one instruction by integrating with the vector registers in the 4 MOSUs.

Instruction Pointer is used to fetch the instructions in the Instruction Pool, and hand it over to the Processing Unit Controller for instruction decoding and circuit control, In addition, the Instruction Pointer also provides zero overhead hardware loop, which can simply construct the loop operation range through LPS (Loop Start) and LE (Loop End), and perform loop jump judgment by hardware, reducing the resources required to operate the loop.

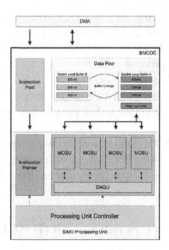

Fig. 1. BMCOC architecture

2) *Data Pool*

It is composed of two sets of Double Local Buffers that can exchange data and a Static Local Buffer. The Static Local Buffer is designed to provide a Local Buffer for SIMD Processing Unit to access and provides SIMD Processing Unit to temporarily store operation results when performing convolution layer operations. The two sets of Double

Local Buffers are used to temporarily store computing data and computing results, and their design utilizes the concept of overlapping computing. When one Double Local Buffer is reading data, another Double Local Buffer can write new operation data. After the operation is completed, the storage data of the two Buffers can be switched directly through the Buffer Change mechanism, thereby overlapping the operation, and reading time, save time waiting for data.

3) *Instruction Pool*

It is used to temporarily store operation instructions. Before operation, the instruction will be transferred from the main memory into the Instruction Pool through DMA. Then, when the operation starts, the instruction corresponding to the address will be sent to the SIMD Processing Unit for operation according to the read request of the Instruction Pointer. The Instruction Pool has a storage space of 1KB, and each time an operation of an operation layer is completed, the instruction of the operation layer of the next layer will be re-fetched through DMA (Fig. 2).

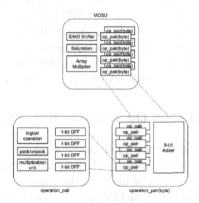

Fig. 2. MOSU architecture

2.2 Zero Overhead Hardware Loop

Zero overhead hardware loop is a loop construction hardware design for the operation rules of the CNN operation process. The zero overhead hardware loop can specify instructions within the range of repeated execution through loop-related instructions. When executing the loop jump back judgment, the judgment can be made directly by the hardware counter, without the need to execute the software comparison Instruction, and the number of operating instructions can be greatly reduced through the zero overhead hardware loop. The zero overhead hardware loop is aimed at CNN. The operation mechanism provides up to two layers of nested loops, and each loop can execute Instruction within the loop range up to 65535 times (Fig. 3).

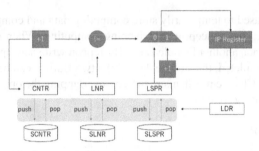

Fig. 3. Zero Overhead Hardware Loop architecture

The zero overhead hardware loop is mainly composed of seven registers, namely CNTR (Loop Counter Register), LNR (Loop Number Register), LSPR (Loop Start Pointer Register), LDR (Loop Depth Register), SCNTR (Stack CNTR), SLNR (Stack LNR), SLSPR (Stack LSPR), of which the first four registers are the registers that are mainly used when the hardware loop is executed. The CNTR register are the registers used to count the number of loop executions. The LNR register that records the maximum execution times of the loop range, the LSPR register that records the loop jump return address, and the LDR that records the loop depth and controls the stack register, and the last three registers are using to save loop parameter. When two layers of nested loops are executed, the temporary registers for recording and temporarily storing loop data are required to be used for temporary storage of CNTR, LNR and LSPR. SLSP.

3 Process Design of CNN Operation in BMCOC

In order to make the CNN operation to be efficiently executed on the BMCOC, this paper rearranges the weight data of the CNN to make it suitable for the operator and combines the BMCOC's operation architecture to design the operation process for the operation layer commonly used in the CNN architecture. to provide highly parallel computing capabilities, the parallel computing process is designed under the Multi-Streaming SIMD architecture, and the next few sections will introduce the design.

3.1 Weight Data Rearrangement

1) *Convolution Layer Weight Data Arrangement Format*

The convolution layer weight data arrangement format is preprocessed and rearranged for the 3*3 convolution kernel weight data. The weight data before rearrangement will first convert the floating-point weight data to 16 bits through the Fixed point 16-bit quantization method. Then, in order to reduce the processing time of the weight data when entering the BMCOC, the convolution kernel of the convolution layer weight will be split, copied and rearranged, as shown in Fig. 4, the rearranged convolution kernel will be changed from the original nine floating-point data become sixteen of fixed-point data, and several pieces of fixed-point data with a value of 0 will be inserted into the sixteen fixed-point data to simplify the preprocessing operation of BMCOC.

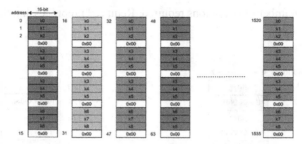

Fig. 4. Convolution layer weight data arrangement format

2) *Fully connected layer weight data arrangement format*

The weight data of the fully connected layer will also be converted into a 16-bit fixed-point number through the Fixed point 16-bit quantization method before the calculation. Then, considering the number of registers of the fully connected layer and BMCOC, in order to make the weight data can be efficiently used when entering the BMCOC, the weights are arranged in the order of the output channels corresponding to the input channels, and because the weight data of the fully connected layer cannot be reused, it will not be copied for the fully connected layer weight data.

3) *Bias Weight Data Arrangement Format*

Since the bias weight data is directly added with the operation result when the operation is performed, after quantization by the Fixed point 16-bit quantization method, in order to allow the bias weight data to match the operation result to expand its fractional, Therefore, when rearranging the bias weight data, it is necessary to additionally record the fractional number of the bias weight data, and the rearranged bias weight data will be stored in combination with its fractional number, and combined with the EXT Instruction

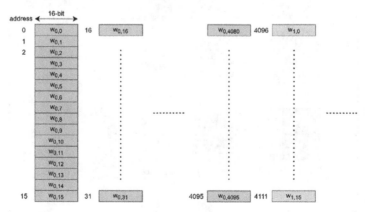

Fig. 5. Fully connected layer weight data arrangement format

can reduce the number of operations required. Required preprocessing time (Fig. 5 and 6).

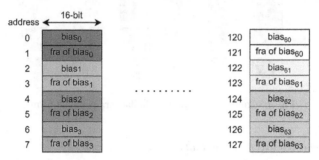

Fig. 6. Bias weight data arrangement format

3.2 Convolutional Layer Operation Process

1) *Overview*

In the design of the convolution layer operation process, this paper assumes that the size of the convolution kernel is 3*3. The image operation of the input channel will be divided into multiple 4*4 blocks, and these 4*4 blocks It will go through the 3*3 convolution operation process, and the operation will generate 2*2 partial operation results. These operation results will be accumulated with the previous operation results,

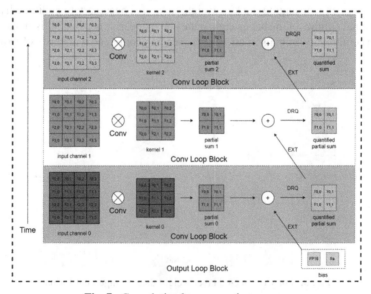

Fig. 7. Convolution layer operation process

and the operation results will be quantized. The same action will repeat the Conv Loop Block in Fig. 7 through the hardware loop, until all input channels are traversed, a 2*2 operation result image in an output channel is generated, and then output The Output Loop Block will switch the image of the input channel to another 4*4 block and execute the operation process again to generate the 2*2 operation result image of the other output channel. When the image of the output channel is generated, all operations of the convolutional layer operation process are completed.

3.3 Maxpooling Layer Operation Process

1) *Overview*

In the operation flow of the maxpooling layer, this paper assumes that the size of the maxpooling filter is 2*2, and the stride is 2 or 3*3 and the stride is 1. In the design of the operation flow, the image of the input channel will be It is divided into multiple 4*4 blocks, and these 4*4 blocks will go through the maxpooling operation process, and the operation will generate 2*2 operation results. These operation results will be directly written back through DMA through Local Buffer in memory.

The same action will repeatedly execute the Maxpooling Loop Block in Fig. 8 through the hardware loop until it traverses all the image data in an input channel and generates all the image data in an output channel, then it will switch to another input channel, and execute the operation process again to generate all output images of another output channel. When the images of all output channels are generated, all the operations of the maximum pooling layer operation process are completed.

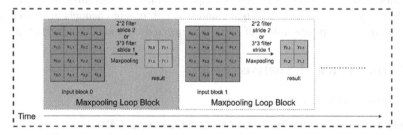

Fig. 8. Maxpooling layer operation process

3.4 Fully Connected Layer Operation Process

1) *overview*

In the design of the operation process of the fully connected layer, this paper cuts the input channels in units of 16 and aims to maximize the use of these 16 input channels to design the operation process of the fully connected layer.

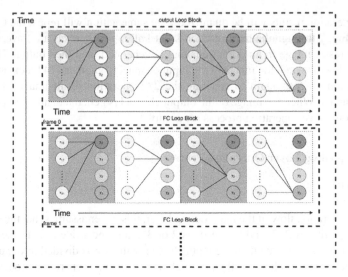

Fig. 9. Fully Connected Layer operation process

In each operation, the image data of 16 input channels will be read first, and the 16 input channels will be used to generate partial results of 4 output channels. When the operation is completed, the next 16 input channels will be read for operation and Accumulate with the 4 output channels from the previous operation, like the FC Loop Block in Fig. 9, and repeat the execution of the block until all input channels are traversed, at this time, 4 output channels will be generated. The output channel that completes the operation will then switch to the next 4 output channels. At this time, the output Loop Block in Fig. 9 will be executed again, and when all output channels have completed the operation, the operation flow of all fully connected layers will be completed.

4   Verification and Analysis

4.1   Functional Verification Platform

In order to verify the correctness of BMCOC function and CNN operation process, this paper builds a Test bench through System Verilog to simulate the operation environment of BMCOC and provides operation data and operation instructions when BMCOC operates CNN by simulating the functions of Data Pool and Instruction Pool.

As shown in the simulation environment architecture of Fig. 10, to enable BMCOC to simulate the operation process of the instruction execution convolution layer, the maximum pooling layer and the fully connected layer, it is necessary to prepare multiple files before the simulation starts, each of which is created by the Instruction Pool. The required Instruction file, which stores the instructions required to run the convolution layer, max pooling layer or fully connected layer, and the Data Pool stores all the required operation data history in the process of running the convolution layer, max pooling layer or fully connected layer, and finally there is a Result file to check whether the result of the comparison operation is correct.

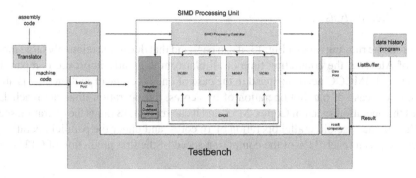

Fig. 10. Simulation environment architecture

4.2 Efficacy Analysis

To evaluate the operation performance of BMCOC, this paper firstly conducts circuit synthesis for the arithmetic unit, selects CPU, Cortex-M55 and graphics processor as the performance comparison objects, and uses five CNN networks of LeNet, AlexNet, VGG16, GoogleNet and MobileNet. The model is run to compare the performance gap between CPU, Cortex-M55, GPU and BMCOC (Fig. 11).

Platform	Operating condition	Data type
BMCOC	100MHz	16-bit fixed point
CPU	Intel Core i7-4790K @3.6GHz	32-bit floating point
Cortex-M55	800MHz	32-bit floating point
GPU	NVIDIA GeForce RTX3070	32-bit floating point

Fig. 11. Simulation Platform Information

1) LeNet Analysis

From Fig. 12, BMCOC can achieve the speed of multiple predictions of GPU with one core, while the speed of GPU is about 8 times different between the first prediction and multiple predictions. The computing speed of Cortex-M55 is presumed to be because the computing volume of the LeNet model is mainly concentrated in the 5*5 convolution core, which makes BMCOC unable to fully exert its data parallel computing capability. Therefore, it is necessary to increase the number of cores to increase the parallel computing capability to achieve Cortex-M55 operation speed, and the CPU only takes about 1ms to complete the operation. It is speculated that because the LeNet model is small, the model can be completely put into the cache, so it does not take a lot of time to wait for data access during the operation process.

2) *AlexNet Analysis*

From the running time of Fig. 13, it can be found that due to the relatively large model size of AlexNet, the computing time of all platform is greatly improved compared to LeNet, and BMCOC needs to spend in the case of one core The execution time is about 20 s, in the case of parallel operation of two cores, the operation time can reach 1.63 times the operation speed of Cortex-M55, and it can reach 1.48 times the operation speed of CPU in the case of parallel operation of 16 cores, and under the parallel operation of 32 cores, it can reach 34% of the computing speed of the first prediction of GPU.

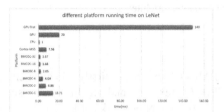

Fig. 12. LeNet Running time

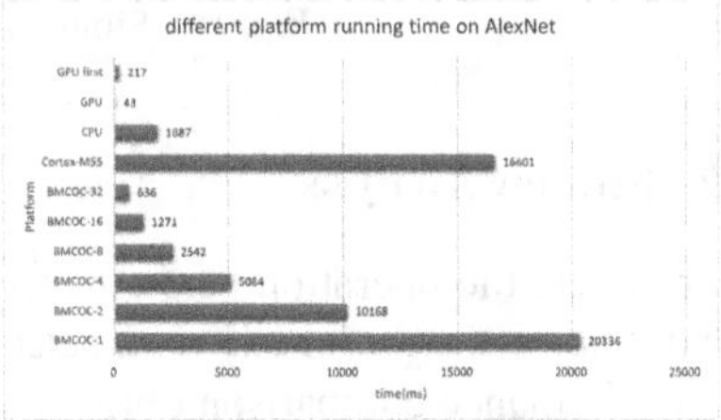

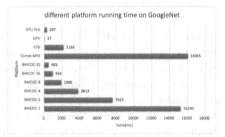

Fig. 13. AlexNet Running time

3) *VGG16 Analysis*

Although the model depth of VGG16 is larger than that of AlexNet, the number of parameters required for its model operation is only about half of that of AlexNet. From Fig. 14, it can also be found that the execution time of VGG16 excluding GPU is much smaller than that required for the operation of AlexNet network model. Execution time, BMCOC takes about 3 s to execute in the case of one core, and can reach about 1.52 times the operation speed of Cortex-M55, and can reach 1.16 times the operation speed of CPU in the case of parallel operation of eight cores, Under the parallel operation of

Fig. 14. VGG16 Running time

Fig. 15. GoogleNet Running time

16 cores, the operation speed similar to the first prediction of the GPU can be achieved, and under the parallel operation of 32 cores, it can reach 32% of the multiple prediction speed of the GPU.

4) GoogleNet Analysis

The number of model parameters of GoogleNet is smaller than that of AlexNet and VGG16, but the execution time required for its model operation is much larger than that of VGG16, and it is quite close to AlexNet. BMCOC takes about 15 s to execute in the case of one core and can achieve a higher execution time than that of VGG16. The 1.05 times operation speed of Cortex-M55 can reach 1.13 times the operation speed of CPU in the case of parallel operation of eight cores, and under the parallel operation of 32 cores, it can reach 61% of the multiple prediction speed of GPU.

5) MobileNet Analysis

The number of model parameters of MobileNet is about twice that of LeNet, but the execution time required for its model operation, excluding GPU, is about 14 to 28 times that of LeNet. As shown in Fig. 15, BMCOC takes about the execution time is 200 ms, and it can reach the operation speed close to the Cortex-M55. Under the parallel operation of 8 cores, the BMCOC can reach 1.17 times the operation speed of the CPU. Under the parallel operation of 16 cores, it can reach the same Compared with 1.65 times the computing speed of GPU multiple prediction speed (Fig. 16).

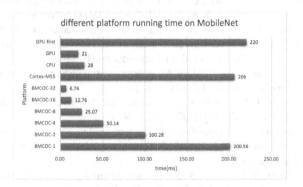

Fig. 16. MobileNet Running time

5   Conclusion

The BMCOC is proposed in this paper, which combines the flexible quantization methods of the CNN algorithm and the characteristics of SIMD to design appropriate data quantization units and quantization related instructions, respectively quantize the operation data and operation results. Based on multi-streaming SIMD concepts, the BMCOC is designed to enable simultaneously manipulate multiple data streams for SIMD instructions to provide high data bandwidth and high parallel computing for the CNN operation. In addition, with the Double Local Buffer in the data pool, it can realize the overlap execution for operations and data loading, thereby improving the overall processing performance. At the same time, the Double Local Buffer mechanism increases the scalability of the processor. Finally, the zero overhead hardware loop mechanism is used in the BMCOC to speedup loop operations, which can favor the execution of the CNN models.

References

1. Yadav, S.S., Jadhav, S.M.: Deep convolutional neural network based medical image classification for disease diagnosis. J. Big Data **6**(1), 1–18 (2019). https://doi.org/10.1186/s40537-019-0276-2
2. Sonata, I., et al.: Autonomous car using CNN deep learning algorithm. J. Phys: Conf. Ser. **1869**(1), 012071 (2021)
3. Rahman, M.M., Barua, P.: A CNN Model-based ensemble approach for Fruit identification using seed, In: 2021 5th International Conference on Electrical Information and Communication Technology (EICT), pp. 1–6 (2021). https://doi.org/10.1109/EICT54103.2021.9733475
4. NVIDA, NVIDA-Amerer-GA-102-Architecture-Whitepapaer (2020)
5. Wen, J., Ma, Y., Wang, Z.: An efficient FPGA accelerator optimized for high throughput sparse CNN inference. IEEE Asia Pacific Conference on Circuits and Systems (APCCAS) **2020**, 165–168 (2020). https://doi.org/10.1109/APCCAS50809.2020.9301696
6. Bouguezzi, S., et al.: An efficient FPGA-based convolutional neural network for classification: Ad-MobileNet" Electr. **10**(18), 2272(2021). https://doi.org/10.3390/electronics10182272
7. Lee, S.J., Park, S.-S., Chung, K.S.: 2018. Efficient SIMD implementation for accelerating convolutional neural network. In: Proceedings of the 4th International Conference on Communication and Information Processing (ICCIP 2018), pp. 174–179. Association for Computing Machinery, New York, NY, USA (2018). https://doi.org/10.1145/3290420.3290444
8. Lai, L., Suda, N., Chandra, V.: CMSIS-NN efficient neural network kernels for arm cortex-M CPUs. arXiv preprint arXiv1801.06601 (2018)
9. Chiu, T.-C., Yang, K.M., Chou, Y.L.: A hyperscalar dual-core architecture for embedded systems. Microprocess. Microsyst. **37**(8), 929–940 (2013)
10. Lin, W.Y.: Design and Implementation of CNN algorithm with flexible quantification and adaptive data arrangement based on BMCD platform. Master thesis, National Sun Yat-sen University, Kaohsiung (2021)
11. Chiu, J.-C., Chou, Y.-L., Hong, S.-X.: A multi-streaming multimedia computing engine. Microprocess. Microsyst. **34**(7–8), 247–258 (Nov.2010)
12. Arm Limited: NEON™ Programmer's Guide. https://developer.arm.com/documentation/den0018/latest
13. Arm Limited: Arm helium technology M-profile vector extension (MVE) for arm cortex-M processors reference book. https://www.arm.com/zh-TW/resources/ebook/helium-mve-reference-book
14. RISC-V "V" Vector Extension. https://github.com/riscv/riscv-v-spec/releases/download/v1.0/riscv-v-spec-1.0.pdf
15. Meng, J., et al.: Automatic generation of high-performance convolution kernels on ARM CPUs for deep learning. IEEE Trans. Parallel Distrib. Syst. **33**(11), 2885–2899 (2022). https://doi.org/10.1109/TPDS.2022.3146257

16. Yang, C., Wang, Y., Zhang, H., Wang, X., Geng, L.: A reconfigurable CNN Accelerator using tile-by-tile computing and dynamic adaptive data truncation. In: 2019 IEEE International Conference on Integrated Circuits, Technologies and Applications (ICTA), pp. 73–74 (2019). https://doi.org/10.1109/ICTA48799.2019.9012913

17. Ioffe, S., Szegedy, S.: Batch normalization: accelerating deep network training by reducing internal covariate shift. arXiv preprint arXiv:1502.03167 (2015)

18. Arm Limited: Arm® Cortex®-M55 Processor Devices Generic User Guide. https://develo per.arm.com/documentation/101273/latest/

19. Lecun, Y., Bottou, L., Bengio, Y., Haffner, P.: Gradient-based learning applied to document recognition. Proc. IEEE **86**, 2278–2324 (1998). https://doi.org/10.1109/5.726791

20. Krizhevsky, A., Sutskever, I., Hinton, G.E.: ImageNet classification with deep convolutional neural networks. Adv. Neural Inf. Process. Syst. **2**, 1097–1105 (2012)

21. Simonyan, K., Zisserman, A.: Very deep convolutional networks for large-scale image recognition. In: ICLR (2015)

22. Szegedy, C., et al.: Going deeper with convolutions. In: 2015 IEEE Conference on Computer Vision and Pattern Recognition (CVPR), pp. 1–9 (2015). https://doi.org/10.1109/CVPR.2015. 7298594.

23. Howard, A.G., et al.: MobileNets: efficient convolutional neural networks for mobile vision applications. ArXiv abs/1704.04861 (2017)

Design and Implementation of the Link-List DMA Controller for High Bandwidth Data Streaming

Jih-Ching Chiu, Yan-Ting Wu, Yung-Chi Liu, and Chi-Yang Hsieh[✉]

Department of Electrical Engineering, National Sun Yat-sen University, Kaohsiung, Taiwan
aa2086607@gmail.com

Abstract. In recent years, the design of artificial intelligence computing system to improve system performance by hardware acceleration has become a trend. High bandwidth, highly compatible data stream for hardware operation flow is a key factor affecting hardware acceleration performance. Therefore, this paper proposes the Link-list DMAC (LDMAC), which can support the linked transfer of three-dimension data block access, high-flexibility data retrieval arrangement. Based on the design concept of establishing high-bandwidth data flow and highly flexible data acquisition, LDMAC has the following design. 1) DMA List: including multiple linked nodes (DMA List Node), each node can be configured with single/multiple channels and single/multiple map data block access mode, access data acquisition and arrangement rules, so as to the LDMAC design that realizes high flexibility and supports linked transfer. 2) PackUnpack Buffer (PUPB): the internal register of LDMAC, supporting highly flexible data arrangement. 3) ABP Buffer: a triple buffer structure with dual data buffers and prefetch data buffer. The buffer data storage and exchange mechanism according to the data access state can improve the storage efficiency of discontinuous data and improve the continuity of data flow. 4) Double-buffering Design: The Ping-Pong mechanism is applied to provide overlapping computing between the LDMAC and the acceleration hardware to improve the system operation performance. In this paper, a synthesizable LDMAC is implemented. With 40 nm library technology of TSMC, a working frequency of 250 MHz is achieved. In terms of simulation verification, by working collaboratively with the CNN accelerator, LDMAC can improve access efficiency by 63% compared to requesting data directly from DRAM.

Keywords: LDMAC · High bandwidth · High flexible · DMA list · PackUnpack buffer · Linked transfer · ABP buffer

1 Introduction

In recent years, the application of artificial intelligence has ushered in explosive development. In terms of image recognition, the deep learning model constructed by the

This paper presents partial results of a long-term research project financed by both NSTC of R.O.C. under contract no. MOST 111-2218-E-110-004 and the industry.

Convolution Neural Network (CNN) has been proposed in large numbers [1–4], and its large-scale data access and computing have become the burden of the CPU. Therefore, it has become a trend to use the CPU and acceleration hardware to work together to improve system performance. For efficient data transmission, such system architectures are equipped with a Directly Memory Access Controller (DMAC), such as IBM CELL [5]. In order to improve the transmission efficiency, the contemporary DMAC design not only supports the link transfer with dynamic address calculation, but also optimizes according to the application environment [6–11] or special computing requirements [12–14] and a few of them support scatter-gather function [15, 16].

In the operation of the CNN model, the operation mode is mainly two-dimensional data space calculation, while the image data and kernel map required for the operation are three-dimensional data space, and the bias is one-dimensional data space, as Fig. 1. In addition, how to arrange the operation data during the operation to improve the operation efficiency is often a difficult problem, so the DMAC must have the ability to capture and arrange the data. In summary, the DMAC design for CNN, requires the ability to have a three-dimensional data space addressing mode, data blocks spanning multiple start addresses, scatter-gather mode ability for data capture and arrangement.

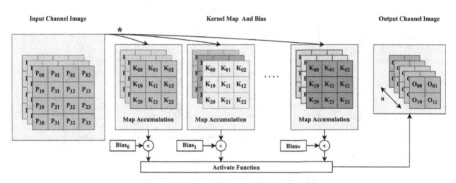

Fig. 1. CNN operation flow

The addressing modes of the current DMAC design mostly only support link transfer of one-dimensional and two-dimensional data spaces, data blocks with a single starting address. In addition, most of them does not provide the flexibility of data arrangement required to accelerate hardware in terms of scatter-gather function in data sets. When faced with the data acquisition mode required for CNN, the CPU must frequently reconfigure the relevant parameters of link transfer, resulting in the loss of the link transfer advantage.

Because the current DMAC design cannot meet the requirements of high bandwidth and flexible data flow for high-efficiency CNN operations, this paper proposes a Link-list DMAC (LDMAC) that combines cache and data buffer. LDMAC will support linked transfer mode with flexible data acquisition and arrangement. Additionally, LDMAC supports three-dimensional dynamic addressing calculation, and it can span data blocks from multiple starting addresses. Therefore, LDMAC can avoid reconfiguration of link transfer parameters in the single-layer CNN operation, thus enabling overlapping computing between LDMAC and accelerator, and achieving the design goal of providing accelerator high-bandwidth data flow.

The rest of this paper is organized as follows: Sect. 2 describes the proposed LDMAC. Section 3 investigates the cache parameter and ABP Buffer mechanism. In Sect. 4, LDMAC implementation cost and access efficiency evaluation are report and discussed. Finally, some conclusions are given in Sect. 5.

2 Proposed Link-List DMAC

2.1 System Architecture

LDMAC is a single-channel, unified access management design, and its application field is a cooperative computing platform composed of CPU and Accelerator. Accelerator has Instruction Pool and Data Pool, which are respectively used to store the operation instructions and data.

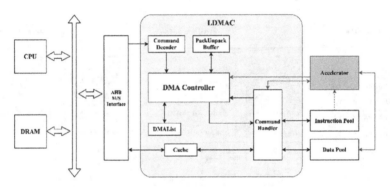

Fig. 2. LDMAC system architecture

As Fig. 2, LDMAC is connected to the CPU and DRAM by AHB Master/Slave Interface. CPU can transmit instructions to LDMAC, configure DMA List of LDMAC through the AHB Slave Interface. LDMAC can send access requirements to DRAM through the AHB Master Interface. In this paper, the bus width is 64 bits, and with burst transmission mode, the total width of the data is 512 bits. LDMAC can receive commands from CPU and Accelerator. It is responsible for tasks such as enabling and resetting the Accelerator, configuring the DMA List, performing link transfer transfers, and constructing the data flow to Accelerator.

During the execution of the link transfer, the DMA Controller will polling the valid DMA List Nodes of DMA List in turn to obtain access-related data such as accessed target memory, addresses. With access-related data, DMA Controller controls the PackUnpack Buffer to perform data scatter-gather function with high flexible. DMA Controller also send access commands to Command Handler to send requests to the system memory, Instruction Pool or Data Pool.

2.2 DMA List

As Fig. 3, the DMA List consists of several independent DMA List Nodes. Considering the flexibility and scalability of the management operation of the linked list node group, it includes List Node Handler and Output Mux to manage the control signal, input and output data of the DMA List Node. List Node Handler can use the "list_nodesel" signal to determine which node is the current incoming control signal should be transferred to, and the Output Mux also uses the "list_nodesel" signal to select which node the stored access information should be sent out.

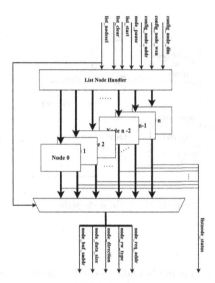

Fig. 3. DMA list architecture

The DMA List architecture enables DMA Controller to easily manage and operate the nodes with high scalability. DMA Controller can configure the content of the specified node by controlling the "list_nodesel" signal, and it can also poll each node to obtain the corresponding access information to execute the link transfer of multiple start address data blocks.

2.3 DMA List Node

A DMA List Node includes three modules: Control, Request Address Generator, and DMA Configuration Register, as Fig. 4. A DMA List Node supports the function of three-dimensional dynamic address calculation, and it has a data register to provide access-related parameters. The DMA List can control the node to start or suspend the calculation of the access address, and it also can clear the node configuration data. Besides, DMA List Node allows the DMA List configures its configuration register directly, and a node status signal for outside is used to indicate whether the node has completed the configured transmission task.

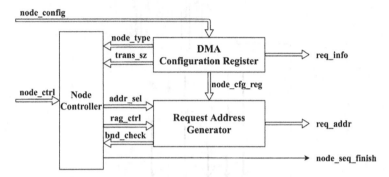

Fig. 4. DMA list node architecture

Node Controller

The Node Controller controls the boundary counter inside the node address generator, the dynamic address calculation mode, and the access address output selection according to the external control signal (node_ctrl), the content of the DMA Configuration Register (node_type), and the access boundary check signal (bnd_check) from the Request Address Generator. In addition, the node controller has a counter inside and generates "node_seq_finish" signal according to the access-related information (trans_sz) from the DMA Configuration Register. It is used to inform the outside whether the node has completed its configured transmission task.

DMA Configuration Registers

The DMA Configuration Register is configured by the "node_config" signal, which includes 10 registers with width of 32 bits. The registers stores access-related information, including access memory, access type, data flexibility, scatter-gather related parameters. With different data access mode configuration, DMA List Node can be configured as single channel mode, multiple channels mode, single map mode, multiple maps mode. The data access flow of each mode is shown in the Table 1.

Table 1. Different data access mode of DMA list node

Data Access Mode	Data Sequence
Not Active	X
Single Channel	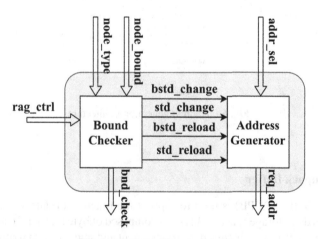
Multiple Channel	
Single Map	
Multiple Map	

Request Address Generator

The Request Address Generator is managed by the Node Controller and performs dynamic address calculation according to the access configuration parameters of the DMA Configuration Register. It consists of two modules, Bound Checker and Address Generator, as Fig. 5.

Fig. 5. Request address generator

Bound Checker

Bound Checker is mainly responsible for the condition detection of the access address across the block, and generates the cross-block condition judgment result signal "bnd_check", so that the Node Controller can control the "addr_sel" signal to select the correct address output. In addition, the Bound Checker also outputs the control signals as the address update signals of the Address Generator across data blocks.

Address Generator

The Address Generator module supports dynamic address calculation in different data access mode. It takes the Master Address as the starting address parameter of the data block, and Stride, Block Stride, and Channel Stride represent address displacement parameters of different dimensions. In order to avoid the use of multipliers for access address calculation, the Address Generator is replaced by an accumulation register. As Fig. 6, the output of the access address will be selected by "addr_sel" signal, and whether to jump across data blocks is controlled by the "bstd_change", "bstd_reload", "std_change", and "std_reload" signals sent by the Bound_Checker.

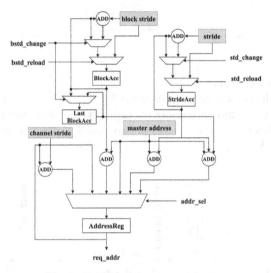

Fig. 6.   Address generator architecture

2.4   PackUnpack Buffer

PackUnpack Buffer (PUPB) is used to support the function of data scatter-gather. As Fig. 7, it has a data storage space of 32 Bytes composed of byte register. To adapt with the cache memory data block, flexible data arrangement and segment data writing functions, PUPB contains 32 Bytes data left shifter and right shifter, 4 Bytes data left shifter, and internal register, data mask generator designed with byte unit. In this paper, responses to the little-endian system of data storage, PUPB equips with a Data Reverse Unit that realizes the high and low bit inversion of 32 Bytes data in Byte units, so that the operation habits and the high and low positions of data storage are the same, as Fig. 8.

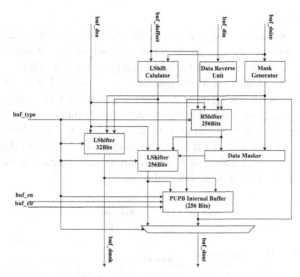

Fig. 7. PackUnpack buffer architecture

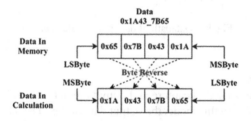

Fig. 8. Data reverse with byte unit

According to the access parameters stored in the DMA List relayed by the DMA Controller, the PUPB operation mode can be divided into four modes: Load Mode, Clear Mode, Pack Mode, and Unpack Mode (Table 2).

Table 2. PUPB operation mode

Access Memory	R/W	PUPB Operation Mode
Data Pool	Read	Data Load Mode
Data Pool	Write	Data Clear Mode
External Memory	Read	Data Pack Mode
External Memory	Write	Data Unpack Mode

Data Pack Mode

Data Pack Mode is used to arrange and store the target segment data of external memory into the PUPB internal registers. In this mode, the output data of the Mask Generator will be used as an enable signal for the internal registers of the PUPB.

The datapath of Data Pack Mode operation is shown in Fig. 9. In terms of data processing, PUPB sends the input data to the Data Reverse Unit, and then right-shifts according to the memory read address, the actual shift number is decide with cache specification. This operation is used to align the address with zero in the PUPB's internal register address. Finally, the PUPB right-shifted data and the output data of the Mask Generator are left-shift according to the externally specified arrangement address to the corresponding block storage of the internal register.

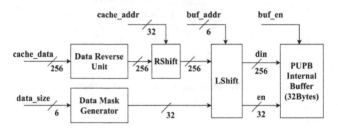

Fig. 9. Datapath of data pack mode operation

Data Unpack Mode

Data Unpack Mode is used to capture and output the data stored in the PUPB internal register to the outside. In this mode, the output data of the Mask Generator will be used as a data mask, and after shifting to the left, it will be used to mark the valid bytes of the PUPB output data.

The datapath of Data Pack Mode operation is shown in Fig. 10. In terms of data processing, PUPB will read the internal register, and then right-shifts the data according to data capture start address parameter. After, the right-shifted data is sent to the Data Masker to mask not interesting data section. Finally, according to the left shift amount calculated by the LShift Calculator, the output data of the Data Masker and Mask Generator are left shifted and sent to the PUPB outputs.

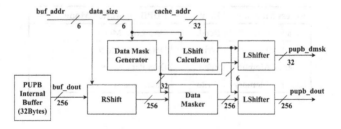

Fig. 10. Datapath of data unpack mode operation

2.5 Double-Buffering Mechanism

The design of DMA List in LDMAC can realize link transfer of single-layer CNN operation data after configuring DMA List once. With this feature, LDMAC supports double-buffering mechanism to implement overlapping computing with accelerator to improve the computational efficiency (Fig. 11).

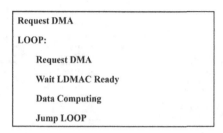

Request DMA

LOOP:

    Request DMA

    Wait LDMAC Ready

    Data Computing

    Jump LOOP

Fig. 11. Overlapping computing mechanism

To achieve double-buffering mechanism, Data Pool is composed of dual-port SRAM. LDMAC, Accelerator can access Data Pool at the same time. In order to separate the LDMAC and the area accessible by the Accelerator, the LDMAC will control the most significant bit of the access address of the Accelerator side, as Fig. 12. After each DMA request is completed, the LDMAC will flip the bit value and exchange the area accessed by the LDMAC and acceleration hardware.

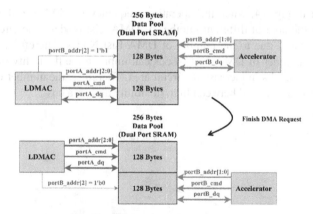

Fig. 12. Double-buffering mechanism

3 Result and Evaluation

3.1 LDMAC Synthesis Result

LDMAC includes modules such as DMA Controller, DMA List, PackUnpack Buffer, Command Decoder. The number of DMA List Nodes in DMA List is parameterized, there is equip 32 DMA List Nodes in synthesis. The synthesis library of LDMAC is TSMC 40 nm. As Fig. 13, LDMAC operating frequency can reach 250 MHz, and the area is 223,792 μm². Because the DMA List contains a large number of configuration registers, and each DMA List Node has its own dynamic address calculation unit, the area of the DMA List occupies most of the circuit area. When number of DMA List Nodes is parameterized to 32, the DMA List will occupy 91% of the total circuit area.

```
Timing Path Group 'clk'                         Area
--------------------------------------          --------------------------------------
Levels of Logic:            54.00               Combinational Area:     140885.891087
Critical Path Length:        3.92               Noncombinational Area:  82906.962725
Critical Path Slack:         0.00               Buf/Inv Area:           17039.710590
Critical Path Clk Period:    4.00               Total Buffer Area:          4344.35
Total Negative Slack:        0.00               Total Inverter Area:       12695.36
No. of Violating Paths:      0.00               Macro/Black Box Area:       0.000000
Worst Hold Violation:        0.00               Net Area:                   0.000000
Total Hold Violation:        0.00               --------------------------------------
No. of Hold Violations:      0.00               Cell Area:              223792.853812
                                                Design Area:            223792.853812
--------------------------------------

Hierarchical area distribution
..............................

                         Global cell area              Local cell area
                         ------------------            --------------------------------
Hierarchical cell        Absolute  Percent   Combi-    Noncombi-   Black-
                         Total     Total     national  national    boxes    Design
------------------------ --------- -------   --------- ---------   -------  ------------------
LDMAC                    223792.8538 100.0    1.3608    0.0000     0.0000   LDMAC
ch                       5386.0462    2.4   2900.3184  2485.7279   0.0000   command_handler
cpu_cmd_dec              273.5208     0.1     64.8648   208.6560   0.0000   command_decoder
dlist                    203819.7122 91.5  61442.3870 77233.1074   0.0000   dmalist
dma_ctrl                 2958.8527    1.3   2178.4140   490.3416   0.0000   dma_controller
pupb                     11353.3811   5.1   8836.0084  2489.1299   0.0000   pack_unpack_buffer
                         ----------- ----- ---------- ----------  -------
Total                                       140885.8911 82906.9627 0.0000
```

Fig. 13.   QoR and area report of LDMAC

As shown in Fig. 14, when the operating frequency is 250 MHz, the LDMAC is matched with the area of different number of DMA List Nodes. The circuit area will be greatly increased due to the number of DMA List Nodes. Therefore, although the increase in the number of DMA List Nodes can improve the flexibility of data access planning, it also results in increase in circuit area. Therefore, the number of DMA List Nodes needs to be balanced between high flexibility and area cost.

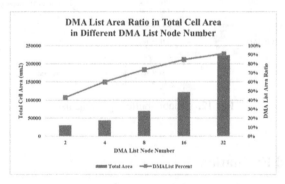

Fig. 14.   Number of DMA list nodes related to design area

3.2 Evaluation

To verify the high-bandwidth and high-flexible data flow of LDMAC to improve the data access efficiency of the CNN acceleration module, we simulate the operation of the CNN Accelerator to execute the VGG16 and obtain its data access trace, which enables LDMAC to perform simulation and analysis with different data storage architectures.

Table 3 is a comparison table of simulation results for LMDAC combined with different data storage architectures. It can be seen from the table that compared with the CNN acceleration module directly accessing data to DRAM, the LDMAC with only cache memory can improve the access efficiency by 49%. For LDMAC equipped with cache memory combined with ABP Buffer, compared with CNN Accelerator sending access requests directly to DRAM, this architecture can improve access efficiency by 63%.

Table 3. DMAC with different data storage architecture

Memory	Data Hit Rate		Access Cycle	Improvement
	Total Data Hit Rate	ABP Hit Rate		
DRAM	X	X	6,248,667,536	0%
Cache Only	99.28%	X	3,170,764,136	49%
Cache + ABP Buffer	99.30%	96.35%	2,309,531,855	63%

4 Conclusion

This paper proposes a Link-list Direct Memory Access Controller (LDMAC) with high bandwidth and high flexibility data streaming. With DMA List and PackUnpack Buffer, link transfer of LDMAC supports three-dimensional data space, multiple data blocks with different starting addresses and flexible data scatter-gather function. LDMAC can perform link transfer on the single-layer CNN computing data with once configuration, thereby realizing overlapping computing and improving the system computing efficiency. In addition, to reduce the impact of waiting for DRAM delay parameters on system operation efficiency, LDMAC combines the cache memory and ABP Buffer, which designed with the data access trace of CNN Models to achieving high hit rate and improve access efficiency, increase data bandwidth. By simulating the operation mode of CNN Accelerator, after adding LDAMC design, compared with CNN Accelerator directly requesting data from DRAM, the access efficiency can be improved by 63%.

References

1. Lecun, Y., Bottou, L., Bengio, Y., Haffner, P.: Gradient-based learning applied to document recognition. Proc. IEEE **86**(11), 2278–2324 (Nov.1998). https://doi.org/10.1109/5.726791
2. Krizhevsky, A., Sutskever, I., Hinton, G.E.: ImageNet classification with deep convolutional neural networks. In: International Conference on Neural Information Processing Systems, pp. 1097–1105 (2013)

3. Simonyan, K., Zisserman, A.: Very deep convolutional networks for large-scale image recognition. In: Proceedings of International Conference on Learning Representations (2015)
4. Howard, A.G., et al.: MobileNets: efficient convolutional neural networks for mobile vision applications. arXiv:1704.04861 (2017) [online]. https://arxiv.org/abs/1704.04861
5. Kahle, J.A., Day, M.N., Hofstee, H.P., Johns, C.R., Maeurer, T.R., Shippy, D.: Introduction to the cell multiprocessor. IBM J. Res. Dev. 49(4.5,), 589–604 (2005)
6. Ma, G., He, H.: Design and implementation of an advanced DMA controller on AMBA-based SoC. In: 2009 IEEE 8th International Conference on ASIC, 2009, pp. 419–422 (2009). https://doi.org/10.1109/ASICON.2009.5351258
7. Ponsard, R., Janvier, N., Houzet, D., Fristot, V., Mansour, W.: Online GPUAnalysis using adaptive DMA controlled by softcore for 2D detectors. In: 2020 23rd Euromicro Conference on Digital System Design (DSD), pp. 436–439 (2020). https://doi.org/10.1109/DSD51259.2020.00075
8. Shirur, Y.J.M., Sharma, K.M.: Design and implementation of efficient direct memory access (DMA) controller in multiprocessor SoC. In: 2018 International Conference on Networking, Embedded and Wireless Systems (ICNEWS), pp. 1–6 (2018). https://doi.org/10.1109/ICNEWS.2018.8903991
9. Morales, H., Duran, C., Roa, E.: A low-area direct memory access controller architecture for a RISC-V based low-power microcontroller, In: 2019 IEEE 10th Latin American Symposium on Circuits & Systems (LASCAS), pp. 97–100 (2019). https://doi.org/10.1109/LASCAS.2019.8667579
10. Nguyen, H., Dong, K., Tran, X-T.: A reconfigurable multi-function DMA controller for high-performance computing systems, pp. 344–349 (2018). https://doi.org/10.1109/NICS.2018.8606841
11. Madhuri, R.A., Hampali, M.W., Umesh, N., Pooja, K.S., Shirur, Y.J.M., Chakravarthi, V.S.: Design and implementation of EDMA controller for AI based DSP SoCs for real-time multimedia processing. In: 2020 Fourth International Conference on I-SMAC (IoT in Social, Mobile, Analytics and Cloud) (I-SMAC), pp. 554–563 (2020). https://doi.org/10.1109/I-SMAC49090.2020.9243535
12. Kashimata, T., Kitamura, T., Kimura, K., Kasahara, H.: Cascaded DMA controller for speedup of indirect memory access in irregular applications. In: 2019 IEEE/ACM 9th Workshop on Irregular Applications: Architectures and Algorithms (IA3), pp. 71–76 (2019). https://doi.org/10.1109/IA349570.2019.00017
13. Ma, S., Huang, L., Lei, Y., Guo, Y., Wang, Z.: An efficient direct memory access (DMA) controller for scientific computing accelerators. IEEE International Symposium on Circuits and Systems (ISCAS) 2019, 1–5 (2019). https://doi.org/10.1109/ISCAS.2019.8702172
14. Ma, S., Lei, Y., Huang, L., Wang, Z.: MT-DMA: A DMA controller supporting efficient matrix transposition for digital signal processing. IEEE Access 7, 5808–5818 (2019). https://doi.org/10.1109/ACCESS.2018.2889558
15. Scatter-Gather DMA Controller Core: Quartus II Handbook Version 9.1, Vol. 5, November 2009
16. IPUG67 - Scatter-Gather Direct Memory Access Controller IP Core User Guide: Lattice Semiconductor, April 2015
17. JEDEC Solid State Technology Association (2012). DDR3 SDRAM Standard (JESD79-3F)
18. Gross. J.: High-performance DRAM system design constraints and considerations. Master's thesis, University of Maryland, College Park, August 2010
19. Chiu, J.-C., Su, K.L.: Design and Implementation of brain memory controller with cache memory. Master thesis, National Sun Yat-sen University, Kaohsiung (2021)
20. Chiu, J.-C., Yang, K.-M., Chou, Y.-L., Chih-Kang, W.: A relation-exchanging buffering mechanism for instruction and data streaming. Comput. Electr. Eng. Kaohsiung 39(4), 1129–1141 (2013)

STEM Education Meets HPC

Hsiu-Mei Chou[1]([✉]), Sugita Norika[2], Ching-Yeh Hsin[2], and Tso-Chung Sung[3]

[1] National Center for High-Performance Computing, Hsinchu, Taiwan
hmchou@nchc.narl.org.tw
[2] National Taiwan Ocean University, Keelung, Taiwan
[3] National Museum of Marine Science and Technology, Keelung, Taiwan

Abstract. STEM education is a teaching approach that combines Science, Technology, Engineering, and Mathematics. Rather than teach the four disciplines as separate and discrete subjects, STEM integrates them into a cohesive learning paradigm based on real-world applications. Based on the STEM approach, we developed a robotics course that engages students in middle school. We adopted the NodeMCU controller, electronic circuits, and free-designed materials to construct a cheap and resilient version of the remote control sailboat. Students design, build and test sailing the boat during the course. Students learn critical thinking, communication, and collaboration skills through the process. A CFD analysis of the model boat was done and demonstrated with augmented reality to help students understand the physics of sailing.

Keywords: HPC · STEM education · CFD

1 Introduction

Starting on August 1, 2014, Taiwan implemented the 12-Year Basic Education Plan. Curriculum Guidelines of the 12-Year Basic Education were developed based on the spirit of holistic education, adopting the concepts of taking the initiative, engaging in interaction, and seeking the common good to encourage students to become spontaneous and motivated learners. The curriculum also urges that schools be active in encouraging students to become motivated and passionate learners, leading students to appropriately develop the ability to interact with themselves, others, society, and nature. [1] There are many innovative designs in the guidelines that mimic the STEM education framework.

The STEM education framework is a teaching approach that integrates Science, Technology, Engineering, and Mathematics (STEM) programs in schools to strengthen students' competence in scientific inquiry and problem-solving skills; and to prepare students for future industrial demands [2]. Researchers have found that robotics courses can significantly increase positive attitudes toward the STEM framework [3]. Practicing STEM in the classroom can also improve test scores in science and mathematics.

To experiment with the STEM framework in marine education, we developed a robotics sailboat course that integrates science, technology, engineering, and mathematics, i.e., STEM, for students in grades 5–12. To better explain the physics of sailing, we computed the flow field with the CFD model. We demonstrated the flow field to the

S.-Y. Hsieh et al. (Eds.): ICS 2022, CCIS 1723, pp. 487–492, 2022.
https://doi.org/10.1007/978-981-19-9582-8_42

students with augmented reality. In the following sessions, we will describe the robotics course and the CFD computation in detail.

2   Method

2.1   The Robotics Course

We developed a robotics course that integrates science, technology, engineering, and mathematics, i.e., STEM, for students in grades 5–12. We adopted the NodeMCU controller, electronic circuits, and free-designed materials to construct a cheap and resilient version of the remote control sailboat. During the course, students are divided into groups; each group designed, assembled, and tested sail the boat in an inflatable pool. At the end of the course, each group presented the result in front of the class. Through the hands-on boat design and assembling process, students learnt the fundamental of naval architecture; and the navigation of the sailboat requires students' concentration and hand-eye coordination. The final presentation not only enhanced students' oral expression skills, but also promoted teamwork (Fig. 1).

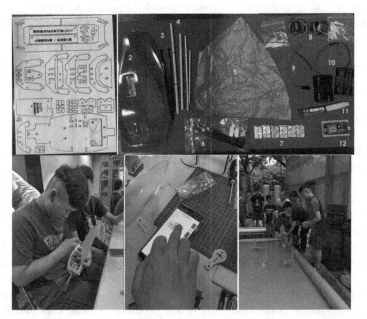

Fig. 1.   Up: the layout and the materials of the experimental sailboat; Down: Students built, coded, and tested sail in a inflatable pool

2.2 The Physics of Sailing

Two questions loom if you start to think about sailing: 1. How is it possible that a sailing ship moves against the direction of the wind, reaching a destination situated windward; 2. How can the speed of a boat be over wind speed, both downwind and upwind? From the point of view of a physicist, a sailing ship is a system made up of two inter-connected hydrodynamic foils, interacting with media of different densities that meet them at different speeds at different angles. Figure 2 depicts a boat sailing close-hauled on the wind (i.e., at an acute angle to the wind direction), illustrating this fact.

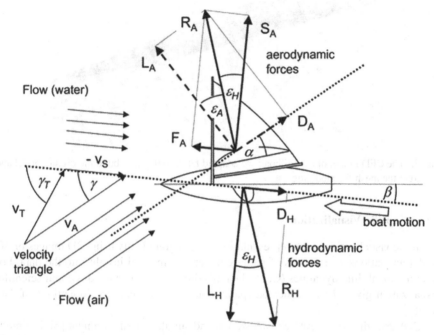

Fig. 2. A boat sailing steadily on the wind. Relative water flow evokes total force R_H, air flow evokes total force R_A. Adapted from [4]. Copyright Wiley-VCH Verlag GmbH & Co. KGaA.

In order to better explain the physics to students, we built a digital model of the sailboat and conducted a CFD analysis on the model. Figure 3 illustrated the mesh of the CFD model. The computation was done using Simcenter *STAR-CCM+* software package [5], and ran on the HPC facilities at NCHC.

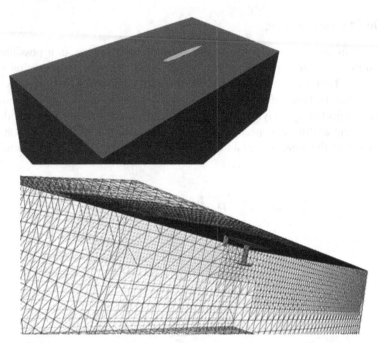

Fig. 3. The CFD model of the sailboat; we adapted DF95 sailboat to build the digital model and construct the mesh for modeling.

2.3   Scientific Visualization

Scientific visualization is the representation of data graphically using 2D images or 3D model animations, as a means of gaining understanding and insight into the data. For computational fluid dynamics (CFD) data, it's difficult to understand without scientific visualization given the complicated spatial data structure and large quantities of data points.

COVISE, the collaborative visualization and simulation environment [6], is a modular distributed visualization system. As its focus is on visualization of scientific data in virtual environments, it comprises the VR renderer OpenCOVER. The development of COVISE is headed by the High-performance Computing Center Stuttgart (HLRS).

In this study, we use COVISE to visualize the flow field of sailboat in different condition. To help students to better understand the spatial relations, we also demonstrated the fluid flow with augmented reality. The visualization of flow field is show in Fig. 4 and Fig. 5 shows the flow augmented to a physical sailboat model.

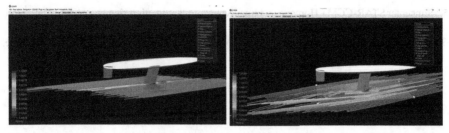

Fig. 4. The flow field around the keel in different attack angels; left: 0 degree; right: 10 degree. The data was visualized using COVISE.

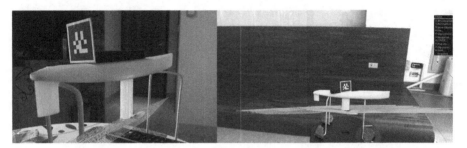

Fig. 5. Flow field around keel was demonstrated with augmented reality

3 Future Work

In this study, we experimented using scientific visualization and augmented reality technology to blend complex engineering application like CFD simulation into middle school STEM education. The visualized unseen physics did bring the WOW effect to the classroom, and triggered students to think deeper. Many students mentioned that the course provided them with a better understanding of the concepts that were previously taught in the other courses such as physics and coding. The integrated STEM course linked abstract science concepts to practical work.

The experiment was done in a small class with only 15 students, and we got to learn the response from students closely. The overall responses were positive, that encouraged us to carry out the course in a larger scale.

References

1. The Curriculum Guidelines of 12-year Basic Education. https://www.naer.edu.tw/eng/PageSy llabus?fid=148
2. Bybee, R.W.: Case for STEM Education: Challenges and Opportunities. National Science Teachers Association, Arlington, VA, USA (2013)
3. Yiching, C., Chi-Cheng, C.: The impact of an integrated robotics STEM course with a Sailboat topic on high school students' perceptions of integrative STEM, interest, and career orientation. EURASIA J. Math. Sci. Tech. Ed. **14**(12) (2018)
4. Püschl, W.: Die Physik des Segelns. Wiley-VCH Verlag, Weinheim (2012). (in German)

5. Simcenter STAR-CCM+ Homepage. https://www.plm.automation.siemens.com/global/en/pro
ducts/simcenter/STAR-CCM.html
6. COVISE Homepage. https://www.hlrs.de/solutions/types-of-computing/visualization/covise.
Accessed 1 Oct 2022

Research on KNN-Based GNSS Coordinate Classification for Epidemic Management

Chi-Yueh Hsu[1], Chun-Ming Kuo[2], Ruo-Wei Hung[3(✉)], and Jong-Shin Chen[2(✉)]

[1] Department of Leisure Services Management, Chaoyang University of Technology, Taichung, Taiwan

[2] Department of Information and Communication Engineering, Chaoyang University of Technology, Taichung, Taiwan
jschen26@cyut.edu.tw

[3] Department of Computer Science and Information Engineering, Chaoyang University of Technology, Taichung, Taiwan
rwhung@cyut.edu.tw

Abstract. As epidemics such as COVID-19 and monkeypox spread, tracing specific people with restricted activities (targets) within administrative areas (targeted areas) is an effective option to slow the spread. Global Navigation Satellite Systems (GNSS) that can provide autonomous geospatial positioning of targets can assist this issue. K-nearest neighbors (KNN) is one of the most widely used algorithms for various classifications or predictions. In this paper, we will use the technique of KNN to classify the areas of the targets and explore the relationship between the density of targets to a area and the accuracy of classifications.

Keywords: GNSS · Infectious disease · Point-in-polygon · Recognition · KNN

1 Introduction

Many infectious diseases are highly contagious such as covid, monkeypox, influenza, … and so on and have been or are seriously affecting human health, economic activities, education, sports and leisure. Restricting, tracing, and even isolating people's movements when an epidemic spreads is an effective option to slow the spread [1]. A satellite navigation is a system that uses satellites to provide autonomous geospatial positioning. GNSS allow a small electronic receiver to determine its position, including longitude, latitude, and altitude (elevation), with an accuracy of a few centimeters to meters, using time signals transmitted by satellite radio along the line of sight [2]. Since GNSS can provide precise location information of targets, it has been widely used in various remote sensing [2, 3] such as epidemic monitoring and geographic information systems.

A targeted area can be represented geometrically as a convex polygon. A target is a geometric point, which is a point with latitude and longitude coordinates. Whether a geometric point is in the targeted area is a Point-In-Polygon (PtInPy) problem. There have been many literatures and their issues are mostly focused on some special conditions between points and polygons that PtInPy can still be handled or can be calculated more

S.-Y. Hsieh et al. (Eds.): ICS 2022, CCIS 1723, pp. 493–500, 2022.
https://doi.org/10.1007/978-981-19-9582-8_43

effective [4]. In simple terms, each of these methods contains a PtInPy function and uses a geometry point and a polygon as its input. Through this PtInPy function, it can confirm the geometry point is a inner point of this polygon or is a outer point of this polygon. When the number of targets is very large and the number of targeted areas is also large, the traditional methods are inefficient to handle this issue. In epidemic management, there may be a large number of targets and a large number of target areas to be managed. Take COVID-19 as an example, the disease spread worldwide, leading to the COVID-19 pandemic. According to the World Health Organization weekly report, as of 22 May 2022, over 522 million confirmed cases and over six million deaths have been reported globally.

The KNN is a non-parametric supervised learning method of machine learning. It is widely used for classification and regression [5]. In both cases, the input consists of the k closest training examples in a data set. The output depends on whether KNN is used for classification or regression. When the eigenvalues of the target are very clear, the KNN technique can be used to obtain high accuracy. The coordinates of GNSS fits this feature. Furthermore, in this proposition, we assume that the number of classifications is large. Under the wide spread of the epidemic, this proposition is reasonable. When the number of classifications is large, it makes the traditional PtInPy method very inefficient. Because these methods have to calculate whether a geometry is in these categories one by one. Therefore, we propose this study. Hope it helps with the epidemic.

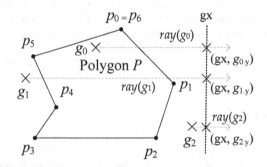

Fig. 1. Polygon with intersections among edges and rays.

2 Research Method

2.1 Point-in-Polygon Algorithm

A target with latitude and longitude coordinate is a geographic point. For a geographical point g, $g_{.x}$ and $g_{.y}$ respectively represent the longitude value and latitude value of point g, i.e. $g = (g_{.x}, g_{.y})$. A targeted area is a polygon. A polygon is composed of edges with geographical points. These edges enclose a measurable interior. Accordingly, a polygon P with n points is defined as $P = \{p_0, p_1, ..., p_{n-1}, p_n\}$, where $p_0 = p_n$, and the straight line segment from point p_i to p_{i+1} is the edge for $i = 0, 1, ..., n - 1$.

A ray of a point is a straight line that starts from this point and goes on to any fixed direction. In this article, $ray(g)$ is the horizontal extension line starting from point g to East direction. If the number of intersections between the edges of polygon P and $ray(g)$ is an odd value, it indicates that point g is the inner point of polygon P. Otherwise, it indicates that point g is an outer point of polygon P. In application, ray(g) can be simplified into a segment from point g to point g', where the latitude coordinate of point g' is the same as point g, and the longitude coordinate of g' can specify a fixed and large enough value g_x.

$$\alpha(g_a, g_b, g_c, g_d) = (g_{a.x} - g_{b.x}) \times (g_{c.y} - g_{d.y}) - (g_{a.y} - g_{b.y})$$
$$\times (g_{c.x} - g_{d.x}); \tag{1}$$

$$\kappa_1(g_a, g_b, g_c, g_d) = ((g_{a.x} - g_{c.x}) \times (g_{c.y} - g_{d.y}) - (g_{a.y} - g_{c.y})$$
$$\times (g_{c.x} - g_{d.x}))/\alpha(g_a, g_b, g_c, g_d); \tag{2}$$

$$\kappa_2(g_a, g_b, g_c, g_d) = ((g_{a.x} - g_{b.x}) \times (g_{a.y} - g_{c.y}) - (g_{a.y} - g_{b.y})$$
$$\times (g_{a.x} - g_{b.x}))/\alpha(g_a, g_b, g_c, g_d) \tag{3}$$

Figure 1 provides an example of a polygon with intersections among edges and rays. This polygon P is composed of points p_0, p_1, ..., and p_6, where $p_0 = p_6$. There are three geographic points g_0, g_1, and g_2 with the corresponding rays $ray(g_0)$, $ray(g_1)$, and $ray(g_2)$. The number of intersections between $ray(g_0)$ and edges of P is 1 (odd number) that g_0 is the inner point of P. The numbers of intersections of $ray(g_1)$ and edges of P and $ray(g_1)$ and edges of P respectively are 2 and 0 that both numbers are even. It means that point g_1 and point g_2 both are the outer points of P. In fact, taking point g_1 as an example, it only needs to calculate the number of intersections between the segment from point g_1 to point (px, $g_{1.x}$) and the edges of the polygon.

Algorithm 1 SegSegInt(point g_a, point g_b, point g_c, point g_d)

1. **if** $\alpha(g_a, g_b, g_c, g_d) = 0$ **then return** 0;
2. **else**
3. $k_1 := \kappa_1(g_a, g_b, g_c, g_d)$;
4. $k_2 := \kappa_2(g_a, g_b, g_c, g_d)$;
5.   **if** $(k_1 \geq 0$ and $k_1 \leq 1)$ and $(k_2 \geq 0$ and $k_2 \leq 1)$ **then return** 1;
6.   **else return** 0;
7.   **end if**
8. **end if**

In [6], a computer-friendly method was proposed to evaluate the intersection between two segments. Accordingly, Algorithm 1 is proposed. Algorithm 1 provides the SegSegInt algorithm. It is a Segment-Segment Intersection algorithm, where its input is 4 points g_a, g_b, g_c, and g_d. The four points compose the segment from g_a to g_b and the segment from g_c to g_d. First, it evaluate α by applying (1). If the value of α is 0, the two lines are parallel. Otherwise, there is an intersection between the two lines.

Next, it evaluates κ_1 and κ_2 by applying (2) and (3), respectively. If the value of κ_1 is between 0 and 1, the intersection is between g_a and g_b. If the value of κ_2 is between 0 and 1, the intersection is between g_c and g_d. In other words, if segment (g_a, g_b) and segment (g_c, g_d) are intersected, the value of κ_1 is between 0 and 1 and the value of κ_2 is also between 0 and 1. Applying this algorithm will result 1 or 0 to represent that the two segments are intersected or are not intersected.

Algorithm 2 PtInPy(point g, polygon P)

1. $count := 0$;
2.   **for** $i := 0$ **to** $|P|$ **do**
3. $g_a := p_i$;
4. $g_b := p_{i+1}$;
5. $g_c := g$;
6. $g_{d.x} := gx$; $g_{d.y} := g.y$;
7.   **if** (SegSegInt $(g_a, g_b, g_c, g_d) = 1$) **then**
8. $count := count + 1$;
9.   **end if**
10. **end for**
11.   **if** ($count \% 2 = 1$) **then return** 1;
12.   **else return** 0;
13.   **end if**

Algorithm 2 provides the PtInPy algorithm. It is a Point In Polygon algorithm, where its inputs are a point g and a polygon $P = \{p_0, p_1, ..., p_n\}$. This algorithm is used to evaluate whether point g is an inner point of polygon P or point g is an outer point of polygon P. Applying it will result 1 or 0 to represent g is an inner point of P or g is an outer point of P. In this algorithm, variable *count* is used to count the number of intersection(s) among the ray of g and the n edges of P. It combines each edge (p_i, p_{i+1}) of P, where $i = 0, 1, ...,$ and $n - 1$ and point g into the segment (g_a, g_b) and the segment (g_c, g_d). If the two segments intersect, the value of *count* is incremented by 1. Finally, if the value of *count* is even (i.e., *count* $\% 2 = 1$), it returns 0. Otherwise, it returns 1.

Algorithm   3. KNN_Calc(point g, training set G_C, KNN k, number of classifications n_C)

1.   **for** $i := 0$ to $n_C - 1$ **do** $V[c] := 0$; **end for**
2.   **for** $i := 1$ **to** $|G_C|$ **do**
3. $x := G_C[i]["x"]$; $y := G_C[i]["y"]$;
4. $G[i]["d"] := \mathbf{pow}((x - g_{.x})^2 + (y - g_{.y})^2, 0.5)$;
5.   **end for**
6.   **for** $i := 0$ to $|G_C| - 1$ **do**
7.   **for** $j := i + 1$ to $|G_C| - 1$ **do**
8.   **if** $G_C[j]["d"] > G_C[j + 1]["d"]$ **then**
9. $T := G_C[j]$; $G_C[j] := G_C[j + 1]$; $G_C[j + 1] := T$;
10.   **end if**
11.   **end for**
12.   **end for**
13.   **for** $i := 0$ to $k - 1$ **do**
14. $c := G[i]["c"]$; $V[c]$++;
15.   **end for**
16. $v := 0$;
17.   **for** $i := 1$ to $n_C - 1$ **do**
18.   **if** $V[i] > V[v]$ **then** $v := i$;
19.   **end for**
20.   **return** v;

2.2 KNN Algorithm

For convenience, if S is a set, $|S|$ represents the number of elements in set S. Assuming that P_A is all of classification set, each classification $P_A[i]$ is a polygon and it also represents the i-th polygon, where $i = 0, 1, 2,...$, and $|P_A|$. Determine whether a point g belongs to the i-th classification can be done via applying PtInPy(g, $P_A[i]$). If its result is 1, then point g belongs to the i-th classification. Moreover, assuming that G_C is a training set that each point of G_C is classified and $G_C[i]$ is the i-th element of set G_C, where $i = 0, 1, 2, ...$, and $|G_C|$. Each element $G_C[i]$ of contains that the coordinate $G_C[i]["y"]$ and $G_C[i]["x"]$ of a point, the classification $G_C[i]["c"]$ of this point, and $G_C[i]["d"]$ is used to store the Euclidean distance of this point to other testing point. Algorithm 3 provides a KNN_Calc algorithm. It is a KNN Calculation algorithm, where its inputs are a point g, a training set G_C, the KNN k, and the number of classifications n_C. Applying it will result the predicted classification v. In this algorithm, it first sets the variable of array V as 0. It next calculates the Euclidean distance of point g and each point of set G_C. Continuing, it sorts set G_C according to Euclidean distance from small to large. Then, it counts the numbers of classifications for the first k points of set G_C. Finally, it evaluates the classification v with largest number of variable V.

2.3 Proposed Method

Here KNN is used to classify the geometric points into the geometric areas. The geometric areas have their spatial range, and it is difficult to have a correspondence based on the number of training samples. The next planning steps is based on the average number of samples per spatial unit to evaluate the performance of KNN. Let P_A be the set of all polygons and k be the value of KNN. The proposed method has 4 steps. Applying the proposed method can be use to evaluate the accuracy with k and the density of testing points.

1) It plans a rectangle R, which can cover the required range, and collects the targeted points G within the range R. It also evaluate the area a_R of rectangle R.
2) It randomly selects $a_R \times d$ points from set G. It also uses PtInPy to calculate the classifications of the selected points. Let G_C be the set of points that have been classified.
3) It randomly selects the set G_T of test points from G, where $G_C \cap G_T = \emptyset$.
4) It takes set G_C as the training samples, set G_T as the test samples and specifying the k value of KNN. The classification v of the test point g can be obtained by using KNN_Calc. Then, the point g and the polygon $P_A[v]$ can be verified by PtInPy(g, $P_A[v]$), that its result is 1 (0) which means the classification right (wrong).

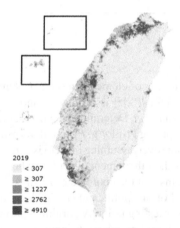

Fig. 2. The distribution of residents per square kilometer by village

Fig. 3. The distribution of the targeted points for simulation

3 Simulation Result

The simulated geographic area is mainly the island of Taiwan located between 120° to 122° east longitude and 22° to 25° north latitude. It covers an area of 35808 km² and has a population of 23.7 million. Figure 2 provides the distribution of residents per kilometer by village [7]. Targeted points for simulation are based on the geographical points of a famous SNS platform that were obtained in January 2017, with a total of 1112188 [8]. Figure 3 provides the distribution of targeted points, which contains 10000 points randomly selected from all targeted points. Through the comparison of Fig. 2 and Fig. 3, it is found that the distribution of the targeted points in this simulation is consistent with the actual population distribution.

There are $a_R \times d$ points, i.e., set where $d = 0.005, 0.01, 0.02, ...,$ and 0.64. This range of this rectangle includes 3 cities and also includes 30 districts. We use 3 cities and 30 districts as classifications, i.e., set P_A, respectively. The k of KNN includes 1, 3, 5, 7, 9, and 11. For each combination of k and density d, 100 test points, i.e., set G_T, are randomly selected randomly as test set G_C each time, and perform a total of 10 times.

Table 1. Accuracy of 3 classifications.

Density	$k = 1$	$k = 3$	$k = 5$	$k = 7$	$k = 9$
0.01	75.6%	60.1%	48.7%	43.7%	44.7%
0.02	84.8%	80.6%	78.6%	69.2%	55.8%
0.04	86.9%	84.8%	80.0%	73.9%	76.1%
0.08	95.0%	88.1%	87.3%	84.8%	83.3%
0.16	95.7%	96.1%	93.0%	91.8%	90.8%
0.32	97.5%	95.9%	97.1%	95.5%	96.2%
0.64	99.0%	98.8%	98.5%	98.3%	96.9%
1.28	99.5%	98.6%	98.3%	99.2%	98.6%

Table 1 provides the accuracy of 3 classifications, i.e., $|P_A| = 3$. It shows over 90% accuracy when $k = 1$ or 3, even if the density is only 0.08. When the value of k increases, the accuracy will decrease because samples with more differences in eigenvalues will also be included in the calculation.

4   Conclusion

As epidemics such as COVID-19 and monkeypox spread, tracing specific people with restricted activities within administrative areas is an effective option to slow the spread. GNSS that can provide autonomous geospatial positioning of targets can assist this issue. When there are many target areas and many targets, it is difficult and time-consuming to calculate the area of each target with 100% accuracy. The results meet the requirements in terms of accuracy. In the future, we will continue to improve the accuracy and performance of KNN.

References

1. Edmond, M.: Isolation. Infect. Control Hosp. Epidemiol. **18**(1), 58–64 (1997)

2. Zhbankov, G.A., Danilkin, N.P., Maltseva, O.A.: Influence of the ionosphere on the accuracy of the satellite navigation system. Acta Astronaut. **190**, 194–201 (2022)
3. Cahyadi, M.N., et al.: Telemedicine technology application for covid-19 patient tracing using smartphone GNSS. Int. J. Geoinformatics **18**, 103–117 (2022)
4. Taylor, G.: Point in polygon test. Surv. Rev. **32**(254), 479–484 (1994)
5. Oh, J., Kim, J.: Adaptive K-nearest neighbour algorithm for WiFi fingerprint positioning. ICT Express **4**(2), 91–94 (2018)
6. Antonio, F.: Faster line segment intersection. In: Graphics Gems III (IBM Version), pp. 199–202. Morgan Kaufmann, Burlington, MA, USA (1992)
7. Demographics of Taiwa [online]. https://en.wikipedia.org/wiki/Demographics_of_Taiwan
8. Chen, J.-S., Lin, C.-B., Yang, C.-Y., Huang, Y.-F.: An efficient Facebook place information extraction strategy. In: You, I., Chen, H.-C., Sharma, V., Kotenko, I. (eds.) MobiSec 2017. CCIS, vol. 971, pp. 131–139. Springer, Singapore (2019). https://doi.org/10.1007/978-981-13-3732-1_10

An Improved Light Weight Countermeasure Scheme to Efficiently Mitigate TCP Attacks in SDN

Yung-Fa Huang[1](✉), Shu-Wai Chang[1], Chuan-Bi Lin[1](✉), Chun-Jung Chen[2],
Shi-Jun Li[1], and Ching-Mu Chen[3]

[1] Chaoyang University of Technology, Taichung 413310, Taiwan
{yfahuang,cblin}@cyut.edu.tw, s10730612@gm.cyut.edu.tw
[2] Chinese Culture University, Taipei 11114, Taiwan
[3] I-Ning High School, Taichung 407, Taiwan

Abstract. The design of Software Defined Networking (SDN) will enable the flexible control of network traffic and handle the large amount of data traffic on the current network. When under a network attack, the control plane will have a heavy load that increases the network connection time and causes the overall SDN network paralyzed. In this study, we investigated the SDN-based lightweight countermeasure for TCP Synchronize (SYN) flooding attacks (SLICOTS) method and further proposed a light weight countermeasure Scheme with reset method to diminish the problems of SDN suffering from TCP SYN flooding. Simulation results show that the proposed SLICOTS based reset (S-RST) algorithms can effectively reduce the impact of malicious traffic after SYN flooding attacked.

Keywords: Software Defined Networking (SDN) · Network security · SLICOTS · Synchronize flooding

1 Introduction

Due to the vigorous development of communication technology brought by smart mobile devices, All-IP network architecture has become the mainstream recently [1]. A large number of mobile devices connected to the Internet come with higher network traffic and attacks. There are many different types of Internet attacks [2] that are not only from limited to desktop devices, but also come from a variety of devices. The Cisco annual security report pointed out that the growth rate of network attacks is getting higher [3]. Software Defined Networking (SDN) can be used for network traffic on the internal network of large enterprises. Google also uses the characteristics of SDN to develop network strategy enhancing the company's internal network usage efficiency and overall service availability [4]. Thus, it shows the importance of SDN in network traffic and security issues [5].

The traffic strategy in the network is concentrated into the SDN control layer. SDN is a comprehensive view of the managed network equipment so that it can flexibly schedule, monitor and manage the overall network situation. It can monitor the characteristics of network traffic and use to block changeable network attacks. Moreover, SDN has been used in many ways to block network attacks [6–9] and to avoid excessive burden on the controller in the control plane to detect attacks. TCP SYN flooding attack makes control plane traffic. That is TCP SYN packets generated by attackers will affect data plane. In short, the SDN-based lightweight countermeasure for TCP SYN flooding attacks (SLICOTS) can efficiently countermeasure to slow down the TCP SYN flooding attack in SDN [6] and is used in the controller for TCP connection requests and blocks hosts been attacked. This paper is based on the SDN architecture to block SYN flooding attacks. It uses its existing methods and collects additional relevant information to send RST packets to reduce the impact of connection delays caused by attacks. The experimental results show that it can effectively reduce the server request delay after the attack and alleviate the controller from the SYN flooding attack.

The amplification attack is that an attacker or a zombie computer sends a large number of requests to a broadcast location in the network protocol [10, 11], and the location will send a network broadcast to all devices on the local area network. Moreover, Smurf attack is especially at switches and servers. ICMP data packets use forged source IP addresses sent to other devices or broadcast so that devices in the same environment use ICMP to respond to the attacker. The attack uses UDP packets instead of ICMP packets [12]. The IP address of the attacker is used as the spoofing source IP address in malicious data packets that allow all parties to respond to UDP requests and were not sent by the attacker. The SNMP amplification attack is used to monitor devices in the network and usually use forged source IP locations to send requests caused the attacker network equipment to respond to a large number of requests, which will eventually lead to a reduction in equipment performance.

The flooding attack sends a large amount of network traffic to the target system through Botnet [11]. The network data transmission and utilization rate of the target system will expand with the increase of burst IP traffic, resulting in unavailability of services. UDP, ICMP, HTTP and SIP packets can all be flooded such as in UDP flooding, ICMP flooding, HTTP flooding and SIP flooding attacks. ICMP flooding attack sends a large number of ICMP requests to the attackers. When sending packets more than 65535 times, the attackers' host will stop working because it exceeds the upper limit. Moreover, a large number of HTTP requests floods the web server. Voice over IP (VoIP) uses SIP call commands during communication. A large number of SIP requests can effectively overflow the bandwidth of the call that causes the call system not able to process real requests.

Internet's communication protocol TCP/IP sends SYN request so that the target computer bears the computational burden [12]. The server sends a SYN-ACK packet to respond to the demand and waits for the ACK packet from the client to respond. If the attacker deliberately responds to the ACK packet, the server will wait for the client to respond to the ACK packet until timeout. If the server's CPU computing resources and memory will be exhausted, or the number of connections that the server can support is full, the incoming normal request will eventually be rejected.

2 Framework of Network Management

Due to the development of the communications industry, network traffic has grown substantially, and network management has become more complex. The traditional network architecture can no longer handle a large amount of network traffic and SDN has changed the tradition. The framework of network management methods is applied to the management of data centers [10, 11].

Mininet is a network simulator based on the Linux core to simulate virtual hosts, switches, SDN controllers and other devices to create a custom virtual network topology. The switch supports the OpenFlow protocol and Mininet is often used as a piece of software in a simulated SDN environment. When the number of attackers exceeds a certain number, attacks will affect the service use of legitimate connections. The TCP queue in the server fills up the attacker's meaningless requests due to reservations. When SDN suffers a SYN flooding attack, it causes an additional burden on the controller in the SDN architecture. Figure 1 shows the flow chart of the impact when SDN suffers a SYN flooding attack as the following lists:

(1) The attacker sends a SYN request packet to the server via OpenFlowSwitch and the OpenFlowSwitch receives it that the flow table does not match.
(2) A packet is sent the information to the SDN controller.
(3) The SDN controller sends the command back to the OpenFlowSwitch, and the packet is processing to the Server.
(4) The Server receives the SYN request from Attacker.
(5) The Server sends the SYN-ACK back to the OpenFlowSwitch.
(6) The OpenFlowSwitch receives the unmatched packet and sends the packet information to the SDN controller.
(7) The SDN controller sends the command back to the OpenFlowSwitch.
(8) The packet is processed back to the attacker.

SYN flooding usually uses forged IP locations to attack. In the SDN environment, the SDN controller needs to install action rules of the OpenFlow switch to ensure the normal operation of the network. When the SDN architecture suffers from a SYN attack, the OpenFlow switch commands are issued to process network traffic. When the SDN environment suffers from SYN flooding attack, there will be a heavy burden on the controller. SDN-Guard is a technology to protect SDN from DDoS attacks [7]. A long time-out method is set through dynamic suspicious network traffic rules to prevent the switch in the SDN from constantly making requests of the controller, and avoids the burden of the controller; However, the malicious network traffic is still forwarded on the network. LineSwitch uses a SYN proxy device to determine malicious network traffic in an SDN environment, and uses probability to calculate and blacklist [8]. This method can reduce the memory and computing resources required.

OPERETTA acts as a SYN proxy through the controller in the SDN [9]. If it is a legitimate connection, it will install the rules to the switch, and send an RST packet to the requesting client at the same time. Hence, the client reconnects the request and records each time with the MAC location. Each linker will record the number of requests. If the

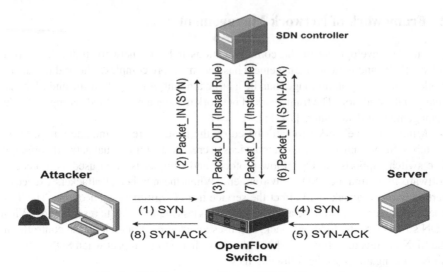

Fig. 1. SDN flow chart suffering TCP flooding attack.

requesting linker exceeds the specified K threshold, the blocking rule of the requester is installed to avoid the consumption of computing resources of the controller and server.

However, the SLICOTS is a technology to prevent the SDN control layer. When the controller and the server of the data layer are attacked [6], it observes all TCP traffic through the controller, installs temporary forwarding rules, and allows SYN requests and ACKs sent normally. When the MAC repeatedly sends the SYN request and the set threshold K is reached, the controller will install the blocking rules according to the device MAC location to prevent the SDN controller from being attacked and avoid the problem of connection delay caused by the SYN proxy. Before the SLICOTS reaches the threshold, some malicious network traffic will pass through and cause problems.

3   Improved SLICOTS

Figure 2 is the flow chart of SLICOTS for TCP packet processing [6]. The C value is defined as a counter. The K value is defined as a threshold. The SLICOTS sends all TCP packet information to the SDN controller for monitoring and judgment in the SDN architecture. Figure 2 shows the processing flow of the SLICOTS program for TCP packets as the following lists:

(1) Determines the TCP packets.
(2) If it is not a SYN request, checks the SYN-ACK. If it is a SYN-ACK request, update the status of MAC as server response and set the Switch to temporary rules. If not, checks the ACK. If it is an ACK, sets MAC = C-1 and the Switch as temporary rules. If not an ACK, sets data sent packets as temporary rules.
(3) If it is a SYN request, checks the MAC address whether or not the detected value C of the MAC exceeds the K threshold. If the C value is greater than the K value, sets the Switch as install temporary rules. If not, updates the MAC as Observe status.

In order to ensure that the server correctly responds to the ACK packet to the MAC position. The C value is increased after the server responds. The block rule is installed when the K threshold is reached, and the RST packet is sent to the attacked server to reduce the burden of the TCP server under the data layer. It can avoid the controller and control layer in the SDN architecture. The huge burden caused by the attack affects the overall network environment and reduces the burden on the TCP server under the data layer.

Figure 3 shows when the SLICOTS method is used, an attacker sends malicious SYN request packets to avoid misjudgment caused by instability in the network. As K is set to a threshold, it allows all clients to connect to the server and observe before reaching the threshold K. The behavior of this device is to determine whether or not it is a malicious attack. This method still has some malicious packets passing through and reaching the server of the data plane in data layer. It affects the performance of the server. There will be a TCP queue form in the server and the number of connections will be affected. It consumes the computing resources and the server will affect the connection efficiency. Servers suffering from SYN flooding will have a large number of meaningless queues. When the server has a large number of waiting to respond the ACKs in the TCP queue table due to SYN flooding attack, it will consume more resources.

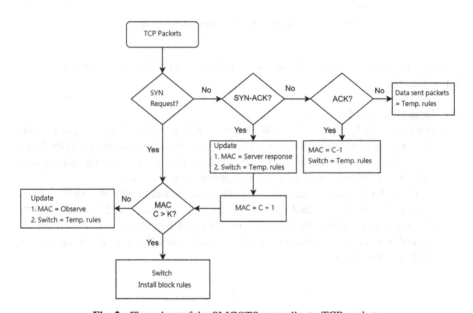

Fig. 2. Flow chart of the SLICOTS controller to TCP packets.

Figure 4 is the flow chart of the S-RST method in this paper. When the attacker is detected, the RST packet is sent to the TCP in the data layer through the previously

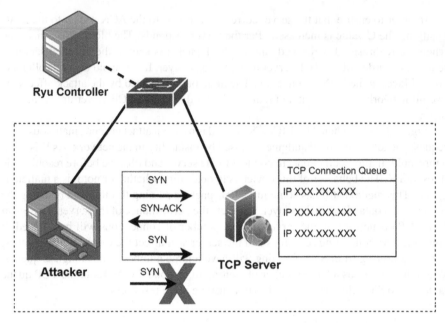

Fig. 3. The SLICOTS before the blocking attacks.

collected information. Figure 4 illustrates the flow chart of the S_RST program as the following lists:

(1) Determines the TCP packets.
(2) If it is not a SYN request, checks the SYN-ACK. If it is a SYN-ACK request, update the status of MAC as server response and set the Switch to temporary rules. If not, checks the ACK. If it is an ACK, sets MAC = C-1 and the Switch as temporary rules. If not an ACK, sets data sent packets as temporary rules.
(3) If it is a SYN request, records SEQ information and checks the MAC address whether or not the detected value C of the MAC exceeds the K threshold. If the C value is greater than the k value, installs blocking rules to the Switch and the controller sends RST packets to server and terminates IO-conn. If not, updates the MAC as Observe status.

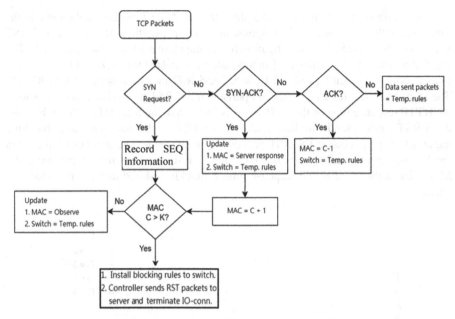

Fig. 4. Controller to TCP packets in the S-RST.

4 Simulation Results

The results show the three attack environments. First, K value is fixed with different attack intensity. Second, K value is different and the attack is realistic. Third, K value is fixed and different attack is simulated. During the experiment, K value is fixed with different attack strengths and the experimental environment is that the threshold K value is set to a fixed value, and the attack strength of each client is adjusted. Moreover, K value is a different attack amount and an attack simulation experiment. The K threshold is set to 10 to 40, which is the number of attackers.

K value is fixed with different attack intensities to compare with different attack volumes. Suppose 19 attackers are set and the attack mode is 1 to 5 attack packets per second. During the experiment, K is fixed to 10. One of the clients regularly observes the HTTP response time. This paper tests the attacker from 1 to 5 malicious packets per second and define different strengths as the attacker's transmission of 1 attack packet per second as $T_A = 1$ and so on. Under different attack strengths, the attacker starts the attack after 20 s of the experiment time, and will collect information such as the number of TCP server queues, and the HTTP response time.

Figure 5 shows the HTTP response time of the S-RST method and the maximum HTTP response time is under different T_A about 30 s as $T_A = 1$, 25 s as $T_A = 2$, 23 s as $T_A = 3$, $T_A = 4$ is also about 23 s; $T_A = 5$ is about 22 s. Since the attacker is blocked at the above time, the number of packets after these time points and the number of packets received by the TCP server will no longer increase. However, HTTP response time also begins to decline after the above time.

The results of T_A equaling 4 and 5 show that the S-RST method is the same at the time point of the maximum HTTP response time. The paper shows the method of S-RST is based on SLICOTS. Attack mitigation lies in the recovery time after the attack. The Fig. 6 shows that the method S-RST in this paper restored to the attacked HTTP response time in about 35 s when $T_A = 4$ and $T_A = 5$. The S-RST method is better than SLICOTS. The recovery is fast for 25 s. After comparison, the S-RST method in this paper shows the HTTP response time of the TCP server is faster than the SLICOTS. This is because the S-RST method sends the RST packet to the TCP on the data plane after blocking the attack. Server receives the RST packet to quickly reduce the number of queues in the TCP server and improves the burden of the TCP server. Therefore, compared to the SLICOTS method, the HTTP response time is quickly restored to the state before the attack.

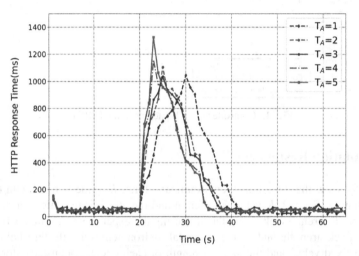

Fig. 5. HTTP response time as $K = 10$ in the S-RST method.

Figure 7 shows the number of TCP queues in the S-RST method and uses S-RST to display the number of TCP queues. The maximum time are: $T_A = 1$ in 30 s; $T_A = 2$ in 25 s; $T_A = 3$ about 23 s; $T_A = 4$ in 23 s; $T_A = 5$ in 22 s. It is the attack occurs after 20 s. According to different attack speeds, the time is set to $K = 10$ officially judged as an attacker and blocked. Sending 1 attack packet S-RST every second will block the attack and send the RST packet to speed up the TCP server's release of queues. Therefore, the number of TCP queues in the TCP server drops rapidly after the attack occurs. When $T_A = 1$ in 42 s, the number of TCP queues has returned to normal.

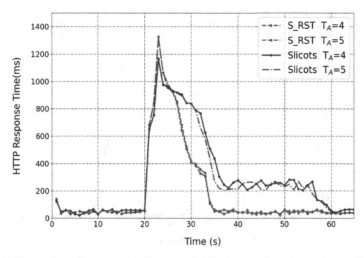

Fig. 6. Comparisons between SLICOTS and S-RST for HTTP response time as $K = 10$.

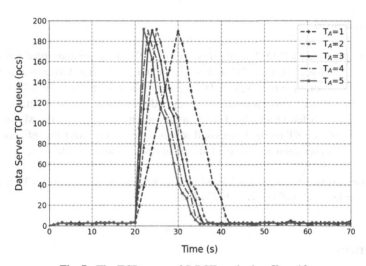

Fig. 7. The TCP queue of S-RST method as $K = 10$.

In Fig. 8, when the S-RST method in this paper recovered on the number of TCP server queues is about $T_A = 4$ in 35 s and $T_A = 5$ also in 35 s to recover. Compared with the SLICOTS method, the TCP server queue number of $T_A = 4$ is about 61 s and $T_A = 5$ is about 62 s to recover. The S-RST method in this paper is the number of queues in the TCP server. The speed of decline is relatively fast. However, the additional RST packets sent by the S-RST method in this paper will release the resources of the accelerated TCP server.

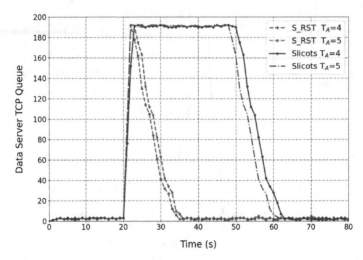

Fig. 8. The TCP queue comparisons between SLICOTS and S-RST as $K = 10$.

5 Conclusion

This paper uses the SLICOTS method based on SDN to record additional information and extends the S-RST method. While blocking attack traffic, it generates and sends RST packets, accelerating the recovery of TCP server in the data plane to be affected by the SYN flooding attack. This paper detects data under different attack volumes, different attack strengths, different thresholds and simulated attacks by using the Mininet. After comparison, the S-RST method proposed in this paper can recover the influence of the attacked TCP server soon and have a balance in environmental protection.

Acknowledgments. This work was funded in part by Ministry of Science and Technology of Taiwan under Grant MOST 111-2221-E-324-018-.

References

1. Olsson, U.U.: Toward the all-IP vision. Ericsson Rev. **82**(1), 44–53 (2005)
2. Zargar, S.T., Joshi, J., Tipper, D.: A survey of defense mechanisms against distributed denial of service (DDoS) flooding attacks. IEEE Commun. Surv. Tutorials **15**(4), 2046–2069 (2013)
3. Cao, L., Jiang, X., Zhao, Y., Wang, S., You, D., Xu, X.: A survey of network attacks on cyber-physical systems. IEEE Access **13**(2), 44219–44227 (2020)
4. Liu, Y., Zhao, B., Zhao, P., Fan, P., Liu, H.: A survey: typical security issues of software-defined networking. China Commun. **16**(7), 13–31 (2019)
5. Nunes, B.A., Mendonca, A.M., Nguyen, X., Obraczka, K., Turletti, T.: A survey of software-defined networking: past, present, and future of programmable networks. IEEE Commun. Surv. Tutorials **16**(3), 1617–1634 (2014)
6. Mohammadi, R., Javidan, R., Conti, M.: SLICOTS: an SDN-based lightweight counter-measure for TCP SYN flooding attacks. IEEE Trans. Netw. Serv. Manage. **14**(2), 487–497 (2017)

7. Dridi, L., Zhani, M.F.: SDN-guard: DoS attacks mitigation in SDN networks. In: 2016 5th IEEE International Conference on Cloud Networking (Cloudnet), pp. 212–217 (2016)
8. Ambrosin, M., Conti, M., De Gaspari, F., Poovendran, R.: LineSwitch: tackling control plane saturation attacks in software-defined networking. IEEE/ACM Trans. Networking **25**(2), 1206–1219 (2017)
9. Fichera, S., Galluccio, L., Grancagnolo, S.C., Morabito, G., Palazzo, S.: OPERETTA: an open flow-based remedy to mitigate TCP SYN flood attacks against web servers. Comput. Netw. **92**(1), 89–100 (2015)
10. Dargahi, T., Caponi, A., Ambrosin, M., Bianchi, G., Conti, M.: A survey on the security of stateful SDN data planes. IEEE Commun. Surv. Tutorials **19**(3), 1701–1725 (2017)
11. Mirkovic, J., Reiher, P.: A taxonomy of DDoS attack and DDoS defense mechanisms. ACM SIGCOMM Comput. Commun. Rev. **34**(2), 39–53 (2004)
12. Douligeris, C., Mitrokotsa, A.: DDoS attacks and defense mechanisms: classification and state-of-the-art. Comput. Netw. **44**(5), 643–666 (2004)

The Effectiveness of Block-Based Programming Learning on the Problem-Solving Skills of the Freshmen

Ah-Fur Lai and Cheng-Ying Yang(✉)

Department of Computer Science, University of Taipei, Taipei, Taiwan
cyang@utaipei.edu.tw

Abstract. Learning computer programming is difficult and complex for most of novices. The block-based visualized programming environments can reduce the learning dilemma in programming syntax and invoke the learners' motivation. This study integrated App Inventor 2 into one course for the freshmen of a public university in Taipei city. The purpose of this study was to facilitate the freshmen to construct concrete advanced organization of programming for learning text-based computer languages in the future, to investigate their perception toward visualized programming environment and the impact on their problem-solving skills when programming. The research results revealed that the freshmen showed positive perception toward App Inventor 2 including helping to be familiar with basic programming concepts, learning transfer from block-based programming to text-based programming, usefulness of project development and programming flows. After guiding the freshmen to learn some algorithms and providing digital simulation-based learning materials in the problem-solving stage, improving ration of their programming skills were very high.

Keywords: Block-based programming · Learning perception · Programming novices · Programming skills

1 Introduction

After the computational thinking was proposed by Dr. Wing in 2006 [14], it become an important education policy all over the worlds. The computational thinker was listed in one of seven educational targets shown in ISTE for students (2016) [1]. Learning programming have great and positive impact on the learners' computation thinking. For example, programming was put into compulsory education in England. That is, the children of England have to learn computer language from 5 years old. In a word, programming is the new literacy.

The current computer languages are multiple and divergent, such as procedure-oriented language and object-oriented language. The tasks in programming processes consist of problem decomposition, planning, coding, debugging and optimization [11]. Based on some literatures [3, 4, 6–10, 12], programming is difficult and complex, especially for programming novices. The learning dilemmas in programming are still unimproved or more serious in the past twenty years [13]. The same learning phenomenon

S.-Y. Hsieh et al. (Eds.): ICS 2022, CCIS 1723, pp. 512–520, 2022.
https://doi.org/10.1007/978-981-19-9582-8_45

appeared in the learners of different age [5]. In order to reduce the learning difficulties, MIT developed Scratch which is a block-based visualized learning environment. Some research showed the positive effectiveness in helping the children to learn coding [2]. In addition, it can enhance the learners' computational thinking. Some researches revealed that Scratch is suitable for the learners to develop coding skills and computational thinking [2]. APP Inventor is also a block-based programming system for offering the learners to design a mobile-based applications. The aforementioned programming systems have the learning advantages including cloud-based, syntax-free, and visualized features, suitable for programming novices. In other words, the block-based programming environments can reduce learning frustration, and promote the learning motivation. Nevertheless, how to promote competency of problem solving, sematic and algorithm in programming relies on suitable instruction design and learning stratedgies.

Based on the previous background, this study integrated App Inventor 2 (AI2 for abbrev.) into a course in a university. Through instructional design and adopting simulation-based learning stratedgy, the purpose of this study was to help the freshmen to construct advanced organization of programming, and to explore the effect of simulation-based system on promoting the students' programming skills and to investigate their perception toward AI2.

2 Methodology

This study adopted one-group experimental design. The subjects were 55 freshmen in a public university in Taipei city, attending a selective course. In this course, App Inventor 2 was used for learning visualized programming. The learning experiment lasted for 18 h in six weeks. The learning content is comprised up of basic programming concepts and algorithms, including variable, array, three procedure-oriented structures, functions, event, interactive form, multimedia and multiscreen control. Learning by doing is an important strategy in the learning activities of this course. The learners were asked to design a series of APP for learning different programming concepts from sequence, selection to iteration application systematically. When the learners encountered the difficulties about problem-solving, this study offered a simulation-based learning system to show some algorithms. Figure 1 is a snapshot of a simulation-based learning module for controlling the process of swapping the max values from three variables to a specific variable. The simulation-based learning system can allow the learners to change values of three variables and to watch the processes by selecting different modes, such as animation or step mode. Figure 2 is a snapshot of a simulation-based learning module for generating a series of randomized and non-repeated numbers and can be operated by the learners in the same manners as Fig. 1 [2]. At the final stage, the leaners were asked to plan and design an APP by ADDIE model. After their projects, they had to present their APPS orally, and attended the peer assessment activities at the same time.

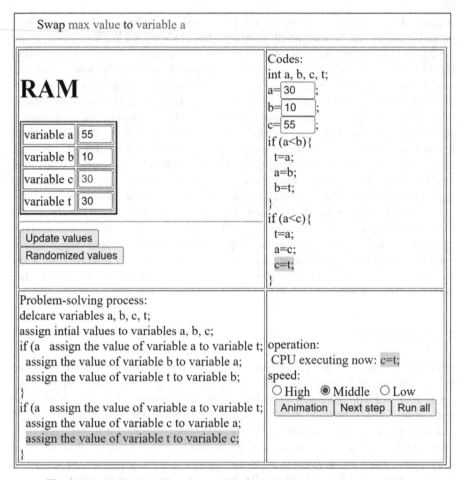

Fig. 1. Simulation-based learning module for swapping max value to variable a.

Table 1. The construct validity and reliability of perception inventory.

Facets	Eigenvalue	Variance explained	Alpha
Usefulness of learning basic programming concepts	7.269	40.383%	.876
Learning transfer of programming concepts	2.115	11.752%	.823
Learning flow	1.807	10.038%	.824
Usefulness for project development	1.352	7.514%	.848
Total		**69.687%**	**.895**

The inventory of learning perception toward AI2 is a kind of self-reported instrument, developed according to Likert 5-point scale, from strongly agree to strongly disagree.

Simulation of flipping-cards algorithm

generating randomized and nonrepeated values with ranging from 0 to n-1

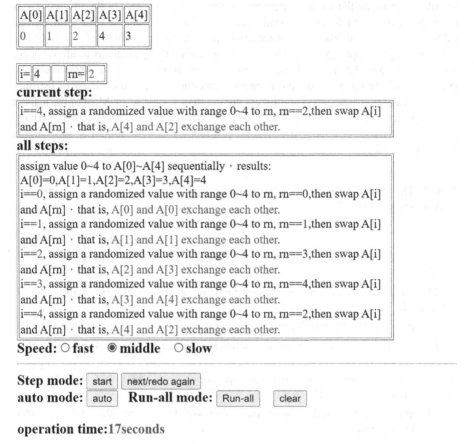

A[0]	A[1]	A[2]	A[3]	A[4]
0	1	2	4	3

i= 4	rn= 2

current step:

i==4, assign a randomized value with range 0~4 to rn, rn==2,then swap A[i] and A[rn] · that is, A[4] and A[2] exchange each other.

all steps:

assign value 0~4 to A[0]~A[4] sequentially · results:
A[0]=0,A[1]=1,A[2]=2,A[3]=3,A[4]=4
i==0, assign a randomized value with range 0~4 to rn, rn==0,then swap A[i] and A[rn] · that is, A[0] and A[0] exchange each other.
i==1, assign a randomized value with range 0~4 to rn, rn==1,then swap A[i] and A[rn] · that is, A[1] and A[1] exchange each other.
i==2, assign a randomized value with range 0~4 to rn, rn==3,then swap A[i] and A[rn] · that is, A[2] and A[3] exchange each other.
i==3, assign a randomized value with range 0~4 to rn, rn==4,then swap A[i] and A[rn] · that is, A[3] and A[4] exchange each other.
i==4, assign a randomized value with range 0~4 to rn, rn==2,then swap A[i] and A[rn] · that is, A[4] and A[2] exchange each other.

Speed: ○ **fast** ◉ **middle** ○ **slow**

Step mode: [start] [next/redo again]
auto mode: [auto] **Run-all mode:** [Run-all] [clear]

operation time:17seconds

Fig. 2. Simulation-based learning module for flipping-cards algorithm.

The data of pilot test was analyzed by factor analysis statistical method. The principal component method and variance-max rotation were adopted for factor analysis. The result of KMO and Bartlett sphere test showed that the sampling is adequate and suitable for factor analysis. The loading criterion of convergent was set as .5. Some of the items in this instrument were deleted due to violating convergent validity and discriminant validity. Finally, the four facets were constructed including the usefulness of learning basic programming concepts, learning transfer of programming concepts, learning flow, and usefulness for project development. The total variance explained is 69.687%, the Cronbach's alpha of total instrument is .895, shown as Table 1, indicating that the formal instrument has great construct validity and high reliability for assessment. The learners were asked to fill out this inventory by Google form at the end of AI2 learning activities.

3   Research Results

3.1   The Learning Perception Toward AI2

In order to examine the learners' perception toward AI2, the data of the inventory was analyzed by means of descriptive statistical method and one-sample t test with the test value 3. The statistical results of learners' perception toward usefulness of learning basic programming concepts are shown in Table 2, indicating that the means of all items are between 3.94 and 3.5, and the one sample t test is significant ($p < .001$) when the test value is 3. In other words, the learners' perception toward usefulness of learning basic programming concepts is significant greater than middle level. Most of the leaners showed positive perception toward learning usefulness of text-based computer language about event driven concepts, structure concepts, loops, methods, and array applications after learning AI2.

Table 2. The statistical results of learners' perception toward usefulness of learning basic programming concepts.

Items	M	SD	t	Sig
11. I became more familiar with event driven concepts after learning AI2	3.81	.816	6.897***	.000
12. I became more familiar with selection structure concepts after learning AI2	3.94	.783	8.296***	.000
13. I became more familiar with loop concepts after learning AI2	3.83	.724	7.970***	.000
14. I became more familiar with modular concepts after learning AI2	3.79	.824	6.656***	.000
15. I became more familiar with array/list concepts and its applications after learning AI2	3.60	.792	5.285***	.000
21. The APPs designed by AI2 are more practical and useful than those by other programming	3.50	.923	3.755***	.000

*** $p < .001$

The statistical results of learners' perception toward usefulness of learning transfer are shown in Table 3, indicating that the means of all items are between 3.88 and 3.6, and the one sample t test is significant ($p < .001$) when the test value is 3. In other words, most of the learners showed positive perception toward learning transfer usefulness from block-based programming to text-based programming about overall concepts and three-structure, problem-solving skills.

Table 3. The statistical results of learners' perception toward learning transfer of programming concepts.

Items	M	SD	t	Sig
3. Coding in AI2 make me more understand the overall concepts and structure of text-based programs	3.83	.996	5.794***	.000
5. Coding in AI2 make me more understand the I/O concepts of text-based programs	3.77	.751	7.115***	.000
6. Coding in AI2 make me more understand the problem-solving skills in text-based programs	3.88	.733	8.271***	.000
7. Coding in AI2 is useful in learning the text-based computer languages	3.65	.729	6.138***	.000
16. Coding in AI2 make me more understand the array/list concepts of text-based programs	3.60	.765	5.474***	.000

*** $p < .001$

The statistical results of learners' perception toward usefulness of learning flow are shown in Table 4, indicating that the means of all items are between 4.15 and 3.81, and the one sample t test is significant ($p < .001$) when the test value is 3. In other words, most of the leaners showed positive perception toward programming flow, programming self-efficacy, and learning intention.

Table 4. The statistical results of learners' perception toward learning flow.

Items	M	SD	t	Sig
8. I intend to master the text-based computer language after learning AI2	3.98	.729	9.305***	.000
10. Only if I work hard, I can master at the text-based computer language in the future	3.81	.915	6.155***	.000
23. I can concentrate on designing APP by AI2	4.15	.850	9.337***	.000
24. I almost forget the time passed so long in coding by AI2	4.04	.944	7.642***	.000

*** $p < .001$

The statistical results of learners' perception toward usefulness of project development are shown in Table 5, indicating that the means of all items are between 3.79 and 3.6, and the one sample t test is significant ($p < .001$) when the test value is 3. In other words, most of the leaners showed that designing APP project by AI2 is useful in project development including analysis, design, development, evaluation competencies in the future.

Table 5. The statistical results of learners' perception toward usefulness for project development.

Items	M	SD	t	Sig
27. he experience of APP project by AI2 is useful in future project development	3.79	.713	7.689***	.000
28. APP project by AI2 inspired my creativity	3.60	.962	4.352***	.000
29. APP project by AI2 enhanced my project and coding skills	3.71	.824	5.955***	.000

*** $p < .001$

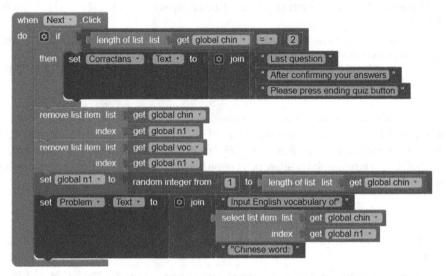

Fig. 3. One example of brute force solution for randomized and non-repeated English vocabulary test APP.

3.2 The Promotion of Problem-Solving Skills in Two Stages of Programming

In the first stage of APP design, many novices employed brute force methods to design mobile APPS. For example, when designing triangle judgement APP, they list all of relational conditions in the selection structures. The percent of their APPs belonging to optimal solutions is 16.3%, belonging to brute force method is 56.4%, and belonging to not-well solutions is 31%. After reviewing the algorithm offered by simulation-based learning system in the second stage, shown in Fig. 1, their solutions had great advancement. That is, the percent of their APPs belonging to optimal solutions is 83%, belonging to brute force method is 0%, and belonging to not-well solutions is 11%. In the other APP assignment, the randomized and non-repeated English vocabulary test APPs had to be designed by adopting array. Nevertheless, many kinds of brute force methods were used, shown as Fig. 3, including using loops to check whether the test item was adopted or deleting the test items when they were adopted. After reviewing the flipping cards algorithm offered by simulation-based learning system in the second stage, shown as

Fig. 2, their solutions had great advancement in problem-solving skills when programming. The percent of their APPs belonging to optimal solutions were promoted from 0% to 81.8%, belonging to brute force method were reduced from 32% to 0%, and belonging to not-well solutions were reduced from 61.8% to 18.2%, shown as Table 6.

Table 6. The progressive percentage of problem-solving model in two stages of programming assignments.

Assignment topic	First stage			Second stage		
	Optimal solutions	Brute force methods	Not well solutions	Optimal solutions	Brute force methods	Not well solutions
Judge triangle types	16.3% (9/55)	56.4% (31/55)	31% (17/55)	87.3% (48/55)	0% (0/55)	11% (6/55)
Randomized and non-repeated vocabulary test APP	0% (0/55)	38.2% (21/55)	61.8% (34/55)	81.8% (45/55)	0% (0/55)	18.2% (10/55)

4 Conclusion and Future Work

This study integrated the block-based programming environment into a course for the freshmen in a public university. The programming novices were guided to learn programming in AI2, and were asked to complete a series of APP design. When they encountered programming dilemma, they were advised to review the simulation-based learning system for improving their problem-solving skills in the programming process. The research results revealed that the learners showed positive perception toward AI2 including the usefulness of learning basic programming concepts, learning transfer of programming concepts, learning flow, and usefulness for project development. The percentage of programming skills enhanced are over 70%. In short, its effect is significantly positive. But the impact of block-based programming on the novices' text-based computer programming learning effectiveness is still unknown, and under exploring in the future.

Acknowledgement. The authors would like to thank MOST for its partially supported under No 111-2410-H-845-002.

References

1. ISTE: ISTE Standards: Students (2016). https://www.iste.org/standards/iste-standards-for-students

2. Lai, A.-F.: The tendency and promise of computer programming education. In: Koa, L. (ed.) Educational Research Tendency in Taiwan, pp. 435–491. WuNan, Taipei City (2012)

3. Gomes, A., Mendes, A.J.: An environment to improve programming education. In: Rachev, B., Smrikarov, A., Dimov, D. (eds.) Proceedings of the 2007 International Conference on Computer Systems and Technologies, Bulgaria, 14–15 June 2007. ACM, New York (2007)

4. Gomes, A., Mendes, A.J.: A study on student's characteristics and programming learning. Accepted for presentation in ED-MEDIA 2008, World Conference on Educational Multimedia, Hypermedia and Telecommunications, Wien, June (2008)

5. Boulay, B.: Programming environments for novices. In: Frasson, C., Gauthier, G., McCalla, G.I. (eds.) ITS 1992. LNCS, vol. 608, pp. 37–37. Springer, Heidelberg (1992). https://doi.org/10.1007/3-540-55606-0_4

6. Hostetler, T.R.: Predicting student success in an introductory programming course. SIGCSE Bull. 15(3), 40–43 (1983)

7. Kelleher, C., Pausch, R.: Lowering the barriers to programming: a taxonomy of programming environments and languages for novice programmers. ACM Comput. Surv. 37(2), 83–137 (2005). https://doi.org/10.1145/1089733.1089734

8. Lahtinen, E., Ala-Mutka, K.A., Jarvinen, H.M.: A study of the difficulties of novice programmers. In: Proceedings of 10th Annual SIGSCE Conference on Innovation and Technology in Computer Science Education, Monte da Caparica, Portugal, pp. 14–18. ACM (2005). https://doi.org/10.1145/1067445.1067453

9. Mannila, L., Peltomäki, M., Salakoski, T.: What about a simple language? Analyzing the difficulties in learning to program. Comput. Sci. Educ. 16(3), 211–227 (2006). https://doi.org/10.1080/08993400600912384

10. Mazlack, L.J.: Identifying potential to acquire programming skill. Commun. ACM 23(1), 14–17 (1980)

11. Robins, A., Rountree, J., Rountree, N.: Learning and teaching programming: a review and discussion. Comput. Sci. Educ. 13(2), 137–172 (2003)

12. Rogalski, J., Samurçay, R.: Acquisition of programming knowledge and skills. In: Psychology of Programming, pp. 157–174 (1990)

13. Simon, S.: Assignment and sequence: why some students can't recognise a simple swap. In: Proceedings of the 11th Koli Calling International Conference on Computing Education Research - Koli Calling, pp. 10–15 (2011). https://doi.org/10.1145/2094131.2094134

14. Wing, J.M.: Computational thinking. Commun. ACM 49(3), 33–35 (2006). https://doi.org/10.1145/1118178.1118215

Behavior Profiling of Role-Playing Game Players Based on Heuristic Event Log Mining

Jason Lin[1]([✉]) [iD], Chia-Wei Tsai[2] [iD], Chun-Wei Yang[3] [iD], and Elie Lafortune[1]

[1] Department of Computer Science and Engineering, National Chung Hsing University,
Taichung 40227, Taiwan
jasonlin@nchu.edu.tw, s108056023@mail.nchu.edu.tw
[2] Department of Computer Science and Information Engineering, National Taichung University
of Science and Technology, Taichung 404, Taiwan
cwtsai@nutc.edu.tw
[3] Master Program for Digital Health Innovation, College of Humanities and Sciences, China
Medical University, Taichung 406040, Taiwan
cwyang@mail.cmu.edu.tw

Abstract. In this paper, we propose a novel player behavior model called the action priority model (APM) for representing player action behaviors. A play log is stored based on the game grammar under analysis, and heuristic filtering rules are applied to eliminate uninteresting events. The proposed model uses sequences and tendencies of event types as the main mining criteria to extract significant player action behaviors. Action sequences reflect the interdependencies of different actions and how a player may use their insights about the game rules to form a (hidden) action priority list (APL) with respect to action types. By mining for significant events from play logs, we aim to produce the APM and APL for different players. In experiments, the fuzzy miner tool was used to analyze a few event logs for the World of Warcraft game to obtain some noticeable discoveries about the structural and timing patterns of effective players. Experimental results show that two players in the same class with similar contributions to encounters will have a similar mined APM and may not have a minimal delay in the timing of actions. Players with a high contribution to an encounter will have an APM like a simulated optimal player along with large thickness edges in the APM to indicate a significant routine of actions.

Keywords: Player behavior · Fuzzy miner · Causal net

1 Introduction

In role-playing games (RPG), there are many situations where groups of players collaborate in an encounter, as each player serves a role in the team to accomplish a team goal. The number of contributions made by individual players aiming to defeat the artificial intelligence (AI) adversary is a fundamental performance metric, which is largely determined by the action strategies in different scenarios. To improve their performance, motivated players routinely crawl through logs and summarize statistics to identify missed

© The Author(s), under exclusive license to Springer Nature Singapore Pte Ltd. 2022
S.-Y. Hsieh et al. (Eds.): ICS 2022, CCIS 1723, pp. 521–532, 2022.
https://doi.org/10.1007/978-981-19-9582-8_46

actions, potential cues for opportunities, effective moves, and assessment of the players' performance. This laborious manual process is difficult and inaccurate to find the underlying behavior patterns of a massive number of time-tagged events. It is often a hit-or-miss process to separate key moves that play pivotal roles in a game's outcomes from those less important ones that require profiling of player activities individually.

To improve the productivity of gameplay performance analysis, this paper proposes a process mining application that uses *timing* and *sequences* for diverse *types* of actions as the primary analytics features. Each player's class, which is of interest to performance and player modeling, is a set of actions and mechanisms that each player has available to them. A novel player model called the action priority model (APM) demonstrates the flow of action sequences and tendencies as the *causal net* for a player's performance. The sequence of actions is related to the dynamics of different actions as they affect subsequent choices based on their action priority list (APL), which is not visible to the analysis. The types of actions correspond to labels of significant actions that have value based on specific preceding or succeeding actions and highly frequent actions in the APL. The APL within these classes is a list of actions and the conditions under which a player should optimally take those actions.

Timing is a key metric that measures how efficient a player uses actions, as it represents the planning of the next action and the use of available actions. It can be used to judge the play performance with respect to the distributions of delay and idle intervals. Time also contributes, in this case, to ensure proper ordering.

Player and opponent modeling have been explored in the context of:

- modeling an opponent's case-based actions or how an opponent reacts to situations [1],
- modeling preferences of players to increase satisfaction by creating a taxonomy on models according to their purpose [2],
- modeling and measuring player features, such as measuring player feedback to actions taken against them, and ways to evaluate player statistical measures of game features [3].

In this work, the modeling approach of player behavior is based on statistical mining of direct casual relations without user feedback.

The APM for player performance profiling can be extracted by the behavior model discovery tools originally developed for business process management (BPM). Some of the most noted process mining algorithms [4] include heuristic miner [5], fuzzy miner [6], and the alpha families [7]. These algorithms fall into various categories, such as ordering-based, frequency-based, semantic-based, evolution-based, trace inductive, and algorithms that yield data perspectives other than the control flow. Among them, the most widely used algorithms are fuzzy miners and heuristic miners, which can produce reasonably desirable and interpretable results.

In this paper, we adopted the *fuzzy miner* tool to mine for significant behavioral patterns using the event logs of the World of Warcraft (WoW) game based on the heuristics of significant event types, timing, and sequences. The general processing steps are organized into: (1) preprocessing of raw logs into minable formats, (2) causal net generation based on the fuzzy and heuristic miners, and (3) player performance metrics analysis of the causal net models. Hence, an abstraction will be established to represent productive or inefficient player behaviors for each player class. It will lead to some noticeable behavior patterns with respect to the game outcomes.

2   APM System Architecture and Its Workflow

The APM for a player is automatically generated by a process mining tool called Disco [8]. It applies fuzzy miner to conduct type classification of the game rules and statistical analysis of the frequency and sequence of action types and their timing. Figure 1 demonstrates the workflow of mining the APM from player logs.

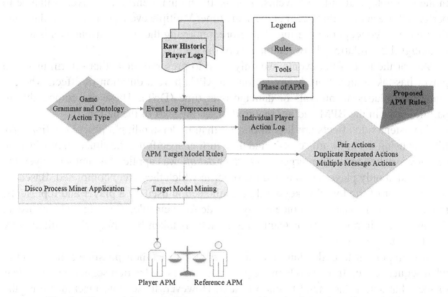

Fig. 1. The workflow to build an APM from historic player logs for an RPG.

Using a heuristic game grammar and ontology of WoW as reference, the game event log is first preprocessed into individual event logs for each player consists of action types and their timestamps are reformatted to be compatible with the fuzzy miner. Filtering rules are based on the proposed APM model, in which the significant actions for this study include (1) duplicate repeated actions, (2) actions that create multiple simultaneous events, and (3) actions that create sequential pairs of events. The resulting APM is a causal net of user behavior based on the player's APL hidden from the analysis.

WoW is an online game that records event logs in encounters and displays them to players for analysis. The event logs for the encounters can be downloaded from the WarcraftLogs [9] database, which consists of many encounters labeled as "successful" and "failure". The first step of process mining is to preprocess the event logs into the proper format and content for the mining tool. In general, an event log consists of two fields: time and event. Here, time should be set to the highest resolution such that two events occurring at the same time have the same time associated, and events are strings that are space delimited.

The structure of the log is as follows: (1) an initial event that specifies current player statistics, class of the player, and additional mechanics for the player; (2) events recorded in chronological order, including player death, player actions taken, and player status changes (i.e., beneficial effects and harmful effects); and (3) a message that informs when an encounter ends with a success/failure specifier.

In this study, a few manual heuristic filtering rules were used to weed out uninteresting event entries. The types of actions that are important to mine are those that can be related directly to player actions. In this encounter, any action that takes place within 0 ms of an action with the most frequent target will be filtered out. This type of action can be found in the chronological order of events. That is, the human-controlled player is unable to perform those actions that occur at the same time. Multiple events that occur at the same time have no concept of ordering. Therefore, removing these concurrent events allows meaningful 2-g relations between the rest of the events.

As for the rest of the events, we only wish to preserve those that inform us that a player has taken an action. Many actions in RPGs have a duration of effect, whereas many take places at intervals or damage over time (DoT). These are comparable to parallel tasks in the BPM and are required to see the start of the action.

Persistent side effects are less important than understanding a player's actions. By filtering using the keyword "casts", and then further specifying the situation in which an action was taken towards a target or a *buff* or *debuff* was applied on another player, the log included only player actions and the order in which they were completed. Based on the grammar of the log, this keyword gives the action used by a player and represents, in many cases, a conscious choice a player made for their role. These include offensive, defensive, or support for their team, and all actions taken by a player are initiated by events containing "casts."

It is important to understand how a player prioritizes their possible actions and in what sequence, i.e., from a node in the graph, to understand action sequences. It is clear to see what action they tend to choose next. However, these state machines miss the context as to why those actions were taken and have a concise representation of short loops. In the resulting model, when an action is repeatedly cast after it appeared in the mined model (an edge to itself), the data structure does not maintain how many times the action was taken in succession. This structure, where an action is preceded and succeeded by itself, exists in process mining as a short loop.

Complex logic on a short loop cannot be represented in many process models due to the model representing all possible actions. These possible actions being mined for are not mined with bounding information. A short loop observed in a log with 0, 1, 2, ..., n iterations is represented by a node having an edge pointing to itself, but an event that always occurs three times consecutively will be represented with the same structure. There is no BPM technique to add any bounded constraints, except duplicate transitions, which relies on a complex context to mine an accurate structure.

RPGs typically include two options that must be mined: (1) an action that incentivizes repeating that action, or (2) no action that provides a higher reward, and taking this action has more benefit than taking no action. Both model structures exist in almost all RPGs, and the BPM technique employed should account for these when attempting to recover performance.

The plug-in is defined as a process that takes an available log after converting it into an algorithm readable format and performing a process mining algorithm on it. After preprocessing, the fuzzy miner can further generate the visualization of a causal net for each player. Here, the fuzzy miner processes the transformed log and generates a model without additional filtering. An example of the causal net is illustrated in Fig. 2, where the shaded nodes represent *significant actions* inferred by the fuzzy miner, and the thickness of each edge represents the frequency of the transition from the source action to the destination action.

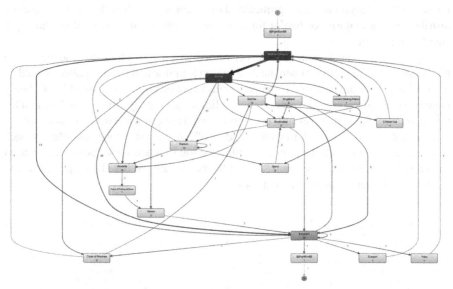

Fig. 2. Example of process model mined using the plug-in approach fuzzy miner of the Disco process mining application.

The plug-in model provides insight into what actions, sequences, and timings are taken, but it is not adequate for understanding the true behavior of a player. There are three issues that exist with this plug-in model: (1) encountering specific actions, (2) duplicating repeated actions, and (3) pairs of actions.

By observing the nodes present in an encounter compared to a different encounter, the intersection of actions demonstrates actions each player has available to them, and the exclusive union results in unique actions for those encounters. The encounter has some unique features, referred to as "mechanics", which is a challenge that a player must address. Some of these challenges include performing a movement, interacting with other players, or using a unique action to a fight provided by the encounter.

Duplicate repeated actions are actions available to the player that have increased weight for the successive casting of that action. From the resources available for each online game, the classes of players that have this feature can be found, but the plug-in model cannot differentiate which step is in repeated use. Pair actions refer to an action a player takes that generates two event messages. A common example in games is a case where a player uses an action with two weapons, and two actions are performed.

For encounter-specific actions, the union of actions across multiple encounters can create a filter for unique actions. This removes references to actions a player takes that are external to their class and are added by an encounter. These encounter-specific events act as noise to understand how experienced players make productive moves. Many actions that perform defensive roles or reactions to stimuli exist and are rarely used by players. However, they must be maintained to understand the player's behavior. By seeing the flow of actions, some unplanned events can be observed that altered their priorities.

To address these issues, where short loops and bounding information exist, we performed a 2-g analysis to find significant short sequences. When the event frequency distribution is a majority of two or three repetitions, the event is labeled as "having a significant pattern."

Figure 3 shows an n-gram analysis performed on a player's logs, and the bias in the histogram can be observed. When the distribution is uniform, the usage pattern would be inferred as a "random pattern." However, a bias in actions, such as "Aimed Shot," being heavily weighted towards two repetitions implies some strategy. A player will search for the action with the highest reward; thus, observing a pattern with two repetitions allows further exploration of the pattern with a window of 3, 4, ..., n size. One possible approach is to rename actions with the numbers within the log for each subsequent execution, as shown in Fig. 3, where subsequent "Aimed Shots" are aliased based on repeated action on the same target in adjacent action uses.

157	1	01:49.8 MÃ-zu	Aimed Shot	Trilliax
158	1	01:49.8 MÃ-zu	Trueshot	MÃ-zu
159	1	01:50.0 MÃ-zu	Cyclonic Burst	Scrubber 2
160	1	01:50.0 MÃ-zu	Windburst	MÃ-zu
161	1	01:50.6 MÃ-zu	Windburst	Deriza
162	1	01:51.0 MÃ-zu	Windburst	Caspz
163	1	01:51.4 MÃ-zu	Aimed Shot	Trilliax
164	1	01:52.0 MÃ-zu	Windburst	Caspz
165	1	01:52.7 MÃ-zu	Aimed Shot	Trilliax
166	1	01:53.9 MÃ-zu	Arcane Shot	Trilliax
167	1	01:54.9 MÃ-zu	Marked Shot	MÃ-zu
168	1	01:55.8 MÃ-zu	Arcane Shot	Trilliax
169	1	01:58.0 MÃ-zu	Aimed Shot	Trilliax
170	1	01:59.2 MÃ-zu	Aimed Shot	Trilliax
171	1	02:00.8 MÃ-zu	Aimed Shot	Trilliax
172	1	02:00.8 MÃ-zu	Marked Shot	MÃ-zu
173	1	02:01.7 MÃ-zu	Arcane Shot	Trilliax
174	1	02:02.7 MÃ-zu	Arcane Shot	Trilliax
175	1	02:04.9 MÃ-zu	Aimed Shot	Trilliax

157	1	01:49.8 MÃ-zu	Aimed Shot#1	Trilliax
158	1	01:49.8 MÃ-zu	Trueshot	MÃ-zu
159	1	01:50.0 MÃ-zu	Cyclonic Burst	Scrubber 2
160	1	01:50.0 MÃ-zu	Windburst	MÃ-zu
161	1	01:50.6 MÃ-zu	Windburst	Deriza
162	1	01:51.0 MÃ-zu	Windburst	Caspz
163	1	01:51.4 MÃ-zu	Aimed Shot#1	Trilliax
164	1	01:52.0 MÃ-zu	Windburst	Caspz
165	1	01:52.7 MÃ-zu	Aimed Shot#1	Trilliax
166	1	01:53.9 MÃ-zu	Arcane Shot#1	Trilliax
167	1	01:54.9 MÃ-zu	Marked Shot	MÃ-zu
168	1	01:55.8 MÃ-zu	Arcane Shot#1	Trilliax
169	1	01:58.0 MÃ-zu	Aimed Shot#1	Trilliax
170	1	01:59.2 MÃ-zu	Aimed Shot#2	Trilliax
171	1	02:00.8 MÃ-zu	Aimed Shot#3	Trilliax
172	1	02:00.8 MÃ-zu	Marked Shot	MÃ-zu
173	1	02:01.7 MÃ-zu	Arcane Shot#1	Trilliax
174	1	02:02.7 MÃ-zu	Arcane Shot#2	Trilliax
175	1	02:04.9 MÃ-zu	Aimed Shot#1	Trilliax

Fig. 3. Log actions renamed based on subsequent actions taken against the same target.

Pair actions are filtered using a black-list approach based on a database of possible actions for each player class. For all cases where one action creates two events, we filter out the second, which are labeled with the common terms "Offhand" and "(2)." By creating a black-list filter, we can filter encounter-specific actions, actions that create two messages for one move, and those extending to defensive actions if the offensive strategy of a player are of interest.

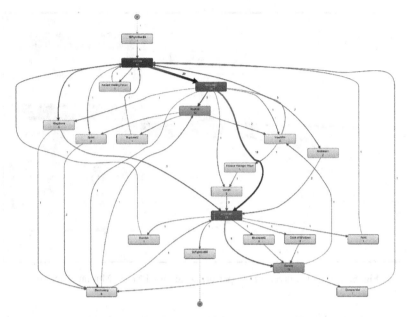

Fig. 4. Target model of a player generated with fuzzy miner from combat log data.

In Fig. 4, the target model is shown with more high-frequency edges and more nodes on paths. There are more significant events with an apparent high-frequency path, as seen with the thick edges between nodes, where two of these significant events are duplicate repeated actions with "maximum duplicates" as two. For example, a sequence of two duplicate actions is more important to understanding player behavior than a possible infinite loop on that action. This target model is our APM, which contains information regarding the actions taken, the relative frequency of each action, the frequency of transition from one action to another, and the timing information detailing how long a player idles between each action.

For measuring timing performance, the state time T_X of an event x can be expressed as $T_X = T_{GCD} + T_{Idle}$, , where GCD is the global cooldown time to activate the use of an action. The idle time is the time that the player is doing nothing related to the action (e.g., strategical waiting or simply doing nothing). In many RPGs, players have limited speed of action with respect to the GCD, where each player can initiate an action once every GCD second. The number of actions initiated in an encounter is directly proportional to the GCD. Dividing the length of an encounter by the GCD gives the total actions possible. Then, a true total action count can be obtained by factoring in latency, reaction time, and many other hidden factors. This number is typically in the high 90 s and helps measure the uptime, or the time for which a player is actively engaged and is performing some goal-oriented action. This is one metric of performance and can be easily extracted from a log by observing the average time a player remains in each state.

A general case would be dividing the duration of an encounter by the player's GCD, where the duration is adjusted to remove any actions that extend beyond the length of the GCD, i.e., casting a spell for 2 s in an RPG.

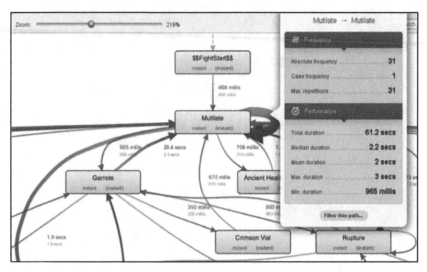

Fig. 5. Example player timing performance on APM of "Mutilate" action.

In Fig. 5, the timing information mined from the log for each action taken by a player can be observed. Each edge displays the time elapsed (in seconds) until the player began the following action and the average time until the player begins the next action.

3   Experimental Results

This section discusses the experimental results of the player model. The generated model is compared to three types of reference models as ground truths, such as peer, simulated, and community ideal player models. The similarity or differences between the actual and expected models will be discussed in this section to explain the results.

When measuring the performance of two players on a team, it is often important to get a sense of why one player is performing better than the other. This can be attributed directly to the player statistics, mechanics the player chose to use, and/or execution of their APL. Two APMs generated from players that play two different classes of players are not comparable as the nodes of each APM will have a small subset of intersecting actions.

Additionally, the actual meaning of those two actions with the same name may be completely different. An action may generate resources for one class of players while costing resources for another. This is true for equipment that provides mechanics to the player, as is common in many RPGs, and what mechanics a player chooses for themselves, as in the concept of traits or talents in many RPGs.

This study focused on exploring an event log for a single target encounter, i.e., an encounter containing one AI adversary with no additional phases where the APL for each player would change. Figure 6 provides two such mined APMs for top players that were the same class of the player in the example encounter. $Player_1$ and $Player_2$ were measured in terms of the extent to which they reduced the AI adversary's health resource over time. This performance was measured relative to every other player that played the same class in the example encounter. $Player_1$ and $Player_2$ performed better than 62% and 72% of the players in the class, respectively. These two players were also measured against players with a similar number of statistics available to them, and $Player_1$ performed better than 17% of players, while $Player_2$ performed better than 28% of players.

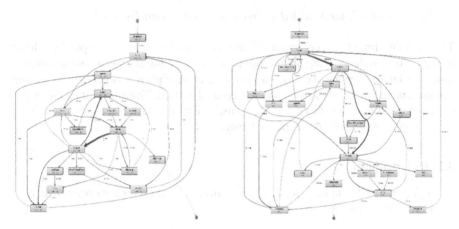

Fig. 6. APM mined using the Disco process mining application displaying time and structure for $Player_1$ and $Player_2$.

Between the two captured APMs, the most significant actions were equivalent, where the frequency of each action was observed to be extremely close in number, which contributes to the visual shading of each node. We observe this from the control flow perspective.

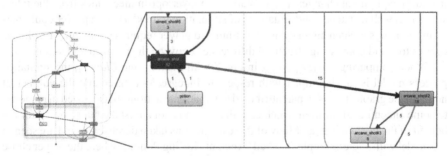

Fig. 7. The mined $Player_{SimCAS}$'s APM using the fuzzy miner within Disco process mining application.

Figure 7 shows an example of this display for another player. $Player_1$ has a clear high-frequency sequence, and $Player_2$ does not have it. However, the relative frequency of each path is present between the significant nodes. There are two main paths present in each player's APM. We infer from the higher performance of the peers that the emphasis on priority listing is correct. One conclusion to infer since the two players have a different root node to their APM is that $Player_1$ may have the wrong priority in mind while executing the encounter.

3.1 Observation 1

"Players with similar APM led to similar encounter contributions."

The transition time between actions is also very similar, and while typically a lower transition time reflects being able to use more actions, this class is a counterexample. Using the internet knowledge base, this example class of players benefits from waiting, and the timing is critical to executing the optimal actions. Transitions time closer to a system-defined limit for the speed of actions, actions that take place closer to 1.5 s in this example, would have better performance.

3.2 Observation 2

"A player's ability to minimize the time between actions does not always lead to the best performance."

Since it is difficult to compare players who play different classes, it is more reasonable to see in the direction of who is performing the closest to their ideal performance to know who has room for improvement and who should be provided more resources for a greater return on investment. In many encounters, there is a situation where one player can focus on one task, as they perform best at their role.

To address this, we experimented with the same analysis technique on the optimal simulated player from the player's profile. This was done using SimulationCraft [10]. This program simulates actual player performance and encodes all player mechanics, including equipment changes, player statistics, player opt-in mechanics from the talent system, as well as latency and situations of simulation to model how a player could perform for analysis. Such an analysis of a simulated player requires a matching resolution of logs to avoid comparing structural differences between the realized and simulated.

When comparing $Player_{SimCMM}$ in Fig. 7 with $Player_3$ and $Player_4$, the simulated process model is much simpler with respect to indegree/outdegree and the number of nodes in the graph. This is in part attributed to situational actions that are used in response to some encounter stimuli, in which case the action is not a mistake but a choice for the benefit of the mission's goal. Many of these are actions taken defensively and are seen in the model with some examples labeled "Ancient Healing Potion," where the player chose to act outside their role to fulfill the mission. Given that each player's log is separate, it is impossible to view what stimuli they are responding to at this resolution.

Figures 8 shows the mining of the event logs of $Player_3$, and the simulated log from $Player_{SimCMM}$ to compare structural differences in nodes, the number of edges between nodes, and the relative significance of each node. $Player_3$'s contribution to the encounter performed roughly better than 68% of others in the same class.

Player₃'s performance with respect to others of similar statistics was in the 33rd percentile. From the shaded nodes, it is visible what emphasis was placed on the ordering of the actions by each player. *Player₃* always performed two "Arcane Shots" before the "Marked Shot".

The simulated model, like *Player₃*, never used only one shot, and the relative weight of the "Arcane Shot" ability and its duplicates "Arcane Shot#2" and "Arcane Shot#3" had similar significance. Furthermore, *Player₃* had no more than four versions of the "Aimed Shot," while the simulation had six versions.

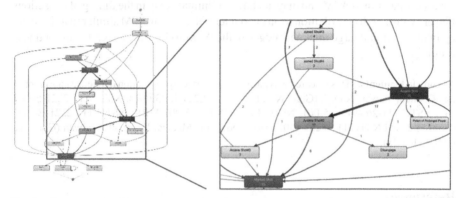

Fig. 8. The APM mined from event logs for *Player₃* to display significant actions and significant sequences.

Many actions did not appear in the simulation for *Player₃*, which can be due to situational actions or mistakes and should be investigated for specific usage. The ordering of actions was also more ambiguous for *Player₃* than in the simulation, as many of the actions were used in multiple orders, such as "A Murder of Crows" was used preceding and succeeding "Aimed Shots."

3.3 Observation 3

"The similarity of player and simulated player APM is indicative of the player's performance."

The fewer additional nodes the player adds to their APM, as well as the edges or additional paths, when compared with the simulated model appears to relate directly to increased performance. If a player's APM appears close to a simulated player's APM, it means that they followed the optimal path and the optimal timing distribution of actions and limited the use of situational actions. Similar weight in the edges implies the relative frequency of action paths matches the optimal one. From an intuitive sense, thicker paths imply that the player follows a better routine in terms of their actions, as they know what action they will take next. Thus, there is less idle time when choosing an action.

4 Conclusions

This paper presents the early results on performance factors and behavior profiles of RPG players based on a novel behavior model called APM which combines game grammar, heuristic noise filtering rules, and typing of actions. Using the Disco process mining tool, we were able to produce noticeable patterns and characteristics of player behavior models, i.e., their action causal net graphs, to give certain interpretations of how certain players can make significant contributions to the WoW game. Experiment results have shown that two players in the same class with similar contributions to encounters will have a similar mined APM and may not have a minimal delay in the timing of the actions. Players with a high contribution to an encounter will have an APM similar to a simulated optimal player and large thickness edges in the APM to indicate a significant routine of actions.

Acknowledgements. This research was partially supported by the National Science and Technology Council, Taiwan, R.O.C. (Grant Nos. NSTC 111-2221-E-039-014, NSTC 111-2221-E-005-048, NSTC 111-2634-F-005-001, NSTC 111-2218-E-005-007-MBK, NSTC 111-2221-E-143 -006 -MY2, and NSTC 111-2221-E-025-010) and China Medical University, Taiwan (Grant No. CMU111-S-28).

References

1. Bakkes, S.C., Spronck, P.H., van Lankveld, G.: Player behavioural modelling for video games. Entertain. Comput. **3**(3), 71–79 (2012)
2. Machado, M.C., Fantini, E.P.C., Chaimowicz, L.: Player modeling: towards a common taxonomy. In: Sharma, M., Mehta, M., Ontanón, S., Ram, A. (eds.) 16th International Conference on Computer Games (CGAMES), pp. 50–57, July 2011
3. Xiaohan, K., Khalid, M.N.A., Iida, H.: Player satisfaction model and its implication to cultural change. IEEE Access **8**, 184375–184382 (2020)
4. Van Der Aalst, W.: Process mining: overview and opportunities. ACM Trans. Manag. Inf. Syst. (TMIS) **3**(2), 1–17 (2012)
5. Weijters, A.J.M.M., van Der Aalst, W.M., De Medeiros, A.A.: Process mining with the heuristics miner-algorithm. Technische Universiteit Eindhoven, Technical report, WP 166, pp. 1–34 (2006)
6. Günther, C., Aalst, W.: Fuzzy mining – adaptive process simplification based on multiperspective metrics. In: Günther, C., Aalst, W. (eds.) International Conference on Business Process Management. 2007, LNCS, vol. 4714, pp. 328–343. Springer, Heidelberg (2007)
7. Van Der Aalst, W.M., Dongen, B.F.V.: Discovering petri nets from event logs. In: Jensen, K., van der Aalst, W.M.P., Balbo, G., Koutny, M., Wolf, K. (eds.) Transactions on Petri Nets and Other Models of Concurrency VII. LNCS, vol. 7480, pp. 372–422. Springer, Berlin, Heidelberg (2013)
8. Disco Homepage. https://fluxicon.com. Accessed 18 Aug 2022
9. WarCraftLogs Homepage. https://www.warcraftlogs.com. Accessed 15 July 2022
10. SimulationCraft Homepage. https://simulationcraft.org. Accessed 15 July 2022

The Impact of Live Streaming on Personal Purchase Behavior

Pai-Ching Tseng[1], Yi-Li Liou[2], Iuon-Chang Lin[2(✉)], and Tzu-Ching Weng[1]

[1] Program of Business, Feng Chia University, Taichung, Taiwan
[2] Department of Management Information Systems, National Chung Hsing University,
Taichung, Taiwan
iclin@nchu.edu.tw

Abstract. This study intends to explore the impact of Live-Stream on user satisfaction and the key to creating purchasing behavior. Therefore, this research will obtain an effective questionnaire from viewers who have watched Live-Stream on the Internet, and successfully use the information system introduced in DeLone & McLean's research [1]. The model is based on the theory, and several new and modified aspects are added as the research model to explore the correlation between live broadcasters, live broadcast platforms, purchase behaviors and recommendation behaviors. The results of this research scale have good reliability and validity. The results of the study found that: (1) Information Quality will positively affect User Satisfaction (2) System Quality will positively affect Business Behavior and User Satisfaction (3) Social Interaction positively affects Business Behavior and User Satisfaction. In "Information Quality", User Satisfaction is the "completely intermediary" variable that promotes Business Behavior; in "System Quality", User Satisfaction is the "partial intermediary" variable that promotes Business Behavior; in "Social Interaction", User Satisfaction is a "partially mediating" variable that contributes to Business Behavior.

Keywords: Live-stream · Purchase behavior · Recommendation behavior ·
Information System Success Model (ISSM)

1 Introduction

1.1 Research Background and Motivation

In recent years, Internet platforms have become more and more mature. According to the 2020 report of the Taiwan Network Information Center (TWNIC), a consortium, the Internet access rate of home networks is 82.8%. Since 2011, the frequency of use has increased in Taiwan. Network Information Center [2], with the development of hardware and software, Live-Stream platforms, media, and social networking sites have also successively cooperated with enterprises to create new business models. In recent years, many domestic researches have focused on the relationship between use intention and Live-Stream platform, and less research has been done on the impact of technology and information on live broadcast rooms, which is the main motivation for this study.

Discuss how the Live-Stream platforms with various types of live broadcasters create what kind of environment and interaction to improve the audience's sensory experience, as well as the layout design and system aspects of the Live-Stream platform, which in turn affect the audience's purchase intention and recommended behavior.

1.2 Research Purposes

In today's society, consumer awareness is on the rise, according to Maslow's hierarchy of needs theory [3]. Basic physiological needs are not so important in today's developed or developing countries. Instead, they pursue the sublimation of quality at all levels. Therefore, among emerging Live-Stream platforms, each Live-Stream platform should consider how to design the user interface to enhance the user experience, how to train their own live broadcasters, and how to influence the audience's feelings with what kind of conversation and environmental atmosphere, thereby increasing the audience. Purchase Intention. Taking the Live-Stream platform as an example, we try to find out: using the Information System Success Model to explore the interaction of Live-Stream social interaction, business behavior intention and user satisfaction.

2 Literature Review

2.1 Live-Stream

In recent years, due to the maturity of broadband networks and wireless networks, as well as the increasingly diversified software and hardware of computer equipment, stronger computing power, lower purchase and use costs, more families and individuals can Unlimited and free use of network resources has also created various models of Live-Stream platforms and enterprises using e-commerce, which are becoming more and more diversified. From the well-known social platforms Facebook, YouTube, Twitter, etc., to online Live-Stream platforms: 17 Live, Up Live-Stream, etc., you can see all kinds of advertisements and Live-Stream content. The online Live-Stream, which can present various interactive forms of different styles according to the different needs of the audience [4]. And live webcasting is also a way of dissemination that is random, broadcast instantly and can be without any purpose. The content provided by the Live-Stream industry is more diversified, including live games, product marketing, topic and song performances, pure companionship, etc. In addition, live broadcasters can also share their personal concepts or products with audiences through charismatic marketing, so as to conduct favorable marketing and promotion of Solomon's research [5].

2.2 Information System Success Model

The Information System Success Model (ISSM) was proposed by DeLone & McLean after synthesizing more than 180 articles related to evaluate the effectiveness of information systems [1]. The model has Six dimensions, including Information Quality, System Quality, System Use, User Satisfaction, Individual Impact, Organizational Impact, etc. From this model, it can be seen that "Information Quality" and "System Quality" have a profound impact on the use of information systems and user satisfaction. There is also an effect of mutual influence between the two aspects of system use and user satisfaction. Through this model, it can be understood that when the quality of an information system is improved, users can be more satisfied with the user experience, and then Increase the frequency of use of the system. When an information system is easier to use, more people will recommend the system, which in turn will increase the number of users of the system and extend its influence to the entire organization. The model is shown in Fig. 1.

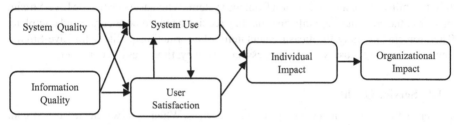

Fig. 1. DeLone & McLean information system success model

DeLone & McLean revised the Information System Success Model and added a Service Quality dimension to the model [6]. The reason is that many scholars such as Parasuraman, Zeithaml, & Berry believe that information systems are important. But for users, the information service is very important [7]. Pitt, Watson & Kavan proposed that if information personnel can communicate with users, start from the needs of users, and then correct and improve, the service quality of information systems will be greatly improved [8], that is, it is necessary to add Consideration of service orientation and customer satisfaction. The revised model is shown in Fig. 2.

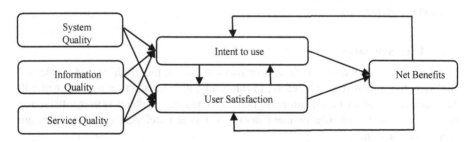

Fig. 2. DeLone & McLean revised information system success model

DeLone & McLean Information system success model [6], which is used in the study of six dimensions (System Quality, Information Quality, Service Quality, Intention to use /Use Behavior, User Satisfaction, and Net Benefits) in the study of Live-Stream platforms. Operational definition as well as measuring item content:

2.2.1 System Quality

It is the processing performance and efficiency of the system interface and the system backend itself. In the Live-Stream platform, its interface needs to be concise and easy to understand, so that users can easily operate and learn to use the Live-Stream interface. Therefore, in this study, the measurement items of system quality in the Live-Stream environment are stability, accuracy, consistency, learnability, and system delay.

2.2.2 Information Quality

It is the ability to obtain information from the system. When users watch the Live-Stream platform, the content of the information they receive needs to be accurate and complete. Therefore, in this study, the measurement items of information quality in the Live-Stream environment are accuracy, completeness, consistency, timeliness, security, etc.

2.2.3 Service Quality

It refers to the evaluation of viewing or users' services. When users watch the Live-Stream platform, the Live-Stream platform can provide viewers with emotional service content, and can enable the viewer to establish several items about the Live-Stream platform. Evaluation Criteria. Therefore, in this study, service quality is defined as social interaction in the Live-Stream environment, and its measurement items are responsiveness, reliability, customization, etc.

2.2.4 Intention to Use/Use Behavior

Whether the user is willing to watch or continue to use the products and services of the Live-Stream platform in the future. Therefore, in this study, the Intention to use is combined with the next fifth dimension (user satisfaction), which is defined as user satisfaction. Before the merger, the measurement items are use intention, recommended use, and use motivation.

2.2.5 User Satisfaction

It is the subjective opinion of viewers or users regarding the products and services of the Live-Stream platform. Therefore, in this study, user satisfaction is combined with the fourth dimension (use intention/use behavior), which is defined as user satisfaction. Before the merger, the measurement items are repeat purchase, repeat viewing, and overall satisfaction.

2.2.6 Net Benefit

It is the substantial return obtained by the Live-Stream platform through various efforts. Therefore, in this study, it is defined as business behavior intention, and its measurement items are to reduce search cost, increase revenue, and expand market.

2.3 Social Interaction

Social interaction is defined as the interaction between people to achieve certain needs and purposes. Maslow mentioned that when people meet their physical and safety needs, they will be expected to belong and be emotionally satisfied, and then they will be recognized by the society through their personal abilities, and by interacting with society Communicate to reflect your own value [3]. In the Social Identity Theory (SIT) proposed by Tajfel & Turner, through social identity, you can not only know which social class you belong to, but also according to various factors such as status and values [9]., this group will not only have a high degree of centripetal force, but also think that the group to which one belongs is superior to other groups, and will contribute to the group's superiority and interests Chen & Li's research [10].

In social media, Wu Bingying & Huang Xiaoting proposed that when viewers watch on the Live-Stream platform, if they are in a relaxed mood, they will achieve good entertainment and interactive effects [11]. Through social media, it is also a method to achieve social interaction. Stern et al. mentioned that when watching social media, it is easy to interact with the live broadcaster, as if it is truly interactive and immersive, and even think the live broadcaster, just like his friend, has no generation gap and can interact and communicate without any grudges [12]. Interactivity is defined as the degree of communication between the communicator and the participant in order to consolidate certain relationships from Roger's research [13], and these interactions will change simultaneously and continuously in the communication environment from Rafaeli & Sudweeks's research [14]. The research results of Jian Yuze show that the level of interaction is highly correlated with the identity of the live broadcaster [15]. Based on the above literature, this study intends to add the dimension of social interaction to the Information System Success Model for discussion.

3 Research Method

3.1 Research Structure

This study explores the related research on the revenue of Live-Stream platforms and user satisfaction, using the Information System Success Model modified from DeLone & McLean's research [6] as the basis of the research structure, and this research is based on the literature content in Sect. 2. Modified and added three dimensions, namely, information quality, system quality, social interaction, business behavior intention, and user satisfaction. The regular and irregular activities of the Live-Stream platform have an impact on the purchase behavior and customer satisfaction of the Live-Stream platform. The proposed research aspect is shown in Fig. 3.

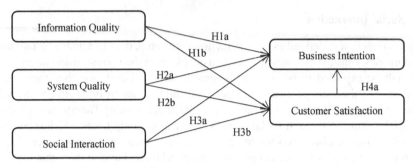

Fig. 3. Research structure

Based on the literature discussion proposed in Session 2, this study modifies and adds three aspects to the Information System Success Model revised from DeLone & McLean [6], and uses the created aspects according to the literature discussion. Content, this study proposes the following hypotheses (Fig. 4):

H1a: "Information Quality" is positively correlated with Business Intention.
H1b: "Information Quality" is positively correlated with Customer Satisfaction.
H2a: "System Quality" is positively correlated with Business Intention.
H2b: "System Quality" is positively correlated with Customer Satisfaction.
H3a: "Social Interaction" is positively correlated with Business Intention.
H3b: "Social Interaction" is positively correlated with Customer Satisfaction.
H4a: "Customer satisfaction" is positively correlated with Business Intention.

Fig. 4. Research hypothesis

4 Data Analysis

The models and research hypotheses constructed based on the content of the questionnaire in Session 2, this research uses SPSS and Amos as analysis tools to conduct statistical analysis on the results recovered from the online questionnaire, including: Statistical Analysis, Reliability and Validity Analysis, Pearson Correlation Analysis, Regression analysis, Structural Equation Model, etc.

4.1 Analysis of Basic Data

The basic information of the pre-study subjects of this study includes: gender, age, occupation, education level, economic income (monthly salary), whether they have watched Live-Streams, whether they have ever purchased and rewarded on Live-Stream platforms, etc., a total of seven items. The statistical status and distribution of the mean and standard deviation between the variables were analyzed through descriptive statistics. This study adopts the method of random distribution of online questionnaires, and mainly studies the correlation between the revenue of the Live-Stream platform and user satisfaction through the Information System Success Model. Subjects filled out the questionnaire content.

A total of 280 questionnaires were collected in this study. This questionnaire needs to meet the requirements of the two items that have watched the Live-Stream, purchased on the Live-Stream platform, and rewarded at the same time, and 27 of them did not meet the questionnaire requirements. Therefore, there were 253 valid questionnaires, and the questionnaire recovery rate was 90.36%. Through descriptive statistics, females accounted for 60.4% of the answers. The age of the respondents was the most in the 30–40 age range (37.5% of the total testers). University graduates are the most educated (accounting for 76.2% of the total testers). The monthly income range of the respondents is 20,001–40,000 yuan (47.8% of the total testers), and the above 253 people are all viewers who "have watched Live-Streams" and "have purchased and rewarded on Live-Stream platforms". It can be inferred from the descriptive statistics that the young and middle-aged population are more financially able to purchase Live-Stream products and have the ability to give rewards; it can be inferred from the gender respondents that women have a higher probability of using Live-Stream platforms than men.

4.2 Reliability and Validity Analysis

4.2.1 Reliability Analysis

This study uses reliability to test the reliability of the questionnaire, and uses Cronbach's α value to measure the reliability level represented by each dimension of the model. There are five dimensions in this study, namely Information Quality, System Quality, Social Interaction, and Business Intention, Customer Satisfaction, etc. Among them, if the value of the dimension is greater than 0.7, it is judged that the questionnaire has a good reliability level [16]. Table 1 below shows the Cronbach's α values for each aspect of this study. The Cronbach's α values of the five dimensions in this table are all greater than 0.7, indicating that the representative questionnaires of this study dimension have good reliability standards, and the dimensions have good consistency and stability.

4.2.2 Validity Analysis

This study uses validity analysis to determine whether it can measure the validity of its dimensions, and uses convergent validity and discriminant validity to test. In factor analysis, this study used the Varimax, this method makes each variable have a higher load in a single factor [17], through the study of Kaiser [18], indicated that in the research aspect, the factor loading of each aspect should be greater than 0.5 or more, the Composite Reliability (CR) needs to be more than 0.6, and the Average Variance Extracted (AVE) value is used for detection, and the AVE value is more than 0.36. The research and analysis results show that the factor loading values of the five dimensions in this table are all greater than 0.6, the combined reliability CR is greater than 0.7, and the average variation extraction AVE is greater than 0.5 except for the Information Quality and Social Interaction dimensions. Although the dimensions of Information Quality and Social Interaction do not reach 0.5, according to scholars Fornell & Larcker's research

Table 1. Cronbach's α results

Research dimension	Number of questions	Number after deletion	Cronbach's α (after deletion)	Results
Information quality	7	3	0.711	Acceptable
System quality	6	2	0.761	Acceptable
Social interaction	8	4	0.792	Acceptable
Business intention	7	5	0.86	Good
Customer satisfaction	7	4	0.829	Good

[16], an AVE value higher than 0.36 is acceptable, indicating that the representative questionnaire of this research dimension has good validity standards and convergence degree.

In terms of discriminant validity analysis, it mainly discusses whether the correlations can be distinguished between each aspect. According to Fornell & Larcker's research [16], the square root value of the average variation extraction amount AVE between each aspect should be greater than the correlation coefficient value of other aspects, and in Table 2, the square root value of AVE in each dimension is in line with the recommendations of scholars, so this study has good discriminant validity.

Table 2. Discriminant validity analysis

	Information quality	System quality	Social interaction	Business intention	Customer satisfaction
Information quality	**0.683**	-	-	-	-
System quality	.411**	**0.82**	-	-	-
Social interaction	.500**	.366**	**0.699**	-	-
Business intention	.427**	.459**	.596**	**0.725**	-
Customer satisfaction	.602**	.425**	.552**	.536**	**0.723**

4.3 Model Fit Analysis

In this study, SEM structural equation analysis was pre-made. The structural equation analysis included a variety of statistical methods such as Factor Analysis and Path Analysis, which was similar to a multiple regression analysis. It is necessary to measure the fit between the model proposed in this study and the hypothetical issues proposed by the model fit analysis index. In this study, three indicators were used as standard measures, namely Absolute Fit Measure, Incremental Fit Measure, and Parsimonious Fit Measure.

The standard values for model fit proposed by the above scholars, and the model fit scale obtained by structural equation analysis in this study, each value in the Absolute Fit Measure, Incremental Fit Measure, and Parsimonious Fit Measure. The comparisons are in line with the values suggested by previous scholars, and the results are shown in Table 3 below.

Table 3. Model fit

Model fit		Suggested	Result	References
Absolute fit measure	X^2/df	<3	2.428	Hair et al. [19]
	GFI	>0.8	0.884	Doll & Xia & Torkzadeh [20]
	AGFI	>0.8	0.884	MacCallum & Hong [21]
	RMSEA	0.05–0.08	0.075	McDonald & Ho [22]; Huang Fangming [23]
Incremental fit measure	NFI	>0.8	0.855	Ullman [24]
	IFI	>0.9	0.91	Zhang Weihao [25]; Huang Fangming [23]
	NNFI(TLI)	>0.8	0.89	Zhang Weihao [25]
	CFI	>0.9	0.908	Hair et al. [19]
Parsimonious fit measure	PNFI	>0.5	0.71	Bagozzi & Yi [26]
	PGFI	>0.5	0.657	Bagozzi & Yi [26]
	PCFI	>0.5	0.754	Bagozzi & Yi [26]

4.3.1 SEM Results

After the validity of this study was proved by the results of the previous reliability and validity analysis and model fit analysis, Amos 23 software was used to carry out the path analysis of the model structural equation to explore the causal influence of each aspect in the model structure. The path coefficients and significance levels are tested against the research hypotheses previously proposed in this study. The analysis results are shown in Fig. 5 and Table 4.

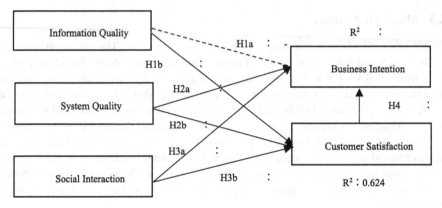

Fig. 5. SEM results

4.3.2 Research Hypothesis Testing

According to the results of the structural equation analyzed by the Amos 23 software, the results were compared and verified with the hypotheses. The obtained data collated the results and found that one of the 7 hypotheses proposed by this research did not hold. The results are shown in Table 4 shown.

Table 4. Hypothesis results

Research hypothesis	Path coefficients	Result
H1a: Information Quality -> Business Intention	−0.166	Invalid
H1b: Information Quality -> Customer Satisfaction	0.575***	Established
H2a: System Quality -> Business Intention	0.27***	Established
H2b: System Quality -> Customer Satisfaction	0.2**	Established
H3a: Social Interaction -> Business Intention	0.58***	Established
H3b: Social Interaction -> Customer Satisfaction	0.253*	Established
H4a: Customer Satisfaction -> Business Intention	0.274*	Established

In the research model, the standardized path coefficient value of Information Quality on Business Intention is −0.166, and the p-value is greater than 0.05, which does not reach a significant level, indicating that "Information Quality" does not affect "Business Intention", the H1a hypothesis does not hold; the standardized path coefficient value of Information Quality on Customer Satisfaction is 0.575, and the p-value is less than 0.001, reaching a significant level, indicating that "Information Quality" positively affects "Customer Satisfaction", the H1b hypothesis is established.

The standardized path coefficient value of System Quality to Business Intention is 0.27, p-value is less than 0.001, reaching a significant level, indicating that "System Quality" positively affects "Business Intention", the H2a hypothesis is established; the standardized path of System Quality to Customer Satisfaction The coefficient value is 0.2, and the p-value is less than 0.01, reaching a significant level, indicating that "System Quality" positively affects "Customer Satisfaction", and the H2b hypothesis is established.

The standardized path coefficient value of Social Interaction on Business Intention is 0.58, and the p-value is less than 0.001, which is a significant level, indicating that "Social Interaction" positively affects "Business Intention", the H3a hypothesis is established; the standardized path of Social Interaction on Customer Satisfaction The coefficient value is 0.253, and the p-value is less than 0.05, reaching a significant level, indicating that "Social Interaction" positively affects "Customer Satisfaction", and the H3b hypothesis is established.

The standardized path coefficient value of Customer Satisfaction to Business Intention is 0.274, and the p-value is less than 0.05, reaching a significant level, indicating that "Customer Satisfaction" positively affects "Business Intention", and the H4a hypothesis is established.

5 Conclusion

This research adopts the Information System Success Model modified from DeLone & McLean's research [6] as the basis of the research structure, and modifies and adds dimensions such as Social Interaction, Business Intention and Customer Satisfaction to this research model. To explore the related research on the revenue and Customer Satisfaction of the Live-Stream platform, through the method of online questionnaire distribution, the audience who "have watched the Live-Stream" and "have purchased and rewarded on the Live-Stream platform" were targeted to fill in the questionnaire, and finally 253 copies were recovered. A valid questionnaire and statistical analysis were conducted. After reliability and validity analysis and structural equation analysis, the five dimensions of the " Live-Stream platform" in the Information System Success Model were obtained. Among the seven hypotheses proposed, one of them did not hold. The research hypothesis and verification results are shown in Table 5 below.

Table 5. Research hypothesis testing

Hypothesis	Result
H1a: "Information Quality" is positively correlated with Business Intention	Invalid
H1b: "Information Quality" is positively correlated with Customer Satisfaction	Established
H2a: "System Quality" is positively correlated with Business Intention	Established
H2b: "System Quality" is positively correlated with Customer Satisfaction	Established
H3a: "Social Interaction" is positively correlated with Business Intention	Established
H3b: "Social Interaction" is positively correlated with Customer Satisfaction	Established
H4a: "Customer satisfaction" is positively correlated with Business Intention	Established

References

1. DeLone, W.H., McLean, E.R.: Information systems success: the quest for the dependent variable. Inf. Syst. Res. **3**(1), 60–95 (1992)
2. TWNIC: 2020 Taiwan Internet Report, Taiwan Internet Information Center (2020)
3. Maslow, A.H.: Motivation and Personality. Harper & Row, New York (1954)
4. Xiaoyi: Interpretation of media technology, China Computer News (2001)
5. Solomon, M.R.: Consumer Behavior. Pearson Education, New Jersey (2005)
6. DeLone, W.H., McLean, E.R.: The DeLone and McLean model of information systems success: a ten-year update. J. Manag. Inf. Syst. **19**(4), 9–30 (2003)
7. Parasuraman, A., Zeithaml, V.A., Berry, L.L.: The SERVQUAL: a multiple-item scale for measuring consumer perceptions of service quality. J. Retail. **64**(1), 12–40 (1988)
8. Pitt, L.F., Watson, R.T., Kavan, C.B.: Measuring information systems service quality: lessons from two longitudinal case studies. MIS Q. 61–79 (1998)
9. Tajfel, H., Turner, J.C.: The social identity theory of intergroup behavior. In: Worchel, S., Austin, W.G. (eds.) Psychology of Intergroup Relations, pp. 7–24. Nelson-Hall, Chicago (1986)
10. Chen, Y., Li, S.X.: Group identity and social preference. Am. Econ. Rev. **99**(1), 431–457 (2009)
11. Wu, B., Huang, X.: A study on the continuous viewing and sharing behavior of Internet celebrities' live video. Chinese Communication Society (2018)
12. Stern, B.B., Russell, C.A., Russell, D.W.: Hidden persuasions in soap operas: damaged heroines and negative consumer effects. Int. J. Advert. **26**(1), 9–36 (2007)
13. Rogers, E.M.: Diffusion of Innovations, 4th edn. The Free Press, New York (1995)
14. Rafaeli, S., Sudweeks, F.: Networked interactivity. J. Comput.-Mediated Commun. **2**(4) (1997)
15. Jian, Y.-Z.: Lonely people cannot live without online streaming? – A study on Livestream continuance watching intentions. Master's thesis, Institute of Information Management, National Central University, pp. 35–37 (2018)
16. Fornell, C., Larcker, D.F.: Evaluating structural equation models with unobservable variables and measurement error. J. Mark. Res. **18**(1), 39–50 (1981)
17. Lin, S., Chen, Y.: Multivariate Analysis: Management Applications, 2nd edn. Double Leaf Book Gallery (2013)
18. Kaiser, H.F.: An index of factorial simplicity. Psychometrika **39**, 31–36 (1974)
19. Hair, J.F., Black, W.C., Babin, B.J., Anderson, R.E.: Multivariate Data Analysis, 7th edn. Pearson, New York (2010)
20. Doll, W.J., Xia, W., Torkzadeh, G.: A confirmatory factor analysis of the end-user computing satisfaction instrument. MIS Q. **12**(2), 259–274 (1994)
21. MacCallum, R.C., Hong, S.: Power analysis in covariance structure modeling using GFI and AGFI. Multivar. Behav. Res. **32**, 193–210 (1997)
22. McDonald, R.P., Ho, M.R.: Principles and practice in reporting structural equation analysis. Psychol. Methods **7**, 64–82 (2002)
23. Fangming, H.: Structural Equation Modeling Theory and Applications, 5th edn. Wunan, Taipei (2007)
24. Ullman, J.B.: Structural equation modeling. In: Tabachnick, B.G., Fidell, L.S. (eds.) Using Multivariate Statistics, 4th edn, pp. 653–771. Allyn and Bacon, Needham Heights (2001)
25. Zhang, W., Zheng, S.: Dancing with Structural Equation Modeling: The Dawn. Future Culture, New Taipei City (2012)
26. Bagozzi, R., Yi, Y.: On the evaluation of structural equation models. J. Acad. Mark. Sci. **16**, 74–94 (1988)

Stochastic-Gradient-Descent-Based Max-Margin Early Event Detector

Hong-Wen Wang, Dai-Yi Chiu, Wei-Chung Chan, and Zhi-Fang Yang[✉]

Department of Computer Science and Information Engineering, National Taipei University, New Taipei City 23741, Taiwan, R.O.C.
zfyang@mail.ntpu.edu.tw

Abstract. Max-margin-based early event detection is first solved by max-margin early event detector (MMED) proposed by Hoai and Torre [10]. In this study, the stochastic gradient descent mechanism is used to replace the quadratic programming solver in [10] to achieve early event detection. Three datasets are tested, including synthetic data, the extended Cohn-Kanade dataset (CK+), and Australian sign language data (ASL). The experimental results show that the proposed approach is feasible, and that the performance is comparable to that obtained in MMED.

Keywords: Early event detection · Quadratic programming · Stochastic gradient descent

1 Introduction

Event detection is one widely researched field in computer engineering [1, 2, 4, 6–10, 13–17]. Generally, event detection can be divided into complete event detection and partial event detection [15, 16]. In partial event detection, early event detection is focused on finding the target event as soon as possible. Early event detection can be applied to many applications, such as facial expression detection [8–10, 15, 16] and sign language detection [10, 15, 16].

Hoai and Torre [10] propose the max-margin early event detector (MMED) based on the structured output support vector machine (SOSVM) which is the generalized support vector machine (SVM) [3, 5]. Later, Huang et al. [4] design the sequential MMED (SMMED) to extend MMED to deal with multi-classes. For MMED, solving the quadratic programming problem is the major work [3]. However, if the number of constraints is very huge, it is too time consuming to be feasible. Thus, alternative solvers may be considered, for instance, Shai et al. [12] propose the primal estimated sub-gradient solver (Pegasos) in which the stochastic gradient descent method is utilized to solve the quadratic programming problem in the support vector machine instead. Furthermore, it is proven to be able to converge efficiently [12].

Thus, due to the huge number of constraints in MMED, about three thousand constraints for one simple synthetic training instance [10, 12], in this study, the stochastic gradient descent method is used to replace the quadratic programming solver in MMED.

S.-Y. Hsieh et al. (Eds.): ICS 2022, CCIS 1723, pp. 545–552, 2022.
https://doi.org/10.1007/978-981-19-9582-8_48

Three data sets are used in the experiments as those used in [10], and comparable experimental results are obtained to verify the feasibility of the proposed approach.

2 Proposed Approach

In order to incorporate the stochastic gradient descent mechanism, Pegasos [12], into MMED [10], the objective function of MMED [10] needs to be rewritten in the gradient-descent style [12]. In this study, for a given training sample $S = \{(x^i, y^i) | x^i \in X, y^i \in Y, i = 1, \ldots, n\}$, where X is the input training instance set, and Y the set of early events, the proposed gradient-descent-style objective function is derived to be:

$$\min \frac{\lambda}{2} \|w\|^2 + \frac{1}{n} \sum_{i=1}^{n} \max \left\{ 0, \mu \left(\frac{|y_t^i|}{|y^i|} \right) \left[f\left(x_{y-y_t^i}^i \right) + \Delta\left(y_t^i, y \right) \right] \right\}, \tag{1}$$

where w is the weight vector of the linear early event detector in [10], λ the trade-off coefficient in [12], y_t^i the early event observed at time t of the complete event y^i in the training instance x^i [10], y a time segment in x^i [10], $\mu\left(\frac{|y_t^i|}{|y^i|} \right)$ the scaling function for soft margin [10], $\Delta\left(y_t^i, y \right)$ the loss function of mistaking y as y_t^i [10], and $f\left(x_{y-y_t^i}^i \right) = f\left(X_y^i \right) - f\left(X_{y_t^i}^i \right)$ the difference of the detection scores of $f\left(X_y^i \right)$ and $f\left(X_{y_t^i}^i \right)$ [10, 12]. The proposed algorithm to achieve the optimization of Eq. (1), denoted as Pegasos-based MMED (PMMED), is as follows.

Algorithm 1: PMMED

input: S, λ, T

```
1.    Set w₁ = 0 ;
2.    for t ← 1 to T do
3.        Choose i ∈ {1, …, |S|} uniformly at random;
4.        Set yᵗⁱ = max f(xᵧⁱ) ;
                  y∈Y
5.        Set ηₜ = 1/λt ;
6.        if f(Xⁱᵧ₋ᵧₜⁱ) + Δ(yᵗⁱ, y) > 0 then
7.              Set wₜ₊₁ ← (1 − ηₜλ)wₜ − ηₜμ(|yᵗⁱ|/|yⁱ|) f′(Xⁱᵧ₋ᵧₜⁱ) ;
8.        else
9.              Set wₜ₊₁ ← (1 − ηₜλ)wₜ ;
10.       end
11.   end
```

output: w_{T+1}

For each iteration in the above algorithm, a training instance (x^i, y_t^i) is chosen randomly, the corresponding gradient is computed, and the weight vector w_i is updated. Note that η_t is the learning rate at iteration t.

As shown in Line 7 of Algorithm 1, the gradient ∇_t is

$$\nabla_t = \lambda w_t + 1\left[f(X^i_{y-y^i_t}) + \Delta\left(y^i_t, y\right) > 0\right]\mu\left(\frac{|y^i_t|}{|y^i|}\right)f'(X^i_{y-y^i_t}). \qquad (2)$$

The derivation of Eq. (2) is as follows. First, recall the objective function of MMED in [10]:

$$\min \frac{1}{2}\|w\|^2 + \frac{C}{n}\sum_{i=1}^{n}\xi^i$$

$$\text{subject to} f\left(X^i_{y^i_t}\right) \geq f\left(X^i_y\right) + \Delta\left(y^i_t, y\right) - \frac{\xi^i}{\mu\left(\frac{|y^i_t|}{|y^i|}\right)}$$

$$\forall i = 1, \ldots, n, \forall t = 1, \ldots, l^i, \forall y \in Y(t). \qquad (3)$$

Since the slack variables $\xi^i \geq 0$, the violated constraint for the objective function shown in Eq. (3) can be rewritten to be the following.

$$0 \leq \xi^i < \mu\left(\frac{|y^i_t|}{|y^i|}\right)\left[f\left(X^i_y\right) - f\left(X^i_{y^i_t}\right) + \Delta\left(y^i_t, y\right)\right] \qquad (4)$$

Based on the hinge loss idea [3], Eq. (4) can be expressed as:

$$\xi^i = \max\left\{0, \mu\left(\frac{|y^i_t|}{|y^i|}\right)\left[f\left(X^i_y\right) - f\left(X^i_{y^i_t}\right) + \Delta\left(y^i_t, y\right)\right]\right\} \qquad (5)$$

By using Eq. (5), Eq. (3) can be rewritten to derive the following equation.

$$\min \frac{1}{2}\|w\|^2 + \frac{C}{n}\sum_{i=1}^{n}\max\left\{0, \mu\left(\frac{|y^i_t|}{|y^i|}\right)\left[f\left(X^i_{y-y^i_t}\right) + \Delta\left(y^i_t, y\right)\right]\right\}. \qquad (6)$$

Finally, change the trade-off coefficient from C in the second term to λ in the first term in Eq. (6), and Eq. (1) is derived. Then, the gradient ∇_t can be derived as shown in Eq. (2).

3   Experimental Results

In this study, three datasets are utilized, including synthetic data, the extended Cohn-Kanade dataset (CK+), and Australian sign language data (ASL) [10]. The ROC curve, the AMOC curve, and the F1-score curve are used to demonstrate detection precision, timeliness, and location ability of the proposed approach, respectively [10].

3.1 Synthetic Data

Following MMED [10], the synthetic dataset is used to check correctness of the proposed approach. One time series contains a target event, two non-target events, and four connecting segments [10]; the total length of one signal sequence is between 160 and 180 numerical values. Some examples of the synthetic data sequence can be found in Fig. 1, in which the green ones are the target events.

In the experiments, one training/testing dataset consists of 100 time series. A total of 100 pairs of training and testing datasets are generated. For each pair, the proposed PMMED and the MMED method [10] are applied, and the testing results are expressed via ROC, AMOC, and F1-score curves.

Some samples of the testing results are given in Fig. 1, in which the target event is shown in green, and the fire frames are marked as red and blue vertical lines for PMMED and MMED, respectively. It can be seen that PMMED detects the target event earlier than MMED.

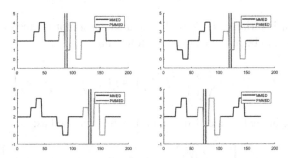

Fig. 1. Samples of testing results of synthetic data. The horizontal axis shows the timing of the time series, and the vertical axis indicates the signal value. (Color figure online)

In Fig. 2, the performance of PMMED and MMED are shown and compared. As shown in Fig. 2(a), all the 200 testing datasets for PMMED and MMED detect the target event with 100% accuracy with the area under ROC curve of 1. In Fig. 2(b), the AMOC curves of the set of the 100 testing datasets for PMMED and MMED are shown by thin red curves and by thin blue ones, respectively; the average AMOC curves are shown by thick ones. It can be found that, for timeliness performance, MMED is a little better than PMMED. The reason may be that the stochastic nature of PMMED selects not-so-good answers sometimes. By using the same illustration style for the F1-score curves in Fig. 2(c), it can be found that PMMED is a little better than MMED on the location ability. The reason may be that required by MMED is the optimal solution, which delays the detection of the event location. However, as shown in Fig. 2, the performance of PMMED and that of MMED are comparable for the synthetic datasets.

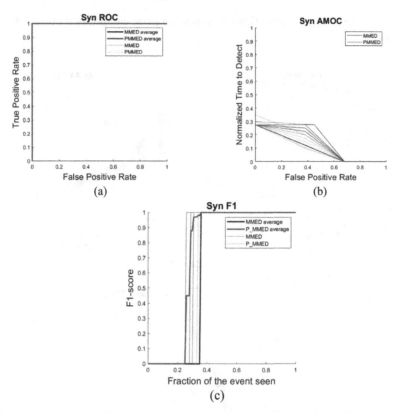

Fig. 2. Performance of synthetic data: (a) ROC curves; (b) AMOC curves; (c) F1-score curves. (Color figure online)

3.2 Extend Cohn-Kanade Dataset

In CK+, there is a total of 327 CAPP facial image sequences from 123 subjects, including 4 kinds of negative emotions and 3 kinds of positive emotions [10]. In the experiments, 100 positive and 100 negative emotion sequences are randomly selected as a training dataset, and the remaining 127 sequences are the testing dataset. The procedure is repeated 100 times to generate 100 pairs of training and testing datasets. Then both PMMED and MMED are applied to all the pairs to get the testing results. Note that the negative emotion is the target.

In Fig. 3, the illustration style is the same as that of Fig. 2, that is, the red curves are for PMMED, the blue ones for MMED, and each thick curve for the average of 100 thin curves. As shown in Fig. 3(a) and Fig. 3(b), the areas occupied by the red curves and the blue ones are almost the same. However, it can be said that the performance of MMED is a little better than that of PMMED if the two average curves in either subfigure are carefully compared. That is, for accuracy and timeliness, the performance of PMMED and MMED are quite comparable on the CK+ dataset. However, as for the F1-score curve shown in Fig. 3(c), the performance of MMED is better than that of PMMED. The reason may be that the strategy of optimal solution finding for MMED is more suitable for event location detection when tackling more complicated events like facial expressions.

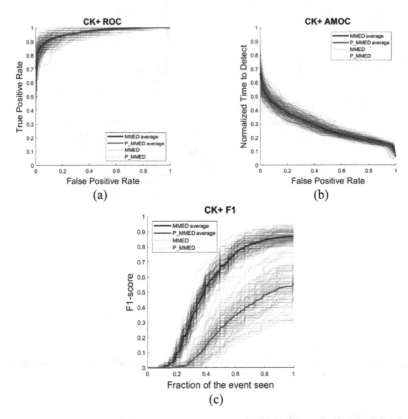

Fig. 3. Performance of CK+ dataset: (a) ROC curves; (b) AMOC curves; (c) F1-score curves.

3.3 Auslan Dataset

The Auslan dataset (ASL) consists of 95 words; for each word, 27 instances can be found, and there are 22 features derived from hands are used to represent an instance [10]. In this study, based on the experimental setting in MMED [10], the target was "I love you", and two sets of 15 randomly chosen words were added before and after the target, respectively. For each word, the first 15 instances were used for training and the remaining 12 ones for testing. The pre-processing of the training/testing data followed that designed in MMED [10].

A total of 100 sentences were generated as the training set, and a total of 200 sentences as the test set. Then PMMED and MMED were applied, and the performance was analyzed. As shown in Fig. 4, all the ROC curve, the AMOC curve, and the F1-score curve indicates that MMED works better than PMMED. Since the stochastic nature of

PMMED is to find a solution based on only one instance chosen randomly, it was natural for MMED to get better results compared with PMMED. However, it is still can be claimed that PMMED and MMED are comparable in terms of accuracy according to Fig. 4(a).

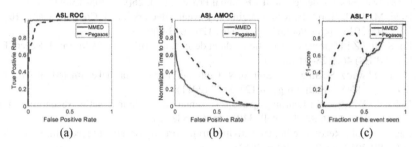

Fig. 4. Performance of ASL dataset: (a) ROC curves; (b) AMOC curves; (c) F1-score curves.

4 Conclusion

In this study, an approach called PMMED has been proposed to achieve early event detection. In order to tackle with huge constraints, the core work of PMMED has been designed to use the strategy of stochastic gradient descent to solve the original quadratic programming problem in MMED [10]. The performance of MMED and PMMED has been compared through the experiments based on three datasets, including synthetic data, CK+, and ASL, and based on the ROC curves, the AMOC curves, and the F1-score curves. According to the experimental results, the performance of PMMED and MMED is quite comparable in terms of accuracy and timeliness, and MMED is better than PMMED in terms of the location ability.

References

1. Shahroudy, A., Ng, T., Gong, Y., Wang, G.: Deep multimodal feature analysis for action recognition in RGB+D videos. IEEE Trans. Pattern Anal. Mach. Intell. **40**(5), 1045–1058 (2018)
2. Tran, D., Yuan, J., Forsyth, D.: Video event detection: from sub-volume localization to spatio-temporal path search. IEEE Trans. Pattern Anal. Mach. Intell. **36**(2), 404–416 (2014)
3. Alpaydin, E.: Introduction to Machine Learning, 4th edn. MIT Press, London (2020)
4. Huang, D., Yao, S., Wang, Y., De La Torre, F.: Sequential max-margin event detectors. In: Fleet, D., Pajdla, T., Schiele, B., Tuytelaars, T. (eds.) ECCV 2014. LNCS, vol. 8691, pp. 410–424. Springer, Cham (2014). https://doi.org/10.1007/978-3-319-10578-9_27
5. Tsochantaridis, I., Joachims, T., Hofmann, T., Altun, Y.: Large margin methods for structured and interdependent output variables. J. Mach. Learn. Res. **6**(2), 1453–1484 (2005)
6. Azorin-López, J., Saval-Calvo, M., Fuster-Guilló, A., Oliver-Albert, A.: A predictive model for recognizing human behaviour based on trajectory representation. In: Proceedings of International Joint Conference on Neural Networks (IJCNN) (2014)

7. Wang, J., Wu, Y.: Learning maximum margin temporal warping for action recognition. In: Proceedings of ICCV 2013, pp. 2688-2695 (2013)

8. Su, L., Sato, Y.: Early facial expression recognition using early RankBoost. In: Proceedings of FG 2013, pp. 1–7 (2013)

9. Xie, L., Zhao, J., Wei, H., Zhang, K., Pang, G.: Online kernel-based structured output SVM for early expression detection. IEEE Signal Process. Lett. **26**(9), 1305–1309 (2019)

10. Hoai, M., De la Torre, F.: Max-margin early event detectors. Int. J. Comput. Vision **107**(2), 191–202 (2013). https://doi.org/10.1007/s11263-013-0683-3

11. Lu, S., Jin, Z.: Improved stochastic gradient descent algorithm for SVM. Int. J. Recent Eng. Sci. (IJRES) **4**(4), 28–31 (2017)

12. Shalev-Shwartz, S., Singer, Y., Srebro, N., Cotter, A.: Pegasos: primal estimated sub-GrAdient SOlver for SVM. Math. Program **127**, 3–30 (2011)

13. Guha, T., Ward, R.K.: Learning sparse representations for human action recognition. IEEE Trans. Pattern Anal. Mach. Intell. **34**(8), 1576–1588 (2012)

14. Cao, Y., et al.: Recognize human activities from partially observed videos. In: Proceedings of CVPR 2013, pp. 2658–2665 (2013)

15. Yang, Z.F., Hung, C.T.: Feedback max-margin early event detector. In: Proceedings of 8th International Conference on Applied System Innovation (ICASI), pp. 115–118 (2022)

16. Yang, Z.F., Lin, Y.C.: Reduction in number of constraints in max-margin early event detectors. Pattern Recogn. **91**, 111–122 (2019)

17. Xu, Z., Yang, Y., Hauptmann, A.G.: A discriminative CNN video representation for event detection. In: Proceedings of CVPR 2015 (2015)

AHP-Based Assessment of Developing Online Virtual Reality Services with Progressive Web Apps

Sheng-Ming Wang[1], Muhammad Ainul Yaqin[2], and Fu-Hsiang Hsu[2(✉)]

[1] Department of Interaction Design, National Taipei University of Technology, 1, Sec. 3, Zhongxiao E. Rd., Taipei 10608, Taiwan
ryan5885@mail.ntut.edu.tw
[2] Doctoral Program in Design, College of Design, National Taipei University of Technology, 1, Sec. 3, Zhongxiao E. Rd., Taipei 10608, Taiwan
{t110859402,t110859008}@ntut.edu.tw

Abstract. The study uses Progressive Web Apps (PWAs) technologies to construct online virtual reality services and utilizes the Analytic Hierarchical Analysis method to evaluate the design and system implementation results. With the development of the metaverse concept, the design and application of online virtual reality services are required. By conducting literature research, semi-structured interviews, and technical application analysis, this study first defines the requirements and framework for developing a prototype virtual reality system with PWAs technologies, following the quality function development analysis and developing the prototype system accordingly. A questionnaire on the prototype system's integration, usability, and cross-platform technology development was then used to evaluate proposed design elements from digital content planning, design, and front-end and back-end engineering experts. Study findings revealed that cross-platform compatibility was a key feature when integrating PWAs with online virtual reality design, especially among experts from all fields. The results of this study can provide a reference for the development of online virtual reality immersive experiences with PWAs in the future. Further research can focus on collecting and analyzing digital footprints generated by users in progressive web technologies and improving the link between user experience and content in the future.

Keywords: Progressive web apps · Web-based virtual reality · Analytic hierarchy process · Quality function deployment · Cross-platform technology development

1 Introduction

This research uses the integrated application of Progressive Web Apps (PWA) and Web-based Virtual Reality (WebVR) technology to provide installable, offline browsing, real-time update, and many other functions. Besides, we are also pursuing the optimization

© The Author(s), under exclusive license to Springer Nature Singapore Pte Ltd. 2022
S.-Y. Hsieh et al. (Eds.): ICS 2022, CCIS 1723, pp. 553–566, 2022.
https://doi.org/10.1007/978-981-19-9582-8_49

of the actual performance and deploying the advantages of WebVR in cross-platform and public sharing to strengthen the current data in navigation service, model framework development of the prototype system. We can be implied to the development and usability purposes. In following the continuous technical evaluation and optimization, we put forward the input indicators and suggestions that meet the needs of end users, as well as future development and design.

Combining the progressive web technology and technical core of WebVR through the integrated application and evaluation function, we can find out the critical elements of development and evaluate the actual development and application. This project first organizes relevant literature to identify critical factors and uses the Analytic Hierarchy Process (AHP) method through pilot interviews and functional analysis. Front-line developers and designers have conducted qualitative questionnaire studies to determine the possible vital factors. This research then proceeds on the importance of the appropriate prototype level, analyzes the performance of the relevant prototypes, and summarizes the results to provide the navigation experience, reference indicators, and suggestions for developers in future system development and design.

In summary, the objectives of this study include the following:

- Propose the development of progressive technology with WebVR, and guide to the prototype to optimize the online experience in the integrating concept.
- Propose primary interface of rendering detection, advanced usage performance model detection, and scoring methods for the in-detailed goals and progressive technical support.
- Put forward suggestions on developing and constructing WebVR by applying progressive technology.

2   Literature Review

This research focuses on evaluating the application of progressive technologies to develop WebVR by investigating "Web front-end components," "WebVR development," "Progressive web technologies," and "Information navigation trend analysis." We disclose related literature, technological trends, and developments to accommodate concrete preliminary evidence.

2.1   Web Front-End Components

The era of multi-screen and cross-platform generates interactive experiences for users on various platforms, including smartphones, tablets, and computers providing multiple user experiences. Nevertheless, the user experience design comes from different devices and needs to support users' demands and satisfaction [1]. The capability of web elements yet also grown and improved in supporting numerous tasks implemented, such as a workable offline system, on-load stability in inadequate connections, and mimicking the performance of the native application in some features [2]. On the other hand, the development of the front-end website no longer relies on static pages. The web system is now extended to the dependency's integration of third-party libraries, automated testing, and packaging and compression code. The conventional front-end development process no longer requires these complex requirements, yet it is now moving to automatic construction. Automatic construction is an automated compilation, merging, refresh, deployment, and synchronization process of the front-end development [3]. It reduces highly repetitive tasks and effectively improves development efficiency. Moreover, a comprehensive treatment on integrating web front-end components in the WebView visualization can leverage lower energy usage evidence [4].

2.2 WebVR Development

Along with the popularization of communication network and mobile devices, "mobility" has become the primary applications of consumers. Based on the vigorous development of WebGL, virtual reality can no longer be operated through a single machine. Still, it is accessible through the WebGL drawing protocol in the web browser. In 2014, developers Mozilla and Google launched the JavaScript API for web virtual reality, which is not limited to a smartphone experience of virtual reality. The new development method of virtual reality devices also provides more advantages, from virtual reality devices such as HTC Vive, Oculus Rift, etc., to smartphone browsers. Numerous WebVR concepts have been explored which try to demonstrate the capability of Web-based systems to enable the enhancement experience of a simulated reality environment. Gunkel (2021) applied the social VR Web-based system with aims to develop, examine, and evaluate the photorealistic experience, yet evidence that the usability of WebVR is acceptable and equally suitable for modern systems [5]. The WebVR advantages allow users to strengthen interactive navigation without requiring them to download additional applications to enhance users' willingness to explore VR. The implication of WebVR has been revealed the interactivity enhancement and motivation [6]. Nevertheless, WebVR performs well in accommodating user support towards comprehensive tasks by adopting interactive and innovative visualization [7].

2.3 Progressive Web Technologies

Progressive web technologies is a webpage built of HTML, CSS, and JavaScript, along with its core technologies, service worker, manifest, application shell, and HTTPS, to provide a progressively enhanced experience awaken of the native and hybrid applications [8, 9]. Current browsers such as Chrome, Firefox, Safari, and Edge can deliver access and optimize mobile-based websites [10]. PWA offers some benefits, such as the ability of the engines to write the command once and then execute it everywhere [11]. Besides, with no internet speed and stability limitation, PWA can leverage its competence in multiplatform access, quick system update, and latest version integration with a more identifiable interface APP under a web-based system [12]. The easy integration of PWA makes the usability of this technology reachable in numerous applications. Shah (2021) performed the notion of combining 3D interactive gaming with the immersive image to accommodate virtual tours for campus visitors, consolidating the PWA; this project has successfully demonstrated better compare results from the regular apps in both hybrid and native systems [13].

2.4 Information Navigation Trend Analysis

The pandemic's impact has accelerated the digitization of information and online virtual tours, gradually moving towards a better in-depth experience. Digital tours today have proven to take advantage of digital technology assistance. The digital information guide breaks the limitations of the traditional guide in terms of region, space, and time and provides the viewer with an online viewing experience at any time. In terms of display and educational functions, digital exhibitions can effectively extend the life cycle of guided tours, utilize sustainable resources, and provide more diverse viewing methods and interactive content (Hong & Shiang, 2020).

Based on the case study analysis, we acknowledged that shifting virtual reality to the webpage mode will interrupt the experience in some browsers. Due to the platform's advantages and interactive navigation, the problem of page switching is optimized by adopting a single-page webpage solution. By means of partial static caching, it solves the performance problems of web virtual reality and improves website functions, which serve as the technical basis for subsequent application service planning.

The rapid development of online information navigation and mobile devices impacts the rapid growth of the economy. The traditional navigation mode has been unable to meet the users' need. Users are beginning to seek a completely online service experience. The integrated application of technology enables end-users to experience an undifferentiated and consistent online information navigation experience anytime, anywhere, and in any situation. Moreover, the cross-platform demonstration work by Lian (2022) has insight into the usage of a cross-platform-based system which can accommodate almost similar performance accuracy compared to the conventional system framework [15]. This concept brings extended more complete cross-platform services to the navigation experience.

3 System Design and Evaluation Methodology

This research focuses on the PWA development of WebVR services, defines the development model framework of the overall system prototype, and evaluates the development of online information navigation services through the integrated application and evaluation function of the application.

This research provides a developer-oriented analysis. Through developer interviews with AT-ONE analysis and characterization scenario simulation, we find the intensive contact points and basic needs among developers and end-users. We then conducted the development process and filtered out the specifications of the prototype system in functional aspects. The following process showed a semi-structured expert interview and AHP expert questionnaires for the feasibility analysis. The overall research process planning is as follows (Fig. 1).

Through the semi-structured interview, we unveiled the conventional development and application process. We divided our process into four stages: planning stage, design stage, front-end, back-end development stage, and testing stage. The development goals and the modular inventory of existing technologies lead to the divergence of development goals and repeated execution. Therefore, through AT-ONE analysis and situational simulation of persona, this research finds the three most intensive and most frequently

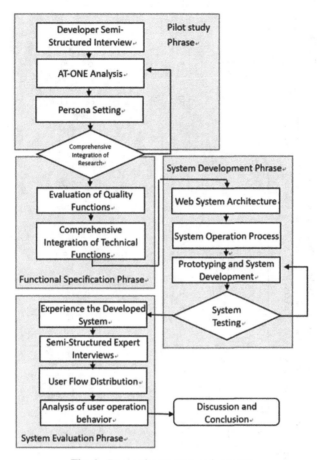

Fig. 1. Research structure and process

interacted touch-points in technology development, as well as the three goals of service usage, immersive service, and cross-platform service.

According to the architecture description, three significant demand aspects of service, functional and technical, are summarized in the overall development process. The domain demand can be divided into three domains: digital content planning, design, and front-end and back-end engineering. This research takes the three major demand-oriented as the basic framework, matches the three major areas as the distinction of technical nature, and finally subdivides the demand and technical aspects by evaluating the quality function, as shown in Table 1.

Table 1. Quality functions deployment analysis

Service requirement	Function requirement											Overall score	Requirement ordering
	Planning-oriented			Design-oriented			Development-oriented						
	Web navigation architecture	Operation guide process optimization	Guided topic positioning	Interface usability	Front-end interactive elements	Web VR	Pre-loading cache process	Cross-platform installation	Site security	User behavior record			
Usability service													
System cross-platform compatibility	1	3		3	3	3	9	9	1			32	1
Lightweight system capacity					1		9	3				13	7
Smooth use process	9	9		9			3					30	3
Immersive service													
Immersive online information tour experience	3	3	3	3	3	9	3	3	1			31	2
Guided image experience			9	3	9	3				1		25	5
Instant installation and uninterrupted experience				3		1	9	9	3			25	5

(continued)

Table 1. (continued)

Service requirement		Function requirement										Overall score	Requirement ordering
		Planning-oriented			Design-oriented			Development-oriented					
		Web navigation architecture	Operation guide process optimization	Guided topic positioning	Interface usability	Front-end interactive elements	Web VR	Pre-loading cache process	Cross-platform installation	Site security	User behavior record		
Cross-platform service	Personal information security						1	1	1	9	1	13	7
	Site tracking									3	9	12	9
	System scalability	3	1		9	3	9				3	28	4
Overall score		16	16	12	30	19	26	34	25	17	14		
Ranking		7	7	10	2	5	3	1	4	6	9		

*9 for Strong Relationship, 3 for Moderate Relationship, 1 for Weak Relationship.

This study uses AHP as the basis for the expert questionnaire design. By calculating the weights of each element factor concerned by the issues of each specialized field, we can understand the problems faced by experts in different fields in practice.

According to the above research method description, firstly, we conduct semi-structured interviews with developers on exploratory issues and conduct a detailed understanding and contextual deconstruction analysis of how developers and end-users import PWA WebVR services. To summarize the results of the comprehensive exploration and problem stage, this research established persona, problem integration, and transformed the problem points in the simulated situation into service requirements. The quality function is the following step to expand the evaluation method in the technical fishbone diagram analysis application, integrate the above service planning, and list the design requirements and technical applications. Besides, we sorted out the overall detailed functional specifications and drew information architecture of system development. Afterward, an AHP expert questionnaire was created to measure the implementation. The final process analyzes and evaluates the overall technical function and end-user behavior.

4 System Integration Design and Development

4.1 Development Lead Analysis

The integrated service system proposed in this study conforms to the cross-platform device application in the terminal vehicle interface. The five levels in the research are visualized as the elements of user experience: user-centered design for the Web and beyond are the main concepts in the development and design. The framework by Garet (2011) is the strategic level for collecting data requirements, the scope level, the structure level, the framework level for implementing the interface and information design, and the presentation level for visual design [16]. Planning analysis and system development are carried out on the contact points of story, the consistency and integrity of online channel service functions are considered. Thus, a system model for innovative experience is proposed.

In formulating the functional architecture, the primary service orientation is drawn regarding the overall operation experience and cross-platform maintenance services. The development process and the practical orientation of the operation requirements are formulated according to the service requirements. This research is trying to obtain the critical areas required for the development needs. The technical aspects of the overall development project include the development process, technical management, interface design, use analysis of system performance, and application requirements. At the strategy level, we defined six target services: functional operation intuition, flow and use, process flow, brand feature experience, real-world preview experience, cross-platform tour, and personal data security.

4.2 System Design and Development Process

In the website system architecture, this research focuses on progressive technology to develop the virtual reality of the webpage. The PWA application technology is the webpage constructed by HTML, CSS, and JavaScript. Its core technologies, Service Worker, Manifest, Application Shell, and HTTPS, provide users with Progressively Enhanced Experiences [17].

Continue to achieve cached data through a service worker. Users can experience virtual experience in offline mode. Through Manifest and Application Shell, settings, and web elements provided, this system can be reliable and instantly process similar experiences to the native app. The WebVR file is accessible on the cloud host, reducing construction and maintenance costs. It is easier for users to experience virtual reality through the search ability of the webpage through a website search. PWA technology will capture some data during the application process. Therefore, all data must have secure HTTPS to ensure website security and user data security. In such an environment, cross-platform web-based services can be provided.

The overall operation stage is mainly distinguished into three major parts: the three major stages of the early essential guidance, the content-guided tour of the mid-term, and entering the VR depth guide. Through the three stages mentioned above interaction, the gradual guidance allows terminal users a profound experience. According to the following operating flowchart, the user can clearly emphasize the initial guidance of critical localization and visual surface through content assistance and mid-term content guidance in this development. The entire station is developed by gradual web technology, as well as at any page of the virtual reality experience, to ensure the stability of the terminal user on the system and experience integrity.

5 System Development and Evaluation

5.1 Web Operation Interface

This research implemented the system on the web-based operation. The user's interface demonstrates guidance for the information entrance as a pre-travel awareness and preliminary information overview, then proceeds to an in-depth VR navigation experience. According to the pre-travel interview and quality function deployment results, the functions of PWA application technology for WebVR services are integrated with a multi-service page system platform developed. Hence, end-users are able to explore the system and operate it efficiently.

On the WebVR interface, this research takes a case study location in Taipei Dadaocheng. On the navigation screen, the user can visualize the location set from the Taipei Dadaocheng as an implemented service platform. The main navigation page provides the choice of scene theme for the user to explore (as shown in Fig. 2). This prototype provides three auxiliary functions: VR and panoramic screen activation, manual field view adjustment, visual screen size, and scene switching. Afterward (as shown in Fig. 3), the user can adjust and optimize the tour experience according to different VR equipment and personal focal length.

Fig. 2. Web VR user interface for information navigation

The overall panoramic theme and VR navigation enhance the user's in-depth navigation experience. The interface is designed to provide directional guidance and information related to key buildings and cultural monuments. The s supplementary functions in the function bar are applied to maintain the scalability of future additions during the design process. A crosshair gaze and point-to-point depth of scene movement are used to improve the overall smoothness of the operation. Regarding auxiliary optimization, the modes provided in the library software allow modularizing the picture correction according to the various VR devices' adjustment and individual focal lengths.

Fig. 3. Web VR interface with cardboard browsing and interaction

5.2 AHP Questionnaire Analysis

Integration and development: According to the majors involved in the project, the objective choice of the questionnaire survey targeted the professional experts in the field as participants. Thus, the topic and area of the participants were set into three major professional fields: digital content planning, design-related, and front-end engineering.

This process analyzed each criterion's weight and order through hierarchical analysis methods. The questionnaire's outcomes, description function, and blurred zone were measured to understand the problematic points during the process. We, therefore, proceed with the questionnaire description and hierarchical project design and complete the key elements in various fields to fulfill the requirement of conducting AHP evaluation methods, as shown in Table 2.

Table 2. The AHP analysis results

First level			Second level			
Facet elements	Relative weights	*Sorting	Evaluate factor	Relative weights	Absolute weight	*Sorting
A. System Integrity	0.55: 0.44: 0.49	1: 1: 1	A-1. Cross-Platform Compatibility	0.55: 0.60: 0.71	0.302: 0.264: 0.347	1:1:1
			A-2. PWA Application	0.22: 0.19: 0.12	0.121: 0.083: 0.058	3:7:8
			A-3. WebVR Integration	0.23: 0.21: 0.17	0.126: 0.092: 0.083	2:4:4
B. System Utility	0.23: 0.36: 0.33	2: 2: 2	B-1. WebApp Installation	0.42: 0.61: 0.48	0.096: 0.219: 0.158	5:2:2
			B-2. System Maintenance and Update	0.37: 0.25: 0.31	0.085: 0.090: 0.102	6:6:3
			B-3. Information Immersion Guide	0.21: 0.14: 0.21	0.048: 0.050: 0.069	8:8:6
C. Cross-Platform Development	0.22: 0.20: 0.17	3: 3: 3	C-1. Offline Operation	0.28: 0.46: 0.44	0.064: 0.092: 0.074	7:4:5
			C-2. Content Update and Expansion	0.51: 0.32: 0.36	0.117: 0.102: 0.061	4:3:7
			C-3. User Behavior Analysis	0.20: 0.22: 0.21	0.046: 0.44: 0.035	9:9:9

* Digital Content Planning Field: Design Field: Front-End and Back-End Field.

The analysis of the domain mentioned above shows that the comparison of absolute weights might be different due to different foremost domains, which led to different results. However, in comparing the three domains at each level, the analysis results prove that "system integration" is the key development orientation at the main level. In addition, "WebVR integration application" and "WebApp installation" are highly recognized in two significant domains, respectively. Still, the results show "cross-platform compatibility" as the core consideration in system integration, then the corresponding weight allocation in "WebVR integration application" and "WebApp installation" can be adjusted according to each domain. The "operation behavior analysis" is prosecutable to be a value-added item when the resources and human resources are sufficient.

6 Discussion and Conclusion

This study uses an immersive WebVR technology visual page platform to achieve multi-platform integration. An offline application through PWA is also provided as a contactless and spatially unrestricted experience. This study focuses on integrating online information navigation with design thinking integration of front-end development. Through the advantages of progressive web technologies and cross-platform, WebVR navigation achieves an active immersive experience in a contactless mode. This research summarized the result and suggestions as the following items:

1. Technical integration and development: This study is mainly based on developing the front-end framework and digital navigation operations. Future work is considering the continuous development of the back-end system and database development so that developers can explore more information and build more flexible operations by establishing a comprehensive back-end management module.
2. The completeness of data collection using Web operations: This study used click events as trigger records to collect data. Therefore, usage data needs to be captured through explicit events, and the details of WebVR usage cannot be thoroughly analyzed. It is suggested that devices such as eye trackers can be used to analyze and enhance the browsing experience of user actions and emotional details in the future.
3. Ease of use of interface design: The evaluation and priorities of the functional and process aspects. It can be deeply integrated and adopted for the continuous process. It is suggested that researchers can further propose design studies on the functional aspects of the user experience towards the scenario context, including the study of motion navigation, emotional interactions, and business model development.
4. The extension of PWA: This technology has been widely supported by browsers in recent years and is actively being developed. This study conducted several functional integration applications and technical evaluations through the advantages of PWA. We suggest further deepening on using each feature, operation application context, and other related service applications to utilize the technical functionality. Thus, this technology can be more closely related to the regular application yet formulate relevant standardized development criteria through evaluating terminal services.
5. Completeness of the business model: This study examines the in-person digital tour's service process and spatial experience. The benefits and impacts can be explored in depth. In the actual implementation, the business model canvas can be employed for analysis and planning so that the design can attain a closer real environment.

Acknowledgement. The authors would like to offer our special thanks to Mr. Bing-Han Yang for supporting the prototype development. We also thank the funding support by the Taiwan National Science and Technology Council (108-2410-H-027-013-MY2).

References

1. Nagel, W.: Four screens. In: Nagel, W. (ed.) Multiscreen UX Design, pp. 11–37. Morgan Kaufmann, Boston (2016). https://doi.org/10.1016/B978-0-12-802729-5.00002-4
2. Leshchuk, S.O., Ramskyi, Y.S., Kotyk, A.V., Kutsiy, S.V.: Design a progressive web application to support student learning, December 2021. http://dspace.tnpu.edu.ua/handle/123456789/25173. Accessed 10 Nov 2022
3. Zhang, N., Cao, Y., Zhang, S.: Research of web front-end engineering solution in public cultural service project. In: 2017 IEEE/ACIS 16th International Conference on Computer and Information Science (ICIS), pp. 623–626, May 2017. https://doi.org/10.1109/ICIS.2017.7960067
4. Huber, S., Demetz, L., Felderer, M.: PWA vs the others: a comparative study on the UI energy-efficiency of progressive web apps. In: Brambilla, M., Chbeir, R., Frasincar, F., Manolescu, I. (eds.) ICWE 2021. LNCS, vol. 12706, pp. 464–479. Springer, Cham (2021). https://doi.org/10.1007/978-3-030-74296-6_35
5. Gunkel, S.N.B., et al.: VRComm: an end-to-end web system for real-time photorealistic social VR communication. In: Proceedings of the 12th ACM Multimedia Systems Conference, New York, NY, USA, pp. 65–79, July 2021. https://doi.org/10.1145/3458305.3459595
6. Glasserman-Morales, L.D., Ruiz-Ramírez, J.A., Estrada, F.J.R.: Transforming higher education using WebVR: a case study. IEEE Revista Iberoamericana de Tecnologias del Aprendizaje **17**(3), 230–234 (2022). https://doi.org/10.1109/RITA.2022.3191257
7. Seiler, R., Widmer, D.: Extended reality in the world wide web: investigating and testing the use cases of WebVR manuals. Presented at the 55th Hawaii International Conference on System Sciences (HICSS), virtual, 3–7 January 2022, pp. 5264–5272 (2022)
8. Behl, K., Raj, G.: Architectural pattern of progressive web and background synchronization. In: 2018 International Conference on Advances in Computing and Communication Engineering (ICACCE), pp. 366–371, June 2018. https://doi.org/10.1109/ICACCE.2018.8441701
9. Roumeliotis, K.I., Tselikas, N.D.: Evaluating progressive web app accessibility for people with disabilities. Network **2**(2), 350–369 (2022). https://doi.org/10.3390/network2020022
10. Malavolta, I., Procaccianti, G., Noorland, P., Vukmirovic, P.: Assessing the impact of service workers on the energy efficiency of progressive web apps. In: 2017 IEEE/ACM 4th International Conference on Mobile Software Engineering and Systems (MOBILESoft), pp. 35–45, May 2017. https://doi.org/10.1109/MOBILESoft.2017.7
11. Frankston, B.: Progressive web apps [bits versus electrons]. IEEE Consum. Electron. Mag. **7**(2), 106–117 (2018). https://doi.org/10.1109/MCE.2017.2776463
12. Gómez-Sierra, C.J.: Design and development of a PWA - progressive web application, to consult the diary and programming of a technological event. IOP Conf. Ser. Mater. Sci. Eng. **1154**(1), 012047 (2021). https://doi.org/10.1088/1757-899X/1154/1/012047
13. Shah, H., Tupe, V., Rathod, A., Shaikh, S., Uke, N.: A progressive web app for virtual campus tour. In: 2021 International Conference on Computing, Communication and Green Engineering (CCGE), pp. 1–5, September 2021. https://doi.org/10.1109/CCGE50943.2021.9776419
14. Hong, H.-Y., Shiang, L.-R.: "Drawing nature: Taiwan as portrayed in natural history illustrations" special exhibition educational activities. Taiwan Nat. Sci. **39**(3), 92–97 (2020)

15. Lian, Z., Yang, Q., Zeng, Q., Su, C.: WebFed: cross-platform federated learning framework based on web browser with local differential privacy. In: ICC 2022 - IEEE International Conference on Communications, pp. 2071–2076, May 2022. https://doi.org/10.1109/ICC45855.2022.9838421
16. Garrett, J.J.: The Elements of User Experience: User-Centered Design for the Web and Beyond. Pearson Education, London (2010)
17. Gambhir, A., Raj, G.: Analysis of cache in service worker and performance scoring of progressive web application. In: 2018 International Conference on Advances in Computing and Communication Engineering (ICACCE), pp. 294–299, June 2018. https://doi.org/10.1109/ICACCE.2018.8441715

From Data of Internet of Things to Domain Knowledge: A Case Study of Exploration in Smart Agriculture

Mei-Yu Wu[1] and Chih-Kun Ke[2(✉)]

[1] Department of Business Management, National Taichung University of Science and Technology, No. 129, Section 3, Sanmin Road, North District, Taichung 404, Taiwan, R.O.C.
mywu@nutc.edu.tw
[2] Department of Information Management, National Taichung University of Science and Technology, No. 129, Section 3, Sanmin Road, North District, Taichung 404, Taiwan, R.O.C.
ckk@nutc.edu.tw

Abstract. Data collected from the Internet of Things (IoT) covers a variety of dimensions indicating some features of a specific monitoring eco-environment. The feature correlation may not easy to identify due to the metadata eliminated between discrete dimensions of IoT data. How to transform discrete IoT data into its domain knowledge becomes an interesting research topic. This paper proposes a novel methodology to formalize the IoT data to the domain knowledge. Through exploring a real smart agriculture case, we understand the deployment of an IoT system in a tea eco-environment. The correlation matrix is produced to present the relationships between IoT sensor data. Principal component analysis reduces the volume of data dimensions. A semantic network is constructed to deploy the associations of discrete IoT data. Multi-criteria decision analysis is used to get recommended domain knowledge from the semantic network. The contribution of this paper is to propose a novel methodology to transform discrete IoT data into its domain knowledge.

Keywords: Internet of Things · Correlation matrix · Semantic network · Multi-criteria decision analysis · Smart agriculture

1 Introduction

Data collected from the Internet of Things (IoT) covers a variety of dimensions indicating some features of a specific monitoring eco-environment [1, 2]. For example, smart agriculture [3–5] may collect feature data from an IoT monitoring system, including atmospheric pressure, carbon dioxide, air temperature and humidity, soil temperature and humidity, ultraviolet rays, pH value, electrical conductivity value (EC), infrared rays and sunlight illuminance, etc. The correlation of feature data may not easy to identify due to the discrete IoT sensors. How to transform discrete IoT data into its domain knowledge becomes a challenge.

© The Author(s), under exclusive license to Springer Nature Singapore Pte Ltd. 2022
S.-Y. Hsieh et al. (Eds.): ICS 2022, CCIS 1723, pp. 567–576, 2022.
https://doi.org/10.1007/978-981-19-9582-8_50

In this study, we set up an IoT monitoring system in the experimental tea plantation [6]. The IoT monitoring system receives various tea environmental feature data from the sensors. Besides, it is connected to a camera to check the current status of the tea farm in real time. Via an Internet VPN router, the system sends back feature data to the database for analysis. Through exploring the real smart agriculture case, we understand the sensor deployment framework of an IoT system in a tea eco-environment. While parsing the collected data, the independence of a single data dimension provides a good understanding for the user. However, when we evaluate multiple dimensions of feature data comprehensively, the absence of dimensions' key association metadata leads to disasters in data analysis. It has no clues to organize different dimensions of feature data. We have to infer feature data associations from the IoT system framework and sensors' properties by ourselves. It makes the data analysis process more difficult.

To improve the above problems, this paper proposes a novel methodology to formalize the IoT data to the domain knowledge. We produce a correlation matrix that presents the associations between feature data collected from IoT sensors. Based on the correlation matrix, the principal component analysis is used to reduce the volume of data dimensions. Then a semantic network is constructed to deploy the associations after principal component analysis. A semantic network is a graphical representation of knowledge [7]. It considers that human knowledge has a hierarchical representation. It is a descriptive model that uses network structure to represent the structure of knowledge, which can be used to explore human associative memory. The actual implementation of a semantic network can build a semantic network via knowledge ontology based on lexical correlation and develop a processing mode similar to human language processing. In this work, we use the semantic network to retain the domain knowledge from a smart IoT monitoring system in a specific eco-environment, e.g., knowledge of tea plants.

The semantic network provides clues for a user making a decision. However, the solution may not be the only one. If there are multiple alternatives are provided, the user needs to evaluate the alternatives. Multi-criteria decision analysis (MCDA) is an analysis method that selects a solution from multiple alternatives [8]. A prioritization of alternatives is generated to assist in the evaluation and selection of an ideal solution that more closely approximates the needs of the decision maker [9]. In multi-criteria decision analysis, multi-attribute decision-making is to consider multiple attributes (criteria) to evaluate alternative solutions, and decide the most suitable solution according to the order of evaluation [10]. The analytic hierarchy process method (AHP) is one of the MCDA evaluation methods that measures through pairwise attribute comparison and relies on expert judgment to deduce the priority of candidate attributes [11–13]. It is mainly used in decision-making problems such as determining priorities, choosing the best solution, predicting results and risk assessment, measuring performance, and optimizing. Each dimension of IoT feature data can be conder as an attribute. Multi-criteria decision analysis is useful to process IoT feature data comprehensively. Our purpose is to transform discrete IoT data into its domain knowledge. We hope to recommend domain knowledge from the semantic network by MCDA. To sum up, the main contributions of this paper are as follows.

- This work preprocesses huge of IoT data from a smart agriculture case to explore an IoT monitoring system deployment in a specific eco-environment and identify the features in IoT data.
- A novel methodology is proposed to transform discrete IoT data into its domain knowledge, including correlation matrix, principal component analysis, and multi-criteria decision analysis techniques.
- A semantic network is constructed to recommend the domain knowledge. The semantic network helps users retain the domain knowledge from a smart IoT monitoring system in a specific eco-environment, e.g., knowledge of tea plants.

The remainder of this paper is organized as follows: Sect. 2 introduces the proposed methodology to transform discrete IoT data into its domain knowledge. Section 3 discusses a smart agriculture case to carry out the proposed methodology. Finally, Sect. 4 presents our conclusions.

2 Methodology

To improve the multi-dimension data preprocessing, feature association discovery in IoT data, and knowledge selection problems mentioned above, this paper proposes a novel methodology to formalize the IoT data to the domain knowledge, the system framework [6] as shown in Fig. 1. This section illustrates a novel methodology, including a correlation matrix, principal component analysis, and multi-criteria decision analysis techniques.

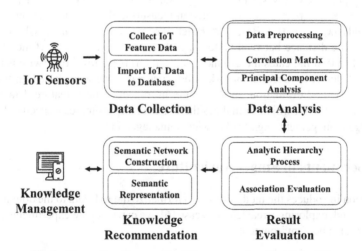

Fig. 1. The system framework of the proposed methodology [6].

In the data collection task, the system collects the IoT feature data through the IoT sensors and sends it back to the database for storage. The data analysis task uses data mining technology to pre-process IoT feature data, including cleaning, integration, and transformation. A utility-based reputation model [14, 15] is used to formalize the features of a IoT monitoring system. Let $S = \{s_1, s, \ldots, s_n\}$ denote the set of sensors, and $s \in S$. Each sensor has associated features of interest, denoted by set FI, which fi are interested in monitoring, and $fi \in FI$. Let $ev_{s,fi}$ denote the expectation of sensor s on feature fi. Let $U\left(ev_{s,fi}\right)$ denote the utility obtained by sensor s on feature fi by obtaining the actual value $ev_{s,fi}$. Function $E : S \times FI \times U \to R$ denotes the expected utility of sensor s for the feature fi that it monitors, where R denotes real numbers. Each expected value ev of specific interest feature fi of a sensor is used to build a comparative utility vertex s_i. Utilities are normalized and scaled to $[0, 1]$. Once the sensor formalization is complete and a relational utility model is applied, the sensor will obtain the expected value of the feature of interest. We evaluate some threshold by comparing with the expected value of the feature of interest to remove some features. Therefore, the utility-based reputation model and principal component analysis method are used to reduce the number of features (data dimensions). Then we calculate the correlation of remaining features through the Pearson correlation coefficient ρ, as shown in Eq. (1).

$$\rho = \frac{\sum_{i=1}^{n}(x_i - \mu_x)(y_i - \mu_y)}{\sqrt{\sum_{i=1}^{n}(x_i - \mu_x)^2 \sum_{i=1}^{n}(y_i - \mu_y)^2}} \tag{1}$$

The result evaluation task is based on the analytic hierarchy process of multi-criteria decision analysis. The CorrelationGain method [16] is designed to get the correlation value from features inferring feature associations to build a semantic network. The CorrelationGain method constructs a connected weight graph $G = (V, E)$ where V means the vertex (IoT feature) and E means the edge (feature association) of the connected weight graph. $\exists$ a vertex set $\{x_1, .., x_n\} \in G$, $n \in N$. If $\nexists \overline{x_i, x_j} \in E$, define that $d(x_i, x_j) = \infty$ where $d(x_i, x_j)$ is a function measuring the distance between vertex x_i and x_j, and $d(x_i, x_i) = 0$. If $\exists \overline{x_i, x_j} \in E$, let $d(x_i, x_j) = \rho$ where $d(x_i, x_j)$ is a function measuring the distance between vertex x_i and x_j, and $d(x_i, x_i) = \rho$. If the value of ρ is larger than 0, it indicates the distance (correlation) is positive, otherwise is negative. The knowledge recommendation task builds a semantic network based on the CorrelationGain method evaluation. In the future, users can identify feature data based on the semantic network which formalizes the IoT data and promotes a specific domain of knowledge management, e.g., tea knowledge management.

3 Experiments in Smart Agriculture

This section introduces the methodology to formalize the IoT data to the domain knowledge. Through exploring a real tea farm case [6], we carry out the experiments of an IoT system in a tea eco-environment.

3.1 Feature Data and Experiment Results

The time interval of the tea feature data collected in the IoT monitoring system [6] is from 2020/05/01 to 2021/10/31. The sampling unit time is per minute. The 15 feature data items are collected through the IoT sensors including atmospheric pressure, carbon dioxide, air temperature, humidity, soil temperature, soil moisture, ultraviolet rays, soil temperature, soil humidity, pH value, EC value, infrared rays, illuminance, spore germination rate and bug eggs of hatching rate, as shown in Fig. 2. The values of spore germination rate (20.13) and bug eggs of hatching rate (47.68) are evaluated as the abnormal status so the tea domain expert uses system strikethrough marking them.

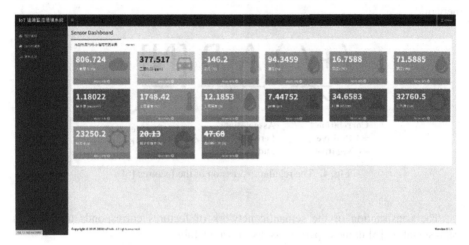

Fig. 2. The IoT monitoring system in smart agriculture [6]

After enforcing the utility-based reputation model [14, 15] and the principal component analysis, we remove 8 features from 15 features and retain 7 features for later experiments, including "air temperature," "humidity," "soil temperature," "soil humidity," "soil temperature," "soil humidity," "pH value," "EC value," and "illuminance." The correlation matrix [6] is produced by Pearson correlation coefficient calculation, as shown in Fig. 3.

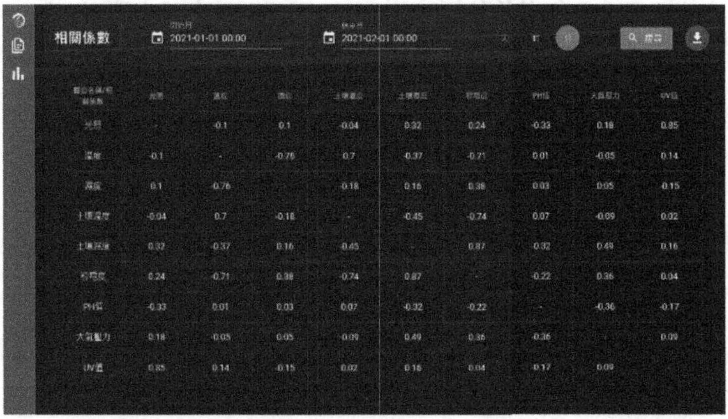

Fig. 3. The correlation matrix produced from the Pearson correlation coefficient calculation [6]

We define a regular expression to analyze the correlation between features, as shown in Fig. 4. If the value of Pearson correlation coefficient ρ is larger than 0, the Correlation-Gain method indicates the correlation between features is positive, otherwise is negative. Besides, the frequency of correlation occurrence is used to define the importance of the feature associations. Various features were analyzed and used to construct a semantic network.

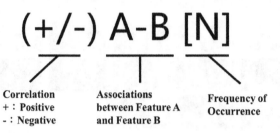

Fig. 4. The regular expression of the features [6]

The construction of the semantic network of features corresponds to the alias representation [6] in the experiments, as shown in Table 1.

Table 1. Corresponding alias for each feature [6]

Illuminance	Air temperature	Air humidity	Soil temperature	Soil humidity	Electrical conductivity	pH
l	t	h	st	sh	ec	ph

Next, we used the analytic hierarchy process method (AHP) of multi-criteria decision-making analysis (MCDA) to show the features based on the tree structure of the hierarchical analysis, as shown in Fig. 5.

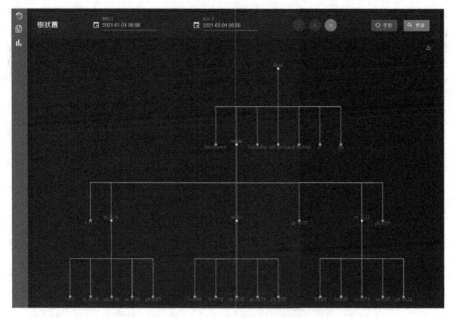

Fig. 5. Tree structure presentation of features based on hierarchical analysis [6]

According to the threshold value (importance), we observe the frequency of correlation occurrence and determine the semantic presentation order (weight) of associations for features, as shown in Table 2.

Table 2. Feature associations via threshold examination [6]

Threshold	Feature associations
0.9	(+)sh-ec[4], (+)st-ph[1], (−)sh-ph[1]
0.8	(+)sh-ec[10], (−)t-h[9], (+)t-st[1], (−)sh-ph[1], (+)l-t[1], (+)st-ph[1]
0.7	(−)t-h[12], (+)sh-ec[11], (+)t-st[5], (+)l-t[3], (−)l-h[2], (−)st-ec[2], (−)sh-ph[1], (−)t-ec[1], (+)st-ph[1], (+)st-sh[1], (+)sh-ph[1]
0.6	(−)t-h[13], (+)sh-ec[11], (+)t-st[5], (−)l-h[5], (+)l-t[5], (−)st-ec[2], (−)sh-ph[2], (−)t-ec[1], (+)st-ph[1], (+)st-sh[1], (+)sh-ph[1]
0.5	(−)t-h[14], (+)sh-ec[11], (+)t-st[8], (+)l-t[7], (−)l-h[6], (−)sh-ph[2], (−)t-ec[2], (−)st-ec[2], (+)st-ph[2], (+)l-st[1], (+)st-sh[1], (+)st-ec[1], (+)sh-ph[1]
0.4	(−)t-h[14], (+)t-st[12], (+)sh-ec[11], (+)l-t[7], (−)l-h[6], (+)sh-ph[4], (−)sh-ph[4], (−)t-ec[4], (−)st-ec[2], (−)st-sh[2], (+)l-st[2], (−)h-st[2], (+)st-ph[2], (+)st-sh[1], (+)st-ec[1], (+)h-ph[1], (+)h-sh[1], (−)h-ph[1]

Based on Table 2 [6], a semantic presentation is built on the feature associations. From the semantic presentation, we examine the causal relationship of various features.

For example, when we examined the threshold: 0.9, the feature association "(+)sh-ec[4]" is found that the "sh: soil humidity" and "ec: electrical conductivity" occur frequently. It indicates the importance of the feature association "(+)sh-ec[4]" is higher than other feature associations, e.g., "(+)st-ph[1]," "(−)sh-ph[1]." Based on different threshold values, so does other feature association examination.

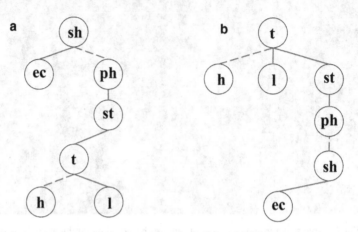

Fig. 6. (a) Semantic presentation generated with "soil humidity" feature as the root node. (b) Semantic presentation generated with "air temperature" feature as the root node

For the associations in the semantic presentation, the solid line indicates that the relationship between features is positive, and the dotted line is negative. The semantic presentation of the AHP hierarchical analysis tree based on a number of features is shown in Fig. 6(a) and 6(b). Figure 6(a) [6] illustrates a semantic presentation generated with the "soil humidity" feature as the root node. Figure 6(b) [6] presents a semantic presentation generated with the "air temperature" feature as the root node. Such a presentation will be translated back into the domain features collected by the original sensor, and the semantic representations that can be understood by the user. The expert can refer to the semantic representations as the basis for verifying the validity of the domain knowledge. This work conducts a study on the knowledge presented by the semantic presentation of the IoT monitoring system. It can transform discrete IoT data into its domain knowledge.

3.2 Discussions

The experimental results [6] illustrated three associations of features that can be classified into tea knowledge management, including:

- When the "air temperature" is high, the "soil humidity" and "electrical conductivity" are insufficient, top dressing and watering are recommended.
- When the "soil humidity" is sufficient and the "electrical conductivity" is insufficient, top dressing is recommended.
- When the "soil humidity" is insufficient and the "electrical conductivity" is sufficient, watering is recommended.

4 Conclusion

This paper uses a novel methodology to formalize the IoT data to the domain knowledge. Through exploring a real smart agriculture case, we understand the deployment of an IoT system in a tea eco-environment. The contributions of the paper are presented as follows. This work processes huge of IoT data from a smart agriculture case to identify the features in IoT data. The proposed methodology transforms discrete IoT data into its domain knowledge, including correlation matrix, principal component analysis, and multi-criteria decision analysis techniques. A semantic network is constructed to recommend the domain knowledge. The semantic network helps users retain the domain knowledge from a smart IoT monitoring system in a specific eco-environment, e.g., knowledge of tea plants. We list some limitations of the paper. This work should continually collect data in long term. Insufficient data collection may produce a low-quality semantic network. Besides, it doesn't consider the adaptive mechanism to adjust the criteria in multi-criteria decision analysis. The key criteria may have different influences due to the eco-environment change. In future work, we intend to investigate the time sequence and deep learning models to strengthen the IoT monitoring system's robustness and effectiveness. Besides, the unified theory of acceptance and use of technology (UTAUT) will be used to verify the user acceptance of the knowledge stored in the semantic network.

Acknowledgment. This research was supported in part by the National Taichung University of Science and Technology, with grants NTCUST111-05 and NTCUST111-22.

References

1. Elijah, O., Rahman, T.A., Orikumhi, I., Leow, C.Y., Hindia, M.N.: An overview of Internet of Things (IoT) and data analytics in agriculture: benefits and challenges. IEEE Internet Things J. **5**(5), 3758–3773 (2018)
2. Sisinni, E., Saifullah, A., Han, S., Jennehag, U., Gidlund, M.: Industrial Internet of Things: challenges, opportunities, and directions. IEEE Trans. Industr. Inf. **14**(11), 4724–4734 (2018)
3. Akbar, M.O., et al.: IoT for development of smart dairy farming. J. Food Quality **2020**, 1–8 (2020)
4. Gupta, N., Gupta, P.P., Pramanik, P., Saikia, A., S.: Integration of geoinformatics and wireless sensors for smart agriculture in tea. In: The International Society for Optical Engineering (2014)
5. Chen, J., Yang, A.: Intelligent agriculture and its key technologies based on Internet of Things architecture. IEEE Access **7**, 77134–77141 (2019)
6. Ke, C.K., Wu, M.Y., Lin, M.D., Pan, J.Z., Qu, K.T.: Semantic presentation of big data for intelligent identification of tea growing environment. In: Proceeding of 2022 Conference on Information Technology and Application in Outlying Islands, Kinmen, Taiwan (2022)
7. Quillian, M.: Semantic Memory in M. Minsky (ed.) Semantic Information Processing, pp. 227–270. MIT Press, Cambridge (1968)
8. Manouselis, N., Costopoulou, C.: Analysis and classification of multi-criteria recommender systems. World Wide Web **10**(4), 415–441 (2007)
9. Büyüközkan, G.: Multi-criteria decision making for e-marketplace selection. Internet Res. **14**(2), 139–154 (2004)

10. Hwang, C., Yoon, K.: Multiple Attribute Decision Making. Lecture Notes in Economics and Mathematical Systems, vol. 186. Springer, Heidelberg (1981)
11. Saaty, T.: The Analytic Hierarchy Process. McGraw-Hill, New York (1980)
12. Saaty, T.L.: Decision making with the analytic hierarchy process. Int. J. Serv. Sci. **1**, 83–98 (2008)
13. Russo, Rosaria de F.S.M., Camanho, R.: Criteria in AHP a systematic review of literature. Procedia Comput. Sci. **55**, 1123–1132 (2015)
14. Silaghi, G.C., Arenas, A.E., Silva, L.M.: A utility-based reputation model for service-oriented computing. In: Priol, T., Vanneschi, M. (eds.) Towards Next Generation Grids, pp. 63–72. Springer, Cham (2007). https://doi.org/10.1007/978-0-387-72498-0_6
15. Yang, I.T.: Utility-based decision support system for schedule optimization. Decis. Support Syst. **44**(3), 595–605 (2008)
16. Ke, C.K., Wu, M.Y.: Smart searching via semantic network for healthcare application. In: Proceeding of International Conference on Frontier Computing Special Forum on AI & Blockchain in Healthcare, pp. 26–31. National Taichung University of Science and Technology, Taiwan (2019)

Physical Layer Coding and Cryptanalysis for the Secure Communications

Cheng-Ying Yang[1], Chuan-Bi Lin[2], Jenq-Foung J. F. Yao[3], and Ming-Hsiang Hwang[4(✉)]

[1] Department of Computer Science, University of Taipei, Taipei, Taiwan
cyang@uTaipei.edu.tw
[2] Development of Information and Communication Technology, Chaoyang University of Technology, Taichung, Taiwan
[3] Department of Computer Science, Georgia College and State University, Milledgeville, USA
[4] Department of Computer Science and Information Engineering, Asia University, Taichung, Taiwan
mshwang@asia.edu.tw

Abstract. The privacy and security are highly requested in the cooperative communication system. The information is sent to the destination with the help of relays. In the system, there might be the eavesdroppers playing the role of the relay. It suffers the system security. Traditionally, the complex and difficult encryption scheme would be applied to a higher network layer. It is not suitable to apply to the equipment with low computing resources. According to Shannon Theory, positive secrecy capacity could support secure communications. In this work, based on the information theorem, the secrecy capacity analysis in the communication is given. Consider the difference between the amount of information at the source and that at the transmitter, the positive secrecy capacity with memory coding scheme under the lossless communication environment might be obtained. Then, the communication security could be implemented with the physical coding scheme. In this work, the physical layer coding schemes are examined. According to the degree of the freedom of the codeword, the secure communication could be achieved. It could be found the secrecy capacity could increase with coding rate decreasing with the multiple code assignments.

Keywords: Secrecy capacity · Secure communications · Physical layer security coding · Cryptanalysis

1 Introduction

Currently, the wireless communications provide amount of multimedia services for the mobile devices. It increases a lot of mobile users and requests more advanced services. Although to access the wireless services is convenient for the mobile users, the degradation characteristics of the radio transmission are signal fading, multipath transmission, signal inferences, bandwidth limitation and so on. Under the limitation of transmission bandwidth, to improve system performance in the wireless systems becomes a significant work. Especially, to use the spatial diversity could be employed to improve the system performance [1]. For example, in the Multiple Input Multiple Output (MIMO) system, it provides a spatial diversity gain to improve the system performance. However, the high implementation cost MIMO is with multiple antennas at both the transmitter and receiver [2]. Instead of MIMO technique, the cooperative communications with a relay channel increase the system capacity without extra antennas [3]. Comparing with multiple carrier modulation schemes and MIMO schemes, the relay stations not only forward the transmitted data but also process the received data. It provides a high throughput performance. The destination station could receive data with a spatial diversity with employing the relay selection scheme. Even though the destination station has no multiple antennas, by employing the relay station as the virtual antenna, it increases the transmission data rate and provides a reliable channel capacity [4]. With a consideration of low cost, the cooperative communication system is a tendency in the future communications.

However, the privacy and security are highly requested in the communication systems. In the cooperative communication system, the information is sent to the destination station with the help of relays. In the system, there might be the eavesdroppers playing the role of the relay. It suffers the system performance in the security. The secrecy capacity analysis and the relay selection strategy according to the secrecy rate in the cooperative system have been proposed in the theoretical solution [5]. Obviously, the improvement of the secrecy performance includes the power control of relay, encryption, relay selection strategy and so on [6]. Among the improving methods, the appropriate relay assignment could improve secrecy rate. In the recent research on relay selection strategy on the secure cooperative system, the results show the secrecy capacity in the system could be improved if the number of relays is larger than the number of source stations [1].

Although the improvement scheme could be found, a fundamental difficulty is on the eavesdropper detection. The practical solution to the eavesdropper detection is to identify the eavesdroppers or to encrypt the information to the eavesdropper. The purpose of the secure communications is to enable the authentic destination station successfully receive the information from the source station. Also, it protects the transmitted information from the eavesdroppers to interpret this information. The secure communication could be held based on the secrecy rate [3]. Traditionally, the encryption scheme is employed in a higher-network layer to provide a secure purpose. Encryption could be complex and difficult without infrastructure. It is not suitable to apply to the equipment with low computing resources, such as IoT (Internet of Things) [3]. Hence, the physical-layer security coding based on the wiretap channel model has been proposed [7].

In the secure cooperative system, the information is transmitted from the source station to the destination station with the help of relay stations [3]. Among the relay stations, the transmitted information is unwrapped in the presence of one or more eavesdroppers. The information could be eavesdropped from the source station or from the relay which the source station adopts in the cooperative communication [3] Hence, the encryption could be employed for the eavesdroppers even if the eavesdropper plays a role in the relay. Many cryptosystems assumed that the attacker has limited resources. Also, the new and unanticipated algorithmic attacks have been conjectured developed. The measure of secrecy was proposed by Shannon [8]. Shannon's perfect secrecy also makes the limited assumption that an attacker has access to an error-free cryptogram. However, this might not be a practical case. The theoretical physical-layer security coding is derived from the wiretap channel model [7]. The purposes of the coding scheme attempt to achieve an arbitrarily low probability of decoding error at the desired destination and to obtain a critical level of security against the eavesdroppers. Hence, physical-layer security coding based on the wiretap channel model should be analyzed at the first stage. Some channel coding schemes, e.g. Low-density Parity-Check (LDPC) Code [9] have the capacity of cryptography.

The physical-layer coding should be coupled with cryptographic schemes for a complete security solution [10]. This coupling commonly assumed the requirement that codes must individually provide secrecy, but rather allows coding to function as a security enhancement in the sense of cryptography. The secure scheme supposes the codewords confuse attackers by providing a positive secret rate in the eavesdropped cryptogram at the attacker. The security of such a code could be characterized through the cryptanalysis of ciphertext. Hence, the cryptanalysis of ciphertext should be realized at the second stage. With the cryptanalysis of stream ciphers, the enhancement of security could be gained when the ciphertext is analyzing the attacks. Finally, a combination of channel coding and cryptanalysis leads to the practical application. This application could provide a large untapped secure source to strengthen cryptography. On the other hand, even if it is without security concern in the physical layer, the higher layer could still work alone for the secrecy. With his combination, the channel codes provide a reliable ciphertext for secret communication and keep the eavesdroppers alike away. It could increase the security strength in the physical layer. Besides, if the secrecy codes are the only source of security in a system, the eavesdroppers might likely obtain information of the transmitted message. Hence, the combination of channel coding and cryptography, physical-layer security coding, obviously outperforms standalone cryptography. It could be practical for the future communication systems. In this work, the analysis of maximum secrecy rate is derived to develop the relay assignment. In Sect. 2, the secure communication model is illustrated. Section 3 Gives the description to physical layer coding scheme. The secrecy capacity analysis and the numerical results are given in Sect. 4. The Sect. 5 gives the conclusion.

2 Secure Communication Model

The security mechanism could be implemented with an efficient cost consideration. According to Shannon theory of perfect secrecy, in Fig. 1, the security could be obtained if the entropy of the codeword is greater or equal to the transmitted information.

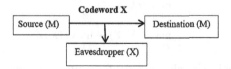

Fig. 1. A peer-to-peer communication with an eavesdropper

It leads to realizing the uncertainty of the transmitted codeword must be at least as larger as the uncertainty of information, i.e. positive secrecy rate,

$$C_{s,d} = I_{s,d} - I_{s,e} \tag{1}$$

where $C_{s,d}$ is the secrecy rate (i.e. secrecy capacity) of transmission is defined as the mutual information difference between the mutual information from the source to the destination and that from the source to the eavesdropper. $I_{s,d}$ and $I_{s,e}$ denote the information between the source and the destination and the information between the source and the eavesdropper, respectively.

With combing both coding and cryptography, the system model is depicted in Fig. 2.

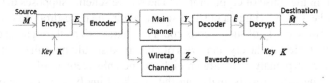

Fig. 2. Secure communication model

In Fig. 2, it assumes the source message M includes discrete symbols. These symbols are generated by a source encoder. Following, it includes a cryptographic encoder and a channel encoder. The destination could decode the received transmitted message in reverse order.

Information theoretic security makes no computational assumption on the attacker and is treated as the perfect secrecy. It assumes that a secret message M is encrypted to form a cyphertext E with secret key K, if

$$H(M|E) = H(M) \tag{2}$$

It means there is no information in the cyphertext, i.e. the cyphertext E is the message equivocation. One-Time Pad is an example to achieve a secrecy communication [12]. In this example, $|K| = |M|$, the length of K is equal to the length of M. In fact, the length of K could be larger or equal to the length of M to achieve the perfect secrecy, i.e.

$$H(K) \geq H(M) \tag{3}$$

A secure communication achieves not only an arbitrarily low error probability but also security against the attackers. Hence, in the wiretap channel model, the secrecy capacity (secrecy rate) is defined based on the previous two purposes [3, 11].

$$C_s = \max_{p(x)} I(X;Y|Z)$$
$$\geq \max_{p(x)} I(X;Y) - \max_{p(x)} I(X;Z) \tag{4}$$

This equation provides a valuable point for secure communication, i.e. the positive secrecy capacity could have security against the eavesdropper. It might be held because of the quality of the main channel.

To minimize the information on the codeword C, it needs the maximum the information on the received C given in X and minimum the information on the codeword C given in Y, as shown in Fig. 3. Hence, the codeword mapping leads the secure transmission.

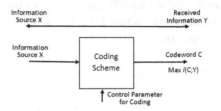

Fig. 3. Code mapping to maximize I(C;Y)

3 Physical Layer Coding Scheme

There are three random variables in the system, information source X, distorted codeword (codevector) C and received information Y. Consider these three random variables X, C, Y to form a chain $X \rightarrow C \rightarrow Y$ (Fig. 4). Let the information source X denote as a space with probability p(x) and the distorted codeword space denote C, i.e. $x \in X$ and $c \in C$.

For the eavesdropper, these nonsense symbols represent the degrees of freedom, D, in the cryptogram space. If the bits in the codeword X are uniformly distributed and independent and identically distributed (i.i.d.), the perfect secrecy is held when $D = K$, where K is the dimension of the encoder, i.e. the length of the secret key. There are 2K equally likely length-k sequences with which to guess the message. The encoder has 2K possible codewords in the code set. Every codeword is equally likely to be the posterior to the eavesdropper.

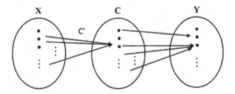

Fig. 4. Mapping of received Codevectors C from the information source X and the Codevectors C to the received information Y

$$P\left(M \,|2^{K_i}\right) = P\left(M \,|2^{K_j}\right) \tag{5}$$

This implies the multiplication of the necessary difficulty to attack the cryptogram with degrees of freedom D. Clearly, if the degrees of freedom are the only factor to confuse to the eavesdropper to release the message, the transmitted message M and the eavesdropper's received data X is related to D. Hence, the degrees of freedom D provides the solution to practical security between the source and the destination.

4 Secrecy Capacity Analysis

The information of the codeword could reach the maximum information if the codeword has the equally probability distribution. In Fig. 5, the slope of curve is larger when the number of the codeword limited within 100 and the slope of the curve goes to smoothly if the number of the codeword goes above 600. This slope could be expected for the changing of the secrecy capacity.

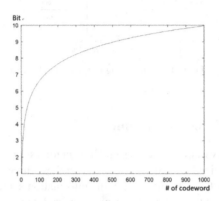

Fig. 5. Maximum of Information if the codeword with equal probability

For example, one-time pad encryption, the scheme meets the requirement for the secret communication. Also, the interleaving coding has the same characteristic, although this coding scheme has the purpose of error controlling [10].

By multiple code assignment scheme, it is expected the secrecy capacity could increase if the number of codeword is larger than that of the source. Figure 6 shows the cases of $i = 1, 3, 7, 15$, respectively.

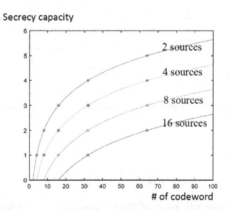

Fig. 6. Secrecy capacity increasing with increasing length of codeword

With the consideration of bandwidth efficiency, the coding rate between the source and the codeword is an important factor to achieve the secrecy capacity. Figure 7 shows the relationship between the secrecy capacity and the coding rate. It could be found that to achieve the same secrecy capacity, coding rate is larger when the length of the source is shorter. For example, to achieve the secrecy capacity of 3 (i.e. $C_S = 3$), coding rate 0.4 (for the source length 2) is smaller than that (for the source length 3.) It leads a higher bandwidth efficiency for the longer length of source.

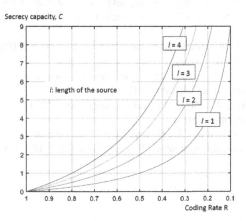

Fig. 7. Secrecy capacity increasing with coding rate decreasing

5 Conclusion

In this research, it could be found that the secret capacity could be expected with the coding rate but without the complex of the coding scheme. The reason is the random degree of codeword depends on the number of codeword only. For one-to-one coding assignment, it could not benefit to the secrecy capacity, but improve the error performance. Hence, multiple code assignment scheme proposed in the research might provide for increasing the secrecy capacity.

Acknowledgement. This work was supported by the Ministry of Science and Technology, Taiwan, under grants MOST 110-2221-E-845-002- and MOST 111-2221-E-845-003-.

References

1. Li, L., Zhou, X., Xu, H., Li, G.Y., Wang, D., Soong, A.: Simplified relay selection and power allocation in cooperative cognitive radio systems. IEEE Trans. Wireless Commun. **10**(1), 33–36 (2011)
2. Harrison, W.K., Almeida, J., McLaughlin, S.W., Barros, J.: Coding for cryptographic security enhancement using stopping sets. IEEE Trans. Inf. Forens. Security **6**(3), 575–584 (2011)
3. Chou, Y., Zhu, J., Wang, X., Leung, V.C.: Improving physical-layer security in wireless communications using diversity techniques. IEEE Network **29**(1), 42–48 (2015)

4. Wang, Y., Noubir, G.: Distributed cooperation and diversity for hybrid wireless networks. IEEE Trans. Mob. Comput. **12**(3), 596–608 (2013)
5. Chen, J.S., Yang, C.-.Y., Hwang, M.S.: The capacity analysis in the secure cooperative communication system. Int. J. Netw. Secur. **19**(6), 863–869 (2017)
6. Shiu, Y.S., Chang, S.Y., Wu, H.C., Huang, S.C.H., Chen, H.H.: Physical layer security in wireless networks: a tutorial. IEEE Wirel. Commun. **18**(2), 66–74 (2011)
7. Ozarow, L.H., Wyner, A.D.: Wire-tap channel II. Bell Syst. Tech. J. **63**(10), 2135–2157 (1984)
8. Atzori, L., Iera, A., Morabito, G.: The internet of things: a survey. Comput. Netw. **54**, 2787–2805 (2010)
9. Kim, K.J., et al.: Low-density parity-check codes for ATSC 3.9. IEEE Trans. Broadcasting **62**(1), 189–196 (2016)
10. Nair, J.V.: A study of secrecy codes and their real-world performance, Master thesis, University of Colorado at Colorado (2017)
11. Bloch, M., Barros, J.: Physical-Layer Security from Information Theory to Security Engineering, Cambridge (2011)
12. Yang, C.-Y., Yao, J.F., Yen, C.E., Hwang, M.-S.: Overview on physical layer security in low earth orbit (LEO) satellite system. In: Proceedings of 2021 IEEE ICCE-TW, pp. 1–2 (2021)

Mobile Computation and Wireless Communication

5G Network Slice Scalability Based on Management Data Analytics Function (MDAF)

Chun Hsiung, Fuchun Joseph Lin$^{(\boxtimes)}$, Jyh-Cheng Chen, and Chien Chen

Department of Computer Science, College of Computer Science, National Yang Ming Chiao Tung University, 1001 Ta Hsueh Road, Hsinchu 300, Taiwan

bearjimbear@gmail.com, fjlin@nycu.edu.tw, jcchen@ieee.org, chienchen@nctu.edu.tw

Abstract. This paper focuses on the scalability of one of the most important VNFs (Virtual Network Functions) in a 5G core slice, AMF (Access and Mobility Management Function). When incoming requests exceed the capacity of a single AMF instance, they will be rejected by the AMF and lead to the failure of user equipment to attach to 5G. To solve this problem, we propose to dynamically scale the number of active AMF instances based on Management Data Analytics Function (MDAF) currently under study by 3GPP by monitoring the loading of AMF. Using Tacker and OpenStack to set up a MANO environment, we design and implement MDAF as a VNF to provide data analytics services required for the scalability of AMF. In addition, we also design a Load Balancer as a VNF between RAN (Radio Access Network) and AMFs to receive the load distribution policy from MDAF and distribute the traffic load from RAN to suitable AMFs. After thoroughly testing two systems, one equipped with MDAF-based scalability and one without, it shows that when the MDAF system encounters a large amount of UE registration requests, it can maintain a higher registration success rate than the non-MDAF system. Moreover, the MDAF system can not only reduce the processing time for individual UEs, but also ensure a stable CPU state of AMF instances.

Keywords: 5G · AMF · MDAF · Scalability

1 Introduction

1.1 5G Introduction

With the evolution of the mobile communications, the 5G technology is gradually gaining attention around the world. In addition to the application of 5G on smartphones, it also focuses on other IoT technologies. For example, emerging technologies such as self-driving cars, VR technology, and remote diagnosis all require 5G technical support. According to the IMT-2020 standard formulated by the International Telecommunication Union Radiocommunication Sector (ITU-R), 5G mainly enhances three application areas, namely enhanced Mobile Broadband (eMBB), Ultra-Reliable Low-Latency

S.-Y. Hsieh et al. (Eds.): ICS 2022, CCIS 1723, pp. 587–598, 2022.
https://doi.org/10.1007/978-981-19-9582-8_52

Communication (URLLC) and massive Machine-Type Communications (mMTC) [1]. In order to meet all these service requirements on the same hardware infrastructure, one of the key features of 5G, network slicing, is a must.

To manage 5G network slices, MANO (MANagement and Orchestration) proposed by ETSI NFV is adopted by 3GPP. MANO divides network services into different Virtual Network Functions (VNFs) and deploys them on different Virtual Machines (VMs). MANO can dynamically monitor each VNF on the 5G slice to meet the diverse needs of the 5G network.

1.2   Research Motivation and Contribution

The mMTC applications in 5G will be used for the interconnection and communication of a large number of devices. To handle this situation, the 5G core network needs to be able to handle a large number of UE registration requests at the same time. As AMF (Access and Mobility Management Function) is the first network function in the core network to connect to the UE, responsible for managing the user's connection control and user device's registration, it is regarded as the bottleneck of the core network. According to the research of [2, 3], if there is only a single AMF in the situation of a large number of registration requests, the AMF will be overloaded and its processing efficiency will drop and cause users unable to connect to the core network smoothly. Hence AMF should be equipped with scalability to deal with this situation.

Our research thus proposes a mechanism of timely scaling out AMF instances by monitoring the loading of each AMF. The goal is to improve the stability and efficiency of processing UE registration requests while maintaining the load balance among multiple AMF instances. Our research uses Tacker [4] and OpenStack [5] to set up the free5GC [6] core network. The data analysis on the AMF in the 5G slice is then performed by implementing the MDAF (Management Data Analytics Function) proposed by 3GPP. Based on the status provided by the AMF, MDAF decides not only when to scale out or scale in the AMF instances but also instructs the Load Balancer how to relay the registration requests to the appropriate AMF for the registration process.

2   Background and Relevant Open Sources

2.1   Scalability of 5G Core Slice

5G Core Architecture. Figure 1 is the basic architecture diagram of the 5G mobile network defined by 3GPP in the TS23.501 [7] standard. The 5G core network adopts Control plane and User Plane Separation (CUPS) and a Service-Based Architecture (SBA). CUPS makes the core network deployment more flexible because the components of the control plane and the data plane can be expanded or reduced according to their specific needs independently without affecting the other. SBA means that the network functions at the control layer adopt a service-oriented architecture and use a unified Service-Based Interface (SBI) to connect with each other. SBI is based on RESTful APIs to reduce inter-dependence among network functions. This makes the system very flexible in adding new network functions, and thus improves the scalability and deployment easiness of the core network.

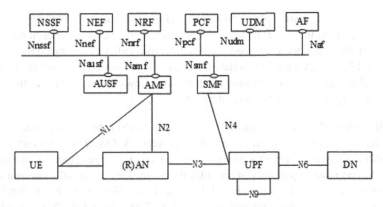

Fig. 1. 5G Core network architecture [1]

5G Network Slice. 5G.co.uk [8] defines network slicing as the provision of dedicated virtual networks with service- or customer-specific functions over a common network infrastructure. It is realized by the Network Function Virtualization (NFV) technology, which allows a Network Service (NS) to be composed of multiple Virtual Network Functions (VNFs), and each VNF can be deployed in a virtual machine (VM) to execute. Through network slicing, a single physical network infrastructure can be sliced into multiple virtual networks, which then can be divided into fully shared, partially shared, or dedicated slices to meet the diverse needs of 5G network services.

5G Scalability. On the 5G network slice, a single network function (VNF) may be overloaded. For example, the AMF may encounter a large number of requests from UEs to connect to the core network or the UPF may receive packets with large traffic that needs to be forwarded. The service-oriented architecture and network slicing characteristics of the 5G core network enable 5G to activate scalability, so related network functions can be expanded in a low-cost environment to solve the overload problem while achieving load balance. It demonstrates the flexibility of 5G at the deployment level.

2.2 5G Management Data Analytics Function(MDAF)

3GPP defines Management Data Analytics Service (MDAS) in TS28.533 [9] as a data analysis service that provides different network-related parameters including load level or resource utilization. MDAF can analyze and predict resource usage information at scheduled future time after data collection. The analysis can also recommend appropriate change settings, such as resource scaling, admission control, traffic load balancing, and more.

2.3 Relevant Open Source Systems

free5GC. This paper uses the free5GC developed by the Wireless Internet Research and Engineering Laboratory (WIRE Lab) of National Yang Ming Chiao Tung University as the experimental platform. Free5GC is a 5G open source core network developed in accordance with the 3GPP R15 standards. The communication between each NF in the control plane adopts a service-based architecture (SBA), and transmits messages through HTTP/2 (H2C) and JSON data structures. This SBA architecture facilitates the addition of any new NF in the future. This feature allows us to add MDAF to free5GC without redesigning the connection interface.

OpenStack and Tacker. Our research also uses the MANO open source systems, Open-Stack and Tacker, as the platform to run the core network. OpenStack is an open source cloud infrastructure system that provides virtualized storage, computing and network resources, and most importantly, it provides the technology to virtualize network functions. OpenStack provides a web-based dashboard that allows users to efficiently configure, manage, and monitor virtualized resources. Tacker is an OpenStack project that provides NFVO (NFV Orchestrator) and VNFM (VNF Manager) functionality to configure, deploy, manage and coordinate individual NSs (Network Slices) and VNFs on NFV infrastructure platforms such as OpenStack. The combination of the two can simulate the actual operating environment of the network slice.

3   System Design

3.1   MANO Architecture

ETSI NFV MANO [10] is an architectural framework that utilizes virtual resources to create network services. MANO is utilized in our research to build the required 5G VNFs and compose the required 5G core network slice. MANO consists of three main components: NFV Orchestrator (NFVO), VNF Manager (VNFM) and Virtualized Infrastructure Managers (VIM).

3.2   MDAF System Architecture Design

Figure 2 depicts the MDAF system architecture designed for this research. First, Tacker is used to create a complete 5G core network slice on OpenStack. Each NF runs on a single VM and has the same resources. It is assumed that the AMF can only be expanded to three instances at most. Since free5GC currently only supports static deployment, three AMF instances will be pre-provisioned to provide subsequent load balancing.

In this system, MDAF is also an NF and is added to the communication interface of SBI. Each AMF will communicate with MDAF one-way regularly via a timer to provide its CPU usage information. On the other hand, MDAF analyzes this information from AMF and dynamically compute the ratio of UE registration requests allocated to each AMF, based on a traffic threshold as the load balance indicator. Finally, this ratio decision is passed to the Load Balancer for execution.

In order to handle a large amount of UE registration requests, we design a Load Balancer as the link between the RAN and the AMFs. The Load Balancer can allocate UE registration requests to different AMFs according to the ratio policy provided by MDAF. It also records the pairing of each UE with its corresponding AMF so that all

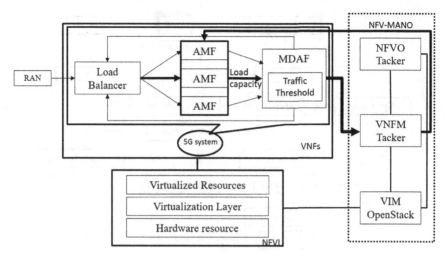

Fig. 2. MDAF system architecture

the information in the registration process can be accurately transmitted to complete the registration process.

From the perspective of RAN, the Load Balancer and the three AMFs are regarded as one virtual AMF under this architecture. All the UE registration messages are sent to the Load Balancer. Likewise, after the registration is processed by the core network, a message reply is obtained from the Load Balancer.

3.3 MDAF Architecture Registration Flow

Next we explain the changes of UE registration flow after using the MDAF architecture. Figure 3 shows the flow of the MDAF architecture, which is the operation process when the entire system is started. The detailed steps of this process are explained as follows:

1. When all NF instances of the core network are started, the three AMFs are also started at the same time, and the HTTP server of each AMF is started to register with the NRF for subsequent communications on the SBI. Also, the SCTP server of each AMF is established to wait for the Load Balancer to connect.
2. The Load Balancer starts the SCTP server and actively establishes connections to the three AMFs. At the same time, the MDAF establishes an HTTP server on the SBI to receive future AMF status messages.
3. After the RAN is powered on, it connects to the Load Balancer according to its own pre-configured connection information, and sends the NG setup request to the Load Balancer. At this time, the Load Balancer will copy the NG setup request and send it to the three AMFs respectively.
4. When the AMF receives the NG setup request, it will start the AMF timer that regulates how often the AMF needs to send its CPU usage information to the MDAF.

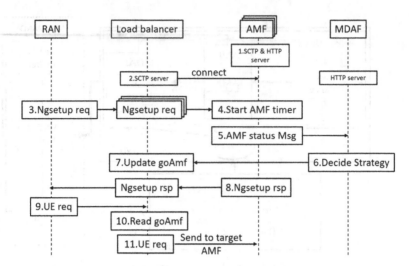

Fig. 3. MDAF architecture initial process flow

5. At the same time the AMF timer is started, the AMF will send its initial status information to the MDAF.
6. After the MDAF obtains the initial information of the three AMFs, it will select one of AMFs as the main AMF, and set the load ratio decision to direct all incoming requests to this main AMF.
7. The Load Balancer will update the goAmf parameter [15] after receiving the load ratio decision from MDAF. This parameter controls how the Load Balancer will distribute traffic to AMFs when receiving the UE registration requests.
8. After the three AMFs store the RAN context information, they will send the NG setup response to the RAN. After receiving the NG setup response, the Load Balancer will send it back to the RAN to complete the NG setup procedure. The subsequent incoming NG setup responses will then be discarded. Consequently, from perspective of the RAN, it only establishes connection with one AMF.
9. The RAN receives the registration request from the UE and sends it to the Load Balancer through the connection established in Step 3.
10. The Load Balancer sends the UE registration requests to different AMFs according to the goAmf parameter [15]. It also records the association between UE's NGAP ID in the registration request and the corresponding AMF to ensure that the same AMF is responsible for the subsequent registration process.
11. The Load Balancer sends the UE registration request to the target AMF and continues to process the messages of the subsequent registration process.

4   System Implementation

This section explains the three major software modules in our implementation: AMF, Load Balancer and MDAF.

4.1 AMF

The implementation of AMF is modified from the AMF module in free5GC v3.0.6. The modified AMF can be scaled horizontally, i.e., it can be scaled to multiple instances to enable the 5G core network to handle a larger number of UE registration messages. It is enhanced with an AMF timer to periodically transmits its own CPU usage to MDAF. This timer is activated after it receives the NG setup request sent from the RAN. The implementation of AMF utilizes the gopsutil [11] library in Golang for recording CPU usage. The AMF status message sent to MDAF includes not only the total CPU usage of AMF but also its specific identification.

4.2 Load Balancer

The Load Balancer is implemented in Golang like other NFs. According to the definition of 3GPP TS 38.412 [12], both RAN and AMF use SCTP as the transport layer. The Load Balancer thus includes an implementation of SCTP in order to communicate with both RAN and AMF. On one side, the Load Balancer needs to receive load ratio policies from MDAF. On the other side, it has to correctly dispatch registration requests to the corresponding AMF. The Load Balancer uses the UE's NGAP ID to effectively distinguish various UEs. Moreover, it uses the Golang map data structure to achieve simple database storage and query functions.

4.3 MDAF

MDAF is also implemented in Golang, and an HTTP server is also established in it on SBI to receive AMF status messages. The main function of MDAF is to accept the CPU usage of three AMFs, and propose a load ratio policy to the Load Balancer after algorithmic analysis. The COOP algorithm in [13] is modified to suit the context of this research, and the purpose is to calculate the optimal load balancing ratio R_i with a total workload of φ according to the remaining available CPU utilization u_i of each AMF [15].

Figure 4 shows the state diagram of AMF scale-out and scale-in controlled by MDAF through the load balancing strategy R[] according to different AMF states. The situations of scale-out and scale-in is described in detail below. Initially, the CPU states of three AMFs are all lower than the threshold (a_0, a_1, $a_2 < C_t$). So MDAF will set the load balancing policy R to [r_0,0,0], indicating that only AMF-0 will process the registration requests. However, as registration requests increase, MDAF finds that a_0 exceeds the threshold after receiving the AMF CPU status message. This implies that AMF-0 has been overloaded and the 5G core needs to expand a new AMF instance. At this time, MDAF will change the load balancing policy R to [r_0, r_1, 0], which means that AMF-1 is added for sharing the load with AMF-0. Similarly, if a_0 and a_1 exceed the threshold, the system will again add a third AMF instance.

On the other hand, when the AMF loading is below the threshold, the MDAF will reduce the number of the AMF instances accordingly after receiving the new AMF CPU status messages. For example, as illustrated in Fig. 4, when R[] = [r_0, r_1, r_2], if a_1 and a_2 decrease below the threshold and only a_0 remains above the threshold ($a_0 > C_t$,

a_1, a_2 < C_t), this means that three AMFs can be reduced to two AMFs to process the current registration messages. Then MDAF will set the load balancing policy R to [r_0, r_1,0], indicating that the 5G core is reduced to use only AMF-0 and AMF-1 for UE registration.

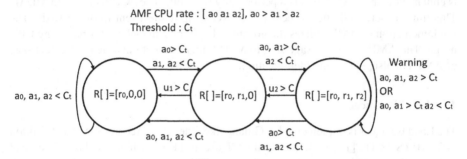

Fig. 4. State Diagram of AMF Scale-Out and Scale-In

5   Experiments and Analysis Results

We verify the proposed MDAF system architecture (as shown in Fig. 2 in Sect. 3.2) with a large number of UE registration requests and compare it with the original core network slice without MDAF-enabled scalability (as shown in Fig. 5). The latter deploys only a single AMF without scalability but still utilizes MANO to simulate a single network slice while the former incorporates MDAF, Load Balancer and multiple instances of AMF in the MANO architecture.

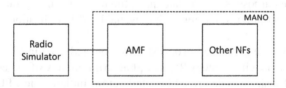

Fig. 5. Baseline architecture

The goal of our experiments is to answer the following questions on the MDAF system:

– Can more UE registration requests be processed?
– Does it make any impact to the registration time for a single UE?
– Is the CPU usage of the AMF instance stable?

To simulate the real situation that the three AMFs may execute other tasks other than processing the UE registration request, our experiments will use the CPU limit command to run some background program in the AMF instance. As a result, the AMF always maintains about 30% of CPU usage. In two experiments conducted below, the maximum number of scalable AMF instances is set to be three. A Radio Simulator [14] is used to drive the tests using different numbers of UE and different rates of registration request arrival.

5.1 Experiment 1

The total number of UEs used in experiment 1 is 100. The UE registration request transmission is divided into three segments with one-third of the total number of UEs in each segment. The first one-third of the UE requests are sent at the rate of 5 per second. In the middle segment, the rate is increased to 10 UE requests per second. Finally, the last third of the UE registrations is reverted back to 5 UE requests per second.

We use the above test to compare the original free5GC architecture with only a single AMF with the MDAF architecture equipped with multiple scalable AMF instances. The objective is to discover how two would react differently when facing the peak and off-peak UE registration. Which one has more stable CPU usage and which one has the quicker registration time? In Experiment 1, we set the CPU threshold of AMF under the MDAF architecture only 40% so that AMF scale-out can easily happen, allowing us to observe whether there is any significant difference in the average CPU usage of AMF.

Figure 6 is a box chart depicting the average registration time of a single UE, obtained after ten tests in Experiment 1. The horizontal axis is the baseline architecture and the MDAF architecture, and the vertical axis is the time required for a UE to complete registration, in milliseconds. It can be seen from the experimental results that the MDAF architecture can effectively reduce the registration time required for a UE. The baseline architecture takes an average of about 1200ms to complete the registration request of a UE, while the MDAF architecture only takes about 500ms. The time is reduced by about three-fifths, which shows that the proposed MDAF architecture can effectively reduce the blocking of UE registration requests. Moreover, Fig. 6 also shows that the MDAF architecture has a more stable average registration time than the baseline architecture.

Figure 7 is a box plot of the average CPU usage of AMF instances after ten tests. The horizontal axis is the single AMF of the baseline architecture and the three AMFs using the MDAF architecture, and the vertical axis is the CPU usage. It shows that the CPU usage of AMF under the baseline architecture is significantly larger due to a large number of UE registration requests. On the other hand, the average CPU usage of the three AMFs in the MDAF architecture can be maintained around 40% of the CPU threshold set in Experiment 1. This proves that the MDAF architecture can more effectively utilize the CPU. The average CPU usage of the three AMFs differs by only 2 to 3%, enabling the AMF instance to handle the UE registration process in a balanced and stable environment, greatly reducing the failure rate of UE registrations.

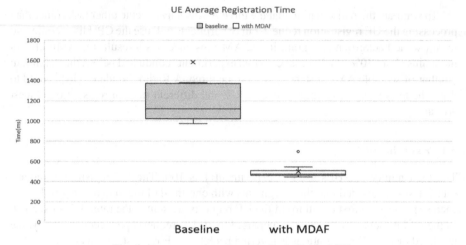

Fig. 6. *Average* registration time for individual UEs

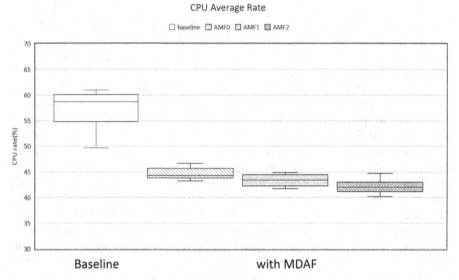

Fig. 7. AMF average CPU usage

5.2 Experiment 2

In Experiment 2, the total number of UEs used is increased to 300. The UE registration request transmission rate is also divided into three segments. Each segment is one-third of the total number of UEs. The first one-third of the UEs are 10 per second UE registration, the middle is increased to 20 UE registrations per second, and the last third of the UEs are reverted back to 10 UE registrations per second. The CPU threshold of AMF under the MDAF architecture is set to 60%.

Figure 8 is a bar graph showing the success rate of registration of 300 UEs in Experiment 2. The horizontal axis represents the results of each experiment, with a total of ten tests, and the vertical axis represents the success rate. It clearly depicts that AMF under the baseline architecture cannot instantly process a larger number of UE registration requests. When there are too many pending UE registration requests, the AMF instance will enter an inoperable state, which will lead to subsequent UE registration failures. The highest UE registration success rate of the baseline architecture is only 23%. In contrast, the MDAF architecture may also fail to register some UEs, but in most cases 300 UE registration requests can be successfully processed. This proves that the MDAF architecture can greatly increase the success rate of UE registration process by scaling AMF instances.

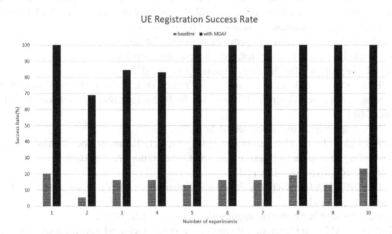

Fig. 8. UE registration success rate

6 Conclusion and Future Work

This research uses Golang to implement the MDAF concept proposed by 3GPP on the platform based on free5GC. The entire 5G core network is setup in the MANO environment to simulate network slices. Through MDAF, the CPU usage of AMF on the network slice is collected and analyzed. MDAF then instructs the scale-out and scale-in of the AMF instances in network slice when needed. Experiments [15] have shown that the core network based on MDAF can (1) process a larger number of UE registration requests, (2) dynamically adjust the load balance policy according to the AMF status, (3) scale out or in the number of AMF instances in a timely manner, (4) effectively reduce about 40% of UE registration time while maintaining stable CPU usage of AMF, and (5) maintain a high success rate of UE registration even when the system is overloaded.

Our future work includes: (1) dynamically add and delete AMF instances using MANO, (2) use MDAF to predict the traffic flow in the near future and activate scalability mechanism in advance and (3) be able to dynamically control the scalability of each NF in 5G core through MDAF as proposed by 3GPP TS 28.533 [9].

Acknowledgement. This work was financially supported by National Science and Technology Council of Taiwan, R.O.C. under NSTC 111-2218-E-A49-023 and NSTC 111-3114-E-A49-001.

References

1. ITU-R M.2083: IMT Vision – Framework and Overall Objectives of the Future Development of IMT for 2020 and Beyond (2015)
2. Alawe, I., Ksentini, A., Hadjadj-Aoul, Y., Bertin, P.: Improving traffic forecasting for 5g core network scalability: a machine learning approach. IEEE Netw. **32**(6), 42–49 (2018). https://doi.org/10.1109/MNET.2018.1800104
3. Alawe, I., Ksentini, A., Hadjadj-Aoul, Y., Bertin, P., Viho, C. Darche, D.: An efficient and lightweight load forecasting for proactive scaling in 5G mobile networks. In: IEEE Conference on Standards for Communications and Networking, pp. 1–6 (2018)
4. OpenStack Tacker. https://docs.openstack.org/tacker/latest/. Accessed 01 Sep 2022
5. OpenStack. https://www.openstack.org/. Accessed 01 Sep 2022
6. free5GC. https://www.free5gc.org/. Accessed 01 Sep 2022
7. 3GPP TS 23.501: 3rd Generation Partnership Project; Technical Specification Group Services and System Aspects; System Architecture for the 5G System; Stage 2 (Release 16), V16.0.0, March 2019
8. 5g.co.uk. https://5g.co.uk/. Accessed 01 Sep 2022
9. 3GPP TS 28.533.: 3rd Generation Partnership Project; Technical Specification Group Services and System Aspects; Management and Orchestration; Architecture Framework; Stage 3 (Release 16), V16.3.0., March 2020
10. ETSI GS NFV-IFA 001: Network Functions Virtualisation (NFV); Management and Orchestration, V1.1.1. (2014)
11. Golang. https://github.com/shirou/gopsutil. Accessed 01 Sep 2022
12. 3GPP TS 38.412: 3rd Generation Partnership Project; Technical Specification Group Radio Access Network; NG-RAN; NG Signalling Transport (Release 15) V15.3.0, September 2019
13. Grosu, D., Chronopoulos, A. T., Leung, M.-Y.: Load balancing in distributed systems: an approach using cooperative games. In: Proceeding on 16th International Parallel Distributed Processing Symposium, April 2002
14. Lin, Y.-J.: Design and Implementation of a Fault Tolerance Mechanism for Access and Mobility Management Function (AMF) in 5G core network. National Yang Ming Chiao Tung University Master thesis, Hsinchu, Taiwan (2021)
15. Hsiung, C.: 5G Network Slice Scalability based on Management Data Analytics Function (MDAF), National Yang Ming Chiao Tung University Master thesis, Hsinchu, Taiwan (2022)

Design and Analysis for Wireless Tire Pressure Sensing System

Shashank Mishra$^{(\boxtimes)}$ and Jia-Ming Liang

National University of Tainan, Tainan 70005, Taiwan
d10982003@stumail.nutn.edu.tw

Abstract. With the expansion of Internet of Things (IoT) technologies, intelligent vehicles are now in increasing public demand, mostly equipped with sensors for measuring various situations, such as distance proximity, driving speed, fuel consumption, and tire anomaly. Nowadays, tire pressure and temperature play an important role in reducing fuel consumption, increasing mileage, improving driving safety, and reducing potential traffic accidents. In this paper, we investigate how to collect the tire data based on the designed sensors and then develop an energy-efficient system, called Wireless Tire Pressure Sensing System (WTPSS), which leverages the energy-saving technique by applying wakeup-sleep operation, while ensuring the data retrieval delay when monitoring. In addition, the worst receiving delay is also discussed and analyzed theoretically. In the simulation, our system has verified that it can have better performance in terms of energy saving.

Keywords: Tire pressure sensing system · Worst-delay · Sensor data transmission · Wireless transmission

1 Introduction

With increasing demands for Internet of Things (IoT) based devices in various fields, intelligent vehicles are now in growing public demand. The automobile industry records a higher number of accidents due to mechanical/technical failures thus safety becomes the first priority [1]. Tire pressure and temperature play an important role in minimizing accidents, reducing fuel consumption and making more convenient driving while minimizing the braking distance and improving tire life [2]. Leakage of pressure from tire and higher temperature if not detected on time, can cause serious problems during running/moving vehicles. To tackle real-time tire pressure and temperature, many wired and wireless technologies using radio frequency (RF) module has been introduced. However, RF module is limited by the antenna coverage range and requires close contact with sensors. Thus, expected to improve the reliability of the system by identifying the transmission delay scenario in the system. In addition, an advanced and latest system architecture is required.

© The Author(s), under exclusive license to Springer Nature Singapore Pte Ltd. 2022
S.-Y. Hsieh et al. (Eds.): ICS 2022, CCIS 1723, pp. 599–610, 2022.
https://doi.org/10.1007/978-981-19-9582-8_53

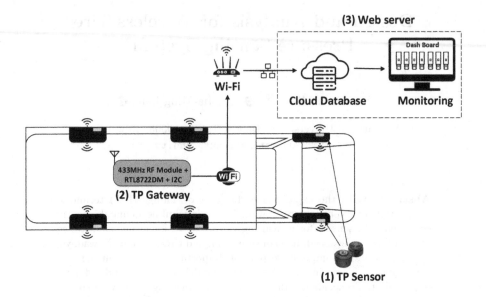

Fig. 1. Wireless tire pressure sensing system (WTPSS).

In this work we considered wireless pressure and temperature sensors, generally used in intelligent vehicle tires these days [3]. These kinds of sensors are usually equipped with RF transmitter modules, a battery and many sensor cells [4]. This allows each sensor to transmit data to the receiver end to decode the real-time pressure and temperature. Based on the observation, we proposed a Wireless Tire Pressure Sensing System (WTPSS) that combines wireless sensor information and RF transmission modules to achieve real-time data monitoring. As shown in Fig. 1, a vehicle consists of (1) TP sensors deployed on each vehicle's tire. (2) TP Gateway placed on each vehicle which includes a 433 MHz RF Module, RTL8722DM development board and Inter-Integrated Circuit (I2C) display. Through the 433 MHz RF Module, it detects each TP sensor and displays the pressure and temperature on the I2C display after processing on RTL8722DM development board. On the other hand, TP Gateway connects with the available Wi-Fi through access points, and the data will be sent to the (3) Web server. To improve the reliability of system and data transmission delay, we found that dimensioning wireless sensor transmission requires formal methods to guarantee transmission performance and delay in various wakeup-sleep conditions. These transmission time delays are general because they can be used in combination to model any complex data transmission traffic scenarios in wireless sensor data transmission.

In order to improve the reliability, we propose a deterministic scheme to identify data receiving delay for sensor transmission to make it highly and precisely real-time to avoid any serious cause. We considered different wakeup-sleep periods to schedule the transmission data on time and save more energy. The scheme includes the number of sensors, wakeup-sleep period, cycle length and transmission delay. A Wireless Tire Pressure Sensing System has been developed and extensive field experiments have been performed in a large parking lot for several months. All the real-time data for vehicle tires can be accessed by the users through the web service.

The rest of this paper is organized as follows. Section 2 is related work; Sect. 3 introduces the system model, including preliminaries, system architecture and problem definition; Sect. 4 describes the proposed scheme; Sect. 5 shows the performance evaluation. Section 6 draws some conclusions.

2   Related Work

Many efforts have been made in previous years to develop tire pressure sensing systems in order to avoid accidents and ensure tire safety [3]. Numerous technologies, including a number of concepts, are proposed to avoid the serious issues caused by sudden changes in tire pressure and temperature [5]. The study [6], proposed a wireless monitoring system for motorcycles that functions as a real-time determinant of tire pressure conditions to improve the experience for bike riders where the system uses input variables in the form of tire pressure and ambient temperature processed on the helmet device. However, the above studies neglect the seriousness of transmission delay. Reference [7], focused on increasing the estimation efficiency of the frequency based on tire-pressure monitoring systems with Wavelet and a Haar Transform based method. Whereas, reference [8] designed an optimized Bayesian estimation data fusion method used to fuse the multi-sensor data to reduce the uncertainty of the pressure measurement. However, transmission loss and reliability have not been considered. The study [9] identified the effect of the tire on the RF signal and system function and compared it to the transmission in an open space in a heavy vehicle environment. Whereas, reference [10] exploited a delay comparison between the wireless experiment and the traditional wired pressure measurement system. However, these works [6–9] and [10] have not considered the issues of energy saving and data receiving delay, which is the key problem identified in our paper.

3   System Model

3.1   System Architecture

Figure 2, shows the system architecture of WTPSS. It basically consists of three parts, including (1) TP Sensor, (2) TP Gateway and (3) Web server. Specifically, wireless inbuilt battery powered TP sensor cell measures the temperature and pressure to send data for preprocessing and transmitting through the RF transmitter. The 433 MHz RF Module receives the output wireless signals from TP sensor. The RTL8722DM IoT development board analyses and controls the received signals and delivers them to the relevant output to show for monitoring on the last part, i.e., Web server. The sensor's transmitted signal, with a fixed cycle length of 32 s, consists of a sensor ID, Pressure, Temperature, Alert, Battery and the Status of sensor (Fig. 3). The RTL8722DM development board then handles the examined signal and adjusts based on the requirements.

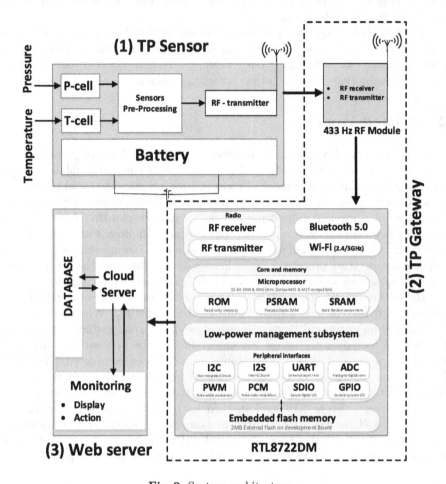

Fig. 2. System architecture.

The structure of the data is reconstructed after retrieving the original sensor data from the transmitted encoded bit values. Figure 3 depicts the packet structure, along with the byte length after decoding. The preamble is a series of Zero and x (i.e., 0x) and the data following the preamble consists of a sequence, with sensor ID, Pressure, Temperature, Alert, Battery voltage and Status of sensor.

Specifically, each component is described as follows.

TP Sensor is battery powered wireless sensor in a combination of pressure, temperature and RF transmitter module inbuilt suitable for Smart Industrial IoT applications. The sensor T_n collects accurate tire pressure, temperature data

Preamble	Sensor ID	Pressure	Temperature	Alert	Battery	Status
0x -	12X35Y67 -	0128 -	025 -	00 -	2 -	3

←03 bytes→←09 bytes→←05 bytes→←———04 bytes———→←03 bytes→←02 bytes→←01 bytes→

←———————————————————————— 26 bytes ————————————————————————→

Fig. 3. Data structure example.

and transmits it periodically in every cycle length C_L (i.e., 32 s) through the RF transmitter.

TP Gateway. Ameba RTL8722DM IoT Development Board integrates the System on Chip (SoC) powered by a high-performance MCU. This SoC also integrates the high-security architecture with ultra-low power consumption suitable for IoT applications. RTL8722DM continuously performs wakeup-sleep period $(W + S)$ and receives the sensor transmission T_n in $C_L^i = \sum_{i=1}^{n}[W + S]$ during the wakeup period W. While the system doesn't update the sensor transmission T_n, it either indicates that the system is in a sleep period S or sensor transmission T_n is not available. Besides the high-performance MCU, RTL8722DM SoC also incorporates wireless equipment such as dual-band Wi-Fi (2.4 GHz/5 GHz) which allows users to access real-time sensor transmission T_n over web server.

The 433 MHz RF module helps to receive the sensor transmission T_n (i.e. 433 MHz frequency data) and sends it to the RTL8722DM development board to decode the data in an appropriate format (Fig. 3). The 433 MHz RF module receives sensor transmissions T_n in the encoded form of signals and transfers them to the data pin, which can later be decoded by using the RT8722DM development board.

Web server is a portrayal of the interface between a physical device and the platform service. It consists of a database for cloud servers which allows access to real-time sensor transmission T_n to user interface. It helps to input and monitor the sensor transmission T_n associated with the vehicle and helps to monitor the real-time event transmitted during wakeup period W.

3.2   Problem Definition

To improve the reliability of system and data transmission delay, we found that dimensioning wireless sensor transmission requires formal methods to guarantee transmission performance, the worst transmission received delay, and energy saving in various wakeup-sleep conditions. These transmission time delays are general because they can be used in combination to model any complex data transmission traffic scenarios in wireless sensor data transmission. The sensor

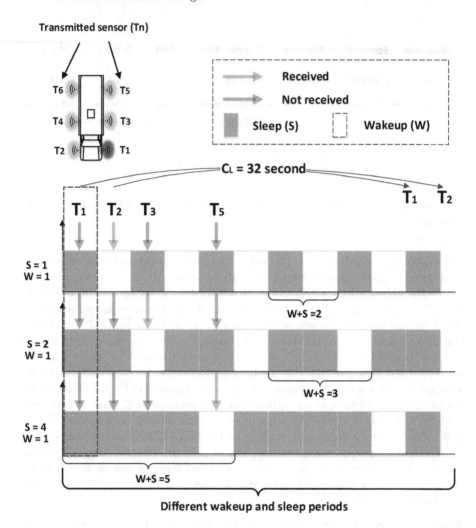

Fig. 4. Formulation of the problem

transmission T_n couldn't assure the successful reception during different wakeup-sleep periods unless the wakeup period W matches with sensor transmission T_n time. The unsuccessful sensor transmission will be considered a delay until it is not received successfully in the system. As shown in the Fig. 4, for different wakeup-sleep periods, sensor transmissions T_2, T_3, and T_5 are received successfully in the system when wakeup-sleep periods are 2, 3, and 5 s respectively. Whereas T_1 is not received successfully in the system during any wakeup-sleep periods (i.e., 2, 3, and 5 s), which costs the least transmission delay of a cycle length C_L. Although each sensor transmits data every 32 s periodically, quantifying the worst sensor transmission T^{max} becomes an important issue in a multiple sensor transmission $T_n, n = 1....C_L$ environment.

In this paper, we try to ask how to identify worst sensor transmission T^{max} received in the system to make it highly and precisely real-time to avoid any serious cause.

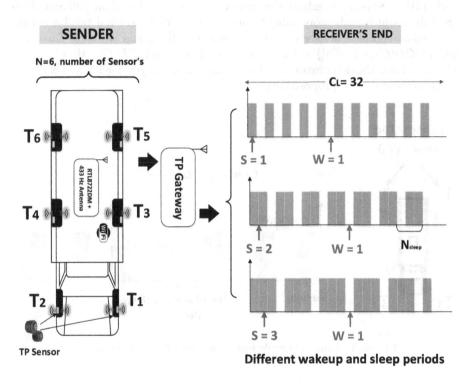

Fig. 5. System model and transmission scenario.

4   The Proposed Scheme

To identify worst sensor transmission T^{max} received, we consider different sleep S and wake-up W (W is fixed as 1 s) to schedule the transmission data on time. The scheme includes number of sensors $T_n, n = 1....C_L$, each transmitting data every 32 s, number of sleep cycles N_{sleep}, cycle length C_L and the worst sensor transmission T^{max} received for each sensor. As shown in the Fig. 5, each sensor transmits data $T_1, T_2, T_3, ...T_6$. On the other hand, 433 MHz RF Module receives the transmission in cycle $C_L^i = \sum_{i=1}^{n}[W + S]$, and checks if the transmission is received during wakeup W period or not.

In this section, we introduce a *deterministic scheme* to show how to derive a worst sensor transmission T^{max} received for any sensor $T_n, n = 1....C_L$ in the system, where C_L is cycle length with a fixed length of 32 s. Which implies that the transmitted sensor T_n can have a minimum/maximum bound of T_1/T_{32}. We considered wakeup-sleep period $[W + S]$ where W is fixed as 1 s and S varies from minimum 1 to maximum 31 s for different wakeup-sleep period. The wakeup-sleep period $[W + S]$ helps to adjust the energy consumption based on different sleep (S) values which adds more value to our scheme. We considered two basic case of Greatest common divisor (GCD) for cycle length C_L and $[W + S]$. *Case 1* is when $GCD(C_L, [W + S]) \neq 1$ whereas *Case 2* is when $GCD(C_L, [W + S]) = 1$. Figure 6 shows the demonstration of transmission with cycle length and wakeup-sleep scenario for the proposed scheme.

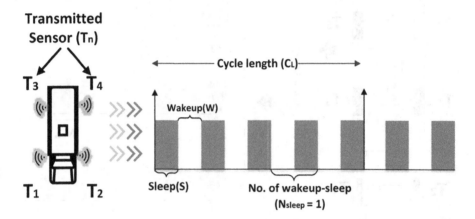

Fig. 6. Transmission cycle length and wakeup-sleep scenario.

4.1   Deterministic Scheme

To identify any transmitted sensor T_n in the system, first we need to identify if the transmitted sensor T_n is received in the system or not. We consider the cycle starting at the first second as a wakeup slot of cycle length. The worst transmission T^{max} is the last sensor to be received in the system with minimum cycle length of C_L^{min} which included minimum number of sleep cycles N_{sleep}^{min}, where $T^{max} = max\{T_n | T_n + C_L^{min} = N_{sleep}^{min}[W + S] + W, n = 1, 2, ..., C_L - 1\}$. We determine C_L and $[W + S]$ to calculate the followings,

$$T^{max} = \begin{cases} \infty & \text{if } GCD(C_L, [W + S]) \neq 1 \\ C_L - S & \text{if } GCD(C_L, [W + S]) = 1 \end{cases} \quad (1)$$

where, C_L is cycle length with a fixed length of 32 s. Note that the larger value of T^{max} implies the worst transmission of the sensor T_n. To quantify the minimum number of sleep cycles N_{sleep}^{min} taken by sensor T_n, we use minimum cycle length C_L^{min} as follows,

$$N_{sleep}^{min} = \begin{cases} \infty & \text{if } GCD(C_L, [W+S]) \neq 1 \\ \frac{C_L + C_L^{min} - [W+S]}{[W+S]} & \text{if } GCD(C_L, [W+S]) = 1 \end{cases} \quad (2)$$

where, $C_L^{min} = C_L * S$, if $GCD(C_L, [W+S]) = 1$. This implies the minimum number of cycle length taken by sensor T_n for worst-case transmission T^{max} in the system.

5   Performance Evaluation

In this section, we develop a simulator in Python and perform real-time experiments to verify the efficiency of the proposed scheme. The parameters of the simulation and experiment are shown in Table 1. For simulation purposes, we used ASUS D320MT platform with Intel Core i7-6700 CPU @ 3.4 GHz, 16 GB RAM, and Intel(R) HD 530 Graphics Card (Intel, Santa Clara, CA, USA). Since the related work is limited to solving a set of different problems, we compare the schemes based on mathematical analysis, simulation and experiment results.

Table 1. The simulation & experiment parameters

Parameters	Values
Total number of sensors	32
Number of iteration (simulation)	500
Cycle length (C_L)	32 s
Wakeup period (W)	1 s (fix)
Wakeup-sleep period ($W + S$)	3, 5, 7, ... 31 (in seconds)

5.1   Worst Transmission Delay

Figure 7 shows the worst transmission delay (in seconds) received in the system for different wakeup-sleep periods. Based on different wakeup-sleep periods, considering mathematical analysis, experiment, and simulation (based on random transmission for 500 iterations), it is shown that the delay is increasing when the number of wakeup-sleep periods increases. This is due to the only availability of wakeup slots (1 s fix) in a wakeup-sleep period, resulting in higher transmission delays when wakeup-sleep period is increasing. Analysis results are efficient due to fixed transmission time and period (32 s), whereas simulation and experiment results are based on random sensor transmission (including collision possibility), causing the higher delay. The worst transmission delay (in seconds) can be calculated by $T^{max} \times N_{sleep}^{min} + W$.

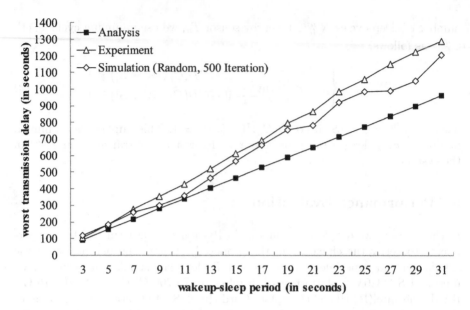

Fig. 7. Comparisons on worst transmission delay for all wakeup-sleep period

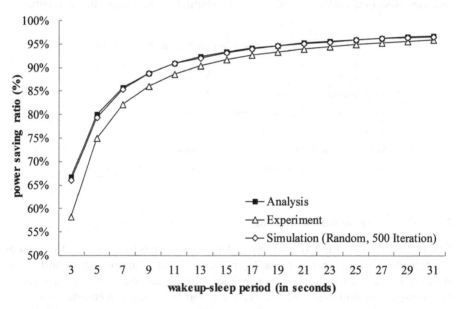

Fig. 8. Comparisons on power saving ratio for all wakeup-sleep period

5.2 Power Saving Rate

Finally, we calculate the power saving percentage based on wakeup-sleep period. Figure 8 shows that all the schemes save more than 55% to 95% of power while considering 3 to 31 s of wakeup-sleep period respectively. As the number of wakeup-sleep periods increases, the power saving increases or power consumption decreases rapidly for all the schemes. This is due to the consideration of a shorter wakeup period (i.e., 1 s) in our scheme for all wakeup-sleep period scenarios.

$$\text{Power saving ratio}\,(\%) = \frac{\text{sleep time length (S)}}{\text{wakeup-sleep period length (W+S)}} \times 100$$

6 Conclusion

In this paper, we have addressed the issue of the worst transmission delay for any sensor received in the system while considering energy consumption. We first identify the factors affecting the transmission and then propose a deterministic scheme to evaluate them. Specifically, we developed the system model for WTPSS and then identified the worst scenario for sensor transmission based on different wakeup-sleep periods with the least wakeup period to improve energy consumption. Experiment and simulation results have verified that our scheme can identify the worst transmission while saving energy.

References

1. Montero-Salgado, J.P., Muñoz-Sanz, J., Arenas-Ramírez, B., Alén-Cordero, C.: Identification of the mechanical failure factors with potential influencing road accidents in Ecuador. Int. J. Environ. Res. Public Health **19**(13) (2022). https://www.mdpi.com/1660-4601/19/13/7787
2. Bachman, L.J.: Do changes in temperature and inflation pressure affect rolling resistance during road and track testing for fuel economy of class 8 tractor-trailers? Tire Sci. Technol. **46**(2), 93–104 (2018)
3. Xiangjun, T.: The design and research of tire pressure monitoring system. In: 2016 International Conference on Intelligent Transportation, Big Data & Smart City (ICITBS), pp. 479–481. IEEE (2016)
4. Javheri, S.R., Sarka, B.K., Patel, B.R.S.: WTPMS: wireless tyre pressure monitoring system for motor vehicles. In: 2017 International Conference on Computing, Communication, Control and Automation (ICCUBEA), pp. 1–6. IEEE (2017)
5. Sharmila, C., Vinod, V.M.: Design of a real-time tyre pressure monitoring system for LMVs. In: 2016 Online International Conference on Green Engineering and Technologies (IC-GET), pp. 1–4. IEEE (2016)
6. Tawakal, M.I., Abdurohman, M., Putrada, A.G.: Wireless monitoring system for motorcycle tire air pressure with pressure sensor and voice warning on helmet using fuzzy logic. In: 2021 International Conference on Software Engineering & Computer Systems and 4th International Conference on Computational Science and Information Management (ICSECS-ICOCSIM), pp. 47–52. IEEE (2021)
7. Marton, Z., Fodor, D., Enisz, K., Nagy, K.: Frequency analysis based tire pressure monitoring. In: 2014 IEEE International Electric Vehicle Conference (IEVC), pp. 1–5. IEEE (2014)
8. Cao, M., You, D.: An application of optimized Bayesian estimation data fusion algorithm in tire pressure monitoring system. In: 2018 Chinese Control and Decision Conference (CCDC), pp. 6564–6568. IEEE (2018)

9. Tawakuli, A.R., Soua, R., Engel, T.: Evaluation of TPMS signal propagation in a heavy commercial vehicle environement. In: 2021 IEEE 94th Vehicular Technology Conference (VTC2021-Fall), pp. 1–5. IEEE (2021)
10. Qing, D., Hongxiang, Z., Lijun, Y.: Design of tire pressure test system based on wireless transmission. In: 2021 IEEE 3rd International Conference on Civil Aviation Safety and Information Technology (ICCASIT), pp. 1025–1029. IEEE (2021)

Ubiquitous Cybersecurity and Forensics

Preserving Collusion-Free and Traceability in Car-Sharing System Based on Blockchain

Tzu-Hao Chen$^{(\boxtimes)}$ (iD), Chit-Jie Chew, Ying-Chin Chen, and Jung-San Lee (iD)

Feng Chia University, Taichung, Taiwan
wilsonchen.tzuhao@gmail.com

Abstract. A car-sharing system has been considered the most promising solution to solve the waste of natural resources, traffic congestion, and greenhouse gas emission in the city. However, the conventional car-sharing system relies on a trusted third party, which is challenging to maximize the benefits of the C2C model. This paper aims to design a decentralized car-sharing system based on the blockchain technique. The demander and supplier can use the smart contract to share the vehicle without the centralized system. In addition, even if the vehicle is damaged, the supplier can track the responsibility for the damage by accessing the order information stored in the blockchain. Simultaneously, the proposed method avoids collusion between the malicious user and the centralized server. Experiments have shown the performance analysis between the centralized car-sharing system and the proposed framework, pointing out the advantages of our new framework.

Keywords: Sharing economy · Car-sharing · Blockchain · Smart contract

1 Introduction

With the explosion development of vehicular ad-hoc networks (VANET), vehicles brought huge convenience for people to travel in a short period, making vehicles inseparable from human life. According to statistics in 2019, there were 1.4 billion vehicles in the world [1]. However, vehicles are idle 95% of the time [2], meaning that a vehicle is only used for 1.2 h a day on average. The waste of natural resources exploitation leads to severe environmental problems, even more, leading to higher resource prices. This could affect economic growth and damage the environment [3]. In order to improve the deteriorating situation, car-sharing services have become a promising solution worldwide [4].

Sharing economy increases utilization and reduces the idle capacity, which makes the vehicle in high productivity to the end of the vehicle lifespan [5]. Through car sharing, people who need vehicles can rent vehicles from suppliers and have the convenience without affording the high budget for having a vehicle. In addition, it reduces the number of vehicles in the city, thereby reducing traffic congestion and greenhouse gas emission [6]. Moreover, the statistical data on the number of car-sharing users worldwide from 2017 to 2024 is illustrated in Fig. 1. The data before 2022 have been gathered from the

© The Author(s), under exclusive license to Springer Nature Singapore Pte Ltd. 2022
S.-Y. Hsieh et al. (Eds.): ICS 2022, CCIS 1723, pp. 613–624, 2022.
https://doi.org/10.1007/978-981-19-9582-8_54

real world, while the rest are predicted. The number of demanders has increased from 36 million in 2017 to 48.5 million in 2022, and the number of demanders has increased by 10 million users in 5 years. Finally, it is predicted that there will be 56.3 million number of demander in 2024 [7]. At the same time, according to the statistics in 2019, the market value of the car-sharing economy approached 2.5 billion, and it is predicted to reach 9 billion by 2026 [8]. All the statics show that the market value and users of the car-sharing economy rise continually.

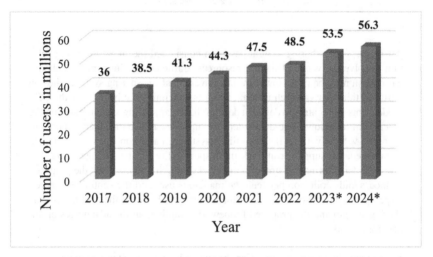

Fig. 1. Number of car-sharing users worldwide from 2017 to 2024.

Consumer-to-consumer (C2C) car-sharing economy creates a win-win situation for both the supplier and demander, but information security issues are challenged. In the traditional C2C car-sharing economy [9], the user's personal information and sharing records are stored in a centralized facility. However, the centralized server suffers from a single point of failure by a malicious attacker. If the server is compromised, the user's private information can be stolen easily, thereby endangering the user's security. In addition, the user needs to pay high taxes to the car-sharing platform provider. Moreover, there is a fairness issue in the centralized car-sharing system. Under the scenario of centralized car-sharing, if the vehicle is damaged, although the server has stored the relevant order information, malicious users can bribe the centralized facility and easily tamper with the stored information. This might result in the actual driving status not being tracked.

To solve the abovementioned problems, we propose a blockchain-based car-sharing platform that immediately solves the problems generated by centralized platforms. In addition, a user uploads order information to the blockchain via VANET. C2C car-sharing can run smoothly in the new proposed framework without a centralized platform. The supplier and demander establish the car-sharing contract through smart contracts without paying the tax rate to a centralized platform. Although the vehicle is damaged, the supplier can track the information stored in the blockchain to trace the incident. According to the performance comparisons, the new framework has better results compared to the related works.

Data Security: Data security includes three properties, that is confidentiality, integrity, and availability. Firstly, confidentiality means that only the authorized user can access the information stored in the system. The new framework provides a secure car-sharing system based on the asymmetric cryptosystem and blockchain technique. To secure the privacy of the demander and the supplier in the car-sharing system, the order information of the supplier and demander not be disclosed by any unauthorized user. Since the proposed scheme is based on a consortium blockchain, only the authorized agency has the right to access it. Secondly, the integrity of the car-sharing system has to be guaranteed. Through the asymmetric cryptosystem, the proposed scheme keeps the order information consistent while transmitting it in the public channel. Finally, the feature of availability means that the system shall guarantee itself available every time and everywhere, avoiding the single point of failure caused by the centralized system. The users contribute computing power to maintain the system. Based on the characteristics of the blockchain, unless 51% of nodes in the blockchain are compromised, the system operates normally. This can achieve the properties of confidentiality, integrity, and availability.

Collusion-Free: Specific users cannot collude with the vehicle sharing platform and then tamper with the order information to escape the responsibility for the vehicle's damage. In the centralized platform, it is easy to bribe the authorized agency to tamper with the information in the system. Since the proposed scheme is based on blockchain, if the malicious attacker cannot bribe 51% of nodes in the blockchain, the information stored in the blockchain will not be tampered with. Therefore, all of the corruption problems of the centralized facilities can be solved.

Tamper-Free: All of the order information shall not be tampered with after being uploaded to the blockchain. Although the malicious attacker can bribe a node in the blockchain if the attacker cannot bribe over 51% of nodes in the blockchain. The order information does not be tampered with. Thus, tamper-free information in the system can be ensured.

Traceability: All of the vehicle statuses can be tracked through the order information recorded on the blockchain. The order information can be used to arbitrate disputes even if the vehicles are damaged. In the proposed scheme, the order information is regularly uploaded through VANET to the blockchain. The supplier can track the history of the vehicle, which contains the vehicle's operation. The authors are able to ensure the properties of traceability.

The rest of the article is organized as follows. In Sect. 2, we introduce the background of the article. The proposed scheme is presented in Sect. 3, followed by the experimental results and analysis in Sect. 4. Finally, the authors conclude the article in Sect. 5.

2 Related Works

We describe related works we use in the proposed scheme, we first introduce the blockchain technique in Sect. 2.1 and smart contract in Sect. 2.2.

2.1 Blockchain

Blockchain is a distributed ledger technology that employs asymmetric encryption, digital signature, and one-way hash function to fulfill the properties of decentralization, tamper-free, traceability, and transparency [10]. Blockchain is maintained by all nodes in the blockchain network. Each block is constructed with the hash value of the previous block, timestamp, merkle root, and nonce. A brief structure is depicted in Fig. 2. The timestamp is the time when the block was established, the block header is calculated from the previous block header with hash function SHA256, and the merkle root is generated from the hash values of all previous transaction.

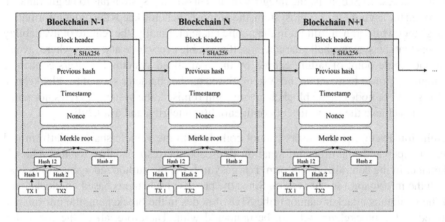

Fig. 2. Blockchain structure

Blockchain can be organized into three categories, public blockchain, private blockchain, and consortium blockchain [11]. In the public blockchain, all of the members in each node keep ledgers and participate in consensus, which makes the consensus faster but has heavier loading. Besides, all of the nodes in the blockchain can join or leave the blockchain easily without permission. On the other hand, the private blockchain is managed by a private enterprise, and it has centralized characteristics [12].

As to consortium blockchain, only the member of the alliance can access the information stored in the blockchain. In addition, the consensus efficiency of the consortium blockchain is intermediated between the public blockchain and the private blockchain. Hence, consortium blockchain is suitable for the car-sharing system.

2.2 Smart Contract

The concept of the smart contract is proposed by Szabo [13] in 1997, which is the contract automatically executed without a third party. The smart contract is the code stored in the blockchain, it will trigger via address and specific regulation, such as the values and status of users. When all of the conditions in the smart contract are satisfied, the transaction will automatically execute. For example, the vending machine will automatically supply different beverages when customers press the button and put a dollar in. Hence, we will leverage smart smarts to achieve a decentralized car-sharing platform.

3 Proposed Scheme

IN this section, we describe the design of the car-sharing blockchain system. The system framework is shown in Fig. 3. The user contains suppliers and demanders. In the beginning, both the supplier and demander have to provide relevant information to the certificate authority (CA) to complete registration, such as the user's e-wallet, driving license, car registration, identification, etc. After registration, suppliers can rent out their vehicles in blockchain, and demanders can rent the vehicles through blockchain and obtain the right to use the vehicle. After the demander completes the rental, it will return the right of use to the supplier. If the vehicle is damaged, the order information stored in the blockchain can be used as the basis for the arbitration of disputes. Notations used in the proposed scheme are defined in Table 1.

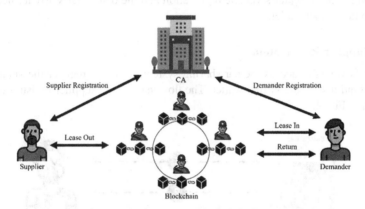

Fig. 3. Car-sharing system blockchain framework

Table 1. Notations

Notations	Description
i	User ith which i can be supplier S_i or demander D_i, $0 \leq i \leq n$.
j	Vehicle jth, $0 \leq j \leq n$.
SK_i/PK_i	The private/public key of i
$E_{SK_i}/D_{PK_i}(.)$	The asymmetric encryption and decryption with SK_i and PK_i, respectively
ID_i	The identification of i
$h(.)$	One-way hash function of SHA256
DL_i	The driving license of i
VIN_j	The vehicle identification number of j

(continued)

Table 1. (*continued*)

Notations	Description
VR_j	The vehicle registration of j, including VIN_j, brand, expiration of the vehicle registration, etc.
DDL_i	The digital driving license of i
DVR_j	The digital vehicle registration of j
$address_i$	The address of the virtual wallet of i

3.1 Registration Phase

In this phase, the supplier's vehicle registration and the demander's driving license are bound to the virtual wallet.

3.1.1 Supplier Registration

Supplier S_i wants to access the car-sharing system. S_i has to register the vehicle with CA and bind it with the virtual wallet. The flowchart of the supplier registration phase is shown in Fig. 4.

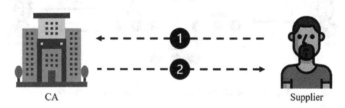

CA   Supplier

Fig. 4. Supplier registration flowchart

Step 1. S_i provides VR_{S_i}, ID_{S_i}, and $address_{S_i}$ to CA through the secure channel in order to bind the vehicle registration with the virtual wallet.

Step 2. If yes, CA accepts the registration request. Then, CA computes $DVR_{S_i} = E_{SK_{CA}}(address_{S_i}\|VIN_{S_i})$ and issues DVR_{S_i} to S_i.

3.1.2 Demander Registration

Demander D_i wants to access the car-sharing system. D_i has to register the driving license with CA and bind it with the virtual wallet. The flowchart of the demander registration phase is shown in Fig. 5.

Step 1. D_i provides DL_{D_i} and $address_{D_i}$ to CA through the secure channel in order to bind the driving license with the virtual wallet.

Step 2. If yes, CA accepts the registration request. Next, CA computes $DDL_{D_i} = E_{SK_{CA}}(address_{D_i})$ and issues DDL_{D_i} to D_i.

Fig. 5. Demander registration flowchart

3.2 Lease Out Phase

Lease out phase is for the supplier to publish the rental contract to the blockchain. The supplier checks the rule block and creates a rental contract, which is verified by the miners and published in the blockchain. The flowchart of the lease out phase is shown in Fig. 6.

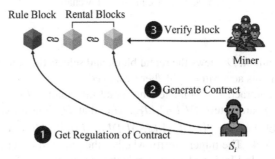

Fig. 6. Lease out phase flowchart

Step 1. Get regulation of contract: S_i has to acquire the rule of blockchain before publishing a rental contract. Then, S_i completes the required information of the rental block for the formulation of the smart contract, such as car plate number, location, rental starting time, rental ending time, mileage fee, deposit percentage, and hourly price.

Step 2. Generate contract: S_i completes the rental information LO_{S_i} and computes the following parameters, $DVR_{S_i}||LO_{S_i}$. Later, S_i signs it $E_{SK_{S_i}}\left(DVR_{S_i}||LO_{S_i}\right)$ and then publishes $E_{SK_{S_i}}\left(DVR_{S_i}||LO_{S_i}\right)||DVR_{S_i}||LO_{S_i}||address_{S_i}||VIN_{S_i}$ to blockchain.

Step 3. Verify block: The miners verify whether the rental information LO_{S_i} complies with the rule block and verifies whether S_i is eligible for leasing out the vehicle. If $D_{PK_{S_i}}\left(E_{SK_{S_i}}\left(DVR_{S_i}||LO_{S_i}\right)\right)$?= $(DVR_{S_i}||LO_{S_i})$ and $D_{PK_{CA}}\left(DVR_{S_i}\right)$?= $address_{S_i}||VIN_{S_i}$ hold, the contract is published in blockchain.

3.3 Lease in Phase

The lease in phase is for the demander to have the need to use the vehicle, the demander can view whether the rental contract meets his/her own needs to rent the car. After the lease in phase, the demander has the right to access the car. The flowchart of the lease in phase is shown in Fig. 7.

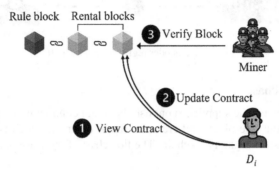

Fig. 7. Lease in phase flowchart

Step 1.   View contract: D_i views the rental block and selects the contract that meets the requirements according to his/her own need.

Step 2.   Update contract: D_i completes the rental information LI_{D_i} and computes the following parameters, $DDL_{D_i}||LI_{D_i}$. After that, D_i signs it $E_{SK_{D_i}}(DDL_{D_i}||LI_{D_i})$ then publishes $E_{SK_{D_i}}(DDL_{D_i}||LI_{D_i})DDL_{D_i}||LI_{D_i}||address_{D_i}$ to blockchain.

Step 3.   Verify block: The miners verify whether the rental information LI_{D_i} complies with the rule block and verifies whether D_i is eligible for leasing the vehicle. If $D_{PK_{D_i}}(E_{SK_{D_i}}(DDL_{D_i}||LI_{D_i}))$?= $(DDL_{D_i}||LI_{D_i})$ and $D_{PK_{CA}}(DDL_{D_i})$?= $address_{D_i}$ hold, the contract is published in blockchain and detains the deposit in the smart contract. The deposit is returned or paid after the end of the rental.

3.4   Return Phase

After the demander finishes the rental, the demander updates the vehicle information to the blockchain. The contract calculates the price or returns the deposit. At the same time, the demander will return the right to use the vehicle to the supplier. The return phase is shown in Fig. 8.

Step 1.   Return vehicle: D_i finishes use of the vehicle and return the vehicle.

Step 2.   Update contract: D_i completes the return information RI_{D_i} then computes the following parameters, $DDL_{D_i}||RI_{D_i}$. D_i signs it $E_{SK_{D_i}}(DDL_{D_i}||RI_{D_i})$ and publishes $E_{SK_{D_i}}(DDL_{D_i}||RI_{D_i})||DDL_{D_i}||RI_{D_i}$ to blockchain.

Step 3.   Verify block: The miners verify the return information RI_{D_i} and the identity of D_i. If $D_{PK_{D_i}}(E_{SK_{D_i}}(DDL_{D_i}||RI_{D_i}))$?= $(DDL_{D_i}||RI_{D_i})$ holds, the contract is updated in the blockchain.

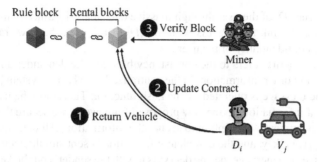

Fig. 8. Return phase flowchart

4 Experimental Results

To highlight the contribution of our proposed scheme, we compare it with a centralized car-sharing system [9], and the performance comparison is shown in Table 2.

Table 2. Performance analysis

Feature		Type	
		[9]	Ours
Data security	Confidentiality	V	V
	Integrity	V	V
	Availability	X	V
Collusion-free		X	V
Tamper-free		X	V
Traceability		X	V

Data Security: IN order to preserve a secure C2C platform, data security plays an essential role in the car-sharing system. Data security considerations include confidentiality, integrity, and availability.

Firstly, confidentiality means that unauthorized users do not access driving information. In the centralized car-sharing system [9], data transmission between PD-KSApp, KS-OBU, and KSMS is protected based on an asymmetric cryptosystem, thus, [9] achieves confidentiality. In our proposed scheme, we leverage the secure channel while user register sharing qualification with CA, which ensures that the user's sensitive information is not exposed. In addition, each phase of the driving information is stored in the consortium blockchain. Therefore, the proposed method guarantees that only authorized agencies can access sensitive information. Moreover, we bind ID_i with the *address*. Although the malicious user camouflages as an authorized agency, they have difficulty knowing the true ID_i of the user through massive data analysis. Since malicious attackers cannot directly link the *address* with the ID_i of the user, the new framework can guarantee the confidentiality of the user.

Secondly, integrity refers to the consistency between the demander and blockchain after transmitting order information. In the centralized car-sharing system [9], the transmission of the message is operated by the hash function. Therefore, the user can verify the integrity of information. In the new proposed framework, we secure the order information with asymmetric encryption to secure the information. All data are signed with the sender's private key, and the complete information is sent simultaneously. After the receiver receives the message, he/she decrypts it with the sender's public key to compare the consistency of the message. We examine the integrity of each phase below.

In the lease out phase, miners verify the ID_{S_i} of S_i. If $D_{PK_{S_i}}\left(E_{SK_{S_i}}\left(DVR_{S_i}||LO_{S_i}\right)\right)$ $?= \left(DVR_{S_i}||LO_{S_i}\right)$ and $D_{PK_{CA}}\left(DVR_{S_i}\right)$ $?= address_{S_i}||VIN_{S_i}$ hold, it means that the lease out information is secured because there is the only supplier S_i has his/her own private key SK_{S_i}, the lease out phase can achieve integrity.

In the lease in phase, miners verify the ID_{D_i} of D_i. If $D_{PK_{D_i}}\left(E_{SK_{D_i}}\left(DDL_{D_i}||LI_{D_i}\right)\right)$ $?= \left(DDL_{D_i}||LI_{D_i}\right)$ and $D_{PK_{CA}}\left(DDL_{D_i}\right)$ $?= address_{D_i}$ hold, it means that the lease in information is secured, which is the same as the return phase. The miners verify the return information RI_{D_i} and the ID_{D_i} of D_i. If $D_{PK_{D_i}}\left(E_{SK_{D_i}}\left(DDL_{D_i}||RI_{D_i}\right)\right)$ $?= \left(DDL_{D_i}||RI_{D_i}\right)$ holds, because there is the only demander D_i has his/her own private key SK_{D_i}, the lease in and return phase has the ability to achieve integrity. Hence, the integrity of the new framework is guaranteed.

Finally, availability refers to the car-sharing system that shall no longer be bounded by space, time, and scale [14]. The system shall guarantee that its service is always available to the user. In the centralized car-sharing system [9], the service might be interrupted if the centralized system suffers from a single point of failure by a malicious attacker, such as DoS and DDoS attacks [15]. In the new framework, we leverage the consortium blockchain to avoid the single point of failure. The users contribute computing power to maintain the blockchain. Even if a single node has been compromised, services can be provided generally. Except for more than 51% of node abnormalities, the system is not breaking down. In fact, it is difficult to disrupt 51% of the user because of the characteristic of the blockchain. Thus, the proposed method achieves availability.

Collusion-Free: The meaning of collusion-free indicates that no one can collude with the system, thereby affecting overall fairness. In the centralized car-sharing system [9], the paper adopts a centralized management architecture. In the aspect of users, they can bribe the system to adjust their reputation values to increase the willingness of other users to rent vehicles, which raises the probability of a collusion attack. In the new framework, we leverage the distributed consortium blockchain. If the malicious user cannot bribe 51% of nodes in the blockchain, the collusion attack will not happen because the malicious attacker cannot tamper with the order information stored in the blockchain. Therefore, there is no collusion issue in our proposed framework.

Tamper-Free: Tamper-free refers to the order information not being tampered with by malicious users after being uploaded. In a centralized car-sharing system [9], the authorized agency can easily tamper with the user's reputation value stored in the system. Moreover, the order information stored in the system could be tampered with by malicious attackers. If the vehicle is damaged, there is no reliable order information to prove the arbitration of disputes. In the proposed framework, all order information is recorded in the blockchain. Suppose a malicious attacker attempts to tamper with the order information in the blockchain. It is hard for a malicious attacker to control 51% of the computing power in the blockchain due to the characteristic of the blockchain. Consequently, the order information has not been tampered with by the attacker.

Traceability: IF the vehicle is damaged in the car-sharing system, it is important that the driving information must be the basis for arbitration disputes. In the centralized car-sharing system [9], the order information is not recorded. Even if the vehicle is damaged, it is difficult to be held accountable for the accident. The new framework uploads the lease in, lease out, and return information to the blockchain. Although the vehicle is missing or damaged, the supplier can trace the responsibility of the vehicle damage through the information.

5   Conclusions

In this article, we have introduced the decentralized car-sharing system based on the blockchain. The properties of decentralization and tamper-free inherited from the blockchain can realize the decentralized car-sharing system, which avoids the tampering of order information stored in the blockchain and the collusion between malicious users and the centralized car-sharing system. The experiment results have demonstrated the strength of the proposed framework over the centralized car-sharing system, which can benefit both the supplier and demander in the car-sharing system.

References

1. Chesterton, A.: https://www.carsguide.com.au/car-advice/how-many-cars-are-there-in-the-world-70629. Accessed 14 Sept 2022
2. Shoup, D.: The High Cost of Free Parking. Updated edn. Planners Press (2011)
3. Dabbous, A., Tarhini, A.: Does sharing economy promote sustainable economic development and energy efficiency? Evidence from OECD countries. J. Innov. Knowl. **6**(1), 58–68 (2021)
4. Ritter, M., Schanz, H.: The sharing economy: a comprehensive business model framework. J. Clean. Prod. **213**, 320–331 (2019)
5. Demaily, D., Novel, A.-S.: The sharing economy: make it sustainable. IDDRI Study **3**(14), 14–30 (2014)
6. Zhou, Q.-H., Yang, Z., Zhang, K., Zheng, K., Liu, J.: A decentralized car-sharing control scheme based on smart contract in internet-of-vehicles. In: 2020 IEEE 91st Vehicular Technology Conference (VTC 2020-Spring), pp. 1–5 (2020)
7. Statista Research Department. https://www.statista.com/outlook/mmo/shared-mobility/shared-rides/car-sharing/worldwide#users. Accessed 14 Sept 2022
8. Car Sharing Market Size by Model (P2P Station-Based Free-Floating) by Business Model (Round Trip One Way) by Application (Business Private) Industry Analysis Report Regional Outlook Application Potential Price Trend Competitive Market Share & Forecast 2020–2026. https://www.gminsights.com/industry-analysis/carsharing-market. Accessed 14 Sept 2022

9. Symeonidis, I., Mustafa, M.A., Preneel, B.: Keyless car sharing system: a security and privacy analysis. In: 2016 IEEE International Smart Cities Conference (ISC2), pp. 1–7 (2016)

10. Zheng, Z.-B., Xie, S.-A., Dai, H.-N., Wang, H.-M.: Blockchain chanllenges and opportunities: a survey. Int. J. Web Grid Serv. **14**(4), 352–375 (2018)

11. Zheng, Z.-B., Xie, S.-A., Dai, H.-N., Chen, X.-P., Wang, H.-M.: An overview of blockchain technology: architecture, consensus, and future trends. In: 2017 IEEE International Congress on Big Data (BigData Congress), pp. 557–564 (2017)

12. Son, S.-H., Lee, J.-Y., Kim, M.-H., Dar, A.K., Park, Y.-H.: Design of secure authentication protocol for cloud-assisted telecare medical information system using blockchain. IEEE Access **8**, 192177–192191 (2020)

13. Magazzeni, D., McBurney, P., Nash, W.: Validation and verification of smart contracts: a research agenda. Computer **50**(9), 50–57 (2017)

14. Lee, J.-S., Lin, K.-S.: An innovative electronic group-buying system for mobile commerce. Electron. Commer. Res. Appl. **12**(1), 1–13 (2013)

15. Peng, T., Leckie, C., Ramamohanarao, K.: Survey of network-based defense mechanisms countering the Dos and DDoS problems. ACM Comput. Surv. **39**(1), 3-es (2007)

Utilization of Theoretical Domains Framework (TDF) to Validate the Digital Piracy Behaviour Constructs – A Systematic Literature Review Study

Nompilo Fakude(✉) ⓘ and Elmarie Kritzinger ⓘ

Science, Engineering and Technology College, School of Computing, University of South Africa (UNISA), PO Box 392, Pretoria 0003, South Africa
42315867@mylife.unisa.ac.za, kritze@unisa.ac.za

Abstract. Changing internet users' behaviors toward digital piracy has been challenging for decades. Therefore, in an attempt to understand digital piracy behaviors, the researchers have included a variety of behavioral psychology theories in their literature. Using theories has resulted in a debate about which theories are relevant in explaining digital piracy behaviors. To address this question, the researchers adopted the Theoretical Domains Framework (TDF) to demonstrate the link between constructs from theories and constructs extracted from the TDF. Following a systematic literature review approach, the researchers reviewed 19 papers related to digital piracy, where various behavioral theories were identified, and from them, numerous constructs were derived. The purpose of the current study is to provide a link between digital piracy behavior and behavioral constructs from theories and to validate them utilizing a Theoretical Domains Framework (TDF).

Keywords: Constructs · Digital piracy · Theoretical Domains Framework (TDF) · Theories

1 Introduction

Online users' behaviors must be examined and understood to reduce the number of digital piracy occurrences and change behaviors. Thus, this paper's key objective is to thoroughly evaluate the behavioral theories and their related constructs as a justification utilizing the Theoretical Domains Framework (TDF). Numerous behavioral theories exist, and there is no standard or methodological way to select them. Additionally, the author-defined constructs modify existing theories. These limitations present challenges when researchers attempt to identify fitting digital piracy behavioral theories for their studies. To alleviate these limitations, this paper consolidates a variety of digital piracy behaviors by mapping out their constructs as found in the Theory Domains Framework (TDF). The layout of this paper is set out as follows: Sect. 2 is the background of this study, Sect. 3 presents the methodology used in this study, Sect. 4 covers the results and findings of the study, and Sect. 5 provides a conclusion to the study.

S.-Y. Hsieh et al. (Eds.): ICS 2022, CCIS 1723, pp. 625–636, 2022.
https://doi.org/10.1007/978-981-19-9582-8_55

2 Background

2.1 Digital Piracy Behaviour

Digital piracy, defined as the illegal copying, downloading, and distribution of digital media, has caused significant financial losses within the creative industry. The phenomenon is global, with many common behavioral constructs regardless of the region. Behavior studies have focused on the psychology domain [14]. It is, therefore, imperative that the psychological principles are examined to understand the digital piracy behavioral constructs.

2.2 What is a Theory?

A theory provides a general explanation for observations made over time; it explains and predicts behaviors to understand the phenomena. A theory is formulated to challenge and extend existing knowledge within the limits of critical bounding assumptions [11, 12]. The theories to be explored in the following sections are existing theories in the area being investigated in this study, i.e., digital piracy.

2.3 What is a Construct?

In a psychology setup, theories are founded from the constructs – the mental abstractions used to express the ideas, people, organizations, events, and objects or things that we are interested in [11, 12]. In this study, the constructs will help explain the different components of theories and measure or observe their behavior. Therefore, it is crucial to investigate which constructs are practical for digital piracy behavior change.

2.4 Theory of Domains Framework (TDF)

In the existing knowledge base, various behavioral theories make it difficult for researchers to select the appropriate theories and constructs for their studies. The Theory of Domains Framework (TDF) was developed for intervention implementation by the health care workers study [7], identifying and summarizing 33 behavioral theories and 128 theoretical constructs. The strength of using the TDF is that it helps to understand behavior change by unpacking the influences on behavior in the context in which they occur [15].

3 Methodology

The Theoretical Domains Framework (TDF) implementation guideline in Table 1 is used as a tool or methodology in this paper.

Table 1. Theoretical domains framework guideline and implementation

TDF guidance steps and study implementation	
Select and specify the target behavior	
Action: Digital piracy behavior	
Actor: Internet users	
Target Behavior: Legitimate usage, i.e., copying and distribution of digital media	
Context: Piracy of digital media such as Software, Games, eBook, Music, and Movies, Film or Videos	
Design Selection	Systematic Literature Review
Sample Strategy Development	
Inclusion Criteria: The publication is in English. The study includes hypothesis testing and is an empirical study utilizing a questionnaire or survey. At least one of the null hypotheses must evaluate the relationship between a construct and the construct's "intention to behave" or the behavior itself. Lastly, the constructs used were either validated by the study or used previously as validated constructs **Exclusion Criteria** Media files acquired via a legitimate acquisition channel contain illegal material, such as child pornography, and no novel data is presented, for example, reviews, opinion pieces, or dual publications	
Search Strategy for Academic Databases:	
The papers were found in Google Scholar, the University of South Africa (UNISA) research repository, and journal databases such as Emerald Insight, ScienceDirect, Springer, and ResearchGate. Most articles were published in the last eleven (11) years, i.e., from 2010 to 2021	
Scoping Keywords:	
Modes of sharing: (File sharing OR file sharing OR DRM OR Digital rights manag* OR digital medi* OR File download* OR Torrent file* OR peer-to-peer OR peer-to-peer OR p2p OR usenet OR freenet OR File transfer protocol OR ftp OR shared directory OR Piracy OR pirat* OR online piracy OR copywrit* OR intellectual property). ***AND: Relevant media*** (software OR video game OR video-game OR game OR gamer OR gaming OR electronic games OR digital game* OR digital music OR Music OR iTunes OR Album OR sound record* OR Music record* OR artist OR record sales OR DVD sales OR music purchas*) ***AND: Behavioral theories' terms (independent variables, constructs, factors, and outcomes)*** (attitude* OR intention OR habit OR individual attributes OR Digital Piracy Theories OR SCT OR Theory of Interpersonal Behavior or General Theory of Ethics OR HVE OR Expected Utility Theory). ***NOT: Noise-inducing keywords*** (Medical OR medicine OR medieval OR Navy or naval or maritime)	
Search Results	

(*continued*)

Table 1. (*continued*)

TDF guidance steps and study implementation
The results from the search using the identified keywords were filtered as follows: Based on the results per search, in some instances, keywords were refined. Results were filtered by article title, by reading the abstracts and looking at keywords, and by reading the entire article to find relevance in the content
Study Material Development
Steps used to map digital piracy construct to TDF: *1) Comparison* of definitions between the TDF construct and literature construct; *2) If* definitions are the same, then the literature construct is placed under TDF construct; *3) Else*, compare survey questions of TDF with literature construct; *4) If* definitions are similar, then place literature construct under TDF construct; *5) Else*, add literature construct to TDF construct list. *Redo* the process starting from the last placed literature construct
Analyze the Data
Questions to answer from the data: Which theories are relevant in explaining digital piracy behaviors? How can the digital piracy behavior constructs be mapped to TDF constructs?

Reporting	A findings write-up

4 Findings and Analysis

The current section provides the results from synthesizing behavioral constructs. The Literature Matrix in Table 2 is a synopsis of 19 articles covering 25 behavioral theories that met all the selection criteria and correlated with digital piracy behaviors. The theories examined by the authors were repeated to a total of 59 frequencies in the identified digital piracy literature. The reviewed papers were downloaded from the cumulative 19 journals across various disciplines related to digital piracy, where different behavioral theories were distinguished, and from them, numerous constructs were extracted. Furthermore, the authors of the reviewed papers researched digital content, software, movies (videos), and online music piracy. Therefore, in analysis, the researchers grouped studies on similar theory contexts and, where possible, attempted to highlight commonalities or differences.

The examination of literature in Table 1 found the Deterrence Theory (DT) of Perceived Punishment, Hunt-Vitell (HV) General Theory of Ethics, and Theory of Planned Behaviour (TPB) to be commonly used behavioral theories in digital piracy literature. Figure 1 presents the top three (3) theories from which the constructs used in this study were extracted.

Table 2. Literature matrix of the digital piracy theories and related constructs

	Articles	Theories examined	Context
1	(Sahni and Gupta, 2019)	Social Learning Theory, Self-Control theory	General
2	(Bethelhem, 2013)	Virtual Ethics Theory, Consequentialist Theories, and Theories of Computer Ethics	Software
3	(Meireles and Campos, 2016)	Theory of Planned Behavior and Deterrence Theory	General
4	(Petrescu, Gironda and Korgaonkar, 2017)	Hunt-Vitell General Theory of Marketing Ethics	General
5	(Byl and Belle, 2008)	Theory of Planned Behavior, Ethical Decision-Making Theory	General
6	(Pham, Dang and Nguyen, 2020)	Theory of Planned Behavior	General
7	(Peace, Galletta and Thong, 2003)	Theory of Planned Behavior and Deterrence theory	Software
8	(Cronan and Al-Rafee, 2008)	Hunt and Vitell's General Ethical Theory	General
9	(Liao, Lin and Liu, 2010)	Risk Cognition Theory	Software
10	(Yoon, 2011a, 2011b)	Theory of Planned Behavior	General
11	(Hoang and Ha, 2014)	Theory of Planned Behavior and Social Cognitive Theory	Software
12	(Vida, Kukar-kinney and Koklič, 2015)	Theory of Planned Behavior	General
13	(Yubero, Larrañaga and Villora, 2017)	Theory of Reasoned Action	General
14	(Nii *et al.*, 2020)	Theory of Reasoned Action, Theory of Planned Behavior, SCT, Social Learning Theory	General
15	(Ahmed, 2020)	Criminological theory	General
16	(Park, 2020)	United Theory of Acceptance and Use of Technology	Music
17	(Belle, Macdonald and Wilson, 2007)	Hunt and Vitell's General Ethical Theory, Theory of Planned Behavior, and Theory of Reasoned Action	General
18	(Eisend, 2019)	Expected Utility Theory, and Perceived Risk Theory	General
19	(Karakaya, 2011)	Equity Theory and Deterrence Theory	Software

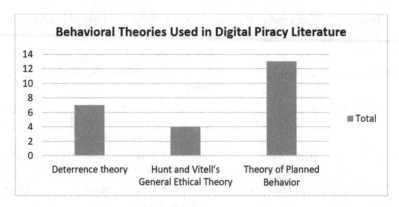

Fig. 1. Top 3 behavioural theories found in digital piracy literature

4.1 Mapping of Literature Constructs to the Theory Domains Framework (TDF)

Evidence suggests that behavior change interventions based on theory are more effective than those without a theoretical base. Therefore, to validate and synthesize the chosen theories and their constructs, the researchers mapped them onto the Theoretical Domains Framework (TDF), as demonstrated in Table 3.

Table 3. Mapping of constructs from theories to their related TDF constructs

1. Deterrence Theory (DT) Constructs	2. Hunt and Vitell's (HT) General Ethical Theory Constructs	3. Theory of Planned Behaviour (TPB) Constructs
Immediate (fast) penalty Certainty of conviction Severity of punishment	Perceived ethical problem, consequences, and alternatives Deontological Norms and evaluation Probabilities and desirability of Consequences Importance of stakeholders Teleological Evaluation Ethical Judgments Intentions Action Control and Actual Consequences	Attitudes Intention Behavioral intention Subjective norms Social norms Perceived power and behavioral control

(*continued*)

Table 3. (*continued*)

TDF Domain Related to DT Constructs: Reinforcement	TDF Domain Related to HT Constructs: Beliefs about Consequences	TDF Domain Related to TPB Constructs: Beliefs about Capabilities
TDF Constructs: Rewards Incentives Punishment Consequents Reinforcement Contingencies Sanctions	TDF Constructs: Beliefs Outcome expectancies Characteristics of outcome expectancies Anticipated regret Consequents	TDF Constructs: Self-confidence Perceived competence Self-efficacy Perceived behavioral control Beliefs Self-esteem Empowerment Professional confidence

This sub-section presents a detailed narration of the theories, their constructs, and related TDF constructs.

4.2 Digital Piracy Behavioural Theories and Connection to TDF

Deterrence Theory

The deterrence theory was first put forth by Bonesana and Beccaria (1764). They suggested that rational human beings will try to avoid pain and maximize pleasure and, in pursuit of such endeavor, will evaluate the costs and benefits of their prospective acts before committing a crime. According to the deterrence theory, individuals weigh the certainty of punishment, the swiftness of the procedure leading up to the punishment, and the severity of the punishment before exhibiting bad behavior [4].

Deterrence Theory Constructs and Connection to TDF

Notably, the three (3) constructs in Table 3 from the Deterrence Theory are related to the TDF Reinforcement domain, which refers to increasing the probability of a response by arranging a dependent relationship, or contingency, between the response and a given stimulus [7]. Under the reinforcement domain are seven (7) constructs shown in Table 3, validated, evaluated, and verified TDF constructs supporting the Deterrence Theory constructs.

Hunt and Vitell's General Ethical Theory

According to Hunt and Vitell's General Ethical theory, individuals engaging in deviant behaviors are influenced by deontological and teleological evaluations (Hunt and Vitell, 2006 [10]). As established by [8], moral obligation is a perception of an individual about a particular behavior influenced by their sense of responsibility and personal obligation [8].

Hunt and Vitell's General Ethical Theory Constructs and Connection to TDF
It is noteworthy that the eight (8) constructs in Table 3 under the General Ethical Theory are related to the TDF Beliefs about the Consequences domain, which refers to the acceptance of the truth, reality, or validity of behavioral outcomes in a given situation [7]. Encapsulated into the beliefs about the consequences domain are five (5) constructs shown in Table 3, which are the validated, evaluated and verified TDF constructs supporting Hunt and Vitell's behavioral theory constructs.

Theory of Planned Behaviour (TPB)
Research has established that the moral obligation and justice component of ethics theory and TPB variables like subjective norms, attitude, and behavioral control influence the intention to commit piracy [18]. A pilot study by [5] involving 20 students contended that the theory of planned behavior could explain significant differences in the intention to share media files (both legitimate and pirated files) over the internet [5].

Theory of Planned Behaviour (TPB) Constructs and Connection to TDF
The TPB comprises six (6) constructs, as reflected in Table 3, that are related to Beliefs about Capabilities and Social Influence TDF domain which refers to the acceptance of the truth, reality, or validity about ability or talent that a person can put to constructive use [7]. The beliefs about the capability's domain comprise eight (8) constructs shown in Table 3: the validated, evaluated, and verified TDF constructs supporting the Theory of Planned Behaviour constructs.

Summary of Behavioural Theories and Connection to TDF
The Theory of Domains Framework validated the 17 constructs extracted from the three (3) commonly cited theories as significant contributors to digital piracy.

4.3   Grouping of Constructs

As observed in Table 4, the list of constructs is further simplified and downscaled to three (3) construct groups.

Table 4. Digital piracy construct groups

Construct groups	Constructs
1. Attitude	1.1 Reciprocal determinism
	1.2 Behavioral capability
	1.3 Observational learning
	1.4 Reinforcements
	1.5 Expectations
	1.6 Action Control and Actual Consequences
	1.7 Self-efficacy

(continued)

Table 4. (*continued*)

Construct groups	Constructs
2. Habit	2.1 Affect
	2.2 Behaviour
	2.3 Intention
	2.4 Roles
	2.5 Self-concept
3. Awareness	3.1 Immediate (fast) penalty
	3.2 Certainty of conviction
	3.3 Severity of punishment

These are crucial and dominant constructs in the theories discussed in Sub-Sect. 4.2 of this article. The categorization of constructs is done for readability and for each construct to be addressed under its appropriate group.

4.4 Construct Groups Defined

AttitudE

The theories examined in Sub-Sect. 4.2 maintained that attitude directs one's intentions so much that it influences behavior [1, 3, 10]. The researchers grouped all attitude-related constructs under the "attitude" construct group, as demonstrated in Table 4. This approach will assist the researchers in investigating digital piracy behavior through a process that resonates with Deterrence Theory (DT), whereby an individual calculates the benefits obtained against the possibility of being caught and the level of punishment [17].

Habit

Most recent research on digital piracy based on TPB [1] suggests that habits mainly impact individuals' behavior. In the context of grouping digital piracy constructs, "habit" [13, 16, 18] is fitting in the psychological and ethical sphere to act as an umbrella or a grouping of the constructs found in Table 4.

Awareness

Investigating the awareness construct group and its sub-constructs shown in Table 4 is essential for the researchers to gauge the level of awareness amongst internet users. The area of investigation will be concerning the digital piracy behavior itself, its legal and illegal platforms, and its dangers and reach the necessary conclusions, thereby closing research gaps in the aspect of digital piracy awareness [1, 2, 6, 10].

4.5 Construct Groups Summary

Identifying the TDF-validated construct groups lays a foundation for future studies where the construct groups will be integrated with the digital piracy super factors previously studied by [9]. Merging the digital piracy super factor groups and construct groups will result in the Proposed Digital Piracy Conceptual Framework, which will enable the researchers to formulate the digital piracy mitigation plans incorporating amendments and implementation of awareness initiatives such as advertisements and persuasive techniques, campaigns, education literature, information security policies, intellectual property (IP) laws, internet usage standards, and guidelines. Additionally, using a proposed conceptual framework and its derivatives, the affected stakeholders will be able to investigate behavior change techniques impacting habit and attitude to be implemented to alleviate digital piracy. Lastly, it is anticipated that the derivatives of the proposed conceptual framework will lead to the implementation of Continuous Improvement Processes (CIPs) such as Lean and or Six Sigma to warrant continuous improvement in the processes and capabilities of any organization to fight digital piracy.

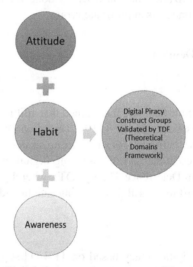

Fig. 2. Digital piracy construct groups validated by TDF

Figure 2 gives a visual representation of the summarized TDF-validated construct groups, which will act as a second building block of the Digital Piracy Proposed Conceptual Framework after the previously investigated first building block - the super factor groups [9].

5 Conclusion

The current paper answers the two research questions, i.e., identifying the most prominent theories relevant to explaining digital piracy behaviors. Finally, the paper aims to answer how the identified digital piracy behavior constructs can be mapped to their related TDF behavioral constructs. To answer the research questions, this paper introduced the top three (3) behavioral theories commonly used in the digital piracy literature to evaluate ethical behavior and the use of IT, specifically digital piracy. The mapping of the behavioral constructs to the Theoretical Domains Framework (TDF) took place to validate the identified constructs extracted from the theories. The identified behavioral domains comprise 17 vital constructs, verified to be the core digital piracy constructs. The long list of constructs was then categorized into construct groups, and a summary of each one was explored. Organized into three (3) groups, the construct groups are 1) Attitude, 2) Habit, 3) and Awareness. These constructs lay a foundation for future studies in the same focus area. They will act as the building blocks on which the researchers will design the Proposed Digital Piracy Conceptual Framework and its derivatives, the mitigation or intervention plans for alleviating the digital piracy phenomenon.

Acknowledgments. The researchers declare no conflict of interest. Professor Elmarie Kritzinger supervised the master's full dissertation, from which this paper was developed. Both authors contributed to all sections of the paper and approved its final version.

References

1. Ajzen, I.: The theory of planned behavior. Organ. Behav. Hum. Decis. Process. **50**(1), 179–211 (1991). https://doi.org/10.1016/0749-5978(91)90020-T
2. Al-Rafee, S., Cronan, T.P.: Digital piracy: factors that influence attitude toward behavior. J. Bus. Ethics **63**, 237–259 (2006). https://doi.org/10.1007/s10551-005-1902-9
3. Armitage, C.J., Conner, M.: Efficacy of the theory of planned behaviour: a meta-analytic review. Br. J. Soc. Psychol. **40**(4), 417–499 (2001). https://doi.org/10.1348/014466601164939
4. Bellamy, R.: Beccaria, Cesare Bonesana (1738–94). In: Routledge Encyclopaedia of Philosophy (2018). https://doi.org/10.4324/9780415249126-t063-1
5. Blake, R.H., Kyper, E.S.: An investigation of the intention to share media files over peer-to-peer networks. Behav. Inf. Technol. **32**(4) (2013). https://doi.org/10.1080/0144929X.2011.558591
6. Butt, A.: Comparative analysis of software piracy determinants among Pakistani and Canadian university students: demographics, ethical attitudes and socio-economic factors, leadership. M.Sc. Computer Science. Hamdard University, Institute of Leadership and Management, Pakistan (2006)
7. Cane, J., O'Connor, D., Michie, S.: Validation of the theoretical domains framework for use in behaviour change and implementation research. Implementation Sci. **7**(1) (2012). https://doi.org/10.1186/1748-5908-7-37
8. Cronan, T.P., Al-Rafee, S.: Factors that influence the intention to pirate software and media. J. Bus. Ethics **78**(4), 527–545 (2008). https://doi.org/10.1007/s10551-007-9366-8
9. Fakude, N., Kritzinger, E.: Factors influencing internet users' attitude and behaviour toward digital piracy: a systematic literature review article. In: Huang, Y.-M., Cheng, S.-C., Barroso, J., Sandnes, F.E. (eds.) Innovative Technologies and Learning: 5th International Conference, ICITL 2022, Virtual Event, August 29–31, 2022, Proceedings, pp. 313–323. Springer, Cham (2022). https://doi.org/10.1007/978-3-031-15273-3_35
10. Hunt, S.D., Vitell, S.J.: The general theory of marketing ethics: A revision and three questions. J. Macromarketing **26**(2), 143–153 (2006). https://doi.org/10.1177/0276146706290923

11. Korner, S.: Encyclopaedia Britannica (1974)
12. Kuiper, K.: The Britannica Guide to Theories and Ideas That Changed the Modern World. Britannica Educational Publishing (2009)
13. Liao, C., Lin, H.N., Liu, Y.P.: Predicting the use of pirated software: a contingency model integrating perceived risk with the theory of planned behavior. J. Bus. Ethics **91**(2), 237–252 (2010). https://doi.org/10.1007/s10551-009-0081-5
14. Lowry, P.B., Zhang, J., Wu, T.: Nature or nurture? A meta-analysis of the factors that maximize the prediction of digital piracy by using social cognitive theory as a framework. Comput. Hum. Behav. **68**, 104–120 (2017). https://doi.org/10.1016/j.chb.2016.11.015
15. Michie, S., et al.: From theory to intervention: mapping theoretically derived behavioural determinants to behaviour change techniques. Appl. Psychol. **57**(4) (2008). https://doi.org/10.1111/j.1464-0597.2008.00341.x
16. Morris, R.G., Higgins, G.E.: Criminological theory in the digital age: the case of social learning theory and digital piracy. J. Crim. Justice **39**(4), 470–480 (2010). https://doi.org/10.1016/j.jcrimjus.2010.04.016
17. Saltzman, L.E., Tittle, C.R.: Sanctions and social deviance: the question of deterrence. Contemp. Sociol. **10**(6), 796 (1981). https://doi.org/10.2307/2067221
18. Yoon, C.: Theory of planned behavior and ethics theory in digital piracy: an integrated model. J. Bus. Ethics **100**(3), 405–417 (2011). https://doi.org/10.1007/s10551-010-0687-7

Domain-Specific Anomaly Detection for In-Vehicle Networks

Edy Kristianto[1]([✉])[iD], Po-Ching Lin[1][iD], and Ren-Hung Hwang[2][iD]

[1] Department of Computer Science and Information Engineering,
National Chung Cheng University, Chiayi, Taiwan
{edy108p,pclin}@cs.ccu.edu.tw
[2] College of Artificial Intelligence, National Yang Ming Chiao Tung University,
Tainan, Taiwan
rhhwang@nycu.edu.tw

Abstract. Connecting components such as electronic control units (ECUs) via an in-vehicle network (IVN) is common in modern vehicles. However, if compromised, the components may send malicious messages to impact the operations of a vehicle and even hurt driving safety. Several in-vehicle intrusion detection system (IDS) solutions based on machine learning have been presented in the literature to detect unknown attacks. Such IDSs are deployed on a central gateway or within each ECU. We note that some vehicles have implemented domain gateways/controllers and automotive Ethernet to support the increasing bandwidth and complexity of the IVN. The domain gateways can take over the computation load from the ECUs. Therefore, each domain gateway can be a promising place to implement an IDS to detect and block malicious messages in its domain. We can optimize the domain-specific IDS model to classify malicious or normal messages in each domain and make it lightweight. In this work, we present two models of lightweight unsupervised IDS solutions for the domain gateway model. Our designs have only 2,708 and 49,454 parameters, fewer than the state-of-the-art designs. Their training and testing time are also shorter, achieving high accuracy from 0.90 to 1.00 in detecting the malicious messages on each domain gateway.

Keywords: CAN bus · Domain-specific · In-vehicle intrusion detection

1 Introduction

Modern vehicles support message exchanges between the components such as sensors, actuators, interconnected electronic control units (ECUs) via the in-vehicle network (IVN) for their essential operations. However, the components in the IVN are known to be vulnerable to various attacks, which can be internal or external. An internal attack can compromise the physical ECUs, e.g., by the owner or vehicle's technician. Examples of typical internal attacks include

Supported by National Science and Technology Council (NSTC) of Taiwan.

flooding, spoofing ECUs, or fuzzing the valid ECU-IDs. The components for the engine and the body functions are more prone to internal attacks [15,17]. An external attack is from the outside of a vehicle, and mostly, oblivious of the vehicle's ECU. However, an attacker can attack via wireless sensors or communication ports (e.g., remote access attack), or flood with random fuzzy attacks, which consist of random ECU-IDs and values of CAN data fields. For example, the components for the chassis, connectivity, and advanced driver assistance system (ADAS) functions are exposed to external attacks [18]. Thus, deploying an intrusion detection system (IDS) to detect malicious messages via the IVN is a common practice in the literature [1,4,7,11,12,16,17,20,21].

The existing IDS solutions for the IVN are commonly based on machine learning, and work with conventional CAN bus in a central gateway, as an ECU, or within each ECU. However, the automotive industry has adjusted from a central gateway architecture to a domain architecture, where related ECUs are connected to the same domain controller. For example, the ECUs for controlling the engine are grouped into the engine domain, and those for controlling vehicle chassis are grouped into the chassis domain [3]. In [10,19], the authors introduced several domains: engine/powertrain, body, chassis, infotainment, ADAS, and connectivity. However, the automotive Ethernet still has security issues, especially in the ADAS and connectivity domains, which have wireless connectivity for wireless sensors and vehicle-to-everything (V2X) communications, and may be compromised from external attackers.

An ECU has fewer computational resources than a central or a domain gateway. Machine learning computation load may interfere the ECU performance if the IDS is implemented in the ECU. The IDS implementation in a central gateway risks a single point of failure. Each domain gateway has its computation resources, and can also host the IDS to detect the malicious messages specific to that domain. Because the domain-specific IDS needs to deal with only specific messages in a domain, it can be optimized for detecting them and become lightweight. To the best of our knowledge, there is no IDS model based on the domain gateway in the literature. The contributions of this work are the following:

1. We propose the IDS for the domain gateway in an unsupervised manner to detect unknown attack types.
2. We show that our models are lightweight, and are proper for devices with limited computation resources.

This work is organized as follows. Section 2 consists of related work of IDS in the IVN. Section 3 briefs our IDS model based on an autoencoder (AE) in each domain gateway. Section 4 presents the experimental results and the discussions, and finally, the conclusion is in Sect. 5.

2   Related Work

The CAN bus is a serial communication protocol still used in modern vehicles for real-time, safety-critical functions and in-vehicle controller applications. However, the CAN bus lacks security mechanisms and may be vulnerable to various attacks [2]. Common CAN bus vulnerabilities are the broadcast mechanism to transmit the CAN data, lack of security mechanisms (e.g., no authentication in ECUs communication), CAN messages are not encrypted, and the arbitration domination status, based on the CAN-ID priority scheme where the lower CAN-ID has the higher priority. The common attacks to IVN are denial-of-service attacks by injecting the highest priority of CAN-ID (e.g., CAN-ID 0x000), fuzzy attacks by injecting spoofed random CAN-ID and its data values, and modifying the values of CAN-ID (e.g., the RPM or gear ECU data values) [17]. These attacks generate malicious messages that trigger false information to the recipient devices, the vehicle can malfunction, and the worst case is to lead to an accident.

An IDS can monitor the messages traffic in-vehicle network for suspicious activities or malicious messages and then issue an alert when they are discovered. Many researchers proposed machine learning models for the in-vehicle IDS to detect malicious messages. We only refer to unsupervised learning because the unsupervised learning is capable of detecting many possible types of attacks in the IVN. An unsupervised learning model only needs to learn from the normal data patterns and does not require data labeling in advance. Moreover, unsupervised learning enables one to recognize unknown attacks. Several researchers have proposed unsupervised IDS based on a convolutional neural network long-short-term memory (CNN-LSTM) [1], the generative adversarial network (GAN) [11,17], clustering [4,16,20], and autoencoder (AE) [7,12,21].

Agrawal et al. [1] proposed a CNN-LSTM model. Their solution could achieve very high accuracy. However, the CNN-based model has a large parameters that may not fit in a central gateway or ECU which has a limited computation resources. Kang et al. [11] proposed the transfer learning IDS between vehicles. Their model was based on GAN and LSTM. After a vehicle was trained with its data, it transferred the pre-trained model to other vehicles. Seo et al. [17] used a GAN-based model to detect malicious messages in the IVN. The proposed IDS was placed as an ECU in the conventional CAN bus, and their model achieved an accuracy between 0.963 to 0.98. However, the GAN needs to convert the CAN data into images, and training the discriminator with known attacks (i.e., supervised learning) is still required. Some researchers, such as [4,16,20], used K-means clustering to categorize the malicious CAN data. However, the K-means model must determine the estimated number of clusters first. Kukkala et al. [12] proposed an anomaly-based IDS. The authors combined the AE and gated recurrent units (GRU) for the IDS model, and the implementation was on each ECU in the conventional CAN bus. In [7] and [21], the authors proposed a similar solution to the IVN IDS for each ECU (CAN-ID); differently, their models were based on the LSTM and AE, namely LSTM-AE. However, the effort of maintaining and implementing the IDS on each ECU may be too much because there are many ECUs in a modern vehicle. The IDS implementation in the ECU may impact an ECU's performance because the learning model needs computation resources whereas the ECU has limited computation resources.

The recent IVN IDS solutions are all designed in a conventional CAN bus which consists of a central gateway. Usually, a central gateway has higher computational resources than the ECUs, enabling it to handle the IDS. However, this implementation is vulnerable to a single point of failure. The domain-based architecture consists of some domain gateways, each having a computational capability similar to a central gateway. We locate the IDS on each domain gateway to detect malicious messages and block them only in their domain. This model can prevent the spread of malicious messages to other domains and avoid a single point of failure.

3   Methodology

In this section, we brief our detection models for the domain gateway IDS, our models, the dataset, and the evaluated performance in our experiments.

3.1   Detection Models

We propose two unsupervised models for the domain gateway IDS. The GRU autoencoder (GRU-AE) model is used for the engine and body domains. The other is the AE for the chassis, connectivity, and ADAS domains. We choose to differentiate the IDS model for the different domain gateway because the engine or body domain has more attack possibilities and variations in the CAN data values than the other domains. Both domains may have more ECUs, sensors, and actuators. The owner may add an after-market ECU, e.g., to improve the engine performance; this can be the attacker's way to access the vehicle. The IDS can use the sequence of CAN-IDs to detect the malicious messages.

The chassis, connectivity, and ADAS domains have wireless sensors. Thus, an attacker can launch attacks via the tire pressure monitoring system (TPMS), Bluetooth or WiFi connectivity, or LiDAR sensors without physical access to the vehicle [14]. The attacker may not know the CAN-IDs in the vehicle, but they can launch random fuzzy attacks with random CAN-IDs and their data values. The normal values in those domains may have static values, and the IDS can use the AE to detect random fuzzy attacks. The attacker also can attack with DoS attack that flood the wireless sensors with the lowest CAN-ID.

Autoencoder. The AE model, in general as seen in Fig. 1, can be trained in unsupervised learning without labels or class information to generate a model for the data. This model extracts essential information from each input feature in the code layer and imposes a bottleneck on the possible representation it can compute. The representation is mapped and reconstructed to the original input features. The main objective of this model is to recover information as much as possible from the original input by minimizing the distance between the inputs

(X_i) and the outputs $(\hat{X}_i)$ [5]. The objective of an autoencoder is to minimize the loss function $L(\theta)$ below:

$$\min_{\theta} L(\theta) = \min_{\theta} \sum_{x \in X} d(x, g_\theta(f_\theta(x))), \tag{1}$$

where x is a set of inputs, θ is the full set of AE's parameters, f is encoder mapping, g is decoder mapping, and d is distance function in the input space.

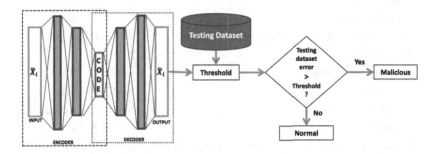

Fig. 1. The autoencoder learning model.

We use this AE model on the chassis, connectivity, and ADAS domains. Our model has a hidden layer with a number of nodes 64 in the encoder and decoder and ReLU for the activation function in each hidden layer. We use the Adam optimizer function with the learning rate 0.0001 and mean absolute error (MAE) for the loss function. The MAE is defined as

$$MAE = \frac{1}{n} \sum_{i=0}^{n} |\tilde{X}_i - \hat{X}_i|, \tag{2}$$

where the n is the total number of data points, and $\tilde{X}$ is the normalized data.

GRU-AE. The IVN traffic data can be seen as a data sequence. The learning model to tackle the sequence data can be recurrent neural network (RNN), LSTM, and GRU. We choose GRU because it has fewer gates and states than the LSTM model. The LSTM uses three gates, input gate, forget gate, and output gate, but GRU uses just two, namely the update gate and reset gate. In [6], the equations for the gates are

$$\begin{aligned}
z_t &= \sigma(W_z x_t + U_z h_{t-1} + b_z) \\
r_t &= \sigma(W_r x_t + U_r h_{t-1} + b_r) \\
\hat{h}_t &= \phi(W_h x_t + U_h(r_t \odot h_{t-1}) + b_h) \\
h_t &= (1 - z_t) \odot h_{t-1} + z_t \odot \hat{h}_t,
\end{aligned} \tag{3}$$

where z_t is the update gate, r_t is the reset gate, $\hat{h}_t$ is the candidate activation vector, h_t is output vector, and x_t is the input vector. $\odot$ denotes the Hadamard product. W and U are the weight parameters and b is the bias. σ is the sigmoid and ϕ is Tanh activation function. For more detail, we list our model parameter in Table 1

Table 1. Hyper-parameters in the models

Hyper-parameters	GRU-AE	AE
Input features	9	10
Hidden layers each decoder/encoder/(nodes)	2/(64–32)	1/(64)
Output classes	2	2
Activation function	ReLU	ReLU
Loss function	MAE	MAE
Optimization function	Nadam	Adam
Learning rate	1×10^{-3}	1×10^{-4}
Decay rate for the first moment estimates (β_1)	0.9	0.9
Decay rate for the second moment estimates (β_2)	0.999	0.999
A small number to prevent any division by zero (ϵ)	1×10^{-7}	1×10^{-8}
Mini batch	1024	512
Epoch	256	384

Moreover, GRU has fewer parameters and a lower memory overhead than LSTM, which makes GRU more efficient in the limited computation resources [12]. The domain-specific architecture has fewer connected ECUs and actuators than conventional CAN buses because the components are grouped into some domain gateway. The fewer connected ECUs also reduce the number of broadcast messages in a domain gateway, as seen in the proposed part of Table 2. The GRU model is more suitable for processing smaller datasets than the LSTM model. We implement the GRU-AE model with nine input features, and two hidden layers with 64 and 32 nodes, respectively, in the encoder and decoder and ReLU for the activation function for each hidden layer. We use the Nadam optimizer function with default parameters and MAE for the loss error. Our model referred to [21] for the layer number and [12] for estimating the node number of each layer. We chose the hyper-parameter values very close to the fitted of loss training and the accuracy with the lowest number of layers and node numbers. The training batch size and epoch also affect the accuracy. The best hyper-parameters can be seen on Table 1. The threshold values for the attack detection are selected from the mean of training loss and its deviation values, the maximum of training loss, or the quartile value of training loss.

3.2   Dataset

We employ the CAN dataset from [13,17]. The authors generated the dataset from Hyundai's YF Sonata. The datasets contain four attacks: DoS, fuzzy, injected revolutions per minute (RPM), and gear attacks. We refer to [8–10] for the domain-based architecture. Our experiment assumes in a vehicle has five domain gateways, and each domain gateway consists of several ECUs. We split the original dataset into five domain gateways to simulate the ECUs grouped

Table 2. Dataset comparison

Paper	Data	Attack	CAN messages	
			Normal	Attacked
[17]	Training test	Normal	1,171,637	N/A
		DoS	3,665,771	17,128
		Fuzzy	3,838,860	20,317
		RPM	4,621,702	32,501
		Gear	4,443,142	29,751
[21]	N/A	DoS	3,078,250	587,521
		Fuzzy	3,347,013	491,847
		RPM	2,290,185	654,897
		Gear	2,766,522	597,252
[1]	Training: testing (65%:35%)	Normal	988,872	N/A
		DoS	3,078,250	587,521
		Fuzzy	3,347,013	491,847
		RPM	3,966,805	654,897
		Gear	3,845,890	597,252
Proposed Engine domain	Training with normal data in each domain	Normal	294,015	N/A
		DoS	618,069	587,521
		Fuzzy (valid)	709,832	1,473
		RPM	904,155	654,897
		Gear	869,551	597,252
Body domain		Normal	235,235	N/A
		DoS	681,803	587,521
		Fuzzy (valid)	767,805	1,536
Chassis domain		Normal	91,678	N/A
		Fuzzy (random)	303,481	5,996
Connectivity domain		Normal	126,658	N/A
		Fuzzy (random)	324,859	7,400
ADAS domain		Normal	136,794	N/A
		Fuzzy (random)	363,190	10,388

into the domain gateways, as seen in Fig. 2. The list of datasets is summarized in Table 2. We group some CAN data based on the CAN identifier (CAN-ID). The engine domain consists of CAN-IDs, which are attacked with spoofing RPM, gear, fuzzy, and DoS attacks. Notably, we select the same CAN-IDs for the normal and fuzzy attacked data for the engine and body domains to simulate the internal attacker on the valid CAN-ID. We use the random fuzzy and DoS attack for the chassis, connectivity, and ADAS domains to simulate the external attacker. The external attacker may not know what kind of CAN-ID is in-vehicle. Therefore they still attack with random CAN-IDs or flood with DoS attack. The dataset has twelve features: timestamp, CAN-ID, data length code (DLC), eight CAN contain data fields, and labels as normal or abnormal data. Our experiment uses only nine features: the CAN-ID and eight data fields for the engine and body domains. We add a feature, the time difference between row data for the chassis, connectivity, and ADAS. The Min-Max re-scaling method is used to re-scaling the values of each feature in each dataset with a range between 0 to 1. The scaling equation to derive $\tilde{X}$ from X is

$$\tilde{X}_i = \frac{X_i - min(X_i)}{max(X_i) - min(X_i)} \tag{4}$$

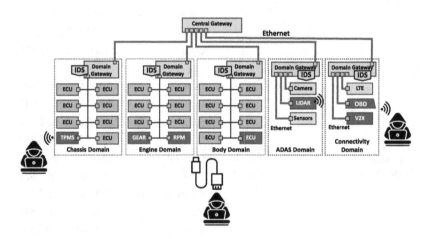

Fig. 2. The domain-specific IDS on each domain gateway.

3.3   Performance Metrics

We evaluate our models with precision, recall, and F1-score, which are defined are follows:

$$Accuracy = \frac{TP + TN}{TP + TN + FP + FN} \tag{5}$$

$$Precision = \frac{TP}{TP + FP} \tag{6}$$

$$Recall = \frac{TP}{TP + FN} \tag{7}$$

$$F_1 = 2 \times \frac{Precision \times Recall}{Precision + Recall}, \tag{8}$$

where FP is false positive, meaning the model has wrongly predicted a negative sample as a positive one; FN is false negative, meaning the model is wrongly predicted a positive sample as a negative one; TP is true positive, meaning the model has correctly predicted a positive sample as a positive one; TN is a true negative, meaning the model is correctly predicted a negative sample as a negative one.

4   Evaluation Results

We trained our models with the normal CAN data on the corresponding domain gateway in each domain. We tested with each testing data that consisted of normal and attack data, as seen in Table 2. Our model accuracy achieved between 0.90 and 1.00, and the models could classify the normal and malicious data with high accuracy. The difficulty was to detect the spoofing gear attack, which got the lowest score because the values from the spoofing gear attack were very close to the normal values. As seen in Table 3, the experiment results are compared with those from [17,21], and [1] for the model performance. Those authors provided the full results of their models' performance.

We added DoS attack to test our AE model in the chassis, connectivity and ADAS domain, the attacker could launch DoS attack to the wireless connectivity. The DoS attack was hard to detect in AE model, the precision our model only achieved around 0.66 to 0.76, some of normal attack detected as the DoS messages (FP). The IDS model with RNN-based is better to tackle the DoS attack. However, our AE model still enable to detect with accuracy between 0.93 to 0.96.

As seen in Table 3, the parameter column, our models were lightweight and had the fewest parameters than the other solution. The training and testing time could compete with the other solutions in the lowest hardware specification, as seen in Table 4. The training time for our GRU-AE model was around 40 to 50 min, and the testing time was around 0.11 s. Our AE model's training and testing had a shorter time, the training time was around 13 to 15 min, and the testing time was 0.06 s. We refer to the testing time in [17], where the authors tested the time for 1,954 messages. In future work, we will experiment with our models with an embedded device, which is likely to be implemented in a domain gateway specification that can simulate the actual performance of our IDS.

The IDS implementation on each domain gateway which has more computation resources can take over the computation load from the ECUs, and the ECUs only need to transmit their data. The training and maintenance of IDS have become more efficient than implemented in each ECU. Therefore, the IDS does not need to be placed in each ECU or a centralized on the central gateway. The IDS in the domain-gateway-based architecture becomes decentralized, and

Table 3. Comparison of the IDS results from the related work and the domain-specific

Paper	Model	Parameters	Placement	Attack	Results			
					Precision	Recall	F1-score	Accuracy
[17]	GAN-CNN-DNN	>500,000	CAN bus	DoS	0.968	0.996	0.982	0.979
				Fuzzy	0.973	0.995	0.984	0.98
				RPM	0.983	0.990	0.986	0.98
				Gear	0.981	0.965	0.973	0.962
[21]	LSTM-AE & DAE	≈65,097	Central gateway for each CAN ID	DoS	0.9997	0.9994	0.9995	–
				Fuzzy	0.9975	0.9991	0.9993	–
				RPM	0.9978	0.9993	0.9995	–
				Gear	0.9998	0.9993	0.9995	–
[1]	LSTM-CNN	>500,000	CAN bus	DoS	0.9997	0.9991	0.999	–
				Fuzzy	0.9999	1.00	1.00	–
				RPM	0.9999	1.00	1.00	–
				Gear	0.9991	0.9990	0.999	–
Domain-specific (proposed)	GRU-AE	49,454	Engine domain	DoS	0.99	0.99	0.99	0.99
				RPM	1.00	1.00	1.00	1.00
				Gear	0.91	0.90	0.90	0.90
				Fuzzy (valid)	1.00	1.00	0.99	1.00
	GRU-AE		Body domain	DoS	1.00	1.00	1.00	1.00
				Fuzzy (valid)	0.95	0.94	0.94	1.00
	AE	2,708	Chassis domain	Fuzzy (random)	1.00	0.95	0.97	1.00
				DoS	0.76	0.98	0.83	0.96
	AE		Connectivity domain	Fuzzy (random)	0.96	0.98	0.97	1.00
				DoS	0.67	0.97	0.74	0.93
	AE		ADAS domain	Fuzzy (random)	0.97	1.00	0.98	1.00
				DoS	0.66	0.96	0.72	0.93

Table 4. Hardware comparison

Paper	Hardware for the model training
[17]	Intel(R) Xeon(R) CPU E5-1650 v4 @ 3.60 GHz; RAM 32 GB; NVIDIA GeForce GTX 1080
[21]	N/A
[1]	Intel(R) Xeon(R) CPU @ 2.20 GHz; RAM 13 GB; NVIDIA Tesla T4
Proposed	Intel(R) Core(TM) i5-1035G1 CPU @ 1.00 GHz, 1190 Mhz; RAM 12 GB

the detection is distributed to each domain gateway to avoid a single point of IDS failure. Moreover, domain gateway-based IDS filter the malicious messages in its domain and avoid them from spreading in the IVN.

5   Conclusion

We propose the unsupervised learning IDS based on the domain gateway architecture. GRU-AE and AE models are trained only with the normal CAN data. Our proposed model can work on each domain gateway with each model parameter and configuration and enable to detect the malicious CAN messages with high accuracy between 0.90 to 1.00 on each domain. Our model parameters are only 2,708 for the AE and 49,545 for the GRU-AE, showing that the models are lightweight. Our solution has fewer parameters and runs on the lowest computation resources than state-of-the-art solutions. The domain gateway replaces the computing load from the ECUs. It distributes the detection load to their respective domains, and this is also to avoid a single point of failure at the central gateway. For future work, we will implement our model to the embedded hardware (ARM-based CPU), compare to the state-of-the-art models, simulating transfer learning between domain gateway, and determine the best fit model to simulate the actual condition of the domain gateway hardware.

References

1. Agrawal, K., Alladi, T., Agrawal, A., Chamola, V., Benslimane, A.: NovelADS: a novel anomaly detection system for intra-vehicular networks. IEEE Trans. Intell. Transp. Syst. **23**(11), 22596–22606 (2022)
2. Aliwa, E., Rana, O., Perera, C., Burnap, P.: Cyberattacks and countermeasures for in-vehicle networks. ACM Comput. Surv. (CSUR) **54**(1), 1–37 (2021)
3. Alparslan, O., Arakawa, S., Murata, M.: Next generation intra-vehicle backbone network architectures. In: 2021 IEEE 22nd International Conference on High Performance Switching and Routing (HPSR), pp. 1–7. IEEE (2021)
4. Barletta, V.S., Caivano, D., Nannavecchia, A., Scalera, M.: A Kohonen SOM architecture for intrusion detection on in-vehicle communication networks. Appl. Sci. **10**(15), 5062 (2020)
5. Charte, D., Charte, F., del Jesus, M.J., Herrera, F.: An analysis on the use of autoencoders for representation learning: fundamentals, learning task case studies, explainability and challenges. Neurocomputing **404**, 93–107 (2020)
6. Chung, J., Gulcehre, C., Cho, K., Bengio, Y.: Empirical evaluation of gated recurrent neural networks on sequence modeling. arXiv preprint arXiv:1412.3555 (2014)
7. Hanselmann, M., Strauss, T., Dormann, K., Ulmer, H.: CANet: an unsupervised intrusion detection system for high dimensional CAN bus data. IEEE Access **8**, 58194–58205 (2020)
8. den Hartog, J., Zannone, N.: Security and privacy for innovative automotive applications: a survey. Comput. Commun. **132**, 17–41 (2018)
9. Jeon, B., Ju, H., Jung, B., Kim, K., Lee, D.: A study on traffic characteristics for anomaly detection of Ethernet-based IVN. In: 2019 International Conference on Information and Communication Technology Convergence (ICTC), pp. 951–953. IEEE (2019)
10. Ju, H., Jeon, B., Kim, D., Jung, B., Jung, K.: Security considerations for in-vehicle secure communication. In: 2019 International Conference on Information and Communication Technology Convergence (ICTC), pp. 1404–1406. IEEE (2019)
11. Kang, L., Shen, H.: A transfer learning based abnormal can bus message detection system. In: 2021 IEEE 18th International Conference on Mobile Ad Hoc and Smart Systems (MASS), pp. 545–553. IEEE (2021)
12. Kukkala, V.K., Thiruloga, S.V., Pasricha, S.: INDRA: intrusion detection using recurrent autoencoders in automotive embedded systems. IEEE Trans. Comput. Aided Des. Integr. Circ. Syst. **39**(11), 3698–3710 (2020)
13. Lee, H., Jeong, S.H., Kim, H.K.: OTIDS: a novel intrusion detection system for in-vehicle network by using remote frame. In: 2017 15th Annual Conference on Privacy, Security and Trust (PST), pp. 57–5709. IEEE (2017)

14. Limbasiya, T., Teng, K.Z., Chattopadhyay, S., Zhou, J.: A systematic survey of attack detection and prevention in connected and autonomous vehicles. arXiv preprint arXiv:2203.14965 (2022)
15. Liu, J., Zhang, S., Sun, W., Shi, Y.: In-vehicle network attacks and countermeasures: challenges and future directions. IEEE Netw. **31**(5), 50–58 (2017)
16. Narasimhan, H., Vinayakumar, R., Mohammad, N.: Unsupervised deep learning approach for in-vehicle intrusion detection system. IEEE Consum. Electron. Mag. **12**(1), 103–108 (2023)
17. Seo, E., Song, H.M., Kim, H.K.: GIDS: GAN based intrusion detection system for in-vehicle network. In: 2018 16th Annual Conference on Privacy, Security and Trust (PST), pp. 1–6. IEEE (2018)
18. Sun, J., Iqbal, S., Arabi, N.S., Zulkernine, M.: A classification of attacks to in-vehicle components (IVCs). Veh. Commun. **25**, 100253 (2020)
19. Wang, D., Ganesan, S.: Automotive domain controller. In: 2020 International Conference on Computing and Information Technology (ICCIT-1441), pp. 1–5. IEEE (2020)
20. Yang, L., Moubayed, A., Shami, A.: MTH-IDS: a multitiered hybrid intrusion detection system for internet of vehicles. IEEE Internet Things J. **9**(1), 616–632 (2021)
21. Zhou, W., Fu, H., Kapoor, S.: CANGuard: practical intrusion detection for in-vehicle network via unsupervised learning. In: 2021 IEEE/ACM Symposium on Edge Computing (SEC), pp. 454–458. IEEE (2021)

LED: Learnable Encryption
with Deniability

Zhe-Wei Lin, Tzu-Hung Liu, and Po-Wen Chi[(✉)]

Department of Computer Science and Information Engineering,
National Taiwan Normal University, Taipei City, Taiwan
{60947043s,40747031s,neokent}@gapps.ntnu.edu.tw

Abstract. User privacy is an important issue in the cloud machine learning service. In this paper, we raise a new threat about the online machine learning service, which comes from outside superior authority. The authority may ask the user and the cloud to disclose secrets and the authority can monitor the user behavior. We propose a protection approach called learnable encryption with deniability (LED), which can convince the outsider of the fake data and can protect the user privacy.

Keywords: Privacy-preserving machine learning · Learnable encryption · Deniable encryption

1 Introduction

Machine learning has gradually become mainstream in recent years. According to its diversified development, model training needs to consume more and more resources. Therefore cloud services become an option for people to train their models. Also, the change in usage and service types let the users take predict services through it. With cloud services, everyone can train, update the model and predict at any time and anywhere.

Nevertheless, with the increase in machine learning based on cloud services, user privacy caught much attention. For example, when a user wants to use the training service, it needs to upload the training data to the cloud service provider (CSP) and undoubtedly, the training data is leaked to the CSP. Moreover, when making a prediction query, the queried data is also known to the CSP and the user loses its privacy. To solve this privacy issue, there are some research fields which are proposed. The first one is the integration of the machine learning service and homomorphic encryption [2,11,16]. This kind of approach simulates a prediction process as a circuit and run this circuit directly over encrypted queried data. So the query answer is also in the encrypted form. However, this approach cannot protect the training data. The other solution is called learnable encryption [13,18]. This approach trains the encrypted data directly and builds models over encrypted data. So the encrypted query can be put into the model and the prediction result is derived. This approach is specific to images, where the encryption is

S.-Y. Hsieh et al. (Eds.): ICS 2022, CCIS 1723, pp. 649–660, 2022.
https://doi.org/10.1007/978-981-19-9582-8_57

based on block scrambling. By scrambling image blocks, the image is kept secret to human but the characteristics can still be found through machine learning.

However, except the above issue which focuses on the CSP, in this era, there is another kind of privacy issue raised by the superior authority. The superior authority generally has power to monitor user behaviors, including learning and prediction. There are some of people and companies facing to this issue such as PRISM in American or internet censorship in China [19]. Even the data is encrypted, the authority can force the user and the CSP to provide secret keys lawfully and common encryption schemes do not work. To preserve user privacy in this scenario, we propose Learnable Encryption with Deniability (LED). With learnable encryption, our scheme can protect data sets and predictive queries from the CSP. As for deniability, LED makes a user to submit fake keys to the outside coercer and to mislead it to a fake behavior, keeping the real behavior secret.

Our contributions about this work is as follows.

- **Learnable encryption with deniability:** LED can make a learnable encryption model have deniability, and it can protect the privacy from superior coercion.
- **Prediction accuracy enhancement:** We predict query with distributional multi-models that make accuracy enhanced.
- **Performance evaluation:** The results are experimentally verified and can also meet expectations.

The rest of this paper is organized as below, we will first introduce related work in Sect. 2, followed by the scheme and technique of LED in Sect. 3, and provide experimental results and explanations in Sect. 4. Finally, in Sect. 5 we will present our conclusions and future works.

2   Related Works

2.1   Privacy-Preserving Machine Learning Schemes

Machine learning is a very powerful tool. In recent years, many cloud services have been launched to allow users to use their machines for training and prediction. Users will provide their training data to cloud service providers, and users' data privacy is An important issue, when users' data privacy is not secure, users will not use cloud training services, and people will lose the benefits of cloud services. This problem is also called *privacy preserving data-mining* by Agrawal and Srikant [1]. To solve this problem means balancing cloud service provider and user data privacy, there are lots of research works and we will introduce some of them.

One kind of solutions is based on fully homomorphic encryption. Homomorphic encryption makes a user can operate data with any circuits in the encryption form. With this feature, it is possible to run a neural network-like network on the encrypted data. Bos et al. [3], Dowlin et al. [8] used this concept to develop a privacy-preserving image prediction service called *CryptoNet*. First, they used lots of images in the plaintext form as the training set and derived a model. Then, they implemented the prediction process with the homomorphic encryption technique. Since the homomorphic encryption is not computationally efficient enough, Dowlin et al. found some properties of the prediction circuit, simplified the prediction process and therefore they could only use some homomorphic operations to improve the service performance. The drawback of CryptoNet is that it cannot protect the privacy of the training dataset because training is operated in the plaintext form. Chabanne et al. [5] proposed another enhancement approach. They used Taylor series as the approximating function and could provide better performance. However, the training data is still open to the service provider.

Another solution is based on the Secure Multi-Party Computation (SMC). The data owner and the cloud service provider work together in the training and prediction phases. Due to the characteristics of SMC, the cloud service provider has no knowledge of the user input data during the calculation. Yao's garbled circuits [20] and the Goldreich-Micali-Wigderson secret-sharing protocol [9] are both SMC technologies. Many studies are based on these two technologies. Rouhani et al. developed a method called DeepSecure based on garbled circuits [17]. Mohassel et al. used Mohassel et al. applied a similar idea with additive homomorphic encryption to speed up operations [14] Liu et al. used a lattice-based additive homomorphic encryption to generate multiplication triples for multiparty computation [12]. Generally speaking, SMC's solution requires frequent interactions between users and cloud service providers, especially for a complex operation like training and prediction. Therefore, it is not a practical solution.

2.2   Learnable Image Encryption

Unlike homomorphic encryption schemes that can process encryption data, Tanaka [18] and Kiya [6, 10] proposed another concept called **learnable image encryption**. This approach is to train and to predict directly over encrypted data instead of considering their plaintext. Generally, a data which is encrypted means that it is randomized and therefore, it is hard to find the patterns. However, Tanaka and Kiya found that if an image is encrypted in a static scrambling transformation, the figure cannot be recognized by the outsider and the figure's characteristics is still maintained.

This study is main introduced by Tanaka's Learnable Image Encryption [18]. Encryption image encryption processing flow is shown in Fig. 1. First, the image is divided into blocks of $M * M$ pixels. Then, each pixel in the blocks is splitted to 6 channels. Every byte of RGB parameter is divided into the first 4 bits and the last 4 bits to obtain 6-channel image blocks. The intensity of the positions of the randomly selected pixels in the third step is reversed. Finally, the pixels in the blocks are shuffled and each block is combined to obtain our encrypted image.

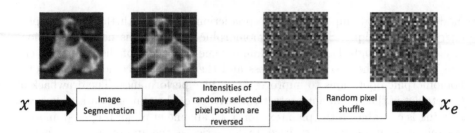

Fig. 1. Learnable image encryption process [18].

2.3 Deniable Encryption

The concept of deniable encryption was originally proposed in [4]. The main feature about deniable encryption is that one ciphertext can be opened to a fake data instead of the original message. Generally speaking, when being coerced, the sender and the receiver will claim the fake with providing convincing proofs. In this paper, we apply this idea on the learnable encryption scheme.

In this work, we make use of two deniable techniques. The first one is proposed by Paolo Gasti et al. [7]. Paolo Gasti et al. creates a redundant space in each ciphertext. The redundant space is claimed to be a random string, where actually is filled with the encryption result of a fake message. When the user is asked to open the encrypted data, the user can open the message in the redundant space so that the outsider will get the fake data. The other technique is called multi-distributional deniable technique, which was first proposed by Waters [15]. Watsers uses two sets of algorithms, one is normal and is claimed to be used while the other one is actually used. The algorithm outputs of corresponding algorithm outputs are computationally indistinguishable. Therefore, the outsider cannot challenge the user's claim and the user can do different things in these two sets of algorithms.

3   Learnable Encryption with Deniability

3.1   Scenario

Here we describe the user scenario, which is shown in Fig. 2. The user wants to predict the label of a given image, which is a dog in Fig. 2. The user first prepares another fake image and form a new image by combining these two images. The user also use a guiding image to indicate the location of the real wanted image. In Fig. 2, we use a triangle to show the real image is on the first part of the image. Then, the user encrypts this composite image, including the guiding image, which is encrypted by a pre-shared key between the user and the CSP, the real image and the fake image, which are encrypted learnably, and sends this encrypted query to the CSP. After receiving the query, the CSP decrypts the guiding image, and answer the prediction result to the user.

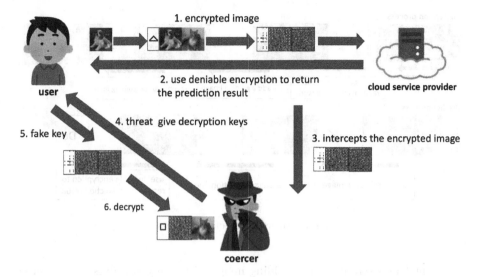

Fig. 2. User scenario.

When being coerced, we assume that the outside coercer gets the encrypted query and asks the user and the CSP to open this query. In this case, the user and the CSP will convince the coercer that the guiding image is a rectangle, which implies the real image is on the second part. After the second image is opened, the coercer will see a cat, which is the real image, is kept secret.

In this scenario, we assume that the CSP is honest-but-curious. This means that the CSP will correctly operate all step defined in our scheme. Because all machine learning operations are over encrypted data, the CSP can know nothing about the training data and prediction queries.

3.2 Learnable Encryption with Deniability

In this section, we show how to provide deniability over learnable encryption. We use a deniable technique called multi-distributional deniability. We build two sets of prediction processes, one is normal, which is claimed to be used, and the other is deniable, which is actually used. We want to make sure that the prediction queries and the opened keys in these two processes are computationally indistinguishable. Therefore, the outside coercer cannot challenge the user claim.

First, we will see how the normal prediction process works, where the process is shown in Fig. 3. First, the user learnably encrypts the training data with a secret key k and uploads it to the CSP for building a model. Note that the CSP does not know k and has no idea about the training dataset. When a user wants to use an online image prediction service for a target image, the user generates a random image with the same size as the target image. The user flips a coin b and form a new image $I = I_0 || I_1$, where I_b is the learnably encrypted target image by k and I_{1-b} is the random image. The user then generates a guiding image to

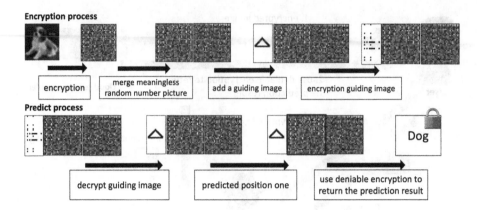

Fig. 3. Normal prediction process.

represent b and scrambles the guiding image with a key sk. sk is a pre-shared key between the user and the CSP. The prediction query will be the scrambled guiding image and a composite image. When receiving the prediction query, the CSP uses sk to recover the guiding image and gets b, finding the correct location of the encrypted target image. The CSP predicts the encrypted target image through the pre-trained model. Next, the CSP answers the query by the answer which is deniable ciphertext from the prediction label and a random label. The user can correctly decrypt the image label by decrypting the answer.

We summarize our notations in Table 1.

Now, we will see how the deniable prediction process works, where the process is shown in Fig. 4. First, the user learnably encrypts the training data with two secret keys k_0, k_1 and uploads them to the CSP for building models. Note that the CSP does not know k_0, k_1 and has no idea about the training datasets. When a user wants to use an online image prediction service for a target image, instead of using a random image, the user prepares a fake image with the same size as the target image. The user flips a coin b and form a new image $I = I_0 || I_1$, where I_b is the learnably encrypted target image by k_b and I_{1-b} is the learnably encrypted fake image by k_{1-b}. The user then generates a guiding image to represent b and scrambles the guiding image with a key sk. sk is a pre-shared key between the user and the CSP. The prediction query will be the scrambled guiding image and a composite image. When receiving the prediction query, the CSP uses sk to recover the guiding image and gets b, finding the correct location of the encrypted target image. The CSP predicts the encrypted target image and fake image through the corresponding models. Next, the CSP answers the query by the answer which is deniable ciphertext from the prediction labels, where one is the target label and the other is the fake label. The user can correctly decrypt the image label by decrypting the answer.

When being coerced, the user should provide sk, k to answer the outside coercer. If the prediction process is deniable and the user wants to hide the queried image, the user can instead provide sk' and k_{1-b} and mislead the coercer

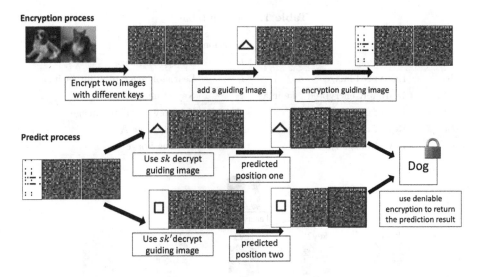

Fig. 4. Deniable prediction process.

that the user queries the fake image. The fake scrambling key sk' is a fake key to convince the coercer that the target image is in the part $1 - b$. The detail about sk' generation is described in the next subsection. Since sk and k are both can be treated as a scrambling mapping, sk, sk' and k_0, k_1 are definitely indistinguishable. Therefore, the coercer has no reason to reject the user claim.

3.3 Deniable Key Generation

In this section, we describe how to generate a deniable key sk'. As mentioned in the previous subsection, we scramble a guide image to a garbled image by sk, which is a scrambling mapping key. Now, we want to find a fake key sk', which can recover the garbled guiding image to a fake guiding image. For example, sk is a key that can scramble a triangle to a guiding image and sk' can be used to recover the garbled guiding image to a square as the fake indication shown in Fig. 4. The steps are as follows, First, we can find the color with the highest proportion of pixels in the garbled image. Then we reshape those pixels into a square. After randomly arranging the rest of the pixels, it will become the fake guide image. The mapping relation will be the deniable key, sk'.

3.4 Prediction Accuracy Enhancement

According to Learnable Image Encryption's work [18], the prediction accuracy of learnable encryption is around Learnable Image Encryption. However, in our experiment, which will be described in Sect. 4.2, the prediction accuracy of our learnable encryption implementation[1] is only around 0.75, which is not

---

[1] Our implementation is based on Learnable Image Encryption work without deniability feature.

Table 1. Notation table.

Notation	Description	Notation	Description
I	New image combine I_0 and I_1	I_0	Encrypted image
I_1	Encrypted image	I_b	Learnably encrypted target image
I_{b-1}	Learnably encrypted fake image	k_b	Key of image I_b
sk	Key of guiding image	sk'	Fake key of guiding image
k_0	Key of image I_0	k_1	Key of image I_1
k_{1-b}	Key of image I_{1-b}	b	Guiding image

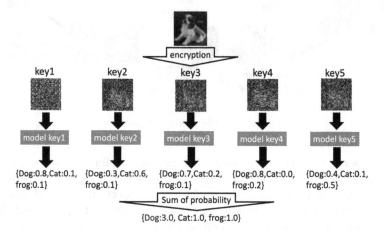

Fig. 5. Multi-models prediction (probabilities in this figure are examples).

acceptable for the practical use. Therefore, we propose an enhancement approach to improve prediction accuracy.

As shown in Fig. 5, Our idea is based on the dependable computing. For each training image, we make the image encrypted n times. So we can get n training sets and derive n models, where each model has its own keys. Then n models predict n results and then sum the predicted probabilities of each model, and the highest probability obtained is our predicted result.

4   Evaluation

In this section, we make some experiments to evaluate the influences caused by learnable encryption and multi-models prediction. We mainly used the CIFAR-10 data set. Its pre-processing part only performs normalization to inputs and one hot encoding to categories. The encryption method is block-wise scrambling proposed by learnable encryption [13]. All experiments are training with 50 epochs, and the batch size is set to 64.

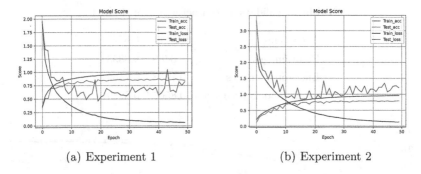

(a) Experiment 1   (b) Experiment 2

Fig. 6. Training history.

4.1 Experiment Schemes

In the following experiments, we will set different parameters to contrast:

1. The model will be set with two different structures to check the consistency. One is a general pyramidal residual network (ResNet) same as learnable encryption. The other will be a simple CNN model with 8 convolution layers which is smaller than the ResNet(half as many params as ResNet).
2. The data set have two types. One is original CIFAR-10 but only does the pre-processing, the other one is encrypted by block-wise scrambling. When training with encrypted data, we will put a block-wise adaptation network before the residual and CNN networks. It can measure the loss of feature and accuracy caused by learnable encryption.
3. We will use the method proposed in this paper. Training 20 models with data sets encrypted by different keys. Then using the prediction to vote the results. And we will check the difference between voting by the predicted label of each model or summing up all the models' predictive probability for each label before outputting the predicted label. And the effect from the model of the number will also perform.

4.2 LED Prediction Accuracy

The training process is shown in Fig. 6. In Fig. 6(a) is the ResNet train with plain images. We can find the training loss went down belong a perfect curve and the training accuracy was close to 1, but the testing accuracy didn't go up after about the 10th epoch. It shows that may have an overfitting problem. And in Fig. 6(b), although the data set used here is encrypted, the training process seems to be the same as Fig. 6(a). The only difference is the accuracy and loss of testing are worse than before. And there are the same circumstances when it comes to CNN. Moreover, we found that a smaller batch-size can make better accuracy, but we still set it to 64 for efficiency.

Table 2. Validation accuracies of cifar dataset

Accuracies	ResNet	CNN
Plain images	0.8469	0.8393
Encrypted images	0.7788	0.7469
Multi-models prediction	0.8507	0.8289

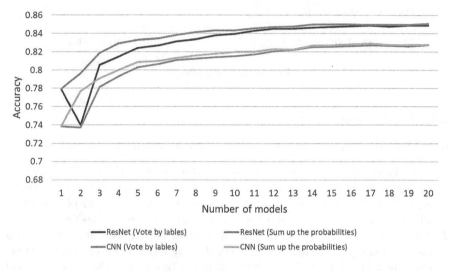

Fig. 7. Model number vs. prediction accuracy.

The results listed in Table 2 are the comparison between the accuracy of two model training by plain images and encrypted images. And the result of multi-models prediction used 20 models to perform. Having an accuracy of 0.847 and 0.840 when training with plain images, the accuracy using learnable encryption reduces by almost 0.1. But with the method we proposed, multi-model prediction, can reduce the feature loss caused by learnable encryption, and make the accuracy return to the almost same level as training with the plain image. And it works on both structures of models.

4.3   Accuracy vs. Number of Models

We also check the impact of the model number. Figure 7 is the evaluation result. We can see that with the model number growing, the prediction accuracy gets improved. And if there are 10 or more models, there are almost the same between voting by labels and summing up the probabilities. Otherwise, if using fewer models, summing up the probabilities will be better than voting by labels. Although the more models made the higher accuracy, it costs more resources. At least 3 or 4 models can make accuracy leap forward, and it will almost reach the limit when using 6 or 7 models. For efficiency, if not emphasized in extremely highest accuracy, 3 to 6 models can be enough to recover the loss. However, the trade-off is the prediction size also grows linearly. Because user privacy is very important, we think that the cost is affordable.

5 Conclusion

In this paper, we proposed new privacy-preserving machine learning service called learnable encryption with deniability. This scheme can not only protect user data from the CSP, but also keep privacy from being coerced. We also propose a multi-models technique to keep privacy and prediction accuracy at the same time.

Currently, this approach can only protect a single prediction query. That is, if the coercer collects lots of past queries, the proof will not be consistent. Therefore, the user needs to change the whole setting at each query. Our next step is to tackle this problem.

References

1. Agrawal, R., Srikant, R.: Privacy-preserving data mining. SIGMOD Rec. **29**(2), 439–450 (2000). https://doi.org/10.1145/335191.335438
2. Ahamed, S.I., Ravi, V.: Privacy-preserving chaotic extreme learning machine with fully homomorphic encryption (2022). https://doi.org/10.48550/ARXIV. 2208.02587. https://arxiv.org/abs/2208.02587
3. Bos, J.W., Lauter, K., Loftus, J., Naehrig, M.: Improved security for a ring-based fully homomorphic encryption scheme. In: Stam, M. (ed.) IMACC 2013. LNCS, vol. 8308, pp. 45–64. Springer, Heidelberg (2013). https://doi.org/10.1007/978-3-642-45239-0_4
4. Canetti, R., Dwork, C., Naor, M., Ostrovsky, R.: Deniable encryption. In: Kaliski, B.S. (ed.) CRYPTO 1997. LNCS, vol. 1294, pp. 90–104. Springer, Heidelberg (1997). https://doi.org/10.1007/BFb0052229
5. Chabanne, H., de Wargny, A., Milgram, J., Morel, C., Prouff, E.: Privacy-preserving classification on deep neural network. Cryptology ePrint Archive, Report 2017/035 (2017). https://eprint.iacr.org/2017/035
6. Chen, G., Chen, Q., Zhu, X., Chen, Y.: Encrypted image feature extraction by privacy-preserving MFS. In: 2018 7th International Conference on Digital Home (ICDH), pp. 42–45, November 2018. https://doi.org/10.1109/ICDH.2018.00016
7. Gasti, P., Ateniese, G., Blanton, M.: Deniable cloud storage: sharing files via public-key deniability. In: Proceedings of the 9th Annual ACM Workshop on Privacy in the Electronic Society, pp. 31–42 (2010)
8. Gilad-Bachrach, R., Dowlin, N., Laine, K., Lauter, K., Naehrig, M., Wernsing, J.: CryptoNets: applying neural networks to encrypted data with high throughput and accuracy. In: International Conference on Machine Learning, pp. 201–210 (2016)
9. Goldreich, O., Micali, S., Wigderson, A.: How to play any mental game. In: Proceedings of the Nineteenth Annual ACM Symposium on Theory of Computing, STOC 1987, pp. 218–229. ACM, New York (1987). https://doi.org/10.1145/28395. 28420
10. Kiya, H.: Compressible and learnable encryption for untrusted cloud environments. CoRR abs/1811.10254 (2018). http://arxiv.org/abs/1811.10254

11. Lee, J., et al.: Privacy-preserving machine learning with fully homomorphic encryption for deep neural network. CoRR abs/2106.07229 (2021). https://arxiv.org/abs/2106.07229

12. Liu, J., Juuti, M., Lu, Y., Asokan, N.: Oblivious neural network predictions via minionn transformations. In: Proceedings of the 2017 ACM SIGSAC Conference on Computer and Communications Security, CCS 2017, pp. 619–631. ACM, New York (2017). https://doi.org/10.1145/3133956.3134056

13. Madono, K., Tanaka, M., Onishi, M., Ogawa, T.: Block-wise scrambled image recognition using adaptation network. CoRR abs/2001.07761 (2020). https://arxiv.org/abs/2001.07761

14. Mohassel, P., Zhang, Y.: SecureML: a system for scalable privacy-preserving machine learning. In: 2017 IEEE Symposium on Security and Privacy (SP), pp. 19–38, May 2017. https://doi.org/10.1109/SP.2017.12

15. O'Neill, A., Peikert, C., Waters, B.: Bi-deniable public-key encryption. In: Rogaway, P. (ed.) CRYPTO 2011. LNCS, vol. 6841, pp. 525–542. Springer, Heidelberg (2011). https://doi.org/10.1007/978-3-642-22792-9_30

16. Podschwadt, R., Takabi, D., Hu, P.: SoK: privacy-preserving deep learning with homomorphic encryption. CoRR abs/2112.12855 (2021). https://arxiv.org/abs/2112.12855

17. Rouhani, B.D., Riazi, M.S., Koushanfar, F.: DeepSecure: scalable provably-secure deep learning. In: Proceedings of the 55th Annual Design Automation Conference, DAC 2018, pp. 2:1–2:6. ACM, New York (2018). https://doi.org/10.1145/3195970.3196023

18. Tanaka, M.: Learnable image encryption. CoRR abs/1804.00490 (2018). http://arxiv.org/abs/1804.00490

19. Wikipedia contributors: Internet censorship in China—Wikipedia, the free encyclopedia (2022). https://en.wikipedia.org/w/index.php?title=Internet_censorship_in_China&oldid=1110094504. Accessed 15 Sept 2022

20. Yao, A.C.: How to generate and exchange secrets. In: 27th Annual Symposium on Foundations of Computer Science (SFCS 1986), pp. 162–167, October 1986. https://doi.org/10.1109/SFCS.1986.25

Module Architecture of Docker Image and Container Security

Guan-Yu Wang[1], Hung-Jui Ko[2], Min-Yi Tsai[1], and Wei-Jen Wang[1(✉)]

[1] Department of Computer Science and Information Engineering, National Central University, Taoyuan, Taiwan
wjwang@csie.ncu.edu.tw

[2] Department of Computer Science Engineering, National Chung-Hsing University, Tai-Chung, Taiwan

Abstract. The security of Docker images has attracted a lot of attention recently, and the lack of content security checks on Docker images has led users to deploy vulnerable systems. In addition, malicious attackers may inject malware when building the image, and once deployed, it may become a cryptocurrency mining node or leak confidential information on the system. Therefore, it is imperative to establish a complete diagnostic process. In this paper, we propose an architecture of DICDS, which consists of four modules: integrity checker module, vulnerability checker module, malware checker module and suspicious behavior checker module. We can ensure that Docker users are using clean images and containers after the process of DICDS.

Keywords: Docker · Container · Cloud security · Malicious · Vulnerability

1 Introduction

The deployment of containerized has been widely increasing in recent year, and Docker is the most representative containerized application in the software development ecology. When it compares Docker to virtual machine, Docker has many advantages. Docker's ability to deploy containers across multiple operating systems solves the problem of deploying applications on different platforms. Docker images are the basis for Docker applications, and users can create images and use these images to run containers. Besides, images can be shared between multiple repository such as Docker Hub, Gitlab, etc. The users can get images directly from the repository and use the applications installed in the image. However, users get an image from the repository, but is unaware of the contents of the image. If an older version or a vulnerable package is installed in the image, the image is vulnerable to various types of attacks. In addition to the vulnerabilities in Docker images, malware in image should not be ignored. For example, researchers at Docker Hub detect some Docker image containing cryptocurrency mining programs [1, 2]. Unfortunately, there is no well-developed Docker diagnostic system can help users to detect the risks of Docker containers and images. In view of this, we propose the Docker

© The Author(s), under exclusive license to Springer Nature Singapore Pte Ltd. 2022
S.-Y. Hsieh et al. (Eds.): ICS 2022, CCIS 1723, pp. 661–669, 2022.
https://doi.org/10.1007/978-981-19-9582-8_58

diagnostic framework of Docker Image and Container Diagnostic System (DICDS). The DICDS can help user to detect the risks in the image and container.

The main contributions of this paper are as follows:

- The proposed DICDS helps users to diagnose the risk level of Docker image or container.
- The DICDS has more thorough progress than previous works.
- The DICDS does not only work for Docker images, but also for Docker containers.

This paper is comprised of the below. The first part of this paper was the preceding introduction. The second part below then introduces the background of Docker and related applications. In the third section, we discuss the related works of Docker images. The fourth section presents an overview of the proposed DICDS. The fifth section then shows how DICDS evaluates Docker images and containers. Finally, the sixth section is our conclusions.

2   Background

2.1   Docker

Since dotCloud Inc open sourced the Docker project and changed the company name to Docker in 2014, more and more developers and enterprises choose Docker to deploy software packages. One of the most important features of Docker is that allows the same applications and services to be deployed on different operating systems. Using Docker to deploy software package is more efficient than virtual machine. Docker is often compared to a virtual machine.

2.2   Docker Image

The Docker image is the base for running container, and it contains the application's environment, dependencies, code, etc. The Union file system [3] is the basis for the Docker image. Based on Union file system, we can create application environments as a thin layer on top of the image and the rest of it can be shared between all the containers. For example, we can install Nginx in Docker image with necessary libraries and files without full-install operating system.

2.3   Docker Container

Container is the instance where Docker executes the application. We can run the Docker image as container by using "docker run" command. Even if the image can be performed static analysis methods, the malicious attackers still can inject commands to download a malicious application or script in a pre-build image. Therefore, the content of containers must be analyzed and monitored thoroughly.

2.4 Image Scanning Tools

Some of the outdated packages in the image often contain numerous unpatched vulnerabilities that can expose the service to various types of attacks (e.g., denial of service, gaining privileges, etc.). In view of this, we have conducted several open-source image scanning tools from [4–6], most of the tools are focused on auditing, tracking Common Vulnerabilities and Exposure (CVE) database and benchmark from CIS, the National Vulnerabilities Database (NVD) [7] and other organizations.

3 Related Work

In [8], Lee and Kwon proposed Docker Image Vulnerabilities Diagnostic System (DIVDS). DIVDS is mainly composed of two modules: IVD and IVE. IVD is based on the open-source detection tool Clair [9] to detect known vulnerabilities in Docker Image, and IVE The work of the IVE module is to calculate the CVSS (Common Vulnerability Scoring System) [10] score of these vulnerabilities found. DIVDS will delete the image which does not pass the score threshold. However, DIVDS only provide static analysis, it's unable to inspect backdoor's hidden in the image or container that executes malware. The other problem of DIVDS is Clair. Clair does not flag vulnerabilities for application-level dependencies currently. Along with increasing ecosystem around application-level dependencies, it would be a great challenge for users. In [11], Sue, Wu and Ye developed proposed a blockchain-based Docker Image detection framework. It uses Clair as CVE detector, ClamAV [12] as Malware & Virus detector and Violation detector to find out the potential risks in the image. Their system will store hash values of image after detectors have done. If the image has found malware, this image will be rejected. The hash value of image on the blockchain can help to identify the image checked or not, but there are always newer vulnerabilities found. The checked image would be vulnerable after a few months later. Therefore, the user must spend more blocks for storing hash values. In [3], Zheng, Dong and Zhao proposed ZeroDVS which based on Clair to detect the vulnerabilities. Besides, ZeroDVS could trace the origin of each layer of the image, but it had the same problem with DIVDS that lack of dynamic detection. In [13], they compared three static detection image tools, Clair, Anchore [14], and MicroScanner (It is deprecated as of 1 Apr. 2021, our recommendation is to replace MicroScanner with Trivy [15]). Although the result shows that Anchore can provide up to 65.7% detection accuracy and can detect both OS and non-OS related vulnerabilities. However, the problem of these detection tools is that they can only perform static programs and lack more comprehensive detection of viruses and containers.

To our knowledge, there are 2 representative vulnerability analysis of images on Docker Hub. Firstly, in [1], Liu et al. collect 2,227,244 Docker images from 975,858 repositories on Docker Hub. They collected three indicators from the dataset, including sensitive parameters, malicious image, and CVE vulnerabilities. In sensitive parameters, they found commands such as "-v" or "–volume" mounted to the Docker host directory, which may allow attackers bypassing the authentication system and attacking the Docker Host. Then, in the indicators of malicious image, they used more than 50 antivirus software to find out that 42 images contain remote execution codes and cryptocurrencies mining programs. At last, regarding vulnerabilities, they use Anchore as a tool to scan for CVE vulnerabilities. They found nearly 3,000 vulnerabilities. They also counted that the average days to patch was 422 days. Second, in [16], Wist, Helsem and Gligoroski investigated 2,500 images on Docker Hub and divided them into four repositories categories: official, verified, certified and community, and found that in verified images, 82% of certified images contain vulnerabilities rated as high or critical, and among all images, only 17.8% of images do not contain any vulnerabilities. Apart from this, in [16] also point out that the security of Docker has two aspects to be concerned: the security of the Docker software in the host, and the security of the Docker container. Lastly, In 2020, Trendmicro stated that they found the presence of both malicious cryptocurrency miners and a distributed denial-of-service (DDoS) bots in the Alpine Linux-based containers [17]. Therefore, it is not only the image security needs to be checked, but also the container should be monitored.

On the above point, we can summarize the risks of Docker image and container as follows:

3.1 Integrity

The source of Docker image should be trusted. When we pulled the image from official registry, the integrity of image should be checked. If the integrity (i.e., Hash value) is not matched, the image cannot be deployed.

3.2 Vulnerabilities

Some images are not maintained any more. The system or the program is outdated and vulnerable. The hackers can compromise these systems easily.

3.3 Malware

Although the image is read-only, we have no way of knowing if there is malware involved. The Trojan horses, virus, cryptocurrencies mining may have existed in the images.

3.4 Suspicious Behavior

The container could be attacked by the malicious users or hackers. When the sensitive files (i.e., password files) are retrieved or a shell is run by a user, we need to be noticed. The suspicious behavior should be monitored.

4 Overview of the System

In this section, we present an overview of the proposed DICDS. The architecture of the DICDS (see Fig. 1).

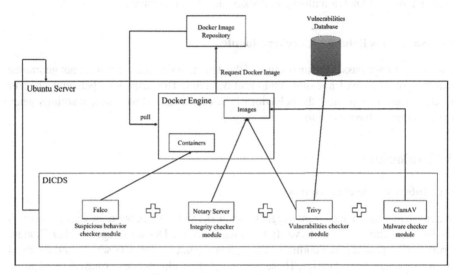

Fig. 1. Architecture of the DICDS

We divide our system into several main modules, Integrity checker module, Vulnerability checker module, Malware checker module, Suspicious checker module.

4.1 Integrity Checker Module

Is the image trustworthy? One of the most important security issues for systems built with containers is to verify that you are using the right container and that it comes from a secure source (or has not been maliciously tampered with). The integrity of image should be verified before running it as a container.

4.2 Vulnerabilities Checker Module

The installed software and the related libraries in the image could be vulnerable. The vulnerability checker module is used to gather the information of installed software and then compare them to the NVD database. We take the CVSS score to quantify the risk of the images and calculate the total vulnerability score of the image. If the score is higher than 9 [11], the image is considered as high risk.

4.3 Malware Checker Module

Apart from the Docker image vulnerability, the malware also needs to concern. The virus, trojan horses, webshell, cryptocurrencies mining could be injected in the images or containers by malicious users. Therefore, malware checker module is used to perform static analysis of known malware in docker image and container.

4.4 Suspicious Behavior Checker Module

Even if the image passes the inspection of the detection system, we still cannot guarantee that the container will not show abnormal behavior. The suspicious behavior checker module is used to monitor the behavior of the container and will issue warnings when the abnormal behavior occurs.

5 Evaluation

5.1 Integrity Checker Method

When we pull the images from a registry, such as Docker Hub, our messages go through the internet. Thus, it's vital to verify the integrity of the Docker image. Docker Content Trust (DCT) provides the ability to use digital signatures for data sent to and received from remote Docker registries. These signatures allow client-side or runtime verification of the integrity and publisher of specific image tags.

Docker currently provides users with a solution called Notary [18]. It is used as our integrity checker method. Notary is a centralized image verification component based on the digital signature mechanism. When the user pulls the image, Notary Server will verify the integrity and origin of the content. It can ensure that the content of the image will not be tampered. We can set up a Notary server for verifying the pulled images, rejecting the unsigned images, and storing the digests of our images.

5.2 Vulnerability Checker Method

To identify OS and non-OS vulnerabilities in Docker images is a very important issue. According to a report, there are over 80% software which uses the open-source software libraries [19]. Therefore, the vulnerability checker does not only need to scan the OS, but also the libraries used by the containers.

We use Trivy as our scanning tool, it uses the NVD as database. Based on the NVD, we can take CVSS as our evaluation standard. CVSS provides a numerical (0–10) representation of the severity of an information security vulnerability. In general, the closer the CVSS score is to 10, the more serious the severity is. The CVEs are evaluated the CVSS score in the NVD. When the CVSS score of CVE is higher than 9, the CVE is considered as high risk. The screenshot of Trivy scan results (see Fig. 2).

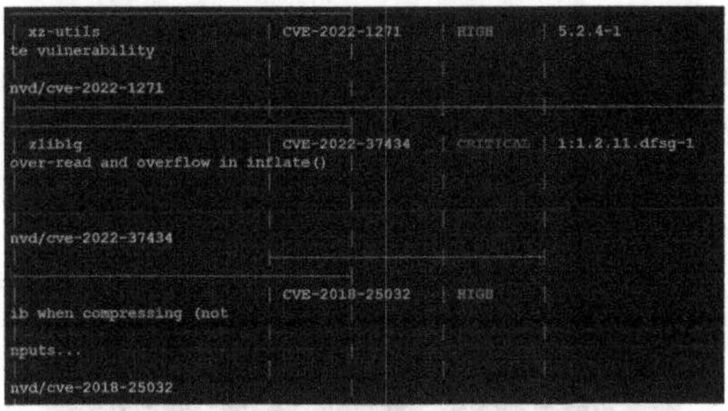

Fig. 2. Trivy scan results

5.3 Malware Checker Method

According to a report, researchers have detected several images containing cryptocurrency mining programs that may perform malicious attacks when containers are running [17]. When these images with malicious code are pushed to public repositories, there is a high risk that users will unwittingly use them and become malicious mining nodes.

ClamAV is an open source (GPLv2) anti-virus toolkit, it is designed to scan files quickly, retrieved to today, its database has nearly 4 million virus species, including viruses, worms, trojans, and other malware. Therefore, we choose ClamAV to be our malware checker and detect the malware in the image effectively. The screenshot of ClamAV scan results (see Fig. 3).

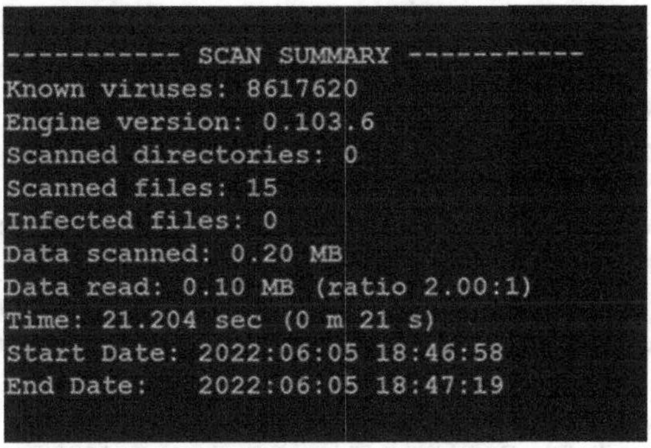

Fig. 3. ClamAV scan results

5.4 Suspicious Behavior Checker Method

When the container appears suspicious behavior, it is possible that the attacker after the intrusion of the doings. Therefore, in addition to the security of the image, the behavior of a running container should also be monitored.

Falco [20] is a tool designed to strengthen container security. It detects threats at runtime by observing the behavior of applications and containers. In detail, Falco uses system calls to protect and monitor containers by alerting on rule violations or parsing Linux system calls. The container monitored by Falco with related information (see Fig. 4).

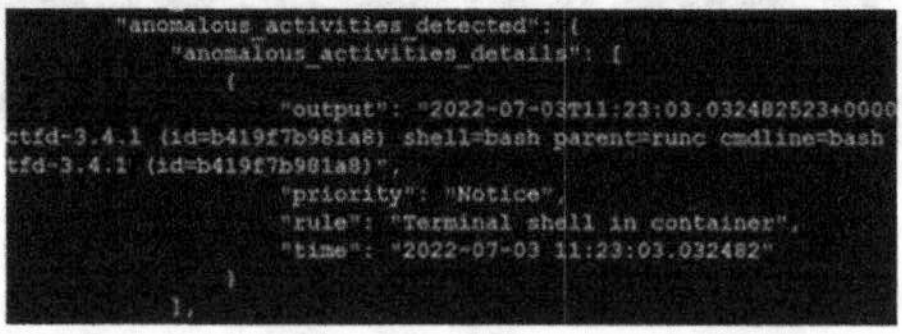

Fig. 4. Falco monitored containers and related information

6 Conclusion

In this paper, we have proposed Docker Image Container Diagnostic System (DICDS) to establish security check methods from Docker image to the container. DICDS is mainly consist of four checker components such as integrity, vulnerability, malware and suspicious behavior detection. The integrity checker verifies the integrity of the image. The vulnerability checker detects vulnerabilities in the image, compares them to the NVD database and uses the CVSS system to evaluate the total score of vulnerabilities. The malware checker uses static analysis to detect the known malware in the image or container. The suspicious behavior checker monitors abnormal behavior of containers. The previous works always focus on static analysis. In DICDS, we consider more aspects of Docker security, not only the static analysis, but also the security of the images source and dynamic analysis. The suspicious behaviors are monitored while the containers are running. As we can see, DICDS takes the static analysis, dynamic analysis and images sources into account, which is more complete and enhances the security of Docker image and container. By performing DICDS, we will further improve each method of DICDS to establish a more comprehensive standard of Docker images security in the future.

Acknowledgement. This research was partially supported by the Ministry of National Science and Technology Council of the Republic of China under the Grant MOST 111-2221-E-008-061.

References

1. Liu, P., et al.: Understanding the security risks of docker hub. In: Chen, L., Li, N., Liang, K., Schneider, S. (eds.) ESORICS 2020. LNCS, vol. 12308, pp. 257–276. Springer, Cham (2020). https://doi.org/10.1007/978-3-030-58951-6_13
2. Karn, R.R., Kudva, P., Huang, H., Suneja, S., Elfadel, I.M.: Cryptomining detection in container clouds using system calls and explainable machine learning. IEEE Trans. Parallel Distrib. Syst. **32**(3), 674–691 (2021)

3. Zheng, Y., Dong, W., Zhao, J.: ZeroDVS: trace-ability and security detection of container image based on inheritance graph. In: 2021 IEEE 5th International Conference on Cryptography, Security and Privacy (CSP), Zhuhai, China. IEEE (2021)

4. Acreman, S.: Container Scanning. https://kubedex.com/container-scanning/. Accessed 30 June 2022

5. Burillo, M.: 29 Docker security tools compared. https://sysdig.com/blog/20-docker-security-tools/. Accessed 30 June 2022

6. Doerrfeld, B.: 10+ top open-source tools for Docker security. https://techbeacon.com/security/10-top-open-source-tools-docker-security. Accessed 30 June 2022

7. NVD. https://nvd.nist.gov/. Accessed 30 June 2022

8. Kwon, S., Lee, J.-H.: DIVDS: docker image vulnerability diagnostic system. IEEE Access **8**, 42666–42673 (2020)

9. Clair. https://github.com/quay/clair. Accessed 30 June 2022

10. CVSS Score. https://www.first.org/cvss/. Accessed 02 Sept 2022

11. Sun, J., Wu, C., Ye, J.: Blockchain-based automated container cloud security enhancement system. In: 2020 IEEE International Conference on Smart Cloud (SmartCloud), Washington, DC, USA. IEEE (2020)

12. ClamAV. https://www.clamav.net/. Accessed 30 June 2022

13. Javed, O., Toor, S.: An evaluation of container security vulnerability detection tools. In: ICCBDC 2021: 2021 5th International Conference on Cloud and Big Data Computing (ICCBDC), New York, United States, pp. 95–101. ACM Digital Library (2021)

14. Anchore. https://github.com/anchore/anchore-engine. Accessed 30 June 2022

15. Trivy. https://aquasecurity.github.io/trivy/v0.28.0. Accessed 30 June 2022

16. Wist, K., Helsem, M., Gligoroski, D.: Vulnerability Analysis of 2500 Docker Hub Images, arXiv:2006.02932, arXiv, USA (2020)

17. Trendmicro: 2020 Exposed Docker Server Abused to Drop Cryptominer, DDoS Bot. https://www.trendmicro.com/en_be/research/20/i/exposed-docker-server-abused-to-drop-cryptominer-ddos-bot-.html. Accessed 30 June 2022

18. Notary project. https://github.com/notaryproject/notary. Accessed 30 June 2022

19. snyk: Open-Source Security Explained. https://snyk.io/series/open-source-security/. Accessed 01 July 2022

20. Falco. https://falco.org/. Accessed 30 June 2022

High-Capacity Double-Layer Data Hiding Technique Based on 3D Magic Cube

Hao-Yu Weng[1], Min-Yi Tsai[1], Wei-Jen Wang[1], and Cheng-Ta Huang[2,3]([✉])

[1] Department of Computer Science and Information Engineering, National Central University, Taoyuan City 320, Taiwan
[2] Department of Information Management, Yuan Ze University, Taoyuan City 320, Taiwan
cthuang2020@saturn.yzu.edu.tw
[3] International Bachelor Program in Informatics, Yuan Ze University, Taoyuan City 320, Taiwan

Abstract. Information technology and the Internet have progressed rapidly in people's lives, the privacy of information has become an important issue due to the accessibility of data. Therefore, to enhance information security and privacy protection, this paper proposes a new high-capacity method for data hiding. The proposed method is based on 3D magic cube with double layers embedding. In the field of data hiding, the reference matrix-based methods attract many researchers because of its high-capacity. Recently, as the needs of the high payloads of the stego-image, the multi-layers-based technique is applied to provide larger embedding capacity. However, the image after data embedding will cause serious distortions, especially on multi-layers embedding, hence, keeping the image at a good visual quality and achieving high-payloads are the main challenges for data hiding. In this scheme, we take advantage of 3D magic cube and 3D reference space with double layers embedding for our data hiding technique to improve the embedding payloads. The experimental results show that our method not only provides good embedding capacity (4.00 bpp) but also keeps the image at acceptable quality (In terms of PSNR > 30).

Keywords: Data hiding · Magic cube · Multi-layers embedding · High capacity

1 Introduction

Information privacy has become the main challenge in people's lives due to the development of the Internet and information technology. The high accessibility of information makes it easy for users to obtain all kinds of information from the Internet, however, this also means that people run the risk of data being leaked, or stolen by malicious people for improper use. To enhance the protection of information privacy, the data hiding technique is a better method to protect data during transmission. Data hiding technique is known as steganography, the main idea is concealing secret data into multimedia files without raising any suspicion of the existence of secret data. The type of multimedia file, such as images, videos or texts or audio files and so on. The files after embedding will be sent to a receiver over the communication channel. At the receiver side, authorized users can extract the secret through the specific algorithm without loss.

© The Author(s), under exclusive license to Springer Nature Singapore Pte Ltd. 2022
S.-Y. Hsieh et al. (Eds.): ICS 2022, CCIS 1723, pp. 670–678, 2022.
https://doi.org/10.1007/978-981-19-9582-8_59

Many existing data hiding methods include least significant bit replacement (LSB) [1, 2], exploiting modification direction (EMD) [3–5], pixel value differencing (PVD) [6–8], and reference matrix-based methods [9–12]. No matter what type of steganographic method, both the visual quality and the embedding capacity are two primary metrics to evaluate the performance of the techniques.

The least significant bit replacement (LSB) technique is a common method among data hiding techniques was proposed by Bender [1], the main idea of LSB replacement is to take the place of the n-bits LSB with the secret bits, receiver can read the n-bits LSB to extract the secret. It is a simple way to conduct data embedding and extraction and it appeals to many researchers. For the higher image quality, Chan et al. [2] proposed the modified LSB replacement to improve the image quality by controlling the $(k + 1)$ bits by 0 or 1, resulting the lower distortion to the image.

Zhang and Wang [3] proposed the exploiting modification direction (EMD) in 2006, this method embeds $(2n + 1)$-ary notational system in n-cover pixels. Only one cover pixel is either increased or decreased by 1 or kept unchanged. Many researchers are devoted to the EMD field due to its good visual quality and trying to improve the embedding capacity. In 2007, Lee et al. [4] proposed the improving exploiting modification (IEMD) to enhance the payloads by modifying extraction function. In 2009, Kuo et al. [5] proposed the generalized improving exploiting modification direction (GEMD), they generalized the EMD extraction function, resulting in larger embedding capacity and better image visual quality.

Wu and Tsai [6] proposed pixel value differencing (PVD) in 2003. The main idea of PVD is to calculate the difference between pixel pairs. The differences d will be classified into a specific range according to the range table, and then determine the number of bits of secret data to embed. According to the feature of PVD, secret bit can be embedded in smooth areas rather than edge areas. For other PVD-based schemes [7, 8], researchers are devoted to modifying the range table in order to improve the image quality and embedding capacity.

The reference matrix-based data hiding methods can be applied to many different types of reference matrix. In 2008, Chang et al. [9] proposed a data hiding method based on sudoku reference matrices and it achieves 1.5 bpp and 44.85 dB on embedding rates and PSNR respectively. In 2014, Chang et al. [10] proposed a data hiding method based on turtle-shell and it can reach 1.5 bpp and 49.4 dB on embedding rates and PSNR. In 2020, Lee et al. [11] proposed a data hiding method based on magic signet, it provides 44.12 dB on PSNR and 2.00 bpp on embedding rates. Afterward, the 3D magic cube-based data hiding method was proposed by Lee et al. [12] in 2020, it turns the reference matrix from 2D into 3D, this method can achieve 2.25 bpp on embedding rates and 44.00 dB on PSNR.

In this paper, we proposed a high-capacity double-layer data hiding method based on a 3D magic cube, we divide the image into blocks and embed secrets according to the cube and 3D reference space, for each layer, we can embed 6 bits secret bits in the cover-image, experiment results indicate that our method can achieve 4.00 bpp on embedding rates and 33.92 dB on PSNR.

The remaining of the paper is organized as follows. Section 2 introduces the overview of related work. Section 3 describes the proposed method in detail. The performance and the experimental analysis of the proposed method are described in Sect. 4. Finally, the conclusion of this paper is presented in Sect. 5.

2 Related Work

IN this section, we briefly introduce the 4-cube based data hiding technique proposed by Lee et al. [12].

2.1 Data Hiding Method Based on 3D Magic Cube [12]

Lee et al. [12] proposed a data hiding technique based on 3D magic cube in 2020. In the method, a $4 \times 4 \times 4$ cube is generated and the value range of the cube is [0, 63]. First, we create a 3D reference space sized $256 \times 256 \times 256$, and fill it up with the created cube. We divide the image into non-overlapping blocks sized 2×2 and 4 pixels can be denoted as (P_1, P_2, P_3, P_4). Next, P_1 will be embedded 3 bits of secret data s_1 by modified LSB method, then stego-pixel Q_1 obtained. Afterward, calculate the absolute differences (d_1, d_2, d_3) between Q_1 and remaining 3 pixels P_2, P_3 and P_4. Thereafter, take $M(d_1, d_2, d_3)$ as the based coordinate to the generated cube M and find the closest position $M(d_1', d_2', d_3')$ where the value equals to the secret data s_2. Finally, modify the cover-pixels by $Q_2 = Q_1 + d_1'$, $Q_3 = Q_1 + d_2'$ and $Q_4 = Q_1 + d_3'$, then the stego-pixels can be obtained. The performance of this method can provide embedding rate of 2.25 bpp and a PSNR of 44.00 dB respectively.

3 Proposed Method

In this section, the proposed double-layer data hiding method based on magic-cube is described in detail. There are 6 bits of secret data that can be embedded in three pixels of each layer, achieving an embedding capacity of 4.00 bpp. The following contents present the way to construct the 3D magic cube and 3D reference space, the embedding process and the extraction process.

3.1 The Construction of 3D Magic Cube and 3D Reference Space

Before data embedding, we must first generate the 3D magic cube C and corresponding 3D reference space M_1 and M_2. The way to generate the cube C and reference space M_1 and M_2 are described as follows.

- **3D Magic Cube:**

In the proposed method, the 3D magic cube of $4 \times 4 \times 4$ is generated from a pseudo-random key, and the range of values is $[0, 4^3 - 1] = [0, 63]$, where all the values in the cube are not repeated. Figure 1 shows the proposed 3D magic cube.

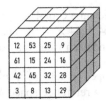

Fig. 1. The 3D magic cube C

- **First and Second Layer of the 3D Reference Space M_1 and M_2.**

In this study, the double-layer embedding technique is applied, there are two different sizes of 3D reference space for each layer. The generated 3D magic cube C will fill up all the 3D reference space M_1 and M_2. For the first layer, the size of M_1 is $64 \times 64 \times 64$. That is because we first down-map the cover-pixel value by dividing 4 before embedding, as we know that the range of pixel value is $[0, 2^8 - 1]$, after the down-mapping process, the maximum value of pixel can be only 63, so the new range will be $[0, 2^6 - 1]$, namely, the range of M_1 is $[0, 63]$. For the second layer, the size of M_2 is $256 \times 256 \times 256$, after the first layer finished embedding, the stego-pixel of the first layer will be mapped into the second-layer by multiplying 4, so the range of the second layer is $256 \times 256 \times 256$. Figure 2 shows the concepts of the 3D reference space M_1 and M_2.

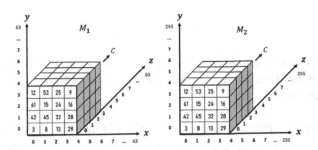

Fig. 2. The concept of the 3D reference space M_1 and M_2 with magic cube C

3.2 Embedding Procedure

Input: Cover-Image CI, Secret Messages s_1, s_2

Output: Stego-Image SI.

Step1. First, divide cover-image CI into non-overlapping blocks sized 1×3 and the three cover-pixels can be denoted as p_1, p_2 and p_3.

Step2. Next, the cover-pixels are down-mapped into smaller values by using Eq. (1), where $\lfloor * \rfloor$ is the floor function, then the first-layer mapped pixels p_i^{FL} are obtained.

$$p_i^{FL} = \left\lfloor \frac{p_i}{4} \right\rfloor, \text{ where } i = 1 \text{ to } 3 \tag{1}$$

Step3. Then, generate a 3D magic cube C of $4 \times 4 \times 4$ by pseudo-random key and fill up the 3D reference space M_1 of $64 \times 64 \times 64$ by repeating the cube C, where the range of value in the cube C is $[0, 63]$ and each value only occurs in one time.

Step4. Take the first-layer mapped pixels p_1^{FL}, p_2^{FL} and p_3^{FL} as the coordinates (x, y, z) in the cube C and the 3D reference space M_1. Thereafter, take the location $M_1(p_1^{FL}, p_2^{FL}, p_3^{FL})$ as the base position.

Step5. Find the surrounding multiple positions $M_1\left(p'^{FL}_{1k}, p'^{FL}_{2k}, p'^{FL}_{3k}\right)$ and their values equal to the secret message s_1, and select a position that is satisfied with the shortest distance to the base position $M_1(p_1^{FL}, p_2^{FL}, p_3^{FL})$, the definition is denoted as Eq. (2), then the stego-pixels of first-layer $p'^{FL}_1, p'^{FL}_2, p'^{FL}_3$ are obtained.

$$M_1\left(p'^{FL}_{1k}, p'^{FL}_{2k}, p'^{FL}_{3k}\right) = s_1, \text{ where } k$$

$$= \arg\min_{k}\left(\sqrt{\left(p'^{FL}_{1k} - p_1^{FL}\right)^2 + \left(p'^{FL}_{2k} - p_2^{FL}\right)^2 + \left(p'^{FL}_{3k} - p_3^{FL}\right)^2}\right)$$

$$(2)$$

Step6. Map the stego-pixels of the first-layer into the second-layer by using Eq. (3) and generate the 3D reference space M_2 of $256 \times 256 \times 256$ and it will be filled up with the Cube C.

$$p_i^{SL} = 4 \times p'^{FL}_i + 2 \tag{3}$$

Step7. The same procedure as Step 4, take p_1^{SL}, p_2^{SL} and p_3^{SL} as the coordinates (x, y, z) in the cube and the 3D reference space M_2. Then, the location $M_2(p_1^{SL}, p_2^{SL}, p_3^{SL})$ is taken as the based position.

Step8. The multiple positions $M_2\left(p'^{SL}_{1k}, p'^{SL}_{2k}, p'^{SL}_{3k}\right)$ in the cube C are found and their values are equal to the secret message s_2, then the position $M_2(p'^{SL}_1, p'^{SL}_2, p'^{SL}_3)$ which is satisfied with the shortest distance to the based position $M_2(p_1^{SL}, p_2^{SL}, p_3^{SL})$ will be selected, where the condition of selecting the shortest distance position can be denoted as Eq. (4). The coordinates of $p'^{SL}_1, p'^{SL}_2, p'^{SL}_3$ are the final stego-pixels. After repeating the steps, the stego-image SI can be obtained.

$$M_2\left(p'^{SL}_{1k}, p'^{SL}_{2k}, p'^{SL}_{3k}\right) = s_2, \text{ where } k$$

$$= \arg\min_{k}\left(\sqrt{\left(p'^{SL}_{1k} - p_1^{SL}\right)^2 + \left(p'^{SL}_{2k} - p_2^{SL}\right)^2 + \left(p'^{SL}_{3k} - p_3^{SL}\right)^2}\right) \quad (4)$$

3.3 Extraction Procedure

Input: Stego-Image *SI*.

Output: Secret Messages s_1, s_2

Step1. First, divide the stego-image *SI* into non-overlapping blocks sized 1×3, three stego-pixels can be denoted as p'_1, p'_2 and p'_3.

Step2. Next, generate the same 3D magic cube *C* by pseudo-random key received from the sender, and then fill up the 3D reference space M_2 of $256 \times 256 \times 256$.

Step3. Take the stego-pixels p'_1, p'_2 and p'_3 as the coordinates in the cube *C* and the 3D reference space, to find the value of M_2 (p'_1, p'_2, p'_3), then the secret data s_2 can be extracted.

Step4. Thereafter, down-map the stego-pixels into smaller values by using Eq. (5), where $\lfloor * \rfloor$ is the floor function, then the down mapped stego-pixels p'^{FL}_i are obtained.

$$p'^{FL}_i = \left\lfloor \frac{p'_i}{4} \right\rfloor, \text{ where } i = 1 \text{ to } 3 \tag{5}$$

Step5. The same process as Step 3 and Step 4, generate the same 3D reference space M_1, and then take the down mapped stego-pixels p'^{FL}_1, p'^{FL}_2 and p'^{FL}_3 as the coordinates and find the value of M_1 ($p'^{FL}_1, p'^{FL}_2, p'^{FL}_3$), then extract the secret data s_1.

Step6. Finally, combining the secret data s_1 and s_2, then the secret messages can be extracted completely without loss.

4 Experimental Results

This section presents the experimental results of the proposed method, which are described in detail. The four grayscale tested images with a size of 512×512 include Lena. Airplane, Peppers, Boat are shown in Fig. 3.

(a)Lena   (b)Airplane   (c)Peppers   (d)Boat

Fig. 3. The four tested images

For the evaluating effect of the proposed method, peak signal-noise-rate (PSNR) and embedding rate (ER) are used to measure the performance, the calculation of PSNR and ER is denoted as Eq. (6) and Eq. (8). The high PSNR indicates that the image has lower distortions and better visual quality of the image. For Eq. (7), the mean square error (MSE) is calculated by the original image and the stego-image sized $M \times N$ pixels. Embedding capacity (EC) is the maximum payload of secret bits hidden in the stego-image, and ER is calculated by EC and the number of pixels in the image. A high-capacity data hiding method can provide more EC and ER at one time.

$$PSNR = 10 \times log_{10}\left(\frac{255^2}{MSE}\right) \tag{6}$$

$$MSE = \frac{1}{M \times N} \sum_{i=1}^{M} \sum_{j=1}^{N} \left[CI(i,j) - SI(i,j)\right]^2 \tag{7}$$

$$ER = \frac{EC}{M \times N}(\text{bpp}) \tag{8}$$

Table 1. The performance of proposed method in the case of single layer and double layers

Method	Single-layer		Double-layer	
Images	PSNR (dB)	ER (bpp)	PSNR (dB)	ER (bpp)
Lena	47.60	2.00	33.91	4.00
Airplane	47.60	2.00	33.92	4.00
Boat	47.58	2.00	33.92	4.00
House	47.59	2.00	33.90	4.00
Average	**47.59**	**2.00**	**33.91**	**4.00**

Table 1 shows the performance of the proposed method both in single layer and double-layer embedding. In the proposed method, the range of PSNR value among 4 tested images is between 47.58 dB and 47.60 dB and 2.00 bpp on ER of single layer embedding. For the double-layer, the average PSNR value can achieve 33.91 dB and the ER can achieve 4.00 bpp. Based on the results, it can be observed that our method provides good image visual quality with high embedding capacity.

Figure 4 and Table 2 present the performance comparison between the proposed method and the 4-Cube + LSB method proposed by Lee et al. [12]. The results show that the proposed method of double-layer can provide the higher ER than the scheme proposed by Lee et al. [12], which can reach 4.00 bpp and maintain image quality at an average PSNR = 33.92 dB. For the single-layer embedding of the proposed method, although the embedding capacity is less than theirs, it can provide good image visual at an average PSNR = 47.59 dB.

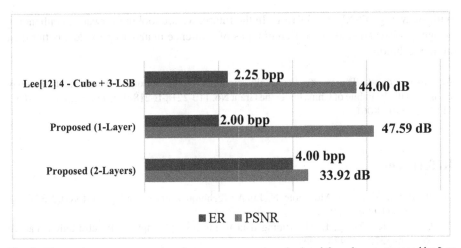

Fig. 4. The performance comparison between proposed method and the scheme proposed by Lee et al. [12] in bar chart.

Table 2. The performance comparison of proposed method with some existing methods

Methods	Lee [12] 4-Magic Cube + 3-LSB		Proposed Method (Single-Layer)		Proposed Method (Double-Layer)	
Image	PSNR	EC	PSNR	EC	PSNR	EC
Lena	43.97	2.25	47.60	2.00	33.91	4.00
Airplane	43.95	2.25	47.60	2.00	33.92	4.00
Peppers	44.00	2.25	47.59	2.00	33.92	4.00
Boat	44.03	2.25	47.58	2.00	33.92	4.00
Average	**44.00**	**2.25**	**47.59**	**2.00**	**33.92**	**4.00**

5 Conclusion

The main challenge of double-layer embedding is how we design an algorithm to ensure the secret messages can be extracted completely and maintain good image visual quality at the same time. In this paper, we propose a double-layer data hiding technique based on 3D magic cube. We divide the image into non-overlapping blocks sized 1×3 and generate a 3D magic cube with a height of 4. Through down-mapping and up-mapping the pixel values, we can take advantage of two reference spaces which are sized $64 \times 64 \times 64$ and $256 \times 256 \times 256$, thus, we can embed the secret twice to achieve high embedding capacity. Moreover, when embedding data, we select the coordinate that has the shortest distance to the based position, so that we can reduce the distortion when adjusting the pixel values. Experimental results show that the proposed method can provide a high embedding capacity (ER = 4.00 bpp) and maintain a good image quality with an average PSNR of 33.91d B. In the future, we are looking forward to enhancing image quality and studying different types of reference matrix to provide a better data hiding technique.

Acknowledgment. This work was partially supported by the National Science and Technology Council of the Republic of China under the Grant No. 110-2218-E-218-001, 111-2221-E-115-038, 111-2221-E-008-061.

References

1. Bender, W., Gruhl, D., Morimoto, N., Lu, A.: Techniques for data hiding. IBM Syst. J. **35**(3–4), 313–336 (1996)
2. Chan, C.-K., Cheng, L.-M.: Hiding data in images by simple LSB substitution. Pattern Recognit. **37**, 469–474 (2004)
3. Zhang, X., Wang, S.: Efficient steganographic embedding by exploiting modification direction. IEEE Commun. Lett. **10**(11), 781–783 (2006)
4. Lee, C.-F., Wang, Y.-R., Chang, C.-C.: A steganographic method with high embedding capacity by improving exploiting modification direction. In: Proceedings of 3rd International Conference on Intelligent Information Hiding and Multimedia Signal Processing (IIHMSP), pp. 497–500 (2007)
5. Kuo, W.-C., Wuu, L.-C., Shyi, C.-N., Kuo, S.-H.: A data hiding scheme with high embedding capacity based on general improving exploiting modification direction method. In: Proceedings pf 9th International Conference on Hybrid Intelligent Systems, Shenyang, China, pp. 69–73 (2009)
6. Wu, D.-C., Tsai, W.-H.: A steganographic method for images by pixel-value differencing. Pattern Recognit. Lett. **24**, 1613–1626 (2003)
7. Tseng, H.-W., Leng, H.-S.: A steganographic method based on pixel- value differencing and the perfect square number. J. Appl. Math. **2013**, 1–8 (2013)
8. Mandal, J.K.: Colour image steganography based on pixel value differencing in spatial domain. Int. J. Inf. Sci. Techn. **2**(4), 83–93 (2012)
9. Chang, C.-C., Chou, Y.-C., Kieu, T.-D.: An information hiding schemeusing Sudoku. In: Proceedings of 3rd International Conference on Innovative Computing Information and Control, p. 17 (2008)
10. Chang, C.-C., Liu, Y., Nguyen, T.S.: A novel turtle shell-based schemefor data hiding. In: Proceedings of 10th International Conference on Intelligent Information Hiding and Multimedia Signal Processing, pp. 89–93 (2014)
11. Lee, C.-F., Wang, Y.-X.: An image hiding scheme based on magic signet. J. Electron. Sci. Technol. **18**(1), 93–101 (2020)
12. Lee, C.-F., Shen, J.-J., Agrawal, S., Wang, Y.-X., Lee, Y.-H.: Data hiding method based on 3D magic cube. IEEE Access **8**, 39445–39453 (2020)

Author Index

Printed in the United States
by Baker & Taylor Publisher Services